MW01096383

THE PEOPLE OF

PLATO

THE PEOPLE OF
PLATO

A PROSOPOGRAPHY
OF PLATO AND
OTHER SOCRATICS

DEBRA NAILS

HACKETT PUBLISHING COMPANY, INC.
Indianapolis/Cambridge

08   07   06   05   04   03   02   1   2   3   4   5   6   7

For further information, please address:

Hackett Publishing Company, Inc.
P. O. Box 44937
Indianapolis, IN 46244-0937

www.hackettpublishing.com

Jacket and interior design by Abigail Coyle

Library of Congress Cataloging-in-Pulication Data

Nails, Debra, 1950-
    The people of Plato : a prosopography of Plato and other Socratics /
Debra Nails.
        p. cm.
    Includes bibliographical references and index.
    ISBN 0-87220-564-9
    1. Plato—Friends and associates.   2. Socrates—Friends and associates.
3. Athens (Greece)—Biography.   4. Plato. Dialogues.   I. Title.

B393.N42 2002
184—dc21   2002068496

Carla Bailey
Bibliothecariae Clarissimae

CONTENTS

List of Diagrams and Maps

PREFACE

This book has a brief and personal history.

In a review of Henry Teloh's *Socratic Education in Plato's Early Dialogues*, Nick Smith suggested that understanding more fully how Socrates interacted with others would require that one know more prosopography. 'Prosopography' was a new word for me in 1990–1991, when I happened to be spending a year as a companion at the Institute for Advanced Study in Princeton. I had long wanted to know more about the people of Plato and had begun a file of notes, so I wondered aloud about the difficulty of collecting such information systematically. My colleagues pointed to the various sources, making the project sound so practicable that the urgency subsided, so I postponed the project and wrote a different book. I could not then have realized that I was for the only time in my life in the only place on the planet where every resource was at my fingertips, even the cheerful and willing guidance of specialists, Christian Habicht and Martin Ostwald.

Returning to Witwatersrand University in Johannesburg, I discovered that no resources were available, that prosopography is not something one can pursue just anywhere. But *apartheid* South Africa meanwhile gave me a deeper sympathy with 5th century Athens: I was teaching in a stratified society labeled 'democracy' by those in power, where the disfranchised majority formed an underclass enduring (economic) slavery, where neighboring countries suffered domination, where women were legal minors, and where religion and violence and political factions fed on one another. Reading Plato's *Republic* with students who thought a merit-based system worth trying against one based on birth and wealth was a change and a privilege.

When I returned permanently to the United States, I joined Mary Washington College's classics, philosophy, and religion department—an intellectual haven in a college demanding a teaching load of four courses per semester. Mehdi Amin Razavi suggested I manage the load by choosing research projects that didn't waste the breaks between classes. I thought again of prosopography, all those people, all those bits of information stacking up. At about that time, I read *Sojourner Truth: A Life, a Symbol* by Nell Painter, from whom I learned the painful lesson crucial to any involvement with Socrates: where heroes are concerned, the world will continue to prefer myth, and academics are of the world.

After years of collecting fragmentary information about the people of Plato, ducking into distant libraries at mealtimes of conferences, keeping the laptop with me, developing a library of photocopies, spending long summer days working out the relations of one person to another, I reached Michigan State University in the fall of 2000. The old urgency returned in a new form: with all the resources of this university at my disposal—time most importantly of all—I realized how impossible it would have been ever to have completed the project as an itinerant scholar. That knowledge entailed the sort of duty academics at land-grant universities welcome: finish it and make it available to others.

Debra Nails
Okemos
15 March 2002

Acknowledgments

The people of Plato led me onto the turf of subdisciplines of classics and history, to mathematics, anthropology, and archaeology, where I trespassed uneasily. John Traill, exemplar of academic openness in the pursuit of knowledge, made available to this perfect stranger his wisdom and his data, gave generously both advice and access that made my task easier and infinitely more pleasant. Slobodan Dušanić read an early draft and made many helpful suggestions, enabling me to prune a project that was sprawling in all directions. Others to whom I am grateful for answering *ad hoc* questions are Luc Brisson, Diane Hatch, John MacIsaac, Bill Morison, Melissa Morison, Michel Narcy, Bruce O'Brien, Chuck Pazdernik, François Renaud, Suzanne Sumner, Holger Thesleff, Paul Woodruff, and, especially, William Levitan, who endured a whole decade of communion with Plato's people, fielded the most anxious questions, and provided the jokes.

Jacob Howland, Jerry Press, and Chuck Young gave me sound advice at the start that set the trajectory of the project. Several colleagues raised my spirits along the way by requesting information about this or that character, this or that dialogue: Jacques Bailly, Betty Belfiore, Ruby Blondell, Gabriel Danzig, Gale Justin, Mark McPherran, David O'Connor, Christopher Rowe, George Rudebusch, and Nick Smith. Ruby, Gabriel, Gale, and Nick provided useful further thoughts, objections and suggestions; and Christopher traded me his delightful Aristodemus for my lackluster Miccus. During the final stages of writing, I benefited from the encouragement and error-spotting of John Cooper, David Reeve, Kent Rigsby, and anonymous reviewers.

I am grateful to a few dear friends who have supported me in so many ways and for so many years that I cannot distinguish the kindnesses that have been specific to this project. Nick Smith and Mark McPherran kept me philosophically engaged when the people of Plato were an occupying army in my brain. Mark lent me a forum at one of the annual revivals of the philosophic spirit, the 2001 Arizona Colloquium in Ancient Philosophy, to present "Prosopography and the Image of Socrates." Ruby Blondell was my brilliant commentator on that occasion, making important points of interpretation explicit that I had overlooked. Lloyd Gerson and Asli Gocer have been steadfast confidantes and sounding boards whose encouragement has been essential and from whom I have drawn strength. Not only did they make me welcome in their home while I played the vagabond scholar, Lloyd intervened directly with crucial practical arguments; and Asli gave me an invaluable gift, reading the penultimate draft from first page to last and making innumerable helpful suggestions. I alone am responsible for the errors that remain in *POP*.

I have admired the principles of Hackett Publishing Company since the late 1970s when Bill Hackett took the time to write a long letter explaining his view of the academic publishing world to one of my teachers, Richard Cole, who recognized it as a document to be shared with graduate students. Hackett Publishing has, over the years, enriched my teaching life in a variety of ways, and I consider myself most fortunate to be included among those who are able to publish there. Deborah Wilkes, able navigator, provided encouragement, anticipated needs, made large and small but always constructive suggestions, and in every way made the process transparent. The staff in Cambridge—with whom I spent a happy morning—consulted with me, kept me abreast of developments, and proved as smart, learned, and attentive to detail as any author could hope.

When time was short, or library collections failed me, it was Shaman Drum Bookshop in Ann Arbor that rescued me, whether by phone or e-mail or in person—like an on-line service, only better. Among the libraries that I used to collect material for the project, the following were especially important: Hekman Library of Calvin College, Alderman Library of the University of Virginia, The University of Arizona Library, Harlan Hatcher Graduate Library of the University of Michigan, the library of the Athenians Project of Victoria College of the University of Toronto, and, of course, Michigan State University Libraries, where Mary Ann Tyrrell went quite out of her way to help me when computers ignored me or, for their various reasons, spat back, "YOUR REQUEST HAS BEEN CANCELED." My greatest debt is to the interlibrary loan librarian of Simpson Library of Mary Washington College. Her skills, prescience, speed, and thoroughness are legendary, and it is to her that I dedicate this book. No matter how arcane, how incomplete or misspelled, how obscure the reference in whatever language I sent her, I doubt I ever even challenged her.

Pat McConeghy and Steve Esquith at Michigan State University encouraged me to take a sabbatical after one year of employment, a boon that had not crossed *my* mind; and the MSU Intramural Research Grants Program provided welcome funding for the year. I heartily thank Ellen White for drawing the maps for *POP*, John Traill for permission to adapt his Organization of Attica map (1986), and the Agora Excavations of the American School of Classical Studies at Athens for permission to redraw the plan of the Athenian agora.

With the kind permission of the following publishers, I quote translations of ancient authors and modern works (see Abbreviations, Ancient Texts, and Translations for full bibliographical citations of the individual volumes): Harvard University Press, and especially Jeffrey Henderson, who sent me corrected galley proofs of the fourth volume of his splendid Loeb Aristophanes; Hackett Publishing Company; and the University of Texas Press.

Audiences at MSU, where I gave "The Social Embeddedness of Plato's Philosophy," and at the Society for Ancient Greek Philosophy conference (Binghamton 1999), where I gave "The People of Plato's *Republic*"—both based on implications of the material in the book—helped me see how others saw Plato and his people.

ABBREVIATIONS, ANCIENT TEXTS, AND TRANSLATIONS

Modern Works

Full bibliographic citations of modern works will be found in the list of works cited and consulted. Superscript numbers identify editions. The texts listed below for ancient authors are those used for Greek citations throughout the prosopography; and the translations listed below are the ones used for English translations of passages of text, except as noted *ad hoc* when other translations are used for comparison. Dates of composition or production, the most recent reliable ones available, are provided whenever possible since these often affect interpretations.

ABV	J. D. Beazley, *Attic Black-Figure Vase Painters*
Agora	*The Athenian Agora. Results of Excavations Conducted by the American School of Classical Studies at Athens*
AM	*Mitteilungen des Deutschen Archäologischen Instituts, Athenische Abteilung*
AJP	*American Journal of Philology*
AO	*Athenian Officials 684–321 B.C.*, R. Develin, ed.
AncPhil	*Ancient Philosophy*
APF	J. K. Davies, *Athenian Propertied Families 600–300 B.C.*
ARV	J. D. Beazley, *Attic Red-Figure Vase Painters²*, 3 vols.
BMCR	*Bryn Mawr Classical Review*
CAH	*Cambridge Ancient History*, D. M. Lewis, John Boardman, M. Ostwald, J. K. Davies, & S. Hornblower, edd., vols. 5² & 6²
CJ	*Classical Journal*
CM	*Classica et Mediaevalia*
CP	*Classical Philology*
CQ	*Classical Quarterly*
CUP	Cambridge University Press
DK	*Die Fragmente der Vorsokratiker⁷*, H. Diels & W. Kranz, edd.
DPhA	*Dictionnaire des philosophes antiques*, R. Goulet, ed.
FGrH	*Die Fragmente der Griechischen Historiker*, F. Jacoby, ed.
FHG	*Fragmente Historicorum Graecorum*, C. Müller, ed.

FRA	*Foreign Residents of Athens: An Annex to the Lexicon of Greek Personal Names*, vol. 2: *Attica*, M. J. Osborne & S. G. Byrne, edd.
GG	*Griechische Geschichte*, J. Beloch, ed., 4 vols.
GRBS	*Greek, Roman and Byzantine Studies*
HCT	A. W. Gomme, A. Andrewes, & K. J. Dover, *A Historical Commentary on Thucydides*
Hell. Oxy.	*Hellenica Oxyrhynchia*, V. Bartoletti & M. Chambers, edd. (cf. P)
Hesperia	*Hesperia. Journal of the American School of Classical Study at Athens*
HSCP	*Harvard Studies in Classical Philology*
HUP	Harvard University Press
IDélos	*Inscriptiones de Délos*
IG	*Inscriptiones Graecae* I³, II², III², IV², XII
IGUR	*Inscriptiones Graecae Urbis Romae*, L. Moretti, ed., 4 vols.
Ind. Acad.	*Academicorum Philosophorum Index Herculananensis*, S. Mekler, ed.
JHS	*Journal of Hellenic Studies*
K	*Comicorum Atticorum Fragmenta*, T. Kock, ed.
Kera.	*Kerameikos; Ergebnisse der Ausgrabungen*, Deutsches Archäologisches Institut
LGPN1	*A Lexicon of Greek Personal Names*, vol. 1 *The Aegean Islands, Cyprus, Cyrenaica* (1987), P. M. Fraser & E. Matthews, edd.
LGPN2	*A Lexicon of Greek Personal Names*, vol. 2 *Attica* (1994), M. J. Osborne & S. G. Byrne, edd.
LGPN3A	*A Lexicon of Greek Personal Names*, vol. 3A *The Peloponnese, Western Greece, Sicily and Magna Graecia* (1997), P. M. Fraser & E. Matthews, edd.
LGPN3B	*A Lexicon of Greek Personal Names*, vol. 3B *Central Greece: From the Megarid to Thessaly* (2000), P. M. Fraser & E. Matthews, edd.
Loeb	Loeb Classical Library
LSJ	*A Greek-English Lexicon*, H. G. Liddell, R. Scott, & H. S. Jones, edd.
ML	*A Selection of Greek Historical Inscriptions to the End of the Fifth Century*, R. Meiggs & D. Lewis, edd.
NIA	M. J. Osborne, *Naturalization in Athens*, 4 vols.
OCD³	*Oxford Classical Dictionary*
OCT	Oxford Classical Texts
OUP	Oxford University Press
P	the historian of *Hell. Oxy.*
PA	J. Kirchner, *Prosopographia Attica*
PAA	J. S. Traill, *Persons of Ancient Athens*
PCG	*Poetae Comici Graeci*, R. Kassel & C. Austin, edd.
PCW	Plato, *Complete Works*, J. M. Cooper, ed.
P. Hib.	*Hibeh Papyri*

Poralla²	P. Poralla, *A Prosopography of Lacedaemonians from the Earliest Times to the Death of Alexander the Great (X–323 B.C.)*
P. Oxy.	*Oxyrhynchus Papyri*
PP	W. Groen van Prinsterer, *Prosopographia Platonica*
PUP	Princeton University Press
PX	C. G. Cobet, *Commentatio, qua continetur Prosopographia Xenophontea*
RE	*Real-Encyclopädie der classischen Altertumswissenschaft*, A. F. von Pauly & G. Wissowa, edd.
SEG	*Supplementum Epigraphicum Graecum*
SSR	*Socratis et Socraticorum Reliquiae*, G. Giannantoni, ed.
Stephanis	I. E. Stephanis, *Dionysiakoi Technitai*
Suda	*Suidae Lexicon*, Ada Adler, ed.
T	Teubners Schulausgaben griechischer Klassiker (classical text series)
TAPA	*Transactions of the American Philological Association*
TGrF	*Tragicorum Graecorum Fragmenta*, B. Snell et al., edd.
TLG	*Thesaurus Linguae Graecae* (E disk)
Tod	*A Selection of Greek Historical Inscriptions*, M. N. Tod, ed., 2 vols.
ZPE	*Zeitschrift für Papyrologie und Epigraphik*

Ancient Authors, Texts, and Translations

Ael.   Aelian (2–3rd c. C.E.), M. R. Dilts, ed., Leipzig 1974. N. G. Wilson, tr., *Historical Miscellany*, Loeb 1997.

> *NA*   *De Natura Animalium* (On the nature of animals)
>
> *VH*   *Varia Historia* (Historical miscellany)

Aen. Tact.   Aeneas Tacticus (4th c. B.C.E.), R. Schöne, ed., T 1911.

Aes.   Aeschines (4th c. B.C.E.), Socratic, frr. in *SSR* 2.VIA, pp. 593–626.

> | | | |
> |---|---|---|
> | *Alc.* | *Alcibiades* | nos. 41–54, pp. 605–10 |
> | *Asp.* | *Aspasia* | nos. 59–72, pp. 611–8 |
> | *Ax.* | *Axiochus* | nos. 55–8, p. 611 |
> | *Cal.* | *Callias* | nos. 73–5, pp. 618–9 |
> | *Mil.* | *Miltiades* | nos. 76–81, pp. 619–21 |

Aes.   *continued*

Rhi.	*Rhinon*	no. 82, p. 622
Tel.	*Telauges*	nos. 83–90, pp. 622–4

Aes. *orat.*   Aeschines (4th c. B.C.E.), orator, M. R. Dilts, ed., T 1997. Chris Carey, tr., *Aeschines*, Austin, University of Texas, 2000.

1	*Against Timarchus*	346/5
2	*On the Embassy*	343
3	*Against Ctesiphon I*	330

Aesch.   Aeschylus (6–5th c. B.C.E.), scholia, W. Dindorf, ed., Oxford 1851.

Pr.   *Prometheus Bound*

Alex.   Alexis (4–3rd c. B.C.E.), *PCG* 2 frr. 1–342, pp. 21–195.

Phae.	*Phaedrus*	frr. 247–8, pp. 159–61	n.d.

Alex. Polyh.   Alexander Polyhistor (1st c. B.C.E.), *FGrH* 273.

Amip.   Amipsias (4–3rd c. B.C.E.), *PCG* 2 frr. 1–33, pp. 196–210.

Con.	*Connus*	frr. 7–11, pp. 200–3	423

Anax.   Anaxandrides (4th c. B.C.E.), *PCG* 2 frr. 1–80, pp. 236–78.

Anch.	*Anchisēs*	frr. 4–5, p. 240	376–349

Andoc.   Andocides (5–4th c. B.C.E.), F. Blass & C. Fuhr, edd., T 1913. D. M. Mac-Dowell, tr., *Antiphon and Andocides*, Austin, University of Texas 1998.

1	*On the Mysteries*	400
3	*On the Peace with Sparta*	391

[Andoc.]   pseudo-Andocides

        4   *Against Alcibiades*

Androt.   Androtion (4th c. B.C.E.), *FGrH* 324.

Antipha.   Antiphanes (4th c. B.C.E.), *PCG* 2 frr. 1–327, pp. 312–481.

Ag.	*Agroikos* or *The Rustic*	frr. 1–12, pp. 314–7	>385
Ant.	*Antaeus*	fr. 35, p. 328	>385
Om.	*Ōmphalē*	frr. 174–6, pp. 408–10	>385

Antiph.   Antiphon (5th c. B.C.E.), orator, Th. Thalheim, ed., T 1914; sophist, frr. in DK 87. J. S. Morrison, tr., *The Older Sophists*, ed. R. K. Sprague, Indianapolis, Hackett 2001 <1972>. Numbering follows Sprague.

3	*Second Tetralogy*	<415
6	*On the Chorus-boy*	412
8	*On the Tribute of the Samothracians* (fr.)	425/4
10	*Defense Against the Indictment of Demosthenes* (fr.)	<413
20	*Prosecution of Erasistratus in a Case about Peacocks* (fr.)	<413
30	*Invective Against Alcibiades* (fr.)	±418

Antis.   Antisthenes (4th c. B.C.E.), frr. in *SSR* 2.VA, pp. 137–225.

Alc.	*Alcibiades*	nos. 36, 198–202, pp. 149, 217–9
Asp.	*Aspasia*	nos. 142–4, pp. 191–2
Me.	*Menexenus*	no. 25, p. 146

Apoll.   Apollodorus (2–1st c. B.C.E.), *FGrH* 244.

        Chr.   *Chronicle*

Ararus   (5–4th c. B.C.E.), *PCG* 2 frr. 1–21, pp. 524–31.

        Hym.   *Hymenaeus*   fr. 16, p. 530   >375

Arch.   Archippus (5–4th c. B.C.E.), *PCG* 2 frr. 1–61, pp. 538–57.

        Fishes   frr. 14–34, pp. 542–9   >403

Aristo.   Aristodemus (1st c. B.C.E.), *FGrH* 104.

Aristoph.   Aristophanes (5–4th c. B.C.E.), F. W. Hall, W. M. Geldart & J. Demiańczuk, edd., OCT 1900–01. Frr. and testimonia in *PCG* 3.2. Scholia in F. Dübner, ed., *Scholia Graeca in Aristophanem*, Paris 1842. Jeffrey Henderson, tr., *Aristophanes* I, *Acharnians*, *Knights*, and II, *Clouds*, *Wasps*, *Peace*, Loeb 1998; III, *Birds*, *Lysistrata*, and *Women at the Thesmophoria*, Loeb 2000; IV, *Frogs*, *Assemblywomen*, and *Wealth*, Loeb 2002. Dates follow Henderson.

Ach.	*Acharnians*		425
Aiol.	*Aiolosikōn*	frr. 1–16, pp. 33–41	>387
Bab.	*Babylonians*	frr. 67–99, pp. 62–76	426
Banq.	*Banqueters (Daitalēs)*	frr. 205–55, pp. 122–48	427
Birds			414
Clouds	(cf. *Neph.*), revised version survives		423, ±418
D. Niob.	*Dramas or Centaur*	frr. 289–98, pp. 164–7	<406
Eccl.	*Assemblywomen (Ecclesiazusae)*		392 or 391
Farmers	*Georgoi*	frr. 100–27, pp. 77–88	424
Frogs			405
Gery.	*Gerytades (Old Age)*	frr. 156–90, pp. 101–15	>409
Hor.	*Horae (Seasons)*	frr. 577–89, pp. 296–303	421–412
Knights			424
Lysistr.	*Lysistrata*		411
Neph.	*Nephelae (Clouds*, add. frr.)	frr. 392–401, pp. 214–9	
Peace			421, >412

Plu.	*Plutus* (*Wealth*), revised version survives		408, 388
Storks	*Pelargoi*	frr. 444–57, pp. 239–44	±398, 389
Tag.	*Tagēnistae (Fry Cooks)*	frr. 504–42, pp. 264–79	<400
Tel.	*Telemessians*	frr. 543–55, pp. 279–85	±402
Thesm.	*Women at the Thesmophoria*		411
Wasps			422

Aristot.   Aristotle (4th c. B.C.E.), *Eu. Eth.*, F. Susemihl, ed., T 1884; *Meta.*, W. Jaeger, ed., OCT 1957; *NE*, I. Bywater, ed., *OCT* 1894; *Pol.*, A. Dreizehnter, ed., Munich, Fink 1970; *Rh.*, R. Kassel, ed., Berlin, de Gruyter 1976; frr. in V. Rose, ed., T 1886. Jonathan Barnes, ed., *The Complete Works of Aristotle: The Revised Oxford Translation*, Bollingen Series 71, Princeton, PUP 1984, 2 vols.

Eu. Eth.	*Eudemian Ethics*
Gen. An.	*On the Generation of Animals*
Meta.	*Metaphysics*
NE	*Nicomachean Ethics*
Phys.	*Physics*
Poet.	*Poetics*
Pol.	*Politics*
Prob.	*Problems*
Rh.	*Rhetoric*
S. Ref.	*On Sophistical Refutations*
Top.	*Topics*

[Aristot.]   pseudo-Aristotle (4th c. B.C.E.), H. van Herwerden & J. van Leeuwen, edd., Leiden, Sijthoff 1891, reissued 1951. H. Rackham, tr., Loeb 1952 <1935, rev. 1938>.

Ath. Pol.	*Athenian Polity* or *Athenian Constitution*	335–322

Aristox.   Aristoxenus of Tarentum (4th c. B.C.E.), *FHG* 2.269.

A. S.   Athanis Siculus (4th c. B.C.E.), *FGrH* 562.

Ath.   Athenaeus (2–3rd c. C.E.), G. Kaibel, ed., T 1985–1992 <1887–1890>.

Callis.   Callisthenes (4th c. B.C.E.), *FGrH* 124.

Cal.   Callias (5th c. B.C.E.), *PCG* 4 frr. 1–40, pp. 38–53.

Atal.	*Atalanta*	frr. 1–4, pp. 41–2	n.d.
Ped.	*Pedētae* (Men in fetters)	frr. 14–23, pp. 46–8	≤429–428

Cic.   Cicero, Marcus Tullius (1st c. B.C.E.), A. S. Wilkins, ed., OCT 1892.

Acad.	*Academicae Quaestiones*
Bru.	*Brutus*
De fato	(On fate)
De fini.	*De Finibis* (On ends)
De invent.	*De Inventione Rhetorica* (On rhetorical invention)
De nat.	*De Natura Deorum* (On the nature of gods)
De orat.	*De Oratore* (On the orator)
Or.	*Orator*
Rep.	*De Re Publica* (On the state)
Tus. Dis.	*Tusculanae Disputationes*

Cle.   Clearchus (4–3rd c. B.C.E.), *FHG* 2.302.

Ctes.   Ctesias (5–4th c. B.C.E.), *FGrH* 688.

Crater.   Craterus (4–3rd c. B.C.E.), *FGrH* 342.

Crat.   Cratinus (5th c. B.C.E.), *PCG* 4 frr. 1–514, pp. 112–337.

Arch.	*Archilochi*	frr. 1–16, pp. 121–30	±430
Chi.	*Chirōnes*	frr. 246–68, pp. 245–57	<430
Cleo.	*Cleobulinae*	frr. 92–101, pp. 167–71	n.d.
Dion.	*Dionysalexandros*	*P.Oxy.* 663, pp. 140–1	
		+ frr. 39–51, pp. 141–7	430 or 429
Pyt.	*Pytinē* or *Wine Flask*	frr. 193–217, pp. 219–32	423
Thr.	*Thraltae*	frr. 73–89, pp. 159–66	±430
Troph.	*Trophōnios*	frr. 233–45, pp. 239–44	n.d.

Dem. Phal.   Demetrius Phalereus (4th c. B.C.E.), *FGrH* 228.

Demos.   Demosthenes (4th c. B.C.E.), C. Fuhr, ed., T 1994 <1914>. J. H. Vince, C. A. Vince, & A. T. Murray, trr., *Orations* etc., Loeb 1936–1949, 7 vols.

4	*First Philippic*	351
9	*Third Philippic*	341
18	*On the Crown*	330
19	*On the Embassy*	343
20	*Against Leptines*	355
21	*Against Meidias*	≥352
22	*Against Androtion*	355
23	*Against Aristocrates*	352
24	*Against Timocrates*	353
27	*Against Aphobos* I	363
35	*Against Lacritus*	n.d.
36	*For Phormio*	351/0
57	*Against Eubulides*	345
60	*Funeral Speech*	338
61	*Erotic Essay*	>355

[Demos.]   pseudo-Demosthenes

25	*Against Aristogeiton 1*	338–324
26	*Against Aristogeiton 2*	338–324

[Demos.] *continued*

40	*Against Boeotus* II	n.d.
47	*Against Evergus and Mnesibulus*	>356
49	*Apollodorus against Timotheus*	>362
50	*Apollodorus against Polycles*	359
52	*Apollodorus against Callippus*	±368
58	*Against Theocrines*	>343
59	*Apollodorus against Neaera*	>369

Did.   Didymus of Alexandria (1st c. B.C.E.), *FGrH* 340.

Din.   Dinarchus (4–3rd c. B.C.E.), F. Blass, ed., T 1888.

Diod. Ath. Diodorus Atheniensis (4th c. B.C.E.), *FGrH* 372.

D. S.   Diodorus Siculus (1st c. B.C.E.), I. Bekker, L. Dindorf, F. Vogel, & C. T. Fischer, edd., T 1888–1906. C. H. Oldfather et al., trr., *The Library of History*, Loeb 1933, vols. 4–7.

D. L.   Diogenes Laertius (3rd c. C.E.), H. S. Long, ed., OCT 1964. R. D. Hicks, tr., *Lives of the Eminent Philosophers*, Loeb 1972 <1925>, 2 vols.

D. H.   Dionysius of Halicarnassus (1st c. B.C.E.), S. Usher, tr., Loeb 1974, 1985, 2 vols.

AR	*Antiquitates Romanae*	*Isoc.*	*On Isocrates*
Dem.	*On Demosthenes*	*Lys.*	*On Lysias*
Isae.	*On Isaeus*	*Thu.*	*On Thucydides*

Eph.   Ephippus (4th c. B.C.E.), *PCG* 5 frr. 1–28, pp. 131–52.

Nau.	*Nauangus*	fr. 14, pp. 142–3	±380–360

Epi.   Epicrates (4th c. B.C.E.), *PCG* 5 frr. 1–11, pp. 153–63.

Ant.	*Antilaïs*	frr. 1–4, pp. 153–6	n.d.
	play uncertain	frr. 9–10, pp. 160–3	n.d.

Eu.   Eupolis (5th c. B.C.E.), *PCG* 5 frr. 1–494, pp. 294–539.

Ast.	*Astrateutoi*	frr. 35–47, pp. 314–20	?429
Auto.	*Autolycus*	frr. 48–75, pp. 320–31	420
Bap.	*Bapta*	frr. 76–98, pp. 331–42	424–415
Dem.	*Demes*	frr. 99–146, pp. 342–76	412
Flatt.	*Flatterers (Kolakes)*	frr. 156–90, pp. 380–98	421
Goats	*(Aiges)*	frr. 1–34, pp. 302–14	<422
Mar.	*Maricas*	frr. 192–217, pp. 399–424	421
Pol.	*Poleis*	frr. 218–58, pp. 424–41	±420

Eucl.   Euclid (3rd c. B.C.E.), J. L. Heiberg, H. Menge, & C. Curtze, edd., *Elements*, T 1883–1916, 9 vols.

Fav.   Favorinus (2nd c. C.E.), *FHG* 3.577.

Gell.   Aulus Gellius (2nd c. C.E.), P. K. Marshall, ed., OCT 1968.

NA	*Attic Nights (Noctes Atticae)*

Harp.   Harpocration (1–2nd c. CE), W. Dindorf, ed., OCT 1853.

Alc.	*Alcibiades*
Asp.	*Aspasia*

Hera. Lemb.   Heraclides Lembus (2nd c. B.C.E.), *FHG* 3.167.

Hera. Pont.   Heraclides Ponticus (4th c. B.C.E.), *FHG* 2.197.

Hermipp.   Hermippus (5th c. B.C.E.), *PCG* 5 frr. 1–94, pp. 561–604.

  Art.   *Artopolides*   frr. 7–12, pp. 565–8   420–419

Her. *hist.*   Hermippus (3–2nd c. B.C.E.), *FHG* 3.35.

Hermog.   Hermogenes (2nd c. C.E.), H. Rabe, ed., T 1913.

  Id.   *On Ideas (Peri Ideōn)*

Hdt.   Herodotus (5th c. B.C.E.), *The Histories*, C. Hude, ed., OCT 1926–1927.

Hier. Card.   Hieronymus Cardianus (4–3rd c. B.C.E.), *FGrH* 154.

Hippo.   Hippolytus (3rd c. C.E.), *Refutatio Omnium Haeresium* (Refutation of all heresies), P. Wendland, ed., Leipzig, Hinrichs 1916, reprinted, Olms 1977.

Hippoc.   Hippocrates (5th c. B.C.E.), W. H. S. Jones & P. Potter, edd., Loeb 1962– 8 vols.

Iamb.   Iamblichus (4th c. C.E.), *VP*, L. Deubner & U. Klein, edd., 2nd edn., T 1975. *CMS*, H. Pistelli, ed., 2nd edn., T 1975.

  CMS   *De Communi Mathematica Scientia* (On general mathematical science)
  VP   *De Vita Pythagorica Liber* (On the life of Pythagoras)

[Iamb.]   pseudo-Iamblichus, V. de Falco & U. Klein, edd., 2nd edn., T 1975.

  TA   *Theologoumena Arithmeticae* (Theology of arithmetic)

Isae. Isaeus (4th c. B.C.E.), Th. Thalheim, ed., T 1963 <1903>.

5	*On the Estate of Dicaeogenes*	390 or 389
18 (fr.)		>357

Isocr. Isocrates (5–4th c. B.C.E.), Friedrich Blass, ed., T 1889–1898. David C. Mirhady & Yun Lee Too, trr., *Isocrates* I, Austin, University of Texas, 2000. Letter: Larue Van Hook, tr., *Isocrates*, Loeb 1945, vol. 3. Dates are those of Mirhady and Too.

5	*To Philip*	346
7	*Areopagiticus*	±357
8	*On the Peace*	355
10	*Encomium of Helen*	370
11	*Busiris*	391–385
13	*Against the Sophists*	390
15	*Antidosis*	354–353
16	*On the Team of Horses* (fr.)	397–396
18	*Special Plea against Callimachus*	402
20	*Against Lochites*	394
Let. 1	*To Dionysius* (fr.)	368

Lycurg. Lycurgus (4th c. B.C.E.), F. Blass, ed., T 1899.

Leocr.	*Against Leocrates*	331/0

Lys. Lysias (5–4th c. B.C.E.), E. Medda, ed., *Lisia, Orazioni: Introduzione, premessa al testo, traduzione e note*, Milan 1992–1995, 2 vols. S. C. Todd, tr., *Lysias*, Austin, University of Texas, 2000. Numbers and dates follow Todd.

1	*On the Death of Eratosthenes*	n.d.
3	*Against Simon*	>394
5	*For Callias*	n.d.
8	*Against the Members of a Sunousia*	n.d.
10	*Against Theomnestus for Defamation*	384/3
12	*Against Eratosthenes*	403/2

Lys. *continued*

13	*Against Agoratus*	≥399
14	*Against Alcibiades 1* (for deserting the ranks)	395
15	*Against Alcibiades 2* (for refusal of military service)	395
18	*On the Property of Nicias' Brother*	≤395
19	*On the Property of Aristophanes*	≥390
21	*On a Charge of Accepting Bribes*	403/2
24	*For the Disabled Man*	>403
25	*On a Charge of Overthrowing the Democracy*	≥400
26	*Against Euandrus*	382
27	*Against Epicrates*	395–387
28	*Against Ergocles*	>389
30	*Against Nicomachus*	≥399
32	*Against Diogeiton*	≥400
fr. 1	*Against Aeschines the Socratic*	>399
fr. 4	*Against Cinesias*	n.d.
fr. 6	*Against the Sons of Hippocrates*	n.d.
fr. 8	*Against Theomnestus*	n.d.
fr. 9	*For Eryximachus*	>402
fr. 10	*Against Theozotides*	>402
fr. 11	*Concerning Antiphon's Daughter*	>403

[Lys.] pseudo-Lysias

2	*Funeral Speech*	>394
6	*Against Andocides*	400 or 399
11	*Against Theomnestus for Defamation* (epitome of 10)	384/3

Mar. Marcellinus (?4th c. C.E.), included in Thucydides OCT (see below).

Maxim. Maximus of Tyre (2nd c. C.E.), M. B. Trapp, ed., T 1994.

Menan.	Menander (4–3rd c. B.C.E.), frr. in *PCG* 6.2.			
	Can.	*Canephorus*	frr. 196–200, pp. 143–5	n.d.

Met.	Metagenes (5–4th c. B.C.E.), in *PCG* 7 frr. 1–20, pp. 4–13.			
	Soph.	*Sophists*	frr. 10–2, pp. 9–10	>400
	Phil.	*Philothytes*	frr. 13–66, pp. 10–2	410–405

Nean.	Neanthes of Cyzicus (3rd c. B.C.E.), *FGrH* 84.

Nep.	Cornelius Nepos (1st c. BCE), E. O. Winstedt, ed., OCT 1904.	
	Alc.	*Alcibiades*
	Arist.	*Aristides*
	Cim.	*Cimon*
	Dion	
	Tim.	*Timoleon*

Pap.	Pappus (3rd c. C.E.), W. Thomson & G. Junge, edd. and trr., *The Commentary of Pappus on Book X of Euclid's Elements*, Cambridge, HUP 1930.

Pau.	Pausanias (mid 2nd c. C.E.), W. Jones, ed., Loeb 1918–1935.

Phae.	Phaedo (5–4th c. B.C.E.), frr. in *SSR* 1.IIIA, with Rossetti (1973, 1980).

Pher.	Pherecrates (5th c. B.C.E.), *PCG* 7 frr. 1–288, pp. 102–220.			
	Chi.	*Chirōn*	frr. 155–62, pp. 178–86	n.d.
	Ip.	*Ipnos or Panuchis*	frr. 64–72, pp. 132–36	≥415
	Sav.	*Savages (Agrioi)*	frr. 5–20, pp. 106–14	420

Philist.	Philistus of Syracuse (4th c. B.C.E.), *FGrH* 556.

Philoch.	Philochorus (4th c. B.C.E.), *FGrH* 328.

Philod.   Philodemus (1st c. B.C.E.), K. Gaiser, ed., *Academicorum Index* (Index of the Academy), Stuttgart-Bad Cannstaat, Frommann-Holzboog 1988.

Philostr.   Philostratus (2–3rd c. C.E.), C. L. Kayser, ed., T 1870, 1871.

> *VA*   *Vita Apollonii*
>
> *VS*   *Vitae Sophistarum* (Lives of the sophists)

Phot.   Photius (9th c. C.E.), *Bibliotheca*, R. Henry, ed., Paris, Société d'édition Les Belles lettres 1959–1977; *Lexicon*, S. A. Naber, ed., Leiden, E. J. Brill 1864–5.

> *Bibl.*   *Bibliotheca*
>
> *Lex.*   *Lexicon*

Phryn.   Phrynichus (5th c. B.C.E.), *PCG* 7 frr. 1–93, pp. 393–430.

> *Con.*   *Connus*   frr. 6–8, pp. 398–9   423
>
> *Mon.*   *Monotropus*   frr. 19–31, pp. 403–9   414

Pl.   Plato (5–4th c. B.C.E.), J. Burnet, ed., OCT 1901–1906; rev. edn. in progress: E. A. Duke, W. F. Hicken, W. S. M. Nicoll, D. B. Robinson, & J. C. G. Strachan, edd., OCT 1995–   ; scholia, W. C. Greene et al., edd., Haverford, American Philological Society 1938; G. M. A. Grube et al., trr., *Plato: Complete Works* (PCW), ed. J. M. Cooper with D. S. Hutchinson, Indianapolis, Hackett 1997.

Ap.	*Apology*	*Mx.*	*Menexenus*
Chrm.	*Charmides*	*Meno*	
Cra.	*Cratylus*	*Phd.*	*Phaedo*
Crito		*Phdr.*	*Phaedrus*
Criti.	*Critias*	*Phlb.*	*Philebus*
Euthd.	*Euthydemus*	*Prm.*	*Parmenides*
Euthphr.	*Euthyphro*	*Prt.*	*Protagoras*
Grg.	*Gorgias*	*R.*	*Republic*
Ion		*Sph.*	*Sophist*
Lch.	*Laches*	*Stm.*	*Statesman*
Laws		*Smp.*	*Symposium*
Ltr.	*Letters 7, 8*	*Tht.*	*Theaetetus*
Ly.	*Lysis*	*Ti.*	*Timaeus*

[Pl.] pseudo-Plato, [Plato]

Alc.	*Alcibiades*	*Hal.*	*Halcyon*
2Alc.	*Second Alcibiades*	*Hppr.*	*Hipparchus*
Ax.	*Axiochus*	*L. Hp.*	*Lesser Hippias*
Clt.	*Clitophon*	*Ltr.*	*Letters 1–6, 9–13*
Def.	*Definitions*	*Minos*	
Dem.	*Demodocus*	*Just.*	*On Justice*
Epgr.	*Epigrams*	*Virt.*	*On Virtue*
Epin.	*Epinomis*	*Riv.*	*Rival Lovers*
Eryx.	*Eryxias*	*Sis.*	*Sisyphus*
G. Hp.	*Greater Hippias*	*Thg.*	*Theages*

Pl. *com.* Plato *comicus* (5–4th c. B.C.E.), *PCG* 7 frr. 1–303, pp. 431–548.

Peri.	*Perialge*	frr. 114–7, pp. 479–82	n.d.
Pis.	*Pisander*	frr. 102–13, pp. 475–9	<412
Syr.	*Syrphax*	frr. 175–81, pp. 502–4	n.d.

Pli. Pliny (1st c. C.E.), "The Elder," L. Jan & C. Mayhoff, edd., T 1967–1996 <1892–1909>.

HN	*Historia Naturalis*

Plu. Plutarch (1–2nd c. C.E.), C. Lindskog & K. Ziegler, edd., *Vitae Parallelae*, T 1960– . C. E. H. Hubert et al., edd., *Moralia*, T 1959–1978. B. Perrin, tr., *Plutarch's Lives*, Loeb 1916, vols. 3 & 4.

Alc.	*Alcibiades*	*Lys.*	*Lysander*
Arist.	*Aristides*	*Mor.*	*Moralia*
Cat. Mi.	*Cato Minor*	*Nic.*	*Nicias*
Cim.	*Cimon*	*Pel.*	*Pelopidas*
Dem.	*Demosthenes*	*Per.*	*Pericles*
Dion		*Phoc.*	*Phocion*
Lyc.	*Lycurgus*	*Th.*	*Themistocles*

[Plu.]   pseudo-Plutarch

                LTO   *Lives of the Ten Orators* (= *Mor.* 832b–852e)

Polem.   Polemon (2nd c. B.C.E.), *FHG* 3.108.

Poll.   Pollux (2nd c. C.E.), E. Bethe, ed., *Onamastikon*, T 1900–1937.

Polyae.   Polyaenus (2nd c. C.E.), J. Melber, ed., *Strategemata*, T 1887.

Procl.   Proclus (5th c. C.E.), E. Diehl, ed., T 1903, 1904, 1906. 3 vols.

                in Tim.   *Commentary on Plato's* Timaeus
                Eucl.   *Commentary on Euclid*

San.   Sannyrio (5th c. B.C.E.), *PCG* 7 frr. 1–13, pp. 585–9.

                Gel.   *Gelōs*   frr. 1–7, pp. 585–7   n.d.
                Dan.   *Danae*   frr. 8–10, p. 588   n.d.

Sat.   Satyrus (3rd c. B.C.E.), *FGrH* 631; *P. Oxy.* 1176 (*Life of Euripides*).

[Socr.]   pseudo-Socrates (4th c. B.C.E.), Rudolf Hercher, ed., Amsterdam, Hakkert 1966 <1873>.

                Ep.   *Socratis et Socraticorum Epistulae*

Speu.   Speusippus (4th c. B.C.E.), Leonardo Tarán, ed. and tr., *Speusippus of Athens: A Critical Study with a Collection of the Related Texts and Commentary*, Leiden, E. J. Brill 1981.

Stes.   Stesimbrotus of Thasos (5th c. B.C.E.), *FGrH* 107.

Stob.   Stobaeus, Johannes (5th c. C.E.), C. Wachsmuth & O. Hense, edd., Berlin, Weidmann 1884–1923.

Str.   Strabo (1st c. B.C.E.–1st c. C.E.), H. L. Jones & J. R. Sitlington, edd., Loeb 1969.

Strat.   Strattis (5–4th c. B.C.E.), *PCG* 7 frr. 1–91, pp. 623–60.

Atal.	*Atalanta*	frr. 3–8, pp. 626–8	n.d.
Cin.	*Cinesias*	frr. 14–22, pp. 631–4	n.d.
Mac.	*Macedonians* or *Pausanias*	frr. 27–33, pp. 636–8	n.d.

Synes.   Synesius of Cyrene (4–5th c. C.E.), N. Terzaghi, ed., Rome, Typis Regiae Officinae Polygraphicae 1939–1944.

Tele.   Teleclides (5th c. B.C.E.), *PCG* 7 frr. 1–73, pp. 667–92.

Them.   Themistius (4th c. C.E.), H. Schenkl, G. Downey & A. F. Norman, edd., T 1965–1974.

Theo.   Theopompus (5th c. B.C.E.), *PCG* 7 frr. 1–108, pp. 708–49.

Kap.	*Kapēlides*	frr. 25–9, pp. 719–21	n.d.
Strat.	*Stratiōtides*	frr. 55–9, pp. 733–5	n.d.

Theop. *hist.*   Theopompus of Chios (4th c. B.C.E.), *FGrH* 115.

Thu.   Thucydides (5th c. B.C.E.), H. Stuart-Jones (rev. J. E. Powell), edd., *The Peloponnesian War*, OCT 1942. S. Lattimore, tr., *The Peloponnesian War*, Indianapolis, Hackett 1998.

Timae.   Timaeus (4–3rd c. B.C.E.), *FGrH* 566.

Tim.   Timonides of Leucas (4th c. B.C.E.), *FGrH* 561.

Xen.   Xenophon (5th c. B.C.E.), C. Hude, ed., T 1985 <1934>. E. C. Marchant, tr., *Memorabilia* and *Oeconomicus*, and O. J. Todd, tr., *Symposium* and *Apology*, Loeb 1923. Carleton L. Brownson, tr., *Hellenica*, Loeb 1918, 2 vols. Carleton L. Brownson, tr., rev. John Dillery, *Anabasis*, Loeb 1998.

Anab.	*Anabasis*		*Mem.*	*Memorabilia*
Apol.	*Apology*		*Oec.*	*Oeconomicus*
Cyr.	*Cyropaedia*		*Symp.*	*Symposium*
Hell.	*Hellenica*		WM	*Ways and Means*

Zos.   Zosimus (5th c. C.E.), L. Mendelssohn, ed., T 1887, reprinted, Olms 1963.

Isoc.	*Life of Isocrates*

Common Abbreviations and Symbols

abbr.	abbreviated		fasc.	fascicle
add.	additional		fem.	feminine form
a.k.a.	also known as		fl.	*flourit*, flourished
anon.	anonymous		fr.	fragment (pl. frr.)
app.	appendix (pl. apps.)		i.e.	*id est*, that is
b.	born		km.	kilometer (0.621371 mile)
B.C.E.	before the common era		lit.	literally
bk.	book		ln.	line (pl. lnn.)
c.	century/centuries		m.	married
C.E.	common era		masc.	masculine form
cf.	*confer*, compare		ms.	manuscript (pl. mss.)
corr.	corrected		n	note (pl. nn)
div.	divorced		n.d.	no date
ed.	editor, edited by (pl. edd.)		no.	number (pl. nos.)
edn.	edition		n.p.	no publisher
e.g.	*exempli gratia*, for example		n.s.	new series
epon.	eponymous		p.	page (pl. pp.)
esp.	especially		pat.	patronymic
et al.	*et alii*, and others		pl.	plural
etc.	*et cetera*, and the rest		r.	reigned, ruled
exc.	excursus		rev.	revised
f.	and the following page/ line (pl. ff.)		s.	singular
			schol.	scholium, scholia

supp.	supplement, supplements		±	*circa*, about
s.v.	*sub verbo*, under the word (pl. s.vv.)		>	after
			≥	in or after
test.	testimonia		<	before
tr.	translator (pl. trr.), translated by		≤	in or before
			=	is the same as
var.	variant spelling		?=	is possibly the same as
viz.	*videlicet*, namely		?	(preceding a name, date,
vol.	volumes (pl. vols.)			or relationship) possibly
*	alive		♀	female, name unknown
†	dead		♂	male, name unknown
§	section (pl. §§)		< >	(enclosing a date) copyright
&	and			right

INTRODUCTION

This book is a concise guide to the persons represented in the Platonic dialogues. It is a prosopography, an account of individuals in their relations to one another and to the major events of their times, the bare bones on which biography and history could be fleshed out. While focusing on the familial and social environment of Socrates and the young Plato, I have included for convenience persons from the Socratica of Xenophon, Aeschines, Antisthenes, and Phaedo, and persons associated with Plato's maturity. I aimed to write a useful book, a one-volume reference to the people of Socrates' milieu that could also assist further research on those individuals. Although the information presented here may be helpful to others, I have written it with one very specific audience in mind, *those who teach and research the philosophy of Plato*, among whom I include myself. We need this book for two reasons.

One is the difficulty of access to the material. The expensive, multivolume sources are not widely available outside the libraries of a few major research universities, where they are most often in noncirculating collections. The basic sources then point to other materials in far-flung places in the familiar variety of languages. And physical lack of availability is only half the problem, for there are disciplinary issues as well. Some of the prosopographical sources, even in hand, are difficult to decipher without expertise that our graduate training in philosophy rarely leaves time for us to acquire. For current information, we must depend on researchers outside philosophy who do not focus on Plato, some of whom consider it a big mistake to focus on Plato. Understandably, when confronted with a character in a dialogue, our practice has been to turn to the history of our own discipline to find out what our august forebears have already concluded. But some of the most respected commentaries are prosopographically out of date, and our continuing to rely on them, or to depend on others who rely on them, perpetuates misidentifications and misinterpretations.

The better reason derives from the nature of the Platonic texts. They are dialogues representing specific, named individuals in conversations with one another. Plato did not invent Athenians with names, demes, and kin; he wrote about real people—some of them still active and living in Athens—people with reputations, families, neighbors and political affiliations, people who show up elsewhere in the existing historical record: lampooned in comedies, called as witnesses, elected to office, being sold, marrying, buying property, traveling, dying. Socrates' society was not only a matter of institutions and ideologies, but a matter of actual people, individuals within a nexus of familial, social, and political relationships, without whom Plato's dialogues would be denatured. I am *not* saying that any specific detail or particular configuration of details—certainly none from Plato's historical context—offers a key for unlocking the meaning of any dialogue. Some of the worst readings of Plato have been grounded on that indefensible assumption. And I am not saying that Plato's philosophy is grounded in the specifics of his social and cultural environment in the sense that it is an inevitable outcome of that environment, interesting only or chiefly as a social construction of that particular time and place. I am saying that the lives of the people of Plato, insofar as they can be reconstructed, need to be read back into the dialogues in an informed and responsible way. It is sometimes important to get the history right. Who a person was can *matter* to the range of plausible interpretations of a dialogue.

Socrates and others make arguments in the dialogues, and arguments can be abstracted from their surroundings and tested for soundness. They stand or fall on their own, regardless of context, regardless of the characteristics of the speaker or the relationships between speakers, as Plato's Socrates often reminds us (*Republic* 1.349a–b, *Gorgias* 473b, *Symposium* 201c–d). It is just as clear, however, that arguments abstracted from context are not what Plato's dialogues provide. Instead, they give us arguments made by specific people with identifiable histories and in determinate relationships with others. In this way, Plato's dialogues instantiate and illustrate the conduct of philosophy. This fact about Plato's dialogues—that they present us with specific individuals in conversation—is something we should take very seriously. Platonic specificity is the unalterable basic condition of not only the dialogues but Plato's conduct of philosophy. I happen to agree with Socrates and Glaucon that philosophy is a yearning for and seeking of Truth of a very particular kind (*Republic* 5.475e), but we cannot reach the universal except by way of particulars; there is no unmediated apprehension of the fundamental principle of the all. So, although arguments can be addressed independently of the text, those arguments are not Plato's dialogues and no longer represent how he conducted philosophy. Plato's dialogues are irreducibly an interplay between specific and universal; understanding the *process* that is philosophy requires us to confront that interplay.

This book can aid in that effort. Whereas previous researchers have addressed discrepancies among Plato and other sources on the assumption that Plato was historically unreliable and should be used only as a last resort, my research shows that there is much to be gained on the opposite assumption: the people of Plato, unless there is strong evidence to the contrary, should be taken as he presents them. Some of the results of that procedure have challenged my previous picture of Socrates' milieu. Stone inscriptions have long given us access to the propertied classes, to the individuals who enjoyed permanent records of their benefactions and achievements, but there were many from the lower classes of Athens as well, and many who supported the democracy. Scholarship has often passed those individuals by, with cumulative effect. Many names, especially those of women, have been lost, contributing to the tendency among scholars to omit females from stemmata altogether, as in Marchant's stemma from his Loeb edition of Xenophon's *Memorabilia*—a tribute perhaps to the Athenian male's uncanny ability to reproduce asexually. But Charmides and Ariston were not brothers, so the

image distorts the relationship. Sometimes, kinship among males is hidden until
the women are reintroduced. In *Protagoras*,
for example, discussions of education and
democracy are given added dimension
with the realization that the central Athen-

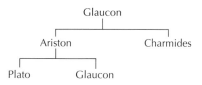

ian figures of that dialogue are all members of Pericles' household or extended
family—something invisible until Callias' mother, the former wife of Pericles, is
added to the family stemma. Similarly, one's understanding of the *Republic* is
increased when more is understood about who the characters really were, especially the long neglected political reed, Clitophon, the sons of the *metic* Cephalus,
and a Thrasymachus made sympathetic through one's knowledge of what his
native city feared from Athens at the time of the actual man's visit. The *Republic*
gathers together a remarkable cross-section of greater Greece, not an aristocratic
few, and not youths. David's painting, *Death of Socrates*, has contributed as much
as anything in the dialogues themselves to the widespread view that Socrates
was surrounded by young male aristocrats, and yet that view is misguided—just
wrong for the *Phaedo* where, apart from "some others" (*Phd.* 59b) whose identities
we do not know, only two of the twenty-three are attested in the Athenian
aristocracy, and at most five are Athenian men under thirty. There are three slaves
and a former slave, a *nothos*, two or three women, three children, and six foreigners,
only one of whom appears to be wealthy.

Apart from filling in information about individuals, this book also takes into
account historical events that impinge on the dialogues. For example, my research
shows that if Plato's *Charmides* is taken literally in light of Thucydides' detailed
account of the siege of Potidaea, many assumptions that have been made about
Plato's family must be abandoned. Surprisingly, perhaps, the resulting picture of
Plato's relations is clearer than the one it replaces, dissolving some existing disputes. On four subjects, the book provides self-contained discussions of historical
material that impinges on several of the dialogues and the people who populate
them: the mutilation of herms and its aftermath from 415, the trial of the generals
after Arginusae in 406, the succession of the Thirty in 404, and the amnesty forged
to effect a lasting peace after 403.

A number of things are outside the scope of this book. Although I do not
discuss the people of Plato as characters in a literary construction, I deeply admire
Ruby Blondell's *The Play of Character in Plato's Dialogues*, which recognizes that
philosophical dialogues require us to confront the question of who the people
were, "Since dialogue form entails the representation of persons, a concern with
human character and its portrayal is literally essential to reading Plato's works
in a way that takes their form into account" (2002: 2). It is one thing to present
characters; it is another to represent persons. The two approaches are complementary within the wider interpretation of Plato, but I am dealing with the latter.
Similarly, I have little to say about persons and affairs of state in the fourth
century, and nothing to say about the dialogues' dates of composition. I offer
nothing whatever on fictional persons, absent persons, symbolism, or the etymolo-
gizing of characters' names. For that approach to Plato, I refer the reader to the
numerous works of Slobodan Dušanić of the University of Belgrade, a former

fellow of the Institute for Advanced Study, Princeton, and historian of the fourth century, who has combined the literary and fourth-century historical subjects over many years.

I have not written a perfect book. There are errors. Of course I do not know where, but a hazard of prosopography is that one cannot get everything exactly right. Each time one reads the material, new questions and new connections present themselves for examination and refinement. To a prosopographer, corrections are "nectar and ambrosia," as John Traill puts it, and he's right. Two implications of that are (a) I deeply appreciate corrections, and (b) I am not being churlish or merely pedantic when I note where other studies have erred on matters of citation or fact. All prosopographies do this. Only by pointing out an error can I save the reader from having to investigate an inconsistency to find out whether it is an error in this book.

The information I present has two aspects: conclusions as bare "facts" about individuals, and more extensive discussions of controversies, i.e., the arguments on which some of the conclusions are based. Readers will be more interested in one or the other as their needs dictate. Those interested in the first may find it useful to jump ahead now to *How to Use This Book* at the end of this introduction. But others will be frustrated—as I was—with prosopographical pronouncements *ex cathedra*, and will want to evaluate the arguments about the persons independently. Since it is impractical to repeat my method and premises at each entry, what I set out in the remainder of this introduction is a basic orientation to this type of research. No doubt there are many issues I have considered settled that others will contest. Good.

On Sources:

I have used and incorporated ancient inscriptions, the work of contemporaneous historians, literary figures, and speech writers, occasional late antique compilations, and inferences from the primary sources in modern secondary sources. The editions and translations of ancient texts that I consulted are listed with their abbreviations in the separate section, Abbreviations, Ancient Texts and Translations. For modern works, and for additional bibliographical material on frequently used sources cited only by abbreviation in the text, see the list of works cited and consulted at the back of the book.

Although I include references to many late sources, I am not comprehensive through the late antique period, and I rarely discuss them except when they seem to color modern conceptions of the people of Plato. I have privileged contemporaneous sources (5th and 4th c. B.C.E.) to a greater extent than have some who have studied these issues from a historical and philological perspective. By doing so, I am leaving as much interpretation and speculation as possible to others, hoping thereby to provide minimal but more reliable accounts of individuals than are offered by the full and rich—if often dubious—biographies of late antiquity.

Consider Madeline Henry: "It is treacherous but obligatory to begin with the most concentrated and connected account of Aspasia's life, that found in chapters 24 and 32 of Plutarch's *Life of Pericles*" (1995: 9). I consider it my obligation to do the opposite *because* our collective view of Socrates' milieu has been distorted by centuries of encrusted interpretation that began early in Hellenistic times. Plutarch, a moralist disowned by historians (Lewis *CAH* 6²: 9, "Sources and Their Uses"), was a marvelous storyteller writing in the 1st and 2nd c. c.e., who used scissors and glue to achieve those concentrated and connected narratives. In my view, if one deliberately begins with lively and memorable but distorted images, one only makes it harder to rid oneself of false beliefs, harder to recognize a challenging anomaly. Yet it is not possible to banish such sources altogether. Not only do they sometimes quote documents and cite contemporaneous material, they are so often used by contemporary historians who debate the past that omitting them would make it almost impossible to lay out for the reader which debates have worn down to consensus and which are still alive. Thus I minimize my use of late sources and accept its consequence for this volume: frustrating fragments, wide gaps, no glue.

A special use of a late source is Diodorus Siculus: contemporary changes in attitude toward him have propelled him into competition with Xenophon's *Hellenica* for the period following the abrupt and premature end of Thucydides' *Peloponnesian War* in 411. Diodorus wrote in the latter part of the 1st c. b.c.e., using Ephorus of Cyme (a 4th c. b.c.e. student of Isocrates) as his chief source for the Socratic period. And Ephorus, in turn, appears to have used the unknown, sober historian nicknamed 'P' who authored a small batch of papyrus fragments discovered in the famous rubbish heap at Oxyrhynchus in Egypt. Where Diodorus' ultimate source is P, he provides a corrective for the sometimes moralizing, often selective, Xenophon. Because "Much recent work on the late fifth and early fourth centuries has been based on a growing preference for Diodorus over Xenophon" (Lewis, *CAH* 5²: 8), I have been obliged to cite Diodorus, but I hasten to add that my arguments have been influenced by the judgment of Rhodes (1993: 419) and Andrewes (1974: 119–20) that P is not Diodorus' source for the period of the Thirty. Another special case is the pseudo-Aristotelian *Athenian Polity* (or *Athenian Constitution*), compiled in the 330s–320s in the school of Aristotle in Athens (Rhodes 1993: 61) which is occasionally our only extant source for particular claims. Controversial is whether *it* uses P as its source, a position that has not found widespread support, and the extent to which it is reliable. For Plato's people, the period of crucial importance is again the period of the Thirty, and the aftermath of their rule, when the *Athenian Polity* conflicts with other sources. I discuss its reliability in context in the primer.

On Ancient Dates:

Through the careful work of historians, there are events that can now be dated precisely to season or month, often when civic duties and religious festivals were involved. A consequence of better dates is a greater understanding of the ages and circumstances of the characters in the dialogues, which in turn provides better grounds than we have previously had for determining the dramatic dates of the dialogues that have them at all. But the determination of ancient dates is a mine-field. Athenians simultaneously used three different and independent calendars in the 5th and 4th c. that were not in use elsewhere in Greece. Each of the calendars was subject to arbitrary official interference, and had in common only an initial reference to the observation or would-be observation of a new moon. The *lunar calendar* is the easy one. Since a lunar month is 29.53 days, the year was divided into full months (30 days) and hollow months (29 days), so each year had 353–5 days (but the same month could be full in one year and hollow in another, depending on astronomical observations at the time). To bring the twelve lunar months into accord with the solar year, an archon could intercalate an extra month—usually a second Posideon—immediately following the first. This occurred irregularly, but produced leap years of 383–5 days when it was used. The months of the lunar calendar listed here (originally the names of festivals)

1. Hekatombaion	5. Maimakterion	9. Elaphebolion
2. Metageitnion	6. Posideon	10. Mounychion
3. Boedromion	7. Gamelion	11. Thargelion
4. Pyanopsion	8. Anthesterion	12. Skirophorion

were also used for the calendar of the festival or archon year, but the two calendars were not synchronous. An archon could manipulate the *archon/festival calendar* by deleting or supplying days for social (*SEG* 14.65), military (Thu. 5.54.3), or other purposes. This led to discrepancies between the lunar and festival calendars of as much as thirty days (*IG* II² 947), and to a few inscriptions bearing two dates: one "according to the archon" and another "according to the god," i.e. the moon. The *prytany calendar* was often used in the dating of public documents and thus is of great value in epigraphical research, but it too was fluid. Until near the end of the 5th c., it comprised ten thirty-seven-day terms, after which the rule was four thirty-six-day, followed by six thirty-five-day, terms of the Prytanes of the Council (*boulē*) which rotated among tribes on a schedule determined by lot. Until 407 (*IG* I² 304B), the new Council could overlap the old set of archons; but, after 407, both the prytany and the archon/festival calendars counted the first day of the year from the first siting of the new moon following the summer solstice. Thus the year changed in midsummer.

In practical terms, when one encounters a date of the form 407/6, a solar year beginning in midsummer is meant. The date 407–406, however, means two solar years from the beginning of 407 to the end of 406. Sometimes it is possible to be more exact: the Arginusae trial, for example, occurred in Pyanopsion (roughly October) of the archon year 406/5, so—because October occurs early in the year—one can write 'October 406' correctly. There are oddities: for example, the greater Panathenaea festival is normally referred to by even years: '450' for the festival when Parmenides visited Athens, more properly designated '450/49,' or August of 450 to be more exact. Similarly, '422' is commonly used for Autolycus' pancratium victory of Hekatombaion (August) 422 of the year 422/1. Attentive readers will notice discrepancies, especially with older sources. Luckily, there are very few such practical implications to worry about in the study of Plato.

Ancient dates herein are B.C.E. unless designated C.E.

AGES AND DATING CONVENTIONS:

Much prosopographical work involves determining who was of the right age and financial standing to be the subject of an inscription or text. To that end, some of the landmarks of Athenian lives in the late 5th and early 4th c. can be useful:

5 days: new infants were carried around the hearth and formally entered into the family in the *amphidromia* ceremony

10 days: new infants received names from their fathers in the *dekatē* ceremony

13–14 years: females became eligible to marry (or a year after puberty), though they were perpetual legal minors

17–18: males reached the age of legal majority: "An Athenian male child seems to have been almost wholly free from parental control as soon as he reached the end of his seventeenth (conceivably eighteenth) year. At that point he was presented by his father or guardian to his demesmen, and, after passing an examination [*dokimasia*] into his qualifications to be a citizen by them and by the *boulē*, he was enrolled among the demesmen" (Harrison 1998: 1.74, citing [Aristot.] *Ath. Pol.* 24.1).

18: males undertook military duties within Attica (Garland 1990: 183, citing [Aristot.] *Ath. Pol.* 42.3–5; the rules were not formalized into the ephebic system until ±370)

20: males became eligible to fight in battle outside the frontiers of Attica

30: males became eligible to serve on the Council (*boulē*), or juries, to be *archon*, general (*stratēgos*), or *trierarch*

30, 40: males became eligible to be *chorēgos* ([Aristot.] *Ath. Pol.* 56.3): 40 by mid-4th c., though 30 was sufficient earlier

40: males became eligible to serve on special commissions (e.g. the *proboulē*)

50: males became eligible to address the Assembly (*ecclēsia*) before younger men (Aes. *orat.* 1.23, 3.4; cf. Lys. 16.20)

In addition, in the modern secondary literature, one finds references to a *flourit* date, the supposed peak of a man's career at age forty. In that same literature, thirty years is taken as the hypothetical interval for generations, applicable in theory to men; it was previously thirty-three years, sometimes seen in older calculations, and more accurate, though still low. A hypothetical generation interval of twenty years is very occasionally used for women as an average childbearing date.

Such a list, however, oversimplifies the difficulties one encounters in the texts. Garland's *The Greek Way of Life*, adds the qualifier: "[T]he problem for this study is that age-related terms are not always used in precisely the same way from one community to the next or even, to cite an extreme case, by the same author within the space of two sentences (cf. Lys. 3.10; Hdt. 3.53; Antiph. 3.4.6 and 8) . . . Scholars remain undecided as to how the Greeks reckoned a person's age in years" (1990: 14). Garland's own admittedly imperfect but preferred solution is to translate ages 'in the nth year' as opposed to 'n years old.' Because the Greeks did not have a zero, and thus were deemed age one at birth, there is the possibility of a year's margin in each sum.

Onomastics:

Conventions of naming differed geographically, culturally, and over time. Five important naming practices are useful to identifications and pointed out in context in the primer. (1) By far the most widespread and ongoing practice was to name the first-born grandson after the paternal grandfather and the second after the maternal grandfather; sons were less frequently named after their fathers. Girls were sometimes named after their mothers, but we so rarely know the names of their grandmothers that we simply cannot infer that a parallel practice existed for girls with respect to their grandmothers. (2) Sometimes, a father's name was embedded in the name of a son, e.g. Critobulus embeds Crito. (3) Certain names were used regularly by the aristocratic classes, as Aristophanes claims (*Clouds* 60–67), e.g. 'Xanthippus' and 'Hippothales'. There does not seem to have been a corresponding set of slave names, though Athenians often renamed foreign slaves (Pl. *Cra.* 384d). (4) Sometimes, a prominent clan (*genos*) would have members with versions of the clan's name, e.g. the Alcmaeonids had male members named Alcmonides. (5) Politically programmatic names showed up from time to time so, e.g. Plato's stepbrother, the son of a prominent democrat, was Demos (people); Themistocles named some of his children for his campaigns, e.g. Asia; and Dionysius I named his daughters Sophrosyne, Dicaeosyne, and Arete, the Greek names for modesty, justice, and virtue. None of these conventions was rigid, and fashion could affect naming too. See Appendix III for the importance in Athens of the surname, i.e. the patronymic and demotic, for making identifications.

Guide to Other Prosopographies:

There are three watershed periods of prosopographical work that are of interest in connection with the Socratic circle. The first group (*PP, PX* and *PA*) predates the development of modern epigraphical and papyrological studies, but the numbers of *PA* mark the beginning of the modern era in prosopography. The second (*APF*) is in a class by itself. The third (*PAA, LGPN,* and *FRA*) incorporates computer databases. Alongside these run encyclopedia articles, arranged alphabetically, and not normally prosopographical: in German, the *Real-Encyclopädie der classischen Altertumswissenschaft* (*RE*); in French, the in-progress *Dictionnaire des philosophes antiques* (*DPhA*); and in English, the *Oxford Classical Dictionary* (*OCD*³). Seen very occasionally in this study are specialist prosopographies on Spartans (Poralla²) and persons from music, theatre, and the arts (Stephanis).

PP	Groen van Prinsterer, *Prosopographia Platonica* (1823, in Latin with Greek): the only existing Platonic prosopography; it includes mythical, legendary, and semihistorical figures that will be found nowhere else in prosopographies.
PX	Carel Gabriel Cobet, *Commentatio, qua continetur Prosopographia Xenophontea* (1836, in Latin with Greek): limited to historical persons in Xenophon.

PA   Joannes Kirchner, *Prosopographia Attica* (1901, 1903, in Latin with Greek): established entries for about two thirds of the names that require discussion from the Platonic corpus.

APF   John Kenyon Davies, *Athenian Propertied Families* (1971, in English with Greek): a model of thoroughness up to about 1969. I owe much to its full discussions. It is out of respect for *APF* that I cite it when disagreeing with its conclusions, for many of the dates I use are those of Davies, sometimes refined (both for persons, and for the events of their familial lives such as marriage). And we all owe to Davies a debt for revealing that group of Athenians Plato names *timocrats* (*Rep.* 8), but whom other authors lump together with aristocrats and oligarchs; *APF* features the liturgical class, the very rich who undertook established *liturgies* for the state as a type of tax, were proud of it, and expected to be honored by the people in return. Yet *APF* treats only about a *third* of the characters who appear in the dialogues and, possibly because of its class orientation, insinuates a bias into accounts of Socratics: "the possession of considerable wealth and adhesion to the party of the City in 404/3 are both characteristics to be expected of a Sokratic associate" (*APF*: 463)—*pace* Chaerephon, the sons of Cephalus, et al. That same bias is found in many ancient historians of the period (despite the useful corrections by, e.g., Rowe 1998, Monoson 2000, et al.). Socrates had a richer life than they imagine, as I expect this prosopography to demonstrate.

LGPN   S. G. Byrne, P. M. Fraser, E. Matthews, Michael J. Osborne, et al., *Lexicon of Greek Personal Names* (3 vols. in 4 published, 1987–in progress, in English with Greek): renumbers, organizes and systematizes known individuals in a clear format with updated epigraphic information, but otherwise simply sends the reader to *PA* and is not usable for locating texts.

FRA   Michael J. Osborne and S. G. Byrne, *Foreign Residents of Athens* (1996, in English with Greek): technically a supplement to the Athens volume of *LGPN*; includes many known slaves, metics, and some foreign visitors, but does not use Plato prosopographically, and has the same limitations as *LGPN*.

PAA   John Traill, *Persons of Ancient Athens* (10 vols. published of 20, 1994–in progress, in English with Greek and Latin) includes many metics, foreign visitors, and Athenians abroad. It is where any reader interested in further information should go for the Greek (and occasional Latin) *texts* of sources cited here, including late sources that I often name without discussion. Its entries are more extensive than those of other prosopographies, it updates the editions and citations of *PA*, and it is undergoing constant database revision as more information becomes available. It has been indispensable as an independent check on the people of Plato.

The advance of computer technology during the third watershed period has made information, and especially ancient inscriptions, more accessible; but it has not yet meant that information about individuals is readily available; material must still be collected from disparate sources; and much of it must be understood in the context of other issues and controversies. Much of the content of the entries (hundreds of thousands of names, fragments, and citations) has been entered by people with no special interest in Plato, and thus with *PA*'s original errors intact. Another oddity encountered with the vast database prosopographies that cannot but strike a philosopher is that, because passages of text are cited and consulted without context, information requiring inference—however valid, however well known—is very often missing because it cannot be proved by citing a particular text. Similarly, no rationales or explanations are provided when a person is split into two (e.g., Euthyphro in *LGPN*) or fused with someone previously thought to be a separate individual of the same name (e.g., Laches and Phaedrus in *LGPN*). For fusions and splittings of entries, and for inferences, one needs the prose explanations of an *APF*, but then one is limited to the upper classes and runs the risk of distorting one's view of Socrates' milieu. I address these issues in *The People of Plato* through discussions of the existing debates in the literature and through bibliographical citations to assist further research.

SPELLING, LANGUAGE, AND PUNCTUATION:

The names of people and places are Latinized here as in Plato: *Complete Works* (PCW). Other Greek words are transliterated by ordinary Hellenizing conventions, and a glossary is provided of Greek terms (as well as a few English terms used technically to translate particular Greek terms, e.g., 'Council' for *boulē*). The convention of referring to Greek works by Latin titles will still be encountered in some bibliographical citations. I have retained the Greek when my argument depends on a particular reading. I have retained original spellings in quotations from the secondary literature, enabling the reader to gain familiarity with the existing and unavoidable variety of spellings in the relatively safe context of a prosopography (e.g., 'Socrates,' 'Sokrates,' and 'Sōkratēs'). However alien it seems to those in other disciplines, philosophers find it useful to observe the use/mention distinction; thus I use single quotation marks for terms, double quotation marks to quote someone else's remarks and, rarely, as "scare quotes."

HOW TO USE THIS BOOK:

The entries in this study have a standard format so readers can see at a glance whether they have found the individual they seek (e.g., the wife of Socrates, the speaker in *Euthyphro*). Normally, entries begin with a person's name in the left-hand column (see *A Sample Entry* following). Athenian males' names include the demotic, i.e., deme of registration (cf. App. III), and the patronymic, i.e. his father's name. When an Athenian's deme is unknown, 'of Athens' is substituted and his tribe is added below. Athenian women and slaves are identified with reference to citizen males. Non-Athenians are identified by *polis* of origin and patronymic. References to the standard prosopographies are followed by the name in Greek, as it is alphabetized there. Dates of birth and death, or period of activity; familial and social relationships; and occupation or identifying fact complete the column. The second column lists the texts in which the person appears or is mentioned (Plato first, followed by the other Socratics, then the person's own works, then inscriptions and contemporaneous historical and literary sources); when '*passim*' is encountered, specific citations appear in the discussion below, and that is where sources from the later tradition are usually added. The right-hand column identifies a person's role in a Platonic dialogue or letter (cf. App. I). A discussion of what is known about the person—dictated by the nature of the extant material— follows in paragraph form with italicized headings to enable the reader to skip to what s/he wants to know. These typically include *Life* and *Career* (or *Political Career*, and/or *Military Career*, et al.), but the variety of information available results in several *ad hoc* headings as well (e.g., *In comedy*). Since the information I provide for each individual is what is extant, what has happened to survive from antiquity, the reader should note that this is not necessarily what was most important about her or him. Similarly, the absence of information of a particular type, e.g., lack of a paragraph on military career, cannot be read as proof that a man had no military career. Rather, it shows that there is no extant evidence of such a career, a weaker claim. What *can* be made consistent across entries without misleading readers has been standardized, but that leaves immense variety.

At the ends of many entries, paragraphs of prosopographical notes are added, as are notes on the later tradition and modern bibliography.

A Sample Entry

At a glance, the information in columns at the top of the entry will usually tell you whether this is the person you're looking for. Skip to whatever topic interests you.

• ancient sources in which the person appears or is mentioned (complete references are normally provided here; for late sources, 'passim,' and complex references, see paragraphs below)

• * and † indicate that the person is represented as alive or dead in the dialogue ('pat.' if mentioned only as someone else's father)

name, deme or *polis*, father [standard prosopographical and dictionary references, name in Greek] tribe (if deme unknown), date of birth, death

known relationships, familial and social

occupation/identifier

what is known or surmised about the person from available data, usually divided into labeled topics

additional labeled paragraphs as required by the nature of the extant material

role in dialogue or letter: present, speaker, addressee (blank if only discussed or mentioned)

genealogical tree, if any

if identification issues are controversial, or there are discrepancies among the principal prosopographical sources, these are discussed separately

when a discussion of modern bibliography is needed to clarify a dispute in the secondary literature, and when much more is known of a person than would be accessed through the prosopographical sources, a separate paragraph of bibliography is included

---

Charmides of Athens, son of Glaucon III [*PA/APF* 15512 (8792.9) *LGPN2* 28 *RE* 2 *DPhA* 102 *OCD³ PP PX* Χαρμίδης Γλαύκωνος] tribe: ?Erechtheis
‡446–403
mother: daughter of Antiphon I
sister: Perictione
ward of Critias IV
lover of Clinias III
member of the Piraeus Ten under the Thirty
See stemma: Plato.

Pl. *Chrm.*   speaker
Pl. *Prt.* 315a   present
Pl. *Smp.* 222b *
Pl. *Ltr.* 7.324b–d,
    unnamed †
[Pl.] *Thg.* 128d
[Pl.] *Ax.* 364a   present
Xen. *Symp., passim*
Xen. *Mem.* 3.6.1, 3.7
Xen. *Hell.* 2.4.19
Andoc. 1.16
SEG 13.28

Life. The record offers no precedent among older relatives for the name 'Charmides'. His birth, into a family of some wealth and influence, is normally set at "about 450 or just after" (*APF*) but that is too early. One consideration for Plato's dialogues is that Alcibiades III s.v., the great beauty of his age, was in 451 and was on campaign in Potidaea with ...

Profanation of the Eleusinian mysteries in 415. When he was about thirty-one, Charmides and three men of Scambonidae—Alcibiades III, ...

Political career. In Xenophon, Socrates has regard for Charmides (*Mem.* 3.6.1) but encourages him to overcome his natural reticence and shyness ...

In inscriptions. An inscription of some interest (*SEG* 13.28) is a fragment of a marble block recovered from the site of the Academy and bearing four names reconstructed by G. Karo in 1934 as Socratic associates (Charmides, Ariston, Axiochus, Crito) and thus to be dated 5th c.:

ΧΑΡΜ . . .
ΑΡΙΣ . . .
ΑΞΙ . . .
ΚΡΙΤΩΝ

Prosopographical notes. There has long been special interest in determining Charmides' deme because one might safely extend the ...

In modern bibliography. A number of modern scholars looking at Andocides IV's *On the Mysteries* in the course of some larger project (e.g., *APF*, *DPhA*, and Kahn 1996: 32) have mistakenly taken all references to ...

PRIMER OF PLATONIC PROSOPOGRAPHY

Addressed here are the genuine and spurious dialogues and letters of Plato and other authors of Socratic *logoi*: Antisthenes, Aeschines, and Xenophon. Included are historical persons who appear or are mentioned as alive or recently deceased, prominent family members of those persons, the homonyms with whom they are often confused, and a few additional individuals whose works or lineage help to clarify aspects of the lives of the others (e.g., women who unite or consolidate families through marriage). Some of these, as legal minors, lack names and are alphabetized at "[unnamed] wife, son, or slave of x" where x is a known person. Historical persons who do not meet the above criteria are treated very briefly in Appendix II, but listed below for convenience. Individuals are identified for cross-referencing purposes by the numbers assigned in *PA* (followed by *APF*), *LGPN*, *FRA*, *PAA*, *RE*, *DPhA*, Stephanis, and Poralla²; and by appearance in *OCD³* and the indexed *PP* and *PX*. When *APF* discussions of individuals occur elsewhere than under *PA* numbers—and in fact they usually cluster at the entry of one prominent family member (thus Plato is discussed in a subsection of the Critias IV entry)—the *APF* discussion is cited in parenthesis after the *PA/APF* reference. Roman numerals are inserted for clarification of related individuals, consistently with *APF*. They are often irrelevant in the Platonic context but are essential for further prosopographical research. In referring to an individual's role in a dialogue as speaker or present, I do not distinguish reported from narrated dialogues, or whether speakers are at one or two or even three removes from the dramatic frame of the dialogue, if any. '[Plato]' is used below to designate the subject of the spurious letters. *See the sample entry in the introduction.*

Acumenus of Athens
[*PA* 477, 478 (cf. *APF* 11907C) *LGPN2* 1
PAA 117065, 117070 *RE* s.v. *PP PX*
Ἀκουμενός]
470s–>415
father of Eryximachus
uncle of Alexippus
physician

Pl. *Phdr.* 227a, 268a,
  269a *
Pl. *Smp.* 176b, pat.
Pl. *Prt.* 315c, pat.
Xen. *Mem.* 3.13.2
Andoc. 1.18

Life. Acumenus was a physician and the father of a physician (*Phdr.* 268a), who advised refreshing walks on country roads rather than city streets (227a–b), and

1

who reportedly advised someone who complained of not enjoying his food to stop eating (Xen. *Mem.*). His very approximate date of birth is set a generation before his son's rather more stable date of birth. Acumenus seems to be roughly of Socrates' generation: Phaedrus, born ≤444, calls him "our mutual friend" (*Phdr.* 227a5), and Socrates speaks of Acumenus' son as Phaedrus' friend as well (268a; cf. *Prt.* 315c). All three—Acumenus, Eryximachus, and Phaedrus—are separately implicated in the accusations and counteraccusations of sacrilege that preceded the Athenian invasion of Sicily in 415 (see Exc. 1). Acumenus was accused by the slave Lydus of profaning the Eleusinian mysteries at Pherecles' house in Themacus, as a result of which Acumenus fled Athens in 415. He was the uncle of an Alexippus who was called as a witness by Andocides IV s.v. in 400 to attest that Andocides IV's evidence, which secured his own release and that of a few others, had not been the cause of Acumenus' exile. It is indeterminate whether Acumenus was alive in 400 but, if he was, he was presumably still in exile: otherwise Andocides IV would likely have called him, rather than his nephew, as a witness.

Prosopographical notes.   Having distinguished *PA* 477 (Pl. and Xen.) and *PA* 478 (Andoc.) at their original separate entries, Kirchner then provides a 'cf.' reference to Andoc. 1.18 when he treats Acumenus' son, Eryximachus, just under four thousand entries later. Such a sea change in a long prosopographical work is evident not only in Kirchner's monumental *PA*, but in Davies' *APF* as well (see Eryxias, s.v.). In *LGPN2, PA* 477 = *PA* 478, but in *PAA, PA* 477 ?= *PA* 478.

Acusilaus of Argos (genealogist) See App. II.

Adeimantus I of Collytus, son of Ariston	Pl. *Prm.* 126a	speaker
[*PA/APF* 199 (8792.10A) *LGPN2* 14 *PAA*	Pl. *R.*	speaker
107935 *RE* 5 *DPhA* 23 *PP* Ἀδείμαντος	Pl. *Ap.* 34a	present

Ἀρίστωνος Κολλυτεύς]
±432–>382
mother: Perictione
siblings: Plato, Glaucon IV, Potone; maternal
 half brother, Antiphon II; maternal
 stepbrother, Demos
stepfather and grand uncle: Pyrilampes
See stemma: Plato.

Life and family.   Adeimantus I was born ≤429, probably ±432, because his mother's father died in that year, leaving Perictione's brother Charmides the ward of their first cousin, Critias IV. She would also have been assigned a guardian, regardless of her age, if she had not already been married; what we do not know is how long she had been married when her father died. Burnet argued, referring to the year 399, that Adeimantus I was among the elders at Socrates' trial, "It is quite clear that Adimantus was much older than Plato, who was about twenty-eight at this time. He stands to him *in loco parentis*" (1924: *Ap.* 34a1n; accepting Steinhart 1873 and *PA*). While it is true that Pyrilampes, the guardian of Perictione's children with Ariston, was dead ≤413, Plato (whose age I dispute s.v.) did not require a guardian in any case by that year. I suspect that Burnet made a mistake common in his own time, and residual now, of thinking of the Athenian family analogously to the Roman family where, regardless of a man's age, he was subordinate to a living father, the *paterfamilias*, unless formally emancipated. In contrast, the Greek male was "emancipated" in his eighteenth year, as Harrison makes explicit in *The Law of Athens*, "There is not a trace of anything comparable with the Roman father's emancipation of his son, without which the latter could not himself become a *paterfamilias* during his father's lifetime" (1998.1: 74). All Perictione's sons had already reached the age of majority by 399, so Adeimantus I's one remaining ward would have been his widowed mother, a minor for life. Besides, Socrates is glossing a long list of persons present at the trial whose ages appear to vary markedly. The point seems to be that fathers and brothers are in a good position to judge Socrates' present *or past* corrupting influence on someone, so even senior status may be irrelevant: Aeantodorus of Phaleron, seated in the same group as Adeimantus I, may have been older or younger than his brother Apollodorus s.v.; either way, he would be in a position to testify. The variety in the list of *Apology* is too great to admit of fine tuning about the ages of individuals.

In his early or mid-twenties, Adeimantus fought at Megara, perhaps in 409, and was eulogized for it (*R.* 368a), perhaps by Critias IV. Adeimantus I is likely to have married and produced offspring himself since Plato's sole heir, named in his will (D. L. 3.41–3), is the boy Adeimantus II (*pais* in 368), presumably the grandson of Adeimantus I. Adeimantus I is still alive in the dramatic frame of *Parmenides*, very crudely dated ±382, so his death must be later than that and may be very much later.

The question arises why this firstborn son was not given the venerable name 'Aristocles' for his paternal grandfather. It was never obligatory to give one's firstborn son the paternal grandfather's name, but there may have been a first-born son named 'Aristocles' who did not survive childhood. 'Adeimantus' was a particularly fashionable name in the mid-5th c.

Adeimantus II See App. II. *See stemma: Plato.*

Adeimantus of Athens, son of Cepis   Pl. *Prt.* 315e   present
[*PA* 194 *LGPN2* 2 *PAA* 107890 *DPhA* 21 *RE* 4
PP Ἀδείμαντος Κήπιος]

Apart from his being among the group gathered around Prodicus, nothing is known of this Adeimantus (or of his father), though he is assumed to have been Athenian. He is introduced in the dialogue, however, as one of "the two Adeimantuses" (τὼ Ἀδειμάντω ἀμφοτέρω) as if he is closely associated with Adeimantus of Scambonidae s.v.; they were possibly first cousins sharing a grand-father after whom both were named. If he was a young man at the time of *Protagoras*, he might well have been killed in the war that was then brewing and might be identified with one of two recorded sepulchral casualties: *PAA* 107860

(*PA* 190) listed at *IG* I³ 1190.114, dated ?412/1; or *PA* 107910 listed in *Agora* 17, 23.392, dated 409.

Adeimantus of Scambonidae, son of Leucolophides
[*PA* 202 (cf. *APF* 11907C, 8792.10An1) *LGPN2* 19 *PAA* 107965 *DPhA* 20 *RE* 3 *PP*
Ἀδείμαντος Λευκολοφίδος Σκαμβωνίδης]
b. 450s–440s, † >405
companion of Alcibiades III
general

Pl. *Prt.* 315e   present
Xen. *Hell.*, *passim*
Andoc. 1.16
Aristoph. *Frogs* 1513
Eu. *Pol.* fr. 240 (K 224)
Demos. 19.191
Lys. 14.38
IG I³ 422, 426, 430
D. S. 13.69.3

Life. Adeimantus' reputation is linked throughout his life to that of Alcibiades III, and his date of birth can only be estimated very roughly by that criterion. Although Burnet (1914: 190) names Axiochus as the uncle of Adeimantus, no basis for that statement has so far emerged (*APF* 8792.10An1); we know even less about his family than about Adeimantus himself. On the eve of the Peloponnesian war, both Adeimantus and Alcibiades III are present in *Protagoras*, though Adeimantus is in the group already gathered around Prodicus when Socrates arrives, while Alcibiades III joins later. Cf. s.v. Adeimantus, son of Cepis.

In 415, Agariste III s.v. accused Adeimantus, Axiochus, and Alcibiades III of profaning the Eleusinian mysteries in Charmides' house by the Olympieum (Andoc.). If Andocides IV is right, all fled except Alcibiades III, but if Diodorus is right, Adeimantus may have been one of those who remained with Alcibiades III, sailed with him, and later escaped with him at Thurii (13.5.2–3). In either case, Adeimantus (with demotic and patronymic) is among the names of the condemned preserved in inscriptions recovered in agora excavations (*IG* I³ 422.191–2). His full name appears on another from the same group of *stelae*, this one recording the sale of his confiscated property; it was erected in the early spring of 413. Such unusually precise dating of a stone record is the result of its content: the sale of "crops on land in the Troad" that, because of the progress of the war, would not have been available after that spring (Lewis 1966: 181). From the inventory on the *stele*, Adeimantus of Scambonidae, son of Leucolophides (*IG* I³ 426.10), is identified as the owner of the following slaves: Apollophanes [*FRA* 7439], adult male, ἀνέρ, 426.12; Aristarchus [*FRA* 7455], shoemaker, σκυτοτ[όμος], 426.14, 24; Aristomachus [*FRA* 7465], adult male, ἀνέρ, 426.44; Charias [*FRA* 8138], maker of iron skewers and spits, ὀβελισκοποιός, 426.13; Phrychs [*FRA* 8132], 426.11; Satyrus [*FRA* 7985–6], shoemaker, 426.15, 430.28; [.....]on [*FRA* 8206], born in the house, οἰκογεν[ές], 426.16. We know from the inventory that Adeimantus was a wealthy man (see *IG* I³ 426.43, 106, 141, 185, 190; and 430.3, 10, 27).

Military career. Adeimantus was a *stratēgos*, one of the generals with Alcibiades III at Andros in 407/6 (Xen. *Hell.* 1.4.21), and Diodorus adds that he was chosen by the men at Alcibiades III's request, not elected by the Athenians. He was again a general in the following year with Conon (*Hell.* 1.7.1, Demos.), and also in the year 405/4 (*Hell.* 2.1.30) when he was among the prisoners taken by Lysander following the naval battle at Aegospotami in 405 (*Hell.* 2.1.32). Adeimantus was the sole Athenian to avoid execution because, in the version of Xenophon, he had previously opposed, in the Athenian Assembly, cutting off the hands of Lacedaemonian captives. Others interpreted his being spared differently, namely as evidence he had betrayed the Athenians to Lysander (Lys.). Aristophanes' *Frogs*, produced in 405, names him among those who ought to be dragged down to the underworld to save Athens; there he's called Adeimantus "Whitecrest" (Λευκόλοφος, 1513) a pun on his father's name (see Stanford 1968: 199). The scholiast notes that Adeimantus' father, Leucolophides, had been satirized fifteen years earlier in Eu. *Pol.* These last known events of his life are taken up in late sources (Pau. 4.17.3, 10.9.11; Plu. *Alc.* 36.4).

Aeantodorus of Phaleron	Pl. *Ap.* 34a	present

[*PA* 291 *LGPN2* 3 *PAA* 112310 *RE* s.v. *PP*
Ἀιαντόδωρος Φαληρεύς]
b. 430s or 420s, † ≥399
brother: Apollodorus

Since his brother, Apollodorus, was the agemate of Glaucon IV (b. ≤429, see Pl. *Smp.* 172a), Aeantodorus was probably of the same generation. ('Acantidorus' at PCW 30 is a misprint.) Aeantodorus is missing from the *PP* index but appears on p. 202.

Aeschines of Sphettus, son of Lysanias	Pl. *Ap.* 33d	present
[*PA* 366 *LGPN2* 84 *PAA* 115140 *RE* 14 *DPhA*	Pl. *Phd.* 59b	present
71 *OCD*³ *PP* Αἰσχίνης Λυσανίου Σφήττιος]	frr. in *SSR* 2.VIA	
roughly contemporary with Plato, † ≥356	Lys. fr. 1	
writer of Socratic dialogues, speeches		

Life. Plato's Aeschines is squarely within the Socratic circle, present for both the trial (with his father) and the death of Socrates. The only other extant contemporaneous reference to him is a fragment of a speech (Lys.) that emphasizes his poverty (cf. D. L. 2.34) and dissolute behavior, preserved in Athenaeus (611d–612f). Aeschines "the Socratic" was the plaintiff bringing suit against an unknown person to whom he owed money, and the fragment does not reveal how this turnabout came to pass. Lysias' speech for the defendant recounts how Aeschines, setting up a perfume business, borrowed money at higher and higher interest rates, eventually asking for a loan from the defendant. Because of Aeschines' speeches about justice and virtue, the defendant trusted him and lent him money. The speech makes a separate accusation: Aeschines, while a mere peddler, seduced the seventy-year-old wife of the perfume seller as a ruse to take the shop from her husband and sons. Without more information, both the meaning and the relevance of the accusation is unclear. Ultimately, Aeschines is dubbed a sophist in Lysias' speech.

Works. Diogenes (2.1) attributes to Aeschines the titles *Alcibiades, Axiochus, Aspasia, Callias, Miltiades, Rhinon,* and *Telauges,* from which frr. of *Alcibiades* and *Aspasia* remain (*SSR*).

His *Alcibiades* is a series of fragments of a conversation about Themistocles between Socrates and Alcibiades III, narrated by Socrates, in which Socrates defends the view that the gods favor the righteous and then abandons Alcibiades III, his head in his hands. 'Rhinon' was the name of a member of the Board of Ten that served under the Thirty (see App. II s.v.) who was involved in the negotiation of the reconciliation agreement after their fall (see Exc. 4). See Aspasia s.v. for a summary of the frr. of that dialogue.

In the later tradition. Aeschines becomes, over time, a rhetorician and teacher of rhetoric who defended clients, notably, Dion and Erasistratus I (D. L. 2.62–4). Diogenes (2.63), citing the first book of Polycritus of Mende's *History of Dionysius,* says that Aeschines lived in Syracuse with the tyrant Dionysius II s.v. until he was expelled, presumably in 356 (a story retold at Plu. *Mor.* 67d and Philostr. *VA* 1.35), but the sustained section on Aeschines in Diogenes (2.60–64) is particularly confused. Diodorus includes him in a list of learned men (15.76.4). In the pseudo-Socratic epistolary tradition, Aeschines writes to Aristippus (10), to Xenophon (1), and to Phaedo (23).

Prosopographical notes. Aeschines is a common name, so there have been confusions in the literature. The Socratic is neither Aeschines (*PA* 354) the rhetorician, whose career was later († 322), nor the Aeschines (*PA* 341) who was one of the Thirty.

Aeschines of Athens (tribe: Kekropis) See App. II.

Aeschines of Cothocidae, son of Atrometus I (rhetorician) See App. II.

Aeschylus of Eleusis (tragedian) See App. II.

Agamedes (builder) See App. II.

Agariste I of Sicyon, daughter of Cleisthenes of Sicyon, wife of Megacles II See App. II. *See stemma: Pericles.*

Agariste II of Athens, daughter of Hippocrates I, wife of Xanthippus I of Cholarges See App. II. *See stemma: Pericles.*

Agariste III of Athens, wife of Alcmonides   Andoc. 1.16
[*PA/APF* 91 (9688.13) *LGPN2* 1 *PAA* 105835
RE 3 Ἀγαρίστη Ἀλκμεωνίδου γυνή]
b. ?450s–440s, † >400
husbands: Damon, then Alcmonides
accused four men of sacrilege

Life and family.   From her name alone, we can fairly safely assume that Agariste III was born into the wealthy and powerful Alcmaeonid clan (*genos*), though it is not possible to determine exactly how closely she might be related to other Alcmaeonids of the time (Pericles I's mother was Agariste II of the same *genos*, and Alcibiades III's mother was Dinomache of the same *genos*; see stemma: Pericles). Agariste III was married first to a member of Pericles I's circle, Damon, through at least 414; he may have been thirty or so years older than she and probably predeceased her. She then married Alcmonides (*PA* 654, 656), whose name also tells his clan, before 400.

There is an interesting bit of history about the Alcmaeonid clan (the *Alcmaeonidae*): a curse against the *genos* followed the murder of suppliants at the alter of Athena, ordered by the archon Megacles I, contrary to his promise to them ([Aristot.] *Ath. Pol.* fr. 8); the curse long had repercussions for the clan's political standing and power in Athens (e.g., forbidding liturgical class functions involving sacred shrines et al.), and fueled the clan's relentless pursuit of dynastic marriages. Other dynasties had other means of consolidating the wealth at their disposal, especially through cults and phratries, that were unavailable to the Alcmaeonids because of the curse. An especially high incidence of intermarriage among Alcmaeonids prevented wealth from dissipating. Agariste III's marriages seem to fit the pattern for which the clan is well known.

The sacrilege charge of 415.   The one thing we know about Agariste III is that she informed against Alcibiades III, Adeimantus of Scambonidae, and Axiochus for performing the mysteries in Charmides' house by the Olympieum in 415 (see Exc. 1). The accusation was probably made before the Council rather than the Assembly (Hansen 1975: 77 & n10, 79n13). That she charged a member of her own *genos*, Alcibiades III, with sacrilege has aroused speculation about her possible motives for informing—political, religious, or personal—and about the means by which she obtained the information that she passed on (cf. Wallace 1992 & references therein; MacDowell 1962: 75). There is another curiosity. Although Andocides IV says they all fled, we know that Alcibiades III did not (i.e. that he remained in Athens and sailed with the fleet), and we know that Axiochus was active in Athenian politics again by 407, that Adeimantus was a general by then, and that Charmides was among the Piraeus Ten in 404. In short, the men accused by Agariste III seem to have overcome their condemnation earlier and more completely than others we can trace. Yet there is no record where we would expect one, namely in Andocides IV's speech, that her evidence was ever officially refuted. By law, had she been found guilty of bringing a false accusation, she would have been executed herself (Andoc. 1.120; MacDowell 1978: 181).

Agathocles of ?Paeania, son of ?Sophroniscus Pl. *Prt.* 316e †
[*LGPN2* 101 *PAA* 103920 *RE* 22   Pl. *Lch.* 180d
PP Ἀγαθοκλῆς Σωφρονίσκου Παιανιεύς] [Pl.] *Alc.* 118c schol.
b. 480s–470s, † <433/2   *IG* II² 7019.1
musician and music teacher   gravestone

Life. Agathocles was a musician of Nicias I's generation (*Lch.*) who was a teacher of Damon (*Lch.*) and, perhaps, of Lamprocles (*Alc.*). Damon's deme of Oe, very recently located, turns out to be just south of Agathocles' deme of Paeania (Kakovoyiannis 1998, with Dow 1963 for Oe, not Oa), convenient for the two musicians if they often resided in their demes of registration. Protagoras remarks to Socrates, "Agathocles, a great sophist, used music as a front" (*Prt.*), so Agathocles was seemingly—like his student, Damon—more than a musician, and dead before the outbreak of the Peloponnesian war (see App. I).

Prosopographical notes. The prosopographical listings above do not cite passages in Plato; they refer only to the Agathocles on an undated gravestone inscription (*IG*); in fact, the musician Agathocles does not yet feature in the prosopographies, even though *Laches* and *Protagoras* are normally considered among the more historically sensitive of Plato's dialogues. Of course it may well be that there is no evidence of this individual outside the dialogues. I hazard a guess, however, that the Agathocles of Plato may be the one from the gravestone based on two pieces of information in combination with one another: Protagoras says "your own Agathocles" (Ἀγαθοκλῆς τε ὁ ὑμέτερος, *Prt.*) to Socrates, meaning at least that Agathocles was Athenian, but perhaps that he was closer to Socrates than that. Recall that Socrates was the son of Sophroniscus. Agathocles of Paeania, son of Sophroniscus, the full name on the gravestone, suggests that Agathocles and Socrates were perhaps related. Their demes and tribes are different—Alopece and Antiochis for Socrates' father, Paeania and Pandionis for Agathocles'—so the connection to a common ancestor would have to be matrilineal on at least one side. The scholiast to [Pl.] *Alc.* 118c writes that Agathocles taught Lamprocles who taught Damon. This late remark has complicated the determination of approximate dates of birth for the three musicians.

Agathon of Athens, son of Tisamenus Pl. *Prt.* 315e2   present
[*PA* 83 *LGPN2* 2 *PAA* 105185 *DPhA* 41 Pl. *Smp.* & schol. speaker
RE 13 *OCD*³ *PP PX* Ἀγάθων Τεισαμένου] [Pl.] Epig. 6
>447–±401   frr. in *TGrF* 39
beloved of Pausanias   Xen. *Symp.* 8.32
tragedian   Aristoph. *Thesm.*
                       28–265, *passim*
                       Aristoph. *Gery.* fr.
                       178 (K 169)
                       Aristoph. *Frogs*
                       83–85 & schol.
                       Aristot. *Eu. Eth.*
                       1232b7

Life.   Nothing that we know about Agathon is incompatible with his having in fact been an adolescent (*neon. . .meirakion*) of apparent good birth and good looks at the time of Plato's *Protagoras*, where he reclines with Pausanias on one of the couches clustered around Prodicus. Lamb (1925: 78) provides his date of birth as "about 447," apparently reasoning that Agathon produced his winning play at about the age of thirty, and that is probably about right, although Aristodemus' description of Agathon as a *neaniskos* in 416 (*Smp.* 198a) might push the date forward a little. Terminology for youths and young men, then as now, has as much to do with physical development and appearance as with chronological age. Given how Agathon is depicted in Aristophanes as delicate or effeminate, he may have continued to look younger than his years.

In the literary and historical record between the dramatic dates of *Protagoras* and *Symposium*, Agathon is mentioned with Pausanias in Xenophon's *Symposium* at Callias III's Piraeus house in August of 422. The main action of Plato's *Symposium* occurs in February of 416, in the archon year of Euphemus (Ath. 216f–217b), when Agathon won his first victory as a tragedian (*Smp.* 173a) at the Lenaean festival. That his household includes women (176e) tells us, probably, that he resided with his mother and/or sisters. No father or brother is mentioned or joins the celebration.

Plato's representation of Agathon is on the whole positive: in *Symposium*, Agathon is quick to say welcoming words and to offer a couch to Socrates' companion, Aristodemus, an uninvited guest who is barefoot and shabby, a self-described "inferior" (174e). Although he is host of the celebration in his home, Agathon is pleased not to act as *symposiarch*, and not even to supervise his slaves (175b). His lover is still Pausanias. In the conclusion of Agathon's rhetorically polished speech (194e–197e), Socrates finds the influence of Gorgias (198c). Agathon manages to stay awake all night with Socrates and Aristophanes (223c), when the others have gone home or fallen asleep.

An anecdote (Aristot.) that Agathon praised Antiphon of Rhamnous' defense speech in 411 suggests to Brown (*OCD³*) that Agathon had "anti-democratic sentiments"; but this is perhaps too hasty a judgment, given that the speech is lost and might have been appreciated for its form as much as its content. Aristotle implies that Agathon is an especially good man—or at least that Antiphon, then in his seventieth year and facing the death penalty, regarded him highly. Aristotle discusses Agathon's plays in the *Poetics, passim.*

Despite his apparently successful career as a tragedian, Agathon left Athens with Pausanias for the Hellenizing court of the infamous Archelaus of Macedonia who reigned 413–399. Henderson (2002: 28–9n9) gives the year 408 for Agathon's departure, and he had certainly been gone for some time before the production of Aristophanes' *Frogs* in 405 in which Dionysus declares, "He's gone and left me; a fine poet and much missed by his friends." *Symposium's* dramatic frame is set in 400, when Agathon has already been abroad for some years (172c, & 172a schol.; cf. Gell. *NA* 13.4), but before his death.

In Aristophanes.   Most of what we know about Agathon's tragedies we infer from other authors' descriptions and imitations of his style: his *Symposium* speech, but much more from Aristophanes' depictions of him during the period of his fame in

Athens. Aristophanes lampooned Agathon at length in 411 (*Thesm.*) and mentioned him again in ±408 (*Gery.*), before paying him tribute in 405 (*Frogs*).

As *Women at the Thesmophoria* begins, the aging Euripides is threatened with a death sentence from the assembled Athenian wives; they are angry that he has revealed their secrets to their husbands in his plays. Agathon, spied from a distance, is neither tanned nor strong nor bearded (31–33; cf. 191–2), but he is promiscuous (33–5):

> EURIPIDES: You've never seen him?
> KINSMAN: Absolutely not, as far as I know.
> EURIPIDES: Well, you must have fucked him, though you might not know it.

Agathon's slave parodies his lyrics while Euripides' kinsman continues making homosexual humor (39–70); then Agathon himself sings (101–29) with "asiatic luxury and effeminacy" (Henderson 2000: ln. 101n). Agathon boasts that playing the female enables him to write about women realistically: "For as we are made, so must we compose" (167, ὅμοια γὰρ ποιεῖν ἀνάγκη τῇ φύσει.). Euripides asks Agathon to dress in drag, infiltrate the gathering of women, and defend him. Although Agathon refuses, he nevertheless oversees the shaving and singeing of the kinsman's face and pubes, and provides from his personal store a razor, a party dress, a brassiere, a wig, a wrap, and pumps for the kinsman to wear in disguise before disappearing from the stage (265).

Agis II of Sparta, son of Archidamus (king) See App. II.

Aglaeon of Athens See App. II.

Aglaophon of Thasos (painter) See App. II.

Alcetas of Macedonia See App. II.

Alcibiades II of Scambonidae, son of Clinias I See App. II. *See stemma: Alcibiades.*

Alcibiades III of Scambonidae, son of Clinias II	Pl. *Prt.*	speaker
	Pl. *Smp.* from 212d	speaker
[*PA/APF* 600 *LGPN2* 23 *PAA* 121630 *RE* 2	Pl. *Grg.* 481d, 519b *	
DPhA 86 *OCD*³ *PP PX* Ἀλκιβιάδης Κλεινίου	Pl. *Euthd.* 275a–b *	
Σκαμβωνίδης]	[Pl.] *Alc.*	speaker
451–404	[Pl.] *2Alc.*	speaker
mother: Dinomache, daughter of Megacles IV	Aes. *Alc.*	

brother: Clinias IV
wife: Hipparete I
father of Alcibiades IV and a daughter who
  married Hipponicus III
ward of Pericles I and Ariphron II
beloved of Socrates
famous and notorious general and politician
See stemmata: Alcibiades, Lysis, Pericles.

Aes. *Ax.* no. 56 (fr.
  12 Dittmar)
Antis. *Alc.*
Xen. *Mem.* 1.2.12–28,
  39–47
Xen. *Hell.* 1–2,
  passim
Critias IV frr. 4–5
Thu. 5–8, *passim*
D. S. 13–14, *passim*
Andoc. 1.11–14, 1.16
[Andoc.] 4
Isocr. 5.58–61; 11.5;
  16
Antiph. fr. 10
Demos. 21.145–7
comedy (see below)
inscriptions (see
  below)

Family.   Alcibiades III's father was a Salaminian and his mother an Alcmaeonid. Thus he was descended on both sides from families that were among Athens' first and most powerful, deploying both wealth and influence. (See Agariste III s.v. for the Alcmaeonid curse.) Of his more immediate forebears, his paternal grandfather, Alcibiades II, was known for having renounced his role as *proxenos* of Sparta in 462/1 (Thu. 5.43.2—where Alcibiades III sought to renew the role; cf. Thu. 8.89.1), and also for being ostracized in 460 (see App. II). The name 'Alcibiades' itself is of Spartan origin (Thu. 8.6.3). Clinias II, Alcibiades III's father, was killed in the battle of Coronea in 446, leaving Alcibiades III legally an orphan in his sixth year, although his mother was still alive. He and his younger brother, Clinias IV, were made wards of Pericles I and Ariphron II though Pericles I appears to have taken primary responsibility for the boys' rearing. It is almost certain that Clinias II wrote a will stipulating this preference, a common practice well established in Athenian law (Harrison 1998: 1.99), and it is not particularly surprising since the boys' mother, Dinomache, was a first cousin to Pericles I and Ariphron II. They were not formally adopted by Pericles I; that is, the boys retained their own deme affiliation, Scambonidae, and such formal responsibilities as the preservation of the *sacra* of their father's house (Harrison 1998: 1.123). The early Platonic tradition provides the information that Alcibiades III's childhood tutor was the elderly Thracian Zopyrus ([Pl.] *Alc.* 122b); and Antisthenes says his nurse was named Amycla (*Alc.* no. 201).

Life.   Antiphon (or his client) accuses Alcibiades III of taking his possessions from Pericles I's house and leaving the city immediately after being presented to his deme in his eighteenth year, but this cannot be taken at face value since eighteen-year-olds were expected to begin their formal military training after being enrolled in their demes. Xenophon retells a story of Alcibiades III at about nineteen, outwitting Pericles I in a conversation about law, persuasion, and force

STEMMA: ALCIBIADES

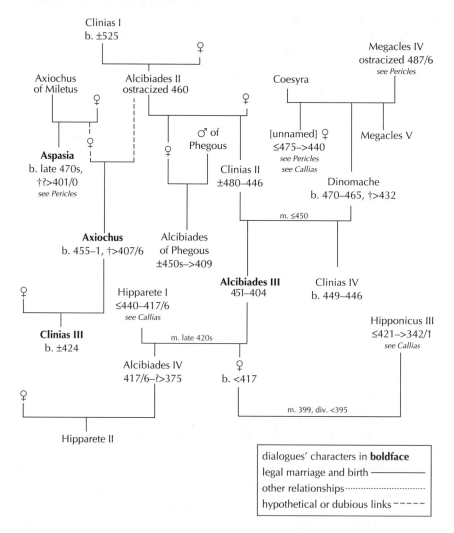

(1.2.40–7), but Xenophon points out at great length that Alcibiades III was no student or disciple of Socrates but, like Critias IV, someone who wanted to use Socrates to advance his own ambitions. Isocrates makes much the same point (11.4; cf. Polycrates s.v.), adding that no one would say Alcibiades III was a student of Socrates. The congruence of views is more interesting because Isocrates was an admirer of Alcibiades III while Xenophon was a critic. (Cf. Aeschines s.v. for that Socratic's dialogue *Alc.*)

When we see Alcibiades III again, in *Protagoras*, arriving at Callias III's house with Critias IV, his beard has grown, and he is Socrates' beloved (*Prt.* 309a). The dialogue is set before he leaves on campaign to Potidaea (Thrace) in 432, either in the summer under Archestratus, or in the fall under Callias (Pl. *Smp.* 219e, Isocrates 16.29—but Isocrates incorrectly identifies Phormion as general), in which Socrates also participated. The long siege kept both men away from Athens until May of 429, under three years, returning to a plague-ridden Athens in which Pericles I would die within four months. By the 5th c., eighteen- and nineteen-year-old Athenian youths were not sent on military campaigns outside Attica ([Aristot.] *Ath. Pol.* 42.3–5 with Garland 1990: 183 on the later formalization of the rules ±370), so Alcibiades III must have been in at least his twentieth year in 432, ruling out 450 as a birth year, and making 451 as certain as is possible, given that, "there is no means of telling whether the interval between a personal birthday and the *dokimasia* counted as a completed year or as a vacuum" (*APF* 600.7). The year 451 fits well with Thucydides' comment on Alcibiades III's exceptional youth for a commander (5.43.2), implying that he was probably just thirty in the spring of 420 and had been elected in the earliest possible year. For his marriage and children, see Hipparete I s.v.

Career in brief.   A complete account of Alcibiades III's political and military career requires a monograph (Hatzfeld 1951 or Ellis 1989). Athens was alternately besotted and infuriated with him, and the later sources seem also to deify or demonize him. In Plato's version of events, Socrates saved Alcibiades III's life and armor when the younger man was wounded at Potidaea, though the generals chose to honor Alcibiades III because of his lineage and wealth (*Smp.* 220e). He served with Socrates again at Delium in 424 where he was in little danger himself: as a *hippeus*, he was on horseback during the retreat; Socrates was the brave one, Alcibiades III said, saving Laches as well as himself (*Smp.* 221a–c).

Alcibiades III was apparently a brilliant leader of men in battle, and a persuasive Assembly speaker. But he was also rich and knew how to use his money to gain a political advantage. For Alcibiades III's financial circumstances and liturgical obligations, see *APF* 600.9 (citing Lys. 14 and 19, [Pl.] *Alc.*, Thu. 6, Isocr. 16, [Andoc.] 4.20, Demos. 21.147, *IG*, et al.). Moreover, he was the ancient equivalent of a record-breaking sports superstar, though winning his victories, not by participation, but by ownership of teams of horses in chariot races, the most expensive of the events. He was an extraordinary victor in the Olympics of 416 (Thu. 6.16.2; Isocr. 16.34; [Andoc.] 4.22, 26; Demos. 21.145), though his legal entitlement to one of the teams of horses he entered was a subject of litigation in 397 (see Alcibiades IV s.v.). Alcibiades III deployed his wealth arrogantly in ways that would bring him the honor and envy of others whom he despised as his inferiors. After he persuaded the Assembly to attack Sicily in 415, he sought election as supreme general for the expedition:

Athenians, I more than others am entitled to command, which must be my first point because of Nikias' attack on me, and I consider myself deserving as well. For the outcry against me involves things that bring glory to my ancestors and myself but also benefit the country. The Hellenes, who had previously expected our city to be exhausted by warfare, believed it to be even greater than its real power because of the splendor of my representation at Olympia, where I entered seven chariots, more than any individual ever had before, and won the prize and also finished second and fourth, and I arranged everything else as my victory warranted. There is honor in this by tradition, and from the accomplishments comes the further inference of might. And again, any brilliance I display in the city by providing choruses or in some other way is only naturally a cause for envy among the citizens, yet for foreigners this too points to strength. This is not useless folly, if a man benefits not only himself but his city through personal expenditure, let alone unfairness for the man to take pride in himself and to be on a different level, since failures do not share their adversity evenly with others; so just as we are not hailed when we are unfortunate, let all submit to the arrogance of the successful, then, or let them demand equality when that is what they bestow. (Thu. 6.16.1–4)

Alcibiades III, Nicias I, and Lamachus were elected to command.

Before the ships could sail, however, Alcibiades III was accused by Agariste III, and separately by Archebiades' slave, Andromachus, of profaning the Eleusinian mysteries (see Exc. 1; cf. *Smp.* 218b). Failing in his demand that he be tried before embarking, he was later recalled from the fleet to stand trial (Thu. 6.53.1, 61.4), but escaped at Thurii and defected to Sparta (Thu. 6.53.1, 6.61.4–6); he was condemned *in absentia* (Andoc.; Thu.; Xen. *Hell.*). He is listed with his demotic and patronymic among the condemned on the *stele* recovered from the Eleusinium (*IG* I³ 370). Dover notes that, unlike the mutilations of the herms, "The identifiable participants in the profanations are connected, directly or through intermediaries" with Alcibiades III: Alcibiades III himself, Axiochus, Adeimantus, Archebiades, ". . . and others who were at least on the periphery, and in some cases near the centre, of the 'Socratic circle' ": Phaedrus, Acumenus, Eryximachus, and perhaps Charmides (*HCT* 4.283). Andocides IV had emphasized the *connections* among those denounced in *both* affairs; despite Dover's own warnings about the hazards of political prosopography, his gloss goes too far: his "identifiable participants" are only eight in number—of thirty-one *named* profaners, not counting the remainder of those accused by Lydus, not listed in Andocides IV, and that is too small a sample for such a generalization about the Socratic circle.

Alcibiades III aided both the Spartans (Thu. 6.88.9–8.26.3, *passim*; D. S. 13.9.2) and the Persians (Thu. 8.45.1–8.47.2, *passim*) until the oligarchy of 411 collapsed, whereupon the Athenian generals in the Hellespont, persuaded by Thrasybulus, urged him to return and take command of the fleet at Samos (Thu. 8.81–2). The action had been opposed by the families with hereditary responsibility for leading and conducting the mysteries at Eleusis, the Eumolpidae and Ceryces (Thu. 8.53.2). Alcibiades III enjoyed naval successes for some years, but avoided the city. When Alcibiades III was finally received in Athens in 407, he immediately reiterated his innocence of the charges brought against him in 415, without objection— though Xenophon remarks that the opposing voices were cowed into silence (Xen. *Hell.* 1.4.20). Diodorus adds that the Athenians threw the *stele* condemning him into the sea and at the same time voted to return his property (3.69.2, Plu. *Alc.* 33.3). It was a bronze *stele*, not the one standing in the Eleusinium, that was thrown into the sea (Lewis 1966: 188–9 with n72). His property, having been sold, could not be returned (see Exc. 4), so it was commuted to a land grant later denied to Alcibiades IV. Alcibiades III's very first, and very dramatic, act upon being vindicated and then enthusiastically "proclaimed general-in-chief with absolute authority" was to undertake a procession of his army to Eleusis by land although the war had previously been forcing a sea journey (Xen. *Hell.* 1.4.20–1; D. S. 13.69.1).

But Athens' expectations may have been unreasonably high. When a subordinate disobeyed his direct order and thereby brought about a naval loss at Notium that same year, the Athenians angrily dismissed Alcibiades III from his command. He retired from the war to his estate in the Chersonese, though the disaster of Arginusae in 406 renewed calls in the city for his return (Aristoph. *Frogs*). In 405, before Athens' calamitous defeat at Aegospotami, Alcibiades approached the Athenian generals to give advice (Xen. *Hell.* 2.1.25–26) or to negotiate for a share in the command in return for Thracian assistance (D. S. 13.104), but was sent away forthwith. We have no contemporaneous account of how he died in 404; what his son says in a forensic speech (Isocr. 16.40) is vaguely compatible with all, that the Lacedaemonians and Lysander were somehow involved. The version of the assassination most often cited is one in which Critias IV tells a diffident Lysander that there can be no peace while the Athenians nurse hopes for Alcibiades III's return, though Lysander reluctantly sends a directive to Pharnabazus only after receiving orders himself from Sparta (Plu. *Alc.* 38–9). Not surprisingly, Plutarch's account gives two versions of what Alcibiades III was dreaming at the time, makes him miraculously immune to the effects of fire on flesh, and puts a courtesan in his bed (or, alternatively, a modest village girl whose brothers kill him in revenge). Although Diodorus says the satrap Pharnabazus seized and killed Alcibiades III for the Lacedaemonians (14.11.1), he immediately tells Ephorus' less glamorous version according to which the satrap's brother and uncle ambushed Alcibiades III to prevent him from warning Artaxerxes that the Lacedaemonians were plotting with his brother Cyrus; Pharnabazus wanted to convey the warning himself to win Artaxerxes' favor (14.11.2–4).

"The recall of Alcibiades."   Anyone who researches Alcibiades III in the secondary literature will encounter references to *the* recall of Alcibiades—as if there were only one. In fact, there were three. (a) In 415, he was recalled from Sicily by the Athenians to answer charges of impiety. (b) In 411, he was recalled by the fleet in the Hellespont to take command. (c) In 407, he was recalled to Athens, where he remained for four months, the Athenians having elected him general while he was still officially in exile (Xen. *Hell.* 1.4.12). This four-month period would likely have been Plato's only opportunity for personal acquaintance with Alcibiades III; Plato would have been perhaps nine when the fleet sailed for Sicily in 415. (See Critias IV s.v. for an elegy in which the leader of the Thirty celebrates himself as author of a proposal to recall Alcibiades III, though it is unclear which recall he means.)

In inscriptions.   Evidence from inscriptions, most of them recovered from the Athenian agora in modern times, is far less readily available than the accounts of the historians, but it is primary evidence at its most solid. Alcibiades III proposed a decree honoring Siphnians in 422/1 (*IG* I³ 227.7 twice named). He was the victor in the chariot race at the greater Panathenaea of 418 (*IG* I³ 370.17), but note that the trophy amphora he won on that occasion shows up again in the record when it is confiscated and sold in 414 (*IG* I³ 422.42). His name appears on pottery *ostraka* dated 417–415 (*Agora* 25.13–17). His election as *stratēgos*, general, for the Sicilian campaign in 415 is recorded in stone (*IG* I³ 370.54, 56), but so is his condemnation following the accusations that he had profaned the mysteries (*IG* I³ 370.49–50, 52, 54, 56), and the confiscation and sale of his property (*IG* I³ 421.12, 422.42, 424.27). There follows a gap in the record that corresponds to Alcibiades III's absence from Athens. But his financial accounts at Eleusis were recorded in the year 408/7 (*IG* I³ 386.134). Like a bookend to his first appearance in the stone record, the decree of 422/1, Alcibiades III's last appearance is with the proposal of honorary decrees in 407 (*IG* I³ 117.4–5, 118.31, 119.3, 120.4–5; & Walbank 1978: 436, 86.31) and in 406 (*IG* I³ 134.2).

In comedy.   Without scholia to the plays, we probably would not have recognized some of the references to Alcibiades III; and imagination has surely multiplied the number of "sightings" of him there (cf. Vickers 1997: xix). In both *Banqueters* of 427 (fr. 205 [K 198]) and *Acharnians* of 425 (716 & schol.), when Alcibiades III would have been twenty-four and twenty-six, Aristophanes spoofed him for his affectations of speech, though in the latter he also described him as "wide-arsed" (εὐρύπρωκτος). By 422, in *Wasps* (44, 46), the affectation seems more like a speech impediment. The next year, Alcibiades III, *qua* womanizer, was one of guests at Callias III's house (Eu. *Flatt.* fr. 171 [K 158]); cf. Pher. fr. 164 [K 155]). Eupolis' *Baptae*, dated between 424 and 415, depicted Alcibiades III and his circle dressed as dancing women, reportedly so annoying Alcibiades III (or his rowdy pals) that the playwright was hauled bodily to the sea and bathed or "baptized" there (Eu. *Bap.* iv and fr. 385 [K 351]). There is little evidence, and none of it contemporaneous, that Alcibiades III was able to effect a law forbidding the naming of names in comedy (through a proposal by Syracusius) in 415, as there had been in 440; the long period when his name is not found in plays or fragments corresponds to Alcibiades III's long absence from Athens. In Aristophanes' *Frogs* of 405 (1422–32), in the underworld, the great tragedian, Aeschylus, asks the visiting god Dionysus what the city—now in a desperate plight from the war, and Alcibiades in voluntary exile—thinks of Alcibiades, and the god replies, "it yearns for him, detests him, and wants to have him" (1425).

In the later tradition.   Later ancient authors provide volumes of further references to Alcibiades III, of which Plutarch's *Alcibiades* has been most influential. The sources used by some of these later writers can be identified with, or traced back to, the contemporaneous sources noted above, but much was apparently conjured to gratify the curiosity of a public that remained fascinated with Alcibiades III long after his death. For example, there are no contemporaneous references to illegitimate children of Alcibiades III though four different such children emerge in later sources. (MacDowell 1998: 160 notes both that the claim that Alcibiades III fathered a child with a Melian woman is impossible in context, and that [Andoc.] 4 was written in later times as an exercise.)

Prosopographical notes.   Much of the prosopographical literature has been preoccupied with late antique references to the familial relationship between Pericles I and Alcibiades III (Nep. *Alc.* 2, stepson; D. S. 12.38.3, uncle and nephew—both undermined in Thompson 1970), used in a variety of explanations of why Axiochus, legally a closer relative to Alcibiades III than Pericles I, was effectively skipped. Since wills were common, no such explanation is needed. For a possible alternative to the family's stemma, see Stanley (1986; also Euryptolemus s.v.).

EXCURSUS 1:
The Sacrilegious Crimes of 415.

Athens was divided in 415 about whether to undertake an invasion of Sicily to ensure her supply line, which had been seriously undermined by the Lacedaemonians. Following fierce debate in which Alcibiades III supported, and Nicias I opposed, the invasion, both were elected to lead it, as was Lamachus. In the period from early summer to early fall, as the Athenian fleet made preparations for the campaign, two different types of crimes of impiety (*asebeia*) were purportedly committed. The first was the mutilation of the city's herms (rough statues of the face and phallus of Hermes that marked boundaries of ordinary homes and public places throughout Attica); the second, the profanation, i.e. parody, or performance without the proper priests etc., of the Eleusinian mysteries on several occasions in private homes by many of the city's rich young men—including Alcibiades III. The second set of alleged crimes came to light after the herms had been defaced, though the profanations were said to have been committed previously. Contemporaneous primary sources are Thucydides (6.27–29, 6.53, 6.60–1), Andocides IV (1.11–1.70), inscriptions on *stelae* found by archaeologists at the Eleusinium in Athens (*IG* I^3 421–430), and Xenophon (*Hell.* 1.4.13–21). Other contemporaneous sources, no longer extant, appear also to have been used in the development of later accounts (Plu., *Alc.* 18–22; D. S. 13.2.2–4, 13.5.1–4, 13.69.2–3).

The ships were almost ready to sail when virtually all the city's herms were smashed in a single night. It is likely that some who opposed the invasion thought a systematic attack on the god of travel would dissuade the superstitious citizens of Athens from embarking on the invasion of Sicily, but Athens was soon awash in accusations. Although the relative and absolute dates of subsequent incidents are controversial, the following events occurred over the next three months, and the persons in the box on the next page (discussed s.vv. with additional details relevant to their particular circumstances) were among those involved.

Events of the three months following the mutilation of the herms.

- A commission, including Diognetus, Pisander and Charicles, was established to investigate the *hermocopidae* and offered rewards for information on all crimes of impiety.

- Euphiletus, leader of the drinking club that had organized the mutilation of the herms, and Meletus of Athens visited the injured club member, Andocides IV, and persuaded him to keep what he knew to himself.
- Dioclides began attempts to blackmail Euphemus, Andocides IV, and others.
- With the fleet on the verge of departure, during a meeting of the generals before the Assembly, Andromachus, slave of Archebiades, in exchange for immunity, accused his master and nine others (including Alcibiades III and Meletus of Athens) of profaning the mysteries in Pulytion's house. Eight fled, one was executed. Alcibiades III demanded a trial to remove suspicion, but was outmaneuvered by his enemies. The fleet sailed.
- The *metic* Teucrus, having first relocated to Megara for safety, sent word that, in exchange for immunity, he would denounce both profaners and mutilators. He returned, and named himself and eleven others (including Phaedrus and Diognetus) who had profaned the mysteries. All fled.

> *Persons implicated who had Socratic connections:*
>
> Acumenus
> Adeimantus of
>   Scambonidae
> Agariste III
> Alcibiades III
> Alcibiades of
>   Phegous
> Andocides IV
> Axiochus
> Charicles
> Charmides, son of
>   Glaucon III
> Critias IV
> Damon
> Diognetus
> Eryximachus
> Eucrates
> Meletus of Athens
> Phaedrus

- Teucrus also named eighteen men who had mutilated herms (including Eryximachus and Meletus of Athens). Some were executed, and others fled. The new year, 414, began at midsummer, rotating many official posts.
- The commission intensified efforts to identify the impious who, it was claimed, formed an organized network bent on overthrowing the democracy. Tensions rose. Agariste III, then wife of Damon, informed against Alcibiades III, Adeimantus of Scambonidae, and Axiochus, for profaning the mysteries in Charmides' house by the Olympieum. Whether all four fled then except Alcibiades III, or all fled later after the fleet sailed, is disputed (Andoc.; D. S.). Alcibiades III was recalled from the invasion to stand trial (he would later escape his state escort at Thurii and defect to the Spartans).
- Lydus, slave of Pherecles of Themacus, accused his master "and others" of profaning the mysteries at Pherecles' house. One avoided prosecution, two fled, other outcomes are unknown.
- Dioclides, after having failed for a month to obtain the blackmail he had been promised, testified that he had witnessed some three hundred men preparing to mutilate herms, had tried to take their money rather than the state's— blackmail instead of a reward—and now named forty-two men including two members of the Council who narrowly escaped torture on the spot. Dioclides was lionized as a savior, and those he had denounced, including Andocides IV and his relatives, were imprisoned. Dioclides' testimony increased fears of a widespread conspiracy against the democracy just as Spartans and Boeotians reached the borders of Attica, so there was a citywide call to arms and general panic.

- Persuaded to save his family by forsaking his already-implicated or executed friends, Andocides IV confessed that Euphiletus' drinking club had instigated the mutilation of the herms, that he had known of it in advance but had tried to prevent it and did not himself participate. Further investigation confirmed Andocides IV's account. Public tensions eased.
- Dioclides confessed at once that he had lied, begged for his life, and named Alcibiades of Phegous and Amiantus of Aegina as the men who had put him up to it. Public suspicion shifted back to Alcibiades III. Dioclides was executed. Other informers were paid rewards at the Panathenaea festival.

Those who saved their lives by fleeing into exile were condemned *in absentia*, and their property was confiscated and sold by the state. Their exiles varied in length and hardship, dependent largely on what foreign holdings and friends they had to sustain them until it was safe to return to Athens. Thucydides (8.97.3) does not specify which exiles, other than Alcibiades III, were recalled after the fall of the Four Hundred in 411. Alcibiades III returned only as far as the fleet at that time, which may be true of Adeimantus of Scambonidae as well. Axiochus returned to Athens itself before 407/6, for he proposed a decree in that year, so one may suppose that all the exiles could have returned by then, their death sentences in abeyance or revoked (cf. Pl. *R.* 553b, 558a, *Ap.* 30c–d). After all, Aristophanes could parody the mysteries publicly by 405, using a chorus of Eleusinian initiates in the *Frogs* (316–459). There was, by the way, no prohibition on the initiation of slaves into the Eleusinian mysteries (Harrison 1998: 1.166), although there is no indication in Andocides IV or elsewhere that the informer and slave, Lydus, or Archebiades' attendant-slave, Andromachus, were in fact initiates. (For a slave initiation, cf. Lysias s.v.)

A set of ten *stelae* recording both the condemnation of those who were believed to have mutilated herms and profaned the mysteries, and the sales of their property was erected at the Eleusinium. A substantial number of fragments from the ten *stelae* have been recovered on the southeast corner of the Athenian agora and published (*IG* I³ 421–430). Altogether, the fragments contain fewer than twenty secure names of about fifty Andocides IV implies would originally have appeared there, but they provide information about the circumstances and property of those condemned for the sacrilege that would otherwise have been lost (e.g. their possessions, and the names and occupations of the slaves of each).

In modern bibliography.   MacDowell (1962: 181–93) is particularly sensitive to political issues in their historical context in his commentary on Andocides IV, though his prosopographical arguments are not always persuasive; Dover (*HCT* 4.278–89, 1970, taking MacDowell into account) is meticulous about historical details, especially but not exclusively in relation to Thucydides, but he is glib about the political issues; Aurenche (1974) is highly speculative but also detailed and systematic; Hansen (1975: 77–9) offers a different chronology from those considered here; Ostwald (1986: 528–50) is prosopographically and legally oriented, reining in Aurenche; and Furley (1996) adds material about Greek religion that has not figured much in previous work; its nine pages of bibliography are supplemented by a large number of other works cited in notes.

Because Andocides IV divided his account into a long section on all aspects of the accusations of profanation (1.11–18), followed later by one on all aspects of the accusations of herm defacement (1.34–47), presumably hoping for rhetorical purposes to place himself as far from any association with the profanation as possible, the impression is generated that Dioclides made his accusations late. Dover holds that the events of the two types of accusations were overlapping, that Dioclides' accusations came early in the process (*HCT* 4.274); and he deploys this premise later when he criticizes the case of those (e.g. Hatzfeld 1940: 193–4) who see Dioclides and the two men who instigated his perjury—Alcibiades of Phegous and Amiantus of Aegina—as motivated by the desire to attack Alcibiades III's enemies. Militating against Dover's view that Dioclides' accusations occurred early in the period, however, is the statement by Andocides IV's cousin that most victims of denunciation had already been dealt with by the time he and his family were imprisoned (1.49).

The mutilation of the herms, which Dover terms a "prank" by "a club of silly young men whose desire for public notice landed them in more trouble than they had bargained for" (*HCT* 4.286), appears to have included a number of older men as well. Troubling is Dover's relentlessly cheerful account of events (e.g., his speculations about how funny it could be to parody the mysteries) in which hundreds of people's lives were being destroyed or at the very least involuntarily redirected by execution, exile, disfranchisement, and confiscation. He downplays the political motivations behind the crime (*contra* MacDowell 1962: App. G). Dover concedes, "No doubt the prevailing feeling in 415 encouraged people to pay off old scores by incriminating personal enemies" (*HCT* 4.282), but he somehow manages to give it all a light touch. This is seen as well in Walter Burkert (*CAH* 5²: 267): "fun turned to hysteria with the mystery scandal of Alcibiades in 415." By comparison, Andrewes (*CAH* 5²: 449) characterizes the unfolding of events as an "inquisition" and Furley associates the mutilation of the herms with the ultimate failure of the Sicilian expedition (1996: 4), Athens' most complete disaster.

Alcibiades IV of Scambonidae, son of Alcibiades III
[*PA*/*APF* 598 (600.8, 10) *LGPN2* 24 *PAA* 121635 *RE* 3 *PX* Ἀλκιβιάδης Ἀλκιβιάδου Σκαμβωνίδης]
417/6–?>375
mother: Hipparete I
sister: woman who married Hipponicus III
father of Hipparete II
See stemma: Alcibiades.

IG II² 7400.2
   gravestone
Isocr. 16
Lys. 14, 15, 19.52
Xen. *Mem.* 1.3.8–15
[Andoc.] 4.15

Life.   The Salaminioi and Alcmaeonids, the families of Alcibiades IV's parents, boasted a number of illustrious members; Isocrates' reference to Alcibiades IV as a *Eupatrid* (16.25)—a descendant of the early ruling caste—may have been programmatic for its forensic context, but it was also correct. Alcibiades IV was born, the second child of Alcibiades III and Hipparete I, the year his father was threatened with ostracism and his mother died. Two years later, his father left Athens for the following eight years, returned for four months, then was gone again permanently. Before the boy turned four, his life had been threatened because of his father. Because his lineage and wealth might someday rally the people, Alcibiades IV was considered enough of a threat to the Thirty that they expelled him from the city when he was thirteen. When democracy was restored after 403, he was denied the property Alcibiades III had been awarded in 407 to compensate for what had earlier been confiscated and sold (Isocr. 16.45–6).

In Xenophon, Socrates, hearing that Critobulus has kissed the attractive "son of Alcibiades" III, advises Xenophon and Critobulus against the dangers of sex (Ἀφροδισίος). Even if Xenophon made up the scene, Critobulus' age—Alcibiades IV's senior by about seven years—is appropriate for the lover-beloved (*erōmenos-erastēs*) liaison. ("Son of Alcibiades" was understood by *APF* to refer to the grand-son of Alcibiades II, implying that Xenophon had confused the lineage of Clinias III—Critobulus' beloved in *Symposium*—who was Alcibiades II's grandson; see Critobulus s.v.)

When Alcibiades IV came of age, he became subject to litigation. In 397, Isocrates wrote a speech for him in which he defended his estate against the charge that his father stole one of the seven teams of horses he entered in the Olympics of 416 (Isocr. 16). The plaintiff, Tisias (cf. Charicles s.v.), claimed that he had contrib-uted at least some of the money used by Alcibiades III to purchase a team of four horses from the city of Argos, and that Alcibiades III had failed to name him as an owner of the team. Accounts differ, between five *talents* and eight, about the amount of money involved, and it may well be that the team cost eight *talents*, of which Tisias contributed five. This would explain why Tisias did not purchase the team himself: he did not have enough ready cash and expected his friend Alcibiades III to make up the remainder. Defending himself where even Isocrates seemed unable to defend his father, Alcibiades IV pointed out that, because he had no money, he would undergo disfranchisement (*atimia*) if found guilty, a terrible price to pay for an action of his father. The outcome of the trial is not known explicitly but, if Lysias' speeches 14 and 15 of later date are genuine, as they probably are (Todd 2000: 162), he won, for he faced the same penalty then. Note that a late confusion of the name 'Tisias' with 'Diomedes' in Diodorus (13.74), pseudo-Andocides, and Plutarch (*Alc.*) is traced to an error in Ephorus (Van Hook 1945: 175).

Lysias' speeches 14 and 15 were written for Alcibiades IV's plaintiffs for another trial, in 495, in which Alcibiades IV was accused of failing to serve as a hoplite when drafted; rather, he followed the orders of the generals by serving in the cavalry instead. What makes the situation peculiar is that the same generals preside over the trial, and some are expected to give evidence in defense of Alcibiades IV. In the midst of a comprehensive attack on the defendant's family, Alcibiades IV is accused of having committed incest with his sister, the wife of Hipponicus III, as a result of which Hipponicus divorced her (14.28). The outcome of the trial is not known, but it can probably be surmised from what we know of Alcibiades IV's later life.

It is common to say that nothing further is heard of Alcibiades IV after 395 (*APF* 600.10; Todd 2000: 161), but he is very unlikely at the age of twenty-two already to have fathered the daughter, Hipparete II, whose name appears on a gravestone with his (*IG* II² 7400.2), and with her presumed husband, Phanocles of Leuconoeum, son of Andromachus; the family plot in Cerameis includes six gravestones preserving several more names, including two sons and a grandson of Hipparete II.

Alcibiades of Phegous   *IG* I³ 428.3–4
[*PA/APF* 599, 601 (600.6C) *LGPN2* 16 *RE* 5   Xen. *Hell.* 1.2.13
PAA 121650 ?= 121652 Ἀλκιβιάδης   Andoc. 1.65–6
Φηγούσιος]
±450s–>409
See stemma: Alcibiades.

Life and career. Alcibiades can be assumed to have been named for his grandfather, Alcibiades II, a daughter of whom married a man from Phegous, a tiny deme of the Erechtheis tribe, probably inland, but of unknown location. He, like Adeimantus of Scambonidae, is so closely linked to Alcibiades III, and so poorly attested elsewhere, that we can only infer tentatively that he was the approximate contemporary of Alcibiades III, his first cousin.

Alcibiades was accused in 415 of instigating Dioclides' false accusations about the mutilation of the herms (Andoc.), apparently to harm the enemies of Alcibiades III. He shared exile with Alcibiades III (Xen.), and was meanwhile condemned *in absentia* (see Exc. 1). The sale of his confiscated property in Oropos is inscribed on a *stele* recovered from the agora (*IG*).

In Xenophon's account, Thrasyllus—on his way to rejoin troops under Alcibiades III in 409—had Alcibiades of Phegous stoned to death (κατέλευσεν), but Andrewes (1953: 11 with n4) finds this incredible, even if Thrasyllus was no supporter of Alcibiades III; thus he welcomes Wade-Gery's suggested emendation κατελε<ήσας ἀπέλ>υσεν, whereby Thrasyllus takes pity on Alcibiades of Phegous and releases him. (Cf. Harp. s.v. for the statement that Antiphon [of Rhamnous] mentions Alcibiades of Phegous in a speech against the general Demosthenes <413 where he is called a guest-friend, ξένος, of Alcibiades III.)

Prosopographical notes. *APF*, followed by *LGPN2*, says of *PA* 601 (Andoc. and *IG*) and *PA* 599 (Xen.) that they are "beyond any serious doubt identical"—but *PAA* separates them tentatively. *PAA* adopted as a deliberate policy "to be as critical and as accurate as possible in the identification of individuals. The result has been a large-scale dismemberment of the traditional identifications in Attic prosopography" (I: xvi). Yet the entries in the *PAA* database offer no place for reasoning about relationships, and little room for citing the record of prosopographical progress in the secondary literature, so the policy poses problems for researchers that cannot be overcome except by supplementing *PAA*. Alcibiades of Phegous appears to be an example of dismemberment without obvious cause.

Alcmaeon I of Athens, son of Megacles I See App. II. *See stemma: Pericles.*

Alcmonides I of Athens, son of Alcmaeon I See App. II. *See stemma: Pericles.*

Alcmonides of Aphidna See App. II.

Alexander, son of Alcetas See App. II.

Alexidemus of Thessaly See App. II.

Alexippus of Athens See App. II.

Amestris, wife of Persian king Xerxes See App. II.

Amiantus of Athens and Aegina See App. II.

Amyclus of Heraclea See App. II.

Amycus (boxer) See App. II.

Amynander of Athens See App. II.

Anacharsis of Scythia (geometer) See App. II.

Anacreon of Teos (poet) See App. II.

Anaxagoras of Clazomenae, son of Hegesibulus
[*FRA* 2895 *OCD*³ *RE* 4 *DPhA* 158 Ἀναξαγόρας Ἡγησιβούλου]
±499/8–428/7
teacher of Pericles I
natural philosopher

Pl. *Phdr.* 270a
Pl. *Ap.* 26d
Pl. *Cra.* 400a, 409a–b, 413c
Pl. *Grg.* 465d
Pl. *Phd.* 72c, 97b–99d
[Pl.] *G. Hp.* 281c, 283a
[Pl.] *Ltr.* 2.311a
[Pl.] *Alc.* 118c
[Pl.] *Riv.* 132a
[Pl.] *Sis.* 389a
frr. in DK 59
Aes. *Cal.* no. 73 (fr. 34 Dittmar)
Isocr. 15.235

Life and career.   In the case of Anaxagoras, almost all the biographical material is derived by Diogenes from earlier sources, which he usually names. There is no contemporaneous allusion to a trial of Anaxagoras for impiety, and that has fed skepticism (Dover 1975); but some have taken Aristophanes' *Acharnians* 703–712 and *Wasps* 946–949 to be references to Thucydides I of Alopece's incompetent prosecution of Anaxagoras. Plutarch (*Per.* 32) says a bill passed by Diopeithes to impeach public officials for atheism and astronomy was an effort to implicate Pericles I because of his association with Anaxagoras (cf. D. S. 12.39.2); and Diogenes (2.7) who cites two sources, Sotion (1–2nd c. C.E.) and Satyrus (3rd c. B.C.E.), who give conflicting "facts" about prosecutor, charges, and outcome. If there was a trial at all, scholars have given two different interpretations of its probable date. According to one view, Anaxagoras went to Athens as a young man, ±480, in which case Pericles I defended him early in his own career, ±450; according to the other, based on Apollodorus (2–1st c. B.C.E., cited by D. L.), Anaxagoras went to Athens in 456/5, putting Pericles I's defense near the time of his own death, given that the only source for how long Anaxagoras remained in Athens is a statement by Demetrius Phalerus (4th c. B.C.E., cited by D. L.) that he was there thirty years. The fact that Plato (*Ap.* 26d) represents Socrates as having known Anaxagoras only through his book, available for a *drachma* at the theatre, suggests that the two did not meet—an implicit argument for the former view. But if Thucydides I s.v. was the prosecutor, the latter date must be correct because Thucydides I was ostracized for ten years from 443. There is some evidence that it became popular, after the execution of Socrates, to compliment other philosophers and sophists by attributing to them at least the threat of a trial for impiety. In Anaxagoras' case, the debate continues (cf. Mansfeld 1979–80; Sider 1981: 1–11). Anaxagoras is said to have died, with great honor, in Lampsacus.

In Plato.   Only once does Anaxagoras appear in a mere list of wise men ([Pl.] *G. Hp.* 281c); and even that notice has a follow-up two pages later to the effect that he went from rich to poor through neglect (283a). References in the dialogues show Plato's familiarity with his work. The longest treatment occurs in a well-known passage of Socratic biography (*Phd.* 97b–99d) that criticizes Anaxagoras' understanding of causation: Socrates had, early on, expected and wanted mind to be the cause of everything but, in a series of steps, had realized to his disappointment that Anaxagoras was a materialist about causes. Elsewhere, however, Anaxagoras is credited with benefiting Pericles I (Pl. *Phdr.* 270a) by passing along his high-mindedness (τὸ ὑψηλόνουν), and for so often discussing mind and mindlessness (νοῦ τε καὶ ἀνοίας) that Pericles I was able to grasp their true nature. Hermogenes (*Cra.* 400a, cf. 413c) agrees harmlessly with Anaxagoras that mind orders nature; and in the same dialogue, Anaxagoras' theory that the moon shines by the sun's light is supported (409a–b). *Gorgias* 465d, like *Phaedo* 72c, shows acquaintance with the beginning of Anaxagoras' book (D. L. preserves its name as *Physica*) where everything is mixed and nothing is distinct. Meletus II appears to confuse Socrates' views with the astronomical views of Anaxagoras (*Ap.* 26d).

In the later tradition.   Anaxagoras is discussed by Aristotle (*passim*), Diodorus (12.39), Plutarch (*Per.* 4–6, 8.1, 16, 32, *Nic.* 23.2) and Diogenes (2.6–2.16). The claim that Archelaus and Euripides were Anaxagoras' students survives from accounts no earlier than the 3rd c. B.C.E. (Alexander of Aetolia). See a large range of testimonia in DK.

Anaximander of Miletus (philosopher) See App. II.

Anaximander (Homeric critic) See App. II.

Andocides IV of Cydathenaeum, son of Leogoras II	Andoc. 1, 2, 3, and fr. 5
[*PA/APF* 828 (828.6–7) *LGPN2* 7 *PAA* 127290	*IG* II² 1138.21–4;
RE 1 *OCD*³ Ἀνδοκίδης Λεωγόρου	1372.3
Κυδαθηναιεύς]	Thu. 6.60.2–5,
≤440–≥391	unnamed
mother: Tisander II's daughter	Philoch. fr. 149
sister: wife of Callias (tribe: Pandionis)	[Lys.] 6
See stemmata: Andocides, Callias.	

Life. This Athenian *not* mentioned by Plato, though related by marriage, is a source of much important information about characters in the dialogues. He was born into the aristocratic and powerful Alcmaeonid clan that had hereditary ties to King Archelaus of Macedonia (Andoc. 2.11). The Alcmaeonids, through intermarriage and marriage alliances, had consolidated a great deal of wealth by the mid 5th c. Andocides IV's paternal grandmother was probably a descendant of the archon Eryxias (*APF*); she was the sister of Critias IV's mother, so Andocides IV was Critias IV's first cousin once removed (Andoc. 1.47). He was also related by marriage to Callias III with whom he fell into a domestic and legal dispute over the surviving daughter of Epilycus II, whom—or whose wealth—both men wanted to claim; as further evidence of the enmity between the two men, Callias III paid the accusers of Andocides IV in 400 (Andoc. 1.110–132; for details of the trial, see Callias III s.v.). Andocides IV's own great wealth is attested by his liturgies listed in his speech 1: *gymnasiarchos* at Hephaistia in 403, *archetheoros* at Isthmia in 403 and again at Olympia in 400, treasurer (*tamias*) of Athena in 401/0 (1.132; the service as *tamias* is corroborated at *IG* II² 1372). *IG* II² 1138 adds a further liturgy, victorious *chorēgos* in the boys' dithyramb at the Dionysia of 403 or 402.

Although traditionally counted among the ten great orators of Athens, there is no evidence that Andocides IV was a professional orator. On the contrary, Andocides IV appears to have been a man of sufficient wealth that he could afford, even from exile 415–403, to engage in business (shipping and import-exporting) without need for profit (Andoc. 2.11; cf. 1.134 for his later concession to collect customs duties). Further, the speeches attributed to him, which are not in chronological order, marked the occasions in his own life when he sought to reinstate himself in Athens. The speeches are thus suspect as sources for his life because—despite his reading public documents, calling witnesses, and in 400

STEMMA: ANDOCIDES

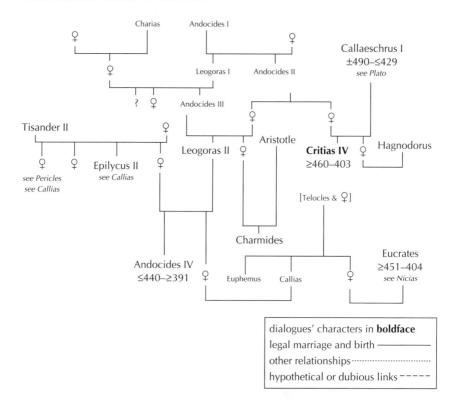

winning his case—they are nonetheless unabashedly partisan accounts, in a context where his life or his freedom was at stake (see below).

On the mutilation of the herms in 415.   Andocides IV was a member of the oligarchic club that, led by Euphiletus, planned and carried out the mutilation of the herms. Marr (1971: 326–38) defends Andocides IV against what he refers to as the anti-Andocides tradition, though he concedes that Andocides IV "was a member of the Euphiletus' club and had made oligarchic propaganda for it" (Andoc. 1.61), that he had had prior knowledge of the intent to mutilate herms, that "[h]e had agreed to share in the crime and fully intended to do so," and that he had remained silent afterwards although the citizenry expected an oligarchic revolution (Andoc. 1.64; Thu. 6.27.3). Andocides IV probably misrepresented the truth in his own defense in 400, for he did not then admit that he had "fully intended" to participate in the crime; rather, he maintained that he had protested against Euphiletus' plans (Andoc. 1.61–63, 1.67) and, implicitly, that he had thwarted those plans successfully until he was himself thrown from a horse and incapacitated, thereby providing Euphiletus with an opportunity to act under cover of Andocides IV's injuries, and to misrepresent Andocides IV's intentions to the other perpetrators.

Andocides IV provides, by describing how Euphiletus persuaded and perhaps deceived members of his "drinking club" to participate in the mutilation of the herms (Andoc. 1.61–64), a useful insight into how some Athenian political clubs may have operated (cf. Socrates at *Ap.* 36b); these oligarchic clubs were to play a pivotal role in the establishment of the Four Hundred in 411 (Thu. 8.54.4).

Andocides IV was among those accused by Dioclides of mutilating herms in 415 as a result of which he and several of his relatives were imprisoned. By incriminating himself and others, and at the instigation of his cousin Charmides (Andoc. 1.51), he was able to gain his own release and that of several of his family—at the cost of becoming, and being labeled, an informer (Thu. 6.60.1–5).

Pseudo-Lysias 6 is a prosecution speech against Andocides IV, accusing him of both mutilating herms and parodying in the mysteries (6.51); the speech is based on a religious fundamentalism that often ignores not only the canons of logography but fact and logic as well. Lamb (1930: 112) suggests it is a "pamphlet composed by one of his [Andocides IV's] many persecutors after hearing or reading of his defence." And Dover (*HCT* 277 and 281n5) in effect dismisses it altogether by omitting to include Andocides IV among those charged with parodying the mysteries (it is not an oversight: Dover had read MacDowell 1962 in ms.). The appearance that Andocides IV is answering pseudo-Lysias 6, point by point (Andoc., after 1.107) fits both accounts since the speech could have been written with the passages following Andoc. 1.107 in mind. MacDowell (1962: 14 with n4, and references therein) argues that the speech is genuine, not a later pamphlet, but spoken by Meletus II, Epichares, or Agyrrhius—and most likely by Meletus II s.v. At one point, the subordinate prosecutor invites the jurors to imagine what parodying the mysteries, and its penalty, involved

This man put on a ceremonial robe. He mimicked the sacred rites and revealed them to the uninitiated, and spoke with his lips the forbidden words: those deities whom we worship, and to those who were not initiates. He gave voice to words that must not be spoken. He mutilated the gods whom we worship, and to whom we sacrifice and pray, honoring them and purifying ourselves. This is why priestesses and priests stood facing the west and cursed him, shaking out their purple robes according to ancient and ancestral custom. ([Lys.] 6.51)

Exile and return. While the various acts of sacrilege were being adjudicated (cf. Exc. 1), the decree of Isotimides was passed, making it a capital offense for anyone who had admitted to impiety to enter temples, the agora, or other public places; Andocides IV thus found life in Athens untenable and went into voluntary exile in 415 or early 414 to pursue his fortunes abroad. On three occasions, he sought legal redress in attempts to return to Athens, succeeding only on the third attempt. He tried in 411 with the Four Hundred, and again, sometime between 410 and 408 (cf. Maidment 1941: 454–8) with the Athenian Assembly of the restored democracy to get around the terms of the decree of Isotimides. On that occasion, with his *On His Return*, Andocides IV elliptically admitted his complicity in an unspecified crime, saying that youthful ignorance had made him susceptible to persuasion into madness (τῶν πεισάντων . . . τῶν φρενῶν, 2.7), and describing his disgrace before the gods (2.15), an apparent reference to an act of impiety, though which particular act is still disputed.

In 403, when democracy was once again restored after the oligarchy of the Thirty, Andocides IV finally succeeded in returning to Athens with his citizen rights restored, taking advantage of the terms of the general amnesty which he later describes in detail (Andoc. 1.71–91). However, in the autumn of 400 (for the precise date, see MacDowell 1962: 204–5, noting that 399 cannot be completely ruled out) he found himself in a court of law, charged with breaking the terms of the decree of Isotimides (Andoc. 1). Opposed covertly by Callias III, with whom the domestic dispute had already begun, but supported by the democratic leaders, Anytus and Cephalus—as well as by fellow tribesmen selected to defend him— Andocides IV was acquitted and returned to public life.

Andocides IV served as a negotiator with Sparta in the winter of 392 (Andoc. 3) but afterwards failed to persuade the Assembly to agree to peace terms he and other emissaries had negotiated with Sparta (Philoch. with Maidment 1941: 487–8; cf. Andoc. 3, though its authenticity is not secure). Callistratus s.v. called the action of the envoys negligence of duty and proposed a successful motion to exile them all. Andocides IV went into exile and apparently never returned to Athens.

In the later tradition and modern bibliography.   MacDowell (1962: Apps. A and C) concludes that Andocides IV was probably guilty of profaning the mysteries, and not of mutilating herms, citing in evidence pseudo-Lysias, *Against Andocides*; Plutarch's *Alcibiades* 21.4–6; Tzetzes, *Historia* 49; and pseudo-Plutarch, *Life of Andocides*, in developing his account of Andocides IV's life and career, addressing further controversies not discussed here.

Andromachus, slave of Archebiades See App. II.

Andromedes of Aegina   [Pl.] *Ltr.* 13.362b
[*RE* 1 Ἀνδρομήδης]
4th c.

Andromedes was wealthy and lent money to Dionysius II. The name is not recorded until the 3rd c. (*LGPN3A*).

Andron of Gargettus, son of Androtion I	Pl. *Grg.* 487c *	
[*PA/APF* 921 (913) *PAA* 129130, 129265	Pl. *Prt.* 315c	present
LGPN2 12 *RE* 2 *OCD*³ *DPhA* 176 *PP* Ἄνδρων	*IG* XII 7.5.17, pat.	
Ἀνδροτίωνος Γαργήττιος]	56, 68	
±445–≥410	*IG* II² 212.8, pat.	
father of Androtion II	Demos. 22.33–4,	
friend of Callicles, Tisander, and Nausicydes	24.125, 24.168	
oligarchic politician		

Life.   Andron's date of birth, ±445, is calculated approximately from that of his well-known son, Androtion II—a man of significant means who studied under Isocrates and was one of the several writers of Attic chronicles, collected under the title *Athides*—born 410–407 (*APF*). Thus Andron was probably among the younger of those present at Callias III's house in 433/2 where Plato represents him in the group including Eryximachus and Phaedrus that had gathered around Hippias (*Prt.*). He was later associated with Callicles, Tisander, and Nausicydes (*Grg.*). Andron was at some time imprisoned for debt (Demos. 22, prosecuting Androtion II in 355). According to Harrison, citing pseudo-Aristotle (*Ath. Pol.* 63.3) for the rule, and Demosthenes (22, 24) for the example, "we find the rule that a public debtor who sat as a juror, and was informed against by ἔνδειξις [indictment] and convicted and fined by a court, was imprisoned until he paid both the original debt and the fine. We have at least one example of a public debtor thus held (and held for a long time) in Andron, father of Androtion" (1998.2: 242). Comparison to modern examples of debtors' prisons is inappropriate: wealthy Athenians did not labor to earn their incomes and thus did not need to be at large to receive revenue from their farms, mines, and businesses. It should be added that Demosthenes was an opponent of this Andron's son, Androtion II; thus the account of Andron as a debtor may have been given a more negative slant than if the account had been written by a disinterested observer.

Career.   Andron was a member of the oligarchy of the Four Hundred in 411. Avery considers the men clustered around Hippias in the passage from *Protagoras* and notes that, of that group, only Antiphon was *not* implicated in the sacrilege of 415 (1963: 165–7); he argues that no one involved in the sacrilege would have been allowed membership in the Four Hundred. After the collapse of the oligarchy, according to pseudo-Plutarch (*LTO* 833d–f), Andron was author of a proposal to prosecute Antiphon of Rhamnous s.v. in 410 (against whom Theramenes s.v. was chief accuser) and, perhaps, Archeptolemus and Onomacles as well (Harp. s.v. Andron)—a denunciation of former colleagues that Dodds describes as aimed at saving his own skin (1959: 282).

Prosopographical notes.   *PAA* separates 129130, the member of the Four Hundred and proposer of a decree against Antiphon in 411 ([Plu.]; Harp. s.v.), from 129265 (Pl., Demos., *IG*). Andron appears as the pat. of Androtion II in a foreign dedication (*IG* XII) dated 387/6, and in a decree (*IG* II²) dated 377/6.

Androtion I of Gargettus, son of Andron See App. II.

Antaeus (wrestler) See App. II.

Anthemion I of Euonymon (tanner) See App. II.

Antimoerus of Mende   Pl. *Prt.* 315a   present
[*RE* s.v. *DPhA* 198 *PP* Ἀντίμοιϱος]
active in 433/2
student of Protagoras

Antimoerus, said to be Protagoras' best student and studying to be a sophist, flanks Protagoras himself at Callias III's house in 433/2. The timing of the visit to Athens represented in the dialogue is plausible: Mende was still under Athenian domination at the time, not revolting from Athens until after the brief general truce of April 423.

Antiphates of Cytherus See App. II.

Antiphon I of Athens   Pl. *Prm.* 126a–c †
[*PA/APF* 1275 (8792.8) *LGPN2* 1 *PAA* 138185   Plu. *Mor.* 581d, pat.
PP Ἀντιφῶν]
b. 510s
father of Pyrilampes
See stemma: Plato.

Antiphon I devoted most of his time to horses (Pl.), but that fact alone tells us that he was almost certainly a very wealthy man, wealthy enough to be required to perform liturgies for the state. There are many inscriptions bearing the name 'Antiphon' that cannot be distributed confidently to any known Antiphon, and the lack of a demotic or patronymic for Antiphon I renders the possibility of positive identifications remote.

Antiphon of Athens   Andoc. 1.15
[*PA* 1279 *LGPN2* 8 *PAA* 138200 Ἀντιφῶν]
active in 415
accused in the sacrilege

Prosopographical notes.   An Antiphon is named among those accused by Teucrus of profaning the Eleusinian mysteries in 415; he fled Athens (Andoc.). Antiphon I was probably already dead. Antiphon II was still a child. Antiphon of Rhamnous is ruled out because the earliest any of those who fled the city were able to return was after the fall of the Four Hundred in 411. Although the remaining two Antiphons are of more plausible ages, the "forest of Antiphons in the late fifth century" (*APF*) precludes any confident fusion on currently available information.

Antiphon of Athens, son of Lysonides   Xen. *Hell.* 2.3.40
[*PA/APF* 1283 (8792.6) *LGPN2* 5 *PAA* 138325,   Crat. *Pyt.* fr. 212 (K
138320 *RE* 3 Ἀντιφῶν Λυσωνίδου]   201)
450s–404/3   Theop. *hist.* fr. 120
executed by the Thirty   Lys. fr. 11

Life.   The execution of Antiphon was one of three examples given by Theramenes, an early leader of the Thirty, of unnecessary and unjust executions of leading citizens that had led the Athenians to oppose the Thirty's rule. Antiphon, he said, had manned and paid for two triremes during the war (Xen.), a heavy financial obligation that was normally shared after ±411 (MacDowell 1976b: 161). So the son of Lysonides was especially wealthy—probably explaining best why he was targeted for execution by the Thirty, who immediately confiscated his property. He was also prominent, mentioned by the comic poet Cratinus in 423. To prevent the Thirty from leaving Antiphon's surviving daughter with nothing (or perhaps for reasons of his own), a man named Epistratus claimed that an estate of Antiphon's was his own. Five months later, when the Thirty realized what was going on, of course they. . .[the papyrus fr. (Lys.) breaks off here]. Under Athenian law, an orphaned daughter without brothers was an heiress (an *epiklēros*) who could be claimed in a special court procedure (an *epidikasia*) by her closest relative, with the father's side of the family first in the legal line (cf. Callias III). The litigant for the heiress in the case of Antiphon's daughter was a Callaeschrus who is assumed to be a relative of Antiphon but cannot be positively identified.

In the later tradition.   Pseudo-Plutarch (*LTO* 832f–833b) tells a confused version of this story, citing the historian Theopompus.

Prosopographical notes.   *PAA* 138322 (the Lysias fragment) ?= *PAA* 138320.

Antiphon II of Athens, son of Pyrilampes   Pl. *Prm.* 126a–c   speaker
[*PA/APF* 1284 (8792.8) *LGPN2* 7 *PAA* 138330   Plu. *Mor.* 484f
RE 5 *DPhA* 210 *PP* Ἀντιφῶν
Πυριλάμπους]
≥422–382
mother: Perictione
maternal half siblings: Plato, Adeimantus I,
  Glaucon IV Potone; paternal half brother:
  Demos
associate of Pythodorus
See stemma: Plato.

Antiphon II was born ≥422 (cf. Perictione s.v.), *pace* the concern that "Pyrilampes' age discourages any much later date" than 425 (*APF*); fifty-eight is not too old for Pyrilampes to beget a child with a new wife who was not yet thirty. As Plato represents his brother, Antiphon II associated with Pythodorus s.v. enough at some time to memorize the bulk of *Parmenides*, indicating at least some interest in philosophy, but by the time of the dialogue's dramatic frame in the late 380s, he resided in Melite and, like his grandfather, spent most of his time with his horses. As is the case with Antiphon I, there are inscriptions that might be assigned to him, but not with certainty. His deme of residence is not a useful guide to his deme of registration—especially since the urban part of Athens was desirable real estate in the early 4th c. and people moved around, even as they kept estates in their demes or elsewhere for income.

Antiphon of Cephisia	Pl. *Ap.* 33e	present
[*PA* 1299 *LGPN2* 45 *PAA* 138545 Ἀντιφῶν		
Κηφισιεύς]		
father of Epigenes		

Antiphon of Rhamnous, son of Sophilus	Pl. *Mx.* 236a *
[*PA* 1304, 1278 *LGPN2* 57, 3 *PAA* 138625,	oratorical *opera*
138190 *RE* 14, 15 *DPhA* 209 *OCD*³ *PP PX*	frr. in DK 87
Ἀντιφῶν Σοφίλου Ῥαμνούσιος]	Thu. 8.68, 8.90–1
±479–411	Xen. *Mem.* 1.6.1–15
student of, or influenced by, Gorgias	Aristoph. *Wasps*
teacher of Thucydides	1270, 1301
oligarchic leader, sophist, rhetorician	Pl. *com. Pis.* fr. 103
	(K 96)
	Lys. 12.67
	Aristot. *Eu. Eth.*
	1232b6–9
	[Aristot.] *Ath. Pol.*
	32.2

Life and career. Antiphon was a successful teacher of rhetoric who composed textbook forensic speeches known as the *Tetralogies* (arguing both sides of a case with equal force), forensic and Assembly speeches for clients to deliver, and treatises on the hot intellectual issues of the day, including the interpretation of dreams, earning enough to cover the costs of the comforts he valued. He had attracted sufficient attention by 422 to be the butt of jokes in Aristophanes ("drunk and disorderly" at *Wasps* 1301), and in the comic poet Plato who accused him of composing his speeches for love of money. Antiphon wrote a diatribe against Alcibiades III, perhaps in 418, which may have been used in a prosecution but may also have appeared as a pamphlet (frr. in Plu. *Alc.* 3.1 and Ath. 525b).

It is common even now to confuse the orator, rhetorician, and sophist—as those ancient professionals are usually translated—partly because their work does not correspond exactly with current professions, and partly because they tended to overlap one another in the same person, as is so often the case in Plato's dialogues. An orator, strictly speaking, was someone who specialized in the excellent delivery of forensic and political speeches—much as the rhapsode performed the works of a poet. Commonly, an orator was also a 'logographer' or speechwriter. Antiphon differed from the norm in that he was a logographer without being an orator as well. He appears to have avoided the limelight and to have written his speeches almost exclusively for others to deliver, though he appears also to have taught public speaking and speechwriting. A rhetorician was someone who not only wrote (and probably delivered) speeches but studied the principles and means of effective oral and written communication. Some developed rhetorical theory further, and some taught rhetorical theory, or at least rhetoric, to others. Socrates shows familiarity with the innovations and technical vocabulary of a number of rhetoricians of his time in *Phaedrus*. Antiphon both advanced rhetorical theory and taught it. But public teachers, professors, were often called sophists in Socrates' time. 'Sophist' is an ambiguous term in that it applied to a professional teacher whose task could be much narrower, or alternatively much broader, than that of a rhetorician. Some sophists (e.g. Euthydemus) were interested in displaying their skills and in teaching the part of rhetoric that deals with valid and fallacious arguments; it is they who developed the reputation for making the worse cause appear to be the better—the shyster lawyer of today. Other sophists (e.g. Protagoras) taught rhetoric within the context of teaching young men to live well generally; and that implied a study of how to live well and what constitutes the good life. The stereotypical sophist was a foreigner who had made himself rich through his itinerant teaching. Antiphon was an *Athenian* who made himself rich through his teaching, and only Xenophon among contemporaneous sources calls him a sophist. Indeed, his *Tetralogies* set him up to be so interpreted, but the label is probably as inappropriate for Antiphon as for Isocrates.

As Antiphon approached the age of seventy, he became the most important leader of the oligarchic faction that established the rule of the Four Hundred, and in that capacity he was an envoy to Sparta to seek peace in 411 (Thu. 8.90.1), a mission that failed owing to a Spartan demand that Athens give up dominion over the sea ([Aristot.] *Ath. Pol.* 32.2). Thucydides (8.68.1–2) says

> the one who devised the way in which the entire enterprise reached this point, after devoting his attention to it the longest, was Antiphon, a man second to no Athenian of his time in ability and a master both at developing plans and at stating his conclusions, and while he was not one to come forward in the assembly or go willingly into any other scene of contention but was regarded with suspicion by the people because of a reputation for cleverness, he was nevertheless the one man most able to help those contending in law courts or in the assembly whenever anyone consulted him. And in addition, after the democracy had been changed back, and Antiphon was brought to trial at a later time when the actions of the Four Hundred had been reversed and were being dealt with harshly by the assembly, it is clear that he in person, on trial for these very actions, as a collaborator, made the best defense on a capital charge of all men up to my time.

The defense, which is not extant, did not save him. Antiphon was condemned to death, and his property was confiscated. Lysias writes in his own voice that Theramenes s.v., who had likewise been a leader of the Four Hundred, betrayed Antiphon and caused him to be executed.

In Xenophon and the later tradition.   When Xenophon introduces the conversations between Socrates and Antiphon, he employs the epithet "Antiphon the sophist," saddling the son of Sophilus with an unsympathetic portrayal so different from that of Thucydides that there have always been those who thought the two could not be referring to the same individual. Yet the character Xenophon sketches—a teacher of rhetoric and lover of money and luxuries—fits the rhetorician well overall. Antiphon in *Memorabilia* is well-known already, has students, and approaches those around Socrates with the idea of drawing them away into his own orbit (1). All three vignettes are about what the young ought to learn from their teachers: Antiphon praises luxuries (2), money (3, 11–12), and turning out success-ful politicians (15); if something is odd for a teacher of rhetoric in Xenophon's characterization, it is that Antiphon never succeeds in getting in another word once Socrates begins to speak.

By the time of Aristotle, Antiphon was an example of magnanimity: "The magnanimous man would consider rather what one good man thinks than many ordinary men, as Antiphon after his condemnation said to Agathon when he praised his defence of himself" (*Eu. Eth.*). Plutarch confirms a number of the above details and adds a few not preserved elsewhere: that Antiphon was a student of his father (*Mor.* 832c), a teacher of Thucydides the historian (832e) and a litigant in suits with Demosthenes and others in 413 (833d). Diogenes reduces Antiphon to a soothsayer who attacked Socrates (2.46). See other testimonia in DK.

Prosopographical notes.   In the list of numbers that heads this entry, the first listed in each pair is Antiphon of Rhamnous, the second is the Antiphon of Xenophon and the sophistic fragments (DK); *LGPN2* notes they are possibly the same individ-ual. They are the same individual, and in spite of Tulin's (1998: 1) observation that the question is "complex—too complex for the elementary reader," I think it is not difficult to see how the separation occurred and then gained a life of its own. There are both historical arguments (Morrison in Sprague 2001: 109–10) and textual ones that can be stated briefly.

Caecilius of Calacte (1st c. B.C.E.), followed by Pseudo-Plutarch, Photius, and Philostratus, conflates the Rhamnousian with a tragic poet and with the son of Lysonides (above). Not surprisingly, *Lives of the Ten Orators* ([Plu.]) and *Lives of the Sophists* (Philostr.) concentrated on different works of Antiphon, paving the way for later authors to suppose there were two Antiphons. Meanwhile, Didymus (1st c. B.C.E.) concluded that the difference between Antiphon's speeches and his treatises could not be accounted for by difference in *genre* alone, so he—and he was first to do so—posited a second Antiphon. In its modern version, based on the old orator-sophist split, difference in political orientation has been held to mark the difference between the two Antiphons: a few papyri of *On Truth* appeared early in the 20th c. that seemed too egalitarian to have been written by the oligarch. But "a new papyrus fragment has forced a revision of part of the text of *On Truth*, eliminating an earlier reconstruction in which the author appeared to challenge the traditional class structure" (Gagarin 1998: 4–5). Additional contemporary bibli-ography for this ancient controversy includes Avery (1982), Pendrick (1987), and Gagarin (1997).

There are a few remaining prosopographical details. An Antiphon of Rhamnous (*PAA* 131500) was treasurer of the other gods in 429/8 (*IG* I³ 383.4) and is thus considered possibly the same as *PA* 1304, though the inscription has been heavily reconstructed; if so, he could be added to the *APF* list of Athens' wealthy elite. *LGPN2* 57 emends the pat. to var. Σωφίλου.

Antisthenes of Athens   Xen. *Mem.* 3.4.1–12
[*PA/APF* 1184 (1194) *LGPN2* 25 *APF/LGPN2*

1184 = 1194 = 1196 = 1197 *PAA* 136760 *PX*
Ἀντισθένης]
late 5th c. ?*chorēgos* and ?*stratēgos*

Life. Nicomachides protests to Socrates that, despite his own military record and war wounds, he has lost the election for general to a businessman with no military experience, Antisthenes (*PA* 1184). Socrates points out, in Antisthenes' defense, that he has won every choral competition he has entered and manages his private affairs well, knowing just when to employ experts.

Prosopographical notes. Here is a textbook case of prosopographical inertia. There is no complete list of the ten generals (*stratēgoi*) elected annually by the ten tribes, and supplementary elections were often required to fill vacancies. Nonetheless, efforts both heroic and foolish have gone into discovering the identity of Xenophon's Antisthenes. A hundred years ago, Kirchner (*PA*) suggested Antisthenes of Cytherus, son of Antiphates (*PA* 1196), who did at least have a choral victory to his credit. But known individuals are like magnets, picking up fresh inscriptions and identifications, and over time this Antisthenes has engulfed the others (*PA* 1194, *PA* 1195, *PA* 1197), becoming also a manumittor of slaves, the owner of mining property at Amphitrope, a priest, twice a *trierarch*, twice a father, and also a brother. The more that is surmised about Antisthenes of Cytherus, however, the more impossible it becomes that he could be Xenophon's general. The earliest this man could have been elected was some twenty years after Socrates' death, and Xenophon, who is in exile, is very unlikely to have known him. Despite this, some have chosen to preserve the momentum of surmise and to use the very difficulties it creates in a sweeping reinterpretation of Xenophon's text, rather than to revisit the original shaky conjecture. "The choice lies between assuming that the Xenophontic Antisthenes is a different man or assuming that Xenophon has taken a gross chronological liberty in order to build up his literary portrait of Sokrates. My own preference is to accept the identification and all that it entails for Xenophon's technique; the evidence for similar distortions in other Sokratic writers is widespread enough for one more example not to cause surprise" (*APF* 1194; accepted by *LGPN2*). For Pete's sake!
   More wisely, *PAA* has dismembered the monster: Antisthenes is again four individuals, and we still have no one who fits Xenophon's description.

Antisthenes II of Athens, son of
   Antisthenes I
[*PA* 1188 *LGPN2* 2 *PAA* 136800 *RE* 10 *DPhA*
211 *OCD³ PP PX* Ἀντισθένης
Ἀντισθένους]
±446–>366
student of Gorgias, Socrates
philosopher, teacher, writer of Socratic
   dialogues

Pl. *Phd.* 59b   present
frr. *SSR* 2.VA
Xen. *Symp., passim*
Xen. *Mem.* 2.5.1–3,
   3.11.17

Life.   Antisthenes II was the wealthy son of a famous father and a mother who was said in the later tradition to have been Thracian. Since Antisthenes II was, in all likelihood, born after the institution of Pericles I's citizenship laws of 451/ 0 (he is listed among the native residents at Pl. *Phd.*), his mother was almost certainly Athenian, though perhaps with Thracian ascendants, and certainly a local resident of Athens (an *astē*). Diogenes (6.1) says Antisthenes II served with distinction in the battle of Tanagra, and Thucydides (3.91) mentions such a battle in 426. It is probable that he had students of his own, and a nominal date of ±396 is sometimes given for the founding of his school—but less certain that he had students before meeting Socrates, afterwards advising them to join him as students of Socrates (D. L. 6.2).

Xenophon describes Antisthenes II as Socrates' constant companion (*Mem.* 3.11.17). In a speech about what he values most—the wealth of soul he acquired from Socrates that makes him eschew material things (Xen. *Symp.* 4.34–44)— Antisthenes II is quite the most talkative and the most contentious person present at Callias III's banquet (3.4, 4.2), quick to take offense and show his temper (4.62, 5.1, 8.6). Xenophon's criticism of Xanthippe is put in his mouth (2.10). Socrates explicitly turns over his "profession" of procurer to Antisthenes, who is said already to have proved himself to be the perfect go-between (4.61; cf. Cephalus' passing everything on to Polemarchus at *R.* 1.331d), as Socrates goes on to demonstrate. And, at a point when Xenophon's *Symposium* begins to look like Plato's (i.e. when the topic of conversation becomes spiritual and carnal *erōs*, heavenly and earthly Aphrodite, lovers and beloveds), Antisthenes is given a bit of Alcibiades III's role from Plato's *Symposium*, complaining that he is in love with Socrates, but that Socrates always refuses him on some pretext or other.

Works.   Despite 88 pp. of *SSR*, almost nothing remains of what Antisthenes II wrote: much of the testimonia collected there consists of long quotations from Xenophon's *Symposium* and from Diogenes (6.1–19), though many anecdotes and maxims reported by various other late authors are provided as well, both the dubious ones (cf. no. 143 & n) and those considered genuine. Diogenes (6.15–18) attributes to Antisthenes II sixty-two titles in ten volumes from which only a handful of direct quotations, if such they are, have survived (quotations from Xen. *Symp.* are treated as frr. of Antisthenes in *SSR*). Most appear to be titles of speeches, and the subjects covered are diverse; but a few (perhaps nine) appear to have been dialogues. Three relevant titles are *Alcibiades*, *Aspasia*, and *Menexenus*.

In the later tradition and modern bibliography.   Aristotle treats Antisthenes II in philosophical contexts (see *Meta.* 1024b32 et al.), but a very large number of anecdotes about him are retailed by a great variety of authors (= the testimonia of *SSR*). Diodorus (15.76) mentions Antisthenes II in a list of philosophers active in the mid 360s. (Cf. also D. L. 6.1–19, 2.31; [Socr.] *Ep.* 8 (Antisthenes to Aristippus); *Suda* α 2723; Plu. *Lyc.* 30.6; and Ath. 157b, 220d, 533c–534b, 589e. D. L. cites Theop. *hist.* fr. 295, Nean. fr. 24, et al.) Monographs include Rankin 1986 and Navia 2001 (cf. Gigon 1953, 1956).

Prosopographical notes.   *LGPN2* 3 (cf. *PA* 1188) is based on Diogenes 6.1.1, repeating that Antisthenes I is the father of Antisthenes II.

Anytus of Euonymon, son of Anthemion I
[*PA/APF* 1324 *LGPN2* 4 *PAA* 139460 *DPhA*
227 *RE* 3 *OCD*³ *PP* Ἄνυτος Ἀνθεμίωνος
(Εὐωνυμεύς)]
≤443–>399
father of an unnamed son
prosecutor of Socrates

Pl. *Meno* 90a   speaker
Pl. *Ap.* 18b, 23e, &
  schol.   present
Xen. *Apol.* 29–31
Xen. *Hell.* 2.3.42, 44
Andoc. 1.150
Lys. 13.78–9, 22.8
Isocr. 18.23–4
D. S. 13.64–6, 14.37.7
Hell. Oxy. 6.2
Aristoph. *Thesm.*
  809, unnamed
Arch. *Fishes* fr. 31 (K
  30)
Theo. *Strat.* fr. 58 (K
  57)
[Aristot.] *Ath. Pol.*
  27.5, 34.3

Life.   Anytus was the son of a self-made man who was highly praised in Plato's *Meno* (90a): Anthemion, son of Diphilus, a *thete* who became a *hippeus* ([Aristot.] *Ath. Pol.* 7.4; Poll. 8.131) "through his own wisdom and effort" (*Meno* 90a). His demotic is virtually certain (Raubitschek 1949). If Anytus was in fact a lover of Alcibiades III (Pl. *Ap.* schol.), his date of birth should be earlier than 451, and nothing that is known about his career makes that early date implausible. If this datum falls away, however, as suggested in detail in *APF*, Anytus' birth would be no later than 443, if he served on the Council in 413/2, and no later than ±440 in any case. Anytus inherited a successful tannery from his father (Xen. *Apol.* 29; Pl. *Ap.* schol.), but the comic playwrights reduced his occupation to one rather more common for slaves, "shoemaker" (Theo.; Arch.). He was also said to have been the father of an unnamed, drunken, son who followed Anytus into the tanning trade, for whom Xenophon's Socrates prophesied a career of vice (*Apol.*).

Career.   The claim that Anytus served as a member of Council in 413/2 rests on the argument of Maas that Aristophanes (*Thesm.*) refers to him; if so, then Anytus was a corrupt member of Council. If he does not, then Anytus' first appearance in the record is his service as general in 409. Pylos, which had been taken in 425 by Athens, was retaken in 409 by Sparta. Anytus led thirty Athenian triremes to retake Pylos but was thwarted by bad weather from rounding Cape Malea ([Aristot.] *Ath. Pol.* 27.5); he was subsequently prosecuted for failing to prevent the loss of Pylos, but escaped punishment by bribing the large jury with his ample inheritance (D. S. 13; [Aristot.] 27); his bribery method, which is not well understood, was later given the special name *dekazein* and was made punishable by death (cf. MacDowell 1978: 173).

Anytus supported Theramenes' faction of the Thirty in 404 ([Aristot.] 34), but was later banished by the Thirty nevertheless; the many slaves his tannery would have employed were presumably confiscated (cf. Lys. 12). Theramenes identifies Anytus, along with Thrasybulus and Alcibiades III, as a capable democratic leader whom it would have been better that the Thirty *not* have banished; doing so had raised the hopes and number of supporters of the democracy (Xen. *Hell.* 2.3.42). Indeed Anytus had been made *stratēgos* of the democrats at Phyle 404/3; there he gave his protection to an informer for the Thirty who later escaped (Lys. 13). Despite that blot, he returned with Thrasybulus to the Piraeus and became one of the political leaders of the newly restored democracy.

In a speech dated 402, Isocrates praised Anytus as a respected supporter of the restored democracy, crediting him with refraining from vendettas: although Anytus had been robbed of much of his wealth at the time of his exile and knew who had betrayed his holdings to the Thirty, he had not brought charges against those enemies because, at least according to Isocrates, he respected the amnesty (18.23–4). In early 402, however, details of the reconciliation agreement were still being worked out, protecting both sides, and it was not until much later that some grudges found their way into court (cf. Exc. 4). In Plato's *Meno* of 402 (cf. App. I), Anytus is introduced as the son of a fine father (90a) who educated Anytus to the satisfaction of the Athenians, who had in turn elected Anytus to Athens' highest offices. Anytus is Meno's host in Athens (*Meno* 90b), and cannot abide sophists (91c, 92e). When the worthiness of Anytus' father is placed in the context of the whole conversation in which Anytus participates with Socrates and Meno, the implicit conclusion is that Anytus is not the man his father was. Plato offers a fair number of examples to show that the sons of the best men do not turn out to be their fathers' equals in virtue. Anytus makes a veiled threat against Socrates, warning him not to be so quick to speak ill of others because it is easy to harm people (94e), whereupon Anytus leaves the scene. Thus "Anytus here will" should be "Anytus will" at PCW 987 (99e).

Anytus appears in the record once more before Socrates' trial; he serves as a character witness for Andocides IV who had been charged with impiety by Meletus of Athens s.v. in 400 (Andoc. 1.150).

In 399, Anytus prosecuted Socrates on behalf of craftsmen and politicians (Pl. *Ap.* 23e; Xen. *Apol.*; D. S. 14), but the *Accusation of Socrates*, said to have been spoken by Anytus at Socrates' trial, was actually written by Polycrates s.v. sometime after 393/2. As in other hagiographic traditions, evil was supposed to have befallen the opponents of the innocent man unjustly executed, so Diodorus tells how Socrates' accusers, Anytus and Meletus II, were put to death without trial by the angry Athenians, in their remorse following Socrates' death (D. S., or his source, appears not to know of Lycon: 14.37.7). Diogenes says the repentant Athenians executed Meletus II and banished the others, meanwhile honoring Socrates with a bronze statue by Lysippus. Further, when the fugitive Anytus reached Heraclea Pontica, the citizens there, having heard the news of Socrates' death, exiled Anytus on the same day (D. L. 2.43)—or stoned him to death (Them. 20.239c). But P describes Anytus as an orator with the party of Thrasybulus and Aesimus address-ing the Assembly in 396, neither dead nor dishonored.

Prosopographical notes.   The name of Anytus' son is considered lost by *APF*—unless the son is the Anytus, *PA* 1322, who was a grain inspector (*sitophylax*) in the Piraeus in 388/7 (*pace* Hansen 1995: 32, who says the inspector was Anytus himself).

Apemantus of Athens
[*PA* 1347 *LGPN2* 1 *PAA* 140520 *PP*
Ἀπήμαντος]
father of Eudicus

[Pl.] *G. Hp.* 286b,
   pat.
[Pl.] *L. Hp.* 363b

An acquaintance of Socrates (*L. Hp.*) who held that the *Iliad* was superior to the *Odyssey*, and Achilles to Odysseus.

Apollodorus of Phaleron
[*PA* 1453 *LGPN2* 177 *PAA* 143280 *RE* 15
DPhA 249 *PP PX* Ἀπολλόδωρος Φαληρεύς]
b. ≤429
brother: Aeantodorus
constant companion of Socrates

Pl. *Smp.*   speaker
Pl. *Ap.* 34a, 38b   present
Pl. *Phd.* 59a, 117d   wailer
Xen. *Apol.* 28
Xen. *Mem.* 3.11.17
P. Oxy. 1608.34

Life. Apollodorus' birth date is set by his statement in Plato's *Symposium* that he was an agemate of Glaucon IV, Plato's brother (173a). He was born into a wealthy and established family, and was a successful businessman early in life, but abandoned business to follow Socrates in ±403; he says in ±400, the year before Socrates' death (cf. App. I), that he has associated with Socrates for less than three years (172c). Yet Xenophon describes Apollodorus and Antisthenes as two men who never left Socrates' side (*Mem.*). Plato represents him in *Symposium* as rather flamboyant, and an unnamed friend refers to his nickname of 'maniac' (173d). Apollodorus was present at Socrates' trial and offered funds for his fine (*Ap.*). Present again in the *Phaedo*, Apollodorus was the most emotional of those gathered at Socrates' execution (117d).

Career. Already in 1901 (*PA*) there were efforts to link the mad Socratic Apollodorus with known individuals. Two further citations have been assigned to the Socratic: a sculptor named Apollodorus (var.–δορος) known from *IG* I³ 898.2 (= *Dedications from the Athenian Acropolis* 146.2, dated ±410–400) and from Pliny (*HN* 34.81, 86). Pliny's "mad" (*insanum*) sculptor is such a perfectionist that he breaks perfect statues in dissatisfaction. It is unlikely that the manic sculptor is the follower of Socrates, so I have not included those references above. The identification seems to be based on nothing more than the coincidence of the name 'Apollodorus' with mania in the two cases. But several points tell against the identification. Apollodorus is a particularly common name (*LGPN2* lists ±263, *PAA* ±340); and, a minor point, its spelling differs between the Socratic and the sculptor. Moreover, while the Socratic Apollodorus, concisely represented by Plato as enthusiastic, loquacious, effeminate and emotional, is indeed called "mad" (μανικός), the context implies he is a Socratic fanatic, not an artist. Nowhere in Plato or Xenophon is there a suggestion that Apollodorus had artistic mania. On the contrary, Apollodorus says his own past resembles Glaucon IV's present (*Smp.* 173a); they are both on the verge of thirty, when Glaucon IV may have had his sights set on a political career (Xen. *Mem.* 3.6), and was turned away from philosophy. A little less directly (173c–d), Apollodorus compares his own wasted past with the lives of the unnamed rich businessmen he addresses; since Apollodorus will, a year later, be among those to offer to pay Socrates' fine, however, there is no reason to think Apollodorus has embraced Socratic poverty. Nor is it unusual, even in the dialogues, to call a person mad (cf. Chaerephon s.v., another close companion of Socrates, who receives that label in Plato and the comic poets). It is conceivable that Apollodorus, still a young man in 400, later became the famous sculptor mentioned by Pliny, and that Plato ignored it, but since the *IG* inscription is dated before Socrates' death, the connection between the sculptor of *IG* and the one of Pliny would thus be lost.

In the later tradition.   Late references include pseudo-Socrates (*Ep.* 14, 21.3), Athenaeus (507a–b), Aelian (*VH* 1.16), Plutarch (*Cat. Mi.* 46), Cicero (*De nat.* 1.34, 1.93), Diogenes (2.35), who says Apollodorus offered Socrates a beautiful garment to die in, et al. in *SSR* 2.VIB.

Prosopographical notes.   LGPN2 queries whether the Socratic 177 = *LGPN2* 9, the sculptor. *PAA* characteristically divides the entry further, querying whether the Socratic 143280 = 141880 (*IG*), and whether either = *PAA* 141985 (Pli.). *DPhA* queries whether *RE* 75 = *RE* 15.

Apollodorus of Cyzicus and Athens   Pl. *Ion* 541c–d *
[*PA* 1458 *FRA* 3062 *PAA* 143545 *RE* 25
DPhA 247 *PP* Ἀπολλόδωρος]
active during the Peloponnesian war
general and naturalized citizen

Apollodorus was originally from Cyzicus, an important commercial seaport on the southern shore of the Propontis, enjoying both east and west harbors, probably linked by a navigable canal (see Map 1). In the period of Athenian empire, Cyzicus was a major contributor, though she rebelled in 411. Osborne (*NIA* 3.30–1) cites the case of Apollodorus' naturalization in ≥410 as "certain or highly probable," on the evidence of *Ion* (Ath. 506a and Ael. *VH* 14.5 are derivative). Osborne appears to be figuring his date from the revolt of Cyzicus and the assumption that Apollodorus would have emigrated to Athens at that time. Since the dramatic date of *Ion* is ≥413, before the Ionic revolt (see App. I), there is a minor anachronism or Apollodorus emigrated earlier. Whereas a *metic* undergoing naturalization would already have a deme of residence in which he was known, the case was different for foreigners; they appear to have kept their original ethnics (see *NIA* 3.31). That demes are not mentioned in the naturalization decrees may suggest that at least some foreigners' admission to demes occurred later than admission to citizenship in the *polis*.   An inscription (*IG* I³ 127.33–4) cited by Whitehead (1986: 103n91) provides a case in which Samian honorees were "allotted amongst the demes and/or tribes"), although that would be a reversal of the virtually universal Athenian practice (see App. III). Contributing to the general uncertainty surrounding individual cases of naturalization, there were degrees of citizenship, sometimes limited to eligibility to speak before the Assembly and be elected to office, implying no deme affiliation. Cf. Heraclides of Clazomenae s.v. and Phanosthenes of Andros s.v. for similar cases from *Ion*.

Apollodorus of Athens See App. II.

Apollophanes, slave of Alcibiades III See App. II.

Apolloniades, slave of Plato See App. II.

Archebiades of Athens See App. II.

Archedemus of Pelekes   Xen. *Mem.* 2.9
[*PA* 2326 *LGPN2* 26 *PAA* 209135, 208885   Xen. *Hell.* 1.7.2
RE 1 *PX* Ἀρχέδημος Πήληξ]   Lys. 14.25
active 424–405   Aristoph. *Frogs*
controversial public figure   420–5, 588
                                                    Eu. *Goats* fr. 9 (K 9)
                                                    Eu. *Bap.* fr. 80 (K 71)

Life.   Two very different pictures of Archedemus emerge from the sources. On the one side, Lysias—charging Alcibiades IV in 395 with desertion and refusing military service—emphasizes the defendant's association with a bleary-eyed (ὁ γλάμων) Archedemus who had embezzled public funds and who, according to the speaker, flouted Athenian mores by lying with Alcibiades IV under one cloak in full view of others (14.25); this Archedemus was already a popular leader, a demagogue, notorious from the comic poets. In a note to the Lysias passage, Lamb describes Archedemus as a "popular leader who pressed for the prosecution of the commanders after Arginusae, 406" (1930: 351n), but this is not easily reconciled with our only extant account of Archedemus' role in the events after the sea battle: having responsibility for the "two-*obol* fund" for relieving the poverty and suffering brought on by the war, Archedemus brought charges against Erasinides, one of the generals, for unspecified mismanagement of public funds (Xen. *Hell.* 1.7.2–3); but this charge was brought in the period before the generals were charged as a group with having failed to retrieve casualties after the battle (see Exc. 2).

Xenophon goes further in his defense of Archedemus, depicting him as a poor but honest public figure and a good speaker (*Mem.* 2.9.1–8; cf. Aes. *orat.* 3.139 remembering him favorably as a speaker and as someone willing to take risks on behalf of Thebes). In Xenophon's story, when Crito complains to Socrates that various false accusations, frivolous lawsuits, are pending against him because some men assume that he will find it less trouble to pay them off than to fight the charges in court, Socrates suggests that, just as Crito has a watchdog to keep wolves from his sheep, he should have a watchdog to keep such men from his money—and suggests Archedemus for the purpose. Crito begins sharing his farming proceeds with Archedemus who, in turn, begins investigating Crito's enemies and bringing countercharges; soon Archedemus is helping Crito's friends as well. Finally, the respected Archedemus becomes not merely Crito's business partner but his friend.

Archedemus must have had noticeably bleary eyes to cause him to be so widely known by that epithet; his condition is likely to have been bilateral ectropion, in which the lower lids turn outward.

Prosopographical notes. *PAA* distinguishes *PA* 2326 into two individuals: *PAA* 209135 (Aes. *orat.*, 3.139, Plu. *Mor.* 575d) and *PAA* 208885 (references above). *LGPN2* 26 cites *GRBS* 28 (1987: 209) in error.

Archedemus of Syracuse — Pl. *Ltr.* 7.339a,
[*DPhA* 306 *PP* Ἀρχέδημος] — 349d *
4th c. — [Pl.] *Ltr.* 2.310b,
Pythagorean associate of Archytas — 312d, 3.319a *

Archedemus was sent by Dionysius II to Plato as a messenger more than once and was Plato's host when Plato was dismissed from the tyrant's household in Ortygia, adjacent to Syracuse. In Italy and Sicily, the –δαμος ending is more common than –δημος, but no instance of either is recorded until the 3rd c. (*LGPN3A*). His homonym, Archedemus of Tarsus, the stoic philosopher, is later.

Archelaus of Athens (philosopher) See App. II.

Archelaus of Macedonia, son of Perdiccas II See App. II.

Archenius of Athens (merchant sea captain) See App. II.

Archestratus of Alopece, son of Crito — Euthd. 306d,
[*PA/APF* 2418 (8823) *LGPN2* 40 *PAA* 211395 — unnamed *
RE 7 Ἀρχέστρατος Κρίτωνος Ἀλωπεκῆθεν] — IG II² 1609.84;
±419–>342/1 — 1611.400 ff.;
mother: daughter of ?Archestratus — 1622.249 ff.
brother: Critobulus
See stemma: Crito.

Life. Archestratus' age is inferred from two data: the remark in *Euthydemus* 306d that he was young and small (νεώτερος ἔτι καὶ σμικρός) when his brother, Critobulus, was approaching manhood, and the likelihood that Socrates' own eldest son (b. ≥416) was younger than Archestratus (cf. Critobulus s.v. for *APF*'s mistake regarding this family, leading to the misidentification of Archestratus as the son of a Crito II and thus the grandson of the Crito of the dialogues). The approximate date of birth I suggest for Archestratus fits the data and puts a six-year gap between the brothers. Archestratus may have been named for his maternal grandfather, given the remark that his mother's lineage was good (*Euthd.* 306d; cf. Crito s.v.).

Archestratus' wealth is attested by his provision of naval equipment sometime before 366/5 (*IG* II² 1609.84), and by his status as sole *trierarch* for the triremes Polynice, Lampas, Pandia, and Cratiste sometime before 356 (*IG* II² 1611.400 ff., and 1622.249 ff.). Archestratus was alive when *IG* II² 1622 was inscribed in 342/1. See Humphreys (1990: 245) for an Archestratus of Alopece who was the son of Spoudides and possibly a relation of the family of Crito (*IG* II² 2345.25, an inscription for a phratry with its main base in Alopece).

Archestratus of Phrearrhi See App. II.

Archestratus, son of Lycomedes (general) See App. II.

Archidamus II of Sparta, son of Zeuxidamus (king) See App. II.

Archilochus of Paros, son of Enipo (poet) See App. II.

Archinus of Coele
[*PA* 2526 *LGPN2* 15 *PAA* 213880 *RE* 2 *PP*
Ἀρχῖνος ἐκ Κοίλης]
active ±405–399
father of Myronides
rhetorician, politician, general

Pl. *Mx.* 234b *
Aristoph. *Frogs* 367
  & schol.
Pl. *com.* fr. 141 (K
  133) = Aristot. *Rh.*
  1.15 (1376a10)
San. *Dan.* fr. 9 (K 9)
Ioscr. 18.2
Aes. *orat.* 1–3
Demos. 24.135
[Aristot.] *Ath. Pol.*
  34.3, 40.1–2
Theop. *hist.* fr. 155

Career in brief.   Known in Plato as a rhetorician, Archinus appears in the record earliest for his proposal to reduce the pay of the comic poets ≤405 (Aristoph., Pl. *com.*, San.) at about the time he was an associate of the moderate oligarch, Theramenes ([Aristot.] *Ath. Pol.* 34.3). In 404, after Theramenes had been assassinated, Archinus joined Thrasybulus in Phyle (Demos., Aes. *orat.* 2.176) and, after the overthrow of the Thirty, was the proposer of a decree voted by the Athenians honoring the heroes of Phyle, including himself, in 403/2 (Aes. *orat.* 3.187; cf. *Hesperia* 10, p. 288, ln. 55, catalogue other). Archinus is known for several decrees in the year 403/2, including the proposal to adopt the Ionic alphabet (Theop. *hist.*;

Phot. *Lex.* Σ 498.15) and others concerning the amnesty: he prematurely terminated the period in which former supporters of the Thirty were permitted to register their intention to leave Athens, thereby forcing some to stay unwillingly ([Aristot.] *Ath. Pol.* 40.2); he supported summary execution for amnesty violators ([Aristot.] *Ath. Pol.* 40.1), and a judicial innovation that enabled the accused to countercharge the prosecutor with having brought an indictment contrary to the terms of the amnesty (Isocr.). Perhaps in the same year, but certainly 403–401, Archinus prosecuted his former comrade, Thrasybulus, for unconstitutional legislation (*graphē paranomōn*) when Thrasybulus proposed to grant Athenian citizenship to *metics*, foreigners, and slaves who had been among those who fought for the restoration of the democracy (Aes. *orat.* 3.195; [Aristot.] *Ath. Pol.* 40.2). Sometime ±403–399, Archinus proposed an assessment decree (Aes. *orat.* 1.163).

In the later tradition. Late sources include Photius (*Bibl.* 260487b–488a), Dionysius of Helicarnassus (*Dem.* 23.57), and pseudo-Plutarch (*LTO* 835–6).

Prosopographical notes. *PA* and *PAA* irregularly count *Mx.* among pseudo-Platonic works. *LGPN2* cites *GRBS* 24 (1983: 162) and 28 (1987: 209–10) in error.

Archippus of Tarentum
LGPN3A 37 *RE* 12 *DPhA* 321 *PP* Ἄρχιππος]
active 450–?420
Pythagorean philosopher

[Pl.] *Ltr.* 9.357d *
frr. in DK 46
Aristox. fr. 11
Iamb. *VP* 250

By about 450, Archippus belonged to a community of Pythagoreans who had achieved some political influence in the southern Italian city of Croton. He was one of the two survivors of a fire deliberately set at the house of Milo in Croton by the associates of a wealthy and prominent local, Cylon, while the Pythagoreans were holding a meeting there (Aristox.). See DK for several quotations from the later tradition.

Archytas of Tarentum, son of Mnesagoras
[*LGPN3A* 2 *RE* 3 *OCD³* *DPhA* 322 *PP*
Ἀρχύτας var. –της, *Ltr.* 7, 13]
r. 366–350
friend of Plato
statesman, general, mathematician,
 philosopher

Pl. *Ltr.* 7.338c 350a *
[Pl.] *Ltr.* 9, 12 *   addressee
[Pl.] *Ltr.* 13.360b *
frr. in DK 47
Aristox. fr. 18

Life and works. Revered in his own time and afterwards, Archytas was an enlightened political leader in the Pythagorean philosophical tradition—at the beginning of a time of prolonged prosperity for Tarentum. Plato introduced him to Dionysius II, apparently in the hope of persuading the Syracusan tyrant to emulate Archytas' just rule. But Tarentum had assisted Sicily as far back as 414–413 when the Athenians invaded, so Bury's (1929: 387) description of the Sicilians' aid to Tarentum against the Lucanians as a "result" of Plato's intervention may be an overstatement. When, in 360, Dionysius II moved Plato out of his private lodgings and into the company of mercenaries who were plotting against his life (which Plato learned from Athenian rowers among them), it was Archytas who arranged for Lamiscus s.v. to take a Tarentine ship to rescue Plato.

Archytas was a man of wide interests and many accomplishments, developing theories in the foundations of mechanics and acoustics. Boethius quotes Archytas' proof against the division of a superparticular ratio into equal parts (*On Music* 3.11); and Eutocius, citing Eudemus, preserves his solution to doubling the area of a cube (*Commentary on Archimedes' Sphere and Cylinder* 84.12–88.2). Porphyry's *Commentary on Ptolemy's Harmonics* gives Archytas' discussion of the three senses of 'mean': arithmetic, geometric, and harmonic (or subcontrary) mean, included among the frr. in DK.

In the later tradition and modern bibliography. Aristotle mentions Archytas several times (*Meta.* 1043a22, *Prob.* 915a29, *Rh.* 1412a12) and is said by Damascius to have written a work on Archytas (fr. 207). Proclus (*Eucl.* 66.15) counts Archytas among the first group of mathematicians of the Academy, a contemporary of Leodamas and Theaetetus. Diogenes purports to preserve the letter written to Dionysius II by Archytas on the occasion of Plato's rescue (3.21; cf. 8.79.82). See also Plutarch (*Dion* 20), who states that Archytas was elected general seven times. Much of the mathematical material is quoted in Thomas (1991: 130–3, 284–9) *Greek Mathematical Works.* Knorr 1975 is an excellent source for further information about the mathematical issues. (DK quotes from Str. 6; Procl. *Eucl.* 2.66.14; Iamb. *VP* 197; Ath. 519b, 545a; Ael. *VH* 12.15, 14.19; Gell. *NA* 10.12.8 et al.)

Prosopographical notes. LGPN3A queries whether he is the son of Mnasagoras, Mnasarchos, Mnasagetas, or Hestiaios.

Arete of Syracuse, daughter of Dionysius I [*LGPN3A* 4 *RE* 2 Ἀρέτη (var. –τα)] b. 397–395, † 353 mother: Aristomache siblings: Nysaeus, Sophrosyne (wife of Dionysius II), Hipparinus II; paternal half siblings: Dionysius II, Hermocritus II, Dicaeosyne (wife of Leptines I) husbands: Thearides, Dion, ?Timocrates son with Dion: Hipparinus III *See stemma: Dion.*

Pl. *Ltr.* 8, unnamed * addressee
Plu. *Dion, passim*

Life. Arete was given by Dionysius I to his youngest half brother, Thearides; but he died when she was, at most, fourteen. She afterwards married Dion, presumably with the tyrant's consent. When Dion was banished by Dionysius II in 366, she remained behind with their only son, Hipparinus III (b. ±373), hoping to persuade her half brother, Dionysius II, to recall Dion. This never happened. Instead, Dionysius II ordered Arete to marry one of his favorites, Timocrates, though it is unclear that the order was ever carried out for she seems still to have been Dion's wife when Ortygia finally surrendered in 455. When Callippus s.v.

had Dion assassinated in 354 and seized power in Syracuse himself, he had both Arete and Dion's sister, Aristomache (Dionysius I's wife) imprisoned. She may there have delivered a posthumous son that Callippus' guards took away. In Plutarch, she and her sister-in-law were then set to sea and either killed first and then thrown overboard, or just thrown overboard.

Arete, daughter of Aristippus of Cyrene (philosopher) See App. II.

Ariphron II of Cholarges, son of   Pl. *Prt.* 320a *
  Xanthippus I   Thu. 4.66.3, pat.
[*PA/APF* 2204 (11811.2) *LGPN2* 3 *PAA* 202330   AM 106.150
PP Ἀρίφρων Ξανθίππου Χολαργεύς]   Lys. 19.52, unnamed
≤495–≥late 430s
mother: Agariste II of Alopece
brother: Pericles I
father of Hippocrates
co-guardian of Alcibiades III and Clinias IV
See stemma: Pericles.

Life. Ariphron II's family was wealthy and prestigious, but he did not himself leave a record of benefactions or accomplishments. Plato's *Protagoras* reports that Pericles I sent Clinias IV to Ariphron II out of fear that the boy would be corrupted by his older brother, Alcibiades III, but that the arrangement only lasted six months, after which Ariphron II sent Clinias IV back to the household of Pericles I. That Ariphron II was co-guardian of Alcibiades III and Clinias IV is not apparent from Plato, though Lysias speaks of Alcibiades III's guardians in the plural, and Plutarch (*Alc.* 1.2) says it explicitly. Davies (*APF*), normally suspicious of Plato's use of dramatic dates, concludes from the evidence of the *Protagoras* that Ariphron II was alive in the late 430s.

In the later tradition. Pausanias repeats that Ariphron II was the father of Hippocrates (3.6.1, 9.6.3); Plutarch tells an anecdote about him in connection with Alcibiades III (*Alc.* 3.1).

Aristarchus of Athens   Xen. *Mem.* 2.7.1–2
[*PA* 1653 *LGPN2* 3 *PAA* 164130
RE 3 *PX* Ἀρίσταρχος]
man impoverished by 404

Life. Aristarchus, once wealthy but in financial straits because of the war, describes to Socrates his chagrin that he can no longer feed his household, now overrun with women left behind as increasing numbers of citizens have abandoned the city for the Piraeus. He cannot figure out how to help himself in the absence of foreign slaves. Socrates advises him to put the women to work—a stratagem that proved a success, according to Xenophon. The scene is set in 404 "since the revolution" in the *polis* (ἐπεὶ γὰρ ἐστασίασεν ἡ πόλις, 2.7.2). With only this passage as a source, *PA* refers to Aristarchus as "favorably disposed" (*favet*) toward the

Thirty who were then in power. That judgment is still common but still misleading—as if all those who "remained in the city" under the oligarchy were implicated
in its host of crimes and offenses. After the execution of Theramenes, the Thirty
began evicting *any* wealthy citizens who were not on their roll of Three Thousand
(Xen. *Hell.* 3.4.1), and Xenophon adds that citizens were similarly driven from
the Piraeus to Megara and Thebes (cf. Exc. 4).

Prosopographical notes.   The name Aristarchus is not uncommon in the late 5th
c., and there are several unassigned liturgical inscriptions bearing the name that
may well refer to this once-wealthy citizen. The most prominent man of that
name, however, the politically active Aristarchus (Thu. 8; Xen. *Hell.* 1, 2; *PA/APF*
1663 *LGPN2* 4 *PAA* 164155), often cited as the probable character in the *Memorabilia*,
is a dubious identification. Not only does the *Memorabilia* say nothing about
a military career, but the identification would imply an obvious anachronism.
Theramenes, speaking of events of 411, says he himself thwarted the plan of
"Aristoteles, Melanthius, Aristarchus, and their fellow generals" (Xen. *Hell.* 2.3.46)
to build a fort overlooking the Piraeus harbor that would admit the Spartans (cf.
Thu. 8.92). In 406, Euryptolemus reminds the people clamoring for the execution
of the generals following the naval battle at Arginusae that they allowed Aristarchus, "the destroyer of the democracy and afterwards the betrayer of Oenoe to
your enemies the Thebans," a day in which to defend himself (Xen. *Hell.* 1.7.28;
cf. Thu. 8.98), implying not only that this Aristarchus was generally viewed as
villainous, but that he had in fact been found guilty and apparently executed
sometime before 406, making him unavailable for a conversation with Socrates
in the era of the Thirty.

Aristarchus, slave of Alcibiades III See App. II.

Aristides I of Alopece, son of Lysimachus I
[*PA/APF* 1695 (cf. 7826.4C) *LGPN2* 32 *PAA*
165170 *RE* 1 *OCD*[3] *PP* Ἀριστείδης
Λυσιμάχου Ἀλωπεκῆθεν]
≤520–±467
mother: a daughter of Callias I
wife: daughter of Callias II
father of Lysimachus II and two daughters
"The Just"—military and political leader
See stemma: Thucydides.

Pl. *Grg.* 526b †
Pl. *Meno* 94a †
Pl. *Lch.* 179a †
[Pl.] *Virt.* 377d †
Hdt. 8.79.2–9.29.1,
    passim
Thu. 1.91.3, 5.18
Aes. *Cal.* no. 75 (fr.
    36 Dittmar)
Agora 25.21–88
IG I[3] 1031.23
[Andoc.] 4.11
Demos. 23
[Demos. 26]
Aes. *orat.* 2.23, 3.258
Eu. *Dem.* frr. 99, 106
[Aristot.] *Ath. Pol.*
    22–4, 28, 41

Life.   Aristides I, known as "the Just," was born to a wealthy family by 520 (*APF* calculates the birth twice, with a ten-year difference between the two conclusions, but 1695.2 is more persuasive than 7826.4C). Aristides I's father, Lysimachus I, had married one of the three daughters of the wealthy Callias I who had allowed them, remarkably, to choose their own husbands (Hdt. 6.122.2). The descendants of Callias I's son, Hipponicus I, went on to become known for their wealth in the 5th c. Lysimachus I's descendants, however, were more likely in the *hippeis* class, despite Aristides I's later reputation for poverty—which might better be understood as austerity. References to Aristides I in Eupolis (*Dem.* frr. 99.78–99.120 and 106 [K 90]) and in Plato fit the just man description. By the time of Aristotle at least (*Rh.* 1398a9, 1414b37), the very name 'Aristides' had become a byword for a respected and just citizen. Nowadays, we are warned against contrasting too strongly the high-minded, aristocratic Aristides I with his sometime rival, the clever democrat, Themistocles. In separate articles for *OCD*[3], *Arisitides (1)* and *Themistocles,* Hornblower and Rhodes, respectively, emphasize cooperation between the two. (Note that Aristides I's ostracism should read "483/2" in the former.)

Family.   Various stories, going back to Aristides I's boyhood, have been debated in the secondary literature, but most are of peripheral interest here. One that appears in [Pl.] *Hal.* 8 is a suggested relationship between Socrates and Aristides I's daughter or granddaughter; I assess it in light of recent scholarship at Myrto s.v. A story preserved by the Socratic Aeschines, however, "written at a time when Kallias' family was still a living entity and when the Socratic writers seem to have been fairly scrupulous in their reporting of the family traditions and relationships of their interlocutors" (*APF* 7826.4C), deserves mention because it is used to cement the claim that Lysimachus I married Callias I's daughter: Aristides I was a relation (ἀνεψιός, usually 'cousin') of Callias II and gave evidence on his behalf (Aes.). It is the orator Aeschines who says that Athens awarded dowries to Aristides I's daughters (3.258), and that story is sometimes debunked as a fabrication (*APF* 1695.4), along with that of a similar decree awarding property and a pension to Lysimachus II (Demos. 20.115). I think it is a mistake to throw out the daughters with the decree, however, and *APF* offers no rationale for having done so, so I retain them here.

Career in brief.   Aristides I may have been a victorious general at Marathon in 490/89, as Plutarch says (*Arist.* 1.1), but he was certainly the eponymous archon in 489/8 (*IG* I[3] 1031.23, catalogue of archons; and the Parian Marble, *FGrH* 239 A 49). His name appears on some 68 *ostraka* in the period 490–482 (*Agora* 25.21–88), and he was in fact ostracized in 482 (schol. Aristoph. *Knights* 855; [Aristot.] *Ath. Pol.* 22.7), although he was recalled from his exile to command Athenian forces victorious at Salamis in September of 480 (Hdt. 8.95; [Demos.] 26.6). He was general again in 479/8 (Hdt. 9.28), proposing a decree about the Eleutherian games after Plataea, and perhaps proposing a decree making all Athenian citizens eligible to administer the state, specifically as archons (Plu. *Arist.* 22.1). Aristides I was something of a mentor to Cimon II (Plu. *Cim.* 5.4), and worked with Themistocles to rebuild Athenian power. He served as ambassador to Sparta in 478/7 (Thu. 1.91.3; [Aristot.] *Ath. Pol.* 23.3), a year in which he may also have served as general but certainly was responsible for assessing tribute under Athenian authority (Thu. 5.18.5; [Andoc.] 4.11; Aes. *orat.* 2.23, 3.258; [Aristot.] *Ath. Pol.* 23.4 et al.). Upon his death ±467, he was buried at Phaleron (Demos. 23.209).

In the later tradition. Both Plutarch and Nepos wrote biographies of Aristides (cf. Plu. *Th.* 11.1). See also Aristotle (*Rh.* and frr. 92, 93, 611); Diodorus (11.29.4, 11.44.2–4 and 11.46.4); Justinian (2.15.16); Aristodemus (fr. 2); Pausanias (8.52.2); Aelian (*VH* 11.9); and Philostratus (*VA* 6.21, and *VS* 2.29).

Prosopographical notes. PAA notes three other sources that possibly refer to the same man. *PAA* 164922: 8 *ostraka* from the Ceramicus dated 487–415 (*AM* 106, p. 149, ln. 1); *PAA* 164930: a "father of" designation at pseudo-Plutarch *LTO* 834e; and *PAA* 165337: an *ostrakon* dated 490–480 (*SEG* 33.28.1, Aristides of Coele, son of Lysimachus).

Aristides II of Alopece, son of Lysimachus II   Pl. *Lch.*   speaker
[*PA/APF* 1696 (1695.3) *LGPN2* 33, 88 *PAA*   Pl. *Tht.* 151a
165185 *RE* 2 *DPhA* 347 *PP* Ἀριστείδης   [Pl.] *Thg.* 130a–e †   speaker
(–δες, *IG*) Λυσιμάχου Ἀλωπεκῆθεν]   IG I³ 1186.174
440s–411
mother: a daughter of Callias II
grandson of Aristides I
student of Socrates
See stemma: Thucydides.

Life. Aristides II was the grandson and namesake of the famous Aristides I. In *Laches*, set in 424 (see App. I), his father is concerned to find the right teacher for him because he hopes that Aristides II will become as distinguished as his famous grandfather. It is decided at the very end of the dialogue (200c–201c) that Socrates will undertake the task of educating Aristides II and Melesias' son, Thucydides II, as well. In *Theaetetus,* set in 399, Socrates describes what happened in Aristides II's case:

> But it is I, with God's help, who deliver them of this offspring. And a proof of this may be seen in the many cases where people who did not realise this fact took all the credit to themselves and thought that I was no good. They have then proceeded to leave me sooner than they should, either of their own accord or through the influence of others. And after they have gone away from me they have resorted to harmful company, with the result that what remained within them has miscarried; while they have neglected the children I helped them to bring forth, and lost them, because they set more value upon lies and phantoms than upon the truth; finally they have been set down for ignorant fools, both by themselves and by everybody else. One of these people was Aristides the son of Lysimachus; and there have been many others. (*Tht.* 151a)

The only extant details of Aristides II's failure as a student appear in the spurious dialogue, *Theages.* Despite Aristides II's having been a quick and able student, he explains to Socrates that he lost his dialectical ability a little at a time after leaving Athens, concluding that Socrates' mere presence had been what had enabled him to make progress.

Prosopographical notes. Aristides (Ἀριστειδες) of Antiochis (tribe of the deme Alopece) was killed in action (*IG* I³ 1186.174, dated 411). *LGPN2* assigns the casualty a separate number, 88; so does *PAA*, 165080.

Aristippus of Larissa
[*LGPN3B* 11 *RE* 1 *PP* Ἀρίστιππος]
active late 5th c.
friend and lover of Meno
student of Gorgias
political leader in Thessaly

Pl. *Meno* 70b *
Xen. *Anab.* 1.1.10,
1.2.1, 2.6.28 *

In Plato's *Meno*, a dialogue set in 402 (cf. App. I), shortly before Aristippus sent Meno against Artaxerxes, Aristippus is identified as a student of Gorgias (70b) and as Meno's friend (ἑταίρου 70b2) and lover (ἐραστής 70b6). Aristippus received financial assistance against his political opponents from his friend, Cyrus, secretly to maintain an army of mercenaries in Thessaly (*Anab.* 1.1.10). In or just before 401, when Cyrus was ready to begin his campaign against his reigning brother, Artaxerxes, he sent word to Aristippus to reconcile with his internal enemies and to send the army to Cyrus' aid (1.2.1). Aristippus did so, under the command of Meno s.v. (2.6.28).

Aristippus I of Cyrene
[*LGPN1* 4 *RE* 8 *DPhA* 356
*OCD*³ *PP PX* Ἀρίστιππος]
>440–>399
father of Arete
grandfather of Aristippus II
founder of the Cyrenaic school

Pl. *Phd.* 59c *
Aes. no. 91 (fr. 49
   Dittmar)
Xen. *Mem.* 2.1, 3.8
test. in *SSR* 2.IVA
Aristot. *Meta.*
   996a32–b1

Life. Aristippus' daughter, Arete, was the mother of Aristippus II, known as "mother-taught" (μητροδίδακτος). Aristippus I is linked to Socrates by three writers of Socratic *logoi*. Xenophon depicts Aristippus as hedonistic, defending the life of seeking pleasure against Socrates' questioning (*Mem.* 2.1.1–34), though the conversation ends with Socrates telling Aristippus Prodicus' cautionary tale of Heracles; at a later date, Aristippus attempts to take on the role of questioner in a discussion of what is beautiful and good and why (3.8.1–10). Aeschines says that Aristippus inquired of Ischomachus about Socrates at Olympia (cf. Ischomachus s.v.). In Plato, there is only that Aristippus was not present in the prison at the time of Socrates' death, but was on the island of Aegina (Pl. *Phd.* 59c).

Career. It is controversial whether Aristippus I himself, or his grandson, was founder of the Cyrenaic school. While Aristippus I, as depicted in Xenophon, champions pleasure, the anecdotes of the later authors very often conflate the two men, making it inconclusive which first had followers or students. And what one means by 'school' and 'founder' also plays a role in the dispute. Aristippus I is generally conceded to have taught his daughter, who taught her son—but is she to be counted as the first student of the Cyrenaic school?

In the later tradition.   In material on Aristippus I, presented in just over a hundred pages of *SSR* 2.IVA (with an addendum following 2.VIB), one finds: references from Plato, Xenophon, and Aeschines; Aristotle's reference to Aristippus I as a sophist who attacked mathematics; lengthy quotations from Diogenes Laertius, who tells a string of anecdotes, mostly unattributed, several of which place Aristippus I at the court of Dionysius I or II in Sicily (2.47, 2.65–104), sometimes with Plato; and a host of other late authors (cf. [Socr.] *Ep.* 12, Simon to Aristippus; 13). But there is not a set of philosophical frr. purportedly written by Aristippus I. Such uncertainty has encouraged abundant speculation.

Aristocles of Athens See App. II. *See stemma: Plato.*

Aristocles of Collytus See App. II. *See stemma: Plato.*

Aristocrates II of Athens, son of Scellius II
[*PA/APF* 1904 *LGPN2* 100 *PAA* 171045 *RE* 2
PP Ἀριστοκράτης (–τες, *ARV²*) Σκελλίου]
tribe: Kekropis
470s–406
father of Scellius III
uncle of Scellius of Chollidae
long-serving general, oligarch, executed after
    Arginusae in 406

Pl. *Grg.* 472a *
Pl. *Ap.* 32b,
    unnamed †
[Pl.] *Ax.* 368d,
    unnamed †
Thu. 5, 8, 9, *passim*
Aristoph. *Birds* 126
    & schol. 125, 126
Aristoph. fr. 591
    (*CGFP* 63)
IG I³ 964.1 (choral
    dedication)
IG I³ 375.35
    (inventory Athena)
Xen. *Hell.* 1, *passim*
Lys. 12.66
[Demos.] 58.67
[Aristot.] *Ath. Pol.*
    33.2
Philoch. fr. 142 with
    Aristoph. *Frogs*
    1196 schol.
ARV² 371.24
    (pottery cup, *kalos*)
D. S. 13, *passim*

Military and political career in brief.   Aristocrates II, a wealthy and well connected Athenian (*IG*) was an ambassador to Sparta for the Peace of Nicias in 421 (Thu. 5.19, 24). We hear of him again when he supported Theramenes in 414 (Aristoph. *Birds*), continuing through 406 (Thu. 8.89.2; Lys.; [Aristot.]), an important period that included his serving among the Four Hundred, then helping Theramenes to replace it with the Five Thousand. In 413/2 Aristocrates II was *stratēgos*, general, at Chios (Thu. 8.9.2; Aristoph. fr.); in 412/1 *taxiarch* at Piraeus (Thu. 8.92.2, 4; [Demos.]); in 410/9 general at Samos (*IG* I³ 375.35); in 408/7 and ?407/6 general at Andros (Xen. *Hell.* 1.4.21, 1.5.16; D. S. 13.74); and in 406/5 at Arginusae (Xen. *Hell.* 1.6.29). But after the battle, he was one of the six generals tried by the Assembly (*ecclēsia*) whom Socrates could not save from execution (see Exc. 2; Pl. *Ap.*; Xen. *Hell.* 1.7.2, 34; Philoch.; D. S. 13.101.5).

Prosopographical notes.   Not all these attributions are certain: *PAA* further divides *PA* 1904 into *PAA* 170785 (Polyae. 5.40, a general attacking a Spartan ally), and *PAA* 171040 (Pl. *Grg.*; *IG* I³ 964). *LGPN2* 100 ?= *LGPN2* 5 (Polyae. 5.40); cf. *LGPN2* 2 (*ARV*² as above but dated 490 instead of as here, 450); cf. *LGPN2* 99 (*IG* I³ 964).

Aristocritus of Syracuse   [Pl.] *Ltr.* 3.319a,
[*LGPN3A* 15 *PP* Ἀριστόκριτος]   13.363d *
associate of [Plato] and Dionysius II

Nothing is known of Aristocritus apart from what the pseudo-Platonic letters say.

Aristodemus of Cydathenaeum   Pl. *Smp.* 173b (†),
[*PA* 1818 *LGPN2* 46 *PAA* 168995 *DPhA* 379   218b   speaker
RE 13 *PP* *PX* Ἀριστόδημος Κυδαθηναιεύς]   Xen. *Mem.* 1.4.2–19
450s–<400

Life.   The person who recalls and repeats the speeches given at the symposium held at the house of Agathon in 416 is this man of apparent low birth and small stature, Aristodemus, a fellow demesman of Aristophanes. Apollodorus (*Smp.* 173b, frame) refers to him as "a real runt of a man, who always went barefoot . . . obsessed with Socrates." Xenophon (*Mem.* 1.4.2) calls him "Aristodemus the dwarf" (Ἀριστόδημον τὸν μικρόν). The very approximate date of birth I assign to him is based on his being already an adult and follower of Socrates in 416 when Glaucon IV and Apollodorus were children (*Smp.* 173a). He describes himself to Socrates, on the way to Agathon's house, "Mine is a case of an obvious inferior arriving uninvited at the table of a man of letters" (Pl. *Smp.* 174c). Once he arrives, he is welcomed, then washed, before taking a seat. Either he does not report his own contribution (180c), or he is passed over, presumably because of his insignificance in the eyes of those present, when they give speeches about *erōs*.

Although not listed as one of Socrates' inner circle (Xen. *Mem.* 1.2.48), Xenophon refers to Aristodemus in the context of Socrates' efforts to improve ordinary people in his "daily talks with his familiar friends" (*Mem.* 1.4.1). When Aristodemus professes to admire artists as wise (1.4.3), and says he neither prays nor sacrifices, figuring that the gods are too great to need humans, he is treated to an extended Socratic argument from design (1.4.2–19).

Aristodemus is remembered at the time of the dramatic frame of the *Symposium*, ±400, as if he has not been around for some time; and he was not present at Socrates' trial and execution, so I take it he was dead before 400.

Aristodorus of Syracuse   [Pl.] *Ltr.* 10.358b *   addressee
[*LGPN3A* 3 *PP* Ἀριστόδωρος]

Aristodorus, supposedly a follower of Dion, is unknown outside this letter.

Aristogiton of Athens (tyrannicide) See App. II.

Aristogiton of Athens, son of Cydimachus (moneylender) See App. II.

Aristomachus, slave of Alcibiades III See App. II.

Ariston of Collytus, son of Aristocles   Pl. *Ap.* 34a, pat. †
[*PA/APF* 2160 (8792.9) *LGPN2* 84 *PAA* 201000   Pl. *R.* 1.327a, 2.368a,
PP RE 11 Ἀρίστων Ἀριστοκλέους   pat.
Κολλυτεύς]   D. L. 3.1–4.1, *passim*
460s–±424
wife: Perictione
father of Plato, Adeimantus I, Glaucon IV,
  and Potone
See stemma: Plato.

Life.   Ariston's father traced his descent from the Aristocles who was archon in the year 605/4. If he claimed descent from Codrus and Melanthus, and thus from Poseidon (D. L. 3.1), that claim is not exploited in the dialogues.

That Ariston was the father of three sons is evident from Plato's *Republic* and *Apology*. Potone s.v., is known but not named until later. If Ariston followed ordinary Athenian practice, he was about thirty when he married in ±432 (cf. Perictione s.v.), allowing a very approximate estimate of his birth in the 460s. Diogenes (3.2) cites a number of earlier sources no longer extant, Speusippus' *Plato's Funeral Feast*, Clearchus' *Encomium on Plato*, and Anaxilaïdes' *On Philosophers* (2), for a story of Ariston's chaste and surpassing love for a Perictione in bloom (ὡραίαν) culminating in the virgin birth of Plato—Apollo having been Plato's real father—retold with relish for centuries.

Diogenes takes from Favorinus a second story offering some possibility of external confirmation: that Ariston and his family were sent by Athens to settle as *cleruchs*, colonists retaining their Athenian citizenship, on the island of Aegina, from which they were expelled by the Spartans after Plato's birth there. (When

APF and *PAA* report that Ariston was a *cleruch* on Aegina in 427, they presumably use Plato's traditional birth date to fasten both the time of the *cleruchy* and Ariston's death.) Since the birth date assigned to Plato s.v. is reassessed at that entry, it is appropriate to reconsider here the information about Ariston. In the first place, there is no record of any Spartan expulsion of Athenians from Aegina during the period from 431 to 411, and such evidence as there is argues in the other direction. Indeed, in 431, Athens expelled the Aeginetans and established a colony of *cleruchs* (Thu. 2.27), so Ariston and his new family—Perictione and perhaps the infant Adeimantus I—could have been among the colonists. The Spartans resettled the Aeginetans in Thyrea, but in 424 Athens burned Thyrea and killed all its inhabitants—after a Spartan garrison had deserted the city as the Athenian fleet approached (Thu. 4.55–57). At the Peace of Nicias, April 421, Aegina was silently left under Athens' control (Thu. 5.18); and it was not until the summer of 411 (Thu. 8.92) that the Spartans, taking advantage of the turmoil of the Four Hundred and the Five Thousand, overran the island. Perhaps Ariston was a *cleruch*, perhaps he went to Aegina in 431, and perhaps Plato was born on Aegina, but none of this enables a precise dating of Ariston's death (or Plato's birth). We can say with certainty that Ariston died after the birth of his four children with Perictione; there is no evidence of a divorce.

Ariston   See App. II.

Aristonymus   See App. II.

Aristophanes of Cydathenaeum, son of
   Philippus I
[*PA* 2090 *LGPN2* 32 *PAA* 175685, 175680 *RE*
12 *DPhA* 404 *OCD³* *PP* Ἀριστοφάνης
Φιλίππου Κυδαθηναιεύς]
±450–±386
father of Philippus II, Araros, Philhetaerus,
   and Nicostratus
consummate comedian

Pl. *Smp.*   speaker
Pl. *Ap.* 19c *
Aristoph. *opera*
IG II² 1740.2
   (Prytanes
   catalogue)

Life and career.   We are fortunate to have Henderson's recent fresh overview of the sources. Regarding Aristophanes' birth, he concludes (1998b: 2), "The exact date of his birth is unknown, but probably fell within a few years of mid-century, for *Clouds* 528–532 imply that he was young and inexperienced when he produced his first play in 427, and by 424 people were wondering why he had yet to produce a play of his own (*Knights* 512–513)." Henderson puts Aristophanes' death at ±386, but makes the date more tentative by adding that "Aristophanes was probably dead when Plato made him a character in the *Symposium* (written c. 380)." Dover (*OCD³*) had previously dated Aristophanes' birth in the 460s and his death ≤386. Among the biographical details Henderson accepts from the ancient and medieval testimonia preserved in *PCG* are that Aristophanes could plausibly be called "bald" by his rivals by the time he was in his twenties, that his detractors could cast doubt on his loyalty and even citizenship by referring to the residence on Aegina that he mentions (*Ach.* 642–644), that his sons Araros and Philippus also became comic poets, that he came from a prosperous family and "moved in elite circles," aligning himself in *Knights* with the cavalry (the playwright appears on stage in *Knights*).

Glossing Aristophanic politics, Henderson (1998b: 3) says, "Throughout his career Aristophanes promotes the views and policies of men on the conservative right and assails their opponents." *PAA* adds "possibly the same as, or grandfather of, 175680" for service as *bouleutēs* in ±389 (*IG* II² 1740.2, catalogue Prytanes or Council). One cannot be certain between grandfather and grandson, but the evidence more than favors the grandfather for member of Council: even if the playwright Aristophanes were born at the beginning of the earlier range suggested by Dover, 469 (rather than Henderson's suggested ±450), the grandson would reach thirty, minimum age for service, as Aristophanes reached eighty. But that would imply short generations for Aristophanes and/or one of his sons. Since it is more likely that Aristophanes was born around 450, it is also more likely that it was he who served as councilman in his early sixties.

Works.   Four of the forty-four comedies attributed to Aristophanes in antiquity were considered spurious then, but only eleven plays and some 976 frr. (*PCG*) survive. About eighty citations from nineteen of the forty-four plays and frr. appear in this prosopography because they mention, or feature as characters, persons from Plato's dialogues (cf. Abbreviations, Ancient Texts, Translations). Of those, the most central plays for an understanding of the Socratic milieu are detailed in the chart below. In passing, Henderson (1998b: 9n19) makes short work of the burning question whether women were prohibited from attending theatrical festivals, an issue that has exercised non-Platonists, and mystified Platonists, for generations: "No ancient evidence supports the modern notion that women must have been excluded, and Plato twice explicitly mentions them among the spectators (*Gorgias* 502b–d, *Laws* 658a–d)."

date	play	synopsis	persons
427	*Banqueters* (*Daitalēs*, frr. 205–255) 2nd prize, ?Lenaea	An attack on rhetorical education: two brothers who have had completely different educations—one in the old style, the other in rhetoric—compete in the presence of their father to demonstrate what they have learned.	Thrasymachus
425	*Acharnians* 1st prize, Lenaea	An honest peasant's private truce with Sparta (a wineskin) is threatened by war-mongering Acharnians, though he ultimately wins them over to the pleasures of peace.	Aspasia Pericles I Alcibiades III Lamachus

date	play	synopsis	persons
423 (rev. ±418)	*Clouds* 3rd prize or worse, Dionysia	An attack on sophistic education: a father seeks to have his gambling son trained by Socrates to outwit creditors, but the plan backfires when the son begins outwitting and beating his father as well.	Chaerephon Socrates Xanthippe Pericles I
422	*Wasps* 2nd prize, Lenaea	An attack on the jury system: a father who favors the democratic leader, Cleon, is besotted with jury service because it puffs him up and pays him. His anti-Cleon son orders him locked up and guarded by two slaves. A contest between father and son results in the old man's giving up his public role for a private one: a domestic trial ensues between two dogs that the father misjudges.	Alcibiades III Chaerephon Pyrilampes Laches Lycon Pericles I Connus
414	*Birds* 2nd prize, Dionysia	Two friends—one confident, one persuasive—abandon the miseries of litigious human society to lead quiet good lives among the birds, metamorphose into birds, and erect a wall between heaven and earth. The persuasive one wins the Princess in the end.	Chaerephon Socrates
411	*Women at the Thesmophoria* Dionysia	When the women of Athens are plotting revenge against Euripides, he decides to send a male spy to the secret women's festival, the Thesmophoria. The effeminate Agathon seems ideal but refuses, so a kinsman is sent instead: when unmasked and threatened, he appeals to Euripides in a series of parodies of Euripides' own plays.	Agathon Euripides
405	*Frogs* 1st prize, Lenaea performance repeated by civic decree (?404)	Divine Dionysus, missing good theatre, goes to the underworld to retrieve Euripides. He attends a poetry contest between the shades of Aeschylus and Euripides, presided over by the shade of Sophocles. Despite his original intention, Dionysus returns to Athens with Aeschylus.	Agathon Alcibiades III Callias III Clitophon Euripides Meletus I
392 or 391	*Assemblywomen (Ecclesiazusae)*	The women of Athens, disgusted with politics as usual, enter the Assembly in disguise and take over the city, instituting the community of women, children, and property, and the abolition of the courts.	Callias III

Aristophanes provides a wealth of appearances by, and even more allusions to, the characters of Plato's dialogues, but—especially in the case of his frr.—moderns are often at a loss to explain the meanings of the allusions. In his 1973 comedy *Sleeper*, Woody Allen explored the problem of understanding an "ancient" civilization from fragments of its written record. When the film premiered, "Albert Shanker"—head of the local teachers' union—was a household name, so a joke at his expense brought down the house, though only in New York City.

In Plato. Plato's treatment of Aristophanes is sympathetic. Only Aristophanes and Agathon are able to stay awake all night with Socrates, for example, discussing comedy and tragedy (*Smp.* 223d). An epitaph for Aristophanes (T 130 among the testimonia in *PCG*) is attributed to Plato: "The Graces, seeking for themselves a shrine that would not fall, found the soul of Aristophanes."

Aristophon of Thasos, son of Aglaophon (painter) See App. II.

Aristotle of Athens   Andoc. 1.47
[*PA/APF* 2053 (828.6) *LGPN2* 4 *PAA* 174675
Ἀριστοτέλης]
† 440s
wife: sister of Leogoras II
father of Charmides
See stemma: Andocides.

This Aristotle died in the 440s, leaving his son, Charmides, to be reared with Andocides IV in Leogoras II's wealthy household. Thus he cannot be identified with any other man of that name in this prosopography.

Aristotle of Thorae, son of Timocrates   Pl. *Prm.* 127d2   speaker
[*PA* 2057, 2055 (cf. *APF* 828.6) *LGPN2* 56 *PAA*   Pl. *Ltr.* 7.324b–d,
174720 *RE* 3 *PP* Ἀριστοτέλης Τιμοκράτους   unnamed †
Θοραιεύς]   Thu. 3.105.3, 107.1
±465–>403   *IG* I³ 285.5, 366.6
one of the Thirty   Xen. *Hell.*, *passim*
                                                     D. L. 5.34
                                                     AM 106.149

Life and career. Plato represents Aristotle as the youngest person present at the conversation at the heart of the *Parmenides*, eager to answer questions; and it is not the first time that Aristotle has conversed with Socrates: Parmenides has witnessed it on at least one previous occasion (*Prm.* 135d). He is probably one of the acquaintances Plato mentions in *Letter 7*.

An Aristotle is named as "treasurer of the other gods" in an inscription of 431/0 (*IG* I³ 285 inventory other). He was commander of twenty ships sailing off the Peloponnesus in 426/5 (Thu. 3.105.3) and was included among the generals Theramenes accused of fortifying Eetionia to admit the Spartans into the city through the Piraeus in 411 (Xen. *Hell.* 2.3.46), a plan thwarted by Theramenes s.v., another future member of the Thirty. By the time the Spartan general Lysander sends Aristotle to Sparta to report to the *ephors* after Athens' defeat in 404, he is described as an Athenian exile (2.2.18). But then he becomes a member of the Thirty (2.3.2) and goes to Sparta on their behalf to ask for Lysander's aid (2.3.13).

Prosopographical notes. *APF* brings together *PA* 2055 (the son of Timocrates) and 2057 (tribe Antiochis, on the Löper hypothesis)—an identification preserved in *LGPN2*—and also adds the demotic Thorae, citing *HCT* (2.417–18) and Lewis (1961: 120–1) with *IG* I³ 366 (inventory Athena). *PAA*, however, assigns 174720 (son of Timocrates) ?= 174760 (Antiochis) and ?= 174910 (of Thorae), implying that we may be dealing with as many as three different individuals here.

Aristotle of Stagira, son of Nicomachus (philosopher) See App. II.

Artaxerxes I of Persia (king) See App. II.

Artaxerxes II of Persia (king) See App. II.

Artemis, slave of Plato See App. II.

Aspasia of Miletus, daughter of Axiochus [*PAA* 222330 (cf. *APF* 11811.4–5) *FRA* 4040 *RE* 1 *DPhA* 460 *OCD*³ *PP PX* Ἀσπασία Ἀξιόχου Μιλητίου θυγάτηρ] b. late 470s, † ?>401/0 *hetaira* of Pericles I wife of Lysicles mother of Pericles II rhetoric teacher of Socrates *See stemmata: Pericles, Alcibiades.*

Pl. *Mx.* 235e–236d,   speaker
  249d–e
Aes. *Asp.*
Antis. *Asp.*
Xen. *Mem.* 2.6.36
Xen. *Oec.* 3.14
Crat., *Chi.* fr. 259 (K
  241)
Cal., *Ped.* fr. 21 (K
  15)
Aristoph. *Ach.*
  515–539
Eu. *Dem.* frr. 110 (K
  98)
Diod. Ath. fr. 40

Life.   One of the reasons so little is known about the individual women of Socrates' time is that, as famously expressed by Pericles I, female excellence and glory belong to the woman "who is least talked of among the men whether for good or for bad" (Thu. 2.45.2)—an unserviceable standard for measuring Aspasia. Aspasia is one of the most written-about ancient personalities, and controversies abound. Aspasia was probably born in the Greek city of Miletus, on the coast of Asia Minor (in present-day Turkey, see Map 1), the daughter of Axiochus of

Miletus. Aspasia was a free woman, not a Carian prisoner-of-war turned slave (*pace* a scholium to the 2nd c. C.E. historian Aristides); the Athenians' decree to legitimize her son with Pericles I would almost certainly have been impossible otherwise; and her later legal marriage to Lysicles (ἐπεγήματο: Cal. = schol. Plato, *Mx.* 235e) equally unlikely, had she been anything less than a freeborn Greek.

The circumstances that took her to Athens are not known, though one plausible theory connects her to Alcibiades II of Scambonidae, who was ostracized from Athens in 460 and may have spent his exile in Miletus. Alcibiades II had already produced a family in Athens; Clinias II and a daughter who married a man from the deme of Phegous were probably already young adults by the time of the exile, and we have no information about Alcibiades II's first wife, for example, whether she was dead or divorced. Bicknell (1982) suggests that Alcibiades II married again during his exile, more specifically, he married a daughter of Axiochus, for he named his son Axiochus, a name previously unknown in Athens that remained very rare. He apparently returned to Athens with his new wife and her younger sister, Aspasia. The hypothesis has several virtues. It explains the presence in Athens of a woman from Miletus in the 450s. It also accounts for the surprising and sudden appearance of the name 'Axiochus' in the Alcibiades family and solves the longstanding problem of Axiochus' age (see s.v.) relative to Clinias II's. Finally, it suggests an origin for the masculine variant of 'Aspasia', 'Aspasius', in a gravestone inscription (*IG* II² 7394) dated >350 naming both an Aspasius of Scambonidae and his ?daughter, an Aspasia—presumably descendants of the original bearers of those names. (I find no evidence to support Bicknell's further suggestions, however, that Alcibiades II fathered an 'Aspasius' after Axiochus or that the Aspasia of the inscription is depicted in the relief.)

Aspasia lived as the *de facto* wife of Pericles I s.v. for about twenty years from >450 until his death in 429. Their son, Pericles II s.v., a *nothos* under the citizenship laws Pericles I had himself advanced 451/0 (cf. App. III), was born ±445. After Pericles I's death, Aspasia married Lysicles (Cal.; Aes. no. 66 [fr. 26 Dittmar]), an Athenian general and democratic leader—labeled only "sheepseller" by the contemptuous—who was killed in action the next year (Thu. 3.19.1–2). Kahn (1996: 27n48), missing Callias' *Pedētae* fr., asserts, "this story should never have been taken seriously by modern historians." But it would have been almost impossible in Athens that Aspasia should remain without a legal guardian (*kyrios*). We cannot be certain what motivated her particular move, though it is probable that Pericles II had not yet come of age, and doubtful that the option of returning to a living Axiochus of Miletus was open to her (he may well have been dead before Aspasia accompanied her sister to Athens). Intermittent political upheaval in wartime Miletus may have presented another obstacle. With Lysicles' death, the contemporaneous record ends. We do not know, for example, whether Aspasia was still alive when Pericles II was elected general, or when he was executed following the Arginusae naval battle (see Exc. 2). The date of her death that I give is the notional date associated with the dramatic date of the *Menexenus* (see App. I).

In Socratic works.   Aspasia's reputation as a teacher and rhetorician derives chiefly from Diodorus Atheniensis and the Socratics (though not from Antisthenes). Plato's *Menexenus* has been the most influential of the sources. In that dialogue,

Socrates identifies Aspasia as his, and Pericles I's, instructor in oratory. But her art was not only the technique of delivery, for Socrates praises her compositions as well. Describing to Menexenus the speech he heard from Aspasia in his lesson the previous day, he credits her with "pasting together some bits and pieces thought up before, at the time when she was composing the funeral oration which Pericles delivered" (236b). Cicero, who attended Plato's Academy, reports that Athenians from Hellenistic times annually recited the *Funeral Speech*—the ancient name of Plato's *Menexenus* (cf. Aristot. *Rh.* 1415b31)—right along with the funeral speech of Pericles I (Thu. 2.34.8–2.46.2), in honor of the war dead (Cic. *Orat.* 151; see Loraux 1986).

Xenophon mentions Aspasia twice. In both cases, her advice is recommended to Critobulus by Socrates. In the *Memorabilia*, Socrates quotes with approval Aspasia's advice to him to tell the whole truth when matchmaking. In the *Oeconomicus*, when Critobulus inquires about how to train his mere child of a wife, Socrates begs off, offering to introduce Aspasia to Critobulus for she is more knowledgeable about the relevant issues, namely the balance of male and female, income and expenditure.

Parts of Aeschines' *Aspasia* are preserved or, more often, reported in a variety of later sources; Athenaeus and Plutarch are the most important ones in Greek. In the dialogue, Socrates advises Callias, probably Callias III, to send his son to Aspasia for instruction. When Callias recoils at the notion of a female teacher, Socrates recounts tales of famous women, noting that Aspasia had favorably influenced Pericles I and, after his death, Lysicles. The only extended text of Aeschines' *Aspasia* is a section preserved in Latin by Cicero (*De invent.* 1.31, 1.51–53): Socrates reports that Aspasia counseled first Xenophon's wife, then Xenophon himself, about acquiring virtue through self-knowledge. Since Xenophon of Erchia was not married during Socrates' lifetime, this may be another Xenophon or an imaginative construction of the sort Xenophon of Erchia himself wrote.

Much less of Antisthenes' *Aspasia* is extant, and what there is has much in common with the hostile tradition of Old Comedy. Athenaeus (220d, 533c–d, 589e) and Plutarch (*Per.* 24.7–8) report attacks on the sexual license of Pericles I's sons, Xanthippus II and Paralus (nos. 142–3; the lurid details are in Ath.); but Antisthenes appears to have attacked the entire household of Pericles I, including Aspasia.

In comedy.   It was the business of the intellectuals we call the comic poets to be scathing when they could; they had a responsibility—and a sacred responsibility at that—to provoke and to criticize, as well as to entertain. They had a large target in Aspasia: a foreign-born woman refusing to observe the norms of the Athenian society into which she had moved, a woman not only linked sexually with the most important citizen of the *polis* but running his household in the presence of his sons, their son, and Alcibiades III and his younger brother. In what follows, I include only the few well-founded texts that say something understandable about Aspasia. I omit the scores of passages that may or may not contain allusions to her; and I likewise omit the countless musings about what the plays of which we have only titles or hypotheses or fragments *may* have said about Aspasia; but I also omit references and possible references to Aspasia that have no context, thus it should be kept in mind that she was used on the comic stage more than we can now recover, and that what was preserved was determined as much by what interested the later writers who copied out the lines as by chance.

Proceeding chronologically, something like an attack on Aspasia in a play (no longer extant) may lie behind Plutarch's well-known remark (*Per.* 32.1) that Hermippus, one of the earlier comic poets of the period, prosecuted Aspasia on the charge of impiety (*asebeia*), was eloquently and passionately defended by Pericles I, and was acquitted, perhaps about 432. This is so similar to stories about charges against, e.g., Anaxagoras and Phidias—also in Pericles I's circle—that it is generally believed that Plutarch, or his source, misunderstood a reference in or to a comedy.

Cratinus is probably first to attack Aspasia <430, when the long war had begun, but Pericles I and his household were still alive. The play was one that damned the present by comparison to a long ago golden age. Evoking comparison to Zeus and Hera, by transforming common epithets, Pericles I's shameful lust has brought him a dog-eyed mistress (*pallakē*). The dog in the remark seems to be one that would steal from the table if one's back were turned, but perhaps it had a physiological point as well. Callias' *Pedētae* is dated formally ≤429/8; the part that concerns Aspasia, however, is preserved in a scholium to Plato's *Menexenus* and communicates information available no earlier than 428, including the fact cited above, that Aspasia married Lysicles after Pericles I's death (235e schol.). Unfortunately for us, it is this same scholium that attributes the fact to Aeschines. But the scholiast also says that the offspring of that union was a son called Poristes (235b schol.). 'Poristes' is not in fact a name but means 'supplier' and is very likely a misunderstanding by the scholiast of some line or lines of Callias. (In a curious error, *FRA* lists Aspasia as marrying Pericles, then Poristes.)

Aristophanes is clearer. His *Acharnians* of 425 gives Aspasia some indirect blame for the war which had, by then, wrecked the economy. The peasant hero of the play, who makes a separate peace with Sparta and enjoys various fruits of peace, says the war began when some drunken rowdies from Athens stole a prostitute (*pornē*) from Megara, prompting the Megarians to retaliate by stealing two prostitutes from Aspasia. Henderson (1998b: 121n70) notes that—in the popular imagination, gossip—Aspasia procured women of free birth for Pericles I, or even that she trained prostitutes.

Eupolis' *Demes* of 412, seventeen years after Pericles I's death, and after the disastrous Sicilian campaign, brings old Athenian political leaders up from the underworld to lead the *polis* to health. In reply to Pericles I's question whether his *nothos* (Pericles II) is alive, he is told "Yes, but he's ashamed to have a prostitute [*pornē*] for a mother."

If anyone should wonder whether the attitude of the comic poets has gained sway in spite of the Socratics, note the emotive language in Simon Hornblower's article on Aspasia for the *OCD*[3]: "After Pericles' death in 429 Aspasia allegedly took up with another demagogue, Lysicles, until he died in 428," oddly suggesting I. F. Stone in his bibliography.

In the later tradition and modern bibliography. The later tradition on Aspasia is vast, but Plutarch's *Pericles* is the source of choice for those who want a brief account of Aspasia within the general context of Pericles I; Athenaeus also mentions her several times (533c cites Hera. Pont.). See also Lucianus' *Imagines* 17, and *de Saltatione* 25; and note the number of later sources cited in the notes to the first chapter of Henry (1995: 132–7). Henry supplements the ancient and contemporary sources for Aspasia with a large number of peripheral and popular studies of ancient women, feminism et al., but there is no particular focus on philosophy (1995: 177–93); Kahn (1963), Coventry (1989), and Salkever (1993) should be added to important contemporary bibliography.

Astylus (athlete) See App. II.

Autolycus of Thoricus, son of Lycon
[*PA* 2748 *LGPN2* 10 *PAA* 569985 *RE* 4 *PX*
Ἀυτόλυκος Λύκωνος Θορίκιος]
±440–404/3
mother: a woman from Rhodes
beloved of Callias III
pancratium winner executed by the Thirty

Pl. *Ap*. 23e schol. =
   Crat. *Pyt*. fr. 214
   (K 203)
Xen. *Symp*.
SEG 34.380.1, 3
Aristoph. *Wasps*
   1169 schol.
Aristoph. *Lysistr*.
   270 & schol.
Eu. *Auto*. frr. 48–75
   (incl. K 42–67)
D. S. 14.5.7

Life.   Autolycus, the son of Socrates' accuser Lycon s.v., was the celebrated winner of the pancratium event of the greater Panathenaea held in the late summer (August) of 422 (*SEG*), enabling an approximate date of birth to be established for him. The pancratium was a particularly grueling athletic contest in the late 5th c., similar to what might be called brawling now, except that biting and gouging were strictly forbidden in Athens. Along with the usual means of overcoming an opponent—boxing and wrestling—the pancratist could break bones, strangle, and kick; he was likely to be a broad and beefy specimen. By the time Autolycus won athletic fame, however, he had already attracted the attention of the comic poets as something of a wastrel: Cratinus' *Wine Flask*, which took first prize in 423, noted his extravagance. A scholiast of Aristophanes' *Wasps* of 422 names him as a referent for the phrase "voluptuous swagger"; and Eupolis' *Autolycus* of 420 exploits the sexual license of his circle (cf. Aristoph., *Lysistr*. 270, directed against the loose behavior of his mother in 411). Diodorus describes him as outspoken and a victim of the Thirty.

Such a description sits ill with Xenophon's characterization of Autolycus. His *Symposium* is set soon after Autolycus' victory, and in celebration of it. In fact, the games are still going on, for Callias III and Niceratus II have been at the horse races with Lycon and Autolycus when they run into Socrates, Antisthenes, Charmides, Hermogenes, and Critobulus on the street and invite them to the banquet at Callias III's Piraeus house. Autolycus is shown as a quiet and modest youth, still too young to recline at dinner (*Symp*. 1.8), who blushes at a compliment

(3.12), and nestles close to Lycon (3.13), next to whom he seats himself. Since we are in no danger of thinking such a victory meal took place (Xenophon says he was there, but he would have been a toddler at the time), the glaring anachronisms need not concern one unduly.

In the later tradition. A number of later sources retell the tale (Ath. 5; Pau. 1.18.3, 9.32.8; Plu. *Lysan.* 15; Pli. *HN* 34.79).

Axiochus of Scambonidae, son of
  Alcibiades II
[*PA/APF* 1330 (600.6B) *LGPN2* 5 = 1 *PAA*
139755, 129725 *RE* 1 Ἀξίοχος Ἀλκιβιάδου
Σκαμβωνίδης]
b. 455–1, † >407/6
mother: ?daughter of Axiochus of Miletus
paternal half siblings: Clinias II and a sister
  (who married a Phegousian)
father of Clinias III
uncle of Alcibiades of Phegous
uncle and cohort of Alcibiades III
See stemma: Alcibiades.

Pl. *Euthd.* 271a,
  275a, pat. *
[Pl.] *Ax.*   speaker
Aes. *Ax.*
IG I³ 101.48
IG I³ 422.193, 202;
  424.10; 426.108,
  125; 427.46, 63, 82,
  85; 430.6, 8, 25, 33
Andoc. 1.16
[Lys.] 2.246

Life. Because Axiochus' son, Clinias III, figures so prominently in the Platonic dialogues and (apparently derivatively) in Xenophon, the date of Axiochus' birth is not a negligible datum, and it has been markedly controversial: the secondary literature of the twentieth century produced a range of dates of birth for this important relative of the famous Alcibiades III from ±480 (*APF*) to ±445 (*PAA*). A later date fits the data better, but 445 is too late. I date Axiochus' birth 455–1 for three reasons: it is likely that he had a foreign mother (see Aspasia s.v. and stemma), which would not have permitted him citizenship status after 451/0; second, a postulated gap of forty-five years between Alcibiades II's two sets of children, even if by different wives, is less plausible than a thirty-five year gap; third, Axiochus was, from what we know, a sidekick of Alcibiades III, making a thirty-year difference in age between them not creditable.

   Discounting pseudo-Lysias' diatribe against both Axiochus and Alcibiades III for debaucheries (recounted in lurid detail) in Abydos in ±433, Axiochus is first heard of when he is accused of profanation of the mysteries by Agariste III in 415 (see Exc. 1 and Charmides, s.v.) when his son, Clinias III, would have been about nine. Although Andocides IV says broadly that all those accused by Agariste III fled Athens ahead of the executioners, it is certain that the co-accused Alcibiades III sailed for Sicily as general in 415, so it is likely that Axiochus went into exile with Alcibiades III. Burnet (1914: 190) names Axiochus as the uncle of another of his co-accused, Adeimantus of Scambonidae, son of Leucolophides, but there is so far no confirmation of the claim in any source.

   Axiochus (with demotic and patronymic) is listed among the condemned whose property was confiscated and sold by the state 414/3 on the *stelae* recovered from the Eleusinium (cf. Exc. 1). The *stelae* are not perfectly preserved, so it is not yet possible to work out, for example, the location of the property Axiochus held. However, he is listed as owner of the slaves Ceph[——], *FRA* 7770 (ln. 26); and Holas, *FRA* 7918 (ln. 7). There is room on the *stele* (*IG* I³ 430) for seven or eight slaves in all.

Axiochus appears to have accompanied his nephew through the period when Alcibiades III was recalled to the fleet in 411 (Thu. 8.97.3) though Thucydides does not specify which other exiles were recalled with Alcibiades III. There is no hint in any source that Axiochus returned to Athens before 407 (*pace APF*), the year that Alcibiades III finally went there and remained for four months, but in that year Axiochus proposed a decree praising Thracian Neapolis (*IG* I³ 101.48). He may have helped Euryptolemus III to defend the generals who led the Arginusae campaign in 406 ([Pl.] *Ax.*; cf. Exc. 2), but not as a member of the Prytanes (*Ap.* 32b).

Axiochus may exemplify a phenomenon Socrates mentions (*R.* 558a): men condemned to death yet walking around the city under a democracy. Since most of the exiles on whom we have later information, including Axiochus, eventually returned to Athens, they were presumably walking around the city wherein still stood the record in stone of their having been condemned for sacrilege. But it is also possible that Axiochus was a special case, i.e. his activity in proposing a decree in 407/6 may be evidence that the other three men accused by Agariste III were exonerated along with Alcibiades III.

Prosopographical notes.   The dozen or so competing stemmata for this family omit females—with the sometime exception of Bicknell (1975), whose suggestion about the connection between Alcibiades II and Axiochus of Miletus (Bicknell 1982) I incorporate in the stemma for the family of Alcibiades. In the selected and abbreviated illustrations below, I standardize spelling and use the Roman numerals that have been standard since *APF*.

Because Axiochus' brother, Clinias II, was born ±480, it was long assumed that Axiochus was of the same generation, born about the same time (most influentially in *APF*), but there are many problems with the assumption. To take one example, mock-performance of the mysteries is an unlikely, though not impossible, diversion for a man of sixty-five. The more Axiochus' activities have been recognized over the years as bound up with those of Alcibiades III, the less plausible an age difference of thirty years between the two men has seemed. After Kirchner planted a tentative family tree (*PA* 1901),

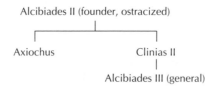

Dittenberger (1902) pointed out problems, including extremely long intervals between fathers and sons, and suggested adding a generation, a suggestion Kirchner immediately accepted and included in the supplement of the second volume of *PA* (1903). Hatzfeld (1940), Alcibiades III's notable biographer, concurred, as did Wallace as late as 1970 (197 & n12).

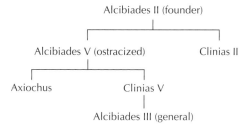

Vanderpool (1952, cf. 1968), arguing from newly discovered *ostraka* that the Alcibiades who was ostracized was the son of a Clinias, not an Alcibiades, inserted yet another generation.

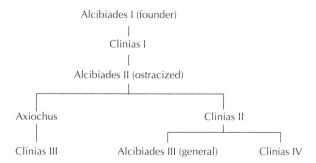

The result, five generations where there were three, had the undesirable consequence that the generations, the intervals between fathers and sons, were extremely short (the supposed precedent for short generations, Crito and Critobulus s.v., has evaporated). Stanley (1986: 179), recognizing that Plato's Clinias III, son of Axiochus, could not be reconciled with Vanderpool's interpretation, suggested yet another that has much to recommend it.

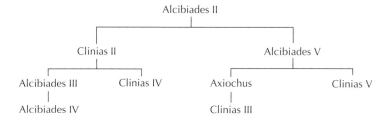

The problem with Stanley's adjustment is that Socrates says explicitly that Axiochus is the son of the "old Alcibiades" (Ἀλκιβιάδου τοῦ παλαιοῦ), so if an Alcibiades V were added, he would be a younger man than the well-known old Alcibiades II, ostracized in 460, and thus still would not be the referent of Socrates' remark, the father of Axiochus. Bicknell (1982) explains the known data without multiplying individuals unnecessarily. He hypothesizes a second marriage for

Alcibiades II, giving him two sets of children, widely separated in age; it is that view that I have incorporated into the Alcibiades stemma.

LGPN2 5 ?= 1, known from IG I³ 101.48 (Ἀχοί–), a decree dated 407/6—an identification already accepted in APF and Dover (1968b: 32), both citing both Dittenberger (1902: 1–13) and Andrewes (1953: 3, 7). Similarly, PAA 139755 ?= 139725, but PAA follows APF in citing Xen. Mem. 1.3.8, 10 in error (see Clinias III s.v.).

Axiochus of Miletus See App. II.

Axiothea of Phlius See App. II.

Bacchius of Syracuse   [Pl.] Ltr. 1.309c *
[DPhA 1 Βακχεῖος]
messenger between [Plato] to Dionysius II

Bacchius' origins are not given in the letter. However, the name is known in southern Italy in classical times, and not in Athens.

Bias of Priene See App. II.

Bictas, slave of Plato See App. II.

Brachyllus of ?Athens See App. II. See stemma: Lysias.

Brasidas of Sparta, son of Tellis (commander) See App. II.

Bryson of Heraclea Pontica   [Pl.] Ltr. 13.360c
[OCD³ DPhA 68 PP Βρύσων]   frr. in Döring 1972
active early 4th c.   Aristot. S. Ref.
student of ?Euclides   171b16, 172a3
associate of Polyxenus   Aristot. Rh. 1405b9
mathematician and sophist   Aristot. An. Post.
                                                     75b4

Heraclea Pontica is on the southern coast of the Black Sea, west of the Bosphorus. Although Aristotle criticizes Bryson (An. Post., S. Ref.) for his claim to have squared the circle, the procedure he used in his attempt was later put to use by Archimedes in measuring the sphere. Aristotle also criticizes Bryson's statement that there is no such thing as foul language because, regardless of the words used, the referent remains the same (*Rh.*), to which Aristotle responds that one word may describe a thing more truly than another. Bryson's attempt to square the circle seems to have been interpreted in later times as eristic and sophistical: Alexander's commentary on Aristotle's *Sophistical Refutations* calls it that (171b7), and criticizes it for using broad principles not specific to geometry. He describes the procedure in such a way that one can see how the accusation might arise. Circumscribe a square around a circle, and another square within the circle; the circle is then *intermediate* between the inscribed and the escribed squares. As Heath points out (1921: 1.223–4), how Bryson proposed to determine the intermediate square— whether with the arithmetic or the geometric mean—is unknown. Even so, Bryson's procedure was an advance over previous efforts.

Callaeschrus I of Athens, son of Critias III [*PA/APF* 7758 (8792.6) *LGPN2* 32 *PAA* 552225 Κάλλαισχρος Κριτίου] tribe: ?Erechtheis ±490–≤429 mother: ?daughter of Glaucon I of Cerameis brother: Glaucon II wife: sister of Andocides IV's paternal grandmother father of Critias IV and a ?daughter who married Hagnodorus of Amphitrope *See stemma: Plato.*

Pl. *Chrm.* 153c, 157e, pat.
Pl. *Prt.* 316a5, pat.
Andoc. 1.47, unnamed

Prosopographical notes. There is no firm information about this individual. *PAA* says "possibly the same as" *PAA* 552220, a leading member of the Four Hundred (Lys. 12.66), but Plato's ancestor would have been rather old to play a leading role in 411 (*pace* Avery 1963: 167n13), though Antiphon may provide a similar case of an aged leader of the Four Hundred. He cannot be the Callaeschrus for whom [Lys.] composed a speech (fr. 11) in 400 or 399. Cf. Plutarch *Alc.* 33.1, pat. and Diogenes (3.1).

Callaeschrus of Eupyridae See App. II.

Callaeschrus of Athens See App. II.

Calliades of Athens See App. II.

Callias I of Alopece, son of Phaenippus See App. II. *See stemmata: Callias, Thucydides.*

Callias II of Alopece, son of Hipponicus I See App. II. *See stemmata: Callias, Thucydides.*

Callias III of Alopece, son of Hipponicus II
[*PA/APF* 7826 *LGPN2* 84 *PAA* 554500 *RE* 3
DPhA 16 *OCD³ PP PX* Καλλίας Ἱππονίκου
Ἀλωπεκῆθεν]
±450–367/6
mother: [unnamed] former wife of Pericles I
siblings: full sister Hipparete I; maternal half
   brothers Paralus and Xanthippus II;
   paternal half brother Hermogenes
wives: (1) daughter of Glaucon II (2)
   daughter of Ischomachus and Chrysilla (3)
   Chrysilla herself
offspring with Glaucon II's daughter:
   Hipponicus III; with Chrysilla: [unnamed]
   of Alopece
student of Protagoras, Hippias, Prodicus
lover of Autolycus
rich host and frequenter of sophists
See stemmata: Callias, Pericles.

Pl. *Prt., passim*   speaker
Pl. *Ap.* 20a–c   speaker
Pl. *Tht.* 165a *
Pl. *Cra.* 391c1 *
[Pl.] *Eryx.* 395a *
[Pl.] *Ax.* 366c *
Aes. *Cal.*
Aes. *Asp.*
Xen. *Hell.* 4.5.13,
   6.3.2 et al.
Xen. *Symp., passim*
Andoc. 1.110–32
Lys. 19.48
Antiph. frr. 33–36
comedy (see below)
inscriptions (see
   below)

Life.   Philosophers have been too quick to write off Callias III as a rich man who spent his money on sophists, for Callias III was a grotesque, if fascinating, figure in Socrates' and Plato's immediate environment, a man controlled by his passions, notably lust and greed, whose reputation was earned while he lived, not contrived later by gossips of the Hellenistic period. He was Socrates' fellow demesman, but lived on for some forty more years after Socrates' death without ever disappearing from full public view. Thus he is a prominent example of Plato's putting well-known living persons into the dialogues; since Callias III remained active in Athenian politics well after the establishment of the Academy, members would have known the man and his character.

   Callias III was familiar first of all as the son of the richest man in Greece (see Hipponicus II s.v.), then from 422 was the richest man in Greece (Lys.). The family wealth was primarily in silver mines, worked with slave labor (Xen. *WM* 4.15) at mining property north of Sunium (*Agora* 19.5.64). But there was also agricultural land in Alopece, perhaps, and cult income from the Ceryces *dadouchia*. Such wealth led to expensive liturgies as well (see *APF* 7826.7 and sources cited there for much more detailed information about Callias III's wealth). The record is one of exceptional wealth for Callias II and Hipponicus II, reduced by the Peloponnesian war and extravagant spending to only two *talents* (Lys. 19.48) after 390 by Callias III. By setting the *Protagoras* in ±433/2, Plato represents Callias III in his late twenties, recently having undertaken responsibility for the family property from the still living Hipponicus II (cf. MacDowell 1978: 91), just before Cratinus makes him infamous for licentious behavior (±430). His household was then, and had

STEMMA: CALLIAS

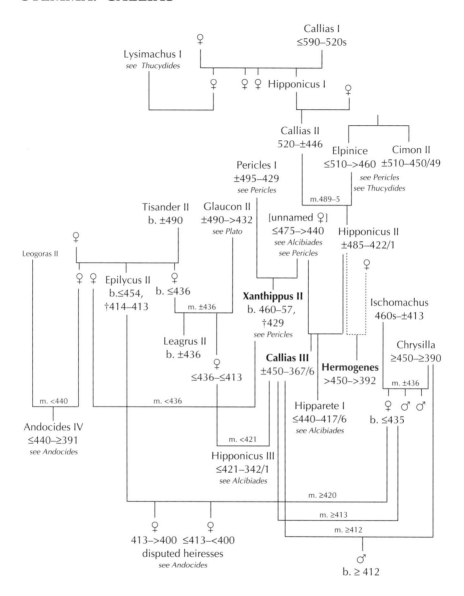

been for at least a decade, receiving some six *talents* annually in revenue from mining operations. He also had agricultural lands which produced income. He still lived in the house that had belonged to his father (*Prt.* 315d), presumably in Alopece, though he acquired a house in the Piraeus in the 420s (Eu. *Auto.*; Xen. *Symp.* 1.2), and another in Melite sometime 420–412 (Aristoph. *Frogs* 501, *Hor.* fr. 583) where larger and more luxurious entertainments could be undertaken. At this point in his life, Callias III's ambition was to make himself wise by buying a sophistical education. He was a student of Protagoras, of Prodicus, and of Hippias, from whom he learned a mnemonic system (*Symp.* 4.62); in 399, Socrates reports that Callias III plans to send his two sons to Evenus for the five *minae* course.

Callias III inherited much more than money from his parents. The money he squandered, but he retained and exploited the connections, the official power, and the prestige—irrespective of reduced financial circumstances. From his mother, Callias III had an immediate connection to the family of Pericles I whose sons were his maternal half brothers, and whose ward, Alcibiades III, married his sister, Hipparete I s.v. (a generation later, their daughter would marry Callias III's son, Hipponicus III). (Sprague's "whose wife Pericles married" of Callias III is a misprint for "whose mother Pericles had married" [2001: 206].) On his father's side, Callias III was a Ceryces. When Xenophon praises him as a *Eupatrid* (*Symp.* 8.40), he implies the Ceryces clan (*genos*) was one of the pre-Solonic ruling elite, "the 'caste' of aristocrats which until 580 held a monopoly of executive political power in Athens" (*APF*). Whether Xenophon's attribution was accurate or an exaggeration, the Ceryces clan, in the late 5th c., maintained its privilege of supplying priests, appointed for life, from among its number for the celebration of the Eleusinian mysteries; Callias III was himself appointed torchbearer, the second most important priest (Xen. *Hell.* 6.3.3–6; Andoc. 1.126). The familial sacred office of torchbearer (*dadouchia*) guaranteed Callias III not only honor in others' eyes, but a cult income as well. Hipponicus II also brought to his son a familial Spartan *proxeny* (Xen. *Hell.* 6.3.4).

By marrying the daughter of Glaucon II of Cerameis, Callias III became related by marriage to the family of Plato, to which his sons would be related by blood. Glaucon II's daughter, born ±436, was well-connected on her mother's side as well, where her maternal grandfather was the rich Tisander II, all of whose daughters married into fame and wealth. Her marriage to Callias III took place 423–421, and they produced a son, Hipponicus III, ≤421, but this first wife of Callias died before 413, when she was between fifteen and twenty-three. See Chrysilla s.v. for the sordid details of Callias III's second and third marriages to Chrysilla's daughter, and then to Chrysilla herself ≥413 and ≥412, respectively. For present purposes, note that Chrysilla's daughter was the widow of Epilycus II and the mother of two daughters—one born in 413 when the other was between the ages of three and seven (see stemma); these daughters will reappear as "heir-esses" (*epiklēroi*) below, where I shall refer to the older as Alpha and the younger as Beta. Callias III's second marriage probably came about after the young widow had returned with her daughters to her father's household (see Ischomachus s.v.); he then agreed to her marriage to Callias III who had also been widowed by then. Moreover, Callias III was at about this time losing the revenues from his silver mining enterprises and may have been attracted to the dowry Ischomachus' daughter would bring with her. Ischomachus appears to have died soon afterwards, at about which time Chrysilla and her sons moved in with her daughter and son-in-law (Callias III may have been named guardian of the sons; cf. Ischomachus s.v.); the arrangement was not amicable: the daughter attempted suicide, then ran away, and Callias III married Chrysilla. We are not told in whose keeping the two girls were during or after this time.

Callias III's third marriage produced a second son ≥412 whose name has not survived, and whom Callias III refused to acknowledge as his own for some years (see Chrysilla s.v., and Protarchus s.v.). After Callias III *had* acknowledged his second son, however, he tried in 400 to arrange a suitable future marriage for him, but proceeded in a clandestine way that apparently backfired in court, according to Andocides IV (1.117–123, who called witnesses to his testimony and also won his case). Callias III's first wife's uncle was the same Epilycus II who was his second wife's first husband (see stemma); Epilycus II died intestate in Sicily 414–3, leaving two daughters and no sons (see below). By law, contested cases were to be settled when the *epiklēros* was in her fourteenth year in a special hearing called a *diadikasia*; and this case was heard in 400. Leaving out Andocides IV's not-disinterested account of his or Callias III's motives, the events seem to have been these: Andocides IV and his first cousin Leagrus II could see that they were their uncle Epilycus II's closest male relatives and would be offered the *epiklēroi*, who were their maternal first cousins; both men were unmarried and discussed the matter between themselves. Since Andocides IV was slightly older, he had the legal right to choose first; he chose Alpha, the older of the two. He and Leagrus II then put their claims before the archon and awaited the court's dispensation in Alpha's fourteenth year. But Alpha then died. Meanwhile, Callias III had persuaded his former brother-in-law, Leagrus II, to drop his claim to Beta, and before Andocides IV learned of it, Callias III had already submitted his claim on Beta to the archon. Beta was the first cousin of Callias III's first wife, who was dead; she was the daughter of Callias III's second wife, from whom he was now divorced; and she was the granddaughter of his third wife, to whom he was still married. In other words, he was not related to her by blood on either side of her family, so he could not claim Beta himself. However, Callias III's second son, the child of his third marriage, was Beta's maternal half uncle, though he was at least two years younger than she, so any marriage would have to be postponed for some years, during which time Callias III would control the estate of Epilycus II. Anticipating that Andocides IV would contest his claim, Callias III paid Cephisius a thousand *drachmae* to charge Andocides IV with impiety and tie him up in court (Andoc. 1.121). Then Callias III planted evidence in an effort to incriminate Andocides IV further, but was caught by the Council, so the original charge of impiety went ahead in 400, with Andocides IV complaining that Beta should already have been awarded to him.

Athenian law regarding *epiklēroi* ('heiresses' is misleading because it implies ownership) was particularly complex (see Harrison 1998: 1.132–8, digested in MacDowell 1978: 95–8), and only a few generalizations can be made here. The institution is appalling by contemporary standards but yields some insight into how daughters were viewed in law when their own interests came into potential conflict with the *polis*' interest in keeping an estate intact for a potential grandson of the deceased. When a man died intestate with a daughter or daughters, and no sons or grandsons, then the daughters became conduits to his estate, in equal portions if there was more than one daughter; they were placeholders until grandsons were produced for the deceased. His widow was meanwhile subject to a different set of regulations and had no claim on her husband's estate (see Perictione s.v.). The law set down a rigid list of male relatives at the various degrees of kinship to the deceased, beginning on the father's side. The archon had responsibility for offering the girl to each male relative in turn, until one was willing to take her; if he reached the bottom of the list, he could compel the deceased's nearest male relative to take her. When an estate was large, there might be competing offers for an *epiklēros* because whoever became her guardian controlled her father's estate until she married and produced a son who came of age; the guardian could of course marry the *epiklēros* himself if he was eligible. In fact, if an *epiklēros* was already married but was childless or had only daughters, the nearest male relative could claim her in marriage anyway, nullifying her previous marriage in the interest of preserving the estate in the family for a potential son; if the nearest male relative was already married himself, he could divorce his existing wife in favor of the *epiklēros* or abandon his claim. A female's preference was at no stage relevant to any part of the process.

Plato's *Laws* introduces an innovative set of regulations regarding marriages of heiresses that is unlike the existing law of Athens or Sparta in his time (see Patterson's compact explanation of the issues 1998: 103–5 and nn).

Career in brief.   Apart from his official priestly duties, and especially as Callias III had fewer resources, he undertook other tasks for the state. He fought or was *trierarch* at Arginusae in 406 (Aristoph. *Frogs* 422–430), and was elected general in 391/0 with Iphicrates during the Corinthian war. Xenophon credits the two with demoralizing and defeating the Lacedaemonians in a regular battle of hoplites, *peltasts* and cavalry (*Hell.* 4.5.13–18). Later, Callias III's familial Spartan *proxeny* was useful to him on three ambassadorships to Sparta to negotiate peace before and in 371 (Xen. *Hell.* 6.3.2–6, *Symp.* 8.39); Xenophon reports one of Callias III's speeches from the final occasion. He was still alive in his mid-eighties in 367/6 (*Hesperia* 10.14.64). And Callias III was a cockfighter (Xen. *Symp.* 4.9; D. L. 2.30).

In comedy.   The comic poets followed the trail of Callias III's money and scandal. *APF* suggests that a passage from Cratinus shows Callias III using the family estate as security for his debts in the 420s, but the fragment has been reassigned and redated in *PCG* (*Thr.* fr. 81 [K 333]), so the activity goes back to ±430, when Callias III was twenty and being sued for adultery. Cratinus calls Callias III *branded* (στιγματίας), marked by his creditors, but the term is itself significant because it is normally used of run-away slaves; it will return below. Cratinus pursues the womanizing theme in another play of about the same date (*Arch.* fr. 12 [K 11]). Eupolis' *Flatterers*, produced in 421, depicts a gathering of sophists and their hangers-on at the house of an improvident Callias III. Guests included Protagoras (frr. 157–8 [K 146–7]) and Alcibiades III (fr. 171 [K 158]). Socrates may have been there in a now-unknown capacity, though that depends on whether the unassigned fr. 386 (K 352) should be assigned to Eupolis' *Flatterers* (which it has not been in

PCG). Eupolis' *Autolycus*, produced in 420, seems also to have featured a sumptuous gathering at Callias III's house, in honor of the pancratist, Autolycus s.v. the
son of Lycon, and to have emphasized the sexual license of the participants. Much
as Plato's *Protagoras* repeats the circumstances of *Flatterers*, Xenophon's *Symposium*
mimics the occasion of Eupolis' *Autolycus*.

In 414, Callias III's mining revenues had dwindled, and he had apparently
mortgaged much of his property; Aristophanes represented him in *Birds* (282–286)
that year as a hoopoe plucked nearly featherless by females and malicious plaintiffs
(sycophants). Aristotle, illustrating the point that both begging and praying are
kinds of asking, preserves a fr. of Iphicrates (*Rh.* 1405a19–24) that refers to Callias
III as a beggar-priest (μητραγύρτης), both a Ceryces torchbearer and a mendicant.
Sometime after 410, but before 405, the comic poet Metagenes makes reference
to Callias III's *nothos* with Chrysilla (*Phil.* fr. 14 [K 13]). Aristophanes' treatment
of Callias III in *Frogs* of 405 recalls Cratinus fr. 81 where he is a branded slave.
At 428–430, the chorus tells Dionysus

> And Callias, we're told,
> that son of Hippocoitus,
> fights at sea in a lionskin made of pussy.

Later in the play, when the slave Xanthias puts on a lionskin, Dionysus tells him
he looks just like that slave from Melite, good only for whipping (μαστιγίας,
reminiscent of στιγματίας)—i.e. he looks like Callias III. Aristophanes gives Callias
III one last jab in *Assemblywomen* (810) where the citizens are turning in all their
possessions to effect community of property; a poor man is described as having
more to turn in than Callias (because he had been through his fortune by then,
392 or 391).

In Socratic writers.   Aeschines' *Aspasia* is a dialogue between Callias III and Socrates (summarized at Aspasia s.v.), in which Socrates advises Callias to send his
son to Aspasia for instruction, and finds himself defending women more generally
to the reluctant Callias. There is less of Callias III to be found in what is preserved
of Aeschines' *Callias*, for the longest fr. is Plutarch's account of Callias II's finding
gold after the battle of Marathon (*Arist.* 5.6–5.8).

In inscriptions.   Callias was apparently *archetheoros* to Delos for a year between
414 and 405 (from his biography, later is rather more probable than earlier, and
APF makes 410/9 and 406/5 look promising): the accounts there show dedications:
IDélos 103.58, 104.116, 104–11B.12, 104–12.90, 104–27B.6, 104–30.10, 104–31.6,
1409Ba2.59, and 1410b.6. He also appears in *Agora* 19.5.64 and perhaps in 19.26.455.

In the later tradition.   See pseudo-Socrates (*Ep.* 6); pseudo-Andocides (4); Athenaeus (169a, 216d, 218b, 220b–c [= Aes. *Cal.* no. 73, fr. 34 Dittmar], and 537b);
and Aelian (*VH* 4.16).

Prosopographical notes.   *PAA* assigns a separate number, ?= 554505, to the owner
of property in Nape at Sunium (*Agora* 19.5.64) who is also the father of a Hipponicus (*Agora* 19.26.455). In the philosophical literature Callias III has sometimes

been confused with his homonyms below, the son of Calliades (Vlastos 1975: app.) and Callias of Athens (Fowler 1925: 291; PCW 398; *DPhA* C16).

Callias of ?Aexone, son of Calliades
[*PA* 7827 *LGPN2* 27, 28 *PAA* 553855 *RE* 6
DPhA 15 *OCD*[3] *PP* Καλλίας Καλλιάδου]
±470–432
student of Zeno of Elea
political leader

[Pl.] *Alc.* 119a
Thu. 1.61–3
IG I[3] 365.5
  (inventory Athena)
IG I[3] 50.3; 52A.2;
  52B.2; 53.8; 54.15
  (*boulē* decrees)
D. S. 12.37.1

Life and political career.   Callias appears in an inscription dated ±435 (*IG* I[3] 50) as the proposer of a decree concerning public works; since he must have been at least thirty by then, I have used that date to figure an approximate date of birth ±470, though he could be a decade older. Zeno was teaching from perhaps the 450s, so the remark in pseudo-Plato's *Alcibiades* I that Callias learned political wisdom from Zeno at a cost of one hundred *minae* is historically possible. Callias proposed another decree in 434/3 (*IG* I[3] 52), concerning repaying money owed to the gods. The two decrees are sometimes together called the "Callias Decrees"— aimed at putting Athens on a war footing. Callias proposed two alliance decrees in 433/2, with Rhegium and with Leontini (*IG* I[3] 53 and 54). He was elected general for 432/1 and sent north to Macedonia, falling in battle at Potidaea in the fall of 432 (Thu. 1.61.1, 62.4, 63.3; *IG* I[3] 365; D. S.). Socrates and Alcibiades III may have served under him, though they may have left Athens earlier with the general Archestratus' contingent.

Prosopographical notes.   I have tentatively accepted Aexone (tribe Kekropis) as the deme for Callias because of the recurrence of the name 'Callias, son of Calliades' in that deme over the 4th c., especially in the family of Lysis s.v., which is independently associated with the dialogue's eponym, Alcibiades III (see Democrates I s.v., Whitehead 1986: 418–9, 421). Lewis (1961: 118–9) suggests an alternative deme, Paeania, and tribe Pandionis; note that a Callias of that tribe (whose sister married Eucrates) married Andocides IV's sister. *PAA* further divides *PA* 7827, the son of Kalliades mentioned in [Pl.] *Alc.*, into *PAA* 553860 (Thu. and *IG* I[3] 365), *PAA* 553855 (proposer of I[3] 53 and 54), and *PAA* 553870 (proposer of I[3] 50 and 52). *LGPN* separates 27 (proposer of I[3] 50, 52–4; cf. Lewis 1961: 118) from 28 (the remainder of the citations).

Callias of Athens
[*PA* 7813 *LGPN2* 22 *PAA* 544040 Καλλίας]
father of Protarchus s.v.

Pl. *Phlb.* 19b5, pat.

Prosopographical notes.   See Protarchus s.v. for the several reasons why this Callias cannot be Callias III.

Callicles of Acharnae
[*PA* 7927 (cf. *APF* 8410, 8443A) *LGPN2* 13
(+ *PA* 7906, 7776) *PAA* 556065, 552978,
552975 *DPhA* 17 *OCD*³ *PP* Καλλικλῆς
Ἀχαρνεύς]
b. 450–445, †404/3
lover of Demos
associates: Andron, Tisander, Nausicydes
young politician

Pl. *Grg.*   speaker
Andoc. 1.127
?Lys. 30.14

In Plato. Because the *Gorgias* is not set in real time (App. I), most of the information that one can normally use to establish a date of birth is not definitive: Callicles, a member of the aristocratic Ceryces clan (see Callias III s.v.), has been in combat already (498a, thus over 18) and is embarking on a political career (515a, thus probably over 30). He is a householder, hosting the important visitor, Gorgias (447b). More promising for identifying him is his deme (495d) and stated association with known persons. He is the lover of Demos s.v. (481d, b. ±440); and he counts among his associates (487c) Andron s.v., most likely born ±445, and a member of the Four Hundred in 411; Tisander s.v., whose father was still active in 403; and Nausicydes s.v., a householder in 404–403. The date of birth I suggest for Callicles is broad to accommodate his associates and his beloved.

Dodds' edition and commentary on the *Gorgias* (1959) is exceptional, and discusses the Callicles of Plato in detail. He takes the view that Callicles was a historical person and makes the most of how Callicles is represented in the *Gorgias*.

> As a politician in a democratic society he must pay court to the δῆμος [people] (481d–e), but his championship of "Nature" against "Law" marks him as anti-democratic in principle. And his contempt for the people is in fact even greater than Socrates': they are in his eyes the "weaklings" (483b), no better than a ["rubbish heap of slaves and motley men"] (489c). These are the sentiments, not of a democrat, but of Plato's "tyrannical man," who is at once a product of democracy and its deadliest enemy (*R.* 565d). (1959: 12–5)

Dodds associates Callicles with Hippias' *physis* doctrine because Andron sits with Hippias in *Protagoras* and Callicles is associated with Andron in *Gorgias* (1959: 282)—something of a stretch. Still, Andron's later membership in the Four Hundred is further evidence for the anti-democratic sentiments Plato and Dodds attribute to Callicles. Noting, however, that "scholarship abhors a vacuum," Dodds also describes efforts by scholars to conceive Callicles as a mask for a variety of better-known characters, efforts that did not abate in the latter half of the 20th c. C.E. (see Taylor *OCD*³ s.v.).

Note that Callicles considers sophists worthless (520a1). Gorgias s.v. is not represented by Plato as a sophist, and the only evidence that Callicles or any of his three associates consorted with sophists is that Andron, as a youth in his mid-teens, was in the group gathered around Hippias in *Protagoras.* Yet sophists, rhetoricians, and orators are not clearly distinct categories in the secondary literature, so one often encounters such broad-brush remarks as, "The appearance of

[Tisander] . . . in late fifth century sophistic circles as an associate of Kallikles and Andron (Plato, *Gorgias* 487c) is indicative enough of his social status and political inclinations" (*APF* 8410), a claim that one might balance with Dover's counsel against facile political prosopography (*HCT* 288). Plato's representation of Callicles is so powerful that Nietzsche was captivated by it (see Dodds 1959: 387–91) and, in May of 1956, the radio series, *Yours Truly, Johnny Dollar,* featured a five-episode "The Callicles Matter" in which Callicles was called the greatest of the Greek philosophers—turnabout to the philosophical literature that questioned his very historicity.

In Andocides and Lysias.   The view embraced by *LGPN2* requires acceptance of a pair of emendations suggested by MacDowell (1962: 153–4): Andoc. 1.127.5 has 'Callides' (Καλλίδης) and Lysias 30.14.6 has 'Calliades' (Καλλιάδης); each is emended to 'Callicles' (Καλλικλῆς). In favor of the first, MacDowell points out that only a well connected Athenian would oppose an influential person's, in this case Callias III's, public attempt to infringe a law (it is ironic that the name 'Callias' had itself been corrupted to 'Callicles' in 3rd c. Delian accounts of Callias III— *APF: 7826.8n*). Further, Andocides IV gives neither patronymic nor demotic, implying the name alone would be easily recognized, yet there is *no* 'Callides' in the record: of the two known instances of the name, the inscription bearing the first (3rd c. B.C.E.) requires restoration of the delta, and the second (3rd c. C.E.) is a fictional person.

As for the 'Calliades' in Lysias, MacDowell says that, despite a few examples of the name in inscriptions (e.g. *IG* II² 1400.46); and ruling out as unavailable the well-known man of that name executed after Arginusae in 406 (D. S. 13.101.5); and *given* what Plato so clearly shows, that Callicles is fearlessly outspoken; then the Callicles of the *Gorgias* is one of those fine and good sort of men (καλοὶ κἀγαθοί, 30.14.7), who would not have outlived the revolution of the Thirty. In this, he agrees with Dodds' (1959: 13) characterization of Callicles as "dangerously frank." Dodds asks, "Why, then, did such a vigorous and richly endowed personality leave no mark whatever on the history of his time?" and answers, "When Socrates is made to say to him at 519a7 σοῦ δὲ ἴσως ἐπιλήψονται, ἐὰν μὴ εὐλαβῇ [they'll get you too, if you're not careful], is not Plato putting in his mouth a prophecy *post eventum?*"

MacDowell explains that a corruption from ΚΛ to ΛΔ or Δ "is not difficult"; we know the kinds of errors of transcription that are common and, one might add, errors are more frequent when, as in these two cases, each name appears only once in its respective manuscript, making a natural cross-check impossible. These are deeply satisfying emendations, though perhaps they do not quite warrant the "beyond reasonable doubt" pronouncement MacDowell gives them—at least not both of them. Yet I would say in favor of MacDowell's Andocides IV argument (and as an aside on the prosopographical power of those who establish the Greek editions of the texts we use) that others have been troubled by the seemingly unique name Callides (Καλλίδης) at 1.127.5. In fact, it will now be found neither in the Loeb edition, except in the *apparatus criticus,* nor in a search of the *TLG*—where, for all its convenience, we miss both knowing the edition we consult, and the essential *apparatus criticus.* Valckenaer long since emended

'Callides' to 'Calliades,' thereby assimilating a unique name to a known name, in effect a unique *person* to one already known. MacDowell, returning to the manuscript, is similarly replacing a unique name with a known one, arguing implicitly that Valckenaer was right to emend, but emended incorrectly. On the other hand, it is useful to note Callias, son of Calliades s.v.—evidence of the two names in one clan in the same era as our Callicles.

MacDowell's Lysias argument is less persuasive overall because there are other men named Calliades who may have been fine and good and executed by the Thirty, particularly if one takes seriously Isocrates' reports that the Thirty executed 1,500 Athenian citizens without trial, not to mention *metics* and others (7.67, 20.11).

Prosopographical notes.   *PAA* preserves the diversity of *PA*, assigning the following equivalents: *PA* 7906 = *PAA* 555885 'Callides' *or* = *PAA* 552978 'Callicles' (dependent on whether the emendation to Andoc. is accepted), both of which ?= *PAA* 556065); *PA* 7776 = *PAA* 552975 (Lys.) ?= *PAA* 552978.

Callimachus of Athens (litigant) See App. II.

Callimachus of Athens (property owner) See App. II.

Callippides (actor) See App. II.

Callippus II of Aexone, son of Philon I   Pl. *Ltr.* 7.333d–334c,
[*PA*/*APF* 8065 *LGPN2* 20 *PAA* 559250 *DPhA*   unnamed
31 Κάλλιππος Φίλωνος Αἰξωνεύς]   *IG* II² 1609.96
≤390–352   (*trierarchy*)
mother: Phanagora   *IG* II² 5432.1; 5433.1,
brother: ?Philostratus   4, 7, 10 (family
father of Proxenus, Philon I   gravestones)
associate of Dion   Plu. *Dion, passim*
assassin of Dion, tyrant in Syracuse   Nep. *Dion* 9.2
                                                          D. S. 16.45.9
                                                          D. L. 3.46
                                                          Demos. 36.53
                                                          [Demos.] 50.47–52

Life and career.   Callippus' family is identified by names on gravestones found in the Piraeus (see above), but they suggest no connections with others of the Platonic milieu, so they need not be discussed. Although the later tradition says Callippus was a student at Plato's Academy and that Dion became acquainted with him there (D.L.; Ath. 508e), Plato denies it. He contrasts his own friendship with Dion, developed "through common liberal culture," with Dion's having met Callippus and his brother "by way of that facile comradeship which is the basis of most friendship, and which is cultivated by hospitality and mystic rites and initiation into secrets." That the two were guest-friends, however, is probably accurate: Callippus was host to Dion in Athens in 365 (Plu. *Dion* 17.1), suggesting that the two men already knew one another before Dion's arrival.

Callippus is attested as sole trierarch on the *Eudoxia* in 366/5 (*IG* I² 1609). Pseudo-Democrates states that Callippus, still a naval officer about five years later, arranged passage for the exile-in-hiding, Callistratus s.v., to Thasos in 361, as a result of which—according to the orator Democrates—Apollodorus prosecuted Callippus, probably in that same year. Possibly to avoid conviction, Callippus and his brother accompanied Dion in 357 on his return to Syracuse (Plu. *Dion* 28.3, 54.1, 58.4; Pl.; D. S.), where Dion returned the hospitality Callippus had shown him in Athens. But the brothers betrayed and were complicitous in the assassination of Dion, at which point Callippus seized control of Syracuse and ruled for thirteen months from late 354 to early 352. During that year, Plato's *Letter* 8 was composed, suggesting a three-kings arrangement that would replace Callippus (quoted s.v. Hipparinus I). Callippus was in fact overthrown by Dion's nephew, Hipparinus II, the son of Dionysius II, but Callippus escaped north to Rhegium, where he survived until 351/0 (the date of Demos. 36). He was killed in Rhegium, supposedly by a Pythagorean named 'Leptines', and with the same sword that killed Dion (Plu. *Dion* 58.6)—though this part of the story smacks of Plutarch's moralism. The story, for what it is worth, suggests that Leptines II s.v. and his companion (Polysperchon) hunted Callippus down.

In the later tradition.   In the *Rhetoric* (1373a19), Aristotle uses Callippus' state of mind when he killed Dion as an example of attitudes toward wrongdoing: it did not feel wrong because of his previous grievance or existing difference. Nepos calls Callippus 'Callicrates' (*Dion* 9).

Callistratus of Aphidna, son of Callicrates [*PA/APF* 8157 = 8129 = 8130 *LGPN2* 50 *PAA* 561015, 561030, 561035, 561125, 561575 *RE* 10 *OCD*³ Καλλίστρατος] 415–355 father of Callicrates prominent 4th c. politician and exile

[Pl.] *Sis.* 388c * Xen. *Hell.* 6.2.39–6.4.10 Philoch. fr. 149 Isocr. 8.24 Demos. 18, 24, 60 [Demos.] 49, 50 inscriptions (see below)

Life.   The Callistratus whose whereabouts are unknown in the pseudo-Platonic *Sisyphus* is Callistratus of Aphidna, a wealthy, prominent, Athenian politician, ambassador, general (serving with Chabrias, in 373/2), advisor, orator, and economist. Among the several decrees he is known to have proposed is the one that sent Andocides IV s.v. and his fellow envoys into exile in 392 when the Assembly disapproved of the peace terms with which they had returned from their negotiations at Sparta. Callistratus lost an impeachment suit (*eisangelia*) in 362 and, sentenced to death, fled into hiding at Methone. Callippus s.v. took him by ship to Thasos where he served as an advisor. He was finally executed by the state in 355. See Dušanić (1980: 125–9, 144; 1995: 342–5).

In inscriptions.   *IG* II 1689 add. p. 813.7 (inventory of Athena, dated ≤368/7); *IG* II 1609.103, 118 (contributor of equipment, *syntrierarch*, naval inventory, dated ≤366/5); *IG* II 1622.185 pat. (naval inventory, dated ≤386); *IG* II 1523.19 and 1524.192 (both inventories to another god, not Athena, undated).

In the later tradition.   Among the more significant contributors are Aristotle (*Rh.* 1364a, 1374b, 1418b), the orator Aeschines (2.124), Diodorus (15, 16, *passim*), Athenaeus (10–12, *passim*, preserving some comic frr.), and Plutarch (*Dem.*).

Prosopographical notes.   For Callistratus, the prosopographical image appears more fragmented than it really is. There is one well known individual—*PA/APF* 8157 (to which *APF* added *PA* 8129, 8130) = *LGPN2* 50. *PAA* 561575 is that same individual ?= four additional entries: *PAA* 561020 was a public lawyer who appears on a curse tablet; *PAA* 561030 proposed an honorary decree <378/7; *PAA* 561035 proposed an honorary decree in 369/8; *PAA* 561125 was a *trierarch* of Lamptrae in 373/2.

Callixenus of Athens
[*PA* 8042 *LGPN2* 2 *PAA* 558605 Καλλίξενος]
fl. late 5th c.
depraved democratic leader

[Pl.] *Ax.* 368d
Xen. *Hell.* 1.7.8–35,
     passim
D. S. 13.103.2

Life.   According to Xenophon (1.7.8; cf. Ath. 5.218a), Callixenus was bribed by Theramenes to bring a formal accusation against the Athenian generals who had won the naval battle at Arginusae but had failed to ensure that the dead, wounded, and shipwrecked were rescued. Callixenus' proposal (1.7.9–10) was to have one vote by tribe, for or against death for the group as a whole (evidence having been heard at the preceding meeting of the Assembly). Whether Theramenes was really behind the motion (for this detail of Xenophon's is uncorroborated), Callixenus succeeded, and the generals were condemned (see Exc. 2).

   When the Athenians had had time to consider what they had done, Callixenus and four others were placed under house arrest, awaiting trial. In a civil disturbance, however, all five escaped. Callixenus returned to the city in 403 when the democracy was restored but "was hated by everybody and died of starvation" (Xen. *Hell.* 1.7.35). Alternatively, Callixenus was tried for deceiving the people and not allowed to speak in his own defense. Although chained in prison, he dug a tunnel and escaped with others, though all Greeks everywhere forevermore scorned him (D. S.).

EXCURSUS 2:
THE ARGINUSAE TRIAL OF 406.

The naval battle of Arginusae, named for small islands between Lesbos and the mainland, was Athens' last triumph of war, a pyrrhic victory. Alcibiades III's celebrated return to Athens the previous year, renewing the city's hopes, had petered out soon after: he had been angrily dismissed after one of his subordinates brought about the loss of the battle of Notium through misjudgment. Alcibiades III s.v. retired to his estates in Thrace rather than return to Athens, and Athens elected a replacement, or a new board of generals (including Aristocrates II, Leon, Pericles II, and Thrasyllus s.vv.) that appears to have remained in place for the 406/5 year. One of the experienced and competent generals, Conon, set about to refurbish the fleet and build the morale of its men. He succeeded in part by reducing the size of the fleet and its crew but, when his seventy ships were confronted by the Lacedaemonians' 170, he avoided battle and raced toward the safety of Mytilene. There he soon found himself with inadequate rations, bottled up in the harbor by the Spartans, with two other generals, Leon and Erasinides. Erasinides appears to have commanded one of the two ships Conon sent urgently to Athens for assistance, for he was tried with the others (while Conon and Leon were exempt). To rescue the fleet, Athens, its manpower seriously depleted already, promised citizenship to *metics* and slaves who would man the 110 ships she could make ready to break the blockade at Mytilene.

Both Xenophon (1.7) and Diodorus (13.98–99) narrate the great clash of ships that led ultimately to an Athenian victory. It is the aftermath of the battle, however, that brings into play a number of persons treated in this prosopography: about twenty-five Athenian ships were wrecked, and—owing to at least three causes— the wounded and dead were not recovered after the battle. The Athenian generals debated among themselves whether to go on immediately to the rescue of Conon, still under siege in Mytilene, or to collect the dead and injured. Two captains, Theramenes s.v. and Thrasybulus, were given the latter assignment, but a storm blew up and prevented both actions. Moreover (D. S. 100.2) the raw crews of the Athenian ships objected to embarking in high seas to collect the dead (recall the large number of *metics* and slaves who did not share the Athenian horror of failing to bury the dead). The generals dispatched a letter to Athens to the effect that the battle had been won but that a storm had prevented the recovery of casualties; and the two captains returned home.

Despite the news of victory, sentiment swelled over the casualties. The generals, hearing this, assumed that the captains must have fomented emotion against them back in the city. They dispatched another letter, this one stating that Theramenes and Thrasybulus had been assigned rescue duty. Diodorus (101.3) cites this letter as a mistake, for it put the captains—who might have been powerful allies to the generals—on the defensive: they described the terrible storm and countercharged that the generals were in effect accusing themselves by implying that rescue had been possible—at least if undertaken earlier. Athens turned against the generals, dismissed all but Conon and Leon, and recalled the other eight to the city to stand trial before the Assembly (*ecclēsia*). Two of the generals fled at once, but six returned to stand trial, among them Pericles II, Thrasyllus, and Aristocrates II s.vv.

To accomplish business under the democracy, where ultimate authority rested with the thousands of the Assembly, there was a Council (*boulē*) of five hundred— fifty from each of the ten tribes—that sat for one year, its members chosen by lot, but afterwards scrutinized for suitability. The Council was the executive of the Assembly, but it too was too large to conduct business efficiently and, besides, outlying citizens could not afford to stay in the city for an entire year. The *prytany* calendar, distinct from the lunar/civic and the archon/festival calendars (see Introduction, *On Ancient Dates*), was divided into ten periods of 37 and 36 days (later 36 and 35 days), allowing each tribe one turn as Prytanes, the presiding committee of fifty; thus at any one time, there were fifty functioning members of the *boulē*. The order in which the tribes would serve was determined by lot. The Prytanes (*prytaneis*) set the agenda for the Council, received ambassadors, dealt with correspondence et al. Socrates' tribe, Antiochis, was serving as Prytanes in October of 406 when the generals were charged, and Socrates was one of its members (Pl. *Ap.* 32b; Xen. *Hell.* 1.7.15); he may also have been the *epistatēs* on that occasion (1.1.18, 4.4.2; cf. *Grg.* 473e), the man chosen by lot to preside over the others, a position that could be held only once.

Returning to the narrative, when the Assembly met, Theramenes spoke powerfully against the generals, several of whom spoke briefly in their own defense, blaming the storm. The telling witnesses in the generals' favor were a number of eyewitness pilots and shipmates who concurred that the storm, and only the storm, was to blame. Darkness fell before a vote could be taken, so the outcome was postponed until the next meeting of the Assembly, after the three-day Apaturia festival. Theramenes attended the Apaturia where he encountered some of his *phratores* and their families dressed in mourning with their heads shaved. He persuaded them to attend the next meeting of the Assembly and to pretend that their relatives had been lost in the sea battle. He then bribed Callixenus s.v. to make a formal accusation of the generals to the Council, preceding the meeting of the Assembly (the Council was responsible for setting the Assembly's agenda for the day). Andrewes (1974: 122) warns: ". . . the charges against Theramenes are found only in Xenophon among the primary sources, and Xenophon's determination to present the generals as innocent stands out clearly. Whatever we make of the rest of Theramenes' career, this particular episode ought not to appear in our books only in the guise which Xenophon has given it."

Callixenus, whether or not at Theramenes' instigation, drafted a motion for the Council to present to the Assembly, calling for the death penalty and an immediate vote by tribe for the guilt or innocence of the generals as a group. He was opposed in the Assembly by Euryptolemus III s.v. and others who entered a complaint that Callixenus' action was unconstitutional, a violation of Athenian law, made explicit in the decree of Cannonus, that individuals charged with capital offenses were guaranteed separate trials. This opposition incensed the crowd. Lyciscus moved to subject Euryptolemus III and his seconders to the same vote as would decide the fate of the generals. When the Assembly overwhelmingly approved Lyciscus' motion, Euryptolemus III was compelled to withdraw his complaint.

At that point, several of the fifty members of the Prytanes supported Euryptolemus III's interpretation of the law and refused to put the question, so Callixenus spoke again, rousing the crowd to greater anger. Socrates alone among the Prytanes was left standing against Callixenus, refusing to disobey the law, but his refusal to allow the vote had the effect of gaining time. Euryptolemus III used that time to make an eloquent speech in defense of the generals that ended with a proposal that a preliminary vote be taken to decide between Callixenus' proposal to vote guilt or innocence at once, and his own proposal to allow separate trials for each man (Xen. *Hell.* 1.7.16–33). The Assembly approved separate trials, but this was quickly followed by a successful maneuver to declare the vote invalid. When the Assembly voted again, it was to decide the lives of the generals up or down. All were condemned.

Xenophon and Diodorus cannot be reconciled here (and [Aristot.] *Ath. Pol.* 34.1 exaggerates in this matter), so in essentials I follow above the likely story surmised in Andrewes' "The Arginousai Trial" (1974), concluding: "This was not a wicked conspiracy against innocent and defenceless men, but something more lamentable and in its beginnings more innocent, a disastrous misunderstanding between two sets of men, separated by a considerable distance, and on the past record understandably nervous of one another" (1974: 122). Andrewes' is the most complete account of the events; although it requires Greek, it can be found digested in *CAH* 5²: 492–3. Lang's "Illegal Execution in Ancient Athens" (1990) is a less technical appraisal of the varying degrees of guilt of the generals and captains. Dodds (1959: 247–8) discusses Socrates' role, concluding that he was probably a *prytanis* but not the *epistatēs*.

Cambyses of Persia, son of Cyrus I See App. II.

Cebes of Thebes	Pl. *Phd.*	speaker
[*LGPN2B* 1 *DPhA* 62 *RE* 2 *OCD³ PP PX*	Pl. *Crito* 45b *	
Κέβης]	Pl. *Ltr.* 7.345a,	
430s–>354	unnamed *	
father of three daughters	[Pl.] *Ltr.* 13.363a	
associate of Philolaus	Xen. *Mem., passim*	
Pythagorean friend of Socrates		

Life.   What we know of Cebes we know from Plato's dialogues. If Cebes was in fact a young man (*neaniskos, Phd.* 89a) in 399, then his date of birth can be established approximately. He was still alive after the summer of 354 when *Letter 7* was written; although not named there, Cebes is referred to as "the Theban" in a reference to his dialect (cf. *Phd.* 62a). Xenophon says only that he was a member of Socrates' inner circle (1.2.48), and that he often visited the *hetaira*, Theodote s.v. in Athens (3.11.17). In the pseudo-Platonic *Letter* 13, from which the occasional detail may be accurate, [Plato] arranges for Cebes' three daughters to receive full-length chitons of Sicilian linen.

In the later tradition.   Diogenes (2.125) attributes three dialogues to Cebes: *Hebdome* and *Phrynichus,* of which nothing is extant, and the *Pinax,* an anonymous work of much later vintage erroneously attributed to Cebes, which survives. The *pinax* ('tablet') was a votive tablet placed in the temple of Cronus describing human life and happiness; it was thought genuine in antiquity and remains available in a number of editions and translations, notably the Renaissance Society of America's 1979 *Cebes' Tablet: Facsimiles of the Greek Text, and of Selected Latin, French, English, Spanish, Italian, German, Dutch, and Polish Translations*. The pseudo-Socratic epistolary tradition includes a letter from Xenophon to Simmias and Cebes (22). See also Aulus Gellius (*NA* 2.18.1–5) and Plutarch (*Mor.* 580e, 590a).

Cephalus of Collytus
[*PA* 8277 *LGPN2* 7 *PAA* 566650 *RE* 11
Κέφαλος Κολλυτεύς]
active 403–377
rhetorician and politician

IG II² 29.6; 34.35, 40;
& add. p. 657.4
Hell. Oxy. 7.2
Pl. *com.* fr. 201 (K 185)
Aristoph. *Eccl.* 248
Andoc. 1.115–6, 1.150
Demos. 18.219, 251
Din. 1.38
Aes. *orat.* 3.194

Political career in brief. Cephalus was prominent in the democratic restoration of 403, winning praise (Aes. *orat.*; Demos.). Because of his reputation, and more generally as a fellow tribesman of Anytus and Thrasyllus (Andoc. 1.150), he assisted Andocides IV in his defense against Callias III (Andoc. 1.115) in 400. After the death of Socrates, he was accused, with Epicrates, of taking bribes in 396/5 (*Hell. Oxy.*). He attracted the notice of Aristophanes in 391 and of Plato *com.* at a less discernable date. Inscriptions show that he proposed a decree in honor of Phanocritus in 387/6 (II² 29), that he was ambassador to Chios in 384/3a (II² 34), and that he proposed a treaty with Thebes & Mytilene in 378/7 (II² add.). The orator Dinarchus attributes another proposed decree to Cephalus, one in support of Theban exiles who captured Cadmea in 378.

Prosopographical notes. Cephalus is a prominent homonym of the men of that name in Plato's dialogues, and the period of his activity coincides with that of Plato rather than of Socrates, but one nevertheless occasionally finds references to this Cephalus as if he were one of the others.

In the later tradition. See Dinarchus (1.76); Harpocration s.v.; Pausanias (3.9.8); Athenaeus (592c).

Cephalus of Clazomenae   Pl. *Prm.*   speaker
[*DPhA* 78 Κέφαλος]
late 430s–>382

Cephalus is represented as a longtime friend of Adeimantus I and Glaucon IV in the late 380s (*Prm.* 126a–127a, 136d–e); he has not seen their younger half brother, Antiphon II, since he was a child though Antiphon II has become grandfatherly (126c) in the interim, so Cephalus is older still, probably about Adeimantus I's age.

Cephalus II of Syracuse, son of Lysanias   Pl. *R.* (330b)   speaker
[*APF* C7 (C9) *FRA* 6986 *PAA* 566667 *DPhA* 79   Pl. *Phdr.* 227a, 263d,
RE 2 *PP* Κέφαλος]   pat.
† 421–415   Lys. 12.4
wives: (1) Syracusan (2) woman still living   Lys. fr. 7, pat.
   >369   [Demos.] 59.21–22
offspring with Syracusan: Polemarchus; with   D. H. *Lys.* 1
   (2): Lysias, ?Euthydemus, and a daughter   [Plu.] *LTO* 835c, pat.
   who married Brachyllus
See stemma: Lysias.

Life.   The chief source for our information about Cephalus II is the report of his son Lysias in the autobiographical speech 12. Pericles I persuaded Cephalus to settle in Athens, probably in the late 450s, when the economy of Athens welcomed foreign residents, and before any backlash. (Pericles I's citizenship laws of 451/ 0 probably had more to do with Athenian men marrying into the families of *metics* than with their bringing home brides from foreign climes.) Cephalus II lived in Athens for thirty years, having established a successful shield factory that had over a hundred slaves by 404. In Plato, Cephalus II is represented as a man who worked hard to build up the family's wealth after his father had diminished it. He estimated his holdings at about what his grandfather, Cephalus I, had established in Syracuse. But Cephalus II remained a *metic* and should not be confused with the aristocratic citizens of Athens with their inherited wealth or "old money" (*pace* Waterfield 1993: 470). *Republic* (562e) provides an instance in which *metics* (e.g. the sons of Cephalus II) are said to be inferior to Athenians (e.g., the sons of Ariston) while superior to foreigners (e.g., Thrasymachus).

It is probable that Cephalus II had two wives. Polemarchus, almost certainly born in Syracuse, was old enough to serve as temporary guardian of Lysias when they, and perhaps also their brother, Euthydemus, went to Thurii as colonists in about 430. Lysias' mother was residing with him >369 ([Demos.]) when, if she was also the mother of Polemarchus, she would have been nearly one hundred years old. That is not impossible but, on balance, a second wife would explain the gap in ages and make the exceptional longevity unnecessary.

There were three houses in Cephalus II's family in 404 (Lys. 12.18), with those of both Polemarchus and Lysias in the Piraeus. In *Republic,* Plato does not represent all the men as living together in the Piraeus (*pace APF*), but as having gathered at Polemarchus' house (*R.* 328b). It is natural, but incorrect, to infer from the fact that Cephalus II is alive and still performing sacrifices that the conversation of *Republic* takes place in the house of Cephalus II (Ferrari 2000: 350; Todd 2000: 4; Howland 1993: 57, 63; Nussbaum 1986: 137). Neither place of residence nor the performing of sacrifices would affect Polemarchus' being the legal owner of the house, as the text describes him. "If a father was getting old and had an adult son, he could retire, handing over control of the *oikos* to his son" (MacDowell 1978: 91; cf. Callias III s.v.).

In modern bibliography.   Working at about the same time, Dover (1968b) and *APF* interpret the evidence of Lysias' speech rather differently. See Appendix I for dramatic date issues for Plato's *Republic* that impinge on the reconstruction of the lives of Cephalus II and his family, and particularly of Cephalus II's death: Guthrie (1975: 437–8) points out, "Taylor [1956: 263] rejects 411 because Cephalus is still alive. He actually refers to pseudo-Plutarch (*LTO* 835e), yet himself favours 421, whereas according to that perhaps dubious authority Cephalus was dead by 443."

Ceph[──], slave of Axiochus of Scambonidae See App. II.

Cephisodorus of Aphidna See App. II.

Cepis of Athens See App. II.

Ceramon of Athens See App. II.

Cercyon (wrestler) See App. II.

Chabrias of Aexone, son of Ctesippus I (general) See App. II.

Chaerecrates of Sphettus   Pl. *Ap.* 21a,
[*PA* 15131 *LGPN2* 2 *DPhA* 89 *PX*   unnamed   present
Χαιρεκράτης Σφήττιος]   Xen. *Mem.* 1.2.48,
b. 360s–50s, † >399   2.3.1–19
brother: Chaerephon

Xenophon (*Mem.* 1) includes this younger brother of Chaerephon s.v. in the Socratic circle which Plato corroborates by placing him at Socrates' trial. Chaerecrates participates in a long conversation with Socrates (*Mem.* 2) about the difficulties of having Chaerephon as a brother. Socrates offers homespun advice and encouragement.

Chaeredemus of Alopece   Pl. *Euthd.* 297e *
[*PA* 15119 *LGPN2* 15 *PP*
Χαιρεδήμος Ἀλωπεκῆθεν]
wife: Phaenarete
father of Patrocles
stepfather of Socrates
See stemma: Socrates.

The attribution of the deme Alopece is based on the assumption that Socrates' maternal half brother, Patrocles s.v., is the Patrocles of Alopece known from *IG* I³ 378.16. Athenian sons took their fathers' demes, so I attribute Alopece to the father through the son. This implies that Phaenarete s.v. married within her former husband's deme, common in the 5th and 4th c.

Chaerephon of Sphettus	Pl. *Chrm.*	speaker
[*PA* 15203 *LGPN2* 21 *DPhA* 109 *RE* 2	Pl. *Grg.*	speaker
*OCD*³ *PP PX* Χαιρεφῶν Σφήττιος]	Pl. *Ap.* 20e8–21a8 †	
≥469, † 403–399	[Pl.] *Hal.*	speaker
brother: Chaerecrates	Xen. *Mem.* 1.2.48,	
close friend of Socrates	2.3.1	
	Xen. *Apol.* 14	
	comedy (see below)	

Life.   Chaerephon, an unusual man by all accounts, seems to have been a slightly younger contemporary of Socrates, who says they have been friends since their youth (Pl. *Ap.*; cf. Xen. *Mem.* 1.2.48), though that need not of course mean childhood. Chaerephon is represented in Plato as an acquaintance or friend of Gorgias (*Grg.* 447b), as a little mad (μανικός, *Chrm.* 153b), and as an enthusiast (σφοδρός, *Ap.* 21a). He proves capable of asking a set of Socratic-type questions of Polus (*Grg.* 447d–448c), though Socrates reenters the conversation with a critique of Polus' answers. It was Chaerephon who consulted the oracle at Delphi and was told that no one was wiser than Socrates (*Ap.*; D. L. 2.37); in Xenophon's version, no one was freer or more just or wiser (Xen. *Ap.*). Despite his supposed advanced age in 404, he chose exile with the democrats, and returned with Thrasybulus in 403. Chaerephon had died by 399 (*Ap.*), but there is no extant contemporaneous evidence for the statement often seen that he was killed fighting for the democracy. Approaching seventy, he may have died of natural causes.

In comedy.   Chaerephon was a favorite of the comic poets for two decades, and it is through them that we get a sense of the man's appearance: he was evidently a tall and very thin man of pallid complexion, perhaps resembling a corpse (half-dead at *Clouds* 502, jaundiced and hovering silently at *Wasps* 1413, arising from the underworld at *Birds* 1562).

In Aristophanes' *Clouds*, produced in 423 when Socrates was about forty-six and Chaerephon perhaps a little younger, Chaerephon appears almost to be the codirector of the Thinkery, except that Socrates was the one on stage (unless Chaerephon was a silent, hovering presence—unlikely, though a medieval ms. gives Chaerephon ln. 1504). A scholiast describes Chaerephon as having great, bushy eyebrows, but we do not know on what authority. In the same year, Cratinus also produced a play that made reference to Chaerephon (*Pyt.* fr. 215 [K 202]) as unwashed and poor. It is one of six texts referring to Chaerephon in comedy that we owe to Arethas, scholiast to Plato's *Apology* 20e, i.e. texts that survive only because Arethas quoted or mentioned them. In none of the frr. does Chaerephon speak.

In the next year, 422, in Aristophanes' *Wasps* (1388–1414) Chaerephon certainly appears on the Athenian comic stage, though only as a silent witness. A year later, Eupolis' *Flatterers* (fr. 180 [K 165]), a play featuring a banquet at the house of Callias III, mentions Chaerephon, as does his *Poleis* of ±420 (fr. 253 [K 239]).

Aristophanes' *Horae* (*Seasons*) cannot now be dated more narrowly than 421–412, but there too a fr. 584 (K 573) includes Chaerephon.

In *Birds*, produced in 414, Chaerephon is one of the Socratic imitators (ἐσωϰϱά-τουν) who show their admiration for the Spartans by wearing their hair long, going hungry, refusing to bathe, and carrying sticks (1280–1283). Clay (1994: 23–5) distinguishes such followers who "Socratize" to the extent that they leave no writings—among whom he includes Apollodorus s.v., as well as Chaerephon, and who may account for Aristotle's likening the genre of Socratic *logoi* to the mimes of Sophron in having as their characters lower-class figures; these would be distinct from other Socratics who wrote Socratic *logoi*, e.g., Antisthenes, Aeschines, Xenophon, and Plato (Aristot. *Poet.* 1447b11).

Chaerephon appears in *Birds* a little later in a short choral ode (1552–1564):

> Far away by the Shadefoots
> lies a swamp, where all unwashed
> Socrates conjures spirits.
> Pisander paid a visit there,
> asking to see the spirit
> that deserted him in life.
> For sacrifice he brought a baby
> camel and cut its throat,
> like Odysseus, then backed off;
> and up from below arose to him,
> drawn by the camel's gore,
> Chaerephon the bat.

Given that the play is *Birds*, 'bat' (νυϰτεϱίς, also at ln. 1296) might also be translated 'night-bird'. Although Greek has a word, νυϰτιϰόϱαξ, for the night-jar or goat-sucker (birds of the genus *Caprimulgus*, of which Greece now has two species), it would not have scanned.

Sometime before 406, Aristophanes refers to Chaerephon as a thief in a context that is lost (*D. Niob.* fr. 295 [K 291]) and yet again in ±402, in his *Telemessians*, Aristophanes makes a joke at Chaerephon's expense (fr. 552 [K 539]). His appearance and reputation must have been strange indeed for the mere mention of him to continue being funny for twenty years.

Prosopographical notes. *PA* queried the deme of Sphettus, but *LGPN2* does not, nor do I. Dover (1968a: 114–5), referring to *Clouds* 156, suggests that the attribution of the deme Sphettus to Chaerephon may be fabricated to effect "a weak pun on σφήξ, wasp, to suit the entomological context," and Henderson (1998c: 27n14) agrees that, without another source for Chaerephon's deme, we should not take Sphettus as certain.

In the later tradition.   See Athenaeus (188c–d, 218e–219a), Plutarch (*Mor.* 116e–f), et al. in *SSR* 2.VIB.

Charias, slave of Alcibiades III See App. II.

Charicles of Athens, son of Apollodorus   Thu. 7.20.1–3,
[*PA/APF* 15407 (13479) *LGPN2* 5 *PX*   7.26.1–3
Χαρικλῆς Ἀπολλοδώρου]   Xen. *Hell.* 2.3.2
tribe: ?Oineis   Xen. *Mem.* 1.2.31–37
† 403   Andoc. 1.14, 36, 101
sister: wife of Tisias   Lys. 12.55, 13.74
member of the Thirty   Isocr. 16.42
                                     Tele. fr. 44 (K 41)
                                     Aristot. *Pol.* 1305b26
                                     D. S. 13.9.2

Life. Charicles' deme is unknown but, in conformity with Löper's hypothesis (see Exc. 3), Charicles' tribe would be Oineis; the hypothesis is unconfirmed. Something of his family's social and financial position can be inferred from the fact that his sister was married to the Tisias who was a one-time friend of Alcibiades III and had five or eight *talents* to spend on a team of horses; he was double-crossed in the transaction, however, and fought his case in court for two decades, beyond the death of Alcibiades III (see details at Alcibiades IV s.v.).

Political and military career. Charicles himself first appears as an ardent democrat in 415, when he investigated the herm mutilation, and concluded that it had been organized to overthrow the democracy (Andoc. 1.36; see Exc. 1). The fragment of Teleclides in which Charicles is mentioned (var. –κλέης) cannot be dated precisely, but Charicles' prominence at the time of the sacrilege may point to this period. He was elected general in 414/3. He took command of thirty triremes and sailed to Argos to demand a contingent of hoplites (Thu. 7.20), which he turned over to Demosthenes for reinforcement service in Sicily. His mission accomplished, he sailed all thirty vessels back home (7.26).

Charicles became one of the Four Hundred in 411, and fled to Decelea after its collapse. He returned in 404 and became one of the Thirty (Xen. *Hell.*). In collusion with Critias IV, Charicles forbade Socrates to speak with men under thirty, men too young to serve on the Council (*boulē*, Xen. *Mem.* 1.2.35). Aristotle refers to Charicles as one of the worst of the Thirty, prompting *APF* to speculate that he may have treated Charicles "as the quasi-eponymous head of the government for the sake of Plato"—an odd thought. What Aristotle says is, "Now, the oligarchical demagogue is of two sorts: either he practises upon the oligarchs themselves (for, although the oligarchy are quite a small number, there may be a demagogue among them, as at Athens Charicles' party won power by courting the Thirty, that of Phrynichus by courting the Four Hundred); or the oligarchs may play the demagogue with the people." Aristotle's description is about demagogues, and Critias IV appears not to have been that particular type of oligarch.

Prosopographical notes. Whitehead (1980: 212), calls the Oineis tribe hypothesis "not unattractive," but also not persuasive in view of more than twenty other homonyms in *PA* alone. Charicles is listed, not by the tribe Oineis, but in the 'Athens' category in *LGPN2. LGPN2* assigns the Teleclides fr. to another individual, otherwise unknown. Dover (*HCT* 284) says "possibly" of the identification between the investigator of the mutilation of the herms and the leader of the Thirty.

Charmantides I of Paeania	Pl. *R.* 328b present
[*PA/APF* 15501 with supp. *LGPN2* 6 *PP*	*IG* I³ 299.39, 324.56,
Χαρμαντίδης (–δες—*IG*) Παιανιεύς]	350.62
±500–≤420	*IG* I³ 1328
father of Chaerestratus	gravestone

Life.   Charmantides I, one of several silent observers of the *Republic* conversation, would have been about the same age as Cephalus. Paeania is a rural deme, so one may assume his wealth derived from agricultural holdings there, though he may have resided anywhere.

Prosopographical notes.   Originally, *PA* identified the character in *Republic* as Charmantides II (see App. II), son of Chaerestratus, grandson of Charmantides I. But, "If Plato was thinking at all clearly when he mentioned Charmantides of Paeania in *Republic* 328b, he must, I think, have meant a grandfather, possibly to be identified with a *tamias* [treasurer] of 427/6" (Lewis 1955: 19; *APF*; Ferrari 2000: 350). There has lately been a return of allegiance to the grandson (see Waterfield 1993: 470; White 1995: 326), which is not impossible, so it is useful to look again at the arguments.

White (1995), making a case for a late dramatic date of 407 for the dialogue, beyond when Charmantides I was likely to have been alive, assigns Charmantides II the part of silent auditor. A wealthy student of Isocrates, and identified as a public benefactor by Isocrates (15.93), Charmantides II, says White, "was roughly Plato's age hence a natural person to join the other young men" in the conversation. White's proposal seems vulnerable on two grounds. First, the gathering at the house of Polemarchus was *not* a gathering of young men. Adeimantus and Glaucon IV were by far the youngest persons named as present, with Niceratus II, b. 445–439, the person nearest to them in age. If Plato had been present, he would have been youngest; and if Charmantides II was roughly Plato's age, he would have been youngest, and then would have been Socrates' interlocutor, for the bulk of *Republic* seems to bear out the rule that the youngest person present should offer replies (explicit at *Prm.* 137b–c).

Second, White (1995: 326) mentions Charmantides II's victory as *chorēgos* some time between 403 and 370 (*IG* II² 1138.25), and that he was a *trierarch* ±370 (*IG* II² 1609.46). White notes that a *chorēgos* had to be at least forty (citing [Aristot.] *Ath. Pol.* 56.3; cf. Aes. *orat.* 1.11). The sources for that claim, however, refer to the period after changes in procedure had been instituted some time before 348/7 (Rhodes 1993: 624–5)—long past any plausible association with the *Republic*. Lewis (1955: 24) cautions against using a forty-year rule outside the 4th c. and finds only one exactly confirming case, in 352/1. In the 5th c., for which we have considerably less evidence, thirty may have been the more common age: Pericles I and Eucrates with victories in 473 and 415, respectively, serve as youthful examples. But the age of thirty, in fact, works better than forty for White's view that Charmantides II was of an age with Plato. Forty would have put his birth as early as 443, on the verge for Charmantides II to be the grandson of a man born in ±500. *APF* gives the *chorēgos* year as <366, implying Charmantides II's birth <406 or <396, making him considerably Plato's junior. Waterfield's suggestion cannot be defended on similar grounds since he judges the dramatic date of the *Republic* to be 420; if that is the case, then the *chorēgos* date needs to be moved back in time thirty-seven years, and the consequence, short generations in the family, accepted—too high a price to pay.

Lewis (1955: 19n21) says "*PA* 15501 is a creation of Busolt from the letters -]μαντ[- in *IG* I² 263.49"; cf. *IG* I³ 324.49. Charmantides I is omitted in error from *APF* Index I, Checklist of Directly Attested Individuals.

Charmantides II of Paeania, son of Chaerestratus See App. II and Charmantides I s.v.

Charmides of Athens, son of Aristotle   Andoc. 1.47–48, 1.51
[*PA/APF* 15510 (828.6) *LGPN2* 5 Χαρμίδης
᾿Αριστοτέλους]
b. ±440
mother: daughter of Andocides I, sister of
  Leogoras II
ward of Leogoras II
first cousin of Andocides IV
See stemma: Andocides.

Charmides was an orphan, reared in the wealthy household of Leogoras II (his mother's brother). Evidently because of his relationship to Andocides IV, Charmides was accused by Dioclides of defacing herms in 415 and imprisoned but, having succeeded in persuading Andocides to incriminate the real culprits, members of Andocides IV's drinking club, was released on Andocides IV's information (see Exc. 1). This Charmides has often been confused with Glaucon III's son, Charmides s.v.

Charmides of Athens, son of Glaucon III	Pl. *Chrm.*	speaker
[*PA/APF* 15512 (8792.9) *LGPN2* 28 *RE* 2 *DPhA*	Pl. *Prt.* 315a	present
102 *OCD*³ *PP PX* Χαρμίδης Γλαύκωνος]	Pl. *Smp.* 222b *	
tribe: ?Erechtheis	Pl. *Ltr.* 7.324b–d,	
±446–403	unnamed †	
mother: daughter of Antiphon I	[Pl.] *Thg.* 128d	
sister: Perictione	[Pl.] *Ax.* 364a	present
ward of Critias IV	Xen. *Symp., passim*	
lover of Clinias III	Xen. *Mem.* 3.6.1, 3.7	
member of the Piraeus Ten under the Thirty	Xen. *Hell.* 2.4.19	
See stemma: Plato.	Andoc. 1.16	
	SEG 13.28	

Life. The record offers no precedent among older relatives for the name 'Charmides'. His birth, into a family of some wealth and influence, is normally set at "about 450 or just after" (*APF*) but that is too early. One consideration for Plato's dialogues is that Alcibiades III s.v., the great beauty of his age, was born in 451 and was on campaign in Potidaea with Socrates. Charmides is represented as some years younger, the great beauty of his own age cohort. If Charmides had been born in 450, he would have been too old, at twenty, to fit the youthful portrait of him in *Charmides*, dated in May of 429 when the siege at Potidaea had ended and the troops had returned (see App. I); in fact, he would have been too old to have required a guardian, though Plato represents Critias IV as having become Charmides' guardian during Socrates' almost three-year absence from Athens from the summer or fall of 432, i.e. between *Protagoras* and *Charmides* (154a, e). Charmides, a young poet (155a), was no more than seventeen the spring of Socrates' return and, because that is so, he was hardly more than an adolescent in the *Protagoras*, where he appears with the sons of Pericles I in the group flanking Protagoras. By 416, however, when Plato's *Symposium* is set, Charmides is mentioned only when Alcibiades III describes him among those whose amorous advances were spurned by Socrates.

Much speculation in the secondary literature has centered on the fact that Charmides was made ward of his first cousin, Critias IV, rather than of his father's elder brother, Callaeschrus I, or his mother's brother (Plato's stepfather), Pyrilampes s.v. In 5th and 4th c. Athens, if a man with minor sons or unmarried daughters of any age died without having stipulated a guardian, it was the archon's duty to appoint one. Athenian law specified in great detail degrees of kinship and their implications for widows and orphans, particularly since access to wealth was often gained or lost that way (see Harrison 1998: 1.143–9; MacDowell 1978: 98–9; Patterson 1998, with clear diagrams; App. III). We can bypass the conjectures about availability and suitability of the uncles on the assumption that Glaucon III, like most fathers, especially when there was considerable property and the dangers of war, had stipulated a guardian for his children in the event of his death (Harrison 1998: 1.99).

Profanation of the Eleusinian mysteries in 415.   When he was about thirty-one, Charmides and three men of Scambonidae—Alcibiades III, Adeimantus, and Axiochus—were accused by Agariste III s.v. of having illegally performed the secret Eleusinian mysteries in the house by the Olympieum belonging to Charmides (see Exc. 1). Charmides' possessions were confiscated immediately and he was condemned to death *in absentia.*

Several texts of Plato, pseudo-Plato, and Xenophon link the persons involved in Agariste III's charges, not only the four accused, but Agariste III's husband, Damon s.v., as well—in part, through ties to Socrates. Charmides, Alcibiades III, and Adeimantus of Scambonidae are present in the *Protagoras* with Socrates. Socrates is linked to Charmides (Pl. *Chrm.*; Xen. *Mem.* 3.6.1, 3.7, *Symp.*), and to Alcibiades III (Pl. *Smp.*, where Alcibiades III mentions Charmides; [Pl.] *Alc.*, where Damon is mentioned, 2 *Alc.*; and Xen. *Mem.* 1.2.40). Damon is praised at some length in *Laches*, and his theories are discussed in *Republic*. Alcibiades III and Adeimantus were *stratēgoi* together in Andros in 407 (*Hell.* 1.4.21–22; cf. Lys. 14.38 for a link in 405). Axiochus, a paternal uncle of Alcibiades III, had a son, Clinias III, who is prominent in *Euthydemus* and the pseudo-Platonic

Axiochus, where he is Charmides' beloved (364a). It is *Axiochus* that most clearly links the profanation group. In the opening scene, Socrates sees Clinias III, Damon, and Charmides running toward Callirhoë, a spring near the Olympieum whose water was used ritually (Thu. 2.15.5), and all four then join Axiochus at home.

Xenophon's *Symposium* depicts Charmides as a poor man, living on public assistance, who now sleeps better than when he was rich and had to worry about burglars digging through his walls (4.31). The dialogue is set notionally in August of 421, but the date, already anachronistic on a variety of grounds, should not detain us. If only it were possible to have more confidence in the erratic Xenophon, we might know more about the situation of the men perhaps formally exonerated of Agariste III's charges years after the event. It is Xenophon wearing his historian's hat (Xen. *Hell.* 1.4.13–21), and well supported on this occasion by Diogenes (13.69.1–3) who describes the city's reversal in 407, when Alcibiades III was recalled to Athens, his sentence overturned, the curse on him retracted, and compensation promised for his confiscated property. The profanation of which Alcibiades III, Charmides, Axiochus, and Adeimantus had been accused by Agariste III (and, presumably those accused with Alcibiades III by Andromachus) was now treated as never having happened at all. But there was, for some of the men at least, a catch: confiscated property that had been sold could be bought back by the *polis* and returned to its original owner—but not property that had been resold by the purchaser. Alcibiades III's compensatory property was still not available when his son was due to inherit it in 404 (see Alcibiades IV s.v., cf. Exc. 4). Charmides, with less clout than Alcibiades III, may well have found himself in 407 back in a city depleted through long years of war, without resources at a time when his cousin Critias IV s.v. was in exile in Thessaly, Pyrilampes s.v. had been dead since <413, Demos s.v. was away on embassies, and others in the family were not yet old enough to be householders.

Political career.   In Xenophon, Socrates has regard for Charmides (*Mem.* 3.6.1) but encourages him to overcome his natural reticence and shyness and become active in public affairs by taking a more voluble role in the Assembly (*Mem.* 3.7.1–9; cf. D. L. 2.29). Charmides did in fact become one of the Ten (Xen. *Hell.* 2.4.19) chosen by the Thirty ([Aristot.] *Ath. Pol.* 35.1) to govern the Piraeus 404–3; thus he is included in the "fifty-one" that Plato mentions as the size of the government (*Ltr.* 7.324c). Burnet (1924: *Ap.* 32c6n) and Bury (1929: *Ltr.* 7.324dn) mistake Charmides for a member of the Thirty, and it is still a common mistake in the literature (Huss 1999a: 400; Wolfsdorf 1998: 130; PCW 639; Kahn 1996: 49n24, 185; Nails 1995: 210; Brickhouse and Smith 1994: 167; Wallace 1992: 329, 331; Sprague 1976: 30; Guthrie 1975: 11). Charmides does not appear in the ancient list of the Thirty (Xen. *Hell.* 2.3.2–3), but he is listed among those killed in the battle of Munychia between the forces of the Thirty and Thrasybulus' group of exiled democrats in 403 (Xen. *Hell.* 2.4.19).

In inscriptions.   An inscription of some interest (*SEG* 13.28) is a fragment of a marble block recovered from the site of the Academy and bearing four names reconstructed by G. Karo in 1934 as Socratic associates (Charmides, Ariston, Axiochus, Crito) and thus to be dated 5th c.:

ΧΑΡΜ . . .
ΑΡΙΣ . . .
ΑΞΙ . . .
ΚΡΙΤΩΝ

The fragment was later redated to the 2nd c. (*SEG* 21.638):

ΧΑΡΜ[- - -]
ΑΡΙΣ[- - -]
ΜΕΝΕΚΡ[ΑΤΗΣ]
ΚΡΙΤΩΝ[- - -]?
[.] Ε[- - -]

Brumbaugh (1992: 171–2) reinterpreted it as the names of "schoolboys" from the dialogues, but only by reading the third name as 'Menexenus' and counting Crito as a schoolboy (cf. Jones 1999: 231n51). It is a lesson in what different reconstructions there may be of a worn stone inscription.

Prosopographical notes.   There has long been special interest in determining Charmides' deme because one might then safely extend the identification to some other males on the maternal side of Plato's family who feature in the dialogues and in history, most notably Critias IV, but also the characters of the *Timaeus* and *Critias*. Since Charmides says he was taxed when he was rich (Xen. *Mem.* 4.31), one might expect to find inscriptions celebrating his liturgies, but so far there is nothing that qualifies. The one suggestion made in *APF*, Charmides of Lamptrae (*PA* 15514) "*tamias* of the Other Gods in 420/19 (*IG* I² 370.11 [cf. I³ 472]), of the right social class and of the right tribe," is unsuitable. Charmides of Lamptrae, to have reached the age of thirty by 420/19, must have been born by 450/49, so he is too old to have required a guardian in 429.

In modern bibliography.   A number of modern scholars looking at Andocides IV's *On the Mysteries* in the course of some larger project (e.g., *APF*, *DPhA*, and Kahn 1996: 32) have mistakenly taken all references to 'Charmides' in Andocides IV to be univocal, leaving unexplained why, after the profaner Charmides is named without demotic or patronymic (1.16)—as if everyone knows him—Andocides IV *later* takes such care to introduce the Charmides, son of Aristotle, who is his own cousin (1.47 and 48), and advisor in prison. Scholars who have dealt with the text directly have assumed naturally that there are *two* men named Charmides in Andocides IV's speech (Maidment 1941, MacDowell 1962, Aurenche 1974,

Dover *HCT*: 277, Wallace 1992: 331, and Ostwald *CAH* 5²: 364). Dover notes that the chronology of events would be affected if there were only one Charmides because he would have to have been released from prison—as a result of Andocides IV's evidence—just in time to flee Agariste III's denunciation (*HCT*: 281). Besides, Andocides IV carefully constructed his speech precisely to distance himself from anything smacking of profanation, so it would have been exceedingly unlikely for him to cite a criminal in so central a way, as his counselor, in his own defense.

On the quite separate matter of whether the first Charmides, the profaner, was also Plato's uncle, only Wallace (1992: 331–5) argues that the case is certain, and I use some of his material above, though Ostwald (*CAH* 5²: 364) says "probably," MacDowell (1962: 76) says "possible," and Dover (*HCT* 283) says "could be" and "perhaps." Both Ollier (1961: 115) and Stanley (1986: 179–81) defend Xenophon against charges of anachronism by suggesting other ways in which Charmides might have gone from rich to poor before 422. (A few sources from the later tradition are occasionally mixed into contemporary discussions; see later testimonia in *SSR* 2.VIB.)

Chilon of Sparta (sage) See App. II.

Chrysilla of Athens, wife of Ischomachus
and Callias III of Alopece
[*PA/APF* 15577 (7826.11–14, 8429.4) *LGPN2* 1
Χρύσιλλα Ἰσχομάχου γυνή ὕστερον δὲ
Καλλίου Ἀλωπεκῆθεν γυνή]
≥450–≥390
husbands: (1) Ischomachus (2) Callias III
offspring with Ischomachus: two sons, a
daughter who married Epilycus II and
Callias III; with Callias III: [unnamed] of
Alopece
See stemma: Callias.

Xen. *Oec.*, unnamed
Andoc. 1.124–7
Met. *Phil.* fr. 14 (K 13)

Life.   Nothing is known of Chrysilla's parents or deme, though they will almost certainly have been both prominent and wealthy, given her marriages; some inferences about her life depend on correctly distinguishing her first husband, Ischomachus s.v., from other men of that name. In that matter I have closely followed the calculations and conclusions in *APF*, occasionally narrowing the range of dates where to do so now seems warranted by the evidence. Chrysilla's birth can be dated ≥450 because her last child was born not earlier than 412, at which time she already had two granddaughters—famous disputed heiresses (Andoc. 1.117–123; cf. Callias III s.v.).

Ischomachus tells Socrates how he trained his young wife to be a good manager of their household (Xen. *Oec.* 7.5–10.13): Chrysilla appears as a quiet child-bride of fourteen (7.5)—whose mother had told her that her only duty was to be modest

(7.14)—taking lengthy instructions from her husband, a rich landowner, on increasing the number of their possessions by adhering to the god-given natures of the male and female, respectively. Her role was to stay busy as a queen bee, superintending servants and caring for them in illness to gain their loyalty; spinning and weaving, and storing food properly. Chrysilla proved capable of learning advanced lessons from Ischomachus as well (8.1): orderliness, interior decoration, choosing and maintaining a good housekeeper, obedience, and personal grooming.

They had three children. Their first child and only daughter, born ≥435, married Epilycus II, the only son of Tisander II, ≥420; *their* daughters were the heiresses (Chrysilla's granddaughters). In all likelihood, the widow returned home with her two daughters, and Ischomachus then arranged her second marriage, this time to Callias III. Chrysilla and Ischomachus also had two sons who were minors at the time of Ischomachus' death, probably ±413 (see Ischomachus s.v.).

Although Andocides IV, facing a possible death sentence at the time of his trial in 400, could be expected to serve his own interest by making Callias III appear the consummate rascal, and although he was already in a separate dispute with Callias III s.v. over who had the greater right to the one surviving heiress (Chrysilla's granddaughter), it has to be admitted that his account of the behavior of Callias III and Chrysilla was supported by witnesses (Andoc. 1.127) and that Andocides IV was in fact acquitted. What he reports is that Callias III, while still married to the daughter, brought Chrysilla to share his bed and thereafter kept both women (1.124). The daughter was so ashamed that she attempted suicide but was caught trying to hang herself; when she recovered, she ran away from her mother and stepfather. Callias III then drove Chrysilla out when she was pregnant with a son he refused to own (1.125). On this point there is some corroboration from the comic poet Metagenes, who refers to Callias III's bastard (*nothos*) sometime between 410 and 405; he is the second of the two sons mentioned in Plato (*Ap.* 20a). Nevertheless, Chrysilla's relatives took the infant and the requisite sacrificial animal to the annual Apaturia festival, intending to register him with the phratry of Callias III who was himself officiating in his priestly role of torchbearer. When the relatives identified the infant as Callias III's son, Callias III denied it, swearing on the altar that he had only one son, Hipponicus III, whose mother was the daughter of Glaucon II of Cerameis (Andoc. 1.126). Some unspecified time later, he took Chrysilla back and presented the boy, now grown large, to the Ceryces himself as his legitimate son by the freeborn woman Chrysilla.

Andocides IV's account is probably roughly correct, though one might surmise that the just-widowed Chrysilla was doing nothing unusual to move with her two sons into the house of her daughter and son-in-law. That the daughter was unhappy with Callias III is not difficult to imagine either. In any case, less than a year after Callias III married Chrysilla's daughter by Ischomachus, Callias III married Chrysilla herself (Andoc. 1.124)—most likely because Ischomachus' death had left an estate that Callias III coveted and could access if Chrysilla's two sons were made his wards (*APF* 7826.14). Ischomachus may even have named his son-in-law, Callias III, guardian of his sons in a will, thereby smoothing the process. (See Callias III s.v. for more about the child-heiresses and Ischomachus s.v. for more about the sons.)

Cimon II of Laciadae, son of Miltiades IV
[*PA/APF* 8429 *LGPN2* 11 *PAA* 569795 *OCD*³
PP Κίμων Μιλτιάδου Λακιάδης]
±510–450/49
mother: Hegesipyle I, daughter of Thracian
    King Olorus
siblings: paternal half brother Metiochus;
    sisters: Elpinice (wife of Callias II), wife of
    ?Thucydides I, and wife of the father of
    ?Olorus of Halimous
wife: Isodice, daughter of Euryptolemus I
father of Cimon III, Lacedaemonius and his
    twin Oulius, ?Thettalus, ?Miltiades V, and
    ?Peisionax
protégé and associate of Aristides I
famous political and military leader
See stemmata: Callias, Pericles, Thucydides.

Pl. *Grg.* 503c–519a,
    passim †
[Pl.] *Thg.* 126a
Hdt. 6–7, *passim*
Thu. 1, *passim*
Stes., *passim*
Theo. fr. 88
IG II² 1388.82,
    1400.66 *tamias* of
    Athena; 1477.16
    tamias of the other
    gods
AM 106.152 *tamias*
    of Athena
Agora 25.592–7
Eu. *Pol.* fr. 221 (K
    208)
[Aristot.] *Ath. Pol.*
    27.3

Family. Cimon II was born into a family already famous for its wealth and political power. His mother was Thracian (Hdt. 6.39; Mar. 11), and he was himself later *proxenos* for both Thrace and Sparta. His father's previous marriage had produced a Metiochus who flourished in Persia and reared his children as Persians (Hdt. 6.41.4). His full siblings present two problems. The first is controversy over whether three of his brothers were historical individuals; the other results from conflicting late traditions that cannot be sorted out, but that reappear from time to time in the literature: (a) that Cimon II was legally married to his sister Elpinice, implying that she too was an offspring from Miltiades IV's first marriage and Cimon II's paternal half sister (marriage between paternal half siblings was legal in Athens), (b) that Cimon II committed incest with his full sister Elpinice (Eu.). See *APF* (8429.10B) for a full discussion of the ramifications of the possibilities. Cimon II married Isodice ±480, thereby uniting the great ruling families of Miltiades I and, on her side, Megacles I. His sister Elpinice's marriage to Callias II was equally dynastic, uniting the Miltiades family with the Ceryces clan of Callias II. Isodice may have been slandered by Stesimbrotus (fr. 6) under the nickname 'Clitoria,' but others have taken the comment as evidence for another wife of Cimon II. Cimon II's death is well attested; he was buried in a family plot much visited in late antiquity.

Career in brief. Cimon II had a long career and was—with his longtime rival, Themistocles—one of the two most influential men in Athens in the 470s and 460s, serving often as ambassador and as general; but he was, by Socrates' time, one of the great men of the past rather than a recently deceased person. He was ambassador to Sparta in the decree of Aristides I in 479. He was a particularly successful general, elected repeatedly (478/7–476/5), in the last year supposedly bringing Theseus' bones back to Athens (Hdt. 7.107.1; Thu. 1.98.1–2). In the period 476–463, with Aristides I, Cimon II supported the Delian League and commanded

most of its operations. He may have prosecuted Epicrates of Acharnae for convey-
ing Themistocles' wife and children to him in exile ±465 (Stes. fr. 3). In the late
460s, his chief rival was Ephialtes, whose close associate was the up-and-coming
Pericles I s.v.; Cimon II was perhaps prosecuted by Pericles I for taking bribes
from Alexander I of Macedonia in 463 or 462; he was acquitted (Plu. *Cim.* 14.2,
15.1). He mixed his wealth with his politics by maintaining a number of members
of his deme, and by leaving his lands unfenced so the needy would have ready
access to his harvest. He also sought to beautify the city with building projects.
He arranged for the planting of plane trees on the agora, was probably responsible
for the so-called painted stoa (see Plan 1), and for a terracotta pipeline (still
partially intact) that carried fresh water to the Academy, transforming it from an
arid area into a shaded grove (Plu. *Cim.* 13.8). As general in 462, he aided Messenia
with four thousand hoplites (Aristoph. *Lysistr.* 1144 & schol.; Thu 1.102.1), but
was unpopular after the Spartans dismissed the Athenians at the siege of Ithome,
and was ostracized in the following year, for which many surviving *ostraka* serve
as evidence (cf. Pl. *Grg.* 516d). He reportedly volunteered, during his ostracism,
to serve in the battle of Tanagra against the Spartans in 458 but was refused (Plu.
Cim. 15.2, 17.2); however, on a motion of Pericles I, he was recalled from exile
four years early, in 457 (Theo.; Plu. *Cim.* 17.6) and arranged a five-year truce
between Sparta and Athens (D. S. 11.86.1; Andoc. 3.3). Cimon II died in 450/49
while serving as general against the Persians on Cyprus (Thu. 1.112.2, 1.112.4; D.
S. 12.3–4).

In the later tradition. Both Plutarch and Nepos wrote biographies called *Cimon*
that augment and corroborate much of what is above; cf. Diodorus 11–12, *passim*.

Cinesias of Athens, son of Meles   Pl. *Grg.* 501e *
[*PA* 8438 *LGPN2* 2 *PAA* 569985 *RE* s.v. *OCD³*   *IG* II² 18.5; 3028.2
Stephanis 1406 *PP* Κινησίας Μέλητος]   Lys. 21.20
±450–390   Lys. fr. 4
minor poet, *aulos* player   comedy (see below)

Life. Before Cinesias had poetic victories of his own to celebrate, he had attracted
the attention of quite a few comic poets of note. His first datable appearance in
a comedy is a scene in Aristophanes' *Birds* (1372–1409), produced in 414, in which
the long and stringy, perhaps emaciated (1378; cf. Plato *com.* fr. 200 [K 184])
composer and choreographer tries to persuade Peisetaerus to give him wings so
he can find new musical preludes in the clouds; but the more Cinesias insists on
singing to demonstrate the quality of his dithyrambs, the more agitated and
ridiculing Peisetaerus becomes. Some of the elements of the scene occur elsewhere
as well. Aristophanes comments again on Cinesias' circular chorus (ln. 1403) in
409 (*Gery.* fr. 156.10 [K 149, 150]), and Pherecrates (*Chi.* fr. 155.8–12 [K 145])
lambastes Cinesias' "new" dithyrambic style. Henderson characterizes the style
as highly emotional with complex music and language (2000: 201n127), qualities
given to Cinesias' lines in *Birds*. On three separate occasions, Cinesias is hammered
in Aristophanes' *Frogs* in 405. The allusions are difficult to make out, but one
refers to a choral dance in armor of which he seems to have been proud (ln. 153);

another, echoed in 392 or 391 (Aristoph. *Eccl.* 330), refers to his having been sick with diarrhea at some public event (ln. 366); the third is a fat man/skinny man team suggested by the character Euripides in which Cinesias would be the skinny man. Sickly skinniness seems also to be the point of Strattis' play *Cinesias* (see esp. fr. 18 [K 19]) where Cinesias is called "chorus-killer".

The logographer Lysias s.v. also had Cinesias in his sights. He mentions him in passing with a backhanded compliment: Cinesias, with his reputation for cowardice, has yet served on more military campaigns than the opponent in the suit (21, dated 403/2). Fr. 4 is an undated one-page diatribe against Cinesias who is said to have offended popular religious sentiment, not only in his poems, but by forming a club with a sacrilegious name that dined on inauspicious days; further, Cinesias was a sycophant.

Nevertheless, at some point in the early 4th c., Cinesias won a victory at the Athenian Dionysia, cited in a choral dedication (*IG* II² 3028). Like Plato and Aeschines among the Socratics, Cinesias may have been approached by the tyrant Dionysius I to visit his court, for he proposed a decree honoring Dionysius I of Syracuse and his family in 394/3 (*IG* II² 18).

In the later tradition. See Galen's *On the Aphorisms of Hippocrates* in which Galen uses scab-covered Cinesias as evidence of the ancients' use of cautery (18.1.149). (Cf. Plu. *Mor.* 348b; Ath. 551c–e; Harp. s.v.)

Clearchus of Heraclea Pontica See App. II.

Cleisthenes of Sicyon (tyrant) See App. II. *See stemma: Pericles.*

Cleisthenes of Athens (reformer), son of Megacles II See App. II. *See stemma: Pericles.*

Cleobulus of Lindos (Rhodes), son of Evagoras (sage) See App. II.

Cleombrotus of Ambracia   Pl. *Phd.* 59c3 *
[*PP* Κλεόμβροτος]
fl. late 5th c.
associate of Socrates, Plato

Life. Nothing is known, so much is conjectured about Cleombrotus. The report that he was on Aegina at the time of Socrates' execution, and therefore not present, has been interpreted in a range of positive and negative ways, for Aegina is very close to mainland Greece. Several persons of this name are known for the latter part of the 5th c. for both Athens and greater Greece (see *PAA* and *LGPN*), but it would be foolish to assign the Cleombrotus of the *Phaedo* to any of the known individuals without more information. Ambracia, a settlement in northwest

Greece, is recorded as Cleombrotus' place of origin no earlier than the 3rd c. B.C.E., when the poet Callimachus uses it without mentioning his source (*Palatine Anthology* 7.471).

In the later tradition.   Besides a pseudo-Socratic letter (*Ep.* 16), there is a remark in passing by Cicero, mistakenly calling him 'Theombrotus' (an unattested name, *Tus. Dis.* 1.38.84), that points back to the brief epigram of Callimachus that gave rise to still later works romanticizing Cleombrotus' suicide after reading the *Phaedo*: " 'Farewell, Helios,' said Cleombrotus of Ambracia / and jumped from a high wall into Hades /—not that anything bad occasioned his death, but Plato's / writing *On the Soul* he had just read."

Cleon of Cydathenaeum, son of Cleaenetus (tanner, general) See App. II.

Cleopatra, wife of Macedonian king Perdiccas II See App. II.

Cleophantus, son of Themistocles See App. II.

Clinias I of Athens, son of Alcibiades I See App. II. *See stemma: Alcibiades.*

Clinias II of Scambonidae, son of Alcibiades II
[*PA/APF* 8510b (600.6) *LGPN2* 22 *PAA* 575375
PP Κλεινίας Ἀλκιβιάδου Σκαμβωνίδης]
±480–446
siblings: sister (who married a Phegousian);
  paternal half brother Axiochus
wife: Dinomache
father of Alcibiades III, Clinias IV
See stemma: Alcibiades.

Pl. *Prt.* 309c, pat.
Pl. *Grg.* 481d, pat.
[Pl.] *Alc.* 105d, 112c
[Pl.] *2Alc.* 141b, pat.
Aristoph. *Ach.* 716
Isocr. 16.28
Lys. 14.39
Agora 25.13–17
IG I³ 421.12, 424.27
  (*ostraka*)

Life.   Clinias II was born into a wealthy and powerful Salaminian family, married the daughter of Megacles IV, from an equally prominent Alcmaeonid family, by 450, and produced two children (Aristoph.) before his death in the battle of Coronea at the age of thirty-four. He was a supporter of Pericles I, his wife's first cousin, and attracted enough attention to appear on a number of pottery *ostraka* before his death.

Prosopographical notes.   Both *PAA* and *LGPN2* divide *PA* 8510 into two individuals, Clinias I (*PAA* 575370, *LGPN2* 21, see App. II) and Clinias II (above). Both also note that Clinias II ?= *LGPN27* and *PAA* 575290, who proposed a decree concerning tribute in 448/7 (*IG* I³ 34.5).

Clinias III of Scambonidae, son of Axiochus   Pl. *Euthd.*   speaker
[*PA/APF* 8511 (600.6, cf. 8823) *LGPN2* 20   [Pl.] *Ax.* 364a–d   speaker
PAA 575380, 575265 *DPhA* 174 *PP PX*   Xen. *Symp.* 4.12–26
Κλεινίας Ἀξιόχου Σκαμβωνίδης]
b. ±424
beloved of Charmides, Critobulus, Ctesippus,
  et al.
See stemma: Alcibiades.

Life. It is surprising that we should know almost nothing about this beautiful youth from the powerful and famous family of Alcibiades beyond what the dialogues tell us. One must wonder whether he may have died before he reached an age when the comic poets could notice him or he could have reason to find himself in the courts. Socrates worries aloud, "He is young, and we are anxious about him, as one naturally is about a boy of his age, for fear that somebody might get in ahead of us and turn his mind to some other interest and ruin him" (*Euthd.* 275b; cf. *R.* 6.494b–c). Clinias III's date of birth, ±424, is established from Plato's very careful description in the *Euthydemus* where he is *meirakion* ≥407 (275e; for the dramatic date, see App. I) and a little younger, though more physically mature, than Crito's older son Critobulus s.v. Clinias III would have been about nine years old when his father, Axiochus s.v., was accused of profaning the mysteries and condemned to death (see Exc. 1). Although Axiochus fled into exile before he could be rounded up, all his property was confiscated for resale by the state, and his condemnation was broadcast on a *stele* for all to read. Some families accompanied the banished into exile, or rather joined them later, particularly if foreign holdings or foreign friends could make the exile's life more livable, but Clinias III and his mother, whoever she was, and if she was alive, almost certainly could not follow Axiochus. He appears to have accompanied his nephew, Alcibiades III, during his exile and to have returned to Athens with him in 407, when Clinias III would have been about seventeen. Unlike Alcibiades III, however, who left the city again after four months, Axiochus appears to have remained in Athens and taken a public role in affairs of state thereafter.

In Plato. In Plato's *Euthydemus*, Clinias III, beautiful and surrounded by lovers, chief among whom is Ctesippus of Paeania, is already acquainted with Socrates (273a–b) on the occasion when he is questioned by the two sophists, Euthydemus and Dionysodorus. Clinias III is first to take a turn in the eristic, followed by a more able Ctesippus, then Socrates. Dover suggests *Euthydemus* 273a as a paradigm for defining terms: Ctesippus and his *paidika*, Clinias III, are both *neaniskoi*, young men or youths of adult height who show early signs of facial hair, suggesting "the possibility of homosexual relationships between coevals" (1989: 85–6).

Xenophon, following the *Euthydemus* rather closely with respect to the physical descriptions of Critobulus and Clinias III, turns the two into lovers in his *Symposium*. In observance of the very mores Dover describes, Xenophon must make them *neaniskoi* in the *Symposium* as well, lingering over the description of how much down covers the fronts of their ears and the napes of their necks (*Symp.* 4.23–24)—but of course the two cannot have been youths in bloom already in the *Symposium*, set some fourteen years earlier than the *Euthydemus*. Xenophon's

Socratic writings are not to be confused with his history. But Xenophon can here be acquitted of one charge of historical inaccuracy: some have thought that Critobulus' lover in the *Memorabilia* (1.3.8–10) is still Clinias III, though he is identified only as "son of Alcibiades"; if so, then Xenophon would be in error to refer to Clinias III as the son—rather than grandson—of Alcibiades (*APF* 600.6B blames the mistake on Xenophon's bad memory). Sons of the old Alcibiades (II), including a Clinias (II) were born in the 480s to 450s, so this is not an error even Xenophon could plausibly make. Rather, "son of Alcibiades" is exactly right and refers to Alcibiades IV, son of Alcibiades III, who would have been a few years younger than Critobulus.

Pseudo-Plato depicts Clinias III as the beloved of Charmides (*Ax.* 364a).

Prosopographical notes. *PAA* assigns the Platonic and pseudo-Platonic passages to *PAA* 575380 and the passage from Xenophon to *PAA* 575265.

Clinias IV of Scambonidae, son of Clinias II	Pl. *Prt.* 320a *
[*PA/APF* 8512 (600.7) *LGPN2* 23 *PAA* 575390	[Pl.] *Alc.* 104b, 118e *
PP Κλεινίας Κλεινίου Σκαμβωνίδης]	
b. 449–6	
mother: Dinomache	
brother: Alcibiades III	
ward of Pericles I and Ariphron II	
See stemma: Alcibiades.	

Younger brother of the famous Alcibiades III (*Prt.*), Clinias IV had illustrious antecedents and wealth on both sides of his family (*Alc.*). His father was killed in the battle of Coronea in 446, whereupon he was made ward of Pericles I and Ariphron II, who were his mother's first cousins, almost certainly because his father had left a will stipulating the arrangement. Other possible lines of relationship—the family intermarried even more commonly than most—may have connected the families of Pericles I and Clinias II. According to the story told briefly in the *Protagoras*, Clinias IV was sent by Pericles I to Ariphron II, so the boy would not be corrupted by Alcibiades III. Ariphron II sent the boy back after six months, saying that he could do nothing with him. In pseudo-Plato's *Alcibiades* 1, Alcibiades III calls his brother a madman (μαινόμενον ἄνθρωπον), prompting *APF* to call him a "psychotic delinquent" (citing *Prt.* and *Alc.*) Clinias IV does not feature in Plutarch's *Alcibiades* and, in fact, is not heard from after pseudo-Plato, though Aristotle remarks, "A clever stock will degenerate towards the insane type of character, like the descendants of Alcibiades [II] or the elder Dionysius; a steady stock towards the fatuous and torpid type, like the descendants of Cimon [II], Pericles [I], and Socrates" (*Rh.* 1390b30).

Clinias of Cnossos	Pl. *Laws*	speaker
[*PP* Κλεινίας]	[Pl.] *Epin.*	speaker
Cretan interlocutor of the *Laws*		

In *Laws*, Clinias is a citizen of Cnossos in Crete (629c), designated with nine others by Cnossos (702c–d) to reestablish a colony at Magnesia (860e). If a real situation is being invoked by the circumstances (see Dušanić 1990a: 363–5), he would be a herald, welcoming "ambassadors" from Athens and Sparta, but the name 'Clinias' is not typical of Crete.

Clito   Xen. *Mem.* 3.10.6–8
[*PX* Κλείτων]
sculptor

Socrates discusses the artist's imitation of the human body and *psyche* with the sculptor Clito. A man of that name of the tribe Antiochis was a casualty in 409, and another, from the Pandionis tribe, appears on a gravestone, but no identification is possible on current information: the Clito of *Memorabilia* may not be a person of whom any record survives.

Clitomachus of ?Athens   [Pl.] *Thg.* 129a *
[*PA* 8539 *LGPN2* 1 *PAA* 575835 Κλειτόμαχος]
brother: Timarchus

Not only does Clitomachus not appear in the prosopographical record of Athens, but neither do any of the others mentioned in connection with the assassination plot of the *Theages*. Dušanić (1990b: 65–70) argues that they are all from Thebes.

Clitophon of Athens, son of Aristonymus   Pl. *R.*   speaker
[*PA* 8546 *LGPN2* 5 *PAA* 576135 *RE* 2   [Pl.] *Clt.*   speaker
DPhA 175 *PP* Κλειτόφων Ἀριστωνύμου]   Aristoph. *Frogs*
≤452–>404   965–7
associates: Thrasymachus, Lysias   [Aristot.] *Ath. Pol.*
oligarchic political leader   29.2–3, 34.3
Cf. stemma: Lysias.   Lys. fr. 32.26

Career.   Clitophon was a person well-known to Athenians for his flip-flopping political affiliations. Aristophanes (*Frogs*) pairs him in 405 with Theramenes s.v. in a context suggesting similar histories of fickle loyalties, and the ability to land on their feet, regardless of change.

　　Pseudo-Aristotle mentions Clitophon twice in contexts that make him appear consistently oligarchic. In the politically unstable aftermath of the Sicilian disaster of 413, general dissatisfaction with a democracy viewed as degenerate or corrupt paved the way for oligarchy (see Ostwald 1986: 475, 478). In the Council (*boulē*) of 412/1, Pythodorus of Anaphlystus moved that "the popular Assembly was to elect twenty persons from among those over forty years of age, who, in conjunction with the existing ten members of the Committee of Public Safety [*proboulē*] ... should then prepare proposals for the public safety"; Clitophon added a rider to the effect that the committee should also investigate the *patrios politeia*, the ancestral constitution ([Aristot.] *Ath. Pol.* 29.3 with Rhodes 1993: 376–7; cf. Thu. 8.1.67). In retrospect, the action can be seen as one of the decisive moves toward what was to be the oligarchy of the Four Hundred in 411. The reestablishment of the ancestral constitution was still his object in 404 when Clitophon was ambassador with Archinus, Anytus s.vv., and Phormisus to Lysander (*Ath. Pol.* 34). That small group is usually taken to be among the "moderates" within the oligarchy who would have preferred a less extreme form of that type of polity than the Thirty.

Clitophon appears with both Lysias and Thrasymachus in the first book of the *Republic*, but is further associated with Lysias (*Clt.* 406a) and Thrasymachus (*Clt.* 406a, 410d), both of whom are connected with the development and teaching of rhetoric, and further associated with one another, in the *Phaedrus* (266c, 269e). Clitophon's few spoken lines in Plato (*R.* 340b) are an offer of aid to Thrasymachus that shows Clitophon to be the one thoroughgoing normative relativist among the speakers. Implicitly, he rejects the distinction between seeming and being already established at 334b–d (cf. Shorey 1930: 31ne), and recommends a more radical relativism, that the advantage of the stronger just *is* whatever the stronger *believes* it is—but Thrasymachus does not take it up (340c). In the pseudo-Platonic *Clitophon*, Socrates submits to a long rhetorical harangue in which Clitophon critiques Socrates' method, concluding, "while you're worth the world to someone who hasn't yet been converted to the pursuit of virtue, to someone who's already been converted you rather get in the way of his attaining happiness by reaching the goal of virtue" (410e).

Prosopographical notes.   This Clitophon ?= *LGPN2* 4 (*PAA* 576140) of Lysias fr. 32—or rather I. Bekker, *Anecdota Graeca* (Berlin 1814–21), who identifies Clitophon as the referent of the fr. (which does not itself mention Clitophon).

In the later tradition.   See Plutarch (*Mor.* 328a–c).

Coesyra of Eretria, wife of Megacles IV See App. II. *See stemma: Pericles.*

Connus of Athens, son of Metrobius
[*PA* 8697 *LGPN2* 1 *PAA* 581470 *PP*
Stephanis 1478 Κόννος Μητροβίου]
active 440s–420s
cithara (lyre) teacher, Socrates' music teacher

Pl. *Euthd.* 272c,
   295d *
Pl. *Mx.* 235e *
Aristoph. *Wasps* 675
   & schol.
Aristoph. *Knights*
   534
Amip. *Con.* frr. 7–11
   (K 7–10, 12)
Phryn. *Con.* frr. 6–8
   (K 6–8)

Although a few frr. remain of the eponymous play or plays of 423, it is not very clear how Connus was featured, or whether Socrates was present or even mentioned as one of his students. (Titles for Amip. and Phryn. are preserved, but there is some suspicion, e.g. Dover's in *OCD*[3], that there was an early confusion, and that only Amip. actually had a play called *Connus*; *PCG* lists the title for both playwrights.) Aristophanes describes Connus in 424 as a has-been who bums drinks off people who remember his earlier fame (*Knights*), and in 422 as one of the old men whose vote can be purchased with such gifts as preserved fish, wine, and honey (*Wasps*)—though Socrates is still studying music with him twenty years later (*Euthd.*).

Conon of Anaphlystus (general) See App. II.

Coriscus of Scepsis	[Pl.] *Ltr. 6* * addressee
[*PP* Κορίσκος]	Aristot., *passim*
brother: Erastus	Str. 13.1.54
father of Neleus	D. L. 3.46
student of Plato	
friend of Aristotle	

Life.   Coriscus was Aristotle's contemporary at the Academy and lifelong friend, often mentioned by Aristotle as an example in making one point or another, though it is difficult to know how many of the attributes applied by Aristotle to Coriscus were accurate (e.g. musical, good, dark). He was a native of Scepsis (see Map 1), near Atarneus where Hermias s.v. was ruler; [Plato] encouraged their mutual friendship (*Ltr. 6*). With Erastus s.v., Coriscus advised Hermias and later established a school at nearby Assos. The later tradition unreliably records that Coriscus' son, Neleus, inherited Aristotle's library from Theophrastus and removed it to Scepsis.

Cratinus of Anaphlystus, son of Conon	[Pl.] *Ltr.* 13.363a *
[*PP* Κρατῖνος Κόνωνος Ἀναφλύστιος]	Lys. 19.36–40,
b. >405	unnamed
brother: Timotheus	
companion of [Plato]	

[Plato] requests that Dionysius II give Cratinus a *hoplite*'s breastplate, an indication that Cratinus was not a wealthy individual; it is his brother s.v. who was an extremely well-known and well attested general. The name Cratinus is not sufficiently attested (appearing only in *Ltr.* 13) to be assigned a number by *PA*, *PAA*, or *LGPN2*—a clear indication of where [Plato's] letters stand in prosopographical studies generally. When Conon died in 389, he had an adult nephew, a wife, and a son in Cyprus (Lys.) whose names are not known. In the secondary literature, it is considered more likely that a forger used this information to generate the name 'Cratinus' than that the letter exposes the previously lost name of a known individual, Conon's son.

Cratistolus of Syracuse   [Pl.] *Ltr.* 2.310c *
[*LGPN3A* 1 Κρατίστολος]
active 4th c.

Cratistolus was allegedly in Olympia when Plato and Dion were there in 360 and
may have slandered them to Dionysius II. *LGPN3A* queries the var. –τόλαος, but
nothing further is known of this person.

Cratylus of Athens, son of Smicrion   Pl. *Cra.*   speaker
[*PAA* 584745 *FRA* 7786 *OCD*³ *PP*   DK 65 (testimonia)
Κρατύλος Σμικρίωνος]   Aristot. *Meta.*
b. 450s–440s   987a32–b1
Heraclitean philosopher

Life.   In a discussion of names as unique signifiers (*Cra.* 429e), Socrates says to
Cratylus, "For example, suppose you were in a foreign country and someone
meeting you took your hand and said, 'Greetings! Hermogenes, son of Smicrion,
visitor from Athens,' would he be speaking, saying, announcing, or addressing
these words not to you but to Hermogenes—or to no one?" Since Hermogenes
is called 'son of Hipponicus' consistently in *Cratylus,* as elsewhere, one must
assume that Socrates' example is, except for the name 'Hermogenes' (i.e., the
unique signifier at issue) a description of Cratylus. Otherwise the philosophical
point would be utterly lost. Thus this Cratylus is Athenian and the son of Smicrion,
the latter an inference drawn inconspicuously by Kirk (1951: 225n1) but unnoticed
in the literature. 'Smicrion' is not a common name in Attica; a Smicrion (–ov) of
the tribe Pandionis (*PA* 12747 = *LGPN2* 7) is of the right era: *IG* I³ 1162.77, dated
447, but there is nothing further to connect our Cratylus with Pandionis; 'Smicrion'
(–ων) appears also in Thebes in the 5th c.

Career and modern bibliography.   Determining even the most approximate dates
for Cratylus involves the statement by Aristotle (*Meta.* 987a32–b1) that the young
Plato became familiar with Cratylus first, implying that Cratylus' views had
reached maturity by the decade before 399. Kirk (1951) took this straightforwardly,
in agreement with the tradition that Cratylus' career was primarily in the latter
half of the 5th c.; Allan (1954: 275n2) argued that "first" (πρῶτον), should be taken
not temporally but logically, and—citing *Cratylus* 429d and 440d for a large age
difference between Socrates and his interlocutors—that Cratylus was no older
than Plato in 399, the dramatic date assigned by Burnet. Cherniss (1955: 184–6),
followed by Guthrie (1965: 359n1), rejected Allan's logical sense of πρῶτον, though
Guthrie goes too far (missing 391c) when he says the *Cratylus* "contains no
indication of when the conversation was supposed to have taken place" (1978:
2), which is not true (see Hermogenes s.v.). Taylor (1956) also opposed Allan by
reducing the presumed age gap between Socrates and Cratylus, pointing out the
mention of a previous conversation with Euthyphro s.v. (*Cra.* 396d; this has grown
into a large prosopographical controversy on its own). Taylor concluded that
Socrates was in his forties in the *Cratylus,* thus that the dialogue is set in the 420s,

a view I find plausible. If Cratylus was young and in his prime (νέος εἶ καὶ ἡλικίαν) in the 420s, then Plato could well have encountered his views, or the Athenian himself, before becoming intimately associated with Socrates, and a birth date for Cratylus in the 450s to 440s would be appropriate.

Creophylus of Samos, son of Astycles (poet) See App. II.

Cresphontes of Messene (legislator) See App. II.

Crison of Himera (sprinter) See App. II.

Critias I of Athens, son of ?Dropides I See App. II. *See stemma: Plato.*

Critias II of Athens, son of Dropides II See App. II. *See stemma: Plato.*

Critias III of Athens, son of ?Leaïdes	Pl. *Ti.* speaker
[*PA/APF* 8791 (8792.5) *LGPN2* 6 *PAA* 585310,	Pl. *Criti.* speaker
585310 Κριτίας Λεαΐδου]	*ABV*² "Leagros
tribe: ?Erechtheis	Group" 33
±520−>429	*Agora* 25.608.1, 609.1
father of Callaeschrus I, Glaucon III	(*ostraka*)
wealthy and influential citizen	Aesch. *Pr.* 128 schol.
See stemma: Plato.	

Life.   An unsettled controversy in Plato studies is the identity of the speaker in the *Timaeus* and *Critias*. Prosopographically, the speaker must be Critias III. Critias III was born into a wealthy, politically prominent family, was a contemporary and opponent of Themistocles s.v., and was a candidate for ostracism in the 480s (two pottery *ostraka* in *Agora*). In Plato's *Timaeus* (21a–b), Critias III tells the company that he was about ten years old when Critias II, his ninety-year-old grandfather, told him Solon's Atlantis story which Dropides II, Critias III's great-grandfather, had passed along to his son, Critias II. That family gathering at the Apaturia festival, by my dating, occurred ±510.

Prosopographical notes.   Until 1949, it was difficult to take seriously Plato's repre-sentation of historical persons in the dialogues when it could be pointed out that he did not, or could not, present even his own ancestors accurately: there were too few known individuals to cover the amount of time Plato described between the days of Solon, a relative (*Chrm.* 155a, missed in *APF*; *Ti.* 20e) and friend of the family, and the days of Critias IV, who was at that time assumed to be the speaker in the *Timaeus* and *Critias* (*Ti.* 20e; cf. *Chrm.* 157e–158a). Yet a passage on inheritance in the *Laws* made it seem unlikely that Plato would get his own ancestry wrong: "the recipient of a holding should always leave from among his children only *one* heir to inherit his establishment. This will be his favorite son, who will succeed him and give due worship to the ancestors (who rank as gods) of the family and state" (740b). Burnet addressed the problem by taking Plato at his word about his ancestors and drawing the obvious conclusion that the speaker was the *grandfather* of Critias IV, Critias III (1914: 338 & app., defended by Cornford 1937: 1–2). Burnet's solution was partial because it was not confirmed by the record: the generations were too long between Dropides II and Critias III. However, Vanderpool (1949; now *Agora*) revealed a previously missing generation (Critias III's father, Leaïdes), an inscription on a single pottery *ostrakon* found in a well near the southwest corner of the agora in 1936 showing that Critias, son of Leaïdes, was a candidate for ostracism in the 480s. Thus the prosopographical record came to conform to Plato's version of events. Critias II, the son of Dropides II, is the *great-great*-grandfather of Critias IV, leader of the Thirty (PCW 644n3 is mistaken; even without Leaïdes, Critias II would be a great-grandfather).

New problems and issues were generated by the new inscription, and by taking Critias III to be the speaker in the dialogues, however: (a) If Dropides I is the father of Dropides II, and Dropides II is the father of Critias II who was born ±600, then the Critias who was eponymous archon ±598 was not Plato's direct ascendant, but an uncle, and that is how I have represented the family on the stemma. (b) Solon's verses were not "new at the time" (*Ti.* 21b) in ±510 although they may have seemed so to ten-year-olds singing them for the first time—but this anachronism would only worsen if Critias IV were the interlocutor. (c) Critias III must have had the longevity of his grandfather to live into the era of the Peloponnesian war. He would be nearly ninety in 432, when the Peloponnesian war broke out. To make matters worse, Socrates was probably out of the city in August of 432 and certainly in the Augusts of 431 and 430, so the earliest possible dramatic date for the dialogue would be 429, when Critias III was ninety-one. A man of that advanced age might well remark of a story heard over eighty years ago, "I don't know if I'd be able to recall everything I heard yesterday, but I'd be extremely surprised if any part of this story has gotten way from me" (26b; cf. *Criti.* 108d). Critias IV would be too young to make such a remark at any point during the war. (d) Hermocrates s.v. would be a man of about twenty-six, Critias III's guest for the Panathenaea (21a)—long before he would advise Syracuse about Athens' expansionist plans. There is a problem that my dating cannot solve: (e) a scholiast's statement that the lyric poet Anacreon (b. ≤570) was the lover of a Critias, for the difference in age looks large, fifty years or more; the uncle Critias who was eponymous archon seems a better bet.

A black-figure vase on which the name 'Kritias' appears (*ABV*[2]) is now housed in the British Museum. Black-figure pottery was well established in Athens by the beginning of the 6th c., but there is not enough information to identify the referent of the vase confidently.

In modern bibliography.   In 1971, *APF* acknowledged the archaeological find, the *ostrakon*, but continued to prefer Critias IV as the speaker—offering two reasons: Plato's literary motivation for telescoping of two generations of his ancestors (*Ti.* 20e–21a); and an admonition that Burnet "makes too much of phrases." But this is a living controversy that shows no signs yet of abatement. In 1997, PCW chose Critias IV; in 1998, Lampert and Planeaux chose Critias III; in 2000, Dušanić chose Critias IV.

Critias IV of Athens, son of Callaeschrus I	Pl. *Chrm.*	speaker
[*PA*/*APF* 8792 (8792.6) *LGPN2* 7 *PAA* 585315	Pl. *Prt.*	speaker
DPhA 216 *OCD*³ *PP PX*	Pl. *Ltr.* 7.324b–d,	
Κριτίας Καλλαίσχρου]	unnamed †	
tribe: ?Erechtheis	[Pl.] *Eryx.*	speaker
≥460–403	frr. in DK 88	
mother: ?descendant of Eryxias	frr. in *TGrF* 43	
sister: wife of Hagnodorus of Amphitrope	Aes. *Mil.* no. 77 (fr.	
guardian of first cousin, Charmides	37 Dittmar)	
lover of Glaucon IV	Aes. *Rhi.* no. 82	
lover of Euthydemus, son of Diocles	schol. (fr. 49	
leader of the oligarchy of the Thirty, "The	Dittmar)	
Tyrant"	Xen. *Mem.*, *passim*	
See stemmata: Plato, Andocides.	Xen. *Hell.*, *passim*	
	Philoch. fr. 143	
	D. S., *passim*	
	Lys. 12.43, 13.55, 74	
	Andoc. 1.47, 68	

Family.   Critias IV could trace his ancestry back six generations to the early ruling families of Athens. Dropides I was archon in 645/4, and both his sons were also archons (see stemma and App. II), and Solon, a friend of Dropides II, was related to the family and composed verses in its honor. Although the later tradition mythologized Solon into a brother of Dropides II and direct ascendant of Critias IV's (and hence Plato's) family, Plato's dialogues claim no closer relationship than kinship with Solon (συγγενείας, *Chrm.* 155a3; οἰκεῖος, *Ti.* 20e1). Critias IV's mother was probably a descendant of the archon Eryxias (*APF*); she was the sister of Andocides IV's paternal grandmother, so Andocides IV was Critias IV's first cousin once removed. Critias IV's sister married Hagnodorus of Amphitrope, a man implicated in some of the excesses of the Thirty (Lys. 13.55). Before the troops returned from the siege of Potidaea in about May of 429, Critias IV had become guardian of his first cousin, Charmides s.v.

Neither the deme nor even the tribe for Critias IV is known with certainty, though a 4th c. descendant of the family, Callaeschrus, suggest the tribe Erechtheis to fit Löper's hypothesis (see Exc. 3) which, if correct, would lead to the same tribal assignment for Critias III, Callaeschrus I, Glaucon III, Charmides, et al. It happens that Erechtheis is a tribe that yields few widely used demotics; as Traill (1975: 38n9) avers at the bottom of a disappointing chart of the evidence for the locations of Erechtheis demes, "There is very little evidence for the trittys affiliation of most of the small demes of Erechtheis" (see Traill 1982: 166–7 and 1986: 125–6).

Early career.   Until 410 or later, i.e., until he was about fifty, Critias IV did nothing much that is known, unless he was at that time producing his literary works. He was in his late twenties when he arrived at Callias III's house with Alcibiades III (Pl. *Prt.* 316a) and about thirty at the time of the *Charmides*. Twenty years of relative obscurity thus need to be accounted for before his notoriety began. In 415, he was arrested for, then exonerated of, mutilating herms (see Exc. 1): he was among the forty-two men accused by the Athenian Dioclides. Andocides IV was at pains to point out that his own relatives had been accused by Dioclides, including Critias IV, and were initially assumed guilty because of their association with Andocides IV, whose drinking club had in fact masterminded the sacrilege. When Dioclides later recanted as a result of Andocides IV's giving evidence against members of his club, Critias IV and all those imprisoned with him were released.

There have been repeated attempts to connect Critias IV with the Four Hundred, a short-lived oligarchic regime of 411 (see modern bibliography below), but they have not been persuasive. The only contemporaneous evidence for it is a remark in a forensic speech against an informer that all the members of the Thirty were former members of the exiled Four Hundred (Lys. 13.74) which is quite an exaggeration (five were, perhaps more). An obscure remark in Xenophon (*Hell.* 2.3.15, see below) that Critias IV had been banished by the democracy is little help since Critias IV's only known absence from Athens was spent helping to set up a democracy in Thessaly. Pseudo-Demosthenes stated that Critias IV meant to admit the Lacedaemonians at Eetionia (58.67; cf. Thu. 8.91.3), but that cannot be accurate: all the members of the Four Hundred involved in that plan either fled the city or were tried after the plan was thwarted; yet Critias IV was not tried and did not flee the city. Further, he is not among those charged by Theramenes with the act (Xen. *Hell.* 2.3.46) though the speech is addressed to Critias IV. The evidence that he was a member of the Four Hundred is poor, but so is the evidence of two proposals he supposedly made soon after the fall of the oligarchy, often adduced to show he was not a member of the oligarchic faction: a proposal to recall Alcibiades III (an elegy preserved in Plu. *Alc.* 33.1), who had not been a part of the oligarchy (*contra* D. S. 13.38.2, stating that Theramenes was the only man to seek the recall); and a proposal to bring to trial for treason the assassinated oligarch Phrynichus who, if found guilty, was to have his bones removed from Attica— the source for which is the rather hyperbolic Lycurgus (*Leocr.* 113). Because membership in the Four Hundred is incompatible with what we can identify as Critias IV's democratic activities in the years soon after 411, these errant claims appear to have been attracted by the vacuum around Critias IV prior to 407.

With the benefit of long hindsight by the time he wrote *Memorabilia*—but also perhaps because that work addressed polemical charges that Socrates had corrupted his "students" Critias IV and Alcibiades III—Xenophon s.v. provided in brief compass a negative account of the tyrant. He accused Critias IV of seeking Socrates' company only to promote his own esteem in the public eye and of never having been Socrates' earnest student.

Political career.   Critias IV's public political career begins with an unspecified accusation against him by Cleophon (Aristot. *Rh.* 1375b32); perhaps as a result of the accusation, but in any case for some reason, he was exiled by the democracy (Xen. *Mem.* 1.2.24, *Hell.* 2.3.15); he spent his exile in Thessaly. Critias IV was there at the time of Alcibiades III's recall in 407, and remained there in 406. Theramenes, defending himself before the *boulē* in 404 against Critias IV's charge he had caused the deaths of the generals after the sea battle at Arginusae, said, "when these events took place, it chanced that he [Critias] was not here; he was establishing a democracy in Thessaly along with Prometheus, and arming the serfs against their masters" (Xen. *Hell.* 2.3.36), a charge Xenophon mentions again in the *Memorabilia* in connection with Socrates: so long as Critias IV sought Socrates' company, he absorbed enough strength from Socrates to behave fairly well but when away from that influence in Thessaly, Critias IV lost his self-control (1.2.24–26). Upon his return, according to Lysias, speaking for himself in 403/2 (12.43), Critias IV had been chosen by the Athenian *hetaireai* to serve as one of the five *ephors* charged with inciting the people to bring down the democratic government.

In this same period, Xenophon reports that, having failed to persuade Critias IV not to make unseemly demands of the son of Diocles, his current beloved, Socrates finally said for all to hear, "Critias seems to have the feelings of a pig: he can no more keep away from Euthydemus than pigs can help rubbing themselves against stones" (1.2.30). This incident caused a rupture between Critias IV and Socrates, according to Xenophon, that was never healed. When Critias IV was empowered as one of the Thirty, he drafted a law with Charicles insulting Socrates by forbidding the teaching of the art of words (λόγων τέχνην). As the situation in Athens worsened under the Thirty, Socrates criticized them, which was reported, and he was called before them. Socrates (in Xenophon) conversed with Charicles to clarify the intent of the law, learning that it prevented his talking to anyone under thirty, and incidentally bringing to light the very comment Socrates had made in criticism of the Thirty (1.2.30–38).

Critias IV was certainly a member and leader of the Thirty in 404/3 (Xen. *Hell.* 2.3; D. S. 14.4.5–6; schol. Aristoph. *Frogs* 541) though Charicles s.v. may also have been a leader (Aristot. *Pol.* 1305b26), for at least part of the eight months in which the Thirty held power. See Theramenes s.v. for Critias IV's leading role in the apprehension and execution of that more moderate member of the Thirty; see Excursus 3 for more on the tyranny of the Thirty as a ruling party. Critias IV appears to have been one of the extreme members and personally to have plotted some of its most reprehensible measures: murders, confiscations, banishments, mass execution of the citizen population of Eleusis. He was killed at Munychia in battle with the returning democratic forces of Thrasybulus in May of 403.

Works.   Critias IV wrote elegiac and hexameter poetry; perhaps he wrote tragedies and a satyr play, *Sisyphus*, purporting to explain how a clever human being had invented the deities to frighten wicked people who would otherwise disobey laws in secret—but the four dramatic fragments attributed to him are elsewhere attributed to Euripides. Two of his poems are of relevance here. One of his elegies is addressed to Alcibiades III s.v., claiming credit for the proposal to recall the general (Plu. *Alc.* 33.1), but it is unclear under what circumstances Critias IV could have done so: it was the fleet, and Thrasybulus in particular, that recalled him in 411; in 407, when the city recalled him, Critias IV was in Thessaly. Critias IV is usually regarded as the author of the verse quoted at *Republic* 368a, "Sons of Ariston, godlike offspring of a famous man" (Schleiermacher 1973). He is also said to have written prose works, several on other polities, aphorisms, and topical essays.

Prosopographical notes.   *APF* (8792.6) rejects Raubitschek's proposed identification "Critias Callaeschrus' son" for the fragment of a dedication to the twelve gods on a statue base found on Salamis: [–]ς Καλαίσχϙο, arguing that the athletic victories commemorated there, which would provide bragging rights to Critias IV, are nowhere mentioned in any extant source. Callaeschrus is an uncommon name, so a brother or cousin of Critias IV, otherwise unknown, is not impossible.

In the later tradition and modern bibliography.   (Cf. Demos. 24.90; Aristot. *Rh.* 1375b32, 1416b26; [Aristot.] *Ath. Pol.* 34–8, unnamed; D. H. *Isae.* 20; Philostr. *VS* 1.16; D. L. 3.1.; and other testimonia quoted in DK.) On Critias IV's role in the recall of Alcibiades III, see Andrewes (1953; cf. *CAH* 5[2]: 477). On his possible membership in the Four Hundred, Wilamowitz (1920) and Avery (1963) argue that he was not; Adeleye (1974) argues that he was, and Krentz (1982: 55) lists Critias IV among known members of the Four Hundred. Avery, by the way, uses the careers of the three men gathered about Hippias in Plato's *Protagoras* to illustrate his view (1963: 167n18). Bicknell makes a case against the view that Critias IV ordered Alcibiades III's assassination (1972: 100 and n35; cf. Alcibiades III s.v.).

EXCURSUS 3:
The Rule of the Thirty 404/3.

There is a widespread tendency to oversimplify both Critias IV and the Thirty he led. From one end of the political spectrum, the renowned journalist, I. F. Stone, uncritically repeats Plutarch's story that Critias ordered the murder of Alcibiades III, and calls Critias an "unrelenting opponent" of democracy, "the first Robespierre. His crimes were the fruit of a cruel and inhumane but consistent logic" (1989: 66–7). "Critias lost his life in an effort to put the Platonic ideal into practice" (166). Equally strident is the famous economist, Friedrich A. von Hayek, who remarks on the Thirty, "the liberty of the subjects was undoubtedly safer under the '30 tyrants' than under the democracy which killed Socrates and sent dozens of its best men into exile by arbitrary decrees" (1978: 15). But the academic literature is also encrusted with later traditions (and political circumstances in various eras and countries), ranging from the Diodorus-inspired view that the Thirty were a mere "puppet-regime" (*CAH* 6[2]: 36) put in place by the Spartans against the wishes of Athenians, to the view that the Thirty were the lawfully elected representatives of the ten traditional tribes: three per tribe, one for each type of *trittys* (Löper 1896).

  The Thirty's authority to rule lies at the root of any discussion of Socrates' disobeying their order. If not a clear act of civil disobedience, which I think it was, at least his action cannot be dismissed with a peremptory, "They weren't a lawful government." That they formed a government that abused and exceeded its authority no one could reasonably deny, but it is against just such governments that acts of civil disobedience are often directed. Four of the persons included here—Isocrates, Lysias, Plato, and Xenophon—lived through the defeat of Athens, the establishment of the Thirty, and wrote accounts that are extant. Regardless of how sharply each criticizes the Thirty, not one questions their authority to rule. Rather, they say the kinds of things one says anywhere when dirty campaigns put the wrong men in office. (See *On Sources* in the Introduction for the judgment that Diodorus is not using the contemporaneous source, P, for this period.)

Isocrates says, "When they took control (παραλαβόντες) of Athens by a vote (ψηφίσματι), they put to death fifteen hundred citizens without a trial, and they forced more than five thousand to flee to Piraeus" (7.67, cf. 20.11 and Aes. *orat.* 3.235). Lysias is precisely consistent in the three passages in which he refers to the Thirty's accession. Speaking against Eratosthenes, a former member of the Thirty implicated in Polemarchus' execution, Lysias says in ±399, "the Thirty, by the evil arts of slander-mongers, were established (κατέστησαν) in the government" (Lys. 12.5, tr. Lamb; Todd's translation [2000: 117] of the second aorist active indicative as "established themselves" is unwarranted). In a speech delivered in the same year but written for a client accusing an informer, the Spartan card is played: "it was just when those persons had been arrested and imprisoned that Lysander sailed into your harbours, that your ships were surrendered to the Lacedaemonians, that the walls were demolished, that the Thirty were established (κατέστησαν), and that every conceivable misery befell the city" (13.34, tr. Lamb). Finally, ≥401/0, Lysias writes for a client undergoing judicial scrutiny, "Neither, again, will anyone prove that, when the Thirty were established (κατέστησαν), I sat on the Council or held any office" (25.14, tr. Lamb). Similarly, Plato (*Ltr.* 7.324c–d) says, "A new government was set up (κατέστησαν)." Plato, however, refers to the episode as a change or revolution (repeating μεταβολή for emphasis), implying an internal cause; but this contrasts with the mildness of *Ap.* 32c: "When the oligarchy was established (ἐγένετο), the Thirty . . . ," where ἐγένετο has the force of *happened* or *occurred*. Xenophon specifies that "the Thirty had been chosen (ᾑρέθησαν) as soon as the long walls and the walls round Piraeus were demolished; although chosen (αἱρεθέντες), however, for the purpose of framing a constitution under which to conduct the government, they continually delayed framing and publishing this constitution . . ." (*Hell.* 2.3.11).

It is not until pseudo-Aristotle's *Athenian Polity*, written in the 330s–20s in the school of Aristotle in Athens (Rhodes 1993: 61), that the charge appears that the Spartan Lysander "set up (καταστῆσαι) the Thirty" (the first aorist connotes appointment) in the following way:

> The peace having been concluded on terms of their carrying on the government according to the ancestral constitution, the popular party endeavoured to preserve the democracy, but the notables who belonged to the Comradeships [*hetairoi*] and those exiles who had returned after the peace were eager for oligarchy, while those notables who were not members of any Comradeship but who were inferior in reputation to none of the citizens were aiming at the ancestral constitution; members of this party were Archi-

nus, Anytus, Cleitophon and Phormisius, while its chief leader was Thera-menes. And when Lysander sided with the oligarchical party, the people were cowed and were forced to vote for the oligarchy. (34.2–3)

Ostwald (1986: 478 and n72) is right to point out that such contemporaneous evidence as we have provides no basis whatever for assuming what is claimed here, namely that an *oligarchical* form of government was approved at the time the Thirty were charged to investigate the ancestral constitution; not even the ardent democrat Lysias mentions oligarchy in connection with their accession though he blames Theramenes and implicates Lysander in a *fait accompli* before the Assembly (12.71–75). The *oligarchy* of the Thirty seems to have grown out of the policies and practices of the group soon after they undertook to restore the ancestral constitution. For a chronology of Athens under the Thirty, based on Xenophon and Diodorus (with Rhodes 1993: 415–39) see Appendix IV.

Löper hypothesized in 1896 that the answer to the question, Why *thirty?* is that one citizen was provided by each *trittys* of the ten tribes (thirty *trittyes* in all). Since the demes or at least the tribes of some of the members of the Thirty were known, proof of the hypothesis lay in mapping men to available slots without overlap, assuming that Xenophon's ordering of the names (*Hell.* 2.3.2–3)—even if that passage is an interpolation—was dictated by the order in which the tribes were traditionally pronounced in festivals and inscribed on monuments (see App. III). Despite some progress in identifying the demes of the thirty individuals, there is still inadequate information to settle the case. See Dinsmoor (1931), White-head (1980), Walbank (1982), and Krentz (1982: esp. 51), who includes a useful chart of the original hypothesis and how it has been augmented. An alternative explanation for, Why *thirty?* suggested originally by Whitehead (1982–3), and much discussed since, is the number's similarity to the Spartan *gerousia,* which comprised twenty-eight members, plus the two Spartan kings. Lewis (*CAH* 6²: 26) downplays the role of the two Spartan kings, noting that power—as opposed to prestige—rested with the *gerousia* and the five *ephors* elected annually, thirty-three persons in all. Another possibility is Ostwald's (1986: 478) observation that Xenophon, taken together with D. S. and Lysias, "suggests that the original model for the Thirty was the board of *syngrapheis* [commissioners] Pythodorus' motion commissioned in 411" though the Thirty were expected to be more than a drafting committee; they were actually to *govern* Athens as well, at least until a new constitution (or a new interpretation of the ancestral constitution, the *patrios po-liteia*) could be formulated. Yet another precedent for the number thirty, from even further back in Athenian history, is the fragmentary first part of [Aristot.] *Ath. Pol.* fr. 3 (= fr. 5 Rhodes) describing clans as consisting of thirty men, with thirty clans for each of the twelve brotherhoods (phratries) before Cleisthenes' reforms of 510.

For the period immediately following the overthrow of the Thirty, see Ex-cursus 4.

Crito of Alopece
[*PA/APF* 8823, 8824 *LGPN2* 18, 19 *PAA*
585850, 585855 *DPhA* 220 *RE* 3 *OCD*[3] *PP PX*
Κρίτων Ἀλωπεκῆθεν]
±469–>399
wife: daughter of ?Archestratus
father of Critobulus, Archestratus
friend of Socrates
See stemma: Crito.

Pl. *Euthd.*   speaker
Pl. *Crito*   speaker
Pl. *Ap.* 33d, 38b   present
Pl. *Phd.*   speaker
Xen. *Symp.* 4.24
Xen. *Mem.* 1.2.48,
    2.9.1–8
IG II[2] 1611.400,
    1622.250 (naval
    inventory), pat.
Aes. *Tel.* no. 84 (frr.
    41, 44 Dittmar),
    pat.

Life. *APF* uses *Apology* 33e, Crito's being a contemporary of Socrates, very broadly, making the two men exact contemporaries for purposes of arithmetic without going so far as to claim that they were in fact born in exactly the same

STEMMA: CRITO

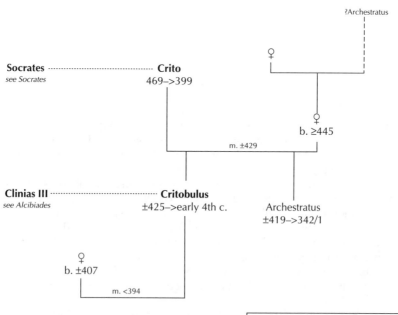

dialogues' characters in **boldface**
legal marriage and birth ———
other relationships ·················
hypothetical or dubious links -----

year; I have adopted the same approach. The dialogues do not describe Crito, as they do so many other characters, as reared in wealth by a powerful or famous family. We never learn his father's name. Crito's considerable affluence was derived from agriculture (Pl. *Euthd.* 291e, Xen. *Mem.* 2.9.4; D. L. 2.31), probably in Alopece rather than in a distant part of Attica, for Crito's wealth appears not to have been diminished significantly during the long war. Alopece was close to the walled city, affording his crops and herds some protection from Lacedaemonian raids (see Critobulus s.v. for details of the family's assets). One gains the impression that Crito made his own way financially to a great extent and, assisted by the luck of having his lands close to the city, was able to build an estate that would make his sons among the richest men in Athens. His farming and herding were likely to have been well established, his prospects clear to any prospective father-in-law, before he turned to the task of locating a woman of good lineage to marry, as he says he found (*Euthd.* 306d). Crito would have married at the proper age for marriage, according to the Athenian conventions of his time; he married after he had turned thirty, and probably when he was closer to forty. His first, or oldest surviving, son, Critobulus, was born in about 425, his second son, Archestratus, about 419 (*Euthd.* 272d, 306d–e). My calculations are at odds with those of *PA/APF*, followed by *LGPN2* and *PAA*—all of which posit a Crito II, of whom nothing is known, as the second son of Crito and *father* of Archestratus. See Critobulus s.v. for my reasoning on that matter. It is more than merely possible that an Archestratus was the father of Crito's wife. There are several known men of that name (or several references to one or two individuals of that name) who are of the right age and status, but having only Crito's statement that he chose a woman of good birth to marry (*Euthd.* 306d), it would be pure speculation to name one as maternal grandfather for Crito's children.

Although Xenophon reports that Crito put Critobulus in Socrates' hands (Xen. *Symp.*), Plato's *Euthydemus*, where Critobulus is described as having reached an age to require a teacher, creates no such appearance. Xenophon, as so often preoccupied with costs and value, also offers a homily in which Crito complains of having to pay to avoid frivolous lawsuits at the hands of false accusers; Socrates effects a solution by introducing Crito to a poor but honest good speaker, Archedemus, who becomes Crito's watchdog: he collects information, then brings a countersuit on Crito's behalf against one of the extortionists who eventually settles out of court. Archedemus is so good at his task that he soon becomes a friend to Crito and to Crito's friends. Xenophon counts Crito among Socrates' inner circle (Xen. *Mem.* 1.2.48), as one would expect from the roles he plays in Plato's dialogues, not only offering funds for Socrates' fine (*Ap.*), but acting as spokesman for the Greeks who arrived from outside Attica after Socrates' trial, in an effort to persuade Socrates to escape from prison (*Crito*). Crito's undertaking to dispose of Socrates' corpse and to perform the sacrifice of a cock to Asclepius (*Phd.* 118a) required no large expenditures and indicate, rather, duties a fellow demesman and friend could be expected to fulfill. Both burial and cremation were customary at the time, and Athenians did not then make a display of funerals and monuments.

In the later tradition.   See Phaedo s.v. for the story that Crito bought Phaedo out of slavery at Socrates' request. Diogenes (2.121) lists titles for seventeen lost dialogues by Crito, of which nothing remains. It is highly unlikely any ever existed: it would be difficult to make the case that Socrates' contemporary, Crito, was producing works in the genre of Socratic *logoi*, a genre that appears to have developed after, or not very long before, Socrates' death, perhaps with Antisthenes, oldest of the known authors. (Cf. Suda; Ael. *VA* 1.16.11, 2.6.11, and fr. 3.2; Cic. *De nat.* 1.54.123; [Socr.] *Ep.* 7, 14; Ath. 220a, et al. in *SSR* 2.VIB.)

Prosopographical notes. LGPN2 gives the year 400 as its date of death for Crito, but that cannot be right; it is incompatible with his role in Socrates' trial and death. Crito appears from Plato to have outlived Socrates, though one cannot say by how long. In contrast to the two sons listed for Crito in *Euthydemus* 306d, four are named by Diogenes (2.121) and reported by *PA*, but rightly rejected in *APF* as reflecting only a misreading of *Phaedo* 59b (Wellmann 1887: 56; Natorp 1913: 865): Hermogenes, Epigenes and Ctesippus (see *DPhA* 217, 220). Archestratus is "son of Crito" in two inscriptions, which would have generated an entry for Crito in the historical record, even if there had never been a Socrates. As it happens, Crito has been divided in two: so long as scholars thought Crito had a son named Crito (II), whose son was Archestratus, a second number was required. The nonexistent Crito II is *PA/APF* 8824, *LGPN2* 19, and *PAA* 585855, in all of which Crito II appears only as the pat. of Archestratus, and all of which should fall away.

Critobulus of Alopece, son of Crito
[*PA/APF* 8802 (8823) *LGPN2* 4, 11 (*APF*
8802 = 8801) *PAA* 585450 ?= *PAA* 585440
DPhA 217 *PP PX* Κριτόβουλος Κρίτωνος
Ἀλωπεκῆθεν]
±425–>early 4th c.
mother: daughter of ?Archestratus
brother: Archestratus
wife: a very young girl
lover of ?Clinias III, ?Alcibiades IV
See stemma: Crito.

Pl. *Ap.* 33e, 38b   present
Pl. *Phd.* 59b   present
Pl. *Euthd.* *
IG II^2 3036.2
Aes. *Tel.* no. 84 (frr.
      41, 44 Dittmar)
Xen. *Mem.* 1.3.8–13,
      2.6
Xen. *Oec.*
Xen. *Symp.*

Life. Critobulus had a well-born mother (*Euthd.* 306d); see Crito s.v. for the possibility that Critobulus' maternal grandfather was an Archestratus.

Usually wisely cautious in inferring anything from the dates provided in Xenophon's Socratica, *APF*, apparently following through on unstated implications of *PA* 2418, makes two mistakes toward the calculation of Critobulus' date of birth: that Critobulus married young, and that he had recently married in 422. The two errors, when combined with the widely accepted date of 469 for the birth of Crito, have had far-reaching consequences for a number of characters in the dialogues and beyond them (see prosopographical notes below); they have also resulted in the creation of an individual, "Crito II, son of Crito I" who did not exist, despite the full set of numbers assigned to him in other prosopographies (see Crito s.v.).

If the premise that Critobulus married young is abandoned, as I argue below it must be, a more natural set of dates and relationships emerges, based initially on Plato's *Euthydemus*. Socrates jokes that Crito's sons could be used as bait for the two sophists of the dialogue (272d). Since Socrates mentions no sons of his own to offer as bait, it might be surmised that his sons would be unattractive because their father would have no money to pay sophists. Perhaps. But we know that Socrates was quite late to begin his fathering career, so his sons were probably too young to serve as bait. Crito mentions that his own younger son is still quite young and small while Critobulus is old enough to require a teacher (306d–e; cf. Xen. *Symp.* 4.24 where Socrates claims to be Critobulus' teacher). So Socrates' own oldest son was most likely younger than Crito's younger son. In 399, Socrates had a son almost of age (*meirakion*), thus born ≥416. Following out the hypothesis, Crito's second son was born even earlier, say 419, in which case he is about eleven at the time the *Euthydemus* is set (dramatic date ≥407: see App. I). Critobulus, though slightly older than the *meirakion* Clinias III s.v., *looks* less mature (*Euthd.* 271b; cf. Xen. *Symp.* 4.23–24). If Critobulus' birth is put at about 425, he could be approaching eighteen at the time of the *Euthydemus*.

Critobulus can be placed within the inner circle of Socrates' associates not only because of his presence at both the trial and death of Socrates, but because he was one of those who offered money for Socrates' fine (33a), and because he appears in both Xenophon and Aeschines as well. If Athenaeus (220a, source for Aes. no. 84) is reporting accurately, Aeschines scorned Critobulus as without learning and uncultured. Critobulus apparently followed in Crito's footsteps as a farmer and herder. Xenophon—who knew something about Critobulus' finances—speaks of Critobulus approvingly, setting his net worth at one hundred times that of Socrates, over 8 *tal.* 2,000 *dr.* (while everything Socrates owned, including his house, Xenophon valued at five *minae* (*Oec.* 2.3). The one inscription that can be securely attached to Critobulus is a record as producer, *chorēgos*, for his tribe Antiochis in the men's dithyramb at the Dionysia (*IG*: Κριτοβου[λος]), dated to the early 4th c.

Evidence for Critobulus' death has previously been inferred from a naval equipment obligation performed by Archestratus s.v., before 366, on the assumption that Archestratus would by then have inherited wealth from a childless uncle Critobulus and from "Crito II." But the assumption is unwarranted. The Athenians did not practice primogeniture; it was common in the case of two surviving sons for one to divide the estate and the other to choose one of the two portions (MacDowell 1978: 93), so Archestratus may be assumed to have been roughly as wealthy as Critobulus, who may but need not have died before 366. We have no evidence about when he died or whether he had offspring.

In Xenophon.   Xenophon's *Symposium* seems to owe much to Plato's *Euthydemus* and *Symposium*, but Xenophon takes the physical descriptions of the near age-mates, Critobulus and Clinias III (271b), and develops them in a different direction, though his dialogue is set some fourteen years earlier. The just-married Critobulus is depicted as the lover of Clinias III (Xen. *Symp.* 4.12–28), so smitten that he keeps talking about his beloved despite Socrates' efforts to quiet him. Socrates offers a caution against kissing, the slippery slope to sex, in reaction to Critobulus' profession of his love (Xen. *Symp.* 4.25–26). Breaking in on the conversation between Socrates and Critobulus, Charmides accuses Socrates of being attracted to

Critobulus, recalling seeing the two of them, heads together over a scroll, with Socrates pressing against Critobulus' bare shoulder. Socrates retorts that the result was his own shoulder's hurting for days as if bitten by a wild beast, and his heart feeling stung (4.27–28). Pursuing the same general theme in the *Memorabilia*, Xenophon describes how Socrates, hearing that Critobulus has kissed the attractive Alcibiades IV, son of the famous general of that name, uses the occasion to advise Xenophon and Critobulus against the dangers of sex (*Mem.* 1.3.8–9; cf. *APF* 600.6B where not Alcibiades IV but Clinias III is taken as the referent for "Alcibiades' son"). The entire scene may be Xenophon's own invention, but the relative ages of the young men—Critobulus about eight years older than Alcibiades IV, by my reckoning—are about right for a plausible liaison.

Prosopographical notes and the later tradition.   Critobulus' youth at the time of his marriage cannot be established from the two pieces of evidence *APF* adduces, both from Xenophon. Xenophon says that Critobulus' *bride* was young (*Oec.* 3.12–13)—probably not yet in her thirteenth year (Garland 1990: 211)—which tells us nothing of Critobulus' age. If his age was unremarkable, he was thirty or older when he married. Xenophon also describes Critobulus as a newlywed in August of 422 when his *Symposium* is set (2.3). As *APF* often has reason to say (e.g. 600.6B), Xenophon had a faulty memory. I agree. It seems to show itself in this case when he depicts both Niceratus II s.v. and Critobulus as recent grooms at *Symposium* 2.3, only Niceratus II as a newlywed at 4.8, and Critobulus as a youth in love with Clinias III at 4.12–24. Xenophon similarly treats Autolycus s.v. anachronistically in the dialogue. To put the best face on it, one might appeal to Momigliano's approval in *The Development of Greek Biography* of Xenophon's creative mixture of fact and imagination—in contrast to Plato. Huss's 493-page commentary on the 50-page *Symposium* makes a virtue of the inconsistencies (1999b), for they reflect Xenophon's sense of humor. Thus a "passage is 'inconsistent' only insofar as the jokes made in it do not need 'consistency'. Xenophon is laughing here. He is not making mistakes or confusing historical facts and the reasoning of his own literary characters" (1999a: 388). For prosopographical purposes, however, it should be recalled that Xenophon's *Symposium* collects an assortment of persons who cannot be fitted together coherently at that date under any construction of their lives yet proposed, so it would be most unwise, not to mention inconsistent with Plato's *Euthydemus* and *Apology*, to take Xenophon literally just this once about just this one individual, Critobulus. Yet the unsupported datum of Critobulus' youth at the time of his marriage is immediately used as a premise for a second error: since Critobulus' "early" marriage implies a date of birth, say, twenty-five years earlier than 422, i.e., 447/6, Crito (b. ±469) in turn must also have married young, at twenty-two or twenty-three, and produced offspring immediately, for Critobulus could not otherwise reach adulthood in the required time.

These two errors are then compounded: *APF*'s calculations make it possible for Critobulus to be "the contemporary and lover" of Clinias III of Scambonidae s.v. (Xen. *Symp.* 4.12–28; but cf. *Euthd.* 271b) by assigning Clinias III a date of birth compatible with the *incorrect* one already calculated for Critobulus (by the same stroke fixing Axiochus' birth in the family of Alcibiades incorrectly at ±480), a generation too early. Potentially affected by the arithmetic are dates of birth for

Archestratus of Alopece, Ctesippus of Paeania, Hippothales of Athens, Lysis II of Aexone, Menexenus of Athens, and all their immediate kin, as well as Critobulus and Clinias III; and dramatic dates for the dialogues *Lysis*, *Menexenus*, and *Euthydemus*; the pseudo-Platonic *Axiochus*; and—though it hardly matters—Xenophon's *Symposium* and *Oeconomicus*. What is more, the secondary literature since 1971 (*APF*) has spread the virus. Typical is, "That Axiochus should have married in his early twenties is nothing unusual. For example, both his son's lover Kritoboulos of Alopeke and Kritoboulos' father Kriton clearly married before the age of 25" (Bicknell 1982: 242, citing not Xen. but *APF*). In fact, we have *no* example of such short generations in the 5th c.—which is exactly why Crito and Critobulus *via* *APF* are almost invariably cited in discussions of the generations. Finally, since Critobulus had a brother (*Euthd.* 272d), and since a wealthy Archestratus of Alopece s.v., son of Crito, is known to have lived until at least 342/1, *PA, APF* and *LGPN2* all posit that Crito's second son was an otherwise unknown Crito II and that Archestratus was *his* son, i.e. Crito I's grandson.

When *APF* (8823) comments broadly, "The marked contrast between the short generations of *c.* 25 years, perceptible here and in Alcibiades' family, and the long generations of *c.* 40 years perceptible in Leagros' family, well demonstrates the variations which were possible within the same city and period in the same social class," two things should be noted. Whereas there are ample cases of very long generations, we are left with no clear examples of short ones in the 5th c. (remembering that our records cover the propertied classes almost exclusively). The Alcibiades family has not yet been plotted satisfactorily, though the balance of evidence is against short generations there too (see examples at Axiochus s.v., affected by the dates assigned to Critobulus). Also, while the actual generations of *males* were rather more than thirty years, the generations of females were barely half that (Garland 1990: 211); and the high incidence of marriages between uncles and nieces means that the widespread use of male generations to describe populations is particularly misleading in the case of Athenians.

PAA 585440 (*PA/APF* 8801, *LGPN2* 11) is assigned only the inscription (*IG*). Because of the practice in classical studies of using quotations, and sometimes reports, as "fragments" from the person quoted, Xenophon's *Oeconomicus* 3.14 = Aeschines' *Aspasia* no. 71 (fr. 32 Dittmar; cf. Xen. *Mem.* 2.6.36 = Aes. *Asp.* no. 72 [fr. 33 Dittmar] et al.). See also Diogenes (2.121), Athenaeus 220a, pseudo-Socrates (*Ep.* 4), et al. in *SSR* 2.VIB.

Croesus of Lydia, son of Alyattes (king) See App. II.

Ctesippus of Paeania	Pl. *Ly.*	speaker
[*PA* 8890 *LGPN2* 11 *PAA* 587515	Pl. *Euthd.*	speaker
DPhA 227 *PP* Κτήσιππος Παιανιεύς]	Pl. *Phd.* 59b	present
b. ±425		
cousin of Menexenus		
lover of Clinias III		

Life. We know very little about Ctesippus, not even his patronymic, though the dialogues reveal some interesting relationships. See Menexenus s.v. for what may be descendants or a collateral branch of the family.

Plato represents Ctesippus as present at the death of Socrates, so we may infer that he was a part of Socrates' inner circle, someone Plato is likely to have known. The dramatic dates of the *Lysis* and *Euthydemus* (see App. I), together with the relationships that are described there, enable an approximate date of birth to be set. This is more important than it may at first seem: Ctesippus links two sets of characters within the dialogues; he is the only one of the playful group in the *Lysis* who is also one of the participants in the *Euthydemus*. The ages of the characters are drawn carefully in both. In the *Euthydemus*, Ctesippus is the lover of Clinias III who is about the same age (see Dover's discussion 1989: 86–7, and Clinias III s.v.), and Clinias III is only slightly younger than Crito's son, Critobulus s.v. (271b); therefore Ctesippus is about the same age as Critobulus. Diogenes is simply confused when he says that Ctesippus is a son of Crito and brother of Critobulus (2.121).

In *Lysis*, the occasion of the festival of Hermes allowed boys of various ages to be grouped together. Ctesippus teases his near agemate, Hippothales, for having an erotic obsession with the younger boy Lysis II s.v.; Ctesippus shows playful familiarity with Socrates (204c–205d), who joins in teasing Hippothales. Ctesippus is himself acquainted with Lysis II because Menexenus, Ctesippus' cousin, is Lysis II's best friend (206d). (At PCW 690, 'nephew' should be 'cousin,' ἀνεψιός.) This explanation makes it appear that both Menexenus and Lysis II are younger boys than Ctesippus and Hippothales.

In the *Euthydemus*, Ctesippus, older now (*neaniskos*, 273a) and youthfully arrogant, is himself fixated on Clinias III (his beloved, *paidika*, 274c), though he is not demonstrative toward his beloved and not nearly so boyishly playful toward Socrates. He does, however, go to Clinias III's aid when the sophists appear to be getting the better of his beloved (283e). Then Ctesippus does a good job of picking up the sophists' technique, winning Socrates' praise (303e). Since the *Lysis* is narrated and the *Euthydemus* dramatic, one cannot make too much of the fuller introduction of Ctesippus that Socrates gives to Crito in the *Euthydemus*.

Prosopographical notes. Because there is no independent evidence of Ctesippus outside Plato, or at least none that certainly refers to *this* Ctesippus, he has not figured much in prosopographical arguments. Yet the literature includes attempts to make Critobulus s.v. some twenty years older, and then to make Clinias III similarly older, and then Clinias III's father, Axiochus, older etc., without noting the implications for Ctesippus. A hypothesis of this study is that there is something important to be gained from taking Plato's representations of Athenians seriously, at least in the first instance. Empirically, there proves to be more consistency and coherence to the genuine Platonic dialogues than has previously been suspected.

Cydias of Hermione (poet) See App. II.

Cypselus of Corinth, son of Aetion (tyrant) See App. II.

Cyrebus of Athens (baker) See App. II.

Cyrus I of Persia, son of Cambyses I (king) See App. II.

Cyrus II of Persia, son of Darius II See App. II.

Damnippus of Athens See App. II.

Damon of Oe, son of Damonides
[*PA*/*APF* 3143, 3133 (8688.13) *LGPN2* 16, 1
PAA 301540, 301415, 301418 *DPhA* 13 *RE* 17
*OCD*³ *PP* Δάμων Δαμωνίδου Οἰῆθεν]
≤485–≤414
wife: Agariste III
student of Prodicus
student of Agathocles
teacher of Nicias I
associate/advisor of Pericles I
musical theorist and thinker

Pl. *Lch.*, *passim* *
Pl. *R.* 400b–c, 424c *
[Pl.] *Alc.* 118c &
  schol. *
[Pl.] *Ax.* 364b   speaker
frr. in DK 37
inscriptions (see
  below)
Aristoph. *Clouds*
  649–651
Pl. *com.* fr. 207 (K
  191)
Andoc. 1.16
Isocr. 15.235
[Aristot.] *Ath. Pol.*
  27.4

Life.   That Damon was born ≤485 is inferred from his influential association with both Pericles I ([Pl.] *Alc.*; [Aristot.] corr. Rhodes 1993: 341) and Nicias I (*Lch.* 200a–b), and from his having been heavily influenced by the younger Prodicus (*Lch.* 197d), and taught music by Agathocles (*Lch.* 180d). Both Socrates and Nicias I praise Damon highly and recommend him as a music teacher because he is also accomplished in other important pursuits (*Lch.* 180c–d, 200b; cf. Isocr.). Alcibiades III also commends Damon and emphasizes Pericles I's dependence on him for advice, but the scholiast of pseudo-Plato's *Alcibiades* is probably confused to insert Lamprocles as the pupil of Agathocles and teacher of Damon. Damon was married to Agariste III s.v., an Alcmaeonid woman of uncertain relation to Pericles I (whose mother was Agariste II); their marriage ended, presumably with Damon's death, sometime after she accused four men associated with the Socratic circle of profaning the Eleusinian mysteries (see Exc. 1), and before 400, by which time she was married to Alcmonides, an Alcmaeonid like herself (Andoc.).

APF faults Raubitschek (1955: 78) for depending on "dramatic dates of the chronologically unreliable Plato" in supposing Damon "still active in the 420s and even later." But to suppose Damon *not* alive and active in his sixties, particularly with his reputation for wisdom, would require the greater stretch of the imagination in this case.

Career. Damon is best known as a music theorist and teacher: both Plato (*R.*) and Aristophanes play around with his views on meter and mode (see Wilamowitz 1921: 59). But Damon appears to have been a private political advisor as well. Not only do pseudo-Plato (*Alc.*) and pseudo-Aristotle testify to that effect, followed by Plutarch, there is contemporaneous evidence in the form of four pottery *ostraka* that the Athenians found Damon's influence too dangerous and ostracized him (*IG* I 912.1; *Kera.* 10, p. 210 100.1; *AM* 106, p. 150.1). The date usually given for the ostracism is 428.

In the later tradition. Damon figures prominently in the later tradition, especially in Plutarch (*Nic.* 6.1, *Arist.* 1.7, and *Per.* 4.1–2, 9.2). It is Plutarch's *Pericles* 4.2 that preserves the comic poet Plato's line, said to have been addressed to Damon, "In the first place tell me then, I beseech thee, thou who art / The Cheiron, as they say, who to Pericles gave his craft." *De Musica* 2 of Aristides Quintilianus (3rd c. C.E.) may be derived from Damon. (Cf. D. L. 2.19 and later testimonia in DK.)

Prosopographical notes and modern bibliography. Two questions have dominated discussions of Damon: Was Pericles I's associate the man who was ostracized? Was Pericles I's associate married to Agariste III? The first has reached a consensus at yes; the second is still open in the literature, though not much discussed. I find no reason to doubt it, and much circumstantial evidence for it.

Damon's deme is incorrectly listed as Oa in *LGPN2* and also at Rhodes (1993: 341), presumably following *PA*; but Dow (1963: 180–1) has shown definitively not only *that* Damon's deme was Oe, but *how* ancient spelling variants of the demotic on inscriptions led to an error in Plutarch (*Per.* 9.2), repeated by Stephen of Byzantium (s.v. *Oa*), and able to be corrected only with the late discovery of the pseudo-Aristotelian *Athenian Constitution*; Dow also shows how Latinization of the Greek obscured the distinction between Oe and Oa for those writing in English (e.g. *CAH* 5, which had five references to Damon, coined the muddled 'Oea' and "solved" the problem in *CAH* 5², removing all reference to Damon). On the demotic, see also Whitehead (1986: 73n30). For Damon, see Raubitschek (1955).

PA 3133 = *LGPN2* 1 = *PAA* 301418 (Andoc. 1.16 only) although *APF* adds that *PA* 3133 = *PA* 3143. *PA* 3143 (references to Pl., Plu. etc.) = *LGPN2* 16 = *PAA* 301540 (ΔΑΜΩΝ) = *PAA* 301415 (var. ΔΑΜΟΝ) ?= *PAA* 301418. *LGPN2*: 16 ?= 1.

Damonides of Oe See App. II.

Darius I of Persia, son of Hystaspes (king) See App. II.

Darius II of Persia, son of Artaxerxes I (king) See App. II.

Datis of Media (commander) See App. II.

Demeas of Collytus (tailor) See App. II.

Demetrius of Athens See App. II.

Demetrius of Amphipolis See App. II.

Democrates I of Aexone, son of Lysis I
[*PA/APF* 3519 (9574), *PA* 3512 *LGPN2* 24,
LGPN2 1 *PAA* 316590, 316595, 316410 *PP*
Δημοκράτης Λύσιδος Αἰξωνεύς]
b. ±460
father of Lysis II and another son
lover of Alcibiades III
See stemma: Lysis.

Pl. *Ly.* 204e, 205c,
    208, pat.
SEG 34.199
    (sepulchral
    sculpture)
Antiph. fr. 30

Life. The determination of Democrates I's approximate date of birth, set between Lysis I and II, is affected by the appearance in Athens for the first time in the 460s of names that reflect the political attitudes of the era; this is the first known bearer of the name. For the fame and wealth of his family, see Lysis I s.v. Democrates I was a lover (*erastēs*) of Alcibiades III, and it was he to whom Alcibiades III ran away from home after becoming Pericles I's ward (Antiph., preserved in Plu. *Alc.* 3). Democrates I's name is on the gravestone of his elder son, Lysis II (*SEG*, pat.).

Prosopographical notes. Although *PA* separately numbers the Democrates in Plato (3519) and the Democrates in Antiphon (3512), *APF* and *LGPN2* have noted that the two entries are possibly the same. *PAA* has made a third division: *PAA* 316410 is the Democrates of Antiphon with cross-references in the database and with Democrates' status as an Athenian questioned; *PAA* 316590 (Pl.) ?= *PAA* 316595 (*SEG*).

Demodocus of Anagyrus
[*PA* 3464 *LGPN2* 3 *PAA* 315130 *DPhA* 72 *RE*
9 *PP* Δημόδοκος Ἀναγράσιος]
<469–>399
father of Theages, Paralius
honored general and office holder

Pl. *Ap.* 33e *
[Pl.] *Dem.*   speaker
[Pl.] *Thg.* 127d–e speaker
IG I³ 1048.24
Thu. 4.75.1
Ael. *VH* 8.1

Life and career. Demodocus' date of birth (older than Socrates at *Thg.* 127d) fits well with the Demodocus who appears in Thucydides (4.75.1) as a general and tribute collector serving with Aristides in 425/4. An unidentified catalogue inscription found in Eleusis and dated to the end of the 5th c. (*IG*) may also be attributed to Demodocus.

Prosopographical notes. *PAA* 315130 (Pl. and Ael.) ?= 315132 (Thu.) ?= 315135 (*PA* 3465, *IG*).

Demophon of Cholarges, son of Hippocrates See App. II. *See stemma: Pericles.*

Demophon of Athens (Menexenus' father) See App. II.

Demos of Athens, son of Pyrilampes
[*PA/APF* 3573 (8792.8) *LGPN2* 1 *PAA* 317910
RE 3 *PP* Δῆμος Πυριλάμπους]
±440–≥390
mother: first wife of Pyrilampes
paternal stepsiblings: Plato, Adeimantus I,
 Glaucon IV, Potone; paternal half brother:
 Antiphon II
See stemmata: Plato, Phaedrus.

Pl. *Grg.* 481d, 513b *
Aristoph. *Wasps* 98
 & schol.
Eu. *Mar.* fr. 227 (K
 213)
Lys. 19.25–26
Antiph. 20
Ath. 9.397c–d

Life and career. Demos enjoys the distinction of being the first attested Athenian with the name that means "people"; his father flourished under the Athenian democracy as an ambassador to the King of Persia, and politically programmatic names had been in vogue since the 470s. The comic poets took notice of him: Aristophanes calls him beautiful, *kalos*, in 422, which helps to establish the year of his birth more or less; but Eupolis found him "stupid" a year later in 421. Because the dramatic date of the *Gorgias* stretches across the Peloponnesian war (see App. I), his being the beloved of Callicles there does not tell us much.

By 413, Demos had inherited his father's peacocks, descendants of an original breeding pair given to Pyrilampes s.v. on one of his embassies to the Persian court. They were such beautiful (εὐοφθάλμως) and expensive birds—a pair valued at a thousand *drachmae* (Ael. *NA* 5.21)—that visitors would arrive from Sparta and Thessaly to see them, and in hopes of obtaining some of their eggs. Apparently Demos continued the tradition his father had begun, more than thirty years previously, of admitting the public on the first day of each month to view the birds. It is Demos' peacocks that somehow feature in the three short fragments of a forensic speech of Antiphon. Demos was apparently the plaintiff in the case, and it has been conjectured that the defendant, Erasistratus II s.v., may have tried to steal the birds or their eggs.

Demos is named in a forensic speech of Lysias, and may have appeared as a witness for the defendant, the prominent but unnamed brother-in-law of an Aristophanes (not the comic poet but the second husband of Phaedrus' wife) who had been executed and whose confiscated estate had turned out to be of less value than had been anticipated. Aristophanes' relatives by marriage were suspected of having secreted away some of Aristophanes' wealth, so Lysias' speech was designed to show that—even while alive—Aristophanes, one of the newly wealthy, was in debt himself and had left no more than the state had already confiscated. To prove his point, the speaker told *inter alia* how Aristophanes had always been willing to lend money in a public crisis and would therefore have lent money to Demos if he had had it to lend. At the time, the late 390s, Cyprus, a pro-Athenian island, was repeatedly fighting with its Persian neighbors and sought aid. Demos was set to go to Cyprus as a *trierarch* and asked the speaker, whom he knew, to present a proposal on his behalf to Aristophanes. Demos had been given a gold cup by the Great King as a pledge. He proposed to leave the cup with Aristophanes in return for sixteen *minae*, an amount adequate to equip his warship and reach Cyprus. Once he had arrived, he promised, he would redeem the gold cup from Aristophanes for twenty *minae* because the cup itself "would enable him to obtain cash and many other benefits throughout the mainland" (19.25). It may be that Demos had made ambassadorial trips of his own to the Great King, but it may be that the cup was a part of his inheritance from Pyrilampes—like the peacocks.

Plato's stepbrother cannot be the Demos of Aristophanes' *Knights*, an *old* codger of a householder with slaves, and a personification of the *dēmos*, the people. *Knights* was produced in 424, two years before Demos was of an age to be called *kalos* in *Wasps*.

Demosthenes of Aphidna, son of Alcisthenes (general) See App. II.

Demosthenes of Paeania, son of Demosthenes (orator) See App. II.

Demostratus of Xyrete, son of Androsthenes See App. II.

Dinomache of Athens, daughter of Megacles IV of Alopece, wife of Clinias II of Scambonidae
[*PA* 3187 (cf. *APF* 600.6–7, 9688.6, 10) *LGPN2* 2 *PAA* 302530 Δεινομάχη Μεγακλέους Ἀλωπεκῆθεν θυγάτηρ, Κλεινίου Ἀλκιβιάδου Σκαμβωνίδου γυνή]
b. 470–465, † >432
mother: Coesyra
?sister: [unnamed] wife of Pericles I and Hipponicus II
brother: Megacles V
husband: Clinias II
mother of Alcibiades III and Clinias IV
See stemma: Alcibiades.

[Pl.] *Alc.* 105d, 123c–d *
Lys. 14.39
Isocr. 16.25
Andoc. 4.34
Plu. *Alc.* 1.1
Ath. 5.219c

Dinomache's father, Megacles IV, was a demesman of Alopece. Her marriage to Clinias II in 451 or 450 is the best indicator we have for her birth, which I have put at 470–465. She was widowed in 446, after the births of her two sons, and there is no record of her having married again. She may have moved with her sons into Pericles I's house when he became the guardian of Alcibiades III and Clinias IV. Dinomache is represented in pseudo-Plato's *Alcibiades* as still alive in 432, the dramatic date of the dialogue (see App. I), actively involved in Alcibiades III's life. See [unnamed] of Athens, wife of Pericles I, and Hipponicus II s.vv. for the controversies surrounding the relationship between Pericles I and Alcibiades III that sometimes involve the unsupportable claim that Dinomache married Pericles I after Clinias II's death and was later given to Hipponicus II. It may be that Dinomache had a *sister* who married Pericles I, then Hipponicus II; but Alcibiades III and Callias III are so close in age that no amount of rearranging can bring Plutarch (*Per.* 24) into conformity with the epigraphical and contemporaneous literary record.

Diocles of Athens See App. II.

Diocles of Phlius (philosopher) See App. II.

Dioclides of Athens See App. II.

Diodorus of Erchia, son of Xenophon See App. II.

Diodorus of ?Athens   Xen. *Mem.* 2.10.1–6
[*PA* 3915 *LGPN2* 6 *PAA* 329535 *PX*
Διόδωρος]

A wealthy friend of Socrates and later, at Socrates' suggestion, of Hermogenes s.v.

Diogiton See App. II.

Diognetus of Cydantidae, son of Niceratus I   Pl. *Grg.* 472a,
[*PA/APF* 3863 = 3850 = 3851 (10808) *LGPN2*   unnamed *
28, 5, 6 *PAA* 327820, 327535, 327540 *RE* 8   Lys. 18, *passim*
Διόγνητος Νικηράτου Κυδαντίδης]   Andoc. 1, *passim*
≥451–<395
paternal half brother Nicias I; brother
  Eucrates
father of Diomnestus
See stemma: Nicias.

Life.   Both brothers of Nicias I, Diognetus and Eucrates, are identified as *chorēgos* victors by the fact that their tripods, dedications to the god Dionysus, are lined up in the precinct of that god (*Grg.*)—which implies they are among Athens' most opulent citizens. Diognetus' choral victory was in dithyramb for the Aigeis tribe at the Dionysia festival (<415). On the relation of the two brothers to Nicias I, see Eucrates, s.v. The context in which they are introduced by Plato is a list of wealthy and prominent Athenians who would, if asked, testify that Polus is right and Socrates is wrong. But that is all we get from Plato. Most of the information we have about Diognetus comes from a speech by Lysias dated ≤395, after Diognetus' death. The speaker is Diognetus' orphaned nephew, the son of Eucrates, who has come of age but was a minor during the period of the Thirty; the aim of his speech is to prevent his property from being confiscated by the state, and he argues that that his ancestors were benefactors of the state.

Career.   Lysias mentions that Diognetus lived in exile for a time (18.9), and that fact is at the root of the controversy surrounding this individual. The speaker of Lysias 18 says that his uncle did not go to Decelea when exiled, eliding the circumstances that prompted the exile except for the vague remark that Diognetus had been slandered by sycophants. Thus it was long hypothesized that the exile resulted from Diognetus' membership in the oligarchy of the Four Hundred (Petersen 1880: 62; Gernet and Bizos 1955: II² 32n1). Decelea, a small deme in the far north of Attica in the foothills of the Parnes mountains, where the Spartans kept a garrison 413–04, was the seat of oligarchic activity in Attica, thus attracting a number of exiles, particularly after the fall of the Four Hundred in 411. Presumably, the most ardent oligarchs sought exile there. But a difficulty with the hypothesis is that there is no independent evidence for the claim that Diognetus was a member of the Four Hundred. While it is well-documented that the whole family was extremely wealthy from silver mining properties and the slaves to exploit them, and that the continuing war with Sparta was not only preventing owners from collecting the profits from such ventures, but increasingly jeopardizing the holdings themselves, it has been suggested that Diognetus' desire for the war to end entailed that the oligarchs be ensconced at the expense of the democracy. The evidence for oligarchic leanings in the family of Diognetus is circumstantial; and weighing heavily against it is Nicias I's military career under the democracy, and the deaths of both Niceratus II and Eucrates at the hands of the Thirty. If Diognetus had been a member of the Four Hundred, Lysias, seeking to present the entire family in the most democratic light possible, might have been expected to offer mitigation for the membership, if it were necessary to mention Diognetus at all under such embarrassing circumstances. But some have interpreted the evidence of Lysias 18.9–10 very differently indeed. Krentz (1982: 100) takes the view that Diognetus was something of a democratic hero, weakening the Spartan King Pausanias' will to establish an oligarchy in Athens by personally making him aware of the suffering caused by the Thirty. The apparent outcome of the case is that the defendants lost; neither they nor their issue, if any, appear in the inscriptions afterward (*APF*)—Krentz may be granting more than the democratic jury was willing to grant.

But if Diognetus was not a member of the Four Hundred, then the question why he was exiled still presses. As MacDowell rightly points out (1962: 75), the mention of Decelea does not require the precipitating event to occur after 413, when the garrison was established; Lysias refers to the entire period of Diognetus' exile, and we have only a hint of how long that lasted. Diognetus, like so many others, may have fled into exile to avoid execution following the events of 415 (see Exc. 1), i.e. this may be the Diognetus accused by the *metic* Teucrus of profaning the mysteries and fleeing to avoid prosecution (Andoc. 1.15).

Two data provide ready support. First, Diognetus' brother, Eucrates, was un-mistakably named by Dioclides in the mutilation of herms: from the evidence of identifiable persons, accusations tended to fall on clusters of closely related individuals, possibly because they tended to be in the same phratries and *hetaerai*. Second, as vague as "slandered by sycophants" may seem, it is far more appro-priate as a gloss to events surrounding the sacrilege than to membership in the Four Hundred: Thu. (6.53.1) blames the Athenians for using the testimony of the unworthy to arrest the worthy in connection with the sacrilege of 415. Another item important to mention is that while one might well suppose *a priori* that the *commissioner* Diognetus (Andoc. 1.14) cannot simultaneously be the *accused* Diognetus (Andoc. 1.15), it is almost impossible to read the text of Andocides IV and come away with any other conclusion. Recall that the board of commissioners on which Diognetus served was initially established by the Council to investigate only the mutilation of herms. This is compatible with the chronologies of both MacDowell (1962: 73, based primarily on Andoc.) and Dover (*HCT* 272, based primarily on Thu.); Maidment (1941: 349n) muddies the issue by failing to point out that the commission's responsibilities were later in the period *extended* to include investigation of charges of profanation of the mysteries, charges came to light only *after* the mutilation of the herms had been publicized and the Council had been called into special session to hear the three generals before the fleet sailed for Sicily. In 400, when Andocides IV delivers his speech, Diognetus *qua* commissioner is called as a witness at Andocides IV's request and verifies the names of ten citizens and three slaves who were charged with profaning the mysteries by the slave Andromachus (1.14); immediately (1.15), the facts surround-ing the *metic* Teucrus are presented, including his *accusation* of Diognetus for profaning the mysteries. To hammer in his point, Andocides IV reminds the jury that all the details are receiving confirmation; the Diognetus standing before them was intimately involved in both aspects of events.

Prosopographical notes and modern bibliography.   *PA* lists Diognetus as three separate individuals: the Diognetus of Plato and Lysias (*PA* 3863 = *PAA* 327820 = *LGPN2* 28), the commissioner of Andocides 1.14, (*PA* 3850 = *PAA* 327535 = *LGPN2* 5), and the accused of Andocides 1.15 (*PA* 3851 = *PAA* 327540 = *LGPN2* 6). *PA* 3863 is the primary listing here because both patronymic and demotic are secure in that passage. *APF* suggested very tentatively a fusion of the three entries, and a number of scholars have addressed the identity of Diognetus before and since *APF*. MacDowell, generally in favor of fusing the three *PA* entries into one individ-ual (1962: 74–5), suggests (1962: 72) another possible Diognetus for the Andocides passages: the secretary of *IG* I³ 104 (cf. Blass, I² 524n4); the date of the inscription (409/8) would make Diognetus among the first of the known exiles to return and—more importantly—to hold office so, though I doubt the inscription should be attributed to the son of Niceratus I, it may be a fourth item in the biography of our one man. Among others who argue for one individual Diognetus (Andoc. 1.14–15) are Plepelits (1970: 147–55) and Storey (1990: 26–7). Nevertheless, both *PAA* and *LGPN2* go back to the separate entries of *PA*, adding "possibly the same as" references among the three. In addition, *LGPN2* 5, the commissioner, ?= *LGPN2* 2, a Diognetus known only from Eupolis (*Dem.* fr. 99.114 [incl. K 108, 130]). *PAA* queries whether Niceratus I is Diognetus' father, and whether the accused Diognetus is Athenian. (It happens that the words "brother of Nicias" are misplaced in the ms., raising doubts.) *LGPN* and *PAA* are marvelous resources, but one almost never knows what arguments have been taken into account by their editors.

Diomnestus of Cydantidae, son of Diognetus See App. II. *See stemma: Nicias.*

Dion of Athens   Pl. *Mx.* 234b *
[*PA* 4490 *LGPN2* 8 *PAA* 369520 *PP* Δίων]
active at the end of the 5th c.
rhetorician

A contemporary of the better-known rhetorician, Archinus of Coele s.v., Dion was considered a plausible candidate for the Athenian Council to choose to deliver a public funeral oration in about 401/0, the dramatic date of the frame of the *Menexenus* (see App. II).

Dion of Syracuse, son of Hipparinus I   Pl. *Ltr.* 7, 8, *passim* †
[*LGPN3A* 64 *RE* 2 *DPhA* 167 *OCD*³ *PP* Δίων]   [Pl.] *Ltr.* 4 *   addressee
±405–354   [Pl.] *Ltr.* 10.358,
siblings: Megacles, Andromache (wife of   13.361d, 362e *
  Dionysius I)   [Pl.] *Epgr.* 3
wife: Arete   *IG* IV² 95.39–40
father of Hipparinus III   (honorary)
brother-in-law and son-in-law of Dionysius I   D. S. 16.5–16.31,
brother-in-law of Dionysius II   *passim*
close friend of Plato, Speusippus   Plu. *Dion*
See stemma: Dion.   Nep. *Dion*

Life. Plato met Dion on his first visit to Sicily in ±384/3 when Dion was about twenty and deeply impressed the forty-year-old philosopher (Pl. 7.324a, 327a, 334b); their friendship lasted thirty years. In a distinctly unsympathetic historical tradition, Dion appears solemn and formal, completely out of place in the raucous court of Dionysius I (Pl. 7.326b–d) where overindulgence was the order of the day, and summary execution and banishment common in the tyrant's court. The same characteristics are evident decades later when Dion negotiates, pardons, and tries to make peace on his return to Syracuse, having suffered the loss of his family and property at the hands of Dionysius II. It appears that the very qualities

STEMMA: DION

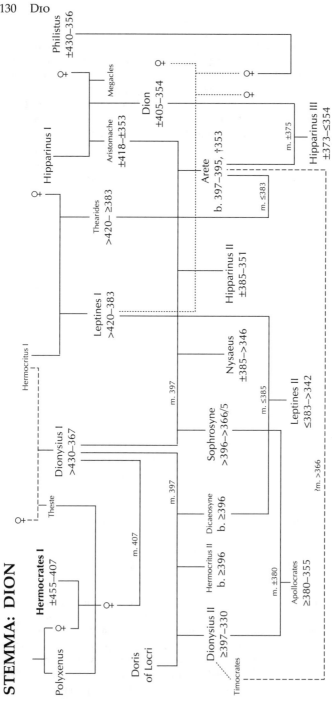

dialogues' characters in **boldface**
legal marriage and birth ——————
other relationships ·····················
hypothetical or dubious links ------

that made Dion attractive to Plato (and to Plutarch and Diogenes) made him an object of suspicion in the Sicily of his day. A few vices might have made him more popular with the citizens (Pl. 7.327b).

It was because of the requests of Dion that Plato was persuaded to return to Syracuse a second time (Pl. 7.327c–d), in 366, in hopes of furthering the education of the new tyrant, Dionysius II, and persuading him to effect reforms (Pl. 7.332c–333b). But Dion's and Plato's efforts were suspect from the start to various of Dionysius II's friends in court (D. S. 16.6.3–4), especially to Philistus s.v., who appears to have been recalled from exile to put a check on Plato's or Dion's influence on the new tyrant (Plu. 11.4). After three months, Philistus revealed to Dionysius II that Dion had been secretly negotiating peace terms with Sicily's enemy, Carthage (Plu. 14.5); and Dion was summarily deported to Italy (Pl. 7.329c). Diodorus reports rather that the tyrant intended the death penalty for Dion, but that Dion was forewarned and escaped with his brother, Megacles, and his friend, Heraclides, a leader of the Syracusan democratic faction, to Corinth (16.6.4–5). Dion was afterwards dispossessed of his wife, son, and a substantial amount of his property. Dion initially went to Athens and was the guest of Callippus s.v. whom he had met previously at a celebration of the Eleusinian mysteries (Pl. 7.333e). But Dion traveled widely in Greece and was welcome wherever he went. Although Athens was his base and provided the opportunity for study at the Academy and friendship with Speusippus, he went also to Corinth, and to Sparta where he was given citizenship. Again Diodorus provides an alternative—and apparently telescoped—version: Dion and Heraclides immediately began raising money to hire mercenaries and buy suits of armor (D. S. 16.6.5).

Plato returned to the court of Dionysius II in the spring of 361 in an attempt to effect a rapprochement between the tyrant and Dion (Pl. 7.338a–b, 339a, 340a). That failed along with Plato's efforts to influence Dionysius II to renounce or reform the tyranny, and Dionysius II made matters worse by stopping the flow of revenue from Dion's estates in Sicily into Greece (Pl. 7.345a). Several months later, when relations with Plato had deteriorated further, he confiscated all Dion's property (Pl. 7.347d–e). When Plato s.v. was finally able to escape from Syracuse (Pl. 7.350a–b), he disembarked at Olympia to apprise Dion (Pl. 7.350b) of the situation as he had left it. Dion and Heraclides were there making plans to liberate Syracuse by overthrowing the tyranny (they are named together as honorees by the sanctuary of Asclepius at Epidaurus, IG).

Hiring mercenaries and arranging for support from other exiles in secrecy took time, so Dion's return to Syracuse was delayed until 357 (Pl. 7.333b; cf. D. S. 16.9.1–3). Only twenty-five (Plu.) or thirty (D. S.) Sicilian exiles were eventually willing to join them in the liberation of Syracuse. While Heraclides remained behind to bring additional troops and triremes, Dion finally left, giving Speusippus his estate. The historian Timonides, a member of the Academy, went along and sent letters back to Speusippus; these historical fragments provide an additional source for the military action that took place. Two Athenians, Callippus s.v. and his brother, also accompanied Dion back to Sicily and helped to retake Syracuse (Pl. 7.333d–e). When Dion's contingent arrived, Dionysius II's army happened to be occupied elsewhere, so the army entered the city unopposed where it was joined by many citizens and cheered as the liberator of the Greeks of Sicily. Dion and his brother Megacles were elected *stratēgoi autokratores* (generals with all powers) and enjoyed the support of all Syracuse—except the tyrant's fort on Ortygia (an island *cum* peninsula off Syracuse, heavily fortified earlier by Dionysius I); but that is where Dion's wife and son were being held, Arete having been given to the tyrant's friend, Timocrates, in marriage. Dionysius II's return was followed by a series of deceptions and military skirmishes (the tyrant said he wished to abdicate, but sent his army to attack during the negotiations). Dion proved heroic in battle.

When Heraclides s.v. joined him at this point, bringing twenty additional triremes and 1,500 mercenaries, there was initial cooperation. The amity deteriorated, however, over Heraclides' official appointment as admiral, the tyrant's escape by sea on Heraclides' watch, and because Heraclides was a more popular leader with the people of the city than was Dion, causing strife among their respective followers. When, in the summer of 356, the assembly voted to redistribute all land and all property, and to stop paying the resident mercenaries, then elected a new board of generals that included Heraclides but not Dion, Dion left with the mercenaries for Leontini (D. S. 16.17.4–5), which welcomed and paid them (see Map 3). A surprise attack on an unprepared Syracuse by forces from the Italian mainland in Dionysius II's employ led to Dion's recall by the Sicilians (D. S. 16.20.1). In the aftermath, although many democratic leaders fled, Heraclides accepted some of the blame for the city's lack of preparedness for attack. He then proposed to the assembly that Dion be appointed *stratēgos autokrator*, and Dion proposed Heraclides as admiral. The attempt at reconciliation, however, soon broke down again over the questions of redistribution of land and property (Nep. 7.1–2), whether there should be a council as well as an assembly, and the advisability of Corinthian advisors.

Meanwhile, on Ortygia, where Dionysius II had left his son, Apollocrates, in command, rations were so low that the troops were mutinous, and an agreement was reached whereby Apollocrates was allowed to sail away to Italy with five vessels. Ortygia was open, and Dion was finally restored to his family after eleven years. Within months, however, Heraclides was assassinated by some of Dion's supporters, which led to Dion's being betrayed by Callipus and assassinated in the summer of 354 (Pl. 7.334d–e; D. S. 16.31.7; Plu. 54–57; cf. Nep. 8–10). Callippus declared himself tyrant.

In modern bibliography.   Historians frequently complain of an unwarranted Academic prejudice in favor of Dion over Dionysius II, and students of Plato will note the opposite bias in historians, though Westlake's account (*CAH* 6[2]: ch. 13) is a notable exception.

Dionysius I of Syracuse, son of Hermocritus I
[*LGPN3A* 284 *RE* 1 *OCD*[3] *PP* Διονύσιος]
>430–367 (r. 406–367)
sister: Theste; half siblings: Leptines I, Thearides

Pl. *Ltr.* 7, 8, *passim* †
[Pl.] *Ltr.* 2.313a,
   13.362b
Isocr. *Ltr.* 1
frr. in *TGrF*
Xen. *Hell.*, *passim*

wives: (1) daughter of Hermocrates I (co-2)
   Doris of Locri Epizephyrii; (co-2)
   Aristomache, daughter of Hipparinus I
offspring with Doris: Dionysius II,
   Hermocritus II, Dicaeosyne (wife of
   Leptines I); with Aristomache: Hipparinus
   II, Nysaeus, Sophrosyne (wife of Dionysius
   II), Arete (wife of Dion)
brother-in-law and son-in-law: Dion
See stemma: Dion.

Timae. frr. 29, 105,
   109
Philist. frr. 57–58, 60
D. S. 13, *passim*;
   15.6–7
Lys. 19.19–20
Nep. *Dion* 2.4–5
Plu. *Dion* 6.2
IG II² 103
   (naturalization)
IG II² 18.5 (praise
   decree)

Family. Although the sources give Dionysius I's father as Hermocrates (the name of his father-in-law), Lewis (*CAH* 6² 132n55) is surely right to suppose that it was Hermocritus, which is what he named one of his sons. An adopted father, Heloris, was banished in 402 and led other exiles in south Italy afterwards (D. S. 14, *passim*). Since Dionysius I reared his younger brothers and had them trained to his own specifications (see below), I think it is likely that his otherwise unknown father married twice, and that he was the child of the earlier marriage. His sister, Theste, married his first wife's uncle, which by itself tells us nothing about her own age. However, since we need not attribute Athenian girls' early marriages to the Greeks in Sicily; and since our only extant account of Theste (Plu. *Dion* 21.7–9) represents her in a face-to-face standoff with the tyrant in a way that the other women of the family are never seen, it is a little more likely that she had the same mother as the tyrant and was closer to his age than their half brothers were. We hear nothing of his training her or marrying her off in an alliance as he did with his younger brothers and his daughters.

Dionysius I's family seems not to have been wealthy and, indeed, he appears to have been an ordinary soldier in the private army of Hermocrates I s.v. before he rose to power, dependent in some ways on the wealth of his close friend, later the historian, Philistus. Dionysius I's first wife, killed in a mutiny incidental to that rise, was Hermocrates I's daughter. Perhaps he had married her upon the death of her father in 407. In any case, Dionysius I famously married two women on the same day in 397, with great feasting and fanfare, taking great care that no one should discover which marriage was consummated first: Doris, to effect an alliance with Locri Epizephyrii, and Aristomache, the daughter of Hipparinus I and sister of Dion. His sons with Doris (Dionysius II and Hermocritus II), were probably both born some years before those with Aristomache (Hipparinus II and Nysaeus).

Dionysius I gave two of his three daughters to his brothers, Leptines I and Thearides, and the third to his son, Dionysius II. Doris' only recorded daughter, Dicaeosyne, even if she was Doris' firstborn after the wedding of 397, could not have produced the four children variously attributed to her before her husband, Leptines I, died in 383. Leptines II s.v. is likely to have been their only son, and I have not included on the stemma the 'Alcetas' (who made no mark in the extant history of the period) or other children attributed to the couple. Another of

Dionysius I's daughters, Aristomache's daughter, Arete, was given to the tyrant's younger half brother, Thearides. Plutarch cannot be right about Aristomache remaining childless for years—not if Arete actually married Thearides before he died in, or very soon after, 383. If Arete was born in the first year of her mother's marriage *and* wed Thearides just before he died, she was wed at fourteen; it would be unwise to insist on a later birth for Arete without giving up the requirement that she wed, rather than was promised to, Thearides. There were no issue from that marriage. Dionysius I gave his third daughter, Sophrosyne, to Dionysius II, her paternal half brother, from which there were no issue.

Career.   When Hermocrates I s.v. was exiled and attempted to reinstate himself by force, Dionysius I was one of his most ardent supporters, but was himself thrown into exile by Hermocrates I's death in the battle to retake Syracuse. He was able to gain power through a series of denunciations, alliances, deceptions, and what appears to have been collusion with Syracuse's enemy, the Carthaginians, in 406. Once in power, he extended his empire in Sicily and southern Italy. In Plato's account, this brought him no joy because, like the tyrant of *Republic* 9,

> after taking over many great cities in Sicily that had been laid waste by the barbarians, he was unable at their resettlement to establish loyal govern-ments in them. For he had no comrades to head these governments, neither among foreigners, nor among his own brothers whom he had raised from private to royal station and from poverty to great wealth. None of these was he able, either by persuasion or by teaching, by benefits conferred or by ties of kinship, to make an associate in his empire. (Pl. *Ltr.* 7.331e–332a)

War with Carthage continued intermittently during his reign, and military cam-paigns of the Punic wars make up an important part of the histories that cover Dionysius I (Caven 1990 and Sanders 1987 are full biographical treatments, both hostile to Plato).

Although the tyrant is remembered chiefly for military exploits, he was inter-ested in learning as well as ruling and pursued lively connections with the intellec-tual life of Athens. Cinesias s.v. proposed a decree honoring him in 393 (*IG* II² 18.5), and he subsequently refrained from sending triremes to assist the Spartans at the request of an Athenian embassy in the summer of that year (Lys.). Titles of a number of his plays are extant. He is said to have invited and received to his court Aeschines and Aristippus as well as Plato, who visited perhaps during the sailing season of 384/3. When displeased with the philosopher, however, Dionysius I turned Plato out, arranging for him to be killed or sold into slavery (see Plato s.v.)—or so the later tradition has it; Caven (1990: 168–9) argues that Plato was not invited to Syracuse and did not meet the tyrant, whom he calls 'the dynast'.

In 368 (*prytany* 10 of 369/8), Dionysius I and his two sons by Doris of Locri, Dionysius II and Hermocritus II, were given honorary Athenian citizenship (*IG* II²). That the tyrant continued inviting famous Athenians to his court is further shown by Isocrates' letter of 368, in which Isocrates apologizes for not appearing in person, as certain flatterers have, and encourages Dionysius I to unite with other Greek states to make a military campaign against Persia possible. Continuing his contact with Athenian culture, Dionysius I's play, *The Ransom of Hector*, took first prize at the Lenaean festival at Athens in February of 367; he received the slow-traveling news probably in April, not long before he died amid rumors of poison and a crisis in the succession. He had chosen Dionysius II to succeed him.

In the later tradition.   Diodorus, Plutarch, Polyaenus, and others had much material from which to draw when they wrote extensively about Dionysius I.

Dionysius II of Syracuse, son of Dionysius I
[*LGPN3A* 285 *RE* 2 *DPhA* 84 *OCD*³ *PP*
Διονύσιος]
≥397–330 (r. 367–357, 346–344)
mother: Doris
siblings: Hermocritus II, Dicaeosyne; half
   siblings: Arete, Nysaeus, Hipparinus II,
   Sophrosyne
wife: his half sister, Sophrosyne
father of Apollocrates
See stemma: Dion.

Pl. *Ltr.* 7, *passim*,
   8.356b
[Pl.] *Ltr.* 1, 2, 3, 13 *   addressee
[Pl.] *Ltr.* 4.320d
Xen. *Hell.* 7.4.12
IG II².103
   (naturalization)
GG 3.2.102–107
Philist., *passim*
Tim., *passim*
D. S. 16.5–16.20
Nep. *Dion, passim*
Plu. *Dion, passim*

Life.   Despite his father's reputed learning and culture, Dionysius II's education appears to have been neglected. As a child, he was not exempt from Dionysius I's order that every person who came into his presence be stripped and searched for weapons, and he appears to have been kept out of sight for the most part. Plutarch uncharitably remarks that Dionysius I feared that his son might meet men of intellect and integrity with whom he might lay plots. Aristotle's judgment was more harsh, calling Dionysius II a degenerate compared to his clever father (*Rh.* 1390b30, quoted in full at Clinias IV s.v.; cf. Aristot. *Pol.* 1312a–b). To contemporary historians (e.g. Westlake *CAH* 6²: 693, whose discussion of sources I follow), Plato's *Letters* 7 and 8 count as "the earliest extant record." Fragments of the Academic historian, Timonides, record some of the details of Dion's campaign of liberation. Plutarch apparently used Timonides extensively; his description of Dionysius II, exaggerated as it likely is, provided the material for Mary Renault's memorable portrait of the tyrant in *The Mask of Apollo* as a nearsighted and reclusive young man absorbed with the carving of wooden toys. Whereas Timonides favored Dion, Philistus and Athanis of Syracuse favored Dionysius II and were probably important sources for Nepos. Other early historians similarly chose sides and argued prejudicially. With the difficulty presented by the sources in mind, I turn to what we know of Dionysius II's life.

Reared in the court of the tyrant Dionysius I, Dionysius II was included in the grant of Athenian citizenship to the tyrant and two of his sons in 368 (*IG*), shortly before he assumed the tyranny himself in 367. His only action reported by Xenophon takes place soon after: Dionysius II sent twelve triremes to Sparta, assisting the Lacedaemonians as his father had on a number of occasions. Apparently under Dion's influence early in his reign, Dionysius II also sent for Plato. There were other crucial influences at court, however, especially the historian Philistus, s.v. banished earlier by Dionysius I, but recalled now to place a check on Dion's and Plato's zeal for reform (D. S. 16.6.3–4; Plu. 11.4). For Plato's visit in 366, see Plato and Dion s.vv.; for present purposes, it is enough to say that it ended with Dion's being banished and further punished for suspected disloyalty, and Plato's offending the young tyrant by his efforts to protect Dion's friend Heraclides s.v., a local democratic leader. Hoping to assuage Dionysius II's suspicions of Dion, Plato parted from the tyrant in an outwardly amicable way.

Dionysius II and his advisors were opposed to Dion's and Plato's ideas for reforming the tyranny, but the tyrant himself appears to have desired something of the cultured life his father led and therefore invited learned men and artists to his court. And he invited Plato back as well, seemingly leaving open the door to Plato's persuading him to allow Dion to return to Syracuse. But the third trip to Sicily, 361–360, was worse than the second (see Plato s.v.), and Plato reported to Dion the apparent hopelessness of the situation, whereupon Dion and Heraclides resolved to take Syracuse by force. This they were able to do in 357, after which Dionysius II was confined briefly to Ortygia during negotiations for his voluntary abdication. After Philistus was killed in battle, however, he slipped away by sea to Locri Epizephyrii (see Map 3). His only son, Apollocrates, remained at Ortygia from 356 until the autumn of 355 when, running short of food, Dion allowed him to sail to Italy.

Several murders and takeovers later, Dionysius II recovered Syracuse from his half brother, Nysaeus, in 346, at which time the Locrians revolted and massacred his family; he was again confined to Ortygia ≥346, surrendering it to Timoleon in 344, then retired to Corinth.

Dionysius   [Pl.] *Riv.* 132a
[*PP* Διονύσιος]
schoolteacher

The name 'Dionysius' was the stock name for schoolteachers in Hellenistic times. 'Dionysus' (PCW 619, 1761) is a misprint.

Dionysius, slave of Plato See App. II.

Dionysodorus of Chios and Thurii   Pl. *Euthd.*   speaker
[*DPhA* 192 *RE* 16 *PP PX* Διονυσόδωρος]   Xen. *Mem.* 3.1
brother: Euthydemus
martial arts teacher, sophist

Life and career.   Dionysodorus and his brother were born in Chios, went to Thurii as colonists, were exiled from Thurii, perhaps in 413, then spent several years around Attica (*Euthd.* 271c), though they are still regarded as visitors in *Euthydemus* (285a) ≤407, the dramatic date of the dialogue (see App. I). Xenophon (*Mem.* 3.1) begins with Dionysodorus' earlier arrival in Athens intending to teach generalship (3.1.1) though he is quite young (*neaniskos*, 3.1.8 et al.). Socrates sends him first to learn what he proposes to teach (3.1.3), then questions him upon his return about what he has learned. When his lessons prove to have been inadequate, Socrates sends him back to learn more (3.1.11). The Dionysodorus of the *Euthydemus* has been in Athens for some years (271c), though he still teaches fighting in arms and has picked up sophistry as well (272a); he is unknown to Crito (271b). Omitted in error by *PA*, *PAA*, and *LGPN1*.

Prosopographical notes. A Dionysodorus who is "cousin and brother-in-law" of the prosecutor in Lysias (13.1) was also one of the "generals and the Taxiarchs" who supported the democracy (13.13) and was informed against by Agoratus— the defendant (Lys. 13). The trial occurred in 399, referring to events in the time of the Thirty (404–3), after many foreign residents had been made citizens for manning ships at Arginusae; and by which time some foreign residents had served Athens as generals (see Pl. *Ion* 541c–d). The prosecutor refers to "your democracy" when addressing the jury (twice at 13.1, *et al.*), which may mean that he was not himself a citizen of Athens, in which case the trial may have been held in a magistrate's court for *metics*.

Diopompus (athlete) See App. II.

Diotima of Mantinea   Pl. *Smp.*   speaker
[*LGPN3A* 1 *RE* 1 *DPhA* 204 *OCD*³ *PP*
Διοτίμα]
active ±440
Socrates' teacher of *erōs*
priestess

Life. The dramatic date of the *Symposium*, 416, and Socrates' claim that Diotima put off the Athenian plague for a decade, push his acquaintance with her back to 440 or so—when Socrates was an unattached young man of thirty. That he might have learned *erōs* from her as he claims (*Smp.* 201d) is no more refuted than confirmed by the evidence in Plato. There is a current and widespread assumption that Diotima is the *one* named character Plato certainly invented. In classical studies generally, "arguments from silence" (i.e. absence of evidence) are used with caution—not only because evidence has a way of turning up unexpectedly in some newly found papyrus or inscription—but because we can be quite certain that we have only a tiny portion of the evidence of antiquity. Yet the argument from silence is the one most commonly employed to the conclusion that Diotima is not historical. Nehamas and Woodruff, however, add another: "Diotima in her speech makes an allusion to the view Aristophanes has just presented at the banquet . . . This . . . suggests that even if Diotima actually existed, what she is represented as saying to Socrates cannot have been composed, as Socrates claims, long before the party during which he relates it" (1989: xii, citing *Smp.* 205d–e, 212c). True enough, but one need not assume that Plato contrived the whole speech of Aristophanes *ex nihilo*. As with the book of Zeno in the *Parmenides*, or the speech of Lysias in the *Phaedrus*, it has often been noted that the change of style and manner may well reflect Plato's ability at mimicry or reconstruction of an existing original. The myth on which Aristophanes based his speech in *Symposium* may be one from a lost play; it may have had a precedent in mythology unknown to us. All extant later references to Diotima are derived from Plato.

Doris of Locri Epizephyrii   [Pl.] *Ltr.* 2.313a
[Δωρίς]   Tod 2.133.20
husband: Dionysius I   Plu. *Dion* 3.3.2
mother of Dionysius II, Hermocritus II,
  Dicaeosyne
See stemma: Dion.

Doris' marriage in 397 to Dionysius I was the result of a matrimonial alliance with Locri Epizephyrii. Dionysius I married Aristomache on the same day, and elaborately concealed which marriage was first consummated. Doris produced sons relatively soon (Tod, dated 368, names both Dionysius II and Hermocritus II), while her co-wife, Andromache, remained without sons for some years.

Dropides I See App. II. *See stemma: Plato.*

Dropides II, son of ?Dropides I See App. II. *See stemma: Plato.*

Echecrates of Phlius   Pl. *Phd.*   speaker
[*LGPN3A* 8, 7 *RE* 3 *PP* Ἐχεκράτης]   Aristox. fr. 11
active 399–mid 4th c.   Iamb. *VP* 251, 267
student of Philolaus and Eurytus of   cf. DK 53
  Tarentum

Life and career. In Aristoxenus' list of the last of the Pythagoreans, nine or ten generations after Pythagoras, Xenophilus of Chalcidice; Phanton, Echecrates, Diocles, and Polymnastus are from Phlius. The Phlius area consisted of a valley with a settlement of the same name on its eastern side; it was something of a Pythagorean refuge, lying on the way from Athens to Elis. Its allegiance was steadfastly to Sparta, so Echecrates' statement to Phaedo that there is very little traffic between Phlius and Athens (*Phd.* 57a–b) is understandable.

Prosopographical notes. This is not the same Echecrates (*pace LGPN3A* 8) as the individual below. Diogenes (8.46) is the source for the Aristoxenus fr. ('8.43' is a misprint in *LGPN3A* 7).

Echecrates, son of Phrynion   [Pl.] *Ltr.* 9.358b *
[*LGPN3A* 8, ?9 *PP* Ἐχεκράτης]   cf. DK 53
Pythagorean youth in [Plato's] care   Iamb. *VP* 267

Prosopographical notes. Perhaps a younger relative of the preceding individual (the Echecrates of the *Phaedo* was already an adult in 399, and *Letter* 9 is dated after 383). This Echecrates may be (while the other cannot be) the same person as *LGPN3A* 9 known from Polybius 12.10.7 (cf. Walbank 1957–1979: 2.346). The catalogue of Pythagoreans (Iamb. = DK 58) lists Echecrates and suggests that the Phrynichus also listed may be a copyist's error for 'Phrynion' (DK 58 n27). Echecrates appears on p. 67 of *PP* (there is a misprint in the index).

Elpinice of Athens, daughter of Miltiades IV of Laciadae, wife of Callias II of Alopece See App. II. *See stemmata: Callias, Pericles, Thucydides.*

Empedocles of Acragas (philosopher) See App. II.

Epeius (boxer) See App. II.

Epicharmus of Syracuse (comic poet) See App. II.

Epicrates of Cephisia   Pl. *Phdr.* 227b *
[*PA/APF* 4859 = 4860 *LGPN2* 4, 70, 71   *IG* II² 6444
RE 3 + supp. 3 *PAA* 393945, 393470 *PP*   *Hell. Oxy.* 7.2
Ἐπικράτης Κηφισιεύς]   Philoch. fr. 149
b. ±440s, active through 390   Aristoph. *Eccl.* 71 &
rhetorician and politician   schol.
     Pl. *com.* fr. 130 (K
       122)
     Lys. 27
     Demos. 19.277–280,
       61.1
     Pau. 3.9.8

Life. Epicrates, who purchased the splendid former house near the Olympieum of the wealthy Morychus s.v., was Lysias' host in Athens at the dramatic date of the *Phaedrus*, 418–416 (see App. I). Each time we meet Lysias s.v. in a Platonic dialogue, he is mentioned in the company of other politically inclined rhetoricians like himself, notably Thrasymachus s.v., but also Clitophon s.v., whose political allegiances, like those of Epicrates, varied over time.

From Demosthenes (19), we know that an Epicrates fought in 403 on the side of the democracy in the Piraeus, as did Lysias. What Lysias says about this same Epicrates, some thirteen years later, is that he was well-known and wealthy (27.6,

9), a persuasive orator (27.2), and a taker of bribes in the 390s, often charged, and as often released, through further bribery (27.1–9). Sources independent of Lysias also testify about Epicrates' Persian ambassadorships and the bribery that resulted (Pau. and *Hell. Oxy.* for 396/5; Pl. *com.*, Aristoph. for the period 394–2; Ath. 229f and 251a; Plu. *Pel.* 30.7). If I am right that this is the same Epicrates ("rhetorician and politician"—*PA*) who was once Lysias' host, then Lysias' words against him at 27.10 provide some insight into the changes of fortune brought about by the war: ". . . those who previously, in peacetime, were not able even to maintain themselves, are now contributing to your war taxes (*eisphorai*) and serving as *choregoi* and building large houses."

Prosopographical notes. That we are in all these cases referring to the same well-known Epicrates might be inferred from the fact that, although the name itself is not uncommon in antiquity, nowhere is there any need to identify the man further by patronymic or demotic. In fact, the demotic ascribed to him by *APF*—and retained at *LGPN2* 70—derives from an early fourth c. gravestone for an Epicrates of Cephisia (*IG* II² 6444). As Davies (*APF*) points out, since the Epicrates so often charged with bribery was sentenced to death *in absentia* after his embassy to Sparta with Andocides in 392/1 to ratify the King's Peace (Demos. 19.277–8; Philoch.), "he must later have been allowed to return to Athens" if he is indeed buried there. The three *LGPN2* references may all refer to the same person. Kirchner says at the end of *PA* 4859, "*Ab hoc diversus est*" (without reasons) immediately before introducing *PA* 4860, to whom he assigns only the *Phaedrus* passage. *APF* does not mention any connection. *LGPN2* splits the original *PA* 4859 into two (giving a "cf. *PA* 4859" at *LGPN2* 71, which cites only *IG* II² 6444), and treats the Epicrates of Plato's *Phaedrus* as a third individual (*LGPN2* 4). There is good evidence for combining at least two of the *LGPN2* three. The Epicrates of Demosthenes' *Erotic Essay* (61) is nominally the same man, Lysias' host, but the essay was written >355, by Demosthenes or someone else, to praise Epicrates and to persuade him to study philosophy.

Epigenes of Cephisia, son of Antiphon	Pl. *Ap.* 33e3	present
[*PA* 4803 (cf. *APF* 4790) *PAA* 391685	Pl. *Phd.* 59b	present
LGPN2 48 *RE* 15 *DPhA* 38 *PP* *PX*	Xen. *Mem.* 3.12.1–8	
Ἐπιγένης Ἀντιφῶντος Κηφισιεύς]		

Life. From Epigenes' presence at both the trial and death of Socrates, one would expect to know more about this "ghost" (*APF*). Xenophon is not much help: Socrates notes that Epigenes is in bad physical condition and advises him at great length to get exercise, asking many questions, but not allowing Epigenes to answer.

In the later tradition. Diogenes mistakes Epigenes for a son of Crito (2.121); see testimonia in *SSR* 2.VIB.

Prosopographical notes. *DPhA* 38 ?= 39 (*RE* 15 ?= 16, the Pythagorean writer of *On the Arts of Orpheus*).

Epilycus II, son of Tisander II See App. II. *See stemmata: Andocides, Callias.*

Epimenides of Crete (prophet) See App. II.

Erasinides of Athens (general) See App. II.

Erasistratus I of Acharnae See App. II. *See stemma: Phaeax.*

Erasistratus II of Acharnae, son of Phaeax See App. II. *See stemma: Phaeax.*

Erasistratus III of Athens
[*PA*/*APF* 5024, 5025, 5028 (13921) *PAA*
400115, 400130 *LGPN2* 3, 5 *RE* 1
Ἐρασίστρατος]
tribe: ?Hippothontis
b. ?440s
mother: daughter of Erasistratus I
uncle: Phaeax I
one of the Thirty
See stemma: Phaeax.

[Pl.] *Eryx.*   speaker
Antiph. 20
Xen. *Hell.* 2.3.2
Aes. *Mil.* no. 77 (fr.
37 Dittmar)

Life. In the pseudo-Platonic *Eryxias*, Erasistratus III has just returned from Sicily, apparently just before Athens' campaign of 415. The only member of the family *known* to have traveled to Sicily and back is Erasistratus III's uncle Phaeax I s.v. (Thu. 5.4) who returned from an embassy to Sicily and Italy in 422. Erasistratus III, a future member of the Thirty, is paired in the *Eryxias* with the Thirty's future leader, Critias IV, and with a member of Critias IV's family, Eryxias (see stemma: Plato). He is preoccupied with the accoutrements of wealth (392d).

Sometime before 413, Erasistratus III seems to have attempted to steal either rare peacocks or their eggs from Plato's stepbrother, Demos s.v. Antiphon's *Prosecution of Erasistratus in a Case about Peacocks* (20) refers to Erasistratus III, or perhaps to another Erasistratus of the same generation, as *APF* suspected, but it cannot refer to Erasistratus I (*pace LGPN2* and *PAA*). Since the peacocks belonged to Demos by the time of the trial, a date following Pyrilampes' death, not much before 413, is probable for the litigation; but Erasistratus I died in 450 (*IG* I³ 1161.14).

As a member of the Thirty in 404/3, by Löper's (1896) hypothesis, Erasistratus III requires the tribe Hippothontis, not the tribe Oineis (the tribe of Acharnae, Erasistratus II's deme). Thus, if Löper is right, Erasistratus III's mother will have been the daughter of Erasistratus I, and Erasistratus III will have inherited his Hippothontid demotic from his presently unknown father—as suggested by *APF* and represented on the stemma of Phaeax. Whitehead (1980: 210) worries that *APF* goes further than the evidence warrants toward confirming Löper, a concern shared by Walbank (1982: 78). Walbank also considers the possibility of restoring the name 'Erasistratus' to lines 5–6 of *stele* 4 of the inscription recording the sale of property confiscated from the Thirty, the Eleven, and the Piraeus Ten after 403. Erasistratus is the only tyrant's name that would fit the space, but the restoration would imply that Erasistratus was from the deme Euonymon rather than Acharnae or some Hippothontid deme (1982: 87 & plate 27b), so Walbank concludes that the property probably belonged to one of the Thirty's associates (many of whose names we do not have). He notes the coincidence that the same restoration could be made on *stele* 5, concerning a property in the Piraeus or an adjacent deme (1982: 89 and plate 28b).

Prosopographical notes. Originally, *PA* assigned 5024 to the litigant in Antiphon, 5025 to the pseudo-Platonic character and 5028 to the tyrant. *APF* collapsed the three, preserving a portion of Löper's (1896) hypothesis that the Thirty were elected three per tribe (see Exc. 3). I have preserved that hypothesis tentatively in the stemma although it is under considerable strain. *LGPN2* identifies Antiphon's litigant, *LGPN2* 6, as Erasistratus III's grandfather of that name, but that is impossible. *LGPN2* 4 is Plato's character ?= 5, the tyrant. *PAA* also preserves *PA*'s separate numbers for the litigant (*PAA* 400110), the character in *Eryxias* (*PAA* 400115), and the member of the Thirty (*PAA* 400130) but 400110 ?= 400115; 400115 ?= 400135 (Erasistratus I).

Erastus of Scepsis
[*DPhA* 49 *RE* 3 *PP* Ἔραστος]
brother: Coriscus
student of Plato

[Pl.] *Ltr.*   addressee
  6.322c–323a *
[Pl.] *Ltr.* 13.362b *
D. L. 3.46
Str. 13.1.54

Erastus lived at Scepsis, near Atarneus, where Hermias s.v. was tyrant; [Plato] encouraged their mutual friendship (*Ltr.* 6). Erastus and Coriscus s.v. advised Hermias, also a former Academy student, and later established a school at nearby Assos. Erastus also went to Andromedes of Aegina s.v. on behalf of [Plato] (*Ltr.* 13).

Eryxias of Stiria
[*PA/APF* 5185 (8792.6Ae) *LGPN2* 2 *PAA*
422640 *RE* 3 *DPhA* 58 Ἐρυξίας Στειριεύς]
kinsman of Critias IV
See stemma: Plato.

[Pl.] *Eryx.*   speaker

The dialogue names Eryxias a kinsman of Critias IV (*Eryx.* 396d). Because an Eryxias was included in the list of ten-year archons (Georgius Syncellus, *Ecloga chronographica*, *FGrH* 251 fr. 15), compiled near the end of the 5th c., and because "the family of a kinsman of Kritias is more likely to be the one concerned than that of the only other known bearer of the name . . .," *APF* suggests tentatively, "It might be worth hazarding the guess that Eryxias of Steiria was a younger member of the hitherto unknown family of Kritias' mother," a little more sanguine about the identification than he had been nearly a thousand entries earlier (*APF* 8792.6Ae; cf. *APF* 828.6).

Mention of Pulytion's house (*Eryx.* 400b; cf. Andoc. 1.12, 14) connotes not only great wealth but the profanation of the mysteries as well. Andromachus, slave of Archebiades, in return for immunity, accused several citizens (including Pulytion, Alcibiades III, Acumenus, and Meletus of Athens) of performing the mysteries in Pulytion's house, in the presence of three slaves, including himself.

Eryximachus of Athens, son of Acumenus	Pl. *Prt.* 315c	present
[*PA* 5187 (cf. *APF* 11907) *PAA* 422650 *LGPN2*	Pl. *Smp.*	speaker
3 *RE* s.v. *DPhA* 59 *PP* Ἐρυξίμαχος	Pl. *Phdr.* 268a *	
Ἀκουμένου]	Andoc. 1.35	
≤448–≥415		
physician		

Life. Eryximachus was a physician and the son of a physician (*Smp.* 214b). He was born ≤448 and was a longtime friend of Phaedrus s.v., who is with him in the group around Hippias at Callias III's house in 433/2, when they would have been in their late teens (*Prt.*). They are still friends 418–416 (*Phdr.*) and at Agathon's house in 416 when they would have been in their early thirties (*Smp.*). Both men, and Eryximachus' father, were apparently implicated in crimes of sacrilege in 415 (see Exc. 1). Unlike the case of Phaedrus, however, there is no independent confirmation that the physician is the Eryximachus accused of defacing herms. The reason for the longstanding assumption that they are identical is not so prosopographical as it is circumstantial: Agathon's victory symposium collects together at the height of Alcibiades III's power and fame, some of the key persons who will, during the following year, suffer exile or death as a result of the mutilation of the herms and profanation of the Eleusinian mysteries on the eve of the Sicilian expedition. At his trial in 400, Andocides IV says of the group of eighteen men, including Eryximachus, accused by Teucrus a.k.a. Teucer: "some of them fled into exile, while others were arrested and put to death on Teucer's information . . . [names are read]. Now, some of those men have returned and are in Athens, and those who were put to death have left a number of relatives" (1.34–35). But it is not clear whether Eryximachus was among the executed or the exiles or, if he was an exile, whether he returned to Athens; and if he was an exile who returned, it is not clear when. If he returned, however, then the question arises whether he might be one of the individuals of that name referenced elsewhere for the period after exiles began returning (see below). If not, then we hear nothing further of Eryximachus after 415.

Dover hesitates to identify Acumenus' son with the herm mutilator because Eryximachus appears in Plato's *Symposium* to be "a doctor of some standing"; he suggests the "prank" was pulled by a cousin or nephew of that name, otherwise unknown (*HCT* 4.284). And *APF* considers the physician wealthy without any independent evidence of his having owned property or performed a liturgy, without anyone complimenting him on his lineage or wealth—although Plato's *Symposium* brings together men from the lowest to the highest classes. For balance, one might recall Plato's *Laws* where physicians were body mechanics who might be citizens or slaves (4.720b, 9.857d).

Prosopographical notes. *LGPN2* 3 ?= 1, exactly as *PAA* 422650 ?= 422652: Lysias fr. 9, a *trierarch*, possibly also *stratēgos*, for whom Lysias wrote a speech >402 in defense of the charge that he "remained in the city" under the Thirty (see Exc. 4), an identification rejected by *APF* on grounds that (a) the physician Eryximachus would have appeared at the trial of Andocides IV in 400 if alive then; and (b) the *trierarch* fails to make any reference to the financial ruin he would have suffered in 415, had he been the physician.

In search of a prosperous Eryximachus to husband one of the daughters of the wealthy Polyaratus and his wife (the daughter of Menexenus of Cydathenaeum), *APF* gives Plato's character an audition but denies him the role because (a) as above; (b) the physician is too old in 395 for a woman born 415–10. But *APF*, missing the *Protagoras* passage, underestimates Eryximachus' age and that of Polyaratus' daughter, who may have been born in 420 into a society where thirty-year differences in age were not remarkable among the propertied elite; but still it is not an optimal match. *APF* has a third reason for rejecting the physician: (c) marginally better husband material is found in the deme of Cydathenaeum in *PA* 5186, a hypothesized son of a known Eryxias (*PA* 5184)—eponym for the pseudo-Platonic dialogue—himself the son of a *chorēgos* Eryximachus (*PA* 5188), known only by patronymic; it is this individual whom Davies (*APF*) incorporates into the stemma for the family. Because of two plausible victory dates for Eryxias, the Eryximachus who is *PA* 5186 has two plausible birth dates. The later, less likely, date would allow Eryxias to be the son of the physician or the *trierarch*; the more likely later date would allow Eryxias' son to have married the daughter of Polyaratus. On present information, the possibilities cannot be narrowed further.

Euaeon of Lampsacus See App. II.

Euathlus of ?Thebes   [Pl.] *Thg.* 129a
[*PP* Εὔαθλος]
runner who harbored Timarchus

The persistent absence from the prosopographical record of Athens of all the characters of the scene described in *Theages* can be accounted for by Dušanić (1990b: 65–70) who argues that they are from Thebes. This particular name, however, is not attested for Thebes in *LGPN3B*.

Euclides of Megara   Pl. *Tht.*   speaker
[*LGPN3B* 19 *RE* 5 *DPhA* 82 *OCD³ PP*   Pl. *Phd.*   present
Εὐκλείδης]
±450–380
friend of Theaetetus, Terpsion
founder of the Megarian school

Life. In the dramatic frame of *Theaetetus*, Euclides says that the conversation his slave is about to read aloud is one he heard from Socrates; to get it right, Euclides afterwards wrote it down and checked the details with Socrates on subsequent trips to Athens (143a). Since the dialogue takes place after the official charge against Socrates had been lodged (210d), Euclides had at least six weeks, and perhaps as long as a few months, to make his trips to Athens (see App. I, *Crito* and *Phaedo* discussions). But he was apparently accustomed to long walks (a detail that sparked a later tradition): as he sits down to rest and to hear the dialogue, probably in the spring of 391, he has just returned from accompanying the wounded and sick Theaetetus from Megara to Erineum, a settlement near the Cephisus River, and a distance of some 15 km., then walked *back* to Megara where Terpsion was waiting (see Map 2). Euclides is best known as founder of the Megarian School of philosophy.

In the later tradition. According to Diogenes (3.6; 2.106), citing Hermodorus, Plato and other Socratics visited Euclides in Megara after the death of Socrates. Cicero connects Euclides with the tradition of Eleatic monism (*Acad.* 2.42.129); and Diogenes adds that the school later became known for eristic, and still later for dialectics (2.106–107). Titles of Socratic dialogues attributed to Euclides are *Lamprias, Crito, Eroticus, Alcibiades, Aeschines* and *Phoenix* (D. L. 2.108). It is Gellius (*NA* 7.10) who adds that, when Athens was hostile toward Megara, Euclides dressed as a woman so he could avoid arrest when walking back and forth to Athens to see Socrates.

Euclides of Athens (gem cutter) See App. II.

Eucrates of Cydantidae, son of Niceratus I
[*PA*/*APF* 5757 (10808) *LGPN2* 36 *PAA* 437715
RE 5 Εὐϰράτης Νιϰηράτου Κυδαντίδης]
≥451–404
paternal half brother: Nicias I; brother:
  Diognetus
wife: sister of Callias (tribe: Pandionis)
father of two sons
See stemmata: Nicias, Andocides.

Pl. *Grg.* 472a,
  unnamed *
Aristoph. *Lysistr.*
  103 & schol.
Andoc. 1.47
Lys. 18

Life. Eucrates' family was exceptionally rich from its silver mining ventures. It is no surprise that Plato should mention the choral dedications that were open to view in the precinct of Dionysus at the time; Eucrates won a *chorēgos* victory (in dithyramb for Aigeis) <415. Since Eucrates and Diognetus are so much younger than Nicias I (the younger brothers born probably ≥451, but Nicias I some twenty-four years earlier (±475), a second marriage for Niceratus I suggests itself (*APF*). Indeed, it would be unusual for a woman to bear one child, then two more after such an interval, though further births and deaths and in-between cannot be ruled out. On the whole, a second marriage seems more likely than the alternative. *APF* adds parenthetically, "If moreover this hypothetical second marriage were to a non-Athenian woman before 451/0, this would give some point to the note of schol. Aristophanes' *Lysistrata* 103 [Eucrates is lampooned as . . . a foreigner] . . . a charge which is never leveled against Nicias I." The line in the play itself is, "My husband's . . . at the Thracian front; he's guarding Eucrates." MacDowell had suggested that the scholiast had confused Eucrates with the demagogue of that name (1962: 97; cf. Aristoph. *Knights* 254), but *PAA* notes that Eucrates, elected general for 412/1, was suspected of corruption in Thrace—and that seems the most straightforward explanation of the line. Eucrates married ≤420s and was the father of two sons who were adults in 395 (though minors in 404).

Career. It is because Eucrates was elected general in 412 that we can be certain that no stain remained after he was exonerated of mutilating herms in the group with Andocides IV in 415 (Andoc.; see Exc. 1).

Lysias 18 is a speech for the defense in 396, when the two sons of Eucrates, having just come of age, are being sued for their inheritance (i.e., Eucrates is being sued posthumously). The inheritance is presumably substantial since *trierarchies* are being paid out of it at the time of the trial though neither young man can yet have reached the age of thirty (18.21). And their case was presumably lost since both and all their issue, if any, are absent from the inscriptions after Lysias 18. A point of the speech itself is to garner support for their case by demonstrating their family's long association with the democracy. When praising their father along these lines, they point out that Eucrates was elected general under the democracy in 405 (18.4), that he refused to join the Thirty when invited (18.4–5), and that he could have preserved his life by joining the oligarchy (the Thirty executed him) but chose rather to perish with the democracy (18.5).

APF nevertheless doubts Eucrates' democratic loyalties because, according even to this speech of praise, it is admitted that he would have been acceptable to the Thirty as one of their number. This seems rather a hasty judgment. Plato serves as another example of someone who turned down an offer of membership in the Thirty (*Ltr.* 7.324d), yet—as Christopher Rowe has argued recently (1998; cf. Monoson 2000)—Plato had more sympathy with the democracy than with the oligarchy, on the whole, his real problem being how to criticize the democracy without undermining it. Diodorus asserts (14.32.5) that the Thirty sent representatives to Phyle, where Thrasybulus was gathering democrats in hopes of mounting a military attack against the Thirty, to offer Thrasybulus Theramenes' vacant place (cf. Krentz 1982: 86–7). Moreover, some of those who were members initially were soon to be executed by their cohorts, Theramenes s.v. most prominently.

Eudicus of Athens, son of Apemantus   [Pl.] *Gr. Hip.* 286c
[*PA* 5422 *LGPN2* 4 *PAA* 429760 *DPhA* 94 *PP*   [Pl.] *L. Hip.*   speaker
Εὐδικος Ἀπημάντου]

Nothing is known of Eudicus independently of the pseudo-Platonic dialogues.

Eudorus of ?Athens   Pl. *Meno* 94c
[*PA* 5447 *LGPN2* 1 *PAA* 430245 *RE* 5 *PP*   [Pl.] *Virt.* 378a †
Εὔδωρος]

Eudorus was a noted wrestler and trainer who taught Stephanus, son of Thucydides I. 'Eudoxus' at PCW 1765 is a misprint for 'Eudorus'.

Eudoxus of Cnidus

[RE 8 OCD³ DPhA 98 PP Εὔδοξος]

≤390–≥340

student of Archytas, ?Philistion

associate of Plato

foremost mathematician of his time

[Pl.] Ltr. 13.360c *

frr. in Lasserre 1966

Philoch. fr. 223

Aristot. Meta.

1073b17–32

Eudoxus was an astronomer and geographer as well a brilliant mathematician. The scholiast of book 5 (280.1–9) of Euclid's *Elements* credits Eudoxus with the development of the general theory of proportion. He also developed a method of approach to the limit, using inscribed polygons, that became the standard method for avoiding infinitesimals; Archimedes, *On the Sphere and Cylinder* (preface to bk. 1) cites Eudoxus' demonstrations, based on that method, that any pyramid (and any cone) is a third part of the prism (or the cylinder) having the same base and equal height. But Eudoxus' most stunning legacy is a geometrical model of the apparent motions of the sun, moon, and planets in homocentric spheres that was able to show retrograde motion (Aristot.) and was not overturned before Kepler. Eudoxus also produced descriptive work on the constellations. He shares credit with Archytas for developing a method for doubling the area of a cube, though the details of Eudoxus' role are obscure. Eudoxus had a school at Cyzicus which he is sometimes said to have combined with Plato's Academy. He is said to have been *scholarch* at the Academy during Plato's Sicilian absence in 366 (Philoch.). 'Eudoxus' at PCW 1765 is a misprint for 'Eudorus', the wrestler of *Meno* 94c.

In the later tradition and modern bibliography. Simplicius' *Commentary on Aristotle De Caelo* (2.12), citing Eudemus, is useful on Eudoxus' spheres. Proclus (*Eucl.* 67.2), probably based indirectly on Eudemus, names Eudoxus among twelve other early mathematicians of the Academy (listed at Theaetetus s.v.). Diogenes' biography (8.86–91) is not considered particularly reliable. See Thomas (1991: 409–15), qualified by G. J. Toomer in *OCD³* s.v.

Euphraeus of Histiaea (Oreos)

[LGPN1 7 RE 2 PP Εὐφραῖος]

†343/2

student of Plato, political advisor

[Pl.] Ltr. 5.321c

    –322a *

Demos. 9.59–62

Ath. 11.506e–508e

Life. Advisor to Perdiccas III, the young ruler of Macedonia. Athenaeus cites the 2nd c. B.C.E. historian Carystius (who supposedly quoted from letters of Speusippus) for the statements that Euphraeus would not allow those ignorant of geometry and philosophy to sit at the table of Perdiccas III; and that it was Euphraeus who persuaded Perdiccas III to put his younger brother, Philip (later Philip of Macedonia), into a position of responsibility. Demosthenes' *Third Philippic* describes how, after Euphraeus returned to Histiaea upon Philip's accession, Philip paid agents within the city to bring it under Macedonian control. Euphraeus opposed the agents and was thrown into prison. The city was soon under Philip's autocratic control, and even the now-former agents were either executed or exiled. Demosthenes praised Euphraeus for committing suicide in prison.

Euphronius of Sunium See App. II.

Euripides of Phlya, son of Mnesarchides I	Aes. *Mil.* no. 77 (fr.
[*PA* 5953 *LGPN2* 13 *PAA* 444585 *RE* 4 *DPhA*	37 Dittmar)
139 *OCD³* Εὐριπίδης Μνησαρχίδου	Euripides' *opera*
Φλυεύς]	*IG* I³ 969.2
480s–407/6	Aristoph. *Thesm.*
mother: Clito	Aristoph. *Neph.* fr.
wives: Melito, Choerine	392 (K 376)
father of Mnesarchides II, Mnesilochus II,	Aristoph. *Frogs*
Euripides II	Tele. frr. 44–5 (K
great tragedian	41–2) schol.
	Cal. *Ped.* fr. 15 (K
	12)
	Aristot. *Rh.* 1416a29

Life.   Euripides took third place for his first play, produced in 455, *Daughters of Pelias*, so his birth is normally figured back thirty years from that, though he may have been a decade younger. He is variously said to have been a student of Anaxagoras and Prodicus (D. L. 9.54; Gell. *NA* 15.20.4, citing the 3rd c. B.C.E. Alexander Aetolus; and Cic. *Tus. Dis.* 3.14); only the very unreliable Suda (ε 3695) calls Socrates his teacher. In 441, Euripides won his first of four lifetime victories at the Dionysia; since he produced over ninety plays, he was not so competitively successful as, for example, Aeschylus or Sophocles. Sometime after 428, he was a litigant against Hygiaenon over exchanging properties in which he is said to have been accused of impiety for writing the line, "My tongue hath sworn; my soul remains unsworn" (*Hippolytus* 612)—which supposedly encouraged perjury (Aristot.). He may well have been a popular personality: Aristophanes s.v. twice makes him a character in his comedies (*Thesm., Frogs*). Euripides, like Agathon s.v., left Athens for the Hellenizing Macedonian court ≥408, where he died in 407/6.

Connection to Socrates.   Such evidence as is available is particularly fragmentary and hardly more than suggestive, but it derives from diverse sources, the comic playwrights, an inscription, and Euripides' ancient biographer. Callias, in his *Pedētae* of ≤429/8, charged Euripides with being aided by Socrates; Teleclides, whose victories began in 445, but whose unassigned frr. we cannot date accurately, accused Euripides of collaborating with Socrates on the *Phrygians*. Aristophanes goes furthest of all, crediting Socrates with having written Euripides' tragedies for him (Aristoph. *Neph.*, a fr. from the first version of the *Clouds* that is not in the extant mss. of the play). Satyrus, Euripides' 3rd c. B.C.E. biographer, also accuses Euripides of getting his ideas from Socrates (*P. Oxy.* 1176 fr. 39), though Satyrus may derive his information from the comic poets.

In the version of the *Clouds* we have, one of Socrates' students first criticizes Aeschylus, then recites approvingly from Euripides. In Aristophanes' *Frogs*, when Aeschylus has already defeated Euripides in an underworld competition, lnn. 1491–1499 (quoted at Socrates s.v.) might be regarded as a description of what has been defeated, again linking Euripides to newfangled Socratic notions. Diogenes (2.44) preserves a line from Euripides' *Palamedes* (fr. 588 Nauck) said to have blamed the Athenians for killing the all-wise and innocent Socrates—but goes on to admit that Euripides died before Socrates' trial (citing Philoch. fr. 221).

In 1965, a choral dedication from a Socrates to Euripides as a producer (*didaskalos*), dated 440–431, was found at Varkiza (*IG*).

ΣΩΚΡΑΤΗΣ ΑΝΕΘΗΚΕΝ / ΕΥΡΙΠΙΔΗΣ ΕΔΙΔΑΣΚΕ

Glaucon of Athens (*PAA* 276750 ?= 277053) is said to have written a dialogue called *Euripides* (D. L. 2.124), but it is not extant.

Euripides of Melite See App. II. *See stemma: Phaedrus.*

Eurybatus (villain) See App. II.

Eurybius of Syracuse   Pl. *Ltr.* 7.348e–349b *
[*LGPN3A* 2 *PP* Εὐρύβιος]   [Pl.] *Ltr.* 3.318c *
fl. mid 4th c.
associate of Heraclides, Theodotes

Eurybius attempted, with Theodotes and Plato, to persuade Dionysius II to stop pursuing the democratic leader, Heraclides s.v. Inadvertently omitted from the index of PCW (1765).

Eurycles of ?Athens   Pl. *Sph.* 252c
[*PAA* 444860 Εὐρυκλῆς]   Aristoph. *Wasps*
active 5th c.   1017–20

This ventriloquist and soothsayer has been long absent from the prosopographical literature but appears now in the addenda of *PAA*. See Plutarch (*Mor.* 414c).

Eurymedon I of Myrrhinus See App. II. *See stemma: Plato.*

Eurymedon II of Myrrhinus, son of ?Speusippus See App. II. *See stemma: Plato.*

Euryptolemus II of Athens, son of Euryptolemus I See App. II.

Euryptolemus III of ?Sunium, son of   [Pl.] *Ax.* 369a
Pisianax II   Xen. *Hell. passim*
[*PA/APF* 5985, 5981 (9688.8, 5985 = 5981)
PAA 445115, 445085 *LGPN2* 8, 3
Εὐρυπτόλεμος Πεισιάνακτος (Σουνιεύς)]
<460–>406
cousin of Alcibiades III
cousin of Pericles I and II
defender of Arginusae generals

Family. Euryptolemus II, Megacles VII, Pisianax II, and Isodice were the four offspring of Euryptolemus I, all born in the decade 510–500, making Euryptolemus II a cousin of Pericles I (vindicating Plu. *Per.* 7.5), and making Euryptolemus III a cousin of Alcibiades III (Xen. 1.4.19)—but both Xenophon and Plutarch must then be using ἀνεψιός not straightforwardly as *first* cousin, but loosely as 'cousin' (*APF* 9688.8, revising *PA* 5985). I have not included Euryptolemus III on the stemmata of Pericles or Alcibiades, but the representation of the relations of this important family occupies a foldout of more than 1.1 meters in tiny type in *APF* (Table 1).

Career. According to Xenophon, Euryptolemus III was Alcibiades III's aide-de-camp in the Hellespont in 408 (1.3.12, 13), and welcomed his cousin back to Athens in 407 (1.4.19). For his prominent role in defending the accused generals after Arginusae (1.7.12–35), see Excursus 2. On that occasion, he attempted to enforce the decree of Cannonus according to which a person accused in a capital crime would be judged by a separate vote. In Xenophon's account, it was Socrates' intervention, as president (*prytanis*) of the Prytanes, that enabled Euryptolemus III to deliver a speech in defense of the generals after Arginusae (1.7.16–33) that almost won them separate trials.

Prosopographical notes. *PA*, *PAA* and *LGPN2*, unlike *APF*, are not certain that the aide-de-camp of Xen. *Hell.* 1.3 is the same Euryptolemus; each assigns a separate number to Xenophon's Euryptolemus: *PA* 5981, *LGPN2* 3, *PAA* 445085 with "possibly the same as" notes to pseudo-Plato's.

Eurysthenes of Sparta, son of Aristodemus (king) See App. II.

Eutherus of Athens   Xen. *Mem.* 2.8.1–6
[*LGPN2* 1 *PAA* 431537 *PX* Εὔθηρος]

With Athens' defeat in 404, a number of Athenian *cleruchies* were lost (cf. Euthyphro s.v. who farmed with his father on Naxos); most of the colonists had no choice but to return to Athens. This impoverished veteran returned to Athens >405, having lost his foreign property and without land in Attica. He decided to work for a living and was advised by Socrates to lower his expectations.

Euthydemus of Athens, son of Diocles   Pl. *Smp.* 222b *
[*PA* 5520 *LGPN2* 5 *PAA* 432175 *DPhA* 169 *RE*   Xen. *Mem.*, *passim*
12 *PP PX* Εὐθύδημος Διοκλέους]
beloved of Critias IV
lover of Socrates

In Xenophon's account, the beautiful (*kalos*) Euthydemus, while still too young to go alone to the agora, already had a large collection of poetry and works by wise men. He stayed around the leather-worker's shop near the agora where Socrates sought him out. While at first reluctant even to speak to Socrates, he was eventually attracted into conversations about justice and knowing oneself, and finally became a devoted student (4.2.1–40). It was this Euthydemus whom Critias IV pursued so openly that he attracted Socrates' public criticism (4.2.29–30). Alcibiades III says nevertheless, in Plato's account, that Socrates spurned Euthydemus' amorous interest. (This may be the same Euthydemus as at Plu. *Mor.* 461d.)

  Errors are common in identifications of the three men named 'Euthydemus' in Plato's dialogues. Brisson (*DPhA*) traces a lacuna in the pseudo-Socratic letter 13 that caused the positing of a Euthydemus, son of Glaucon; this was corrected by Wilamowitz in 1879, but missed by others who continued to speculate through at least 1973. Late references are collected in *SSR* 2.VIB.

Euthydemus, son of Cephalus II   Pl. *R.* 328b   present
[*APF* C3 (C9) *FRA* 6982 *PAA* 432410 *PP PX*   D. H. *Lys.*
Εὐθύδημος Κεφάλου]   [Plu.] *LTO* 835d
b. ?440s
full or half siblings: Lysias, a sister who
  married Brachyllus, Polemarchus
See stemma: Lysias.

Euthydemus is not mentioned by his brother Lysias in the autobiographical speech 12; and there is no contemporaneous corroboration for Plato's mention of him as present at Polemarchus' house in the Piraeus. Dionysius and Plutarch may have used Plato's *Republic* as a source for the name. It has been assumed that Euthydemus went with his brothers to Thurii as a colonist (D. H.), but there are other possibilities as well. Whether Cephalus II had died by the time the colonists set out or not, Euthydemus may have remained in the Piraeus to manage the family's shield factory, or for other reasons.

  Waterfield mistakes this Euthydemus for the son of Diocles above (1993: 471).

Euthydemus of Chios and Thurii
[*PAA* 432415 *LGPN1* 1 *RE* 13 *DPhA* 172 *OCD*³
PP PX Εὐθύδημος]
brother: Dionysodorus
sophist and martial arts teacher

Pl. *Euthd.*   speaker
frr. tr. in Sprague
2001
Aristot. *Rh.* 1401a26
Aristot. *S. Ref.*
177b12

Euthydemus and his brother traveled from their home in Chios to Thurii, and thence to Athens (see Dionysodorus s.v. for that period of their lives). It is Euthydemus who developed an independent reputation as a sophist. Aristotle refers twice to a fallacious argument that does not appear in Plato, naming Euthydemus as its source: "a man knows that there is a trireme in the Piraeus because he knows each of the two things ['a trireme' and 'in the Piraeus'] separately" (*Rh.*; cf. *S. Ref.*). *PA* 5520 distinguishes this Euthydemus from the son of Diocles but does not assign him a number.

Euthyphro of Prospalta
[*PA* 5664 *LGPN2* 7, 12 *PAA* 434065 *RE* 1 *PP*
Εὐθύφρων Προσπάλτιος]
b. late 440s
diviner-priest

Euthphr.   speaker
Cra. 396d *
D. L. 2.29

Life.   Euthyphro was twenty or so at the time of *Cratylus* (dramatic date, ≤422; see App. I), so he was in his mid-forties in *Euthyphro*, and his father likely in at least his mid-seventies (cf. *Euthphr.* 15d). Additional evidence that Euthyphro is not a youth includes his having spoken before the Athenian Assembly (2c) more than once in the past, and his acquaintance with Socrates' habits, sufficient that he can comment on them confidentially (2b). Euthyphro of *Euthyphro* is a prophet (μάντεσιν, 3e) who farmed on Naxos with his father (4c). Athens, at the instigation of Pericles I, established its *cleruchy* on Naxos by sending five hundred Athenian colonists there (Plu. *Per.* 11.5) before the spring of 447 (*CAH* 5²: 128). While many Athenians owned property outside Attica that they leased, farmed, mined, or grazed for income and that also served as a recourse in the event of exile, *cleruchies* were exceptional in that they were established on conquered or rebellious territory; and *cleruchs* were resident there partly as a buffer against further rebellion. An incentive for providing land to Athenian settlers—not that Naxos had any choice in the matter—was a sharp reduction in the tribute assessment for the island. These aspects of the *cleruchy* arrangement make it unlikely that Euthyphro's father just happened to own farmland on Naxos, and unlikely that Athenians remained there after Athens was forced to relinquish it in 404. We do not know when Euthyphro's father joined the *cleruchy* or under what circumstances, but Euthyphro may well have helped his father informally at peak periods without himself being a *cleruch*. He would already have passed his *dokimasia* in Prospalta before the date of the *Cratylus*, where his demotic is used, so he was of age to act independently of his father. Although Euthyphro's demotic is not used in *Euthyphro*, his speeches to the Assembly attest to his Athenian citizenship in 399.

See Appendix I (s.v. *Euthyphro*) for Burnet's explanation of factors that may have delayed the trial of Euthyphro's father from <404 to 399 or later. Euthyphro sees Socrates waiting in the stoa of the king archon. Euthyphro already has a case (*dikē*, 2a3) before the king archon, so he appears to have indicted his father at some point in the past. Euthyphro's abrupt departure, as well as the absence of his father, makes it appear that he was not there for the pretrial hearing.

Prosopographical notes.   LGPN2 splits *PA* 5664 into two individuals: 7 ?= 12 where 12 is the Euthyphro of ?Athens or Naxos in *Euthyphro* and 7 is the Euthyphro of Prospalta in *Cratylus*; but this is an unsupportable division. In 399, Euthyphro listened more than he spoke in the conversation with Socrates, who declares at the dialogue's end that Euthyphro is abandoning him without having made him wise (15e). Socrates listened to the Euthyphro of the *Cratylus* for a long time on the morning of that dialogue and was so inspired (ἐνθουσιῶν, 396d) that he suggests using Euthyphro's divine wisdom to complete the inquiry into names (396d–e). Whether ironic or not, this is not a description of the *Euthyphro* discussion that we have. Since Socrates is represented in the dialogues as conversing with some of the same people repeatedly over his lifetime, two or many more discussions with Euthyphro would not be surprising. What would be surprising is a second Euthyphro with the same mantic bent as the first, and the same claimed expertise in father-gods: Uranus, Cronus, and Zeus (*Cra.* 396b and *Euthphr.* 5e). The evidence is that there is one Euthyphro who spoke to Socrates more than once. And even if *LGPN2* 12 were a Euthyphro of Naxos, he would have to be designated "Athens and Naxos" because *cleruchs* retained their Athenian citizenship, and because Naxos held no Athenians after 404.

In the later tradition.   In Diogenes, the conversation with Socrates diverts Euthyphro from pursuing the indictment of his father (2.29).

Evenus of Paros   Pl. *Ap.* 20a–c *
[*LGPN1* 4 *RE* 7 *PP* Εὔηνος]   Pl. *Phd.* 60c–61c *
active in the late 5th c.   Pl. *Phdr.* 267a
poet and rhetorician   frr. ed. Bergk

Such frr. of Evenus as are extant are of elegiac verse (tr. J. M. Edmonds, Loeb *Elegy and Iambus* I), somewhat imitative of the better known Theognis, but Evenus appears in his time to have been noted for his wide learning. In Plato's *Apology*, Callias III s.v. says that he plans to put his two sons into the care of Evenus of Paros, whose course costs five *minae*, reasonable by comparison to the fees Callias III was paying to sophists twenty years before, but still an expensive course (see Xen. *Oec.* 2.3 where five *minae* is given as the net worth of all Socrates' property, including his house). So Evenus was an itinerant teacher, present in Athens in 399, but no one in Plato refers to him as a 'sophist' (*pace* PCW 52n4, 543n49) and, on the contrary, he is treated with relative respect in the dialogues. Simmias calls him a philosopher (*Phd.* 61c6), though Socrates appears to doubt that characterization and refers to him rather as a poet (60d9). In the *Phaedrus*, he is said to have introduced some rhetorical devices or terms for them (267a3).

Gelon of Syracuse and Gela, son of Dinomenes (tyrant) See App. II.

Glaucon I of Cerameis See App. II. *See stemma: Plato.*

Glaucon II of Cerameis, son of Leagrus I See App. II. *See stemmata: Callias, Plato.*

Glaucon III of Athens, son of Critias III	Pl. *Chrm.* 154a †
[*PA/APF* 3013 (8792.7) *LGPN2* 42 *PAA* 276785	Pl. *Prt.* 315a, pat.
DPhA 21 *RE* 8 *PX* Γλαύκων Κριτίου]	Pl. *Smp.* 222b, pat.
tribe: ?Erechtheis	[Pl.] *Thg.* 128d, pat.
?480s–≤429	[Pl.] *Ax.* 364a, pat.
mother: daughter of ?Glaucon I of Cerameis	Xen. *Hell.* 2.4.19,
brother: Callaeschrus I	pat.
wife: daughter of Antiphon I	Xen. *Mem.* 3.6, pat.
father of Perictione and Charmides	Ael. *VH* 8.1, pat.
nephew: Critias IV	Procl. *in Tim.* 25–6,
See stemma: Plato.	pat.

From the name 'Glaucon,' *APF* surmised that Glaucon III was a grandson of the wealthy and prominent Glaucon I of Cerameis, but since Leagrus I was Glaucon I's only known son, Glaucon III was assumed to be the son of Glaucon I's otherwise unknown daughter. Glaucon III married the daughter of his first cousin, Antiphon I, i.e., he married his first cousin once removed.

Glaucon IV of Collytus, son of Ariston	Pl. *Prm.* 126a	speaker
[*PA/APF* 3028 (8792.10B) *LGPN2* 24 *PAA*	Pl. *Smp.*	speaker
277053, 276750 *RE* 7 *DPhA* 21 *PP PX*	Pl. *R.*	speaker
Γλαύκων Ἀρίστωνος Κολλυτεύς]	Xen. *Mem.* 3.6	
≤429–>382	Aes. no. 43 (fr. 2	
mother: Perictione	Dittmar)	
siblings: Plato, Adeimantus I, Potone;		
maternal half brother: Antiphon II;		
maternal stepbrother Demos		
stepfather and grand uncle: Pyrilampes		
See stemma: Plato.		

Life. Two crucial pieces in the puzzle of Glaucon IV's birth year are provided in a single passage of the *Republic*; Socrates says, addressing both Adeimantus I and Glaucon IV, "You are the sons of a great man, and Glaucon's lover began his elegy well when he wrote, celebrating your achievements at the battle of Megara, 'Sons of Ariston, godlike offspring of a famous man' " (368a). As Dover (1968b: 31) rightly puts the issue, "Plato's brothers ... are old enough to have distinguished themselves in 'the battle at Megara,' but Glaukon was not too old at that time to have had a 'lover' who composed elegiacs in his honour." The (a) old-enough criterion is twenty; the (b) not-too-old criterion is harder to specify since it was related to his height and the growth of his beard.

(a) An Athenian male, i.e. a citizen registered through his deme, was expected to serve in the militia (train, muster, maintain gear, etc.) from the age of eighteen; this fact is very widely known and frequently used in establishing ages roughly; but it is a partial fact, and thus widely misused: eighteen- and nineteen-year-olds fought only within Attica, and Megara is outside Attica. Those who believe there is a definite dramatic date for the *Republic* of 421, during the Peace of Nicias (see App. I) require a battle in Megara before that date, which Thucydides (4.72) accommodates with a battle in 424. However, Glaucon IV must then have been born by 444, generating a gap of sixteen years between Glaucon IV and Plato by the traditional dating of the latter (twenty years by my dating of Plato s.v.), and making Plato's brothers so old that some scholars have posited that they were in fact his uncles (see Shorey 1930: 144–5ne). If so, Perictione was not their mother, and Plato could have been her firstborn (the later myth of Plato's virgin birth would then be up and running). An additional consequence of choosing an early battle date is that the Glaucon of the *Republic* cannot be the Glaucon of the *Symposium* frame (see App. I) because a Glaucon born by 444 was no child in 416 (*Smp.* 173a). Another famous battle at Megara, favored by those who give a definite dramatic date of 411 to the dialogue, is the slightly anachronistic one of 409 (D. S. 13.65.1–2), making Glaucon IV's birth date 429 and, by the traditional dating, only one year senior to Plato. Dover (1968b: 31) notes that there were several battles mentioned by one historian or another, and that one cannot simply assume that the battle in question was one for which we have extant evidence.

(b) Glaucon IV's erotic orientation is toward males at the time of the *Republic*. His lover (*erastēs*, *R*. 368a) has reasonably been identified as Critias IV s.v. (Schleiermacher 1973), and nothing shameful about the relationship is hinted at in the passage. Glaucon IV was an *erōmenos* at the time the elegy was composed, some time before the action of the *Republic*. Glaucon IV's sexual orientation is presumably more marked than that of others present because he is singled out for teasing; he is the lover (*erastēs*) of boys: "You praise a snub-nosed one as cute, a hook-nosed one you say is regal, one in between is well proportioned, dark ones look manly, and pale ones are children of the gods. And as for a honey-colored boy, do you think that this very term is anything but the euphemistic coinage of a lover who found it easy to tolerate sallowness, provided it was accompanied by the bloom of youth?" (*R*. 474d–e). But the mores of Greek society at the time established that a youth was not to be called an *erōmenos* after he was fully bearded—a standard that varied by individual maturity.

Dover's *Greek Homosexuality* is indispensable for the vocabulary of Greek propriety:

> The junior partner in homosexual eros is called *pais* (or, of course, paidika) even when he has reached adult height and hair has begun to grow on his face, so that he might more appropriately be called *neaniskos, meirakion* or *ephebos*. There is a clear distinction between *paides* and *neaniskoi* . . . Once the beard was grown, a young male was supposed to be passing out of the eromenos stage . . . One could be erastes and eromenos at the same stage of one's life, but not both in relation to the same person. (1989: pp. 85–7)

It is unclear whether Dover would still put this last point quite so strongly, however, since his 1989 postscript adds of the 1978 original, "I underrated the evidence against the assumption . . . of Plato and Xenophon that the eromenos does not derive pleasure from copulation" (1989: 204). At the time of the battle, Glaucon IV could be an *erōmenos* proudly, but he could not age much past twenty and still be without a beard, so there is nothing in this bit of evidence to persuade us away from a battle in 409, and Glaucon IV's birth in 429.

In matters of Plato's own family and agemates, and those of his brothers, I attribute to Plato more accuracy in drawing characters in roughly correct chronological relations to one another than for people who were already old or dead in his youth. Rather surprisingly, *APF* goes to some lengths to preserve the accuracy of Xenophon (*Mem.* 3.6), according to whom a brash Glaucon IV, not yet twenty, is dissuaded from premature political activity by Socrates, who acts out of regard for Adeimantus I and Plato. But Diogenes 3.6 reports that Plato knew Socrates only from the age of twenty; on this evidence, Glaucon IV would be Plato's *younger* brother (Moors 1987: 13–6). Davies (*APF*: 8792.10B) tweaks twenty down to eighteen for Plato's meeting Socrates, noting that the biographical tradition for Plato is flawed and thus subject to such minor adjustments; the result "would allow Plato to have met Sokrates at the age of 18 [b. 428/7] before an elder brother was 20. Very tentatively, then, Glaukon's birth can be placed in or before 428." Glaucon IV and Plato, that is, were born a scant year apart (*APF*). Since neither Xenophon nor Diogenes is reliable for dates, since both are far removed from events by comparison to Plato, and—most importantly—since a number of episodes of Plato's life would be rendered problematic by assigning him the traditional date of birth, the *APF* compromise is not worth the ingenious effort.

In the later tradition.   Nine dialogues are attributed to a Glaucon of Athens (*PAA* 276750 ?= 277053): *Phidylus, Euripides, Amyntichus, Euthias, Lysithides, Aristophanes, Cephalus, Anaxiphemus,* and *Menexenus* (D. L. 2.124), from which nothing is extant. (Cf. D. L. 2.29, 124; 3.4; 13.65; Plu. *Mor.* 484f; [Socr.] *Ep., passim*; et al. in *SSR* 2.VIB.)

Glaucon (rhapsode) See App. II.

Glauconides (cockfighter) See App. II.

Gobryas of Persia (sage) See App. II.

Gorgias of Leontini, son of Charmantides	Pl. *Grg.* speaker
[*LGPN3A* 19 *OCD³ RE* 8 *DPhA* 28 *PP PX*	Pl. *Ap.* 19e *
Γοργίας]	Pl. *Phdr.* 261c
±485–±380	[Pl.] *G. Hp.* 282b, d
siblings: Herodicus, and a sister (who	frr. in DK 82
married Dicrates)	Xen. *Symp.* 1.5
renowned rhetorician with far-reaching	Xen. *Anab.* 2.6.16
influence	D. S. 12.53.1

Isocr. 10.3; 15.155–6,
268
Aristoph. *Wasps* 421
Aristoph. *Birds* 1701

Life and career.   Ancient Leontini, where Gorgias was born, was located in eastern Sicily ±79 km. northeast of Syracuse and ±19 km. from the sea (see Map 3). Gorgias' visit to Athens on an ambassadorial mission in 427 (D. S.) appears to have had a far-reaching impact on the practice of rhetoric in Athens. It was so widely imitated that various men have been identified as his students who may well have learned elsewhere what came to be called the Gorgian figures: antithesis most of all, but also "tropes and metaphors and figurative language and hypallage and catachresis and hyperbaton and doublings of words and repetitions and apostrophes and clauses of equal length" (Suda; cf. Pl. *Phdr.* 238d). Isocrates, Antiphon of Rhamnous, Thucydides, Polus, and Agathon s.vv. (see *Smp.* 194e–197e for a Gorgian parody) were all affected. Athenians generally seem to have been enchanted with the Sicilian novelty practiced by an expert, but those who later tried and failed to reproduce Gorgias' style saw their prose deemed bombastic and overly contrived. Dodds, whose brief introduction to Gorgias (1959: 6–10) is ideal, accepts ancient descriptions of Gorgias' public appearances in his purple robe (Ael. *VH* 12.32) and his dedication of a solid gold statue of himself at Delphi (Pau. 6.17.9; Ath. 505d)—both of which may argue, if true, that he was at least as vain and pompous as he appears in the *Gorgias*.

The distance between rhetoric and philosophy can be seen in Gorgias' own description of his art: "All who . . . persuade people of things do so by molding a false argument" (*Encomium on Helen* 13). Plato speaks of Gorgias as a rhetorician (*Grg.* 449a). Only pseudo-Plato refers to him as a sophist (*G. Hp.* 282b5), and even that reference has an honorific ("wise man") context with Bias and others. He (*Ap.* 19e) gives him a context with Prodicus and Hippias, often called sophists, but without any pejorative sense whatever. He is often mentioned in the dialogues without discussion (*Phlb.* 58a, *Smp.* 198c, [Pl.] *Thg.* 127e–8b).

Gorgias lived at least a hundred and five years, perhaps a hundred and nine; and his is not at all the only case of extreme longevity in ancient times (Lucian wrote a treatise called *Long-Lived Men* that includes Gorgias). One of the Greek practices that contributed to long lives was the mixing of wine with water (the underlying principle was understood by medical doctors at the end of the 19th c. c.e.). Both white and red wines contain malvoside which, even in 50–50 mixtures with water, kill typhoid and cholera bacilli, *E. coli*, staph, strep, et al. in time periods related to the density of the polyphenols in the wines tested, minutes to hours, regardless of alcohol concentrations (Majno 1975: 186–8). In fact, the bactericidal effect persists even when all the alcohol has been removed from the wine. People could drink *water* safely because they had, however inadvertently, disinfected it against the deadly epidemic diseases and against what are still the major causes of high infant mortality in the developing world.

In comedy.   With the *Wasps* of 422, five years after Gorgias' embassy to Athens, Aristophanes is already criticizing an imitator of Gorgias. In 414, he identifies Gorgias as a foreign cause of the litigious society that the two Athenians of *Birds* have left behind. (The last line alludes to tongues used in sacrifices; see Henderson 2000: 245n153.)

> They're a race of barbarians,
> Gorgiases and Philippuses.
> It's from these philippic
> Thrive-by-Tongues
> that all over Attica
> the tongue is specially excised.

In the later tradition.   In addition to the later authors cited above, scores of ancient sources retail tales about Gorgias (see Aristot. *Rh.* 1404a24; Philostr. *VS*; Pliny, *NH*; [Plu.] *LTO*; D. L. 8.58–9; Apoll. fr. 33; Cic. *Cato, De Orat.* and others quoted in DK).

Gryllus I of Erchia See App. II.

Gryllus II of Erchia, son of Xenophon See App. II.

Gyges of Lydia (king) See App. II.

Hagnodorus of Amphitrope See App. II. *See stemma: Plato.*

Hagnon of Stiria, son of Nicias of Stiria See App. II.

Harmodius of Aphidna (tyrannicide) See App. II.

Hegesippus, son of Ariston   [Pl.] *Ltr.* 2.314e *
[*PP* Ἡγήσιππος Ἀρίστωνος]

Hegesippus—if there was such a person—was probably an Athenian: the name 'Hegesippus' is not known in ancient times in Sicily but is common in Athens and other parts of Greece. [Plato] had some unstated obligation to him, although he was under Dionysius II's protection.

Hegias of Athens See App. II.

Helicon of Cyzicus   [Pl.] *Ltr.* 13.360c *
[*DPhA* 25 *RE* 3 *PP* Ἑλικών]   Plu. *Dion* 19
student of Eudoxus
associate of Polyxenus, Bryson
scientist

Letter 13 introduces and recommends Helicon to Dionysius II as a potential teacher. If Dionysius II had not yet the leisure for learning, then Helicon could teach a colleague who could later teach the tyrant. Helicon remained for some years in Syracuse, predicting a solar eclipse there during Plato's final visit in 360, for which, according to Plutarch, he was paid a *talent* of silver by Dionysius II.

Heraclides of Clazomenae and Athens   Pl. *Ion* 541d *
[*PA* 6489 *PAA* 486295 *FRA* 2901 *PP*   Thu. 4.50
Ἡρακλείδης]   Andoc. 3.29
active 424/3–390s   [Aristot.] *Ath. Pol.*
general, benefactor, naturalized citizen   41.3
                                                   inscriptions (see
                                                     below)

Life.   Heraclides of Clazomenae, a port city of Asia Minor east of Chios and south of the Hermus River (see Map 1), was a *proxenos* and benefactor (*euergetēs*) to Athens. He was honored for both, and granted certain privileges, in a Council decree dated 424/3 (*IG* I³ 227.8; *IG* I³ 227.19; *SEG* 32.10.26–27). In particular, Heraclides assisted Athens with a treaty negotiated with the Persians in 424/3 by Epilycus II, uncle of Andocides IV (Andoc.; Thu.).

   Osborne's discussion of Heraclides' naturalization (*NIA* 3.45) cites Plato's statement as evidence that Heraclides was granted Athenian citizenship in the category of extraordinary beneficence to the city, and gives the date of the naturalization as "early 390s" (dated 404–396 in *PAA*), adding that the first of the two decrees (*IG* I³ 227.2) is likely to be Heraclides' naturalization decree (*NIA* 3.47). That Heraclides was granted Athenian citizenship is beyond dispute. We have the testimony of pseudo-Aristotle (*Ath. Pol.* 41.3) that Heraclides (nicknamed 'the king') proposed increasing the payment to those attending the Assembly under the democracy to two *obols* a day. The proposal must have been made before 391 because two *obols* was the rate being paid in 492 or 491 when Aristophanes' *Assemblywomen* was produced. Since no noncitizen could make such a proposal, there is no doubt that Heraclides was a citizen by then. However, many scholars have doubted that *IG* I³ 227.2 actually refers to the naturalization of Heraclides because—but for two words (ἀναγράψαι τὸν)—the inscription consists of a suggested restoration by Köhler (1892) on the same stone, but higher than the commendation of 424/3 (see Moore 1974: 433–5 & nn). I share the concern that so complete a reconstruction does not inspire much confidence, but it also seems very odd that Heraclides' citizenship should have been granted so very late. By the 390s, so many foreigners, *metics,* and slaves had been granted citizenship in return for their services to the *polis* that Heraclides' being passed over for a decade or two is difficult to credit. Perhaps we do not have his naturalization decree.

It is especially interesting that, after having been granted Athenian citizenship, Heraclides continued to be referred to by his ethnic. That is, he remained "the Clazomenian" to others. Osborne (*NIA* 3.31) comments, "Clearly in these early instances at any rate, the original ethnics of these prominent figures remained standard in Athenian parlance."

In the later tradition.   Athenaeus (506a) summarized, and Aelian (*VH* 14.5) repeated, Plato's statement about Heraclides.

Heraclides of Syracuse	Pl. *Ltr.* 7.348b–349c *
[*LGPN3A* 135 *RE* 24 *PP* Ἡρακλείδης]	[Pl.] *Ltr.* 3, 4,
† 354	*passim* *
father of one son	*IG* IV² 95.39–40
associate of Dion	A. S. frr.
democratic leader	D. S. 16.5–20
	Plu. *Dion, passim*

Life and career.   Heraclides was the leader of the democratic movement in Sicily under the tyrant Dionysius II, but he appears to have had an official role in the regime (*Ltr.* 7.348b) as well. During Plato's third trip to Syracuse, 361–360, Dionysius II attempted to reduce the pay of the older mercenaries he maintained on Ortygia, causing a near mutiny that backfired: the tyrant raised their pay. When blame for the debacle fell on Heraclides, he went into hiding, and Dionysius II sent soldiers to find him. At that point his friend Theodotes s.v. made an agreement with the tyrant for which Plato was a formal witness: if Heraclides would return to the acropolis and face charges, and if it was decided he should be exiled, then he could have safe passage to the Peloponnese with his wife and son, and receive the income from his property in Sicily (7.348c–d). The tyrant angered Plato by reneging on the agreement, but Heraclides was meanwhile able to escape to the Peloponnese where he joined Dion (already in exile since 366). The two were honored together by the sanctuary to Asclepius in Epidaurus (*IG*). During the Olympic games of 360, Plato joined them on his way back to Athens from Syracuse, delivering the news of the tyrant's further intransigence in the face of five years' effort, in effect, the news that there was no further hope under Dionysius II of either reforming the tyranny or reuniting Dion with his family. Diodorus (16.6.4–5), as so often, telescopes five years into one: in his account, Heraclides and Dion escaped Sicily together (presumably in 366) and immediately began trying to raise an army.

Heraclides and Dion determined to attract other exiles and funds for ships and mercenaries, and to mount a full-scale military operation to free Sicily from tyranny. Dion was to return to Syracuse first, with Heraclides bringing triremes and other craft later (D. S. 16.6.5, *contra* Plu. *Dion* 32.4; see Westlake *CAH* 6²: 698–702). For those events in Syracuse after Heraclides' return and until his assassination in 354, see Dion s.v.

Heraclides of Athens See App. II.

Heraclides of Pontus, son of Euthyphro (historian) See App. II.

Heraclitus of Ephesus, son of Bloson (philosopher) See App. II.

Hermias of Atarneus	[Pl.] *Ltr.* 6 *	addressee
[*OCD³ DPhA* 80 *PP* Ἑρμείας]	Callis. fr. 2	
† 341	Theop. *hist.* frr. 201,	
student of Plato's Academy	242, 291	
friend of Aristotle	D. S. 16.52.2–7	
ruler of Atarneus and Assos in the Troad	Str. 13.1.54–57	
	Aristot. fr. 675	

Life. Hermias may have visited at the Academy in the 350s, and may have heard Plato (Str. 13.1.57 *contra* [Pl.] *Ltr.* 6) or met Aristotle there, but Aristotle was independently connected to Atarneus through his guardian, Proxenus of Atarneus. After his return to Atarneus from Athens, Hermias appears to have been advised by two former students of Plato that [Plato] introduces in *Letter* 6, Coriscus and Erastus, of nearby Scepsis s.vv. (described as *Socraticoi* by Str. 13.1.54), who later founded a philosophical school at Assos. Upon Plato's death, a number of philosophers of the Academy, including Aristotle, Xenocrates, and Theophrastus, went to Assos; there Aristotle became Hermias' close friend. Hermias was later captured by Mentor of Rhodes and tortured to death by agents of the Great King for his Macedonian sympathies. Aristotle had a cenotaph dedicated to Hermias at Delphi and wrote a hymn to his excellence (fr. 675) preserved not only by Diogenes but in frr. of papyri as well. Aristotle then married Pythias, Hermias' adopted daughter and niece. (Hermias is missing from the *PP* index but appears on p. 153.)

In the later tradition. Hermias is a favorite subject in late antiquity, but much of that tradition builds on the hostile statements of Theopompus (frr. 201, 242) who said Hermias was a eunuch and had been a slave before inheriting power. The latter fr. also alludes to the friendship of Hermias with Coriscus and Erastus.

Hermocrates I of Syracuse, son of Hermon	Pl. *Ti.*	speaker
[*LGPN3A* 12 *RE* 1 *OCD³ PP PX* Ἑρμοκράτης]	Pl. *Criti.*	speaker
±455–407	Thu. 4, 6–8, *passim*	
father of a daughter who was the first wife	Xen. *Hell.* 1.1.27,	
of Dionysius I of Syracuse	30–1, 3.13	
statesman, general	D. S. 13.18.3, 13.34.4	
	Procl. *in Tim.* 20a	

Plato represents Hermocrates as a young man of about twenty-eight, attending the Panathenaea and hosted by Critias III. Although he is expected to present the final discussion in the series *Timaeus-Critias-Hermocrates* (*Critias* 108c), there is no trace of that third dialogue.

Hermocrates was a prominent Sicilian leader; he warned the Sicilian *poleis* against Athenian expansionist plans as early as 424 (Thu. 4.58), and his command was central to the defeat of the Athenians 415–413. He was head of the aristocratic party and an opponent of radical (i.e. lawless) democracy. When the democratic party gained control in Syracuse in his absence in 410, Hermocrates was exiled *in absentia*. When he hired a private army, with funding from Pharnabazus, and attempted to take Syracuse by force in an effort to return, he was killed and his supporters banished. Dionysius I, future tyrant of Sicily, was one of those supporters and married Hermocrates' daughter, probably in 407. There are a number of later accounts of these events: see Dionysius I s.v.

Hermocritus I of Syracuse (cf. 'Hermocrates') See App. II. *See stemma: Dion.*

Hermodorus of Syracuse (biographer) See App. II.

Hermogenes of Alopece, son of	Pl. *Cra.*	speaker
Hipponicus II	Pl. *Phd.* 59b7	present
[*PA/APF* 5123 (7826.16B), 5119 *LGPN2* 23, 4	Xen. *Mem.*, *passim*	
PAA 420340, 420015 *RE* 21 *DPhA* 94 *PP*	Xen. *Hell.* 4.8.13	
Ἑρμογένης Ἱππονίκου Ἀλωπεκῆθεν]	Xen. *Smp.*	
>450–>392	Xen. *Apol.*	
paternal half brother: Callias III	Aes. *Tel.* no. 83 (fr.	
member of the Socratic circle	40 Dittmar)	
See stemmata: Callias, Pericles.	[Socr.] *Ep.* 14.9	

Life. Hermogenes, like his paternal half brother, Callias III, was a son of the "richest man in Greece," Hipponicus II, but Hermogenes' mother is unknown to us. And we do not know whether Hermogenes was older or younger than Callias III, though the texts provide a few hints. What is clear is that he was a *nothos*, acknowledged by his father and often called by his patronymic. If Hipponicus II had been married to Hermogenes' mother, even if she died, or he divorced her and then married Pericles I's [unnamed] former wife, Hermogenes would not have been a *nothos* and would have been entitled to a share in Hipponicus II's estate equal to Callias III's—which it is abundantly evident he did not receive. He may have been born outside a legal marriage before 450 or after. After is more likely—and it was probably closer to 440—because he seems to be a young man ≤422, the dramatic date of the *Cratylus* (383a; see App. I). Moreover, he was not one of those participating in Callias III's world congress of philosophy in ±433/2 (*Prt.*, see App. I). Another known member of Pericles I's extended household (see stemma) not mentioned at that great event is the other *nothos*, Pericles II (b. ±445). Although one participant, Agathon (b. >447), is of a similar age, he is represented as *notably* young (*Prt.* 315e) in that company.

In Plato, Hermogenes is an able interlocutor (*Cra.*) and is one of those present at Socrates' death (*Phd.*). Hermogenes' statement on naming beginning, "when we give names to our domestic slaves" (*Cra.* 384d) does not sound like the words of an impoverished man who depends on "charity from his friends" (*pace APF*, citing Xenophon). The Hermogenes of Xenophon is hardly recognizable as the same man, for Xenophon makes something of a fetish of Hermogenes' poverty and superstition—which is quite absent from Plato's dialogues.

Hipponicus II (†422/1) is still alive when Socrates addresses Hermogenes at *Cratylus* 391c: "since you haven't yet come into any money of your own" (ἐπειδὴ δὲ οὐκ ἐγκρατὴς εἶ τῶν πατρῴων), implying that Hermogenes had some just expectation of inheriting from his father. As Harrison points out in *The Law of Athens*, a *nothos* was allowed to receive bequests and also to receive gifts *inter vivos* (1998.1: 67). Since no author represents Hermogenes as money-grubbing, let us turn to the more important issue of citizenship rights, which is more controversial, and on which views range from "*nothoi* were also excluded from participation in the Athenian polis" (Patterson 1990: 70) to "*nothoi* had full rights of citizenship" (Stroud 1971: 299). Arguments very often take the form, "if a man was a member of x was he a citizen of the *polis*," or "membership in x was a necessary but insufficient condition for membership in the *polis*" where x is the household (*oikos*), the phratry, or the deme. Each has its adherents and, although I privilege deme membership, I would nonetheless emphasize two further points: that any of the three could be routes to citizenship when presiding locals felt favorably inclined toward a candidate; and that practices differed across geographical regions and time, frustrating all efforts to reduce the issue to a simple rule or to claim certainty in the absence of an explicit text. Hermogenes was a *nothos*, but he was a part of Hipponicus II's household; Hipponicus II, as torchbearer for the phratry, had some influence over phratry membership; and demes appear to have been more flexible about membership than either of the other groups (which was probably one of the reasons Pericles I sought to standardize procedures in 451/0). Even Patterson concedes, "We should not exaggerate the extent to which Athenian society conformed to formal, legal structures." I view it as very likely that Hermogenes *was* registered in the deme of Alopece and enjoyed such citizen rights as he wished to exercise, and such obligations as he was required to bear. Thus I take the son of Hipponicus II to be the Hermogenes who served as ambassador to the Persian King in the summer of 392 (Xen. *Hell.*).

In Xenophon.   Hermogenes appears to be Xenophon's chief source for the period at the end of Socrates' life when Xenophon s.v. was serving as a mercenary in Persia. Not only is Xenophon's *Apology* evidently based on the report of Hermogenes (*Ap.* 1)—who, by the way, is not among the named persons at the trial—Hermogenes supposedly tells Xenophon (*Mem.* 4.8.4–11) that he himself tried to persuade Socrates to think about his defense in advance of the trial, but Socrates tells him that his whole good life had been lived as a preparation for trial (4.8.4). However, Xenophon's Socrates also chips in that his *daimonion* forbade his thinking about what to say to the jury (4.8.5); that he would not want to grow old and decrepit (4.8.8); and that posterity will judge him, who suffered injustice, better than those who acted unjustly toward him (4.8.9–10). Also in the *Memorabilia*, Xenophon offers a homily in which Socrates advises Diodorus to assist Hermogenes financially (*Mem.* 2.10.1–6), but the anecdote is told at such a level of generality that it lacks the sort of persuasive power that would challenge Plato's representation of the same character.

According to Xenophon's *Symposium*, Callias III found Hermogenes walking in the Piraeus with Socrates, Charmides, Critobulus, and Antisthenes, after the horse-racing event at the greater Panathenaic games in August of 422. He invited all five to join him and Niceratus II as last minute guests to a banquet in honor of Lycon's son, Autolycus. Hermogenes proves on that occasion to be quite super-stitious—though less so than Xenophon s.v. himself—saying that he reads the gods' messages to him in dreams and bird entrails (*Symp.* 4.48).

Prosopographical notes and the later tradition. APF states that 5123 = 5119 is "con-ceivable," but *PAA* 420340 carries no cross-reference to 420015 (the ambassador); similarly, *LGPN2* 23 carries no cross-reference to 4 (the ambassador). Diogenes (2.121), misreading *Phaedo* 59b, takes Hermogenes to be a son of Crito; a few other late testimonia are collected in *SSR* 2.VIB.

In modern bibliography. The literature on *nothoi* has grown in recent years, espe-cially as Pericles I's citizenship laws of 451/0 have been reinterpreted, but there is no consensus. See MacDowell 1976b, "Bastards as Athenian Citizens," Rhodes 1978, "Bastards as Athenian Citizens," and Patterson 1990, "Those Athenian Bas-tards" (including a detailed history of the debate) for focused studies. See, for the legal context, Harrison (1998.1: 63–5); for orphan *nothoi*, Stroud 1971; for differing interpretations of the citizenship laws, Patterson 1981, Whitehead 1986: 97–109 (emphasizing deme membership), and Cohen 2000; and for phratry mem-bership, Lambert 1993.

Herodicus of Selymbria   Pl. *Prt.* 316d–e *
[*LGPN3B* 1 *RE* 2 *PP* Ἡρόδικος]   Pl. *Phdr.* 227d
teacher of ?Hippocrates of Cos   Pl. *R.* 3.406a
active early 5th c.
physician and trainer

Life. Herodicus, an athletic trainer in Selymbria, on the northern coast of the Propontis, is credited in medical history with having understood how diet affected both health and illness, and with having originated one of the three branches of ancient therapeutics: dietetics, alongside pharmacology and surgery. Athenians, however, seem to have taken a dim view of his strict regimen. In Plato's dialogues, Socrates uses a bit of Herodicus' physiological theory in describing the bulky pancration athlete, Polydamus, who needs the meat that would harm a normal person (*R.* 1.338c–d). Later, Herodicus is criticized personally for "nursing" his own illness with the result that instead of being cured of it, the illness remained with him throughout his too-long life (*R.* 3.406a–c). Protagoras describes him as formerly from Megara, and as a great sophist *cum* sage (*Prt.*; cf. *Phdr.*).

In the later tradition. By the time of Aristotle, Herodicus seems to have had an almost exclusively negative reputation for promoting what sounds very like an ascetic way of life (*Rh.* 1361b4). (Cf. Plu. *Mor.* 554c.)

Prosopographical notes. This is not Gorgias' brother of the same name.

Herodicus of Leontini, son of Charmantides (doctor) See App. II.

Heroscamander of ?Thebes See App. II.

Hesiod of Ascra (poet) See App. II.

Hestiaeus of Perinthus See App. II.

Hiero I of Gela and Syracuse, son of
  Deinomenes
[*RE* 11 *OCD*³ Ἰέρων]
r. 478–466
brother: Gelon
wife: daughter of Anaxilas
tyrant of Syracuse

Pl. *Ltr.* 7.336a †
[Pl.] *Ltr.* 2.311a
Xen. *Hiero*

Hiero I (also 'Hieron') was known both for his martial successes, especially against Carthage, and for his patronage of Greek festivals and poets. From 485, he was regent in Gela for his brother, Gelon, upon whose death Hiero became tyrant of Syracuse. Xenophon's dialogue is between Hiero and the lyric poet Simonides.

Hieronymus of Athens See App. II.

Hipparchus of Athens, son of Pisistratus (co-tyrant) See App. II.

Hipparete I of Athens, daughter of
  Hipponicus II of Alopece
[*PA*/*APF* 7590 (600.8A, 7826.9) *LGPN2* 1 *PAA*
537550 Ἱππαρέτη Ἱππονίκου Ἀλωπεκῆθεν
θυγάτηρ]
≤440–417/6
mother: [unnamed] former wife of Pericles I
siblings: full brother, Callias III; maternal half
  brothers, Paralus and Xanthippus II;
  paternal half brother, Hermogenes
husband: Alcibiades III
mother of Alcibiades IV and a daughter who
  married Hipponicus III
See stemmata: Alcibiades, Callias, Pericles.

Isocr. 16.31, 45,
  unnamed
[Andoc.] 4.13–15,
  unnamed

Life.   Hipparete I's birth has usually been set soon after 450 on grounds that she was born soon after her brother, Callias III (b. ±450), after her mother had already had two sons with Pericles I 460–455. If that were accurate, she would have married Alcibiades III very late indeed for an Athenian woman, when she was approaching thirty; and he would have been unusual both in marrying before he turned thirty and in marrying a woman his own age. These peculiar consequences are unnecessary because there is no reason to confine Hipparete I's mother's childbearing span to ten years. Hipparete I's birth was very likely much closer to 440 than 450. (For an alternative solution to the consequences, positing a second wife for Hipponicus II s.v., see Bicknell 1982 and Cox 1998.)

Hipparete I's marriage to Alcibiades III occurred in the late 420s (Isocr. 16.31; cf. [Andoc.] 4.13). Her father († 422/1), may therefore have been living when she married, but her dowry would in any case probably have been promised and paid by Callias III because Hipponicus II s.v. appears to have passed control of family affairs to Callias III as early as the beginning of the Peloponnesian war. The terms of the dowry of twenty *talents*, with half to be paid upon the birth of a child, are given by the speaker of pseudo-Andocides, possibly Phaeax (4.13–4). But he is not well informed about other family matters, confusing Hipparete I's father with the general Hippocrates, thus mistaking Hipponicus II for the casualty at Delium (4.13), so the exact terms are perhaps not reliable. Nevertheless, he presents an upstanding Hipparete I who, embarrassed by Alcibiades III's bringing a variety of lovers into their house, approached the archon to seek a divorce, which was her legal right, whereupon Alcibiades III had her carried bodily from the *agora* (4.14–15). The speaker might have added that the ongoing war had caused Callias III to fall deeply into debt himself by the late 420s. While Alcibiades III may well have been in such financial straits that he could not afford the consequences of a divorce, namely, that he would be required to return the dowry, he may not have been able to collect the remaining half either. The couple produced a daughter who would later marry her first cousin, then they produced a son, Alcibiades IV; Hipparete I died at or very soon after the son's birth.

Hipparete I's reputation for modesty is confirmed by Isocrates (16). While the two sources approach the family of Alcibiades III from opposite directions—the one defends Alcibiades IV, in part by defending the reputation of his family (Isocr. 16.31), the other attacks Alcibiades III ([Andoc.] 4.13–15)—they agree in their praise of Hipparete I. See *APF* and Cox (1998: 222–9) for alliances among wealthy families in which Hipparete I was more pawn than player. Plutarch (*Alc.* 8.1–4) mainly follows pseudo-Andocides.

Hipparete II of Athens, daughter of Alcibiades IV of Scambonidae See App. II. *See stemma: Alcibiades.*

Hipparinus I of Syracuse
[*LGPN3A* 3 *RE* 1 Ἱππαρῖνος]
5th–4th c.

Pl. *Ltr.* 8.353b, 354d,
    355e, unnamed †
IG IV² 95.39

father of Dion, Megacles, Aristomache (wife   Nean. fr. 31
   of Dionysius I)
father-in-law and counselor of Dionysius I
See stemma: Dion.

Prosopographical notes.   *Letter* 8 has an ancient history of causing confusion because
its famous "three kings passage" mentions all three men named Hipparinus, but
not by name:

> . . . first, my son [Hipparinus III], in double gratitude for my father's [Hippar-
> inus I's] services and my own (as my father in his time saved the city from
> the barbarians, I have twice freed it from tyrants, as you yourselves can
> bear witness); secondly, him [Hipparinus II] who has the same name as my
> father and is the son of Dionysius [I], in gratitude for the help he has just
> rendered your cause, as well as because of his upright character; for though
> he is the son of a tyrant [Dionysius I], he is voluntarily liberating the city
> and gaining for himself and his house undying honor in place of an ephem-
> eral and unjust tyranny. Thirdly, invite him who is now head of the army
> of your enemies—Dionysius [II] the son of Dionysius [I]. . . . (Pl. *Ltr.* 8.355e–
> 356a)

Hipparinus I, Dion's father, is missing from the index of PCW (1772), where there
is the additional confusion that the Hipparinus labeled 'I' is also labeled 'tyrant
of Sicily' when the son of Dionysius I—a separate entry—was in fact the 'tyrant
of Sicily'.

Hipparinus II of Syracuse, son of Dionysius I   Pl. *Ltr.* 8.356a,
[*LGPN3A* 4 *RE* 2 *PP* Ἱππαρῖνος]   unnamed, 356c *
±385–351   *GG* 3.2.102–7
mother: Aristomache
siblings: Nysaeus, Sophrosyne (wife of
   Dionysius II), Arete (wife of Thearides and
   Dion); paternal half siblings: Dionysius II,
   Hermocritus II, Dicaeosyne (wife of
   Leptines I)
uncle: Dion
tyrant of Sicily
See stemma: Dion.

Hipparinus II successfully led Dion's party from exile in Leontini to make a
surprise attack on Syracuse in Callippus' absence in 353, beginning his own rule
early in 352 and remaining in power for two years, until the end of 451. His
successor was his younger brother, Nysaeus. Hipparinus II was proposed for the
triple kingship (*Ltr.* 8.356a, quoted above) with Hipparinus III and Dionysius II.

Hipparinus III of Syracuse, son of Dion   Pl. *Ltr.* 7.324a *
[*LGPN3A* 5 *RE* 3 *PP* Ἱππαρῖνος]   Pl. *Ltr.* 8.355e,
±373–≤354   unnamed *
mother: Arete   Plu. *Dion* 31.3
See stemma: Dion.

Prosopographical notes.   Plato proposed Hipparinus III for the triple kingship (*Ltr.* 8.355e, quoted above) with Hipparinus II and Dionysius II. Plutarch (and Nepos) report that Hipparinus III died before Dion, making it implausible for Plato to propose this son of Dion for the shared kingship, leading others to posit a posthumous child of Dion, an Aretaeus et al. Bury sensibly (1929: 569) proposed that, if *Letter* 8 is genuine, Plato wrote it before he learned of Hipparinus III's death. Harward (1932: 10) understands 'Aretaeus' to be an alias for Hipparinus III, but lists an unnamed posthumous son of Arete and Dion as well. *LGPN3A* lists them separately as two sons. The index of *PP* lists Hipparinus once, but the text (p. 152) takes both II and III into account.

Hippias of Elis, son of Diopeithes   Pl. *Prt.*   speaker
[*LGPN3A* 11 *RE* 13 *DPhA* 145   Pl. *Ap.* 19e *
*OCD*³ *PP PX* Ἱππίας]   Pl. *Phdr.* 267b
±470s–>399   [Pl.] *G. Hp.*   speaker
polymath, sophist, diplomat   [Pl.] *L. Hp.*   speaker
                                                 Xen. *Mem.* 4.4.5–25
                                                 frr. in DK 86

Life and career.   Plato is the chief source for the life of Hippias, including his date of birth: Protagoras says he is old enough to be Hippias' father (*Prt.* 317c), and Hippias himself describes Protagoras as an older man in the comic and pseudo-Platonic *Greater Hippias* (282d–e), so he was an approximate contemporary of Socrates. Hippias, who often served Elis as an ambassador, especially to Sparta (*G. Hp.* 281a–b), is represented as supremely self-confident, eager to display or to teach "arithmetic, astronomy, geometry, music, and poetry" (*Prt.* 318e), astronomy, geometry, arithmetic, grammar, music, genealogy, ancient history, and ethics (*G. Hp.* 285b–286c), a craftsman who made his own clothing, jewelry and implements (*L. Hp.* 368b–d), a polymath who could memorize fifty names on one hearing (*G. Hp.* 285e)—but also as a sophist who taught his students how to win arguments (*G. Hp.* 287b) and had already made himself very rich by teaching public speaking to the young (*G. Hp.* 282d–e). Socrates' discussion of justice and law with Hippias in Xenophon (*Mem.* 4.4.6) is very like a sequel to the conversations of the *Greater Hippias* and *Lesser Hippias*, offering no additional biographical information; but Xenophon attributes a system of mnemonics to Hippias that Callias III paid to learn (Xen. *Symp.* 4.62). Because Plato brings in Hippias' knowledge of mathematics all three times he introduces the character (see *L. Hp.* 367a–e), it is probable that Hippias of Elis was the mathematician who discovered the curve called the *quadratrix* for trisecting an angle (Procl. *Eucl.* = DK 86 fr. 21, without specifying which Hippias), which Dinostratus used later to "square the circle." The *quadratrix* was the first curve to be plotted point by point (using a sliding apparatus) rather than with a compass and straightedge.

In the later tradition. Aristotle's Hippias of Thasos (*Poet.* 1461a21–3) may be a confusion with Hippias of Elis (Freeman 1978: 144). Two titles supposed to be of works by Hippias derive from later authors, *Nomenclature of Tribes* (named by a scholiast of Apollonius of Rhodes), and *Synogogē* (Ath. 608f), a compilation of what Hippias had read. Woodruff (1982: 134–135nn1, 13), assessing the ancient evidence independently, warns against the fuller but unstable constructions of Hippias' life in Dümmler (1889: 52 ff.) and Untersteiner (1954: 272–303). (Cf. Philostr. *VS* 1.11.1–8; Ath. 218c; 506f; et al. from DK.)

Prosopographical notes. The tradition that Isocrates married Hippias' widowed daughter is a late one, "legally and chronologically impossible" (*APF*). Dušanić (1991: 82–3, 2000: 30 with n59) notes that Tertullian (*Apology* 46.16) says Hippias was killed in an Elean *coup d'état* in ±385.

Hippias of Athens, son of Pisistratus (co-tyrant) See App. II.

Hippocrates of Athens, son of Apollodorus
[*PA* 7630 *LGPN2* 7 *PAA* 538420 *PP*
Ἱπποκράτης Ἀπολλοδώρου]
?late 450s–>411
mother: ?Pericles I's sister
brother: Phason
See stemma: Pericles.

Pl. *Prt.* 310b, 316b,   speaker
    328d
Aristoph. *Thesm.* 273
& schol.

Life. The Hippocrates of the dialogue, at most about twenty, is not an outsider to the other participants: he knew in advance of Protagoras' anticipated arrival, and he does not need to be introduced to the local persons present. Hippocrates is introduced to Protagoras as a local (Athenian), and a member of a "great and wealthy family" (316b9), a family wealthy enough that Hippocrates has a slave serving as a personal attendant. Satyrus, the slave, had run away to Oenoë, and Hippocrates had just brought him back (310c) as the *Protagoras* began.

There is some evidence that the Hippocrates of the dialogue is a nephew of Pericles I. Besides the preponderance of persons of Pericles I's family and household named as present in the dialogue (see stemmata for Pericles I and Callias III, related through Pericles I's first wife), note that Socrates makes it a point to single out the absent but living Pericles I and Clinias IV (and no one else) at 319e–320b. Socrates brings up Pericles I again at 329a. With the stemma for the family, and the date and participants of the *Protagoras* in mind, it may well be that Pericles I's sister, a victim of the plague of 429, had married an Apollodorus—a common name—and named a son after her maternal grandfather, exactly as her full brother Ariphron II had done. The name 'Hippocrates' goes back further in the Alcmaeonid family than the stemma shows; the father of Pisistratus is the first one of note. Without such a strong familial connection, it is difficult to justify the praise of Hippocrates' family in *Protagoras*, and difficult to explain his very presence there. Cf. the root 'Hippo-' in names of Pericles I's family at Xanthippe s.v.

There is another reason, an independent one, to suppose that Socrates' companion may be a nephew of Pericles I. In Aristophanes (*Thesm.* 273), Euripides' kinsman shouts, "You might as well swear by Hippocrates' Apartment House!" A scholium states that of the passage refers to the father of three rowdy young men identified in Aristophanes' *Clouds* (1001), i.e. Hippocrates, the nephew of Pericles I. Thus *PA* assigns the line to the only known nephew of Pericles I named Hippocrates, the famous general (*PA* 7640). But *that* Hippocrates had been dead for some twelve years at the time of the play. *APF* (11811.2) suggests that the scholiast "conflated" the two; I suggest rather that the Hippocrates still living in 411, the nephew of Pericles I, is the Hippocrates who takes Socrates to the house of Callias III.

Prosopographical notes.   Socrates mentions Hippocrates' father, Apollodorus, in the dialogue as if he is already well known to both the friend who listens to Socrates' narration (310a9), and to the company in Callias III's house—that is, Socrates finds it unnecessary to distinguish this Apollodorus by demotic or patronymic (although the name itself is a particularly common one). Hippocrates' father, Apollodorus, cannot be the Socratic one because that Apollodorus s.v. says explicitly that he has been associating with Socrates for less than three years (Pl. *Smp.* 172c5–6) in ±400, the dramatic date of the frame, whereas the dramatic date of Plato's *Protagoras* is ±433/2, when Socrates was in his mid-thirties. Moreover, the Socratic was about the age of Plato's brother, Glaucon IV (*Smp.* 173a5), and thus had not been born when Callias III brought together the illustrious intellectuals of his day.

Nor can Hippocrates' father be the Apollodorus s.v. of Plato's *Ion* (541c–d) for that Apollodorus had not yet been made a citizen of Athens in 433/2. Because the Hippocrates of the *Protagoras* is Athenian, his father must also have been Athenian because Pericles I's citizenship laws, limiting Athenian citizenship to those with two Athenian parents, had been in effect since 451/0 and are still nearly two decades from breaking down under manpower pressures at the end of the Peloponnesian war.

Hippocrates I of Athens See App. II.

Hippocrates II of Athens, son of Megacles II See App. II. *See stemma: Pericles.*

Hippocrates of Chios (mathematical astronomer) See App. II.

Hippocrates of Cholarges, son of Ariphron II	Thu. 4, *passim*
	Xen. *Mem.* 3.5.4
[*PA*/*APF* 7640 (11811.2) *LGPN2* 18 *PAA*	*IG* I³ 369.3
538615 *RE* 3 *PX* Ἱπποκράτης Ἀρίφρονος	(inventory other)
Χολαργεύς]	Aristoph. *Clouds*
±460–424	1001 & schol.

father of Telesippus, Demophon, and Pericles
    III
See stemma: Pericles.

Family. Although Hippocrates must have been born by 456 to have been elected general in 426, he died in 424 leaving three sons; since Athenian men married at about the age of thirty, and because he is not mentioned as a young general, it is more likely that he was born ±460. He was Pericles I's nephew, a member of a wealthy governing family of Athens. His sons were apparently a very ill-behaved lot (Aristoph.).

Hippocrates appears in an inscription noting his election as general in 426/5 (*IG*) and is heard of first in Thucydides as one of two Athenian generals who received entreaties from the democratic party in Megara in the summer of 424 to collude with them in a "surprise" Athenian attack on Megara (Thu. 4.66.3), the success of which would be ensured by the party's leaving open a city gate. The conspiracy was hatched, and Hippocrates attacked (4.67.1), but someone revealed the plot to the rival party within Megara in time to prevent an easy Athenian victory. After some skirmishes, Megara remained in the hands of its oligarchic faction (4.74.3–4). At about this same time, Hippocrates entertained entreaties from Boeotians for Athenian assistance in establishing an Athenian-style democracy in Boeotia (4.76.2), again with promised help from the inside (4.77.1).

Hippocrates' Delium campaign is of some interest because Socrates was one of the hoplites serving in the action. In Delium, Hippocrates' troops fortified the temple of Apollo and headed homeward (4.91.1), though Hippocrates remained with a hoplite contingent in Delium (4.90.4). Boeotian troops about equal in strength to the Athenians arrived and prepared to attack the Athenian hoplites who were formed "eight-deep." In the midst of Hippocrates' speech to his troops (4.95.1–3), the Boeotians suddenly attacked, followed soon by a surprise cavalry attack, generating such panic that the Athenians retreated in great disorder (4.96.1–6). Although Delium was able to hold out for seventeen days, casualties were double those of the Boeotians, and Hippocrates was killed (4.101.1–2), making the attempted penetration into Boeotia a disaster for Athens (*CAH* 5²: 425). In Xenophon (*Mem.* 3.5.4), Pericles II mentions Hippocrates to Socrates as one of several examples of crucial losses suffered by the Athenians during the Peloponnesian war.

In the later tradition. Hippocrates appears also in some late sources: Pausanias (3.6.1, 9.6.3); Diodorus (12.66 Megarian episode, 12.69 the Delium battle); Plutarch (*Nic.* 6.3 Delium mentioned). His sons are known from their appearance in comic poets (cf. *APF* 11811.2).

Hippocrates of Cos, son of Heraclides
[*LGPN1* 11 *DPhA* 152 *RE* 16 and supp. 3, 6,
13 *OCD³ PP* Ἱπποκράτης]
±469–399
mother: Phaenareta or Praxithea
father of Dracon, Thessalus
student of Herodicus and Gorgias
famous physician

Pl. *Prt.* 311b–c
Pl. *Phdr.* 270c–d
Pl. *Chrm.* 156e
Hippoc. *opera*
Aristot. *Pol.* 1326a14

Life. By convention, the physician Hippocrates is given a lifespan virtually identical to that of Socrates. Hippocrates was well-known by the time of Plato, and Plato has the distinction of providing the only contemporaneous passage on Hippocratic method from outside the Hippocratic corpus (*Phdr.*). By the time of Aristotle (*Pol.*), Hippocrates is the byword for greatness among physicians. Although there is no shred of evidence in any contemporaneous source that Hippocrates visited Athens, much less lived there, it is not uncommon in the literature to see Hippocrates represented as a resident of the city. But in fact there are a great many inconsistent stories about the life of Hippocrates, about whom there is little information available. Controversy continues over which parts of the enormous Hippocratic corpus, if any, he may have written.

In the later tradition.   Galen takes up Plato's discussion of Hippocrates in his *De methodo medendi* 1.2.7 et al.

Hippodamus of Miletus (city planner) See App. II.

Hipponicus II of Alopece, son of Callias II
[*PA/APF* 7658 (7826.9) *LGPN2* 13 *PAA* 538910
RE 3 *PP* Ἱππόνικος Καλλίου
Ἀλωπεκῆθεν]
±485–422/1
mother: Elpinice of Laciadae
wife: [unnamed] former wife of Pericles I
offspring with [unnamed]: Callias III,
  Hipparete I; son with unknown woman:
  Hermogenes
"richest man in Greece"
See stemmata: Callias, Pericles.

Pl. *Prt.* 314e5,
  315d2 *
Xen. *WM* 4.15
Aes. *Asp.* no. 61 (frr.
  16, 20 Dittmar)
Aes. *Tel.* no. 84 (frr.
  41, 44 Dittmar)
Aes. *Cal.* no. 73 (fr.
  34 Dittmar)
IG I³ 455.5
IDélos 104–30, 10;
  104–31, 7
Thu. 3.91.4
D. S. 12.4.5, 12.65.5
Isocr. 16.31
Andoc. 1.115, 130
Lys. 19.48
comedy (see below)

Family.   The marriage between Hipponicus II's parents, Callias II of Alopece, a Ceryces, and the Alcmaeonid Elpinice, paternal half sister of the wealthy Cimon II of Laciadae, was probably contracted in the early 480s when political circumstances encouraged the consolidation of wealth within leading Athenian families (*APF* 7826.6, Cox 1998: 222–4). At *Cimon* 4.3, Plutarch remarks that Elpinice, Hipponicus II's mother, was buried among Cimon II's family. Kirchner's inference (1896: 258–9, 1617) has been generally accepted that Elpinice's marriage to the wealthy Callias II of Athens ended in divorce sometime after the birth of Hipponicus II (see Meyer 1899: 27–31, Hignett 1952: 194, *APF* 7826.6). Cox (1989: 35n2, 1998: 222–9) has been a holdout against the divorce hypothesis, supported by

Humphreys' evidence that a married woman could choose to be buried with the family into which she had been born (1983: 111–5). But there is another piece of evidence for an estrangement between Hipponicus II's parents. Although *APF* notes that reliable biographical information about Elpinice (8429.10B) does not exist following her marriage to Callias II, a later association with Polygnotus (Plu. *Cim.* 4.6) is noted. Osborne (*NIA* 3.23–4n) puts the date of Polygnotus' arrival in Athens ≥463, and his naturalization at ±460. Elpinice, born ≤510, would have been at least fifty in 460; but Callias II would still have been alive, since his death is put at ±446. A divorce from Callias II is required to make the association with Polygnotus plausible.

Life and career.   By the time of Hipponicus II's birth ±485, Callias II had already amassed a legendary fortune, having been among the first to exploit slave labor for mining silver on the cape at Laurium. Thus Hipponicus II was famous as the "richest man in Greece" (Isocr., Andoc., Lys.). In *Ways and Means*, Xenophon states, Hipponicus II was working six hundred slaves in his mines and thus bringing in six *talents* per year from that source alone (4.15). Hipponicus II also had cult income from the priestly office to which he had been appointed as a Ceryces (Andoc. 1.115), and probably other resources as well.

    After 455, Hipponicus II married the former wife of Pericles I who was a close relation of Pericles I (see [unnamed] s.v.). With her, Hipponicus II had two children, Callias III ±450, and Hipparete I ≤440. Nothing is known of the mother of Hipponicus II's other son, Hermogenes s.v. A typographical error with the potential to do mischief both to the stemma and to the record of who was present in the *Protagoras* appears in PCW (752) at 314e5: "On one side were Hipponicus and . . ." should be "On one side were Callias, son of Hipponicus, and. . . ."

    In 445/4, Hipponicus II was secretary of Council (*IG*). He was still an active man in ±433/2, the dramatic date of *Protagoras* (see App. I), but we may assume that he had passed control of the household to his adult son, Callias III (as Cephalus s.v. did with Polemarchus in *Republic*; see MacDowell 1978: 91 on this common practice). Hipponicus II served as general for Athens in Tanagra in 426/5 (Thu., D. S.), and probably died in 422/1 (Ath. 218b, citing Eu. *Flatt.* of 421). The inscriptions from Delos are posthumous.

In comedy.   Hipponicus II is not much heard of in comedy compared to his son, Callias III; the ridicule he suffers at the hands of the Socratic Aeschines is comparable. However, both Cratinus, >430 (*Thr.* fr. 81 [K 339], and fr. 492 from an uncertain play [K 336]), and Eupolis, in the late 20s (*Flatt.* fr. 156 [K 154], and *Sav.* fr. 20 [K 19]), mention Hipponicus II variously as a tightwad, red-faced or red-haired.

In the later tradition.   See Athenaeus (218b, 220b, 328e, 537b); Aelian (*VH* 14.16); and Nepos (*Alc.* 2.1).

Hipponicus III of Alopece, son of Callias III
[*PA*/*APF* 7659 (7826.15) *LGPN2* 14 *PAA*
538915 *RE* 4 Ἱππόνικος Καλλίου
Ἀλωπεκῆθεν]

Pl. *Ap.* 20a *
Lys. 14.28
Andoc. 1.121, 126
Agora 19.26.455

≤421–>342/1   Harp. s.v.
mother: daughter of Glaucon II
sibling: [unnamed] paternal half brother
wife: daughter of Alcibiades III
See stemmata: Alcibiades, Callias, Pericles.

Life. Hipponicus III's mother died when, or perhaps a few years after, he was born ≤421; his father, Callias III s.v., remarried ≤413 and a third time about a year later. Although Callias III's loss of his silver mining income during the Peloponnesian war much reduced Hipponicus III's inheritance, such changes of fortunes were widespread in Attica, so he was still relatively wealthy as a young man and could expect to contract a favorable marriage. Moreover, in addition to wealth, he had the familial Spartan *proxeny* (Xen. *Hell.* 6.3.4) and his honorable Ceryces heritage (Andoc. 1.126) to make any offer of marriage more attractive. In 399, Hipponicus III married his first cousin, the daughter of Alcibiades III. In about 395, however, according to a speech of Lysias, Hipponicus III not only divorced her, but publicly denounced her before witnesses for incest with her brother, Alcibiades IV.

Other expectations also failed to pan out: Hipponicus III was not appointed torchbearer by the Ceryces clan upon the death of Callias III in 367/6 (see Androt. fr. 30, Philoch. fr. 155). Hipponicus III probably litigated against Autocles <360 (Harp.); he was still active in 342/1 at about the age of eighty, buying two workshops in Melite for 1,500 *drachmae* (*Agora*). The family appears never to have regained anything like its former wealth or influence.

Prosopographical notes.   APF mistakes Hipponicus III for the son of Callias III who, through his father's intervention, sought to claim the surviving heiress daughter of Epilycus II (who was Hipponicus III's first cousin once removed). As Andocides IV explains (1.124), Callias III was acting on behalf of his other son, Hipponicus III's unnamed half brother (who was maternal half uncle to the surviving heiress)—though Andocides himself muddies the water by implying that Callias III wanted to marry the girl himself (1.122, 128).

Hippothales of Athens, son of Hieronymus   Pl. *Ly.*   speaker
[*PA* 7613 *LGPN2* 1 *PAA* 538065 *DPhA* 158   D. L. 3.46
PP RE s.v. Ἱπποθάλης Ἱερωνύμου]
b. ±425
lover of Lysis II

In the *Lysis*, Hippothales is called *neaniskos* (203a), and is fixated on the apparently slightly younger Lysis II. Diogenes (3.46) names a Hippothales of Athens as a pupil of Plato, perhaps on the basis of this dialogue, but he may also have been an associate, given the similarity in their ages.

Holas, slave of Axiochus of Scambonidae See App. II.

Horomazes of Persia See App. II.

Iatrocles of Athens and ?Syracuse   [Pl.] *Ltr.* 13.363e *
[*LGPN3A* 3 *FRA* 7722 *PAA* 531065
Ἰατροκλῆς]

If manumitted by [Plato], as the letter states, Iatrocles qualifies as a foreign resident of Athens, having been a slave there, and also as a resident of Syracuse if, as alleged, Dionysius II intended to employ him for wages in ≥365. *LGPN3A* queries Syracuse; *FRA* says "probably fictitious"; *PAA* says "name doubtful."

Ibycus of Rhegium (poet) See App. II.

Iccus of Tarentum (athlete) See App. II.

Ion of Ephesus   Pl. *Ion*   speaker
[*FRA* 1604 *PAA* 543175 *RE* 13
Stephanis 1305 *OCD³ PP* Ἴων]
active late 5th c.
rhapsode

Ion claimed that, as a rhapsode, he knew the business of a general, so Socrates suggested he make himself available to Athens for service as a general. The dramatic date of *Ion*, 413 (see App. I), is a time of manpower shortage after the Athenian fleet had been utterly lost on the Sicilian campaign. When Ion claims that Ephesus, his home city on the coast of Asia Minor, is under Athenian control and that Athens would not be likely to choose a foreigner as general (541c), Socrates quickly provides three examples of foreign generals Athens has already chosen (see s.vv.)—examples that have since been borne out by evidence from inscriptions.

Ion of Chios, son of Orthomenes   frr. in DK 36
[*FRA* 7317 *LGPN1* 1 *PAA* 543185   frr. in *FGrH* 392
DPhA 20 *RE* 11 *OCD³* Ἴων]   frr. in *TGrF* 1²:
b. 485–480, † ≤421   95–114
father of Tudeus   Aristoph. *Peace*
tragedian, Pythagorean philosopher, historian   834–7 & schol.

Life and works. Ion's birth is calculated from a trip to Athens he says he made while still a youth (*meirakion*) at which time he met Cimon II. That meeting can be dated to ±465, and Ion's birth within the range 485–480. Ion appears to have visited Athens frequently thereafter. He began producing tragedies in the late 450s or early 440s. Soon after his death, Aristophanes paid him a straight compliment in

Peace, dated 421, "Ion of Chios, who some years ago on earth composed *The Dawn Star*. When he arrived up there, everybody dubbed him Dawn Star right away!" It is the scholiast of these lines who provides much of what we surmise about Ion: that he wrote satyr plays to accompany his tragedies, epigrams (the few that survive under his name are spurious), lyrics of various types (some survive), encomia, and elegiac poems. A dithyrambic victory is recorded in the same scholium, along with the story that Ion sent a gift of Chian wine to celebrate his victory, enough for every Athenian. Ion's prose works (*FGrH*) included an *Epidemiae* or *Visits* in which Socrates is mentioned (frr. 4–7), a *Foundation of Chios*, and a *Cosmology*. His *Triagmos* was apparently a Pythagorean philosophical work attributing a threefold principle to nature (DK). What is recorded as *Memoirs* is probably his *Epidemiae* under another name.

The scholiast also says, however, that Ion of Chios appears in Plato's dialogue *Ion*, which is historically improbable: Ion was probably dead in 421, although a revival of *Peace* after 412 provides an alternative date for his death. Plato's Ion was from Ephesus, however, a fact emphasized in the dialogue.

In the later tradition.   The philosophical frr. are preserved at Harpocration (s.v.); Diogenes (8.8); and Plutarch (*Mor.* 316d). See testimonia in Suda (ι 487); Strabo 14.1.35; Athenaeus (3f, the Chian wine story; 35d–e, 436f; 447d; 463a; 603e); Plutarch (*Cim.* 9.1); Euripides (*Hipp.* hypothesis ii, that Ion placed when Euripides won); and many others. The Loeb *Greek Lyric* IV (1992) collects a large number of the testimonia with notes about their reliability; DK has fewer testimonia and no such notes.

Iphicrates (?general) See App. II.

Ischomachus of Athens   Xen. *Oec.*, *passim*
[*PA/APF* 7725 (7826.13–4) *LGPN2* 1   Aes. no. 91 (fr. 49
PAA 542585, 542570, 542575 *DPhA* 26 *PX*   Dittmar)
Ἰσχόμαχος]   Lys. 19.45–6
460s–±413   Lys. fr. 32
wife: Chrysilla (who later married Callias III)   (Thalheim)
father of two sons, and a daughter who   Andoc. 1.124–7
  married Epilycus II, then Callias III   Crat. fr. 365 (K 328)
See stemma: Callias.   P. Oxy. (see below)

Life.   In a masterful winnowing of wheat from chaff, Davies (*APF* 7826.13–4) draws a consistent Ischomachus, "Xenophon's ideal landowner," against a background of prosopographical complexity generated both by Ischomachus' daughter's marriage to Epilycus II <420, then to Callias III ≥413, and by his widow Chrysilla's marriage to Callias III ≥412 (s.vv.)—altogether involving at least five minor children and large fortunes in wartime. In what follows, I have incorporated *APF* dating except to tighten the range of a few dates where the evidence permits. Ischomachus was probably born in the early 360s, married ±436, and produced three children before his death ±413. *APF* offers 413–04 as the period in which Ischomachus died, a range I have narrowed because there is less than a year between Callias III's second and third marriages, and it is overwhelmingly more probable that Epilycus II died with his fellow citizens in the Sicilian expedition than that he died on some later visit to Sicily (Andoc. 1.117); moreover, each additional year of life for Ischomachus would increase Chrysilla's childbearing span from the current twenty-three years between first and last child to as much as thirty-one years.

Ischomachus is known primarily from Xenophon, who provides neither his parents' names nor his deme (typical in Xen.; cf. Whitehead 1983 on *Hell.*). Xenophon gives some other important details, e.g., Ischomachus' father was the landed farmer from whom Ischomachus learned how to make estate management a profitable business. Ischomachus proudly tells Socrates his secret of success: purchase only uncultivated land, then improve it, increasing its value a hundredfold, then sell it and use the proceeds to buy more uncultivated land (Xen. *Oec.* 20.22–6). The comic poet Cratinus lampooned Ischomachus <420 as a "tightwad"—an epithet that well fits the attitudes Xenophon reports. Ischomachus, for example, is as serious about housekeeping as he is about husbandry, detailing to Socrates the instructions he gave his fourteen-year-old bride on orderly estate management, abundantly illustrated with Ischomachus' military experiences (*Oec.* 7.5–10.13; cf. Chrysilla s.v.). Socrates compliments him, "you are considered one of our best horsemen and wealthiest citizens" (*Oec.* 11.20)—evidence that Ischomachus was a *hippeus* who evidently undertook liturgical responsibilities (7.3), though there are no direct attestations. Aeschines (no. 91) also connects Ischomachus with Socrates' circle: upon meeting in Olympia, Aristippus s.v. inquired of Ischomachus about Socrates. Such a meeting took place—if it actually took place—in either 420 or 416 since an Athenian would not have been welcome there earlier, and Ischomachus was most likely dead before the next set of games.

By the time of Ischomachus' death, the war had diminished his seventy-*talent* fortune; he reportedly left only one *talent* each for his two minor sons (Lys. 19.45–6, repeated as common knowledge in ≥390 though it may have been an exaggeration, or may not have included wealth in property). Apparently, Callias III s.v., in similar financial straits as a result of the war, had been attempting to improve his financial situation by arranging to marry Ischomachus' daughter, Epilycus II's widow, who happened also to be the mother of two heiresses too young to be married off for some years. If Ischomachus agreed to an arrangement whereby Callias III would become their guardian as well as their mother's, then Callias III had the use of their father's estate until they married. He married the widow, and one can only speculate about the reasons for what happened next. Ischomachus died, perhaps having named Callias III, his new son-in-law, as guardian of his wife, Chrysilla, and their two sons (see below). In any case, Chrysilla (and probably her two sons) moved in with Callias III. Callias III's wife attempted suicide, then ran away. Callias III divorced the daughter and married Chrysilla (Andoc. 1.124). Although Andocides IV adds a number of lewd details to put Callias III in as unfavorable a light as possible, thereby to plead in his own favor, he called witnesses (1.127) to these statements, and the court ruled in his favor against Callias III.

Prosopographical notes.   If the date of Ischomachus' death is correct, then two other texts refer to a man of the same name who was likewise rich, but younger and of a different nature: one who lost his money to flatterers (Ath. 12.537c) and maintained parasites (Ararus fr. 16). But I concede that one must be careful in dealing with comic poets: the Cratinus comment that Ischomachus was a tightwad may have been funny precisely because it was the opposite of the truth, in which case only Xenophon's portrait would be out of sync with the other references. And one could argue that the early date of Cratinus' fr. 365 leaves some time for a change in personality over the years. But if there are two men of that name, the younger Ischomachus might also be mentioned by Isaeus (fr. 18) after 357; pseudo-Demosthenes (58.30), referring to a man who died in the late 340s; and the councilor/s named Ischomachus in 421 (*Agora* 15.411). MacDowell (1962: 151–2), named as a source in *APF*, had earlier reasoned that a second and later rich Ischomachus was a less plausible scenario than that one Ischomachus married more than once, and lived into his eighties. It favors MacDowell's view that Ischomachus' wealth was in land, less likely to be affected by loss of revenues in wartime than, for example, Callias III's income from Laurium silver mines; on the other hand, we do not know where Ischomachus' property lay or how subject it was to being raided and burned during the war. A crucial but controversial piece of evidence is a speech of Lysias extant only as a title and hypothesis (see *APF* 7826.13D, interpreting the fr. with *P. Oxy.* 31.2537 *verso* lnn. 8–11, and Lys. fr. 32 Thalheim): the estate of the sons of Ischomachus had been leased by a Callias to someone unknown in an attempt to deprive the boys of their inheritance. If this Callias is Callias III, it appears that Ischomachus may have stipulated in his will that his then son-in-law, Callias III, would be their guardian in the event of his death. MacDowell's hypothesis of a long-lived Ischomachus—not revisited in Gagarin and MacDowell (1998: 133n100), where a divorce from Chrysilla is still deemed possible—implies that the sons of Ischomachus became wards of no one since their father lived to a ripe old age.

PA's three individuals (7725, 7726, 7727) are combined into one by both *APF* and *LGPN2*, but *PAA* brings the distinctions back: *PAA* 542570 ?= *PAA* 542575 (the Ischomachus of Xen. *Oec.* and [Plu.] *Mor.* = *PA* 7727); *PAA* 542585 (the Ischomachus of *P. Oxy.* and Lys. fr. 32 = *PA* 7725).

Ismenias of Thebes See App. II.

Isocrates of Erchia, son of Theodorus
[*PA/APF* 7716 *LGPN2* 13 *PAA* 542150 *DPhA*
38 *RE* 2 *OCD*³ Ἰσοκράτης Θεοδώρου
Ἐρχιεύς]
±436–338
mother: Hedyto
siblings: Theodorus, Telesippus, Diomnestus,
   and a sister
wife: Plathane, former wife of Hippias
adopted son: Aphareus
friend of Timotheus of Anaphlystus

Pl. *Phdr.* 278e *
Isocr. *opera*
Strat. *Atal.* fr. 3 (K 3)
Demos. 35, 61
[Demos.] 47, 52
Zos. *Isoc.*
[Plu.] *LTO* 836e–9c
D. H. *Isoc.*

student of Gorgias, ?Prodicus, ?Tisias,
  Socrates, Theramenes
teacher of Androtion II, Charmantides II,
  Philomelus II

Life.   Apart from what Isocrates himself imbeds about his life in his speeches, especially the *Antidosis* (15), most of his biographical details derive from late and uncertain compilations, though pseudo-Plutarch (*LTO*) appears to report on the family burial ground at Cynosarges, from which the names of his immediate family are preserved. Isocrates' maternal aunt, Naco, had a son named Socrates buried with her (see stemma in *APF*). The exceptional affluence of Isocrates' family, owing to its *aulos* factory employing slave labor, enabled Isocrates to be lavishly educated (15.161) and to pursue the expensive pastime of horsemanship as a youth ([Plu.] 839c)—but the later sources probably overestimate the number of his teachers (see below).

More evidence—

Like so many other aristocratic families, Isocrates' family suffered a financial decline during the final decade of the Peloponnesian war; Thucydides mentions the escape of twenty thousand slaves from Athens by 413, and many of them artisans (7.27.5, with Isocr. 15.161–2). It would presumably have been during the war that Isocrates was one of Socrates' companions (Pl. *Phdr.*; cf. Pl. *Euthd.* 305c with PCW 708). By the end of the war, Isocrates found himself without income and turned briefly to forensic speech writing, logography, for clients. But he was able to open a school of rhetoric in about 390 that flourished (15.30, 41, 87) and made him once again a rich man required to perform liturgies for the *polis*. With his income secure, he could write "orations" (not for presentation, but distributed in their written form) privately in his own name. Isocrates' school may have had a hundred pupils ([Plu.] *LTO* 837c) paying as much as a thousand *drachmae* each (Demos. 35.15, 35.42; [Plu.] *LTO* 387d, 838e), though the round numbers arouse suspicion. In pseudo-Plutarch's account, Isocrates never demanded fees from a fellow citizen (838f), a claim difficult to judge at this distance. Isocrates' known students included sons and grandsons of persons in this prosopography: Androtion II of Gargettus, son of Andron; Charmantides II of Paeania, grandson of Charmantides I; and Philomelus II of Paeania, son of Philippides I. His *Against the Sophists* (13) of 390 is an interesting overview of education in Athens in its time.

More evidence that Isocrates achieved considerable wealth is provided by his own account. He describes himself as having voluntarily undertaken three *trierarchies* (15.145). He was subjected to *antidosis* twice, winning on the first occasion in 356/5 (D. H. *Isoc.* 18; [Plu.] 839c) and losing on the second in 354/3 (15.9); cf. Mirhady and Too (2000: 201–2), calling the second fictional. Another indicator of his wealth is a one-*talent* gift from the general Timotheus, who may also have been a friend of Plato's. A fragment of Lysias preserved by Athenaeus (592b) states that he had *hetaira* expenses for two women, Metanira and Lagisca.

At about the age of fifty-six, ≤380, Isocrates married Plathane, widow of an otherwise unknown Hippias who cannot have been the famous polymath Hippias—a marriage *APF* describes as "legally and chronologically impossible"— though the desire to connect Isocrates by marriage to the polymath persists unabated (e.g., Guthrie 1971a: 280; Mirhady and Too 2000: 2), lately with the chronological amendment that Isocrates' wife was the widowed *daughter*, not wife, of the famous Hippias. In pseudo-Plutarch's version of the story, Plathane already had two children and produced a third child, the son Aphareus, with Isocrates. *APF*, however, citing the date of pseudo-Demosthenes (52.14), argues that Isocrates must have adopted Plathane's third child by her former marriage, Aphareus— and that view seems preferable. Aphareus and Isocrates performed joint liturgies for the city (15.145) until Isocrates established his son independently in the liturgical class, which must have involved great expense. After Isocrates starved himself to death at the age of ninety-eight upon hearing the news that Philip's army had defeated the Athenians in 338 ([Plu.] 837e, 838b), both his son and Timotheus erected statues by Leochares, and other memorials ([Plu.] 838c–d, 839b–c).

Works.   Isocrates wrote orations throughout his long career, twenty-one of which are extant; there are in addition nine letters. He is the source for our knowledge of Periandros' naval law of ±357 which established a panel of 1,200 men who provided funding to the fleet (15.145); it stayed in force until Demosthenes' naval law of 340. Isocrates was himself on the list, as was Philippides I s.v.

In the later tradition.   Besides the well-known pseudo-Plutarchian *Lives of the Orators* (= *Mor.* 832b–852e), and the biographies of Dionysius and Zosimus, both called *Isocrates*, see Cicero (*Or.* 52.176), and Pausanias (1.18.1). Socrates is later said to have been Isocrates' teacher on the basis of Pl. *Phdr.*, Theramenes on the basis of D. H. and [Plu.].

Isodice of Athens, daughter of Euryptolemus I; wife of Cimon II of Laciadae See App. II. *See stemma: Thucydides.*

Isolochus of Athens See App. II.

Laches of Aexone, son of Melanopus	Pl. *Lch.*	speaker
[*PA* 9019 *LGPN2* 25 *PAA* 602280 *RE* 1 *PP*	Pl. *Smp.* 221a	
Λάχης (–χες) Μελανώπου Αἰξωνεύς]	IG I³ 75.4 (treaty)	
±475–418	Thu. 3–5, *passim*	
father of Laches and at least one other son	Aristoph. *Wasps*	
general	Androt. fr. 41	
	D. S. 12, *passim*	

Life and military career.   Laches is represented in Plato as older than Socrates (*Lch.* 181d, 186c), which is helpful in establishing his date of birth because—using the conventional method of adding thirty years to the date he is known to have been general—he could have been more than a decade younger. He is paired in the dialogue with Nicias I, and both of them are enough older than Socrates to make the matter worth commenting on twice. Laches had at least two sons whom he describes as of the wrong age to require sophists or Socrates (*Lch.* 200c) in 424, the dramatic date of the dialogue (see App. I), one of whom was also named Laches

(Demos. 24.126–7). Inscriptions tell us that the names of Laches and Melanopus continued to be used in the family for several generations: Whitehead (1986: 419.89) notes a Laches of Aexone, son of Melanopus on a deme decree of ±330. In the context of *Laches'* several references to demes, demesmen, and demotics, note that Laches describes himself, after an outburst, as "a typical Aexonian" (197c); the scholiast to the passage notes that Aexonians were aggressive speakers (κακολόγος), citing Menander's comedy (*Kan.* fr. 200, K 222) in which an old woman is so labeled.

Laches was elected general (*stratēgos*) in 427/6 and 426/5 and commanded the fleet in Sicily, then Locri and Rhegium (Thu. 3.86.1, 3.90.2, 3.103.3; D. S. 12.54.4). He was almost certainly charged with misconduct by Cleon in 425 (Aristoph. *Wasps* 240–4, 894–5) and acquitted. Laches was with Socrates on the retreat from Delium in 424 (Pl. *Lch.* 181b) where, according to Plato's Alcibiades III, Socrates was more effective than the general and saved them both by swaggering so fiercely that enemy soldiers did not dare to approach (*Smp.* 221b). Laches is named in several pacts: a treaty with Haleis ±424/3 (*IG*), the famous Peace of Nicias with Sparta in 421 (Thu. 5.19.2), and the fifty-year alliance with Sparta in 421 (Thu. 5.24.1). He was a hoplite commander in Argos in 418 (Thu. 5.61.1; D. S. 12.79.1), and died in the battle of Mantinea in 418 (Thu. 5.74.3; Androt.).

In comedy.   Aristophanes' *Wasps*, produced in 422, introduces Laches, a cheese-stealing dog from Aexone called "Grabber" (Λάβης, ln. 836), accused by a guard dog from Cydathenaeum, Cleon's deme. In 423, Cleon—something of a war monger—had advised the Athenians against accepting a peace treaty with Sparta that Laches, among others, had proposed (Thu. 4.119.2 with *CAH* 5²: 428n146). In revenge, Cleon had charged Laches with embezzling funds while on campaign in Sicily in 427–425, though Laches was acquitted. In the play, a Cleon-loving father, enamored with jury duty, must decide the case between the dogs. As in real life, Laches is acquitted, but there's a monkey wrench: Laches was a good dog because, although he stole, he stole to help the people, while Cleon was a bad dog because he took the people's money for doing nothing (Aristoph. *Wasps* 835–43, 891–1002).

Henderson suggests that "one of those who betrayed the Thracian front" (note to *Wasps* 285) may also be a reference to Laches. In early 422, treachery at the border fort of Panactum had caused the Athenians to lose to the Boeotians. The reference is unclear partly because this charge is not mentioned in the later and private trial of Laches in the play.

Prosopographical notes.   *LGPN2* 25 combines *PA* 9019 with references from *PA* 9010. *PAA* 602280 ?= 602185. Laches son of Laches is *PA* 602375.

Lamachus of Oe, son of Xenophanes
[*PA* 8981 *LGPN2* 7 *PAA* 601230 *RE* s.v. *OCD*³
PP Λάμαχος Ξενοφάνους Οἰῆθεν]
±470–414
father of Tudeus
long-serving general, killed in Sicily

Pl. *Lch.* 197c *
Thu. 4, 6, *passim*
Aristoph. *Peace* 304,
   1290–4
Aristoph. *Ach.*,
   passim

> Aristoph. *Thesm.* 841
> schol.
> Aristoph. *Frogs* 1039
> Andoc. 1.11
> Lys. 13.65
> *IG* I³ 370.50, 52, 54,
> 56
> D. S. 12, 13, *passim*

Life.   Lamachus is approximately contemporary with Socrates (MacDowell 1962: 68–9, *contra HCT* 3: 537, argues for a birth year of ≤365). The phrase "Lamachus son of Gorgasus" (Aristoph. *Ach.* 1131) refers to the gorgon on his shield, not to his father.

Military career in brief.   Lamachus is mentioned only once in Plato: Nicias I praises his courage (*Lch.*). He may have been a commander under Pericles I in about 436 (Plu. *Per.* 20.1), but was a general (*stratēgos*) in 425/4 when he lost ten ships at anchor to a flood of the river Calex (Thu. 4.75.1–2; D. S. 12.72). In 425, he is satirized for seeking personal benefit from his prosecution of the war (Aristoph. *Ach.*). He was a signatory to two treaties with Sparta in 421, the Peace of Nicias (Thu. 5.19.2), and the fifty-year alliance (Thu. 5.24.1). He was elected general in 416/5 (schol. Aristoph. *Ach.* 270) with Nicias I and Alcibiades III for the disastrous Sicilian campaign (*IG*, Thu. 6.8.2; D. S. 12.84, 13.2); his flagship was the first to leave the harbor (Andoc.). He advocated sailing directly for Sicily and winning the upper hand through a surprise attack (Thu. 6.49.1–4), but supported Alcibiades III's plan instead (6.50.1). After Alcibiades III's defection, Lamachus shared command with Nicias I. Apart from the central account of events in Sicily (Thu. 6), we hear of his bloodless crucifixion of a traitor (Lys.). But Lamachus was killed in action in the summer of 414, leaving sole command to Nicias I (Thu. 6.101.6). Aristophanes is negative in his portrayals of the living Lamachus (*Ach.* in 425, *Peace* in 421), but more sympathetic after Lamachus' death (*Thes.* in 411, *Frogs* in 405).

In the later tradition.   Lamachus appears also in Plutarch (*Per., Nic.,* and *Alc.*).

Lamiscus of Tarentum   Pl. *Ltr.* 7.350a *
[*LGPN3A* 20 *RE* s.v. *DPhA* 12 *PP* Λαμίσκος]
associate of Archytas
Pythagorean

Lamiscus commanded the thirty-oared Tarentine ship that rescued Plato from danger at the court of Dionysius II in 360.

Lampido, daughter of Spartan king Leotychidas II, wife of Spartan king Archidamus II See App. II.

Lamprocles I of Athens, son of Midon
[*LGPN2* 1 *PAA* 601565 *RE* 1 *OCD*³ *PP*
Λαμπροκλῆς Μίδωνος]
5th c.
?father of Xanthippe the wife of Socrates
student of ?Agathocles
teacher of ?Damon
musician
See stemma: Socrates.

[Pl.] *Alc.* 118c schol.
Aristoph. *Clouds* 967
  & schol.
P. Oxy. 1611.172

Life. Lamprocles' father's name is given in three scholia to Aristophanes' *Clouds.* That Lamprocles was the name of Xanthippe's father is posited from nothing more than the widespread practice of naming sons for grandfathers together with the aristocratic style of both names (see Xanthippe s.v.), so it is far from certain that it happened in this case, and unusual for a firstborn son not to receive the name of the paternal grandfather. It is equally uncertain that the musician Lamprocles, well-known in the 5th c., and the only presently available candidate, was the same individual as Xanthippe's father. *If* Lamprocles was Socrates' father-in-law, then they were of roughly the same generation, in which case *Laches* 180d, where Agathocles is said to have been Damon's teacher, is preferable to the scholiast of pseudo-Plato's *Alcibiades* where Lamprocles is identified as the pupil of Agathocles and teacher of Damon s.v.

Works. In *Clouds* and its scholia, Lamprocles is linked to staid old patriotic songs, including a hymn to Athena (Παλλάδα περσέπολιν δεινάν, ln. 367) still known in the late 5th c. He composed dithyrambic verse and was an innovator in harmonics (Ath. 491c; cf. Plu. *Mor.* 1136d).

Lamprocles II of Alopece, son of Socrates
[*PA* 8993 *LGPN2* 3 *RE* 2 *PX*
Λαμπροκλῆς Σωκράτους Ἀλωπεκῆθεν]
b. ≥416, *meirakion* in 399
mother: Xanthippe
brothers: Sophroniscus II, Menexenus
See stemma: Socrates.

Pl. *Ap.* 34d *
Pl. *Phd.* 116b   present
Xen. *Mem.* 2.2.1–14
D. L. 2.29

Xenophon is the contemporaneous source for Lamprocles' name, and for the statement that he was the eldest son of Socrates. In the *Memorabilia*, where Lamprocles is still a child (*pais*), Socrates finds him annoyed with his mother and counsels him didactically on the duties of parents and offspring, a story retailed later (D. L.).

Lamprus of Athens (musician) See App. II.

Laodamas (Pl.) or **Leodamas** (Procl.) of
  Thasos

[Pl.] *Ltr.* 11 *   addressee
Procl. *Eucl.* 66.18

[*LGPN1* 12 *RE* 3 + supp. 7 *DPhA* 35   D. L. 3.24
Λαοδάμας]
fl. early 4th c.
mathematician

Leodamas was one of the first generation of Academic mathematicians, said by Diogenes and Proclus to have learned the analytic method from Plato. In *Letter* 11, Laodamas represents a group of colonists seeking advice from [Plato]. It has been conjectured that the colony being planned might be Crenidae or Datos, both of which were founded about 360–59 (a nod to [Plato's] comment that he is too old to travel).

Prosopographical notes. 'Laodamas' appears to be pseudo-Plato's incorrect name for Leodamas of Thasos.

Lasthenia of Mantinea See App. II.

Leagrus I of Cerameis, son of Glaucon I See App. II. *See stemma: Plato.*

Leagrus II of Cerameis, son of Glaucon II See App. II. *See stemmata: Callias, Plato.*

Leaïdes of Athens, son of Critias II See App. II. *See stemma: Plato.*

Leochares of Athens   [Pl.] *Ltr.* 13.361a *
[*LGPN2* 4 *RE* 2 *OCD³ PP* Λεωχάρης]   [Plu.] *LTO* 838d
active ±370–320   inscriptions (see
sculptor   below)

A pupil of Scopas, Leochares worked mostly in bronze, though some of the Amazon slabs now in the British Museum (1013–15) are attributed to him. A few copies of some of his statues remain. Inscriptions include *IG* II² 2825.13, 2831, 4367, 3829, 4270, 4330, 4899, 4900; *IGUR* 1571, 1572; *SEG* 15.285.3. The Apollo purchased by [Plato] is not known.

Leodamas I of Acharnae, son of Phaeax I See App. II. *See stemma Phaeax.*

Leogoras II of Cydathenaeum, son of Andocides III See App. II. *See stemmata: Andocides, Callias.*

Leon of Salamis and Athens
[*PA* 9100 *LGPN2* 4, 5, 66 *FRA* 6468 *RE* 12 *PP*
Λέων]
471–404
father of Pantaleon, speaker of Lys. 10,
  another sibling
general executed by the Thirty

Pl. *Ap*. 32c–d †
Pl. *Ltr*. 7.324e–5a,
  unnamed †
Thu. 5, 8, *passim*
Xen. *Hell*. 1, 2,
  passim
Andoc. 1.94
Lys. 10, 13.44,
  unnamed

Life.   Leon's date of birth is established by his son's remark that Leon was sixty-seven when executed in 404. Leon was an Athenian citizen who resided in Salamis, probably as a *cleruch*, and served Athens as general. Since his citizenship has been controversial in the literature, note three points: Plato refers to Leon as a citizen (*politēs*) and as a friend of the democratic exiles (Pl. *Ltr*. 7.324e–5a); Leon is grouped with the citizens Niceratus II and Antiphon—and not with the resident aliens—in Theramenes' speech (Xen. *Hell*. 2.3.39–41); and Lysias makes contemporaneous references (12.52 and 13.44, dated 403/2 and ≥399, respectively) to the Thirty's destruction of citizens living on Salamis (McCoy 1975: 196n45). Leon's children included the speaker of Lysias' speech 10, another sibling, and their older brother, Pantaleon, who became their guardian when Leon was killed in 404, when the speaker was thirteen (10.4–5, 27). Onomastic practice often embedded a father's name within a son's (e.g., Pantaleon, Antileon). Leon was, by all accounts, a man of impeccable character who passed every audit without ever being fined for fraud (10.27). The story of Leon's execution, beginning with Socrates, Meletus of Athens, and three others being summoned to the Thirty and ordered to seize Leon, is known from other sources besides Plato's *Apology* (Xen., Andoc.), but Plato and Andocides IV refer to Leon without specifying Salamis, presumably because there was only one famous Leon at the time whom they could mean, and that has led to confusion.

Military career.   Thucydides records that Leon signed the Peace of Nicias (Thu. 5.19.2) and fifty-year alliance—both with Sparta in 421 (Thu. 5.24.1). He took reinforcements to Lesbos in 412 (8.23.1), and fought three victorious battles against the Chians (8.24.2–3). Later that year, as the Athenians began sliding toward oligarchy, political intrigues resulted in the democratic Leon's being sent to replace Phrynichus in command of the fleet (8.54.3). He soon attacked the Rhodians successfully and moved his base of operations to Chalce (8.55.1). His friendliness to democracy is seen in his opposition to the establishment of a Samian oligarchy (8.73.4). When the Four Hundred took power in Athens, Leon was deposed (8.76.2). According to Xenophon, after the Athenians lost the battle of Notium in 407, blaming Alcibiades III, they elected ten new generals for the year 406/5, including Leon (*Hell*. 1.5.16). He was one of three generals originally blockaded at Mytilene by the Lacedaemonian general, Callicratidas (1.6.16), who captured and detained Leon until the battle of Aegospotami in 405, after which Leon returned heroically to Athens.

In modern bibliography.   Andrewes and Lewis (1957: 179n10—but page citations of this source are incorrect in *LGPN2* and *FRA*)—reasserted by Lewis (*CAH* 6²:

35n53), identified the general with the man Socrates was ordered to apprehend and with the father of the speaker of Lysias 10. MacDowell (1962: 133n94), not fully persuaded, argued that a capture by the Spartans in 406 is incompatible with the speaker's remark that his father was never captured by the enemy (Lys. 10.27). McCoy (1975: 187–99) then made it difficult to avoid the conclusion that one must subordinate that lone remark: he adduces evidence (Thu., Xen., and D. S. or Ephorus) for Leon's capture, replacement, and eventual release.

Prosopographical notes. The father of the speaker of Lysias 10 is unnumbered because he is not named, but Pantaleon is *PA* 11599 and *LGPN2* 3. *PA* 9100 is the general and "perhaps" the signatory of 421; *LGPN2* 5 (?= 66) is the general, but *LGPN2* 4 is separately assigned to the signatory of 421 with "cf. *PA* 9100"; the man Socrates was ordered to apprehend is *LGPN2* 66 (?= 5) and *FRA* 6468 although *FRA*, like Burnet (1924: *Ap.* 32c6n), makes none of these links to the Leon of Plato. There is a 4th c. Leon, student of Neoclides—both of whom were among the first group of mathematicians in Plato's Academy (see Theaetetus s.v.).

Leontius, son of Aglaeon	Pl. *R.* 439e *
[*PP* Λεόντιος Ἀγλαῖωνος]	Theo. *Kap.* fr. 25
	(K 24)

According to the comic dramatist, Theopompus, Leontinus—emended to 'Leontius' because of the *Republic* passage—was attracted to boys with the complexion of corpses (Aristoph. *Birds* 1406). 'Aglaion' is an alternative spelling of Leontius' patronymic (an oversight in PCW 1071).

Leosthenes of Athens See App. II.

Leotychides II of Sparta (king) See App. II.

Leptines I of Syracuse, son of Hermocritus II	Pl. *Ltr.* 7.332a,
[*LGPN3A* 14 *RE* 2 Λεπτίνας]	unnamed
>420–383	*GG* 3.2.102–7
brother: Thearides; half siblings: Dionysius I,	Tod 2.108
Theste	Plu. *Dion* 11.6.1–4
wife: Dicaeosyne (daughter of Dionysius I	Philist. fr. 60
and Doris)	Polyae. 5.8.1–2,
offspring: two daughters by an unknown	6.16.1
woman, one of whom married Philistus;	D. S. 14.48.4–15.17.2,
Leptines II with Dicaeosyne	*passim*
brother-in-law and uncle of Dionysius II	
See stemma: Dion.	

Family.   Plato describes Leptines I as having been reared and trained by his older brother, Dionysius I s.v., though without trust between them. Consolidating the family in power, Dionysius I gave Leptines I his daughter by Doris to marry, Dicaeosyne. We know little about the birth order of Doris's three children but, even if Dicaeosyne was firstborn, she was at most fourteen when Leptines I was killed in action in 383.

Military career.   In 397, Sicily and Carthage were at war, with the Spartans assisting Sicily. Leptines I enters the historical record there as the capable commander of a siege engine operation against Motya, a forward base of the Carthaginians. He had a celebrated military career across two wars between Sicily and Carthage, and became a more popular leader than his tyrant brother. He was sacked, however, in 390, when he negotiated peace between the Lucanians and Thurii against Dionysius I's larger scheme; their younger brother, Thearides, was given command. See Philistus s.v. on the exile of Leptines I with Philistus in 386. Leptines I was reconciled later with the tyrant and served again as a general, but was killed (heroically, as usual in these accounts) at the battle of Cronium in 383.

Prosopographical notes.   *LGPN3A* lists at the entry for Leptines I a son, Alcetas, and a possible son, Leptines, but not the earlier daughters; but it gives no entry for Alcetas.

Leptines II of Syracuse, son of Leptines I   [Pl.] *Ltr.* 13, *passim* *
[*LGPN3A* 12, 13 *RE* 3 Λεπτίνας]   Plu. *Dion* 57.6
≤383–>342   Iamb. *VP* 267
mother: Dicaeosyne   D. S. 16.45.9
See stemma: Dion.

Life and career.   Neither the origins nor the career of Leptines II is known certainly. Because Dicaeosyne was no more than fourteen when Leptines I died in 383, it is unlikely that she had any other children with Leptines I. In Plato's letter, Leptines II is represented as the tyrant's trusted aide ≥365. The Leptines II of the letter paid [Plato] back the expenses [Plato] had incurred fitting out a Leucadian ship (13.361a–c), and also lent a sum to [Plato] (362b–c) that Dionysius II was asked to repay (363d). He seems a responsible young man, not a youth—adding further evidence to the view that the letter is a piece of pseudo-Platonica and that its author was not well informed about the Sicilian family of Dionysius I.   The writer of *Letter* 13 may simply have used the name 'Leptines' to suggest a vague familial connection to Dionysius II, or may have intended readers to assume that Dionysius II's uncle (Leptines I) was the referent, not realizing that he had been dead for nearly twenty years when Plato paid his second visit to Sicily.

Prosopographical notes and modern bibliography.   The evidence beyond *Letter* 13 for a Leptines II is not very firm, but does not require that he reach maturity so soon as 366, strengthening the possibility of direct descent from Leptines I. Harward (1932: 231), citing Diodorus, says that Leptines, jointly with Callippus, seized Rhegium; that would have been after Callippus was deposed by Hipparinus II in 352. Apparently following Plutarch, Bury notes (1929: 616n3) that a Pythagorean

by the name of Leptines [var. –νης] killed Callippus in Rhegium; he might have
added that the avenging Pythagorean used the very sword that had killed Dion—
vintage Plutarch. Westlake (*CAH* 6² 712–3 & n17) accepts both accounts: the
onetime associate of Callippus (D. S.) later murdered him (Plu.); and Westlake
adds for the same Leptines: he was tyrant of Engyum and Appollonia in 342 and,
moreover, "may have been a nephew of the elder Dionysius" [I]. The profiles of
as many as three different individuals may well be buried here.

Leucolophides of Scambonidae See App. II.

Lichas of Sparta, son of Archesilaus See App. II.

Licymnius of Chios   Pl. *Phdr.* 267c
[*LGPN1* 1 *RE* s.v. *DPhA* 68 *OCD³PP*   Aristot. *Rh.*
Λικύμνιος]
teacher of Polus
dithyrambic poet and rhetorician

Licymnius was Polus' rhetoric teacher (Pl.), having himself written an *Art of
Rhetoric* in which he coined what Aristotle called "pointless and silly" rhetorical
terms (*Rh.* 1414b15). Licymnius intended his poems to be read rather than performed orally (*Rh.* 1413b14–5).

Lycon of Thoricus   Pl. *Ap.*   present
[*PA* 9271 *LGPN2* 19 *RE* 8 *PP PX*   Xen. *Smp.*
Λύκων Θορίκιος]   Aristoph. *Wasps*
±470–>399   1301
wife: a woman from Rhodes ("Rhodia")   Aristoph. *Lysistr.*
father of Autolycus   270 & schol.
democratic politician and accuser of Socrates Crat. *Pyt.* fr. 214 (K
                                                   203)
                                                Eu. *Auto.* frr. 58, 61
                                                   (K 58, 53)
                                                Eu. *Pol.* fr. 232 (K
                                                   215)
                                                Eu. *Flatt.* fr. 295 (K
                                                   273)
                                                Metag. *Soph.* fr. 10
                                                   (K 10)

Life. Lycon's birth year, roughly established from his son's victory as a pancratist
in the Panathenaea of 422, might be brought down as far as 460, but he is nevertheless a man of Socrates' generation. In comedies of the late 420s, his wife, a Rhodian
woman, recurs as sexually forward (Eu.), and is referred to in Aristophanes with

the same implicit slur, though as Lycon's wife (*Lysistr.*). Lycon is among the "drunk and disorderly" (Aristoph. *Wasps*); he and his son are named for living extravagantly (Crat.; Eu. *Auto.* 61) despite poverty (Crat.), and of having a foreign origin (Eu. *Auto.* 61; Metag.). After the fall of the Four Hundred, Lycon emerges in the more respectable role of democratic politician, appearing again in comedy to be accused of treachery, of betraying Naupactus to the Lacedaemonians in 405, (Metag.; cf. D. S. 14.34). In 404/3, his son was executed by the Thirty. In 399, he joined in Meletus II's prosecution of Socrates though Socrates did not address Lycon or even criticize him directly, as he did both Meletus II and Anytus.

It is Xenophon who rehabilitates the character of Lycon, representing him and his son as especially devoted to one another at Callias III's banquet in August of 422; at the time of Socrates' trial in 399, Autolycus' execution was relatively fresh in memory. Lycon may have believed that Socrates had been aligned with the oligarchy responsible for his son's death, which the amnesty forbade mentioning, but which may help explain both Lycon's participation in the prosecution and Socrates' silence toward him. Hansen (1995: App. 3) seeks to exonerate Lycon altogether from the charge of treachery, noting that there were other men of that name; and Hansen also denies that the Lycon of Xenophon and the comic poets was Socrates' accuser, arguing that it would be "completely out of character" for Xenophon to suppress the fact that Lycon was Socrates' accuser by allowing the character to praise Socrates (*Smp.* 9.1). Against Hansen's defense are the twenty years of foreign and civil war that elapsed between the praise and the accusation, and Socrates' remark that the participation of Anytus and Lycon was all that prevented Meletus II's being fined for bringing a frivolous accusation (*Ap.* 36a), implying the public prominence of those two men.

Lycophron
[*LGPN3A* 33 *RE* 10 + supp. 14
DPhA 135 *PP* Λυκόφρων]
active late 5th–early 4th c.
student of Gorgias

[Pl.] *Ltr.* 2.314d *
frr. in DK 83

In the later tradition. Lycophron was a sophist (Aristotle's term) who was a student of Gorgias; he is often cited by Aristotle, most memorably, perhaps, in the *Physics*: "Even the more recent of the ancient thinkers were in a pother lest the same thing should turn out in their hands both one and many. So some, like Lycophron, were led to omit 'is,' others to change the mode of expression and say 'the man has been whitened' instead of 'is white,' and 'walks' instead of 'is walking,' for fear that if they added the word 'is' they should be making the one to *be* many—as if 'one' and 'is' were always used in one and the same way" (185b25). All the fragments in DK are collected from Aristotle (cf. *Meta.* 1045b10, *Pol.* 1280b8, *Rh.* 1405b34, *S. Ref.* 174b32, and fr. 91) and there are no testimonia.

Lycurgus of Sparta (legislator) See App. II.

Lydus, slave of Pherecles of Themacus See App. II.

Lysander of Sparta, son of Aristocritus (general) See App. II.

Lysanias of Sphettus   Pl. *Ap.* 33e1   present
[*PA* 9324 *LGPN2* 53 *PP* Λυσανίας Σφήττιος]
probably born mid 5th c.
father of Aeschines

Lysanias of Syracuse See App. II.

Lysias of Thurii and Athens, son of
  Cephalus II
[*APF* C9 *PAA* 614240 *FRA* 6988 *DPhA* 146 *RE*
13 *OCD³ PP* Λυσίας Κεφάλου]
±445–>380
paternal half brother: Polemarchus; ?full
  siblings: Euthydemus, woman who married
  Brachyllus
wife: his niece, daughter of his sister and
  Brachyllus
associates: Thrasymachus, Clitophon
hetaira: Metaneira
famous orator
See stemma: Lysias.
	Pl. *R.*
	Pl. *Phdr.*
	[Pl.] *Clt.* 406a, 410e *
	Lys. 12
	Lys. fr. 7
	Lys. *opera* ed.
	  Medda
	[Demos.] 59.21–2
	P. Oxy. 13.1606
		present
		speaker

Family.   Lysias, born in Athens, was the son of a wealthy *metic* originally from Syracuse, Cephalus II. When Lysias was about fifteen, he went with his older brother, Polemarchus, as his guardian to join the colonists at Thurii; that was probably in about 430. Lysias was thus older than Isocrates, as Plato's Socrates says (*Phdr.* 279a), but the gap was more likely ten years than twenty. The difference in age between Polemarchus and his younger brothers, together with the fact that Lysias' mother was alive and living with him >369 ([Demos.] = Apollodorus), suggests that Cephalus II married twice. An older tradition (D. H. *Lys.*, followed by Lamb 1930) puts Lysias' birth 459–457, but that estimate has not panned out: it depended on Lysias' being fifteen when the colony at Thurii was first established in 444/3. Lysias and Polemarchus returned permanently to Athens at some unspecified time, though certainly by 412, following the general expulsion of all Athenian colonists after the failed Sicilian expedition of 415–413. But Lysias had visited Athens 418–416 when the *Phaedrus* is set (227b; see App. I), by which time he already had a reputation as an orator. Lysias may have studied rhetoric with Corax and Tisias (or a Nicias) while in Thurii ([Plu.] *LTO* 835d); in any case, he did not turn to philosophy (*Phdr.* 257b).

STEMMA: LYSIAS

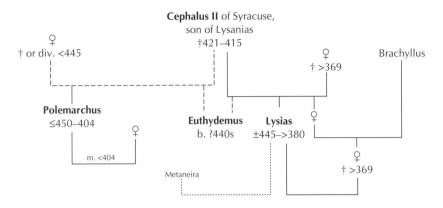

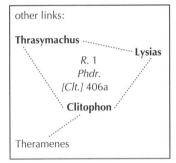

other links:

Thrasymachus .... **Lysias**
R. 1
Phdr.
[Clt.] 406a
Clitophon
Theramenes

dialogues' characters in **boldface**
legal marriage and birth ————
other relationships ·····················
hypothetical or dubious links – – – – –

His family derived its wealth partly from its armory that produced shields in the Piraeus, employing over a hundred slaves, but Lysias must have had other sources of income elsewhere for him to have been able to provide extensive financial backing for the exiled democrats after the Thirty had confiscated the factory. Lysias and Polemarchus were, by 404, among the wealthiest people in Attica, sponsoring choral performances, paying war taxes (*eisphorai*), and ransoming citizen prisoners of war (Lys. 12.20). By 404 Lysias had acquired a house in the Piraeus adjacent to the shield factory (Lys. 12.9). The rule of the Thirty forced Lysias from Athens (see below). After his return to the Piraeus with Thrasybulus in 403 ("we" at Lys. 12.53), he became a successful speechwriter, and married his niece, the daughter of his sister and Brachyllus ([Demos.]). Plato does not mention him in connection with the trial and death of Socrates, but a story is preserved according to which Lysias wrote a defense speech for Socrates that the philosopher found fine (*kalos*) but "unsuitable for me," to which Lysias is supposed to have replied, "How, if it is a fine speech, can it not be suitable for you?" Socrates' rejoinder is to the effect that noble clothing and shoes would likewise be unsuitable for him (D. L. 2.40–1). In the 380s, but while his wife and mother were still living in his house, Lysias kept a *hetaira*, Metaneira, who was a slave whom he took to

Eleusis for initiation ([Demos.]), reasoning that her owner, the freedwoman Nicarete would take from Metaneira any gifts or money Lysias might give her, but
that her initiation would be inalienable.

For Lysias' connections to Thrasymachus, including the possibility that *Against
the Members of a Sunousia* (8) may also be autobiographical, see Thrasymachus s.v.

Political career.   Soon after the Thirty were established in 404, Theognis and
Peison, two of their number, argued to the others that some resident aliens opposed
their administration (12.6) and that the cash desperately needed by the Thirty
could be confiscated from those *metics* under the pretext of punishing them for
opposition to the regime. Lysias' speech 12 of 403/2 accuses a former member
of the Thirty, Eratosthenes, of causing Polemarchus to be executed (it was uncon-
tested that Eratosthenes had arrested Polemarchus). The Thirty were excluded
from provisions of the amnesty but each had the right to seek exemption from
the exclusion by successfully defending himself at a *euthunai*, a public examination
of his conduct. Lysias' speech was probably used on the occasion of Eratosthenes' *euthunai*.

According to Lysias, he was entertaining guests when three members of the
Thirty—Peison, Melobius, and Mnesitheides—assisted by a number of other men,
apprehended him in his house (12.8). Leaving Peison to guard him, the others
went into the factory attached to his house and began to list the slaves (12.9).
Lysias attempted to bribe Peison with a *talent* of silver (12.9), but Peison saw that
Lysias had in his safe three *talents* of silver, four hundred Cyzicene *staters*, one
hundred Persian *darics*, and four silver cups (12.11), so he took it all, refusing to
give Lysias even enough cash for his journey (12.12)—but leaving intact the
promise to help Lysias escape. Promising to rejoin Lysias later, Peison handed
him over to Melobius and Mnesitheides who took him to the house of Damnippus,
where Theognis, another member of the Thirty, was guarding other men (12.13).
Lysias knew Damnippus and asked him for help, which was promised, but
Damnippus thought it best to bring Theognis into the escape plan by bribing him.
Taking advantage of Damnippus' brief absence in conversation with Theognis,
and familiar with Damnippus' two exterior doors from a previous visit, Lysias
escaped to the house of a sea captain, Archenius (12.16), who went back into
town on Lysias' behalf to inquire about Polemarchus s.v. Lysias then sailed to
Megara (12.17). From the factory, the Thirty had confiscated seven hundred shields
and 120 slaves; from the brothers' houses, they had taken copper, jewelry, furniture, and women's clothing (12.19). In spite of losing the armory and the income
derived from it (*pace* Ferrari 2000: xii), after fleeing Athens, Lysias was able to give
substantial material assistance—three hundred mercenaries, currency in excess of
two *talents*, et al. (fr. 7)—to the exiled democrats who were seeking to topple the
Thirty, an indication that he had access to assets elsewhere.

Citizenship status.   On the thorny issue of naturalization generally, Lysias is both
a recipient and a source for information about other recipients (see App. and
sources cited there). Whether Lysias was ever made a citizen or granted *isoteleia*
probably depends on what his role was in the defense of the democracy. Because
he was a prominent figure in Athens, it is possible, though not probable, that he
was singled out in a decree no longer extant. It is more likely that those (e.g.

[Plu.] *LTO* 835f–6a) who mention Lysias individually do so because they extrapolate from the general case. I am not sanguine about accepting pseudo-Plutarch's version of events *tout court*. Let us take the general situation first.

Thrasybulus proposed a decree, probably soon after the restoration of the democracy in 403, to give citizenship to all (*metics*, foreigners, and slaves) who had supported him in the overthrow of the Thirty. The decree was passed but immediately challenged for constitutionality by Archinus s.v. and ultimately annulled. A separate decree of 401/0, probably also moved by Thrasybulus, and also passed (recorded and known from archaeological findings, *IG* II^2 10, Stroud 1971), granted different degrees of citizenship to three groups of men proportional to their degrees of participation in the campaign of the democrats (*NIA* 2.26–43, *contra* Krentz 1980: 289–306). The three groups on the *stele*—appearing in the order of the tribes to which they were then being assigned—happen to correspond to Xenophon's division of the actions of the democrats (*Hell.* 2.4.2–43). Group 1, to whom full citizenship was granted, begins with about seventy men following Thrasybulus, including foreigners, who seized Phyle in the winter of 404 or early spring of 403; they were joined by others bleeding out of the city until they had about a thousand for their ±12-mile march to the Piraeus in the spring of 403. Group 2, to whom *isoteleia* was granted, fought in the battle of Munychia in 403, where the Thirty were defeated; this included many men without armor, some of whom were *metics* and foreigners who had joined Thrasybulus. Group 3, to whom *isoteleia* had been promised in advance and was hereby granted, included still more men of non-hoplite status, and more foreigners, who anticipated civil war and would have fought if required (reconciliation with the city intervened). There is room on the *stele* for ±70–90 men in group 1, ±290 in group 2, and ±560–80 in group 3.

Pseudo-Plutarch (*LTO* 836a) tells a remarkably similar story that begins with a version of the first two sentences of the previous paragraph—except that Lysias is the *sole* beneficiary of the decree. He is then said to have had *isoteleia* status to the end of his days. Maybe. But commentators have to go to great lengths to explain away what appear to be cases of Lysias' speaking in his own voice rather than writing a speech for someone else to deliver, which they do on the assumption that, without citizenship, he could not prosecute in a court of law. Todd (2000: 114, but apparently unaware of *IG* II^2 10) suggests, for example, that the autobiographical prosecution of Eratosthenes for Polemarchus' murder (Lys. 12) may have been circulated as a pamphlet. What Lysias himself says (12.53) leaves ambiguous whether he marched into the Piraeus with Thrasybulus or joined him after he arrived—and the difference is what would decide his group. I incline to the view that Lysias was among those made citizens.

Lysias' speech in Plato.　Some commentators, and even some editors, have included *Phaedrus* 230e–234c as an authentic speech of Lysias (35). The majority, however, take it to be an imitation of Lysias. If so, it is an excellent specimen. Stylometric testing has shown that the speech behaves anomalously in a range of computer tests, that it "differs substantially from the main mass of Platonic material" (Ledger 1989: 104, cf. 117), and has more affinity with works of the rhetoricians than with the remainder of Plato's *Phaedrus*.

In the later tradition and modern bibliography. There are late ancient sources as well (D. H. *Lys.*; Cic., *Bru.* 63). Among modern works, Dover's detailed study (1968b, comparing Lys. 12 with Pl., [Demos.], and D. H.) is not a source for *APF*, and some of the available information is sifted differently by the two, though many of their conclusions are similar.

Lysicles See App. II. *See stemma: Pericles.*

Lysiclides of Sicily   [Pl.] *Ltr.* 2.315a *
[*LGPN3A* 1 *PP* Λυσικλείδης]

Praised for not misrepresenting [Plato's] relationship with Dionysius II in Athens, as others previously had, Lysiclides is not otherwise known. His is the only instance of the name in Sicily in ancient times.

Lysimachus I of Alopece See App. II. *See stemma: Thucydides; cf. Socrates.*

Lysimachus II of Alopece, son of Aristides I   Pl. *Lch.*   speaker
[*PA/APF* 9505 (1695.3) *LGPN2* 37 *RE* 4 *PP*   Pl. *Meno* 94a
Λυσίμαχος Ἀριστείδου Ἀλωπεκῆθεν]   [Pl.] *Virt.* 377d †
480s–≥423   Demos. 20.115
father of Aristides II and ?Myrto
See stemma: Thucydides.

Life. By his own admission in *Laches* (179c), and by Socrates' description in conversation with Anytus in the *Meno* (94a, virtually quoted at [Pl.] *Virt.* 377d), Lysimachus II was the undistinguished son of a famous father who had provided Lysimachus II with the best teachers. Lysimachus II is nowhere represented as a bad man, only as no better than other men for all his fine education. He acknowledges being the oldest of the group in the *Laches* (201b), old enough to have been the friend and fellow demesman of Socrates' father, Sophroniscus I, of whom he speaks admiringly (180e). See Myrto s.v. for considerations that she was the sister, daughter or niece of Lysimachus II.

Prosopographical notes.   A variety of misidentifications have resulted from the text at *Laches* 179a where Lysimachus says of himself and his friend Melesias II, "we have these two sons here" (ἡμῖν εἰσὶν υἱεῖς οὑτοί), then introduces Aristides II and Thucydides II, respectively. This does not mean Lysimachus II himself had two sons, so the youth Lysimachus (*PA* 9506) depicted on a 5th c. gravestone (*IG* I³ 1326) with his sister, Polycrite (*PA* 12028), was not the son of Lysimachus II (*pace PA*). The only son of Lysimachus II apparent from the record was Aristides II (*pace APF*, which otherwise does a superb job of disentangling several myths about the descendants of Aristides I).

Lysimachus of Athens See App. II.

Lysis I of Aexone
[*PA*/*APF* 9573 (*APF* 9573 = 9567) *LGPN2* 7
Λῦσις Αἰξωνεύς]
b. ±490
father of Democrates I
See stemma: Lysis.

Pl. *Ly.* 205c †
ARV² 1597–8
(pottery-*kalos*)

Life and family.   The three sorts of evidence available—physical, literary, and social—seem to point to the same Lysis I, grandfather of the Lysis in Plato. The physical evidence is a large number of red-figure vases, of a type dated to the 470s and 460s, that say "Lysis is beautiful" (Λῦσις καλός), suggesting a popularity that agrees with the literary evidence: "the whole city goes around singing—poems about . . . the boy's grandfather Lysis." The family was well-known for its great wealth and athletic victories in chariot and horseback racing, and had been celebrated in poems for generations (Pl.). In addition, Athenians had a tendency, also in the 470s and 460s, to give politically charged names, of the type of which 'Democrates' is a token, to their sons. In this period, however, men did not normally marry before the age of thirty. The problem arises that "this youth's period of popularity would then have coincided with the birth of his putative son" (Stroud 1984: 357n7, *contra APF*). The chronological difficulty does not present an insurmountable obstacle: if the Lysis *kalos* vases are from early in the period, Lysis I could have been born ±490, becoming *kalos* <470 and fathering Democrates I ±460.

Lysis II of Aexone, son of Democrates I
[*PA*/*APF* 9574 *LGPN2* 8 *RE* 3 *DPhA* 156 *PP*
Λῦσις Δημοκράτους Αἰξωνεύς]
≥422–≤350
brother: [unnamed] younger brother
wife: daughter of Isthmonicus
father of Timoclides and Isthmonice
beloved of Hippothales
See stemma: Lysis.

Pl. *Ly.*   speaker
SEG 29.203, 34.199
IG II² 7045.5
D. L. 2.29

Family.   We know far more about the family of Lysis II than about Lysis II himself, but he is another of those characters in Plato who was very likely to have been known personally by early members of the Academy since the archaeological evidence, still turning up in new inscriptions in the 1980s, shows that he grew up, married, had children and grandchildren in Athens before his death. His approximate date of birth can be determined from the dramatic date of the *Lysis*—where Lysis II is still an adolescent: he is described both as a young man (*neaniskos*) and as a boy (*pais*) at *Lysis* 205b–c. We meet characters in the *Lysis* who appear also in *Euthydemus* and *Menexenus*, so the dramatic dates of those two dialogues (see App. I) also help to establish dates of birth for Lysis II and his friends. Lysis

STEMMA: LYSIS

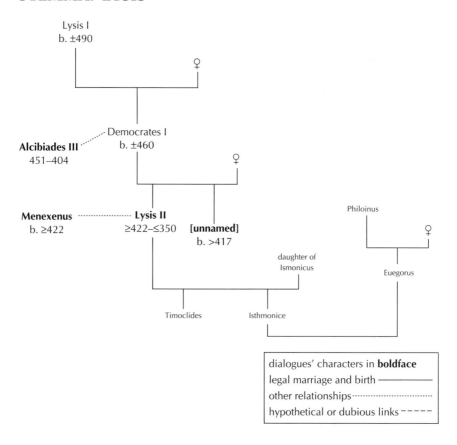

II was a younger contemporary of Plato, born into a widely renowned and affluent family (*Ly.* 205c–d; cf. Lysis I s.v.), the elder of the two known sons of Democrates I (204e, 223a).

Lysis II's wife's father was very likely the Isthmonicus who is known to have signed the Peace of Nicias and fifty-year alliance with Sparta in 421 (Thu. 5.19.2, 24.1) and to have had or built a bathing room known from another inscription (*IG* I³ 84.37). It is probable that Lysis II's clan held the hereditary priesthood of the cult of Heracles in Aexone (*APF* on *Ly.* 205d). Not much is added in the later tradition, only that Socrates exhorted him successfully to become exceptionally virtuous (D. L.). His death is best seen in the archaeological context.

In inscriptions.   The gravestone of Lysis II's daughter and her husband was recycled, built into the Dipylon gate, where it was discovered in 1912. In 1974, the gravestone of Lysis II himself and his son was found in a construction trench northeast of the Piraeus, broken in two. The gravestone is white marble in the shape of a vase (*loutrophoros*), 0.95 m. high and 0.41 m. wide (*SEG*). It bears a beautifully preserved relief sculpture, 0.30 meters high, of three figures, two of whom are identified with labels above their heads. The elderly and bearded Lysis II sits in the middle, shaking hands with his standing, bearded son, Timoclides. Behind Lysis II's chair stands a very young woman, unidentified, who might be Timoclides' daughter, sister, wife or stepmother. The familiar handshake motif (*dexiōsis*) and the lettering on the monument show that Lysis probably died by the end of the second quarter of the 4th c.; it is a very modest grave marker for its time. The fact that Timoclides' epithet ("Timoclides, son of Lysis, of Aexone") is less well carved than that of Lysis II

ΑΥΣΙΣΔΗΜΟΚΡΑΤΟΣ
ΑΙΞΩΝΕΥΣ

("Lysis, son of Democrates, of Aexone") probably means that Lysis II died first, and that the stonecutter had to work *in situ* to add the second epithet some time later. Curiously, the initial lambda of Lysis II's name in the inscription, but not in the label above his head, was incorrectly carved as an alpha. The family's gravestones have now been reunited in the Piraeus Museum. For the archaeological details with illustrations of the monument, the relief, and a squeeze (impression worked into special paper) of the inscription, see Stroud (1984).

Megacles II of Athens, son of Alcmaeon I See App. II. *See stemma: Pericles.*

Megacles IV of Alopece See App. II. *See stemmata: Alcibiades, Pericles.*

Megacles V of Alopece, son of Megacles IV See App. II. *See stemma: Alcibiades.*

Megacles VI of ?Alopece, son of ?Megacles V See App. II.

Megacles VII of ?Sunium, son of Euryptolemus I See App. II.

Megillus of Sparta
[*LGPN3A* 2, 3, 4 Poralla² 513, 514
RE 1 *PP* Μέγιλλος]
fl. late 5th, early 4th c.
Spartan negotiator

Pl. *Laws*   speaker
[Pl.] *Epin.*   present
Androt. fr. 44
Xen. *Hell.* 3.4.6

Career. In the quasi-diplomatic atmosphere of *Laws*, Megillus is the taciturn representative of Spartan views, but he is also a *proxenos* to Athens (642b). A

Spartan peace commissioner of that name is known (or perhaps two of them, though that prospect in the space of a decade seems unlikely): the 4th c. chronicler of Athenian history, Androtion, records a mission to Athens undertaken at some time 410–7 by the Spartan envoys Megillus, Endius, and Philocharidas to ransom prisoners of war and discuss peace. This Megillus, because he is listed first, though youngest of the three envoys, has been assumed to have headed the embassy, and perhaps to have been an Athenian *proxenos* (see Dušanić 1990a: 363–5, dating the embassy to 408). The chronology of those years is controversial (see Andrewes *CAH* 5²: 503–5). Xenophon's reference to a Spartan peacemaker negotiating with Tissaphernes in 396 is surely the same ambassador as Androtion's, and both should be identical with the Megillus represented in *Laws*. There is a further catch: the Androtion mss. say 'Metellus' (Μέτελλος) which, because that would be a unique name, was emended (Usener) to 'Megillus'.

Prosopographical notes.   *LGPN3A* 3 notes "fictional?" of the Megillus of *Laws*. However, *LGPN3A* 2 (*RE* 1, Androtion's Megillus) ?= *LGPN3A* 4 (Poralla² 513, Xenophon's).

Melanippides of Melos (poet) See App. II.

Meles of Athens, son of Pisias (lyre player) See App. II.

Melesias I of Alopece (wrestler, trainer) See App. II.

Melesias II of Alopece, son of Thucydides I	Pl. *Lch.* 179c speaker
[*PA/APF* 9813 (7268.3) *LGPN2* 8 cf. *RE* 2 *PP*	Pl. *Meno* 94b–d
Μελησίας Θουκυδίδου Ἀλωπεκῆθεν]	[Pl.] *Virt.* 378a–c †
≤475–>403	Thu. 8.86.9
mother: sister of the wealthy Cimon II	Agora inv. no. I
brother: Stephanus	627b
father of Thucydides II	
one of the Four Hundred	
See stemma: Thucydides.	

Life and career.   For the calculation of Melesias II's date of birth (*pace APF*), see Thucydides I s.v. Like his close friend Lysimachus II, Melesias II is the unremarkable son of a remarkable father (*Lch.* 179c); but Melesias II's grandfather, Melesias I, was also notable—a wrestler famous in his time. Melesias II is noteworthy in two ways: he was taught wrestling by the great Xanthias (*Meno* 94c); and he lived to be a very old man ([Pl.] *Virt.* 378a). At the dramatic date of *Laches*, 424, Melesias II was already about fifty, and putting his hopes in his adolescent son, Thucydides II. In 411, Melesias II was one of the Four Hundred who briefly replaced the Athenian democracy, and was one of the envoys to Sparta seized by the crew of the *Paralus* and handed over to the Argives (Thu. 8.86.9). After 403, he appears again in the record, as a purchaser of property confiscated from the Thirty and their adherents on an installment plan at a total cost of 3,255 *dr.* plus 55 *dr.*, 5 *obols* tax (see Walbank 1982: 82–3 and plate 27b). Most of the properties of the Thirty were sold to neighbors of the original owners.

Meletus of Athens	Xen. *Hell.* 2.4.36
[*PA* 9825 *LGPN2* 4, 5, 6 Μέλητος]	Andoc. 1.12–3. 35,
b. early 430s	63, 94
associate of Andocides IV	[Lys.] 6

Life.   Meletus and Andocides IV were both members of Euphiletus' club which, in 415, planned and carried out the mutilation of herms as Athens made ready to invade Sicily (see Exc. 1). Andocides IV named Meletus as the member who accompanied Euphiletus to ensure Andocides IV's complicitous promise of secrecy after the event (Andoc. 1.63). Despite Andocides IV's silence, Meletus was accused by the slave Andromachus of profaning the mysteries (1.12–3) and by the *metic* Teucrus of defacing herms (1.35). Apparently, Meletus was one of the many convicted of sacrilege who returned to Athens after 411 or, more likely, 407, and began an active public life again. He was among those ordered by the Thirty to arrest Leon of Salamis s.v. in 404 (1.94), when Socrates refused to carry out the order. In 403, he was a member of an embassy to Sparta with Cephisophus to negotiate on behalf of the moderate oligarchic faction (Xen.). We hear of him for the last time in 399 when he prosecuted Andocides IV.

Pseudo-Lysias 6 is most likely Meletus' speech on that occasion; he was a subsidiary prosecutor and assumed Andocides IV's guilt instead of arguing for it; the religious views he espouses are inadequate to allow his identification with the prosecutor of Socrates over the objections of MacDowell (below) and the further argument that this Meletus is *opposed* by the democrat Anytus (Andoc. 1.150) whom Andocides IV calls as a witness. It hardly seems likely that the oligarchic Meletus of Andocides IV would, within a year, team up with the democratic Anytus to prosecute Socrates. (For a discussion of the authenticity of [Lys.] 6, see Todd 2000: 63–4.)

In modern bibliography.   Meletus is a particularly contentious name. We owe the best analysis so far of the prosopographical issues to MacDowell (1962, App. M; 1976a) whose main interest is in the Meletus of Andocides IV's speech. MacDowell undertakes to distribute some eight different accounts among as many as eight different men named 'Meletus'; he canvasses the evidence, concluding that there are at least four distinct men of that name. Against MacDowell's view, and especially in the philosophical literature, those who have reviewed the issues have cited Burnet's statement that the accuser of Socrates is the Meletus who arrested Leon (1924: *Ap.* 32d6n). A circumstantial argument in Xenophon has been adduced to support Burnet: Xenophon mentions the Leon incident, then immediately mentions Meletus' role in charging Socrates (*Mem.* 4.4.3–4), mentioning neither Anytus nor Lycon (he mentions only Meletus again at 4.8.4). This could be an implicit acknowledgement that the two references are to the same individual, but it may only show that a confusion already existed a few decades after Socrates' death; and the order of the names may be merely coincidental. In any case, a number of scholars have lined up behind Burnet: e.g., Dover (1968b: 78–80), Blumenthal (1973: 169–78), and McCoy (1975). Maidment (1941: index) had previously distinguished the Meletus who was accused in 415 from the Meletus who both prosecuted Andocides IV and arrested Leon, though without explanation. Saunders (1970, citing *PA*) distinguished the Meletus accused in 415 from the Meletus who prosecuted Socrates, implying—*contra* MacDowell—that there is only one Meletus in Andocides IV's speech.

In reply, MacDowell has pointed out that if Andocides IV's accuser arrested Leon, then Socrates met Andocides IV's accuser (Pl. *Ap.* 32d). But Socrates says that his own accuser is "young and unknown" (Pl. *Euthphr.* 2b); the passage implies that Socrates "had not met his own accuser before 399. There remains some room for doubt" (1976a: 226). Even if one doubts that Socrates met his accuser only at the preliminary hearing, the more important point is that the Thirty did not implicate young and unknown citizens in their actions. Their tactic, and it is why they chose Socrates, was to implicate people who were well-known and, preferably, had the respect of others—though there is still room for doubt. Addressing another aspect of the controversy, MacDowell (1976a: 226) criticized Aurenche (1974) for failing to consider that—if Andocides IV's prosecutor were the Meletus denounced in 415—then Andocides IV would have pointed out in his own speech that his prosecutor had been more deeply involved in the sacrilege than himself. The argument has merit, but I find it equally implausible that Andocides IV would fail to distinguish a second man with the same name as someone he had already mentioned—as he takes pains to do when he distinguishes the Charmides (Andoc. 1.16) accused of profaning the mysteries (Plato's uncle), from his own cousin Charmides (1.47). The evidence phase of the case, no longer extant (though indicated at 1.18, 1.28, 1.46, etc.) may well have allowed Andocides IV to identify Meletus—whom he had already named in two indictments (1.13, 35)—as the Meletus there in the court and thus the Meletus who had arrested Leon (1.94). If so, it would go some distance toward explaining Andocides IV's acquittal in the trial.

A remaining loose end is Andocides IV's statement (1.94) that Meletus was not protected under the amnesty but under an additional decree limiting enforcement to laws passed after midsummer of 403 (i.e., since the archonship of Euclides). Taken together with Xenophon's account of the embassy to Sparta, this has sometimes been taken to mean that Meletus had been a member of the Board of Ten under the Thirty and thus was not covered by the amnesty unless he underwent a judicial scrutiny and proved he had not acted improperly while in office. MacDowell (1962: 133) explains the same passage by arguing that Meletus is covered by the amnesty because he did not kill Leon with his own hands.

Prosopographical notes.   *PA* 9825 cites all the references above and Plato's *Apology* as well, so *LGPN2* 4, 5, and 6, all refer to *PA* 9825: *LGPN2* 4 (Andoc. 1.94, prosecutor of Meletus); *LGPN2* 5 (remainder of Andoc. citations, found guilty of sacrilege); *LGPN2* 6 (Xen.).

Meletus I of Pithus
[*PA* 9829 *LGPN2* 13 *OCD*³
Μέλητος Πιτθεύς]
b. 460s?
father of Meletus II
tragic poet, songwriter

Pl. *Ap.* 18b schol.
frr. in *TGrF* 1².186–8
Aristoph. *Frogs* 1302
Aristoph. *Farmers*
  117 (K 114)
Aristoph. *Storks* fr.
  453 (K 438)
Aristoph. *Gery.* fr.
  156 (K 149, 150)
Epi. *Ant.* fr. 4
D. L. 2.40, pat.

Life. Diogenes cites Favorinus for the attribution of the name 'Meletus' to the father of Socrates' accuser, but the patronymic is not in the contemporaneous record. His birth is calculated partly from the age of his son, and partly from his established reputation, necessary for the comic poets to be able to lampoon him for more than twenty years before Socrates' trial. Aristophanes' *Farmers* was probably produced in 424, and the *Frogs* definitely in 405, so Meletus I could not have been described as young or unknown (Pl. *Euthphr.* 2b) in 399. Further, the Meletus of Aristophanes' *Frogs* must be mature enough for Euripides to be accused of having borrowed his drinking songs—which were probably bawdy (Epi.). Meletus I is called a tragedian in fragment 156 (where he is noteworthy for his skinniness), a worthless (φαῦλος) tragedian in fragments 114 and 438, the latter fragment attributing to him Thracian origins—for which there is no other extant evidence. Such a description ill befits a Meletus "young and unknown" in 399 (Pl. *Euthphr.* 2b). Some have used Plato's *Apology* 23e describing Meletus II as "vexed on behalf of the poets" as evidence that the songwriter-tragedian, Meletus I, is Socrates' accuser (e.g., Lattimore, in a note to his translation of the *Frogs*, calls the accuser of Socrates "a poet of indifferent reputation"; cf. *PX*). Such an identification will not work chronologically. Besides, as Derenne pointed out long ago (1930), the father of Socrates' accuser need not *be* a poet for the accuser to act on behalf of the poets.

In the later tradition. Confusion of father and son goes back at least to the scholia of the Platonic dialogues. The source for Aristophanes' *Farmers* fr. 114, in which a Meletus is mentioned with a Callias, is the scholiast of Plato's *Apology* 18b, who mistakes the tragedian for Socrates' accuser. There are other puzzles about the passage: the rich Callias III would be ±26 in 424, too old to have lovers in the traditional sense—but perhaps that is the source of the remark's humor, if the rich Callias was meant; but Socrates' accuser would have been a boy in 424, so fr. 114 cannot refer to him. Some who have argued that Andocides IV's accuser was also Socrates' accuser have pointed to the mention of Callias in fr. 114 for support (Callias III was behind the accusation of Andocides IV s.v.). But this is a wild goose chase: a connection between Meletus I and Callias III tells us nothing about the enmity between Callias III and his relative, Andocides IV (Andoc. 1.112–32), one of whose accusers was Meletus of Athens s.v. who arrested Leon (1.94).

Meletus II of Pithus, son of Meletus I
[*PA* 9830 *LGPN2* 14 *RE* 3 *OCD*³ *PP PX*
Μέλητος Μελήτεύς Πιτθεύς]
b. ≤429
Socrates' prosecutor

Pl. *Euthphr.*, *passim* *
Pl. *Ap.*   speaker
Pl. *Tht.* 210d *
Xen. *Mem.* 4.4.4,
   4.8.4
Xen. *Apol.* 11, 19–20

Life.   It is rare to have a physical description of a person in Plato, so let us note Meletus II's long hair, scraggly beard and somewhat hooked nose (*Euthphr.* 2b). Meletus II was the primary plaintiff in Socrates' prosecution (Pl. *Tht.*; Xen. *Mem.*) and is said to have brought charges on behalf of the poets (Pl. *Ap.* 23e); it is probable that his father was a poet, but not that Meletus II was himself. At the time of the trial, Meletus II was young and unknown (*Euthphr.* 2b). At *Apology* 36a–b, Socrates says of him, ". . . it is clear to all that, if Anytus and Lycon had not joined him in accusing me, he would have been fined a thousand *drachmae* for not receiving a fifth of the votes."

In the later tradition.   Aristotle cites Plato's *Apology* (27c) as an example of interrogation used well (*Rh.* 1419a8); Diodorus preserves from Favorinus the indictment naming Meletus II's father and giving the charges (2.40, quoted at Socrates s.v.); and Diodorus makes the false claim that the Athenians were so angry at the death of Socrates that they put Meletus II and Anytus to death without trial (14.37.7). In Diogenes' equally false version of the tale, the Athenians repented, executed Meletus II, and banished Anytus and Lycon, meanwhile commissioning Lysippus to cast a bronze statue in Socrates' honor (D. L. 2.43).

Melissus of Samos (philosopher) See App. II.

Menedemus See App. II.

Menedemus of Eretria See App. II.

Menexenus of Athens, son of Demophon
[*PA* 9973 *LGPN2* 1 *DPhA* 173 *OCD*³
RE 8 *PP* Μενέξενος Δημοφῶντος]
b. ≥422
brother: [unnamed] younger brother
cousin: Ctesippus of Paeania
See stemma: Lysis.

Pl. *Mx.*   speaker
Pl. *Ly.*   speaker
Pl. *Phd.* 59b   present

Life.   We know very little about this Menexenus, though it is natural to wonder whether he might be related to Socrates' family since one of Socrates' sons also bears the name. Of his relatives, we know only that his cousin is Ctesippus of Paeania (*Ly.* 206d: at PCW 690, 'nephew' should be 'cousin' [ἀνεψιός]). His father cannot be the Demophon who is a son of Hippocrates (stemma Pericles) because that Demophon was probably only a little older than Menexenus, suggesting—at best—some collateral relationship between the families.

Menexenus is in his early teens in *Lysis* and is already acquainted with Socrates (207a–b). By the time of the *Menexenus*, he is older and has completed his schooling (234a). Socrates teases, "At your age, my prodigy, you're undertaking to govern us older men, so that your family may carry on with its tradition of providing someone to look after us" (234b), implying that members of Menexenus' family had held public office. It transpires that Menexenus has not been to the Council Chamber for any such reason, but because he aspires to be chosen as a public speaker by the Council. Since he will be counted among those present at Socrates' death (*Phd.*), his being perhaps temporarily enamored of rhetoric should not be damning: he insists he would not attempt to govern without Socrates' consent.

Prosopographical notes. Together with the coincidence of father-son pairs that Lewis observes (1955) and about which Habicht expresses caution (1990), one sometimes finds a whole *cluster* of names in one family, virtually all of which have homonyms in the Platonic dialogues; sometimes the names are repeated over several generations.

For example, the wealthy Polyaratus of Cholarges (*PA/APF* 11907) who held two public offices, married a daughter of Menexenus of Cydathenaeum (*PA/APF* 3773, b. <470) in about 420, and probably died in 399/8. He had a litigious son, Menexenus of Cholarges (*PA/APF* 9981, b. <420), and a daughter (b. ?420s) who married (±395) an Eryximachus (possibly but probably not Eryximachus s.v.). Note too that both Cydathenaeum and Paeania are of the Pandionis tribe. This is much too flimsy for positive identifications, but it yields intriguing repetitions: Menexenus of Cydathenaeum's daughter and Eryximachus certainly had one child, a daughter who married a possible associate of Plato, the general Chabrias (s.v. App. II; cf. Philoch. fr. 223; Dušanić 1980) in the 370s and produced a son, Ctesippus, making Ctesippus the nephew of Menexenus of Cholarges. They may also have had a son, Eryxias. Repetition of the uncommon names 'Menexenus' and 'Ctesippus' suggests an association (perhaps a common ancestor) with a branch of the family that includes Socratic characters of those names known to have been cousins in the late 5th c. (Pl. *Ly.* 206d). There are other links as well, though they may of course be coincidental: a defense of Chabrias by Plato (D. L. 3.23–4; cf. Sealey 1993: 87, 290n55), and the statement that Chabrias and his lieutenant were Academy regulars (Plu. *Mor.* 1126c, Plu. *Phoc.* 4.2). Tantalizing though such tidbits may be, on present information, they are no basis for identifications.

Menexenus of Alopece, son of Socrates   Pl. *Ap.* 34d *
[*PA* 9975 *LGPN2* 7 *RE* 1   Pl. *Phd.* 116b   present
Μενέξενος Σωκράτους Ἀλωπεκῆθεν]
b. ≤402
mother: Xanthippe
brothers: Lamprocles II, Sophroniscus II
See stemma: Socrates.
Menexemus is probably Socrates' youngest
  son

Meno of Thessaly, son of Alexidemus	Pl. *Meno*	speaker
[*LGPN3B* 54 *RE* 4 *PP PX* Μένων]	Xen. *Anab.* 1.2.6–	
±423–400	3.1. 47, *passim*	
student of Gorgias	Ctes. frr. 27–8	
mercenary general	D. S. 14.19.8–9,	
	14.27.2–3	

Life. Both Plato (76b) and Xenophon (2.6.28) remark on Meno's physical beauty in the bloom of his youth, and on his several lovers, both noting in particular that Meno is the beloved of Aristippus of Larissa s.v. Xenophon adds what he regards as a curiosity, that the beardless Meno had a bearded beloved, Tharypus. These observations determine the date of birth I estimate above. The *Meno* is set in early 402 (see App. I), when Meno visits Athens and stays with Anytus s.v. before leaving for Persia on the campaign chronicled in Xenophon's *Anabasis* from March of 401. Plato represents Meno as a wealthy and outspoken young man, attended by several slaves (82a), and as recently having been under the influence of Gorgias (70b, 71c), whom Thessaly had especially welcomed. Thessaly itself, Socrates remarks to Meno, is noted for its horses and wealth (70a–b), but Socrates notes elsewhere its lawlessness (*Crito* 53d).

It is Xenophon who depicts Meno as so thoroughly scurrilous as to deserve his end: whereas other generals were beheaded, Meno was tortured alive for a year before being tortured to death (*Anab.* 2.6.29). Having himself been on campaign with Meno, Xenophon goes on for forty-three lines, remarking *inter alia* that Meno

> was manifestly eager for enormous wealth—eager for command in order to get more wealth and eager for honour in order to increase his gains; and he desired to be a friend to the men who possessed greatest power in order that he might commit unjust deeds without suffering the penalty. Again, for the accomplishment of the objects upon which his heart was set, he imagined that the shortest route was by way of perjury and falsehood and deception, while he counted straightforwardness and truth the same thing as folly. Affection he clearly felt for nobody, and if he said that he was a friend to anyone, it would become plain that this man was the one he was plotting against . . . he thought he was the only one who knew that it was easiest to get hold of the property of friends—just because it was unguarded . . . those who were pious and practised truth he would try to make use of, regarding them as weaklings. And just as a man prided himself upon piety, truthfulness, and justice, so Menon prided himself upon ability to deceive, the fabrication of lies, and the mocking of friends; but the man who was not a rascal he always thought of as belonging to the uneducated . . . (2.6.21–7).

Military career. Xenophon mentions Meno's generalship under Cyrus only to criticize it, with the exception of specifying, from time to time, whether he commanded the right or the left wing of the advancing army. Meno led from Thessaly 1,500 hoplites and *peltasts* hired by Aristippus and sent at Cyrus' request (*Anab.* 1.2.6). Meno's first reported assignment was to escort home the Cilician queen, Epyaxa (1.2.20), who had met with Cyrus and provided him with sufficient funding to pay his troops four months' wages (1.2.12). On the way, however, Meno lost some hundred hoplites in circumstances never made clear: either his men were caught plundering and were therefore killed by Cilicians, or they had been left behind and wandered about until they perished (1.2.25–6). In anger, the remainder of Meno's army plundered Tarsus and its palace. (Xenophon later remarks that Meno made his soldiers obedient by participating in their injustices, 2.6.27.)

Cyrus had originally deceived the troops about the aim of their campaign, which was ultimately directed at unseating his brother, King Artaxerxes of Persia, and usurping the throne. When the men began to suspect the real nature of their mission, they rebelled against their commanders (1.3.1). Meno appears again at this point in Xenophon's story, taking his own men aside and promising them special favors from Cyrus, light assignments and promotions, if they will be first to march onward across the Euphrates River, which they do to Cyrus's delight (1.4.13–7).

When Cyrus was killed at the battle of Cunaxa, stranding the army deep in Persian territory, Meno offered to accompany messengers in an effort to persuade Ariaeus, a Persian who had led troops under Cyrus, to accept the crown from the army. Meno was the "intimate and guest-friend" of Ariaeus (2.1.5; cf. 2.6.28, that Ariaeus loved boys in general and Meno in particular); Meno then remained with Ariaeus after the messengers returned to the Greek army to announce that Ariaeus had declined the offer of the throne (2.2.1). Clearchus then met on friendly terms with the Persian leader Tissaphernes, who had opposed Cyrus. Following pledges of mutual friendship, Tissaphernes asked that Clearchus return, accompanied by the other generals and captains, for a public exchange of the names of spies and slanderers on both sides. Knowing that Meno had had meetings with Tissaphernes in the company of Ariaeus, Clearchus assumed that Meno was the slanderer. When five generals and twenty captains, accompanied by two hundred soldiers, reached Tissaphernes' tent, the generals were seized within, the captains killed outside, and soldiers killed wherever they could be found, causing panic among the Greeks (2.5.24–34). Whereas Xenophon says the generals were beheaded (2.6.1), his account is modified in the case of Meno to the torture-death mentioned above (2.6.29). In a departure from the outline of Xenophon's narrative, Diodorus reports that Meno was spared the beheading because, having quarreled with the other commanders, Tissaphernes thought him ready to betray the Greeks (14.27.2). (Cf. the frr. of Ctes., which do not present Meno as the complete scoundrel of Xenophon's account.)

Menon of Athens (tailor) See App. II.

Metaneira, slave of Nicarete (*hetaira*) See App. II. See *stemma Lysias.*

Metrobius of Athens See App. II.

Metrodorus of Lampsacus (rhapsode) See App. II.

Miccus of ?Athens   Pl. *Ly.* 204a *
[*PP* Μίκκος]
friend and admirer of Socrates
wrestling teacher

Prosopographical notes. *LGPN2* lists the three *PA* persons of this name, two of whom are much too late to be compatible with a dramatic date for the *Lysis* of ±409. *FRA* adds a Miccus of Torone, son of Calliclides, known from a funerary monument dated 450–20, which is too early. *PA* 10193 = *LGPN2* 1 (= *NIA* 3 T26) is the 5th–4th c. father of an Alcaeus who was a comic poet (writing mythological burlesques, and known from Aristophanes' *Plutus* schol., for having composed a *Pasiphae* in 388 that competed against *Plu.*). *LGPN2* includes the *Suda* reference "Α 1274 Ἀλκαῖος" which identifies the son as "a Mytilenian, then an Athenian," prompting *FRA* to accept that the son of Miccus must have been a naturalized citizen of Athens. *PP* (p. 197) mentions Miccus only to list him among prefects of various types of schools.

Midias   [Pl.] *Alc.* 120a *
[*PP* Μιδίας]

Midias was a cockfighter with a slave boy haircut who took an active role in government (*Alc.*). Diogenes may confuse the reference, making Midias into a barber whose fighting cocks display in defiance of those of Callias III (2.30).

Miltiades IV of Laciadae, son of Cimon I   Pl. *Grg.* 503c †
[*PA/APF* 10212 (8429.8) *LGPN2* 13 *RE* 15   Hdt. 6, *passim*
*OCD*³ *PP* Μιλτιάδης Κίμωνος Λακιάδης]   Thu. 1.98.1, 1.100.1,
≤550–489   pat.
brother: Stesagoras II   *IG* I³ 1031.19; 1472
wives: (1) a kinswoman of ?Hippias (2)   *ARV*² 1601
  Hegesipyle I, daughter of Thracian King   *Agora* 25.592–7
  Olorus   *AM* 106.152
offspring with (1): Metiochus; with (2):   D. H. 7.3.1
  Cimon II, Elpinice, and two other daughters
famous political and military leader
See stemma: Thucydides.

Life. Miltiades IV was eponymous archon in 524/3; thus he should have been born no later than 554, but he was named *kalos* by Paseas 520–10 (*ARV*²) when he would have been about a decade older than youths to whom such tributes were usually paid. Upon his brother's death in 516/5, Miltiades IV was sent to the Chersonese by the tyrant Hippias, but he had probably already married (and certainly had married by 514) for his son, Metiochus, was old enough to be commanding a ship in 493 when, as Herodotus recounts, he was captured by the Phoenicians. Metiochus was released and given lands and a Persian wife by Darius (6.41.2–4), never returning to Athens. To explain Metiochus' treatment in Persia, *APF* suggests that Miltiades IV's first wife was a relation, perhaps a daughter, of the tyrant Hippias, who was in that year an exile in the Persian court where he could wield influence.

Miltiades IV had married again ≤510, this time to Hegesipyle I, daughter of King Olorus of Thrace. The children of that marriage, and especially Cimon II, carried on the family's dynastic tradition of marriage alliances (see stemmata: Callias, Pericles, Thucydides).

Career in brief.   Miltiades IV's military exploits were many and, although perhaps inflated, account for the reverence that his name was likely to evoke in the late 5th c. When Callicles mentions Miltiades IV in the *Gorgias*, it is in company with his son, Cimon II, and Pericles I—i.e. renowned dead leaders—all of whose greatness Socrates goes on to question. The main elements of Miltiades IV's career, for which Herodotus is the chief source, began with his temporary success in the Chersonese (he was later driven out by the Scythians). He served Darius I for a time, then joined the "Ionian revolt"; when it was subjugated, Miltiades IV returned to Athens where he was tried and acquitted of tyranny in the Chersonese and promptly elected general in 490/89. At this point, some exaggeration probably enters the picture, but Miltiades IV is credited with a decisive role in the Athenian decision to fight the Persians at Marathon. The further claim, that he was responsible for the particular phalanx strategy that ensured Athenian victory is not credible, given his relative lack of military experience. He died of wounds received in a military effort to seize Paros soon after Marathon, but not before the Athenians could fine him fifty *talents* for failure to capture the town. His son, Cimon II s.v., inherited and paid the debt.

Miltiades VI of Laciadae, son of Stesagoras III
[*PA/APF* 10207 (8429.15) *LGPN2* 15
Μιλτιάδης Στησαγόρου Λακιάδης]
±470–>404
contemporary of Socrates

[Pl.] *Ax.* 368d
Aes. *Mil.*
Lys. 12.72

Life.   The life and career of Miltiades VI is partially conjectured (*APF*) to explain the appearance of a Miltiades in the Socratic literature who cannot be any of the other known bearers of the name. Aeschines' dialogue *Miltiades*, of which six short fragments remain, three on papyri, appears to have been named for Miltiades VI whose patronymic is given only by Aeschines, and who is an approximate contemporary of Socrates; since his father is otherwise unknown, neither can be fitted onto the several stemmata of Miltiades IV and Cimon II, famous presumed ascendants. This may be the same Miltiades (and there is not another known one of the right age) who went with Philochares to Lysander in 404 as a sympathizer with the oligarchic faction and returned with him to Athens for the Assembly debate that resulted in the establishment of the Thirty. (Todd 2000: 131 describes

Miltiades as a subordinate "in command of the Spartan fleet," but I have been unable to substantiate a basis for that alternative possibility.)

Socrates is the speaker of at least *Miltiades* no. 76 (missing from Dittmar). Also present are Euripides (nos. 76 and 80, also missing from Dittmar), and Hagnon, Theramenes' father (no. 76). Miltiades VI is depicted as especially devoted to physical training (no. 77 = fr. 37 Dittmar) at some time long after the family held sway in Athenian political life.

Mithaecus of Syracuse (pastry cook) See App. II.

Morychus of Thria, son of Lachemorus	Pl. *Phdr.* 227b &
[*PA* 10421, *PA/APF* 10423 (*LGPN2* 3, 4	schol. *
Μόρυχος Λαχεμοίρου Θριάσιος]	*IG* I³ 1032.409
	(naval catalogue)
	IG II² 4882
	(dedication)
	Aristoph. *Ach.* 887
	Aristoph. *Peace* 1008
	Aristoph. *Wasps* 506
	Pl. *com. Peri.* fr. 114
	(K 106)

Life. The rich Morychus mentioned in Plato's *Phaedrus*, who needs neither demotic nor patronymic for further identification, is unlikely to be anyone but the individual who was both *syntrierarch* of a ship that fought at Arginusae (*IG* I³) and the author of an Acropolis dedication (*IG* II²), well-known also from comedy in the period 425–421 for his extravagance. At one time he owned a house near the Olympieum in which its new owner, Epicrates, hosted Phaedrus sometime 418–16.

Prosopographical notes. *PA* 10421 lists *Phaedrus* and the comic frr. only; *LGPN2* 4 queries whether Morychus is an Athenian (and adds a citation, *TGrF* 1 p. 148.30). *PA/APF* 10423, followed by *LGPN2* 3, lists the inscriptions only.

Myronides of Athens and Syracuse	[Pl.] *Ltr.* 13.363e *
[*LGPN3A* 2 *FRA* 7877 Μυρωνίδης]	

Myronides was manumitted by [Plato] and sailed with Iatrocles from Athens to Syracuse to be employed by Dionysius II. If there is any substance to the letter, Myronides was a foreign resident of Athens by virtue of being a slave, and a resident of Syracuse by virtue of his later employment. *LGPN3A* queries Syracuse, and *FRA* says "probably fictitious."

Myrto of Athens, [?grand]daughter of	[Pl.] *Hal.* 8
Aristides I of Alopece	Aes. *orat.* 3.258
[*PA* 10500 (*APF* 1695.4) *LGPN2* 4	Aristot. frr. 92, 93
Μυρτώ Ἀριστείδου Ἀλωπεκῆθεν θυγάτηρ]	

440s–>399
See stemma: Thucydides.

Family. Myrto, known only from fragmentary references, was the daughter or granddaughter of Aristides I, "The Just." The orator Aeschines reports that the Athenians awarded dowries to the daughters of Aristides (3.258), a report augmented with two later specifications: the amount of 3,000 *dr.* apiece (Plu. *Arist.* 27.1); and the addition that they were to be maintained with meals in the Pryteneum at state expense (Nep. *Arist.* 3.3)—dubious at least because communal meals were a male institution. Although the whole plan is generally viewed as a Hellenistic fabrication, I retain the detail from Aeschines that Aristides had two daughters, one of whom may have been Myrto. It is more likely, however, that one of those daughters, or Lysimachus II, was the parent of Myrto, i.e., that she was Aristides' granddaughter. Although, theoretically, a daughter of Aristides I could have been born right up until the time of his death ±467, making Myrto Socrates' near agemate, Lysimachus II (b. 480s) describes himself a fellow demesman and friend of Socrates' father, Sophroniscus I (*Lch.* 180); again, theoretically, Lysimachus II could have a sister some twenty years younger than himself, but it is more likely that Myrto was of the next generation, the generation of Aristides II.

Of Socrates' household? Perhaps because Phaedo of Elis tells Echecrates of Phlius that the women of Socrates' household were brought to him in prison (*Phd.* 116b; cf. Xanthippe s.v.), there grew up a story that Socrates had had a second wife, Myrto, a late version of which is mentioned in [Pl.] *Hal.* 8, written sometime between 150 B.C.E. and 50 C.E. If Plutarch, writing in the late 1st or early 2nd c. C.E. is reporting his own sources accurately, then he had four for his claim that "Myrto, grand-daughter of Aristides, lived with the sage Socrates, who was married to another woman but took Myrto under his protection when she was widowed because she was poor and lacking in the necessities of life" (Aristot. fr. 93, in part = Plu. *Arist.* 335): Demetrius Phalerus, *Socrates,* writing in the 4th c. B.C.E., but known as a poor source for prosopographical material (cf. *APF* 1695.4); Hieronymus of Rhodes, who resided in Athens in the 3rd c. B.C.E.; Aristoxenus, a 4th c. B.C.E. writer on music and debunker of the Socratic legend; and Aristotle's fr. from the lost *On Good Birth,* also dated to the 4th c. B.C.E. Plutarch did not believe the story. In the 2nd–3rd c. C.E., Athenaeus attributes to Aristotle the story that Socrates married twice, to Xanthippe and to Myrto, citing the same Demetrius and Aristoxenus, but adding Callisthenes and the 3rd c. B.C.E. historian Satyrus. Diogenes tells a more elaborate version of the story in the 3rd c. C.E., that Socrates "had two wives, first Xanthippe from whom he had Lamprocles, and secondly Myrto, the daughter of Aristides the Just, whom he took without a dowry and from whom he had Sophroniscus and Menexenus" (Aristot. fr. 93, in part = D. L. 2.26). All these versions have been summarily dismissed by most scholars (but cf. Winspear and Silverberg 1960, Fitton 1970, Woodbury 1973, and Bicknell 1974b for more details, texts, and the conclusion that Xanthippe was a citizen *pallakē,* a concubine). Because our contemporaneous sources, Plato and Xenophon, say with one voice that Xanthippe was Socrates' wife, I do not accept a second marriage to Myrto. Nevertheless, it is worthwhile attending to the social conditions in Athens that make the first version of the story—that Socrates, while married to

Xanthippe, took the widowed and indigent Myrto under his guardianship—both plausible and unremarkable.

Under Athenian law, women were perpetual minors who, upon the death of a husband who had not provided a will, were immediately made wards of a male guardian, determined by degree of kinship. The Peloponnesian war had produced thousands of casualties, and war widows had become a social problem of some magnitude. One sees it in Aristophanes' female-dominated plays (*Lysistr., Thesm.* and *Eccl.*); when Xenophon's Aristarchus s.v. complains to Socrates that his house has grown full of women (*Mem.* 2.7); and perhaps in the prominence given women in *Republic* 5.451b–457b. However, a guardian appointed in the will of the deceased married the widow only if he was not already married, having the right to marry her off to someone else, or to keep her in his household. There was a loophole in the law, interesting if not applicable here: if his living wife had not produced issue, he was allowed to divorce her and marry the widow in her stead (MacDowell 1978: 96). (On these issues more generally, see Harrison 1998: 1.38; MacDowell 1978: 88–9.) Thus there is no reason to posit a marriage between Socrates and Myrto. She was his neighbor in the deme of Alopece already, and Socrates' special debt to her family is established in the dialogues. Lysimachus II, Myrto's uncle or father, tells Socrates, "you have a duty . . . because you are my friend through your father. He and I were always comrades and friends, and he died without our ever having had a single difference" (*Lch.* 180e); and "I myself would be willing to do a great many things for him [Socrates] which I would not be willing to do for practically anyone else" (200d).

What seems to account for the later fixation on marriage is the decree passed by the Athenians in the face of its unprecedented manpower shortage: the population had fallen precipitously, and there were few men available as husbands. According to the decree, Athenian men could, while legally married to one woman, produce *legitimate* children with a *pallakē*, a concubine—they could already produce *nothoi*, illegitimate ones (D. L. 2.26; Ath. 556a; Gell. *NA* 15.20.6). Neither Harrison (1998.1: 17) nor Osborne (*NIA* 3.35 and n68) doubts the decree was passed, but MacDowell (1978: 90) notes that it must also have been repealed for, in the 4th c., legitimacy was as it had been before the decree.

Myson of Chen (sage) See App. II.

Nausicydes of Cholarges
[*PA*/*APF* 10567 (8443) (*APF* 10567 = 10571)
LGPN2 5 *PP PX*
Ναυσικύδης Χολαργεύς]
† >392
father of ?Nausimenes
associates: Callicles, Andron, Tisander

Pl. *Grg.* 487c *
Xen. *Mem.* 2.7.5–66
Aristoph. *Eccl.*
424–6

Xenophon's Socrates says of Nausicydes, a miller and holder of foreign slaves and who remained in the city under the Thirty, that Nausicydes so prospered in making barley flour that he could keep herds of pigs and cattle and still have a remainder for the expenses of liturgies etc. Aristophanes, however, implies in 392 or 391 that there was something discreditable about his dealings, perhaps only that he was reluctant to perform the liturgies for which he was obliged, having risen to the liturgical class through successful trading. But it may also have been extortion: Athens was largely dependent on foreign trade for the grain essential to make bread, so grain trading was a highly regulated enterprise: several sets of commissioners were charged with various aspects of the business, ensuring a fair system of weights and measures to protect consumers. A passage in Xenophon's *Symposium* (2.20) implies that regulations extended to the requirement that baked loaves of bread be weighed against a standard measure as well.

Niceratus I of Athens See App. II. *See stemma: Nicias.*

Niceratus II of Cydantidae, son of Nicias I	Pl. *R.*	present
[*PA/APF* 10741 (10808) *LGPN2* 26 *RE* 1 *DPhA*	Pl. *Lch.* 200d *	
s.v. *PP PX* Νικήρατος Νικίου Κυδαντίδης]	Xen. *Symp.*	
b. 445–439, †404	Xen. *Hell.* 2.3.39	
father of Nicias II	D. S. 14.5.5	
See stemma: Nicias.	Lys. 18.6–10, 19.47	
	Aristot. *Rh.* 1413a7	
	inscriptions (see below)	

Life. Niceratus II, named for his paternal grandfather, must have been born by 439 to have been *trierarch* at Samos in 409 (*IG* I³ 375.36), but could as easily be a few years older. He grew up in the extreme wealth made possible by his father's, and grandfather's, silver mine holdings, worked by slave labor. Xenophon describes him as overly fond of money (*Symp.* 4.45, 4.51).

Of Niceratus II's education, both Plato and Xenophon are informative. At the dramatic date of the *Laches*, 424 (see App. I), Nicias I had already asked Socrates on more than one occasion to take Niceratus II under his wing, but Socrates had always suggested other possible teachers (200c–d; both Damon and Prodicus had already been mentioned). In Xenophon, Nicias I is described as having been so eager that Niceratus II should become a good man that he required his son to memorize both the *Iliad* and the *Odyssey* (*Symp.* 3.5–6), which he could still recite in their entirety in August of 422 (the nominal dramatic date of Xen. *Symp.*)— appropriate to the discussion of Homeric poetry in *Republic* 2, 3 and 10. Aristotle makes a further connection between two *Republic* characters, Niceratus II and Thrasymachus, linking them both to rhapsodic competition: ". . . Niceratus *is like* a Philoctetes stung by Pratys—the simile made by Thrasymachus when he saw Niceratus, who had been beaten by Pratys in a recitation competition, still going about unkempt and unwashed."

Niceratus II married and had a son, Nicias II, between 413 and 409. Xenophon depicts Niceratus II as newly wed in 422 (an anachronism), in love with his wife and she with him (Xen. *Symp.* 2.3, 8.3). It may be this image that inspired the later tradition that she committed suicide upon his death (Hieronymus Cardianus, *Jovinianum* 1.310, in the 4th–3rd c. B.C.E.). We have a full account of Nicias II's becoming the ward of his paternal great uncle, Diognetus s.v., in 404 (Lys. 18), but a child was considered an orphan if his or her father was dead, regardless of whether the mother was alive. The further implication of the speech, however, that Nicias II was an infant in 404 (laid on the knees of Pausanias, king of Sparta) is an exaggeration: he had grown up to marry a daughter of the democratic hero Thrasybulus of Steria s.v. in 389/8 (*IG* II² 2409.21 with Lewis 1955: 27–8). He was younger than his cousins, the sons of Eucrates (Lys. 18.10) who had recently come of age in 396 (having been born, presumably, <414). Nicias II's birth year can be put at 413–09, but the later date carries with it the consequence that he will have married early for an Athenian, so a date closer to 413 is more likely.

In Xenophon's *Hellenica*, Theramenes uses the execution of Niceratus II at the hands of the Thirty as an example of the regime's having gone too far, identifying Niceratus II as a wealthy man who, like his father, had never sought popular acclaim. (The claim is patently untrue of his father, Nicias I; see below.) Diodorus, however—similarly praising Niceratus II's wealth and reputation, but calling him just and humane as well—puts his execution after Theramenes' death. Xenophon's account tallies better with such evidence as there is (see Rhodes 1993: 446).

In the later tradition. See Plutarch (*Mor.* 998b; Niceratus II is not mentioned in Plu. *Nic.*). Aristophanes' *Knights* 358 has been emended to accommodate a reference to Niceratus II, but Davies (*APF*) argues compellingly against both the proposed emendation and the consequent reference.

Prosopographical notes. LGPN2 26 ?= 3 (known from *P. Oxy.* 2537.12, 14 *verso*).

Nicias I of Cydantidae, son of Niceratus I	Pl. *Lch.*	speaker
[*PA/APF* 10808 *LGPN2* 95 *DPhA* 104 *RE* 5	Pl. *Grg.* 472a *	
OCD³ PP PX Νικίας Νικίου Κυδαντίδης]	Xen. *Mem.* 2.5.2	
±475–413	Xen. *WM* 4.14	
paternal ?half brothers: Eucrates and	Thu. 3.51.1–7.86.2,	
Diognetus	*passim*	
father of Niceratus II, Stratippus	D. S. 12.65.1–13.33.1,	
associate of Pericles I	*passim*	
longtime general and political leader	Andoc. 3.8	
See stemma: Nicias.	Lys. 19.47	
	inscriptions (see	
	below)	
	in comedy (see	
	below)	

Life. Nicias I was somewhat older than Socrates (*Lch.* 186c). The point is not adequately addressed by putting Nicias I's birth at 470 (commonly used), for that is a difference not worth noticing in the conversation. The gap of five or six years that I suggest, together with Nicias I's having married and pursued a public

STEMMA: NICIAS

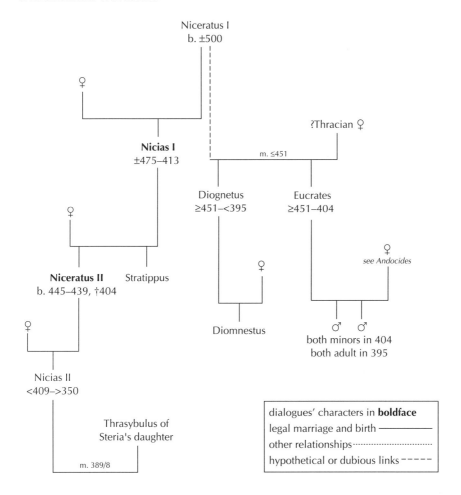

Niceratus I
b. ±500

♀

Nicias I
±475–413

?Thracian ♀

m. ≤451

♀

Diognetus
≥451–<395

Eucrates
≥451–404

♀
see Andocides

Niceratus II   Stratippus
b. 445–439, †404

♀

♀

Diomnestus

♂   ♂
both minors in 404
both adult in 395

Nicias II
<409–>350

Thrasybulus of
Steria's daughter

m. 389/8

dialogues' characters in **boldface**
legal marriage and birth ————
other relationships·······················
hypothetical or dubious links – – – –

career so much earlier than did Socrates, makes more sense of the text of *Laches*. Nicias I was *not* from a prominent aristocratic family, not from an aristocratic family at all. The family's wealth began only with Niceratus I, Nicias I's father, who exploited the possibility of using slaves to mine silver, and made a fortune. Xenophon writes of his thousand slaves (*WM*), managed by Sosias, a Thracian he had purchased for a *talent* (*Mem.*). *APF* calculates that Nicias I's mining income, on a return of one obol per day per slave (*WM*), would have been ten *talents* annually. Lysias, looking back from ≥390, put Nicias I's capital accumulation at about one hundred *talents*. Nicias I used his extraordinary wealth to win influence, and he succeeded with moderates of both oligarchic and democratic allegiance. He was often *chorēgos*, performed the task in sumptuous style and, if Plutarch is believed (*Nic.* 3.3), was never beaten (cf. Pl. *Grg.* 472a for his dithyramb victory for Aigeis <415). Inscriptions (below) support his lavish expenditures.

The description of Nicias I's wealth—as *APF*, sharply attuned to class divisions, has pointed out—places him among slave-owning demagogues such as Cleon and Hyperbulus, rather than among such landowners as Pericles I. If one examines the Platonic dialogues now believed genuine as a group, and considers the persons who appear in them in person, the men who are noteworthy for the wealth they derive from the exploitation of slaves are Nicias I and his son Niceratus II (1,000 slaves in silver mining), Callias III (600 slaves in silver mining)—where mining was considered the harshest form of slavery—Cephalus II and his sons (120 slaves in an armory), Anytus (unspecified number of slaves in a tannery). Others certainly owned slaves, but these were the ones whose revenues most depended on slaves; they might reasonably be contrasted not only with Pericles I but with Crito and his son Critobulus, whose wealth appears to have been substantial, but who were also landowners.

Military career in brief.   Nicias I was repeatedly elected general, implying that the Athenians found him competent for the task. He had a reputation for caution, however, which he appears to have deserved, for he fought in many campaigns without significant defeat before the Sicilian disaster. His caution, his reluctance to take risks, however, prevented the Athenians from lionizing him as a great general; their preference was the Alcibiades type, a general who won heroic victories against high odds.

Nicias I is previously unknown (*pace* Plu. *Nic.* 2.2) when he appears as general in 427. He undertook successful campaigns in Minoa (Thu. 3.51.1) and Melos (Thu. 3.91.1–6; D. S. 3.80.5). By late July of 424, however, when the beleaguered Athenians were blockading a stranded Peloponnesian force off Pylos, the pro-war Cleon advised the Assembly to "sail against the Lacedaemonians. He pointed to Nikias, one of the generals, putting personal hostility into the criticism that with the right preparation it was easy—if the generals were men—to sail and capture the troops on the island, and that he himself would certainly do it if he were in command" (Thu. 4.27). Nicias I replied by calling Cleon's bluff, handing over his Pylos command to a Cleon Thucydides describes as frightened and reluctant (Thu. 4.28). In Aristophanes' *Knights*, produced at the following Lenaean festival in 424, the vulgar Sausage Seller representing Cleon boasts that he will harass Nicias I (ln. 358). Lewis (*CAH* 5²: 417) points out that, prior to Cleon, the position of general (*stratēgos*) had been reserved for men of birth and wealth, but that the Assembly promptly ratified Nicias I's action, and Cleon proceeded to victory in Pylos. (Cleon's glorious return to Athens with Spartan prisoners of war prevented a Lacedaemonian invasion of Attica in the summer of 424.) But Nicias I had not resigned his generalship along with his Pylos command; he soon gained his own victories against Corinth (Thu. 4.42.1), Cythera and Nisaea (Thu. 4.53.1–2; D. S. 12.80.5), and Mende (Thu. 4.129.2–5)—all in his cautious way. But Nicias I is remembered as Thucydides says he wished to be remembered (5.16.1), as a peacemaker. He was involved in the negotiations for an armistice in 423 that held in most places; the treaty finally settled in April of 421 that lasted fitfully until 416 was called the Peace of Nicias (Thu. 5.19, 24). He opposed the Sicilian expedition (D. S. 12.83.5–6; Thu. 6.9–14, 6.21–25), but was nevertheless elected one of three generals to lead it, and dutifully took command. His co-general, Alcibiades III, left the fleet at Thurii (see Exc. 1), and his other co-general, Lamachus, was killed in action in the summer of 414; so Nicias I inherited sole command (Thu. 6.101.6) at a time when his health had deteriorated markedly from what is now believed to have been kidney disease. After some initial successes in Sicily, Nicias I wrote to Athens of the coalition that was forming against the Athenians and urged that he should be either reinforced or recalled at once (D. S. 13.8.6; Thu. 7.8.2–3, 7.10–15). Ultimately, all help was too little or too late, and the Athenians were driven to defeat, surrender, and enslavement. Nicias I—his antiwar and peacemaking efforts acknowledged—was put to death by the Syracusans over the objections of their Spartan allies (Thu. 7.86.2; D. S. 13.33.1).

In comedy. A number of frr. are preserved by Plutarch, whose desire to emphasize Nicias I's virtues may have skewed the selection. Although Nicias I paid off informers, it was not because of any previous wrongdoing on his part but because he was an easy mark for rogues: Eupolis (*Mar.* 193 [K 181], dated 421) and Teleclides (fr. 44 [K 41])—not unlike Crito s.v. Phrynichus (fr. 62 [K 59]) makes Nicias I so timid that he cowers when he walks. In 414, Aristophanes first praises his clever strategy (*Birds* 363), then takes it back in a reference to his characteristic delays (ln. 639, μελλονικιᾶν; cf. *Farmers* fr. 100 of 424).

In inscriptions. Nicias I's military career accounts for a number of inscriptions, e.g. the Sicilian campaign of 415–3: *IG* I³ 369.20; 370.20, 50, 53 et al.; 371.11; 470.?13; 1474. His liturgies for others: *archetheoros* to Delos (*IDélos* 104–11B.13; 104–12.91; 104–27.7) + *APF*: [*IG* II² 1638.46]; 1640.8; 1652.11; [1653.8]; *IDélos* 41; *IG* XI 164A.39; 203B.56.

In the later tradition and modern bibliography. See pseudo-Aristotle (*Ath. Pol.* 28.5) and Plutarch's *Nicias*, which has been particularly influential (cf. Plu. *Alc.* 13, 17); see also Diogenes (1.110, anachronistic), and Isaeus (6.14). On controversial military dating issues involving Nicias I (including inscription information), see Lewis (1961), and on other epigraphical issues Lewis (1955: 27–31). On the period of the Peace of Nicias, see Seager (1976); for Nicias I's virtue as a general, strategic expertise, see Lewis (*CAH* 5²: 406, citing Gomme *HCT* 2.333–6).

Nicias II of Cydantidae, son of Niceratus II See App. II. *See stemma: Nicias.*

Nicias of ?Thebes, son of Heroscamander   [Pl.] *Thg.* 129b
[*PA* 10784 *LGPN2* 5 *PP*
Νικίας Ἡροσκαμάνδρου]
assassination target

Dušanić (1990b: 65–70) argues that most of the persons mentioned in *Theages* are from Thebes, including Nicias, the assassination target of Timarchus and Philemon s.vv. This would account for their leaving no record in Athens.

Nicomachides of Athens   Xen. *Mem.* 3.4–12
[*PA* 10931 *LGPN2* 1 *PX*
Νικομαχίδης]

Nicomachides, a commander who displays his war wounds with pride, complains that the Athenians have passed him over and elected an inexperienced business-man to be general (*stratēgos*). Socrates launches into a defense of men who transact their personal business well, "For the management of private concerns differs only in point of number from that of public affairs" (3.12).

Nicostratus I of Athmonon, son of   Pl. *Ap.* 33e   present
   Theozotides I   *IG* XII 5.542.35, pat.
[*PA* 11033 (cf. *APF* 6915) *LGPN2* 51 *RE* 24 *PP*
Νικόστρατος Θεοζοτίδου Ἀθμονεύς]
b. ±418
brother: Theodotus
father of Theozotides II

IG II² 944 (cited in error by Burnet) is properly attributed to Nicostratus II, the grandson of this Nicostratus.

Nysaeus of Syracuse, son of Dionysius II and Aristomache See App. II. *See stemma: Dion.*

Oenopides of Chios (mathematical astronomer) See App. II.

Orthagoras of Thebes (*aulos* teacher) See App. II.

Paralius of Anagyrus, son of Demodocus   Pl. *Ap.* 33e   present
[*PA* 11611 *LGPN2* 1   *IG* II² 1400.3
Παράλιος Δημοδόκου Ἀναγράσιος]
b. >420
brother: Theages

Treasurer in 390/89 (*IG*). The Plato mss. have 'Paralus' which Kirchner amended to 'Paralius' with *IG*. On current information, this family would merit inclusion in the *APF* register of directly attested individuals.

Paralus of Cholarges, son of Pericles I   Pl. *Prt.* 315a   present
[*PA/APF* 11612 (11811.3) *LGPN2* 1 *RE* 5 *PP*   Pl. *Meno* 94b
Πάραλος Περικλέους Χολαργεύς]   [Pl.] *Alc.* 118d–e &
<455–429   schol. *

mother: [unnamed] kinswoman of Pericles I
  who later married Hipponicus II
siblings: full brother Xanthippus II; maternal
  half brother Callias III; maternal half sister
  Hipparete I; paternal half brother Pericles II
See stemma: Pericles.

[Pl.] *Virt.*
  377d–378a †
IG I³ 49.13
Plu. *Per.* 24, 36.4

Paralus is the younger of Pericles I's two sons by his first wife. He walks with his brother, flanking Protagoras in the dialogue (*Prt.*). The brothers are undistinguished in Plato, but have reputations as wastrels in the later tradition (Plu.). Paralus died, unmarried, about three years later in the plague that struck Athens at the outbreak of the Peloponnesian war (Plu.).

Parmenides of Elea, son of Pyres
[*LGPN3A* 1 *DPhA* 52 *RE* s.v. *OCD*³ *PP*
Παρμενίδης]
b. ±515
teacher and ?adoptive father of Zeno
philosopher

Pl. *Prm.*   speaker
Pl. *Smp.* 178b, 195c
Pl. *Tht.* 152e,
  180e–4a
Pl. *Sph.* 216a3–58c6,
  passim
Speu. fr. 1
frr. in DK 28
SEG 38.1020.4

Life and career. Parmenides' father's name is given by Apollodorus (cited in D. L. 9.21 and 9.25). An inscription for a Parmenides, son of Ouliades, has been found as well (*SEG*, cited in *LGPN3A* along with Pyres), but 'Ouliades' was Parmenides' later cult name in Elea where he was associated with healing. Parmenides' date of birth is fixed by his age of sixty-five at the time of the greater Panathenaea in Athens in August of 450 of the year 450/49 (*Prm.* 127b). The meeting between Parmenides and Socrates in Plato's dialogue would have occurred, if it occurred, then (see *Tht.* 183e and *Sph.* 217c, referring to a meeting between Parmenides and Socrates). Diogenes provides information incompatible with Plato's account of Parmenides' age, however, citing either *On Philosophers* by Speusippus (not in the catalogue of Speusippus' works) or a work of Speusippus on philosophers (perhaps *Philosopher*, or *On Philosophy*, or some other work about philosophers). Diogenes (9.23) says Parmenides flourished in the 69th Olympiad, 504–500—a claim that would make him closer to ninety than sixty-five in 450. Extant fragments of Speusippus do not include Diogenes' reports.

    Still citing Speusippus, Diogenes says Parmenides was a legislator for Elea, founded in 540 (9.23). The legislator story was told by both Strabo (6.1) and Plutarch (*Mor.* 1126a–b), the latter adding that the citizens of Elea began each year by swearing to abide by Parmenides' laws. Diogenes reports on *teachers of* Parmenides, but any such claims are so intertwined with considerations of *influences on* Parmenides that they are better considered in a philosophical than a historical context; I will not retail them here. Plato, the extant source closest to events, reports a rumor that Parmenides was once Zeno's lover (*Prm.* 127b), but that does not in itself preclude the possibility that Zeno was Parmenides' adoptive son.

In the later tradition and modern bibliography. A few additional testimonia are quoted in DK. There is no evidence to support Burnet's conjecture (1920: 171n2, 311) that Timaeus of Tauromenium was the source of the story that Parmenides was the Elean lawgiver, and none for Gigon's conjecture, based on an emendation of Plutarch's text, that the lawgiver was Democritus (1947: 220). Tarán (1981: 237–8), whose arguments I have abbreviated, is essential for a full discussion of these issues.

Parrhasius   Xen. *Mem.* 3.10.1–5
[*PX* Παρράσιος]
painter

Parrhasius was a painter famous for his outlines, which were used as models for centuries. In his home, Parrhasius agrees with Socrates that good paintings depict the subject's emotions, as well as outward appearance.

Patrocles of Alopece, son of Chaeredemus   Pl. *Euthd.* 297e *
[*PA* 11697, 11691 *LGPN2* 8, 9, 4 *RE* 4 *PP*   *IG* I³ 378.16
Πατροκλῆς Χαιρεδήμου Ἀλωπεκῆθεν]   Isocr. 18.5–8
±450–>402
mother: Phaenarete
half brother: Socrates
See stemma: Socrates.

Life. Socrates says he has a brother (*Euthd.*); but the brother has a different father and is much younger than Socrates. If he was the Patrocles of Alopece who was treasurer of Athena in ±406/5 (*IG*),

ΔΔΔ ᵛ ἀθλοθ[έταις ἐς τὰ] Παναθήν[αια ------------------------]
[λ]ηρεῖ, Πατρο[κ]λ[εῖ Ἀλωπε]κῆθεν· τρίτ[ηι --------------------]

he was a wealthy Athenian; and only if he was that Patrocles do we know his deme with certainty. Socrates, like his father, was registered in Alopece, and resided there as well. If, as postulated at Phaenarete s.v., Socrates' mother was widowed after Socrates had reached the age of majority, then he was responsible for arranging any further marriage. Other factors of Athenian social life increase the chances that Phaenarete s.v. married within her husband's deme: Alopece was one of the larger demes, and marriages were relatively more common within demes (see App. III) than between demes.

Career after the Thirty. A more interesting question is whether Socrates' wealthy brother may have been one of the Board of Ten archons, the king archon in fact, elected by the Three Thousand in the period immediately following the fall of the Thirty to govern in their place and negotiate a peace between the parties (see Exc. 4).

The Patrocles who was king archon (*PA* 11691 *LGPN2* 4) was a friend of the speaker of Isocrates 18. The speaker, a wealthy former *trierarch*, was originally the defendant but was countersuing the democrat Callimachus for illegally pursuing a case that had already been settled, i.e. harassing him (see Archinus s.v. for the legal innovation that made such a countersuit possible). Because the speaker does not hesitate to call Patrocles his friend, we can safely infer that Patrocles had already presented his accounts, been successfully scrutinized, and made subject to the amnesty himself (members of the Board of Ten were probably initially exempt from the protection of the amnesty but were allowed to redeem themselves by judicial scrutiny). In the same speech, Rhinon—another former member of the Board of Ten, and eponym of a dialogue of Aeschines—was called as a witness (18.8); since he was soon after elected general, we can assume that it was not necessarily deadly to one's career to have been an archon immediately after the reign of the Thirty.

The facts of the case, albeit from the speaker's perspective only, are these. Patrocles, during the period of the Thirty, 404/3, accused Callimachus of being in possession of money belonging to a member of the exiled democratic party. The Board of Ten referred the case to the Council (under both the Thirty and later the Ten, the Council assumed judicial responsibilities normally borne by juries), and the Council confiscated the money. When the democracy was restored in 403, Callimachus brought suit, winning a settlement that included a fine of ten *minae* paid by Patrocles, and two *minae* paid by a Lysimachus. Under arbitration, the speaker also paid two *minae*. Dissatisfied, Callimachus tried to sue again, but the defendants were able to argue successfully that the dispute had already been settled. When Callimachus brought suit a third time, in 402, it was for a hundred *minae* against the speaker who argued *inter alia* that it was Patrocles who had originally brought the accusation. For a contemporary assessment of this affair, see Loening (1987: 124–8).

Prosopographical notes. *PA* 11697 provides Patrocles' demotic and patronymic, the reference to *Euthydemus*, and the treasurer inscription (*IG*). *LGPN2* splits that entry into Patrocles 8, Socrates' half brother ?= Patrocles 9, treasurer of Athena. *PA* 11691 (= *LGPN2* 4) is a reference to the Patrocles of Isocrates 18.5. *LGPN2* 4 consists only of the reference in Isocrates (18.5) where no demotic or patronymic is given.

EXCURSUS 4:
THE AMNESTY OF 403–402.

The defeat of the Thirty on the Piraeus hill of Munychia in which both Critias IV and Charmides were killed in May of 403 did not end the tyranny. Although a herald of the Eleusinian mysteries among the democrats, Cleocritus, made a beautiful conciliatory speech (Xen. *Hell.* 2.4.20–2), the remnants of the Thirty returned to the city to consider their options. The Three Thousand, increasingly suspicious of one another, deposed the Thirty and replaced them with a Board of Ten, elected one per tribe (Xen. *Hell.* 2.4.23). The Thirty began abandoning the city for Eleusis, which they had earlier secured for themselves by putting to death the population on charges of supporting democracy (Xen. *Hell.* 2.4.8–10; D. S. 14.32.5). Here the story forks: Pseudo-Aristotle (41.2) and Diodorus (14.33.5–6) call the Ten another tyranny, and Lysias says they were worse than the Thirty (12.55, 58–60); all three agree that the Ten, instead of bringing an end to the civil war, which had been their primary responsibility, sent immediately to Sparta for aid in case the democrats, still holding out in the Piraeus, should attack the city (Lys. 12.55, 58–60). In Xenophon's version of events, it was the Three Thousand who asked Sparta for help, but Xenophon does not mention any responsibility of the Ten to settle the war. The Spartans arrived in two contingents, under Lysander and Pausanias, and, after some additional skirmishes, the Spartan king Pausanias encouraged a settlement between the city and the Piraeus, the oligarchic and the democratic factions. Thus a reconciliation agreement was negotiated by the Ten, ten democrats, and several (ten or fifteen) Lacedaemonian arbitrators. The agreement had several different features and was negotiated over a period that lasted well into 402. An important part of that agreement was the declaration of amnesty for both oligarchs and democrats, something that had been attempted in 410 after the previous oligarchy of Four Hundred had fallen, but that had failed and left mistrust all around. Yet there were exclusions this time too: excluded from its protections were the Thirty, the Eleven, the Piraeus Ten, and perhaps the Board of Ten archons, though the possibility of undergoing judicial scrutiny against malfeasance was available even to these—or at least to most of them—a procedure by which they could demonstrate innocence individually. Many of the characters of Plato's dialogues were affected by the amnesty, so widespread were its implications for the populace; and understanding it is essential to any account of the political atmosphere in which Socrates was tried and executed.

The overall salutary effect of the reconciliation agreement was to separate the parties during the period when acts of vengeance were most likely, and to move property disputes into the courts. Under its terms, persons could not be prosecuted for crimes committed during the period of the Thirty—except for murder as distinct from execution. The democrats who had fought with Thrasybulus were readmitted to the city in peace; the Thirty, the Eleven, the Piraeus Ten, and any of their supporters who felt unsafe with the democrats among them could choose to govern themselves in Eleusis (where many had already gone) with full political rights there, while retaining control of their property in Athens and all its earnings ([Aristot.] *Ath. Pol.* 39.1–6). But Athens and Eleusis were to be isolated from one another; only during the annual celebration of the mysteries would Athenians be allowed in Eleusis—though the sanctuary itself would remain permanently open to all—and the emigrants could visit Athens only for the performance of the lesser mysteries there. This isolation provision was abandoned in late 402/1 or early 401/0 when the oligarchs began hiring mercenaries, seemingly to retake Athens; the Athenian democracy then annexed Eleusis, killing the remaining oligarchs. Lysias (fr. 7b.38–43) includes an aspect of the amnesty not noted elsewhere:

property confiscated by the Thirty that had become public property was to be restored to the owner, but property confiscated and later sold to individuals could be disputed. In the latter case, the shaky claims of original purchasers, i.e. those who bought property during the rule of the Thirty and thereby profited from unjust confiscations, were distinguished from the more secure claims of those who later purchased the property from the original purchasers. Another distinction made in the latter case was between fixed and movable property.

The Thirty had in its time drawn up a citizen roll of Three Thousand (see App. IV); and it often appears in the sources that, during the period of the amnesty, no fine distinctions were made among those who remained in the city, those actually named on the citizen roll, and those who actively supported the Thirty. As Rhodes (1993: 421) puts it, "In spite of the amnesty of 403, what a man had done in 404–403 was a topic regularly raised in the lawsuits of the next twenty years" and "inevitably cited as his δοκιμασία [scrutiny] if he was appointed to any office under the restored democracy" (1993: 472). Thus Eryximachus s.v. (Lys. fr. 9), who remained in the city, denies what he can: "nobody can prove that I served as a member of the Council, or that I held any public office; nor that I took revenge on any of my enemies . . .; nor that I obtained an arbitration against anybody or put anybody's name on the list of those with Lysander; nor that I was one of the Three Thousand" (Lys. fr. 9.110). Todd (2000: 379n2) notes in Lysias the courtroom jargon for "remained in the city" (ἐν ἄστει μείναντες, 18.19; ἐν ἄστι μείνασι, 25.1; ἔμειναν ἐν τῷ ἄστει, 25.18; ἐν ἄστει μεινάντων, 26.16; and in the new papyrus fr. 9 where the phrase appears as part of the title: "On Behalf of Eryximachus, Who Remained in the City," dated >402); see "those from the city" contrasted with "those from the Piraeus" in Lysias (τούς τε ἐξ ἄστεως καὶ τοὺς ἐκ Πειραιῶς, 12.92; and at length in 13.88–90), meaning oligarchic and democratic sympathizers, respectively.

Loening (1987) is indispensable on the reconciliation agreement (see also Kuehn 1967). Rhodes' (1993: 462–81) commentary on *Athenian Polity* 39–40 is a satisfying treatment of that problematic text in relation to the contemporaneous accounts already mentioned, adding a few remarks from other sources that cannot be fitted into any coherent picture, and a few later references presumably based on contemporaneous sources no longer extant; Rhodes, throughout, finds Cloché (1915) still reliable on matters related to the amnesty, but he cites the new work by Loening as well. MacDowell (1962: App. I) provides a thorough analysis of the parts of the amnesty cited by Andocides IV whose speech (1.71–91) is a chronological account of various agreements. Andocides IV quotes the decrees of Patroclides (1.77–79) and Tisamenus (1.83–84); three additional laws (1.85, 87); and from three oaths respecting the amnesty: the one sworn by all citizens, and the bouleutic and dicastic oaths, i.e. the pledges given by members of Council (*boulē*), and by jury members, not to bear malice.

There is a respectable minority opinion, however, that I have not mentioned. A number of scholars think pseudo-Aristotle—late, and alone among sources— was correct to say that the Board of Ten elected after the fall of the Thirty was replaced by a second Board of Ten shortly afterwards. Walbank (1982: 93–94 n. 47) accepts pseudo-Aristotle's claim (*Ath. Pol.* 38.1; cf. D. S. 14.33.5–6) that there *was* a second, accepting the consequence that Isocrates, Xenophon, and Lysias all write as if unaware that there was a second; his view finds support from Krentz (1982: 97) and Loening (1987: 44–47), though Loening's position is rather more subtle: there was one board, but its membership changed during the period. Lewis (*CAH* 6²: 36n59) and Rhodes (1993: 30), who charges pseudo-Aristotle with political bias, doubt the second Board of Ten existed, favoring "all the contemporary evidence."

Pausanias of Cerameis

[*PA* 11717 *LGPN2* 20 *PP PX*

Παυσανίας ἐκ Κεραμέων]

lover of Agathon

sitting with Prodicus (*Prt.*)

active late 5th c.

Pl. *Prt.* 315d   present

Pl. *Smp.*   speaker

Xen. *Symp.* 8.32 *

Strat. *Mac.*

TGrF I p. 329, no.

255

The dialogues represent the relationship between Pausanias and Agathon s.v. as enduring 433/2 to 416 (the dramatic dates of *Prt.* and *Smp.*; see App. I). On the earlier occasion, both Pausanias and Agathon are represented as reclining with Prodicus s.v.—of the three sophists present, the most consistently admirable in Plato. In 416, it is Pausanias, pleading a hangover from the previous night's celebrations, who proposes that the celebrants of Agathon's victory avoid drunkenness on their second night (Pl. *Smp.*176a). In his speech, he contends that extravagant behavior, intolerable or contemptible in practical matters, is blameless in a lover, and that both the gods and Athenian laws protect lovers (182e–183c), commenting on the constancy of the noble lover (183e). In Xenophon, within a prolix speech by Socrates on the superiority of spiritual to carnal *erōs*, Pausanias is criticized for his defense of his own version of homosexuality, that "the most valiant army, even, would be one recruited of lovers and their favourites!" (*Symp.* 8.32–3; Socrates' speech continues through 8.41). But Xenophon appears to be misremembering a passage in Plato (*Smp.* 178e) where Phaedrus makes the same martial point just before Pausanias' speech begins. (Cf. Ael. *VH* 2.21; Ath. 216e.)

The *Suda* records the title *Pausanias* for the comic poet Strattis (*Mac.* with *PCG* 1), whose victories are >408, but the title's being out of alphabetical order has caused some confusion and several rival explanations, some of which imply other men of this name. *PCG* treats *Pausanias* as identical to the play also known as *The Macedonians*, suggesting that it may be about Pausanias and Agathon once they have joined the court of Archelaus of Macedonia.

Pausanias I of Sparta, son of Cleombrotus (general) See App. II.

Pausanias II of Sparta, son of Lamedon (king) See App. II.

Perdiccas II of Macedonia (king) See App. II.

Perdiccas III of Macedonia, son of Amyntas   [Pl.] *Ltr.* 5 *   addressee
[*RE* 3 *PP* Περδίκκας]   D. S. 15–16, *passim*
r. 365–360   Aes. *orat.* 2
mother: Eurydice
siblings: Alexander, Philip, Eurynoë (wife of
  Ptolemy of Alorus)
King of Macedonia

In Diodorus' account, Perdiccas III ascended the throne by assassinating the regent (who was also his brother-in-law), Ptolemy of Alorus, three years after Ptolemy had assassinated Perdiccas III's older brother, Alexander (15.77.5). Perdiccas III died in battle five years later (16.2.4) at which time his younger brother, Philip, became king. Plato's student, Euphraeus s.v., was one of his advisors.

Periander of Corinth, son of Cypselus (tyrant) See App. II.

Pericles I of Cholarges, son of Xanthippus I   Pl. *Prt.*, *passim* *
[*PA/APF* 11811 *LGPN2* 3 *RE* 1 *OCD*³ *PP PX*   Pl. *Grg.*, *passim* †
Περικλῆς Ξανθίππου Χολαργεύς]   Pl. *Phdr.* 269a–70a
b. ±495, † Aug.–Sep. 429   Pl. *Smp.* 215e, 221c
mother: Agariste II   Pl. *Mx.* 235e
brother: Ariphron II   Pl. *Meno* 94a–b †
wife: [unnamed] kinswoman who later   [Pl.] *Virt.* 377d–e †
  married Hipponicus II   [Pl.] *Thg.* 126a
hetaira: Aspasia of Miletus   [Pl.] *Alc.* 104b, 118 *
offspring with first wife: Xanthippus II,   Xen. *Mem.* 1.2.40–7,
  Paralus; with Aspasia: Pericles II   2.6.13
associate of Damon   Aes. *Alc.* no. 46 (fr.
associate of Pyrilampes   5 Dittmar)
See stemma: Pericles   Aes. *Asp.* nos. 66–7
                                                     (frr. 23, 26, 29, 30,
                                                     25 Dittmar)
                                                   comedy (see below)
                                                   inscriptions (see
                                                     below)
                                                   Philoch. fr. 88
                                                   Thu. 1–2, *passim*

Life.   Pericles I's parents' marriage—Xanthippus I's alliance with Agariste II, Cleisthenes' niece, of the politically powerful Alcmaeonid clan—was important enough for Herodotus (6.131.2) to cover. The family was of the liturgical class, though not notably wealthy, with holdings of productive land and stock in Cholarges; Pericles I's sons, however, rose to *hippeus* status (Pl. *Meno* 94b). Pericles

STEMMA: PERICLES

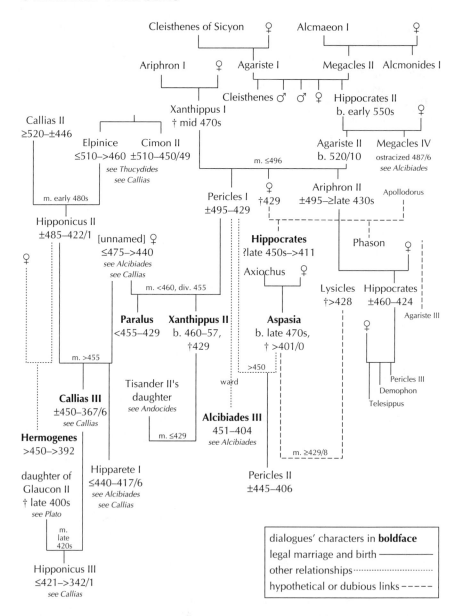

Cleisthenes of Sicyon ♀   Alcmaeon I   ♀

Ariphron I   ♀   Agariste I   Megacles II   Alcmonides I

Cleisthenes ♂ ♂ ♀ Hippocrates II
Xanthippus I   b. early 550s   ♀
† mid 470s

Callias II
≥520–±446

Elpinice   Cimon II   Agariste II   Megacles IV
≤510–>460 ±510–450/49   m. ≤496   b. 520/10   ostracized 487/6
see Thucydides   see Alcibiades
see Callias

Ariphron II   Apollodorus
Pericles I †429   ±495–≥late 430s
m. early 480s   ±495–429

Hipponicus II
±485–422/1   Hippocrates   Phason
[unnamed] ♀   ?late 450s–>411   ♀
♀   ≤475–>440
see Alcibiades   Axiochus   ♀
see Callias
m. <460, div. 455   Lysicles   Hippocrates
                                                            †>428   ±460–424
Paralus   Xanthippus II   Aspasia   Agariste III
<455–429 b. 460–57,   b. late 470s,
†429   † >401/0   ♀

m. >455   >450   Pericles III
Tisander II's   ward   Demophon
Callias III   daughter   Telesippus
±450–367/6   see Andocides
see Callias
Alcibiades III
Hermogenes   451–404
>450–>392   m. ≤429   see Alcibiades

m. ≥429/8
daughter of   Hipparete I   Pericles II
Glaucon II   ≤440–417/6   ±445–406
† late 400s   see Alcibiades
see Plato   see Callias
m.
late
420s

Hipponicus III
≤421–>342/1
see Callias

| dialogues' characters in **boldface** |
| legal marriage and birth ————— |
| other relationships ···················· |
| hypothetical or dubious links ‑ ‑ ‑ ‑ ‑ |

I's attested activity as *chorēgos* for the trilogy including Aeschylus' *Persians* in 472 (*IG* II² 2318.9–11) occurs before his political ascendancy and suggests that he may have produced the play voluntarily, perhaps to win public notice, because he was not nearly thirty, the minimum age for *chorēgos* in the 5th c. He married a close relative (see s.v. [unnamed]) with whom he had two sons. Sometime after the birth of the second, probably ±455, they divorced, and she married Hipponicus II (s.v.). Kahn (1996: 8) is not the first to treat Pericles I as having discarded his first wife for Aspasia, but the ancient evidence is against it—especially because of the gap of some five years between the divorce and the beginning of the relationship with Aspasia ("at least five years"—*APF*). It is not only that Plutarch (*Per.* 24.8) says Pericles I gave his wife to another man with her own consent, but that few scholars have been willing to concede that Pericles I would have advanced the citizenship laws of 451/0 (see App. III) if Aspasia had been on his horizon at that time: she was not Athenian and no issue of theirs, even if they were married, could be counted a citizen of Athens. Pericles I's ex-wife was already married to Hipponicus II by then because her son, Callias III, was born ±450. Pericles I continued in his relationship with Aspasia until his death parted them (Thu. 2.65.6).

Political career in brief.   Pseudo-Aristotle's *Athenian Polity* (26.3.4–28.3.1) is the primary, though not contemporaneous, source for Pericles I's early career. In the late 460s, the chief political rivalry in Athens was between Cimon II and Ephialtes, whose close associate or protégé was Pericles I. When Cimon II was audited and his books did not balance in 463/2, he was tried for taking bribes, and Pericles I was elected to prosecute him, but Cimon II was acquitted. In the following year, Pericles I helped Ephialtes to strip the Areopagus of some of its judicial power, thereby promoting a more democratic system. During the period of rivalry with Cimon II, Pericles I instituted payment for jury duty, a response to Cimon II's broad philanthropy with private funds ([Aristot.] *Ath. Pol.* 27.4; cf. Pl. *Grg.* 515e). In the power vacuum that appeared after Cimon II was exiled and Ephialtes murdered, Pericles I emerged as Athens' most influential democratic leader, and he maintained that position of prominence until his death, being elected general every year, and often commanding troops. For his relatively brief rivalry with Thucydides I, see s.v. Critics of the Athenian democracy use Pericles I's thirty years of dominance in Athenian policy to argue that power could be concentrated in fewer hands under the democracy than under the variety of oligarchical schemes that were attempted after Pericles I's death. Against this, one might note the opposition Pericles I faced in getting his policies implemented, including democratic opposition, in the 430s.

   Among Pericles I's more important policies was his effort to bring other Greek *poleis* into alliance under Athens' leadership; his ambitious architectural and sculptural undertakings on the Athenian acropolis (see Phidias s.v.) were at least in part a demonstration of Athenian preeminence among Greek *poleis*. It was Pericles I's expansionist and imperialist measures undertaken in the 430s that led to the outbreak of the Peloponnesian war, at which point the historian Thucydides takes up Pericles I's story and devotes much of the first book and a half of his history to it. Apart from describing several military operations, Thucydides reports Pericles I's funeral oration (2.34.8–2.46.2), describes the plague that wiped out

Pericles I's family before killing him as well, and the Athenians' ambivalence about his leadership, once they were faced with the hardships of war, leading them first to depose him from his generalship, then to fine him, then to reelect him. Thucydides does not dilate on the fine, but Plato says it was for embezzling funds (*Grg.* 516a)—which we may read, as with Cimon II above, as Pericles I's failure to pass an audit of his books when deposed from the generalship. Thucydides depicts Pericles I as a great and incorruptible man, and attributes Athens' ultimate defeat to her failure to follow his advice (2.65.8),

> he, influential through both reputation and judgment and notable for being most resistant to bribery, exercised free control over the people and was not led by them instead of leading them, because he did not speak to please in order to acquire power by improper means but, since he had this through his prestige, even contradicted them in their anger. Certainly, whenever he perceived that they were arrogantly confident in any way beyond what the situation justified, he shocked them into a state of fear by his speaking, and again, when they were unreasonably afraid, he restored them to confidence. And what was in name a democracy became in actuality rule by the first man.

Plato never mentions Thucydides, but his account of Pericles I as a political leader makes an interesting contrast to the historian's view, for Plato's Socrates tells Callicles (516b),

> A man like that who cared for donkeys or horses or cattle would at least look bad if he showed these animals kicking, butting, and biting him because of their wildness, when they had been doing none of these things when he took them over. Or don't you think that any caretaker of any animal is a bad one who will show his animals to be wilder than when he took them over, when they were gentler?

Yet Plato joins Thucydides in praise of Pericles I's oratorical ability, "Pericles was in all likelihood the greatest rhetorician of all" (*Phdr.* 269e; cf. 269a, *Smp.* 215e).

In comedy and inscriptions.   The favorite topic for Pericles I in comedy of his own time—or at least the favorite of the later authors who preserved fragments from comedies of his time—was the peculiar shape of his head. Cratinus puns on a familiar epithet of Zeus: κεφαληγερέταν "head-gatherer" <430 (*Chi.* fr. 258 [K 240]; see *Thr.* fr. 73 [K 71] for his odd-shaped head and helmet ±430; but also Crat. *Dion.* that he was a warmonger in 430 or 429). After the Sicilian disaster, in 412, Eupolis calls Pericles I up from the underworld in *Demes*—along with Solon, Miltiades IV, and Aristides I—to testify in person to the glories of the past (fr. 110 [K 98], quoted at Aspasia s.v.). Pericles I's head is a joke again (by now a stale one?) a little later in the play (fr. 115 [K 93]). The precedent for finding Pericles I in Aristophanes is ancient, despite the difficulty that Aristophanes' first play was produced some two years after Pericles I's death: a mere handful of direct references in the plays translates into eighty-seven references in the *scholia* (see *Ach.* 530—discussed at Aspasia s.v., *Knights* 283, *Clouds* 213, 859, *Peace* 606, and *Lysistr.* 1138).

A number of further inscriptions attest to Pericles I's status: *IG* II² 3546.6; 3679.3 f.; *IG* I³ 48.43–4; 49.13; 884 (decrees); *Agora* 25.651–2; *AM* 106.155.

In the later tradition.   Xenophon, who mixes and matches generations and dates, does not represent Socrates in conversation with Pericles I; in the *Memorabilia,* he provides a dialogue between Alcibiades III and Pericles I. Socrates says in the *Gorgias* that he heard Pericles I give his recommendations about the city's middle wall (455e), but he does not claim to have known the man. Much that appears in Plutarch's influential biography, *Pericles,* finds its way into what is called the contemporaneous literature on Pericles I because, when Plutarch cites his sources, what he then reports becomes a part of the "fragments" of that source. For example, a reference to the *Aspasia* of the Socratic Aeschines is reported by Plutarch and thus preserved as a fragment of Aeschines (Aes. *Asp.* no. 66 = Plu. *Per.* 24.4–5). Pericles I is hardly mentioned except in passing in Diodorus (11.39, 12.42.8; 12.45.4–12.46.2; 15.88.2). See also Pausanias (1.25.1, 1.28.2), Strabo (9.395), Andocides (3.7–3.9) and Pliny (*HN* 34.74).

Pericles II of Cholarges, son of Pericles I
[*PA/APF* 11812 (11811.4) *LGPN2* 5 *RE* 2 *PX*
Περικλῆς Περικλεοῦς Χολαργεύς]
±445–406
mother: Aspasia of Miletus
paternal half brothers: Xanthippus II, Paralus
general, executed after Arginusae
See stemma: Pericles.

Pl. *Ap.* 32b,
    unnamed †
Pl. *Mx.* 235e, schol.
[Pl.] *Ax.* 368d,
    unnamed †
IG I³ 375.8, 11, 13, 18
Xen. *Hell.* 1.7.16, 21
Xen. *Mem.* 3.5.1–28
D. S. 13.98–99
Eu. *Dem.* 110 (K 98)

Life.   Pericles II, perhaps called "The Olympian" in his own time (D. S. 13.98.3), one of his father's nicknames, is often called "Pericles junior" in today's secondary literature. His service as treasurer (*hellenotamias, IG*) in 410/9, when he had become at least thirty, means he was born before 440, but he is usually figured to have been born earlier, about ten years after Pericles I s.v. divorced his first wife amicably, and within a few years after Pericles I's liaison with Aspasia of Miletus s.v. began >451/0. Thus Pericles II's two paternal half brothers were ten to fifteen years his senior. Pericles I's wards, Alcibiades III and Clinias IV, also growing up in the household, were about five and two years older, respectively, than Pericles II. Plato represents all but Pericles II in *Protagoras* at the home of Callias III s.v., who was the maternal half brother of Pericles I's older sons.

    The Athenians noted two types of *nothos*: the son of a citizen not legally married to the mother; and (after 451/0), the son of a citizen with a non-Athenian woman, regardless of marriage status. Pericles II was of the second type. *Nothoi* were known and acknowledged by their fathers, but they had inferior rights of inheritance under the law. In the early days of the Peloponnesian war when a large part of the population of Attica sought refuge inside the walls of Athens, and especially between the long walls leading to the Piraeus, overcrowding led to an outbreak of plague in which both of Pericles I's sons, Xanthippus II and Paralus, died. In 429, before his own death from the same cause, he requested and received dispensation from his own citizenship laws of 451/0 to naturalize his son with Aspasia. Osborne's comments on this event are instructive for broader issues:

> The ancient sources speak of Perikles junior as a *nothos,* and there is a common disposition in modern works to speak of Perikles senior as seeking the 'legitimation' of his son by Aspasia. But this obscures the point that Perikles junior was a *nothos* by virtue of being a *mētroxenos* [son of a foreign mother] and so was a ξένος [foreigner]. Thus it was not just a case of legitimization but one of naturalization, and the Assembly must have passed a decree declaring Perikles junior an Athenian and granting him permission to seek entry into a deme, tribe, and phratry. (*NIA* 3.27–9)

Pericles II entered his father's deme, Cholarges, of the tribe Akamantis. See Hermogenes s.v. for modern bibliography on *nothoi.*

Career. Xenophon (*Mem.* 3.5.1–28) sets a conversation between Socrates and Pericles II in about 406, when Pericles II had just been elected general (*Hell.* 1.5.16). They discuss how to make both Athens and the Athenians better by emphasizing the superiority of the era of their ancestors. Pericles II praises some Spartan institutions, but concedes Socrates' praise of Athenian ones and professes to see the value of Socrates' suggestion that the mountains around Athens be fortified with lightly armed soldiers, a pet idea of Xenophon's (see *Anab.* 2.5.13).

Pericles II saw action in the battle at Arginusae in the fall of 406. Xenophon's and Diodorus' accounts are incompatible in detail, with Diodorus lionizing the "Olympian": when the Spartan general, Callicratidas, rammed Pericles II's ship, Pericles II bound the two ships together so his own men could board the Spartan ship and slay its crew, including Callicratidas (13.99.4–5). In Xenophon's account, the Spartan general fell overboard and drowned when his own ship was rammed (*Hell.* 1.6.33). Xenophon (*Hell.* 1.7) and Diodorus (13.101–103) give reasonably complementary accounts of parts of the aftermath of that battle. It ended with Pericles II's execution in Athens (see Exc. 2), which Socrates attempted, but was unable, to prevent. For late elaborations, see Plutarch (*Per.* 24.1–2, 25.1, 37.2, 37.5).

Pericles III of Cholarges, son of Hippocrates See App. II. *See stemma: Pericles.*

Perictione of Athens, daughter of Glaucon III [*PA/APF* 11813 (8792.9) *LGPN2* 1 *DPhA* 95 *RE* 1 Περικτιόνη Γλαύκωνος θυγάτηρ] ≥450–>365
mother: daughter of Antiphon I, sister of
  Pyrilampes
husbands: Ariston, then Pyrilampes
offspring with Ariston: Plato, Adeimantus I,
  Glaucon IV, Potone; with Pyrilampes:
  Antiphon II and stepson Demos
See stemma: Plato.

[Pl.] *Ltr.* 13.361e,
  unnamed *
D. L. 3.1
Procl. 1.82

Life. Perictione married Ariston ≤429, probably ±432 (for Hellenistic embellishments of their love affair, see Ariston s.v.). By Athens' rules regarding degrees of kinship, she, like her brother Charmides s.v., would otherwise have been made ward (or wife) of Critias IV when her father died. She was probably born ≥450. The traditional version of Plato's life span is almost ubiquitously taken as an anchor for this branch of his family, yielding, for Perictione, a narrow and rather implausible cluster of births: Adeimantus I and Potone born between 432–430, Glaucon IV in 429/8, Plato in 428/7, and—with a new husband—Antiphon II ≤425; *APF* extends the period by two years, setting 435 as the earliest year in which she might have given birth. If her firstborn was an 'Aristocles' who did not survive childhood, then her productivity was all the more remarkable—or dubious. I suspect, rather, and I shall pursue this below, that her life was supplied with the default dates that suited the biographical tradition of Plato s.v., and are in need of revision.

Under Athenian law, in which women were perpetual minors, a husband had the power to bequeath his wife, along with her dowry, to another husband or guardian, in the event of his death. In the absence of a will, however, a widow who had sons could choose between remaining in her deceased husband's house or returning to that of her father. If she remained, she was under her sons' tutelage, if they were of age, and under the tutelage of *their* guardian if not; her dowry either went with her back to her father (or his heirs), or went to her sons (or their guardian) to provide for her maintenance. A childless widow—or one with only daughters, perhaps—passed along with her dowry to her original guardian or his heir, unless her husband had bequeathed her to someone else; under special circumstances, such as pregnancy, the eponymous archon became the widow's official guardian. A guardian could arrange for a widow to remarry, marry her himself if he was eligible, or keep her as a part of his household, though the archon was obliged to provide protection (Harrison 1998: 1.1.38; MacDowell 1978: 88–9).

At the time of Perictione's being widowed the first time, she would have been twenty-seven or so and the mother of at least four children. Her mother's brother, Pyrilampes, who then married her, may be assumed to have been a widower since he was available to marry; he was in his mid-fifties and had recently been wounded in the battle of Delium; his son from his first marriage, Demos, would have been about seventeen at the time. (One may think of Euripides' *Hippolytus* of 429/8, exploiting the social upheaval caused by the increasing need to place young war widows and plague survivors in established households.) When she was widowed a second time <413, her eldest son, Adeimantus I, appears to have become her legal guardian; he would have reached the age of majority by 414.

Phaeax I of Acharnae, son of Erasistratus I
[*PA*/*APF* 13921 *LGPN2* 1 *RE* 4 *OCD*³
Φαίαξ Ἐρασιστράτου Ἀχαρνεύς]
b. ±455
father of Erasistratus II, Leodamas I
nephew: Erasistratus III
politician

[Pl.] *Eryx.* 392a
Thu. 5.4–5
Aristoph. *Knights*
  1377–1381 & schol.
Eu. *Dem.* fr. *116
  (K 95)
Antiph. 20

See stemma: Phaeax.   *Agora* 25.653–6
                                             AM 106.155
                                             [Andoc.] 4.41–42

Life.   Phaeax I, the uncle of the character Eryxias in Plato's dialogue of the same name, was probably of the Salaminian clan since his name refers to its hero. In 425, he was acquitted of a homicide charge that Aristophanes puts into the *Knights* of 424. The passage may imitate Phaeax I's rhetorical style while commenting explicitly on it. He talks too much and says too little, as Eupolis states more economically in 412. Thucydides records Phaeax I's heading an embassy to Sicily and Italy in 422, which argues against putting his birth much after 455.

STEMMA: PHAEAX

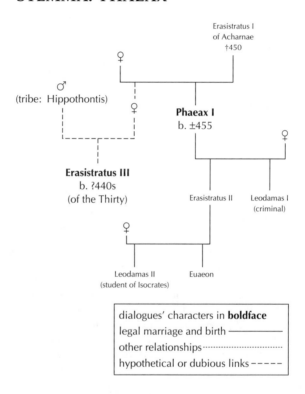

dialogues' characters in **boldface**
legal marriage and birth ─────────
other relationships ·······························
hypothetical or dubious links ─ ─ ─ ─ ─

In the later tradition.   Pseudo-Andocides 4, an attack on Alcibiades III, is not by Andocides and not by the Socratic Aeschines (who wrote from the 360s) though it has been attributed to both and remains anonymous. It is written as if its speaker is Phaeax I, and as if it is intended to promote the ostracism of Alcibiades III, but the speech appears to be a logographic exercise written some time later and should not be trusted for information about Phaeax I.

Prosopographical notes.   Pottery *ostraka* (one from *Kera.* 3.78.149 and four from *Agora*) would establish his father's name and his deme, but if their date of 447–445 (*PAA* 400135) holds up, then everything else about this family will need to be recalculated by a generation. *LGPN2* mentions the unpublished Paros *stele* (David M. Lewis) at its entry for Phaeax I, but nothing about it.

Phaedo of Elis
[*LGPN3A* 1 *FRA* 1645 *RE* 3 *OCD*³ *DPhA* 118
PP PX Φαίδων]
b. ±419/8
student of Socrates
teacher of Menedemus the Eretreian
founded school of philosophy at Elis

Pl. *Phd.*   speaker
frr. in *SSR* 1.IIIA &
   Rossetti (1973,
   1980)

Life.   Phaedo of Elis, a town in the northwest Peloponnese, is young enough in 399 that Socrates could, as was his habit, stroke Phaedo's hair, apparently worn long in the Spartan style, during the conversation marked by the dialogue *Phaedo* (89a–b). His presence in Athens in 399, despite recent hostilities between Athens and Elis, is explained by Diogenes, citing Hieronymus Cardianus (4th–3rd c. B.C.E.) and unnamed others: Phaedo was a youth of aristocratic parentage who was brought from Elis as a prisoner of war and sold into slavery as a catamite but redeemed, perhaps at Socrates' request of Crito (D.L. 2.31). Although the story is later elaborated to more than one moral effect (by church fathers, *inter alia*; see testimonia in *SSR*), McQueen and Rowe (1989) put firmly to rest the claim that there was no recorded capture of Elis that could have accounted for such an enslavement (*pace* Kahn 1996: 9n17), pointing out that both Xenophon (*Hell.* 3.2.21–31) and Diodorus (14.17.4–12, 34) write of a Spartan-Elean war in which Athens became involved. McQueen and Rowe date the war 402–1 and Athens' involvement 401; they argue plausibly that, if Phaedo was captured while performing outpost duties, when he was in, say, his eighteenth year, in 401, he would have had two years with Socrates and been in his twentieth year at the time of the dialogue.

In the later tradition.   Diogenes notes that Phaedo founded a school of philosophy in his native city of Elis, and gives names for some of those who succeeded Phaedo at its head (2.105); one notable early head of the next generation was the philosopher Menedemus (D. L. 2.125–144). Diogenes cites eight titles for Phaedo (2.105); though none is extant, there is some further evidence for a *Simon* and for a *Zopyrus* (see s.vv.). Diogenes (2.64) also repeats the 2nd c. B.C.E. stoic Panaetius' doubts that the dialogues attributed to Phaedo were genuine. The Roman emperor Julian (r. 361–363 C.E.), known as 'the Apostate,' believed that an original dialogue by Phaedo had survived into his own time (Phae. no. 2), but we have no way of knowing whether what the emperor read was in fact Phaedo's. (Cf. Gell. *NA* 2.18.1–5; Plu. *Mor.* 776a; Poll. 3.18; Cic., *De fato* 5.10, *De nat.* 1.33.93, and *Tus. Dis.* 4.37.80–81; Synes. *Dion* 14; [Socr.] *Ep.* 12, 13; there is more from the Christian tradition assembled in *SSR*.)

Phaedondas of Thebes	Pl. *Phd.* 59c	present
[*LGPNB2* 1 *PP* Φαιδώνδας]	Xen. *Mem.* 1.2.48	

According to Xenophon, Phaedondas was a member of the Socratic circle, which his presence at Socrates' execution appears to confirm.

Phaedrus of Myrrhinus, son of Pythocles	Pl. *Prt.* 315c	present
[*PA/APF* 13960 (5951), 13950, 13951	Pl. *Smp.*	speaker
LGPN2 19, 1 *RE* 7 *OCD*³ *PP*	Pl. *Phdr.*	speaker
Φαῖδρος Πυθοκλέους Μυρρινούσιος]	[Pl.] *Epgr.* 4	
≤444–393	Lys. 19.15	
wife: his first cousin	Lys. 32.14	
See stemma: Phaedrus.	Andoc. 1.15	
	IG I³ 422.229;	
	426.102	

Family and life. Enough is known of the family of Phaedrus to produce an approximate birth year for him, but the details are rather complex and best understood with reference to the stemma for the family. The son of Euripides of Melite was the general Xenophon of Melite (see App. II), who had a daughter who married the father of a client of Lysias (i.e., the speaker of Lys. 19) in the 420s without a dowry. That speech provides the rudiments for reconstructing the family tree. By 404, the speaker's sister had married her first cousin, the Phaedrus of Plato's dialogues (Lys. 19.15), with a dowry of 4,000 *drachmae,* implying an approximate date of birth for Phaedrus that puts him in his mid-twenties at the time of the *Phaedrus.* (Upon Phaedrus' early death in 393, his widow married Aristophanes, son of Nicophemus.) Davies (*APF*) laments that the name of the speaker, Xenophon's son-in-law, is unknown, speculating that he, like Phaedrus, may have been a member of the Socratic circle, though they are a generation apart; there is another connection to the Socratic circle—or at least to Plato—unnoticed in *APF*: the speaker's friend (19.25–26), who asks the speaker to intercede with Aristophanes, is Plato's stepbrother Demos, s.v. The speaker's father-in-law seems to have been extremely wealthy, and to have had something discreditable to hide (Lys. 19.60). Since he is Phaedrus' uncle (19.15), Phaedrus' father or mother was his sibling; since a brother would probably also have been an extremely rich man, and Phaedrus' father left no record of wealth, it is more likely that Phaedrus' mother was the sister of his father-in-law.

In Plato, Phaedrus is linked closely to Eryximachus s.v., who stands with him in the group around Hippias at Callias III's house in ±433/2, when Phaedrus would have been in early adolescence and Eryximachus in his mid- to late teens (*Prt.* 315c), and again at Agathon's house in 416 (*Smp.*; cf. *Phdr.* 268a, where Eryximachus is mentioned as Phaedrus' friend).

The sacrilege of 415. Phaedrus was accused by the *metic* Teucrus of sacrilege in profaning the Eleusinian mysteries (Andoc. 1.15) and fled into exile, whereupon his possessions were confiscated and sold. That he was accused is especially

STEMMA: PHAEDRUS

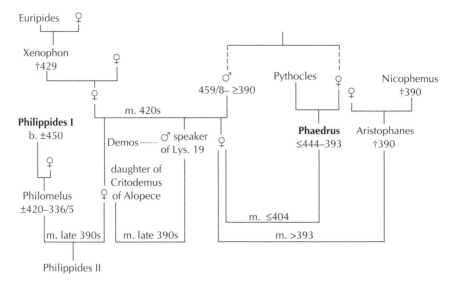

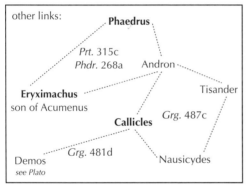

dialogues' characters in **boldface**
legal marriage and birth ————
other relationships ··························
hypothetical or dubious links -----

well attested for there are three independent sources. Not only is he named by Andocides IV, he is listed with some of his possessions among the condemned on the *stelae* recovered from the Eleusinium (see Exc. 1), and also named as the owner of the house into which Diogiton moved from Collytus with his brother's three orphans while Phaedrus was in exile after 415 (Lys. 32)—the fate of Andocides IV's house as well.

But Phaedrus was not accused of mutilating herms; on that count, he has been the subject of repeated or compounded errors in the literature that can be easily explained: Andocides IV, for reasons related to the charges against him, separates his accounts of the mysteries (1.11–29) and the herms (1.34–70). When Dover (*HCT* 4.273) justifies this order of exposition, he inadvertently reverses it, though he then presents the evidence in correct order. But *APF* misreads Andocides IV, saying Phaedrus was "guilty both of profanation and of mutilation" (5951C) which is false. Philosophers might never have noticed except that Nussbaum (1986: 212–3 and nn. 24–5a) wrote an unforgettable and moving portrait of Phaedrus based on the mistaken assumption that he was a mutilator of herms (and also that no dramatic date for the dialogue *Phaedrus* is possible), so it is important to set the record straight. In the section of his speech exclusively devoted to the profanation of the mysteries, Andocides IV says the *metic* Teucrus offered, in exchange for immunity, both to name his coparticipants in the profanation and to tell what he knew about the herms affair; having said only this, Andocides IV asks the bailiff to read a list of names, which includes Phaedrus, adding that everyone listed fled the city (Andoc. 1.15). If that were all, it might indeed seem—despite the formal structure of the speech—that the listed men were guilty of both crimes; but that is not all. When Andocides IV takes up Teucrus' accusations again, having formally ended his account of the profanation (1.29), it is to name the eighteen individuals responsible for mutilating herms (1.34), a list that does not include Phaedrus. Some of the eighteen fled, and others were seized and executed.

In the later tradition.   Fragments of Alexis' comedy, *Phaedrus* (frr. 247–8 = [K 245–6]), about a man philosophizing on the nature of *erōs*, cannot have spoofed the living Phaedrus of the dialogues since he was dead by 393 (while victories of Alex. are recorded 350s–30s). If the play refers to a contemporary of that name, he could be a descendant or collateral member of the family, otherwise unknown (see [Pl.] Epig. 4 mentioning both an Alexis and a Phaedrus). But it is also possible that Plato's dialogue was attracting interest at the time; Demosthenes' *Erotic Essay*, written >355, is addressed to Epicrates s.v., at whose house, according to Plato's dialogue, Phaedrus heard Lysias' speech. Diogenes (3.29, 3.31) identifies Phaedrus as Plato's favorite. Cf. pseudo-Socrates (*Ep.* 27), et al. in *SSR* 2.VIB.

Prosopographical notes and modern bibliography.   LGPN2 1 (Lys. 19 only) ?= LGPN2 19 (all other citations), but this should no longer be treated as controversial; the two are one. Cf. Parmentier (1926: 17), Hatzfeld (1939: 13–8), and MacDowell (1962: 74).

Phaenarete of Athens, wife of Sophroniscus I of Alopece
[*PA* 13971 *LGPN2* 1 *RE* 2 *PP*
Φαιναρέτη Σωφρονίσκου Ἀλωπεκῆθεν γυνή]
±484–>407
husbands: Sophroniscus I, then Chaeredemus
offspring with Sophroniscus I: Socrates; with
   Chaeredemus: Patrocles
midwife
See stemma: Socrates.

Pl. *Tht.* 149a
Pl. *Euthd.* 297e,
   unnamed *
[Pl.] *Alc.* 131e
D. L. 2.18

Life.   Phaenarete's inexact date of birth is calculated by adding fifteen years to Socrates' date of birth, and keeping in mind that she gave birth again about twenty years later. The order of Phaenarete's marriages was almost certainly Sophroniscus I, then Chaeredemus, making Patrocles Socrates' younger brother (*Euthd.* 297e). Although we do not know how old Socrates was at his father's death, Lysimachus—friend and fellow demesman of Sophroniscus I—expresses mild surprise that Socrates should still be using the patronymic of his deceased father (*Lch.* 181a), as if that death were far in the past. In 424, the dramatic date of the *Laches* (see App. I), Socrates would have been about forty-five in the year before the premier of two prizewinning plays featuring him—Aristophanes' *Clouds*, and Amipsias' *Connus*. The career of Patrocles s.v. is altogether later, evidence of a rather wide gap between the two sons of Phaenarete. That gap makes it unlikely that Sophroniscus I left a will, bequeathing Phaenarete to someone else immediately upon his death. As a widow with a son, she was in a position unique within the Athenian legal code, allowed to *choose* whether to return to her father's household (or that of his heirs), or to remain in Sophroniscus I's house under the tutelage of Socrates, if he was of age, or of *his* guardian, if Socrates was still a minor when his father died. Whatever she chose, her dowry went with her to provide for her maintenance. If she returned to her father, he was free to give her in marriage again, but the distance between the births of her sons argues against that possibility as well. If Socrates was not yet of age, Phaenarete would have been under the tutelage of Sophroniscus I's nearest male relative, under Athens' well defined rules about degrees of kinship, who would have had the power to give her in marriage, to marry her himself if eligible (i.e., if he was unmarried, or if he was married but childless and preferred to divorce his existing wife). These considerations point to the likelihood that Socrates had already come of age when his father died. (Cf. Harrison 1998: 1.38; MacDowell 1978: 88–9.)

If Phaenarete was in fact a midwife, that career was not undertaken until she had passed childbearing age herself, perhaps in the 430s. Plato's Socrates demonstrates some familiarity with the range of the midwife's knowledge, including the use of drugs (*pharmakeia*) and incantations for easing and causing pain, inducing birth, aborting the fetus, and cutting the umbilical cord (*Tht.* 149a–150b; cf. *Laws* 5.740d–e). It should be noted that, in a society where infanticide was permissible for five days after birth, prohibitions on abortion would have made little sense (see Riddle 1992: 7 on abortions and the Hippocratics, 10–11 on infanticide, 18 on *Laws* and *Tht.*). Until an infant was publicly acknowledged by its father in the *amphidromia* ritual that admitted the infant to the household (*oikos*), it had no status under law (Garland 1990: 93–4). Because Phaenarete seems still to have been alive at the dramatic date of the *Euthydemus*, I have set her date of death later than that, though such imprecision cannot bear much weight.

Phanosthenes of Andros and Athens
[*PA* 14083 *LGPN1* 1 ?= 2 *RE* 1 *FRA* 538
RE s.v. *PP* Φανοσθένης]
b. ?450s
naturalized citizen and general

Pl. *Ion* 541c *
Xen. *Hell.* 1.5.18–19
Andoc. 1.149
IG I³ 182.1, 14, 18–9
Ath. 506a

Life and military career.   Phanosthenes is likely to have emigrated to Athens ≤411, when Andros revolted during the Peloponnesian war, but the early date attached to his grant of citizenship is evidence that he may well have served the *polis* already in other capacities for some time before emigrating. Such service would, by the way, be consistent with Socrates' words at *Ion* 541c–d (see App. I). Phanosthenes was a military commander (*praetor*) in 408/7, an office that did not require Athenian citizenship, and was a general replacing Conon at Andros in 406 (Xen. with *CAH* 5² 490). Citing Plato's *Ion*, Osborne (*NIA* 3.12, 31–3 with Andrewes 1953: 1–2) puts the naturalization ≥410, pointing out that the democrats of Athens had difficulty identifying good candidates for general because of the estrangement of the *polis* from the fleet leaders based on Samos in the years after the fall of the Four Hundred and the Five Thousand. This is certainly plausible though the earlier period after the loss of the fleet in Sicily, and the later period after the *polis* executed almost all its remaining generals (see Exc. 2), were equally difficult times.

The citizenship decree, *IG* I³ 182, praises Phanosthenes for a variety of benefactions: he had already served Athens on campaign and had already provided oars for the fleet. Osborne (*NIA* 3.33 & nn) adds, "The date of the preserved decree has been disputed, but it seems best set in the years 410–407. It clearly honours Phanosthenes as a foreigner, so that it is the *terminus post quem* for his naturalization. The *terminus ante quem*, of course, is his generalship of 407/6." Although I think Phanosthenes may have been granted citizenship before 410, it is worth noting that he could be a general without being a citizen (see Dover *HCT* 4. 391–2). See Moore 1974: 434–6) for a range of reservations and possibilities.

Andocides is negative about the many Andrians granted citizenship ±403 and may have had Phanosthenes in mind among others (see Osborne *NIA* 3.33).

Prosopographical notes. LGPN3A: the naturalized Athenian is 1 ?= 2 (all other citations).

Phason of Athens, son of Apollodorus   Pl. *Prt.* 310b *
[*PA* 14122 *LGPN2* 2 *PP*
Φάσων Ἀπολλοδώρου]
?mother: sister of Pericles I
brother: Hippocrates

See Hippocrates s.v. for the identification of this Phason with the great and well-to-do family of Pericles I.

Pherecles of Themacus (Athens), son of Pherenicaeus See App. II.

Pherecrates of Athens (comic poet) See App. II.

Phidias of Athens, son of Charmides   Pl. *Prt.* 311c *
[*PA* 14149 *LGPN2* 1 *RE* 2 *OCD*³ *PP*   Pl. *Meno* 91d †
Φειδίας Χαρμίδου]   [Pl.] *G. Hp.* 290a–d *
b. ±490, active 465–425   Philoch. fr. 121
brother: Panaenus   Plu. *Per.*
sculptor

Life. 'Phidias' in Plato, and perhaps to Plato's generation, was synonymous with the master sculptor. He belonged to the inner circle of Pericles I, who supported Phidias' building project on the Athenian acropolis from 447 until 438. Phidias was charged by enemies of Pericles I with impiety and embezzling in 438. One cannot but suspect contamination among the three stories that have come down to us, in *each* of which Pericles I's enemies brought false accusations against someone dear to him (Anaxagoras, Aspasia s.vv., and now Phidias), and the democratic leader himself undertook the defense. Of the three, the best case can be made for Phidias' having actually been prosecuted. In his case, in Plutarch's version, Pericles I had foreseen the possibility that Phidias would be victimized and warned the sculptor long in advance to fashion wrought gold so that it could be detached and weighed. The actual weighing at the trial proved Phidias innocent of embezzling. However, apparently related to the impiety charge, someone argued that Phidias had used himself and Pericles I as models for two of the figures on the shield of Athena depicting the battle against the Amazons. Philochorus gives the likely version of what happened next: Phidias left Athens for Olympia where he completed the colossal Zeus that counted as one of the seven wonders of the ancient world. Indeed Phidias' workshop has been uncovered in Olympia and dated to the 430s; the find includes his cup (Cf. Simon s.v.), tools, and huge terra-cotta molds. Philochorus goes on to say that Phidias was killed by the Eleans; Plutarch, that he died of illness, or perhaps poisoning, in prison.

Works.   We cannot be certain of the extent of Phidias' involvement in the acropolis enterprise but, since he was absent after 438, and it was virtually complete by 432, he cannot have done everything himself. He is usually given credit for oversight of the project, the master sculptor working with other excellent sculptors and painters. That he probably directed the exterior sculpture of the Parthenon is argued from the fact that the themes treated there are repeated on his two statues of Athena. Pseudo-Plato's description (*G. Hp.*) is of the Athena commissioned for the cella of the Parthenon, the one at issue in Phidias' trial. It was made of ivory and over a ton of gold mounted on a wooden core, and finished with precious stones, other metals, enamel, and paint; and the goddess's shield depicted the battle against the Amazons. Standing outside the Parthenon and facing the Propylaea was Phidias' bronze Athena, 39 feet high, reputedly visible all the way to Sunium. See Stewart (1990: 257–63) for information about other works and techniques of Phidias.

Prosopographical notes.   There is no known connection between Phidias' father's name and the family of Plato's mother.

Phidostratus of Athens   [Pl.] *G. Hp.* 286b *
[*PP* Φειδόστρατος]
grammar school teacher

See Miccus s.v.; *PP* treats the two together.

Philaedes   [Pl.] *Ltr.* 13.363b *
[Φιλαίδης]

Philaedes was an ambassador to the king of Persia: he lauded both Dionysius II and [Plato]. The name is attested nowhere else in Sicily or Athens in ancient times (*LGPN2, 3A*). 'Philaides' at PCW 1676 is a misprint.

Philagrus   [Pl.] *Ltr.* 13.363b *
[Φίλαγρος]

Philagrus was an ambassador who praised Dionysius II and [Plato] ≥365. The name is attested in both Sicily and Athens in the 4th c. (*LGPN2, 3A*).

Philebus of ?Athens   Pl. *Phlb.*   speaker
[*LGPN2* 1 Φιλήβος]

The name is not known in Greece in ancient times except for a fictional instance in the 4th c. C.E. in the epistolographer Alciphro (3.50). Philebus receives a number from *LGPN2* strictly on the basis of his appearance in Plato's dialogue.

Philemon of ?Thebes, son of Philemonides   [Pl.] *Thg.* 129b
[*PA* 14271 *LGPN2* 1 *PP*
Φιλήμων Φιλημονίδου]

According to the dialogue, Philemon plotted the assassination of Nicias, son of Heroscamander, with Timarchus. He is not heard of outside the dialogue, which Dušanić (1990b: 65–70) attributes to his being from Thebes.

Philemonides of Athens See App. II.

Philesia, wife of Xanophon of Erchia See App. II.

Philippides I of Paeania, son of Philomelus I   Pl. *Prt.* 315a   present
[*PA/APF* 14360 (14670) *LGPN2* 14 *RE* 6 *PP*   Isocr. 15.93
Φιλιππίδης Φιλομήλου Παιανιεύς]   Lys. 19
b. ±450   *IG* II² 1740.43
father of Philomelus II
See stemma: Phaedrus.

Life.   Philippides I appears flanking Protagoras himself in Plato's dialogue. His family was wealthy (Lys.), probably from silver mining (*APF*), wealthy enough that Philippides I's son, Philomelus II, could pay Isocrates' high fees. Philippides I was a councilor, but at an unknown date (*IG*).

Prosopographical notes.   ?= *LGPN2* 15: *Agora* 15.12.54.

Philippus   Xen. *Symp., passim*
[*LGPN2* 13 *PX* Φίλιππος]
clown

Philippus was a comic (γελωτοποιός) by profession, uninvited, so he said (1.13), to Callias III's house to provide entertainment. Apart from puns and other short witticisms, his repertoire included pretending to weep until that brought a laugh (1.15–16), and mimicking the moves of dancers who had earlier jumped over swords and through hoops (2.21–22). When it was his turn to tell what about his profession made him proud, he remarks on the superiority of the comic to the tragic actor: one makes the audience laugh, the other makes it weep (3.11). Athenaeus (20a–b) lists Philippus among the three most famous clowns of antiquity.

Philippus I of Athens See App. II.

Philippus of Chollidae See App. II.

Philippus of Mende = Philip of Opus (astronomer) See App. II.

Philistion of Locri Epizephyrii	[Pl.] *Ltr.* 2.314d *
[*LGPN3A* 17 *RE* 4 *OCD*³ *PP* Φιλιστίων]	frr. in Wellman 1901
teacher of ?Eudoxus	Epi. frr. 9–10 (K
physician	10–11)
	D. L. 8.86

Philistion was a noted ancient physician, apparently at the court of Dionysius II, whose views appear to have been influenced by those of Empedocles, and who influenced Galen. If he ever visited Athens at Plato's request, he may have been the Sicilian physician at Plato's Academy in Epicrates' comedy (fr. 10, lnn. 27–29). His theory of pathology may be evident at *Timaeus* 81e–86a (Taylor 1928: 599). In *Letter* 2, [Plato] requests that Dionysius II allow Philistion to go to Athens where Speusippus s.v. is said to need him.

Philistus (Plu.) or **Philistides** ([Pl.]) of	[Pl.] *Ltr.* 3.315e *
Syracuse, son of Archomenidas	frr. in *FGrH* 556
[*LGPN3A* 28 *RE* 3 *OCD*³ Φίλιστος]	*SEG* 26.1123.3B
±430–356	Plu. *Dion* 11.6, 13,
wife: daughter of Leptines I	19
See stemma: Dion.	D. S. 13.91.4,
	13.102.3; 15.6–7

Life. Philistus was instrumental in establishing the tyranny of Dionysius I in 406/5; he was already wealthy and independent enough at the time to offer to pay Dionysius I's fines (D. S. 13.91.4), so he cannot have been born much later than the traditional date that I give above. He commanded the tyrant's citadel, Ortygia, until exiled in ±386 for reasons variously reported. According to Plutarch (preferred by Lewis *CAH* 6² 152), Leptines I offered his daughter to Philistus without first consulting Dionysius I, causing the tyrant to fear an alliance against

him (see Philist. fr. 60) and to retaliate by banishing both. A difficulty with that
account, however, is that the only daughters Leptines I had in 386 were two by
a married woman that Plutarch says he debauched (11.6), and who was imprisoned
by the tyrant. Leptines I's wife (Dionysius I's daughter), Dicaeosyne, would have
been *at most* eleven years old in 386; and any daughters by her would have been
hypothetical. Since Philistus writes about the sufferings of Leptines I's daughters,
it may well be that he married one of the illegitimate ones, but the reason for his
exile might better be found elsewhere. In one early account (Aen. Tact. 10.21–22
in 350 B.C.E.), Philistus' absence from Syracuse is deviously arranged, but it is not
an exile. Diodorus (15.6–7) says simply that the tyrant killed and banished a
number of people in a mad rage.

Whatever the real circumstances of the banishment, Philistus did not return
to Syracuse during the lifetime of Dionysius I. He was later recalled by Dionysius
II—perhaps, as *Letter* 13 implies and Plutarch states, to act as a counterweight
during Plato's second visit to Sicily. He successfully opposed Plato's and Dion's
attempts to reform the tyranny and died in a sea battle over Ortygia when Dion
retook it in 356 (committing suicide out of fear of torture when it appeared he
would be captured, according to D. S. 16.16.3–4).

Works.   'Philistides' is pseudo-Plato's incorrect name for this known and well
regarded historian, an imitator of Thucydides, and an eyewitness source for events
in the time of Dionysius I and Dionysius II. He is thought to be a source behind
the better known historians Timaeus and Ephorus. Philistus wrote thirteen scrolls
in two parts on the history of Sicily from its mythical beginnings to 363/2. His
account is so favorable toward both Dionysius I and II that later writers comment
on his love for tyrants.

Philolaus of Croton (philosopher) See App. II.

Philomelus of Paeania, son of Philippides I See App. II. *See stemma: Phaedrus.*

Philonides of Tarentum   [Pl.] *Ltr.* 9.357d *
[*LGPN3A* 58, 59 Φιλωνίδης]   Iamb. *VP* 267 = DK
associate of Archytas, Archippus   58A
Pythagorean philosopher

Prosopographical notes.   Philonides is not distinct from other associates of Archytas
in the Pythagorean community of Tarentum. Iamblichus covers the whole Pythagorean school, and other DK testimonia and fragments are likewise not specific
to Philonides. *LGPN3A* assigns no. 58 to the known 4th c. Pythagorean philosopher
(DK) and no. 59 to the subject of *Letter* 9, dating him in the latter *half* of the 4th
c.—but there is really no question that the two are the same. Homonyms include
the Athenian comic poet of the late 5th c. and the later Epicurean philosopher.

Philostratus of Aexone, son of Philon I
[*PA*/*APF* 14723 (8065B) *LGPN2* 29 *RE* 4
Φιλόστρατος Φίλωνος Αἰξωνεύς]
mother: Phanagora
brother: Callippus II

Pl. *Ltr.* 7.333e,
   334a–c
IG II² 5433.10–12
   (gravestone)
Nep. *Dion* 9.1–2
Plu. *Dion* 54–6

Accompanied his brother to Sicily, and betrayed Dion s.v. to Dionysius II s.v.

Phocylides of Miletus (poet) See App. II.

Phoenix, son of Philippus
[*PP* Φοῖνιξ Φιλίππου]

Pl. *Smp.* 172b *

Prosopographical notes.   The name is unusual but not unknown; two instances
from the 4th c. are possible (see *LGPN2*), but both lack patronymic and demotic.

Phrychs, slave of Alcibiades III See App. II.

Phrynichus of Athens, son of Polyphrasmon (tragedian) See App. II.

Phrynichus of Athens, son of Eunomides (comic poet) See App. II.

Phrynichus of Diradiotae See App. II.

Phrynion of Phlius See App. II.

Phrynondas (villain) See App. II.

Pindar of Cynoscephalae (poet) See App. II.

Pisander of Acharnae, son of Glaucetes
[*PA* 11770 *LGPN2* 3 *OCD*³
Πείσανδρος Γλαυκέτους Ἀχαρνεύς]
460s–≥411
Athenian oligarchic leader

Xen. *Symp.* 2.14
IG I³ 174.4–5;
   472.3–4
Thu. 8, *passim*
Andoc. 1.27, 1.36
Aes. *orat.* 2.176
   schol.

Lys. 7.4, 12.66
comedy (see below)
Aristot. *Rh.* 1419a27
[Aristot.] *Ath. Pol.*
32.2

Career.   Pisander appears to have been with the Athenians who marched on Chalcidice in 429 (Thu. 2.79) because he was soon afterwards lampooned on the comic stage as spineless (Eu. *Ast.* fr. 35 [K 31]). In the fall of 422, he was a part of the expedition to Thrace, soon after which Aristophanes assigned a chorus the line, "if you feel any loathing for Pisander's crests and brows" (*Peace* 395), implying that he was, besides being a coward, one of the advocates of war (see Eu. *Mar.* i with Aristoph. *Birds* 1556 schol. and *Bab.* fr. 84 [K 81]). It is at about this time that Xenophon set the dramatic date of the *Symposium*, in which Pisander is mentioned as a coward and a demagogue; and shortly afterward, 420–419 that Hermippus called Pisander a pack-ass (*Art.* fr. 7 [K9]). In or before 421, his wealth is attested by an appearance on the register (*IG* 472); and sometime between 425 and 410 that he appeared in an honorary decree (*IG* 174).

Under the democracy in 415, Pisander served on the commission to investigate the profanation of the Eleusinian mysteries and, with Charicles s.v., offered a reward for evidence (Andoc.). In the next year, in Aristophanes' *Birds*, he was linked to Socrates in a choral ode (quoted in full at Chaerephon s.v.) where he is depicted as visiting Socrates in an attempt to recover his courage by persuading Socrates to conjure up "the spirit that deserted him in life" (1556–1558). In the same year, Phrynichus called him a big ape (*Mon.* fr. 21 [K 20]), and at about this time the comic poet, Plato, produced a play called *Pisander*.

Pisander continued his opposition to the Athenian democracy in 412/1, seeking help from the Persian king and the recall of Alcibiades III to lead the Athenian military forces (Thu. 8.49.1, 8.53.1–3). Among his actions in that effort were a false accusation of Phrynichus, resulting in the democracy's replacement of that general with Leon s.v.; and a return to Athens to solicit aid from the oligarchic clubs (*synōmosiai*) in the overthrow of the democracy (8.54.3–4). It is at this point in Pisander's career that Aristophanes characterizes Pisander as motivated by greed to hold office (*Lysistr.* 490–1). Henderson (2000: 256) uses facts about Pisander's activities then apparently not yet known in Athens to establish that the *Lysistrata* was produced at the Lenaean festival in February, not at the Dionysia later in the year. Pisander was a leader in the oligarchic coup (Thu. 8.68.1; [Aristot.] *Ath. Pol.* 32.2), proposing the resolution describing the mechanics of the rule of the Four Hundred: five men were to be elected who would, in turn, elect one hundred; each of the hundred would elect three more, making a total of four hundred; this group would convene the Five Thousand whenever they wished (8.67.3). During the rule of the Four Hundred, Pisander was honored more than Theramenes (Lys. 12.66). When the Four Hundred fell, Pisander fled to Decelea (8.98.1) where the Spartans had a garrison, and was condemned to death *in absentia*. His confiscated property is under discussion in Lysias 7.4.

Pisianax II of ?Sunium, son of Euryptolemus I See App. II.

Pisias of Athens See App. II.

Pisistratus, son of Hippocrates See App. II.

Pistias   Xen. *Mem.* 3.10.9–15
[*PA* 11822 *LGPN2* 2 *PX*
Πιστίας]

Pistias was a maker of armor whom Socrates visited in his armory, and with whom Socrates discussed the importance of properly fitting breastplates and other armor. (Cf. Ath. 5, referring to him as Pistona, Πίστωνα.)

Pittacus of Mytilene (sage) See App. II.

Plato of Collytus, son of Ariston   Pl. *Ap.*   present
[*PA/APF* 11855 (8792.11C–12D) *LGPN2* 24   Pl. *Phd.* 59b *
RE 7 *DPhA* 216 *OCD*³ *PP PX*   Pl. *Ltr.* 7, 8 *
Πλάτων Ἀρίστωνος Κολλυτεύς]   [Pl.] *Ltr.* 1–6, 9–13 *
424/3–348/7   Xen. *Mem.* 3.6.1
mother: Perictione   *AM* 51.21–2
siblings: Adeimantus I, Glaucon IV, Potone; Eph. *Nau.* fr. 14 (K
  maternal half brother: Antiphon II;   14)
  maternal stepbrother: Demos   Epi. fr. 10 (K 11)
stepfather and grand uncle: Pyrilampes   Antipha. *Ant.* fr. 35
philosopher and academician   (K 33)
See stemma: Plato.   D. S. 15.7.1
                                             D. L. 3

Life.   Because the Greek practice of naming sons for grandfathers was strong, a tradition developed according to which Plato's given name was 'Aristocles,' and 'Plato' was a nickname he earned either from the physical breadth that made him a good wrestler, or—implausibly—the breadth of his style (D. L. 3.4, citing Alex. Polyh.), a tradition soundly refuted by Notopoulos (1939).

   APF (like Gilbert Ryle, but more solemnly) warns about the variety of mythologizing influences on calculations of Plato's life: one was the desire that Plato be born in the year of Pericles I's death, 430/29 (Nean. fr. 20). Another was to give Plato an Apolline life span of eighty-one years and a precise Apolline date of birth, 7 Thargelion of the 88th Olympiad (Apoll. *Chr.* fr. 37, and D. L. 3.2) where even the 88th Olympiad is a back-calculation from the certain date of Plato's death with the desideratum of eighty years in mind. For a full discussion of the ancient tradition, see Jacoby (1902); *APF* brings the account forward to 1971; both include citations they rightly reject, not repeated below. I would love to sidestep

STEMMA: PLATO

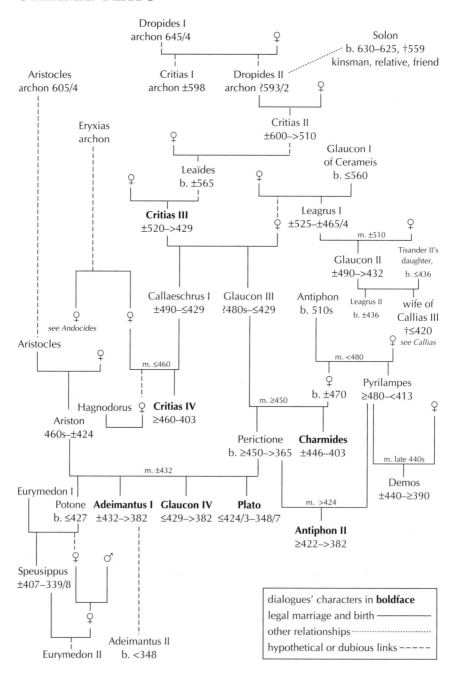

Dropides I
archon 645/4

Solon
b. 630–625, †559
kinsman, relative, friend

Aristocles
archon 605/4

Critias I
archon ±598

Dropides II
archon ?593/2

Critias II
±600–>510

Glaucon I
of Cerameis
b. ≤560

Eryxias
archon

Leaïdes
b. ±565

Critias III
±520–>429

Leagrus I
±525–±465/4

m. ±510

Glaucon II
±490–>432

Tisander II's
daughter,
b. ≤436

Callaeschrus I
±490–≤429

Glaucon III
?480s–≤429

Antiphon
b. 510s

Leagrus II
b. ±436

wife of
Callias III
†≤420
see Callias

see Andocides
Aristocles

m. ≤460

m. <480

Hagnodorus   Critias IV
Ariston   ≥460-403
460s–±424

b. ±470

Pyrilampes
≥480–<413

m. ≥450

Perictione
b. ≥450–>365

Charmides
±446–403

m. late 440s

Demos
±440–≥390

Eurymedon I

Potone
b. ≤427

Adeimantus I
±432–>382

Glaucon IV
≤429–>382

Plato
≤424/3–348/7

m. >424

m. ±432

Antiphon II
≥422–>382

Speusippus
±407–339/8

Eurymedon II

Adeimantus II
b. <348

dialogues' characters in **boldface**
legal marriage and birth ———
other relationships ··················
hypothetical or dubious links – – – –

the mythologizing of Plato, but I cannot. For centuries, most discussions of Plato's life have taken for granted not so much the original texts or their immediate historical context, but claims that grew up from them in Hellenistic and late antique times.

We have one comfortably firm bit of evidence, (a) Plato's death in 348/7, in the first year of the 108th Olympiad, in the thirteenth year of the reign of Philip, based on a number of fragmentary historical sources (Theop. *hist.* fr. 294, Her. *hist. FHG* 3.43, Philoch. fr. 223, et al.; cited in D. L. 3.2 and 3.40, relying in part on Her. *hist.* and Fav., respectively). One's next step is paramount, and *APF* stumbles, "The basic *datum* can be now seen to be the statement of Plato's pupil Hermodoros that when Plato left Athens for Megara after Sokrates' death Plato was aged 28" (D. L. 3.6). But we do not have Hermodorus; we have Diogenes, who wrote some six centuries later. I suggest that the datum, which I happen to accept, appears *basic* only with contaminated hindsight, and I will return to it below. Meanwhile, I suggest that we turn *in the first instance* to the texts of Plato in relation to events that can be verified independently.

There are two pertinent autobiographical details from the dialogues: Plato's brothers, Adeimantus I and Glaucon IV, were eulogized after a battle at Megara (*Rep.* 368a), but Plato apparently was not, so (b) Plato was almost certainly younger than both his brothers, and no older than nineteen at the time of that battle outside Attica. (c) Plato is old enough, at least eighteen, in 399 to have some independent control over his finances (*Ap.* 38b–c). Historical details are also helpful: Athens fought at Arginusae in 406, and at Aegospotami in 405, the last two battles before the siege of Athens that ended the war; so desperate was the manpower shortage at that stage, even with the citizens fully deployed, that slaves and *metics* were promised citizenship in return for serving (*NIA* 3.33–7). (d) If Plato was twenty by 405, he probably would have been required to serve. Here we encounter a text that will lead to three options: Aristoxenus of Tarentum, a 4th c. B.C.E. musicologist, is said by Diogenes (3.8) to have said somewhere that Plato served in the battles of Corinth, Tanagra, and Delium; but those battles of the mid-420s play havoc with any reasonable chronology; and there is no mention elsewhere of any military service. Our three options are accept, deny, and withhold judgment. If we accept the text, we infer that, although Aristoxenus was wrong about the details, he was probably right about the underlying point that Plato served somewhere in some capacity (perhaps in Corinth in 391 when Theaetetus was mortally wounded). If we deny it, we infer that Plato probably did not serve, since Aristoxenus was wrong about the details; after all, we have his information secondhand, uncorroborated, and reported six centuries after he wrote it. I suggest option three, withhold judgment pending further evidence. And I offer the further evidence of Plato's *Letter 7* which, if not genuine, enjoys almost universal recognition as having been written by someone very close to the events of Plato's life in the period under discussion—a recommendation that cannot be given to Diogenes:

When I was a young man [νέος] I had the same ambition as many others: I thought of entering public life as soon as I came of age. And certain happenings in public affairs favored me, as follows. The constitution we then had, being anathema to many, was overthrown; and a new government was set up consisting of fifty-one men, two groups—one of eleven and another of ten—to police the market place and perform other necessary duties in the city and the Piraeus respectively, and above them thirty other officers with absolute powers. Some of these men happened to be relatives and acquaintances of mine, and they invited me to join them at once in what seemed to be a proper undertaking. My attitude toward them is not surprising, because I was young. I thought that they were going to lead the city out of the unjust life she had been living and establish her in the path of justice, so that I watched them eagerly to see what they would do. (*Ltr.* 7.324b–d)

Plato makes his coming of age congruent with the ascendance of the Thirty. In one sense, Plato could be regarded as "coming of age" at eighteen since that is when he would be presented to the demesmen of Collytus, undergo scrutiny, and be registered as a citizen; he would begin military service by training and maintaining his gear, and would be expected to defend Attica within her borders. But a youth under the age of twenty made himself a laughingstock if he attempted to enter the political arena (Xen. *Mem.* 3.6; cf. [Pl.] *Alc.*). It thus appears that (e) Plato is turning twenty as the Thirty take control of Athens; and that he does not immediately accept the invitation to join them is unexceptional, given his youth. Hence I date Plato's birth 424/3, without coming into conflict with (a)–(e), or, incidentally, with (f) below.

To address (b), there is a well-known battle at Megara in 409 (D. S. 13.65.1–2) when, by my calculations, Plato would have been fifteen (Adeimantus I perhaps twenty-three, and Glaucon IV at least twenty). The traditional dating would make Plato eighteen or nineteen, a year younger than Glaucon IV, in 409. (For other candidate battles, see Glaucon IV s.v.) The criterion of (c) is also met: because I take Plato to have been twenty-five at the time of Socrates' trial and death, he would have reached an age when he could join in an offer to increase the amount of the fine Socrates could offer to pay; but the same is true for the traditional dating. Regarding (d), Plato would not have been eligible to serve in the battles of Arginusae and Aegospotami because he would not have reached the age of twenty until 404; here the traditional dating fails us because Plato would have been twenty-two and twenty-three, prime military age. The traditional dating also has difficulty explaining away (e), the evidence of *Letter 7*, for Plato would have been of an age, in his mid-twenties, to join the Thirty at once.

Claims considered in the text:

(a)   Plato died 348/7
(b)   Plato was ≤19 when brothers fought at Megara
(c)   Plato was ≥18 in 399
(d)   if Plato was 20 ≤406/5 he served at Arginusae/ Aegospotami
(e)   Plato was turning 20 in 404
(f)   Plato was 28 when he left Athens for Megara
(g)   Plato left for Megara in 399
(h)   Plato was 20 when he began to follow Socrates
(i)   Plato knew Socrates for 10 years

Now I return to *APF*'s basic datum: (f) Plato was twenty-eight when he went to Euclides in Megara after Socrates' death (D. L. 3.6), an age Philodemus gives as twenty-seven (col. X.7, p. 6). This datum, however plausible, led to the invalid inference that (g) Plato set out for Megara immediately upon Socrates' death, i.e., in 399, and consequently to the much-repeated *further* inference that Plato was born in 428/7 (Apoll. *Chr.* fr. 37 [cf. Jacoby 1902: 304–9], Philoch. fr. 223, and Hippo. 1.8.13). This flawed reasoning has in turn provided a convenient way of dating Ariston's death, with its implication that Perictione's childbearing career was highly consolidated. What Diogenes actually reports is, "When [Socrates] was gone, [Plato] joined Cratylus the Heraclitean and Hermogenes, who philoso-phized in the manner of Parmenides. Then, at twenty-eight, Hermodorus says, [Plato] went to Euclides in Megara with some other Socratics." The text itself gives no reason to infer that Plato left immediately for Megara and implies the very opposite. Thus, I continue to hold that Plato was about twenty-five when Socrates was tried in 399; and, if one allots two years or so of respite for Plato to seek other philosophical companions (whether or not they were Cratylus and Hermogenes) before his departure for Megara, he could well have been twenty-seven or twenty-eight then. Thus (g) can be abandoned.

Diogenes (3.6), apparently drawing from Alexander Polyhistor's *Successions of Philosophers*, says that (h) Plato was twenty when he began to follow Socrates (τοὐντεῦθεν δὴ γεγονώς, φασίν, εἴκοσιν ἔτη διήκουσε Σωκράτους); and *APF*, citing the anonymous *Life of Plato* and the Suda, provides the wider context: "Diogenes' statement that Plato met Sokrates when he was 20 is evidently part of the tradition that Plato was 30 at Sokrates' death and had been with him for ten years." That (i) Plato was with Socrates for ten years thus forms the second part of the popular datum. Neither my proposed birth year of 424/3, nor the traditional birth year of 428/7 can accommodate both (h) and (i) simultaneously. It is, however, far more likely that Plato knew Socrates for ten years than that he did not meet Socrates until he was twenty. Plato shows his own older brothers associating with Socrates (*R.*, *Smp.*, *Ap.*; cf. Xen. *Mem.* 3.6), he shows Socrates in public places with young boys (e.g. *Ly.*; cf. Xen. *Symp.* 4.27), and he shows older Athenian males accompanied by younger relatives in public places (e.g., brothers in *Ly.*, fathers and sons in *Lch.* 187d–e). It would be very surprising indeed if Plato did not know Socrates for *at least* ten years.

Career.   It is normally assumed that Plato traveled for some years before returning permanently to Athens, but the transition to the academic phase of his life requires that he somehow gain a reputation prior to 387 that would attract the attention of Dionysius I, then tyrant of Syracuse, and account for Plato's being invited to his court. There is contemporaneous confirmation (Isocr. *Let.* 1) of Dionysius I's having invited a variety of intellectuals to Sicily by 368, perhaps including Ae-schines and Archippus; but Plato's visit is supposed to have been much earlier. One possibility is Caven's (1990: 168–9): Plato received no invitation to Sicily but went there and to southern Italy "as an enquiring tourist," and never even met the tyrant. Caven's view makes it difficult, however, to understand how Plato could have met Dion on that visit since the tyrant's family resided in the fortress of Ortygia, apart from the citizens. Another possibility is to put the beginning of Plato's writing career into the period of his travels after Socrates' death. A few suggestions about this possibility could be derived from the discussion of the dramatic date of *Republic* (see App. I). Since Plato says he was about forty when he first visited Syracuse (*Ltr.* 7.324a), he went there in 384/3, having had ample time to attract an invitation.

Scholarship moves back and forth about how Plato's first visit to Sicily ended. Details differ in the accounts of Diodorus (15.7) Plutarch (*Dion* 4–5, whose source may be Timaeus) and Diogenes (3.18–21), none of whom is contemporaneous, but all report that Plato angered the tyrant by speaking frankly, and that the tyrant had him sold into slavery for twenty *minae* (D. S.; D. L.) either at the slave market in Syracuse (D. S.) or by the Spartan emissary, Pollis, in Aegina which was then allied with Sparta against Athens (Plu., D. L.). Plutarch, who adds that Dionysius I gave Pollis the alternative of killing Plato, drops the story in Aegina, but Diodorus and Diogenes go on to describe Plato's further purchase, probably by Anniceris of Cyrene, who set him free. When Plato's friends, perhaps Dion, tried to refund the money, Anniceris refused it and purchased for Plato the garden that was to be incorporated into the Academy (D. L.). It is not entirely clear what the founding of the Academy meant in concrete terms, but the traditional date of 387 should also be revised to 383, after Plato's return from Sicily. The best evidence for the earliest days is that the Academy was an open area where one might go to study mathematics with others of like mind as a propaedeutic to dialectic (see Theaetetus s.v.). It probably never had rooms in Plato's lifetime. We might infer that there were a handful of associates in the early days who, by the time Aristotle arrived, were doing as much teaching as learning, but the beginnings are murky and it is difficult not to impose current categories (teacher, student) anachronistically—as in other centuries such terms as 'master' and 'disciple' were deemed appropriate.

Plato's second trip to Sicily, after the death of Dionysius I, cannot realistically be dated 367 because the timing is wrong: news of the tyrant's February 367 Lenaean victory had to travel from Athens to Sicily, an unspecified time had to pass afterwards before the tyrant died, and news of his death had to reach Athens, making possible Plato's departure—and news did not travel fast outside the sailing season in the ancient world—so the *earliest* Plato could have left Athens was April of that year, and months later is more likely. The year changed in midsummer, so the second trip is better dated in the early months of 366. Thus the story that Plato was absent when Aristotle arrived at the Academy in 367, if that is when he arrived, should probably be rethought. While Plato was in Syracuse, Dionysius II, who had succeeded his father and accepted Dion's counsel, became suspicious of Dion's loyalties and had him banished, confiscating a portion of his property (see Dion & Dionysius II s.vv.). Plato attempted to effect a reconciliation, and the restoration of Dion's property, but repeatedly failed. He returned to Athens and, over the next several years, continued to maintain cordial relations with Dionysius II, possibly still hoping to see Dion restored.

Plato returned to Sicily a third and last time in 361, staying over the winter (*Ltr.* 7.347a–c) and well into the sailing season of 360. But Dionysius II was without interest in philosophy and, this time, kept Plato a virtual prisoner, putting his life in jeopardy outside the fortress, forcing Plato to appeal to friends in Tarentum to be rescued. He was able to return to Athens only with the intercession of Archytas s.v. (7.349e–350b; D. L. 3.21–22). Dion was assassinated in the summer of 354, ending their thirty-year friendship, but Plato remained in contact with Dion's family and friends, assuming *Letters* 7 and 8 to be genuine.

The dialogues and the productions of other early Academics are evidence of the success of the Academy, which apparently never charged fees in Plato's time. (D. L. lists nineteen students who became well-known, with four others as probable, but adds "and many others"; the names are given in App. II.) Plato died in 348/7, in his seventy-sixth year, and was buried at the Academy, which lies northwest of the city in the grove of the hero, Hecademus, between the rivers Cephisus and Eridanus (see Plan 1). The site can still be visited and has resulted in some interesting archaeological finds (see below, and Charmides and Cimon II s.vv.).

In comedy.   Three fragments demonstrate that the students of Plato's Academy were subjects of the comic poets as Socrates' young associates had been (see Aristoph. *Birds* 1280–1283). But whereas the young men around Socrates tended to imitate him by neglecting their appearance, Ephippus' *Nauangus* fragment of 13 lines depicts the affectations of a young member of Plato's Academy who might better be described as a dandy; it cannot be dated more precisely than 380–360. The most famous sketch to reach us from antiquity is a 37-line fragment from an unnamed, undated play of Epicrates in which two Academy students are bent over a pumpkin, discussing its genus in a parody of the method of collection and division, reminiscent of a scene in Aristophanes' *Clouds* (186–194). Antiphanes' six-line fragment from *Antaeus* is in the same vein: two Academy students "doing" philosophy.

Property.   That Plato was *chorēgos* in boys' dithyramb with Dion's financial backing (D. L. 3.3–3.4) is the only evidence we have of a liturgy performed by Plato. When he died, Plato was not a wealthy man, but a self-sufficient one. Plato seems to have arranged for the Academy separately from his estate, possibly having established, or accepted from Dion, an endowment for it. It is not mentioned in his will (D. L. 3.41–43):

These things have been left and devised by Plato: the estate in Iphistiadae, bounded on the north by the road from the temple at Cephisia, on the south by the temple of Heracles in Iphistiadae, on the east by the property of Archestratus of Phrearrhi, on the west by that of Philippus of Chollidae: this it shall be unlawful for anyone to sell or alienate, but it shall be the property of the boy Adeimantus to all intents and purposes: the estate in Eiresidae which I bought of Callimachus, bounded on the north by the property of Eurymedon of Myrrhinus, on the south by the property of Demostratus of Xypete, on the east by that of Eurymedon of Myrrhinus, and on the west by the Cephisus; three minae of silver; a silver vessel weighing 165 drachmas; a cup weighing 45 drachmas; a gold signet-ring and earring together weighing 165 drachmas and three obols. Euclides the lapidary owes me three minae. I enfranchise Artemis. I leave four household servants, Tychon, Bictas, Apollonides and Dionysius. Household furniture, as set down in the inventory of which Demetrius has the duplicate. I owe no one anything. My executors are Leosthenes, Speusippus, Demetrius, Hegias, Eurymedon, Callimachus and Thrassippus.

North of the city, and east of the Cephisus River, Plato owned properties in the demes of Iphistiadae and Eresidae, both city *trittyes* of the tribe Akamantis (see Map 2). Plato's tribe was Aigeis, and that of his brother-in-law Eurymedon was Pandionis, evidence that one's place of residence and one's deme were not necessarily the same by the second half of the 4th c. (see App. III).

The Iphistiadae property, perhaps 10 km. north-northeast of the ancient city wall, and 2 km. from the banks of the Cephisus, appears to have been inherited since no mention is made of a sum paid for it. The land can be precisely located, since Plato describes it as bounded on the south by the temple of Heracles, a boundary stone for which was found in 1926 (*AM*). The land at Eresidae, however, was purchased from a Callimachus who serves as one of the named executors of the will; its location is not known precisely, but the deme of Eresidae is tentatively located (Traill 1986: Table I and map), from Diogenes' description and from one grave marker discovered in 1963, west of Colonus: that puts the property about 3 km. north of the city wall, on the east bank of the Cephisus. Plato's nephew, Eurymedon II, another of the executors, owned the adjacent properties to the north and east. Plato leaves everything to the boy (*pais*) Adeimantus II, presumably the grandson of one of Plato's brothers, most likely Adeimantus I.

It is not surprising that Plato would not have land in his own deme of Collytus since his two brothers, at least one of whom married and reared a family (accounting for Adeimantus II, not known in Potone's line), may also have desired so centrally located and valuable an urban plot. Divisions of estates among heirs, in the absence of a will, was usually decided by an initial apportionment of the assets of the estate (property in land and structures, herds, precious metals, cash etc.) into equal portions; when the portions were agreed to be equal, the brothers might draw lots or choose their inheritance (see MacDowell 1978: 93). In Plato's *Laws*, the father may stipulate in a will who will inherit what (*Laws* 11.923c, see App. III).

In inscriptions.   A controversial archaeological find known as the Academy Tablets was unearthed in 1958 on the site of Plato's Academy by Phoibos Stavropoullos (*SEG* 19.37 and 22.61; Vanderpool 1959) and dated 450–early 4th c. The find included some hundred slate tablets, sixteen of which are inscribed, but inscribed with such poor orthography that Stavropoullos believed them to be the work of young schoolboys learning to write. Lynch (1983), with a number of doubts about the interpretation of the find, disputed the early date as well, preferring the 2nd c. C.E. If authentic, the tablets would challenge not only what is known of the work of the Academy, but the Greek primary education system, and the history of the pronunciation of Greek—too much to ask of these "suspicious tablets" in Lynch's view. Balatsos (1991), agreeing with most of Lynch's objections to the original interpretation of the find, reiterated a date of "by the end of the 5th century" B.C.E., noting that everything retrieved from the stratum on which the tablets were found, and everything from higher strata, had been dated in the archaic or classical period. All have called for more archaeological work in the area of the Academy.

Polemarchus of Thurii, son of Cephalus II   Pl. *R.*   speaker
[*FRA* 6993 *APF* C11(C9) *DPhA* 236 *PP*   Pl. *Phdr.* 257b
Πολέμαρχος Κεφάλου]   Lys. 12
≤450–404
half or full siblings: Lysias, Euthydemus, a
  sister who married Brachyllus
philosopher executed by the Thirty
See stemma: Lysias.

Life.   Polemarchus was probably born in Syracuse at about the time his parents, or just his father, immigrated, at Pericles I's request, to Athens. It is likely that the mother of the other children in the family was Cephalus II's second wife. Polemarchus was temporary guardian for at least Lysias and perhaps Euthydemus as well when Cephalus II's sons went to Thurii in ±430 as colonists. Thurii, in southern Italy (see Map 3), was a panhellenic colony originally settled in 444/3, planned by Hippodamus of Miletus and supported mainly by Athenians. After the Sicilian expedition and campaign 415–413, however, there was substantial anti-Athenian sentiment. The Thurians sent ten ships of mostly free men, which was unusual, to help Hermocrates s.v. of Syracuse defeat the Athenian fleet (Thu. 8.26.1, 8.35, with Lewis *CAH* 6²: 126); Cephalus II's sons returned to Athens at least by that time, but probably before then. They were an exceptionally wealthy family by any standard, but certainly the wealthiest *metics* in Attica. Polemarchus married (12.19) and was the legal owner of the house in the Piraeus where the conversation of the *Republic* is set (*R.* 328b). See Cephalus II s.v. for references to the "retirement" of an old man whose son was of age and capable of undertaking responsibility for the family.

In the period of the Thirty.   Polemarchus is said to have turned to philosophy (*Phdr.* 257b) before he was executed by the Thirty in 404 (Lys. 12.17). Lysias gives an account of the events that led to Polemarchus' death at their hands, though of course Lysias cannot be counted an impartial reporter, and does not claim to have been a witness to much of what he reports (see his own story s.v.). Nevertheless, he says that after he escaped his guards, Archenius, his sea captain host, returned to the city to reconnoiter Polemarchus' situation: Eratosthenes (a member of the Thirty and the defendant in Lys. 12) had arrested Polemarchus on the street and taken him to prison (12.16–17). Lysias does not name his source for the additional detail that when Melobius, one of the Thirty, entered Polemarchus' house, he snatched the earrings of wound gold from the ears of Polemarchus' wife (12.19).

   Although saying "we" throughout his account of the funeral of Polemarchus (12.17–19), Lysias had already fled the city and could not have been present himself. He reports that the Thirty ordered Polemarchus to drink hemlock without informing him of any charges, and without trial. Afterwards, they forbade that a funeral be held in any of the three houses belonging to the family (12.18), forcing a shed to be hired for laying out the body. With all the family's goods in the hands of the Thirty, neighbors contributed whatever they could spare—a cloak for a shroud, a pillow—for the interment.

Polus of Acragas (Sicily)
[*LGPN3A* 7 *RE* 3 *OCD³ PP* Πῶλος]
b. ?440s
student of Licymnius of Chios and of
  Gorgias
rhetorician

Pl. *Grg.*   speaker
Pl. *Phdr.* 267b
[Pl.] *Thg.* 127e–128b
frr. in Stob., *passim*

Life and works.   Only an approximate and tentative date of birth can be assigned to Polus, partly because the *Gorgias* has so fluid a dramatic date (see App. I). Although Polus is the youngest of the speakers in the dialogue, young enough to be Gorgias' or even Socrates' son, born perhaps in the 440s, Polus is not a youth in the dialogue—far from it: Socrates had read Polus' treatise on the art of rhetoric (*Grg.* 462b11) already. So the Polus of the dialogue is an adult who still behaves rather childishly (463a, 467b, 473e). As no one fails to mention, his name means 'colt' (Aristot. *Rh.* 1400b20). When discussed in the third person, Polus emerges as a generator of rhetorical terms. Socrates asks Phaedrus, "And what shall we say of the whole gallery of terms Polus set up—speaking with Reduplication, Speaking in Maxims, Speaking in Images—and of the terms Licymnius gave him as a present to help him explain Good Diction." The passage may contain a title of one of Polus' treatises, something like *Word Sanctuaries of the Muses* (Sprague 2001: 17), or "shrines of learned speech" (Fowler 1914: 539).

In the later tradition and modern bibliography.   Aristotle attributes to Polus the saying "Experience made art, inexperience luck" (*Meta.* 981a4); cf. Suda s.v. Stobaeus preserves frr. at *Anthologium* 3.5.56.27, 3.9.51.1, 4.4.31.9, 4.4.31.22, 4.33.28.9–10. Dodds (1959: 11–2) characterizes Polus in relation to other persons and issues in *Gorgias*.

Polyaratus of Cholarges See App. II.

Polyclitus of Argos (sculptor) See App. II.

Polycrates of Athens
[*PA* 12005 *LGPN2* 1 *RE* 7 Πολυκράτης]
440–370
rhetorician

Isocr. 11
Lys. frr. 220–224
Sauppe

Life.   Polycrates wrote rhetorical exercises ('paradoxical encomia') defending villains and attacking heroes, including a *Defense of Busiris* and an *Accusation of Socrates*, neither of which is extant. (Busiris was an Egyptian said to sacrifice strangers on Zeus' altar.) From Isocrates' letter, it appears that Polycrates proposed for himself a career teaching "philosophy" conceived as rhetoric (11.1–2). Isocrates sought to discourage him by severely criticizing both discourses, but especially the former. *Accusation of Socrates* purports to be the speech Anytus delivered at Socrates' trial but was not in fact written until after the reconstruction of Athens' long walls 393/2. Xenophon probably answers its charges (*Mem.* 1.1–2), and Lysias may have as well; Libanius certainly does in *Declamations*, written in the 4th c. c.e.

In the later tradition and modern bibliography.   See Athenaeus (335d) and Diogenes (2.38). Dodds (1959: 28–9) is excellent.

Prosopographical notes.   This is not the Polycrates of Xenophon's *Anabasis* (*PA* 12006).

Polycrates of Samos, son of Aeaces (tyrant) See App. II.

Polydamas of Thessaly (athlete) See App. II.

Polygnotus of Thasos and Athens, son of Aglaophon (painter) See App. II.

Polyxenus	[Pl.] *Let.* 2.310c,
[*LGPN3A* 31 *RE* 7 *DPhA* 267 *PP* Πολύξενος]	314c, 13.360c *
associate of Bryson, Helicon	

In *Letter* 13 of ≥365, Polyxenus is mentioned as an associate of Bryson (a well-known sophist) and of Helicon (who is being sent to Dionysius II as a mathematics teacher). In *Letter* 2 (>360), Polyxenus is represented as suspect in two ways: he is one of two people who may have slandered [Plato's] friends to Dionysius II; and he is said to be inferior in intelligence and argumentative competence to Dionysius II. Nevertheless, and crucial to the homonym below, if Polyxenus was in fact sent by Plato to Dionysius II, as both letters allege, he cannot be the husband of Dionysius I's sister, Theste.

Polyxenus of Sicily	Xen. *Hell.* 5.1.26
[*LGPN3A* 30 *RE* 7 *PP* Πολύξενος]	Tod 2.108
active 480s	D. S. 13.96.3
sister: wife of Hermocrates I	Plu. *Dion* 21.7–8
wife: Theste (sister of Dionysius I)	
advisor to Dionysius I	

Three different relationships between Proxenus and Hermocrates I s.v. are encountered in the literature. He was (a) the brother of Hermocrates I's wife (D. S., *CAH* 6² 143, 151), or (b) the son of Hermocrates I (Harward 1932: stemma facing p. 10), or (c) the brother of Hermocrates I (*CAH* 6² 130—perhaps just an oversight for 'brother-in-law'). He is both the brother-in-law of Hermocrates I and of Dionysius I, because he was married to the tyrant's sister, Theste. Polyxenus acted as a successful emissary to Greece and Italy for Dionysius I in the wars with Carthage, bringing home thirty ships and their Spartan commander to help in the defense of Sicily against the invasion; over several years he appears to have been Dionysius

I's most trusted and useful advisor. But he, like Dionysius I's other advisers, appears to have had cause to flee in fear of the tyrant at some point (Plu.).

Potone of Athens, daughter of Ariston of Collytus
[*PA/APF* 12153 (8792.11D) *LGPN2* 1 Ποτώνη (Ποτώ–) Ἀρίστωνος Κολλυτεύς θυγάτηρ]
b. ≤427
mother: Perictione
siblings: Plato, Adeimantus I, Glaucon IV;
  maternal half brother: Antiphon II;
  maternal stepbrother: Demos
husband: Eurymedon I of Myrrhinus
mother of Speusippus I and a daughter
stepfather and grand uncle: Pyrilampes
See stemma: Plato.

[Pl.] *Ltr.* 13, unnamed
D. L. 3.4, 4.1
[Iamb.] *TA* 82.10

Life.   Potone's name appears perhaps as early as a papyrus fragment of Philodemus from the Herculaneum (see Tarán 1981: 203), but twice in Diogenes (3.4, 4.1); she is still often omitted from discussions of Plato's immediate family (see e.g. Ferrari 2000: 346, 353). The birth of Potone can be confidently dated 432–424, but is traditionally refined with reference to the birth of her son Speusippus s.v. in ±407. The inference from ±407 to the date of Potone's own birth as ≤427 is merely an application of the standard default of twenty years in the face of ignorance of further details. Potone is then Plato's elder sister, as Wilamowitz held (1919: 1.35–6). Speusippus was probably her first born son, because Eurymedon I was most likely the son of a Speusippus. It is very likely that Potone also had a daughter, whose own daughter married Speusippus (as Potone's mother had married her maternal uncle).

Potone's son, Speusippus s.v., became the second head of the Academy. He and Potone's probable grandson, Eurymedon II, were named among executors of Plato's will (D. L. 3.43); the property of Eurymedon II, on which she was probably living, bordered that of Plato on two sides (D.L. 3.42). Accounting for the property's already having passed to Eurymedon II when Speusippus was still alive has given rise to suggestions that the two were not son and father but nephew and uncle, or perhaps even brothers. We do not know what counted as the family's principal plot, but there is ample precedent for an elderly man's passing responsibility for his estate to his son before his death (cf. Cephalus and Hipponicus s.vv.).

Procles of Sparta, son of Aristodemus (king) See App. II.

Prodicus of Ceos
[*LGPN1* 2 *RE* 3 *DPhA* 325 *OCD³ PP PX* Πρόδικος]
5th c.

Pl. *Prt.*   speaker
Pl. *Phdr.* 267b–c
Pl. *Lch.* 197d
Pl. *Euthd.* 277e

teacher of Damon	Pl. *Smp.* 177b
teacher of Theramenes	Pl. *Ap.* 19e
revered teacher of semantics, rhetoric	Pl. *Cra.* 384b
	Pl. *Tht.* 151b
	Pl. *Meno* 75e, 96d
	[Pl.] *G. Hp.* 282c
	[Pl.] *Eryx.* speaker
	[Pl.] *Ax.* 366c
	Xen. *Mem.* 2.1.21–34
	Xen. *Symp.* 4.62
	Aes. *Cal.* no. 73 (fr. 34 Dittmar)
	frr. in DK 84
	Aristoph. *Birds* 685–692
	Aristoph. *Tag.* fr. 506 (K 490)
	Aristoph. *Clouds* 358–363 & 361 schol.

Life and works. Protagoras says he is old enough to be Prodicus' father (*Prt.* 317c), and Prodicus seems still to be alive in 399 (*Ap.*), so—for want of more exact information—he has been viewed as an approximate contemporary of Socrates. Prodicus appears to have had the respect of Plato's Socrates, who sends him the students he does not expect to be able to help himself (*Lch., Tht. Ap.*), and counts himself as learning about the exact use of terms from Prodicus (*Meno* 96d), though not the advanced course (*Cra.* 384b). Plato is the most important source of information about Prodicus available to us. From Plato, we learn of his deep, resonating voice (*Prt.* 315d), his writing on Heracles and other heroes (*Smp.* 177b), his diplomatic missions for Ceos and how those enabled him to travel to where young men would pay high fees ([Pl.] *G. Hp.*; to which Aristot. adds that he dazzled sleepy audiences with "a bit of the fifty-*drachma* show-lecture," *Rh.* 1415b15); and perhaps most importantly, that his special skill and emphasis as a teacher, or 'sophist' in its neutral sense, was the exact use of words (*Prt.* 337a–c, 340a–341b, *Euthd.*; cf. Aristot. *Top.* 112b22). Moreover, Prodicus had the respect of Athenians in his time. "Prodikos was the most distinguished and respected intellectual of the day, and achieved in his lifetime (as Einstein did, uniquely, in this century) something like the 'proverbial' status of Thales" (Dover: 1950: lv)—implied in Aristophanes as well. Athenaeus reports that Aeschines' dialogue *Callias* abuses Prodicus for being the teacher of Theramenes s.v. (cf. Aristoph. *Clouds* 361 schol.). The long story of Heracles' choice that Socrates tells in Xenophon's *Memorabilia* (cf. Pl. *Smp.* 177b) may be based on Prodicus' original book which was perhaps called *Seasons* (*Horai*). But it is the later tradition that insists he was a hedonist, a claim that may be based on Aristotle's statement that he distinguished three types of pleasure (*Top.* 112b22).

In addition to the sources cited above, Prodicus is mentioned a few times in passing by Plato (*Chrm.* 163d, *R.* 600c) and pseudo-Plato (*Thg.* 127e–8b).

In the later tradition.   A number of later sources confuse and decorate what appears originally in contemporaneous sources (see Philostr. *VS* 12; Ath. 220b; Gell. *NA* 15.20.4; D. H. *Isoc.* 1; Mar. 36).

Protagoras of Abdera	Pl. *Prt.*	speaker
[*FRA* 4 *DPhA* 331 *RE* 1 *OCD*[3]	Pl. *Cra.* 391b–c	
PP PX Πρωτάγορας]	Pl. *Phdr.* 267c	
±490–420	Pl. *Tht.* †	speaker
renowned sophist	[Pl.] *Gr. Hp.*	
	frr. in DK 80	
	Eu. *Flatt.* fr. 157 (K 146)	
	Apoll. fr. 71	

Life and works.   Protagoras was born in Abdera on the northern shore of the Aegean Sea but lived in Athens for perhaps as long as forty years, teaching rhetoric and, he said, virtue. Plato's representation of the household and extended family of Pericles I in the *Protagoras*, including his sons Paralus and Xanthippus II, and their half brother, Callias III—all following closely behind Protagoras and hanging on his every word (*Prt.* 315)—suggests that Protagoras may have been in some way responsible for the educations of some of the persons present (see Plu. *Per.* 36). Protagoras wrote a work called *Truth* (*Cra.*), and probably much more. Diogenes lists twelve titles, all but the first of which he implies had survived to his own time in the 3rd c. C.E. (*On the Gods, The Art of Controversy, Of Wrestling, On Mathematics, Of the State, Of Ambition, Of Virtues, Of the Ancient Order of Things, On the Dwellers in Hades, Of the Misdeeds of Mankind, A Book of Precepts,* and the two-scroll *Of Forensic Speech for a Fee*). Two stories of later provenance, that Pericles I asked Protagoras to write a constitution for the panhellenic colony of Thurii, and that he was charged with impiety in Athens, cannot be corroborated in contemporaneous sources, and the latter is routinely assigned to philosophers by later authors, almost as an honorific, after Socrates. Protagoras seems to have lived seventy years, if the date of his death in the 84th Olympiad (D. L. 9.56) is correct.

Plato represents Protagoras memorably in the dialogues: his speech in defense of the Athenian democracy is still marked a masterpiece by many (*Prt.* 320d–328d); and he is conjured by Socrates in the *Theaetetus* to speak of the proper way to philosophize (*Tht.* 166a–168c). In addition, Plato mentions him in passing at *Cra.* 386a, *Euthd.* 286c, *Meno* 91d, *R.* 600c, *Sph.* 232e, and *Laws* 4.716c. The secondary literature offers a wide range of opinions on Protagoras' influence, or lack of influence, on Plato, but a prosopography ought not to dictate philosophical interpretation.

In Eupolis' *Flatterers* of 421, or in the frr. we have, Protagoras is negatively presented, called *alitērios*, amoral or full of guilt. When Diogenes discusses him at 9.50–6, it is clear that the biographer struggled with more intermediate sources for Protagoras than for most of the other ancients whose biographies he wrote; he cites a number of previous sources by name, freely mixing fact with fiction.

There are many other later references about his life as well (Philostr. *VS* 1.10.1–4; Ath. 218b, 505f) though many are concerned with his theories, and in particular with his relativism immortalized with the line, "Man is the measure of all things: of the things which are, that they are, and of things which are not, that they are not" (*Tht.* 152a). Aristotle, for example, discusses his views in a number of different contexts (see *S. Ref., Meta. NE, Rh., Poet.* and frr.). DK collects some other later testimonia.

Protarchus of Athens, son of Callias   Pl. *Phlb.* 19b   speaker
[*PA* 12289 *LGPN2* 4 *DPhA* 333 *PP*
Πρώταρχος Καλλίου]

Prosopographical notes.   Nothing is known about this Protarchus, but he cannot be some early and otherwise unknown son of Callias III s.v. though that is what has most often been assumed in the philosophical tradition (Fowler 1925: 291; PCW 398; *DPhA* C16). Two sons of Callias III are mentioned often, e.g. at Plato's *Apology* 20a; they are known and relatively well documented: Hipponicus III s.v. and an unnamed *nothos-cum*-citizen with Chrysilla s.v., born ≥412 and therefore too young for such a conversation in Socrates' lifetime. Further, Callias III was so constantly in the public eye, and so many times the object of extant criticism in the theatres and the courts, that his having had a third son must be considered an extremely remote possibility. Further, there is no known Protarchus in the family tree of Callias III or of his wives to provide a known onomastic precedent for this one. Since the *Philebus* is virtually free of dramatic content—perhaps because its introduction has been lost, perhaps because it is a patchwork hastily assembled, the view Nussbaum (1986: 459n21) attributes to Owen—it would be unwise to identify Protarchus' father with Callias III in the absence of any trace of confirmation.

Note that Protarchus is later called "son of that man" (*Phlb.* 36d) with no clear referent. Fowler canvassed the possibilities: "son of Philebus" because Protarchus was his student, or "son of Gorgias" because Gorgias is a great figure discussed later in the dialogue, or "son of [some man of mark]." In the Clarendon series of analytic translations, Gosling (1975) hides the issue from view by deleting the reference to Callias at 19b, and by translating "as your master's pupil" at 36d.

There are other men of the same period named Protarchus who may be this Protarchus, or may be homonyms, though there is no known instance of a Protarchus-Callias pair. 'Callias' too was a very common name, even at the end of the 5th c., so common that even the famous Callias III s.v. is elsewhere given an identifier ("the rich" or "son of Hipponicus") to distinguish him from others.

Pulytion of Athens See App. II.

Pyrilampes of Athens, son of Antiphon I   Pl. *Chrm.* 158a *
[*PA/APF* 12493 (8792.8) *LGPN2* 1 *RE* 1 *PP*   Pl. *Grg.* 481e, 513b *
Πυριλάμπης Ἀντιφῶντος]   Pl. *Prm.* 126b–c †
≥480–<413   Lys. 19.25

offspring with first wife: Demos; with	Antiph. 20
Perictione: Antiphon II	Aristoph. *Wasps* 98
guardian of Perictione's children:	& schol.
Adeimantus I, Glaucon IV, Potone, and	Plu. *Per.* 13.10
Plato	Plu. *Mor.* 581d
friend of Pericles I	Ath. 397c
many times emissary to the Persian court	
See stemma: Plato.	

Life and diplomatic career.   Pyrilampes' date of birth is figured roughly from his having been very active politically from 449. Noted for beauty of face and form (*Chrm.*), he appears to have married his first wife in the late 440s since his first son, Demos s.v., was born ±440. Pyrilampes was many times ambassador to the Persian court (*Chrm.*), and was a friend of Pericles I (Plu. *Per.* 13.10). It is interesting, in connection with the democracy under which Pericles I and Pyrilampes both flourished, that Pyrilampes named his son Demos, "people"—a name without precedent in the record (see Democrates I s.v.). Pyrilampes was wounded at Delium in 424 when he was in his mid-fifties (Plu. *Mor.*), and he had probably already been widowed since he was free to marry his niece, Perictione s.v. ≥423 when she was widowed. He added his seventeen-year-old son Demos to Perictione's four offspring. Pyrilampes and Perictione then had a son together, named Antiphon II for Pyrilampes' father.

Pyrilampes raised and showed peacocks, gifts he had received on his Asian embassies. A character in Aristophanes' *Acharnians* implies that the gift, presumably a breeding pair, was not uncommon: he says he's sick of bragging Asian ambassadors returning with their peacocks (62–63). It is possible that Pyrilampes was an ambassador on the 449 mission that negotiated the controversial Peace of Callias, for the dates are right. Evidence for the embassy is provided by Antiphon's speech, *Prosecution of Erasistratus in a Case about Peacocks*, dated <413: the peacocks, birds as expensive as racehorses, had been displayed for over thirty years on the first of every month, so Pyrilampes had received the first breeding pair before 443 ("forty years" is a misprint in Sprague 2001: 210). Plutarch accused Pyrilampes of using the peacocks to procure freeborn women for Pericles I (*Per.* 13.10). The fact that the peacocks had passed to Demos by 413 (or the date of Antiph. 20) provides a date by which Pyrilampes had died, but it could not have been much before 413: Adeimantus I appears to have become his mother's guardian upon Pyrilampes' death, and he would have reached the age of majority ≤414.

On absent fathers.   Plato's father was dead, and his stepfather often away on state business in Asia while he was growing up. At *Laws* 3.682d–e and 3.694e–695a there are examples of how the absence of fathers leads to the ruin of governments. Lysimachus II, son of Aristides I "The Just," speaks for himself and for Melesias II, son of Thucydides I, when he tells Nicias I and Laches: "we blame our fathers for allowing us to take things easy when we were growing up, while they were busy with other people's affairs" (*Lch.* 179d). "We watched our children growing without our guidance," Nelson Mandela said of his prison years; "my children said, 'We thought we had a father and one day he'd come back. But to our dismay, our father came back and he left us alone because he has now become the father of the nation' " (1994: 523).

Prosopographical notes. *PA* cites Plutarch's *De genio Socratis* (= *Mor.* 575a–598f) incorrectly: 518d should be 581d.

Pythocles of Myrrhinus See App. II. *See stemma: Phaedrus.*

Pythoclides of Ceos   Pl. *Prt.* 316e
[*LGPN1* 1 *FRA* 2812 *RE* s.v. *DPhA* 366   [Pl.] *Alc.* 118c, schol.
Stephanis 2173 *PP* Πυθοκλείδης]
active mid-5th c.
teacher of Pericles I and Sophocles
musician

Protagoras says Pythoclides disguised his wisdom (sophistry) as music (*Prt.*; cf. Damon s.v.). He is praised by Alcibiades III in pseudo-Plato (*Alc.*). Plutarch mentions him (*Mor.* 16).

Pythodorus of Athens, son of Isolochus   Pl. *Prm.*   speaker
[*PA* 12399 *LGPN2* 6 *RE* 7 *DPhA* 370   [Pl.] *Alc.* 119a
PP Πυθόδωρος Ἰσολόχου]   Thu. 3–6, *passim*
≤479–>414   Philoch. fr. 104
friend and student of Zeno
Athenian commander

Life. Pythodorus is represented as a householder of some status already in August of 450, so he was probably at least thirty when he hosted Parmenides' and Zeno's visit to Athens at the time of the greater Panathenaea (see App. I). He was a friend (*Prm.* 126b–c) and perhaps a student (*Alc.*) of Zeno. Although Pythodorus resided in the area in which pottery was produced, Ceramicus (*Prm.* 127c), his deme of registration is unknown. That he was an Athenian, however, is well established.

Military career. Pythodorus was a commander (*praetor*) in 426/5, and was sent by Athenians to Sicily where he superseded Laches s.v. in command of the fleet. Near the end of the fighting season, he led a contingent of ships on an unsuccessful attempt to retake a Locrian fort that Laches had previously taken (Thu. 3.115.2, 4.2.2–3). Upon his return to Athens, he was banished for having been defeated (Thu. 4.65.3).

Prosopographical notes. Pythodorus may also have been the *epistatēs* of the Assembly in 445 whose deme was Phlya (IG I³ 433.44; *PA* 12433; *LGPN2* 83) and/or the eponymous archon of 432/1 (*AO*; *PA* 12387; *LGPN2* 8), compatibly with the dates assigned above, but the name is not uncommon, and there is no compelling reason to assign these other offices to the Pythodorus of Thucydides and Plato. Basing his date of birth on the *Parmenides*, however, reduces the possibility that he was also the Pythodorus who was again a *praetor* in 414, when this man would have been sixty-five.

Python of Aenus See App. II.

Rhinon of Paeania, son of Charicles See App. II.

Sannio of Athens   [Pl.] *Thg.* 129d *
[*PA* 12552 *LGPN2* 1 *PP* Σαννίων]
>435->404

Sannio was an attractive Athenian soldier who survived the Sicilian campaign and later joined Thrasyllus s.v. on an Ionian campaign during which Socrates feared Sannio might be killed or wounded.

Sappho of Mytilene (poet) See App. II.

Sarambus of ?Athens   Pl. *Grg.* 518b *
[*LGPN2* 1 *PP* Σάραμβος]
wine merchant

Satyrus, slave of Hippocrates   Pl. *Prt.* 310c *
[*FRA* 7984 Σάτυρος]
runaway

Satyrus, slave of Alcibiades III See App. II.

Scellias II of Athens, son of Aristocrates I See App. II.

Scopas of Thessaly, son of Creon See App. II.

Simmias of Thebes   Pl. *Phd.*   speaker
[*LGPN3B* 5 *DPhA* 92 *OCD³ RE* 4   Pl. *Crito* 45b *
PP PX Σιμμίας]   Pl. *Phdr.* 242b
b. 430s   [Pl.] *Ltr.* 13.363a
Pythagorean friend of Socrates   Xen. *Mem.* 1.2.48,
                                                 3.11.17

Life. Simmias' birth can be calculated only roughly from the statement that he, like Cebes, was labeled *neaniskos* in 399 (*Phd.* 89a). Apparently, from what Socrates says of him in the *Phaedrus*, Simmias was fond of words. Xenophon puts him in the circle of friends closest to Socrates (Xen. *Mem.* 1.2.48), supported both by his having arrived from Thebes with money to help in Socrates' prison escape (*Crito*), and by Plato's representation of him as present at Socrates' death (*Phd.*), where he presents the argument for the *psyche*'s being like the harmony of the lyre. Xenophon also lists Simmias among friends and acquaintances of Socrates who visit the *hetaira*, Theodote s.v. (*Mem.* 3.11.17).

In the later tradition. Diogenes (2.124) attributes twenty-three dialogues to him, but since they are said to have been in one volume (*biblion*), these were relatively short pieces with names such as "On Philosophy" and "On Music"; none is extant. The pseudo-Socratic epistolary tradition includes a letter to Simmias and Cebes from Xenophon (22). Attributed to him in the *Palatine Anthology* are two verses on Sophocles (probably those of Simmias of Rhodes), and an epitaph for Plato of unknown province, giving his name as 'Aristocles'.

Simon of Athens
[*PA* 12688 *LGPN2* 8 *DPhA* 93 *RE* 6 *OCD*³
Σίμων]
active late 5th c.
cobbler and ?Socratic

Agora 21.86
Phae. nos. 2, 8,
16–18 & Rossetti
(1973)

Life. All we know for certain about Simon is that he owned a black-glazed cup (*kylix*) that declared itself in scratched-on letters of 5th c. style: "Simon's" (ΣΙΜΟΝΟΣ). But more can be inferred from the results of the archaeological dig in the southwest corner of the Athenian agora that unearthed the cup. Found together with it were a great number of hobnails (short iron tacks with wide rounded heads) and bone eyelets—both used in bootmaking—and a whetstone for sharpening knives required to cut leather accurately. The site is a 5th c. cobbler's shop of two rooms; at the base of its northeast terrace wall, a stone still says for all time, "I am the boundary stone of the agora" marking the southwest corner of the ancient market area.

   Whether this Simon is the cobbler of Phaedo's lost dialogues, the Simon immortalized in many wisdom-of-the-cobbler stories in later antiquity, is a separate question. Perhaps Phaedo wrote about the very Simon whose shop stood beside the agora; or perhaps it is sheer coincidence that Phaedo should choose the name 'Simon' for his cobbler character-type, one of the "creatures of Phaedo's imagination" (Kahn 1996: 10). Contemporary studies of Plato stand at what may not be the end of a long and elitist tradition of rejecting the notion that any artisan *other* than Socrates was capable of philosophical labor. Since nonaristocrats were not likely to leave records of themselves in stone inscriptions, they have been more likely to fade with time, even to be labeled fictions, and it has been easy to imagine a Socrates and his aristocratic young companions with leisure to spare, in the company of—but not engaging—craftsmen. Simon's cup is a lucky find, suggesting something of the breadth of associations Socrates may have enjoyed.

Those who credit Simon's historicity point out that, in Xenophon (*Mem.* 4.2.1–40), Euthydemus s.v., the son of Diocles, frequents the leather-worker's shop near the agora, and that a cobbler might well cut leather into reins for bridles as well as boots (*'hēnia'* refers equally to a bootlace, a rein, or any leather thong). Lysias adds, "Each of you is accustomed to visit tradesmen: the perfume seller, the hairdresser, the leather cutter, and wherever you might happen to go. Most of you visit the tradesmen who have set up shop nearest to the Agora, and very few visit those that are furthest away from it" (24.20).

In the later tradition.   Diogenes devotes a section to a citizen of Athens, a cobbler named Simon whose shop Socrates often visited (D. L. 2.122–3). This Simon noted down on leather what he could remember of Socratic conversations he heard in his shop, altogether making up thirty-three titled excerpts of discussions, dialogues (e.g., On the beautiful; On law; On virtue, that it cannot be taught; etc.), collected on one roll or book (*biblion*). One of the titles of the dialogues attributed to Phaedo s.v. is *Simon* and another is *Cobblers' Tales* (D. L. 2.105, noting that the latter has also been attributed to the Socratic Aeschines). One or the other may have featured Alcibiades III along with Socrates and their friends (cf. Ael. *VH* 2.1); Antisthenes too may have been present. See also the pseudo-Socratic *Epistles* (9.4, 12, and 18.2) among Simon, Aristippus and Antisthenes (see Hock 1976); Plutarch (*Mor.* 776a); et al. in *SSR* 2.VIB.

In modern bibliography.   Excavation reports appear in H. Thompson (1954: 51–4; 1955: 54; 1962: 112), popularized but abundantly illustrated in D. Thompson (1960), Lang (1978) and Camp (1986: 145–7). Among the range of views on the historicity of Simon, some (e.g., Lang 1978: 12; Vander Waerdt 1994: 2) take seriously not only that Simon wrote Socratic dialogues, but that he was *first* to do so, and thus was the originator of the genre. Others (e.g. Kahn 1996: 10 & n18), are adamant: "optimistic archaeologists digging in the Athenian agora claim to have found traces of Simon's workshop. . . . I can see no good reason to believe in his historical reality. This is one of the many examples where the imaginary creation produced by a Socratic author has become the source of a pseudo-historical tradition."

Prosopographical notes.   This is not the Simon accused of stealing public funds and perjuring himself in Aristophanes' *Clouds* (391–399).

Simonides of Ceos, son of Leoprepes (poet) See App. II.

Sisyphus of Pharsalus	[Pl.] *Sis.*	speaker
[Σίσυφος]	Theop. *hist.* frr. 18,	
active early 4th c.	356	

Sisyphus was a political leader in Pharsalus (Thessaly) at a time of Spartan and other aggression against the city.

Smicrion of Athens See App. II.

Socrates of Alopece, son of Sophroniscus I
[*PA* 13101 *LGPN2* 30 *RE* 5 *DPhA* 104 *OCD*³
PP PX Σωκράτης Σωφρονίσκου
Ἀλωπεκῆθεν]
469–399
mother: Phaenarete
maternal half brother: Patrocles
father of Lamprocles II, Sophroniscus II,
  Menexenus
wife: Xanthippe
student of Connus, Aspasia, Diotima
See stemma: Socrates.

Pl. *opera*   speaker
[Pl.] *opera*   speaker
Xen. *opera*
Antis. frr. in *SSR*
2.VA
Aes. frr. in *SSR*
2.VIA
Isocr. 11.5–6
D. S. 14.4.5–14.5.4,
  14.37.7
comedy (see below)

Family and property. Plato's Socrates says something about each of his parents, beyond their names (see Sophroniscus I s.v., Phaenarete s.v.), mentioning also his mother's second husband, Chaeredemus s.v., and his own maternal half brother, Patrocles s.v. (*Euthd.* 297e). He speaks of his three sons in the dialogues, but unnamed (*Ap.* 34d, 41e2, *Crito* 45c, 48c, 54a1b; Nehamas *OCD*³ "two sons" is an error). Nor does Socrates name Xanthippe, though Plato does (*Phd.* 60a). Indeed,

STEMMA: SOCRATES

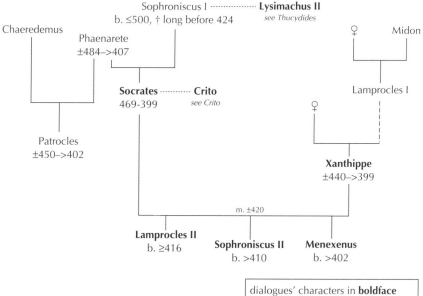

Xanthippe and all three sons are present in the *Phaedo* (60a, 116a–b). With respect to names, *Laches* (179a–181c) makes a number of points that bear on debates in the literature concerning the use of demotics and patronymics—e.g., that demotics were favored by democrats and patronymics by oligarchs—and reiterating the common Greek practice of naming a son after his grandfather. In two brief but implicit defenses of the use of patronymics, the dialogue articulates the fathers' hope that their sons will prove worthy of their names, and praises Socrates for continuing to use his long dead and excellent father's name. The dialogue also praises the demesman relationship (187d–e). Further, the dialogue suggests that the name 'Socrates' was often bandied about by youths who used neither his patronymic nor his demotic (181a), explaining why Lysimachus II—who has been hearing of a Socrates from his son and his son's friend—had not realized this was the same Socrates who was his fellow demesman in Alopece and the son of his own friend, Sophroniscus I. On Socrates' poverty, consider Xenophon's remark that everything Socrates owned, including his house, was worth five *minae* (*Oec.* 2.3).

Life.   Since it is unusual to learn much detail about the physical appearance of the ancients, it is worth noting that Socrates was said to have resembled the satyrs that one finds represented on clay pots of the classical period (Pl. *Smp.* 215a–c, 216c–d, 221d–e; Xen. *Symp.* 4.19); his physical description appears in Plato's *Theaetetus* (143e), Xenophon's *Symposium* (5.5–7) and Aristophanes' *Clouds* 362: Socrates went about barefoot and unwashed; had bulging eyes that darted sideways and enabled him, like a crab, to see not only what was straight ahead, but what was on the sides as well; a flatish upturned nose with wide-open nostrils that sniffed all around; large fleshy lips like an ass; an arrogant expression; and an intimidating swagger—which could be misinterpreted as condescending, as when other soldiers looked askance at Socrates' walking barefoot over the ice on the retreat from Delium: "they thought he was only doing it to spite them" (Pl. *Smp.* 220b). Aristoxenus, a part of the anti-socratic tradition, describes Socrates' anger vividly (frr. 54–9) on the authority of his father's personal recollections of Socrates.

There are persistent hints—but mere hints—that Socrates was related to the Athenian aristocracy, despite his own poverty and his refusal to use the Assembly as a forum. If so, and if such relations were generally known, they may have contributed to the general climate of hostility that ended with Socrates' execution. Indications appear elsewhere in this prosopography: See Patrocles s.v. for the wealth and possible archonship of Socrates' younger brother in the period of the Thirty. See Xanthippe s.v. for the suggestion that his wife's background was elite (perhaps related to Pericles I's family). See Excursus 3 and Theramenes s.v. for the period of the Thirty and its citizen roll of the Three Thousand. See Excursus 4 for the amnesty that was in effect when Socrates was tried. Not one of these hints—and not even all of them taken together—gives evidence that Socrates was himself complicitous with the Thirty.

Military career.   Socrates' service as a hoplite, a heavily armed foot soldier, included Potidaea, Amphipolis, and Delium. Potidaea revolted in April of 432, and Socrates, aged about thirty-seven, was among Athenian troops deployed that summer under Archestratus s.v., or in the fall under Callias s.v., to Potidaea; so was Alcibiades III s.v. There was a "battle of Potidaea" in June (Gomme *HCT*) or the fall (Planeaux 1999), followed by an extended siege that did not end until the population had been reduced to cannibalism (Thu. 2.70.1). Potidaea surrendered in the winter of 430/29 to three Athenian generals (including Xenophon s.v., son of Euripides) on terms that the population abandon the city. When this was accomplished, the Athenians set out for home but were detained near Spartolus (Thu. 2.79.1–7) where they were delivered a severe defeat, losing 430 men and all three commanding generals; this is where Socrates saved the wounded Alcibiades III and his armor (Pl. *Smp.* 220d–e). What was left of the army reached Athens only in May of 429 (Pl. *Chrm.* shows Socrates' return), having been away nearly three years. The exact dates are those of Gomme (*HCT* 1.222–4, 421–5 on Thu. 1.64–66, 2.58, 2.70) and Planeaux (1999: 74 on Thu. 2.79). The battle of Delium, fought in 424 under the joint leadership of Hippocrates s.v. and Demosthenes, began with Hippocrates' successful two-day fortification of a shrine to Apollo at Delium (Thu. 4.90.1–4). As the army withdrew, however, it was attacked by a buildup of Boeotian footsoldiers, then surprise-attacked by cavalry; when night fell, the Athenians fled (4.96.1–6). It is Socrates' heroic behavior during the retreat that Laches (Pl. *Lch.* 181b) and Alcibiades III (Pl. *Smp.* 221a) commend. Two years later, in 422, Socrates fought at Amphipolis, another Athenian disaster: though the Lacedaemonians under Brasidas and the Athenians under Cleon were relatively well matched, again the Athenians were surprised by an attack, losing about six hundred men in an overwhelming defeat that saw the deaths of both commanders (Thu. 5.6–5.11 with *CAH* 5²: 430). It was, in part, the losses at Delium and Amphipolis that prepared the Athenians to accept the Peace of Nicias in April of 421. Socrates' active military career appears to end when he is forty-seven, though his participation in campaigns other than these three defeats cannot be ruled out.

As president of Council after Arginusae.   It happened that Socrates was a *prytanis* (Pl. *Ap.* 32b; Xen. *Hell.* 1.7.15), and possibly the *epistatēs* (Xen. *Mem.* 1.1.8, 4.4.2; cf. *Grg.* 473e) for his tribe Antiochis on the day in October of 406 when six of the ten elected generals who were accused of failing to collect the wounded and dead after the sea battle at Arginusae were sentenced (see Exc. 2). The generals were being tried for a capital crime in one day—a flaw in the Athenian legal code which Socrates would later criticize (Pl. *Ap.* 37a–b)—but, what was worse, they were being tried as a group, in direct violation of the Athenian law of Cannonus requiring each defendant in a capital crime to receive a separate trial. Socrates, having sworn an oath to apply the law, attempted on that occasion to uphold the law, but succeeded only in winning some time for a defense speech by Euryptolemus III. All the generals were executed. By the following February, the people had begun to regret their haste (see Callixenus s.v.).

   In the twenty-four-hour period of Socrates' service, if he was in fact *epistatēs* as well as *prytanis*, he took office after the drawing of lots at dawn, and dined in the *tholos*, the round building adjacent to the *bouleutērion* where meetings of the Council (*boulē*) were held (see Plan 1). Because the new *bouleutērion* was probably first used 409–405 (Camp 1986: 91), we cannot be certain in which building Socrates

served. He had responsibility for presiding over the Assembly (*ecclēsia*) and Council, which condemned the generals that day, and he retired with one third of his
fellow tribesmen, those of one *trittys*, to the *tholos* for the night. Apart from
presiding, he guarded the symbols of the *polis* for the entire period: the keys to
the treasuries and archives, and the state seal used in official correspondence.

In comedy.   Socrates' earliest known mention in Athenian comedy is Callias' claim
in the *Pedētae* of ≤429/8 that he helped Euripides write his tragedies (fr. 15 [K
12]; cf. Euripides s.v. for similar accusations at Aristoph. *Neph.* fr. 392 [K 376] and
Tele. frr. 41–42 [K 39–40]). In 423, Socrates was a *kōmōidoumenos*, a person ridiculed
in comedy, in two of the three plays of the year's Dionysian festival. Because the
Clouds of Aristophanes is extant and marvelous, it is easy to forget that it placed
third that year behind Cratinus' *Wine Flask* and, more significantly, Amipsias'
Connus, a play about Socrates' music teacher, Connus s.v. (whose name was
possibly used as the title of a play by Phryn. as well). Socrates is "barefoot" in
one of Amipsias' extant fragments (*Con.* fr. 9 [K 9]), but we are not in a position
to know the extent of Socrates' role or, indeed, whether he appeared on stage at
all in that comedy. Taking *Connus* together with *Clouds,* however, one can be
fairly certain that, after the spring of 423, it would not have been possible for
Socrates to have had the sort of anonymity in Athens that is attributed to him at
Laches 181a.

Aristophanes' Socrates in the *Clouds* is, against the explicit protests of Plato's
Socrates (*Ap.* 18a–b, 19c), a plausible caricature of a natural scientist and sophist
who introduces new gods. On stage, Socrates appears suspended from the god-
walk in a basket and explains why he's there: "Why, for accurate discoveries
about meteorological phenomena I had to suspend my mind, to commingle my
rarefied thought with its kindred air. If I had been on the ground and from down
there contemplated what's up here, I would have made no discoveries at all: the
earth, you see, simply must forcibly draw to itself the moisture of thought"
(227–233). His school is represented as teaching other subjects as well: cosmology,
music, grammar, entomology, astronomy, and geometry. But only initiates into
the Cloud cult, reminiscent of the Eleusinian mystery cult (252–274 with note in
Henderson 1998c), receive instruction, for the traditional gods of Athens are
irrelevant in the Thinkery: "What do you mean you'll swear by the gods? First
of all, gods aren't legal tender here" (247–248), and "Zeus doesn't even exist!"
(367). The *real* gods are "this Void, and the Clouds, and the Tongue, and only
these three" (423–424). But the Clouds are important contributors to sophistry,
". . . they're heavenly Clouds, great goddesses for idle gentlemen, who provide
us with judgment and dialectic and intelligence, fantasy and circumlocution and
verbal thrust and parry" (316–318); ". . . they nourish a great many sophists . . ."
(331). However, Dover's thoughtful essay on Socrates' role in *Clouds* (1950: xxxii–
lvii) argues that the philosopher serves as a token of the 5th c. intellectual in
general; thus many of the gags should not be taken literally as representing the
Socrates of, for example, Plato or history. Dover uses contemporaneous citations
to show that some specific passages in the play apply not to Socrates, but to
Anaxagoras, Diogenes of Apollonia, and Hippias—other intellectuals altogether.
Dover also examines the anti-Platonic tradition (Aristox. frr. 54–9, Aristippus I

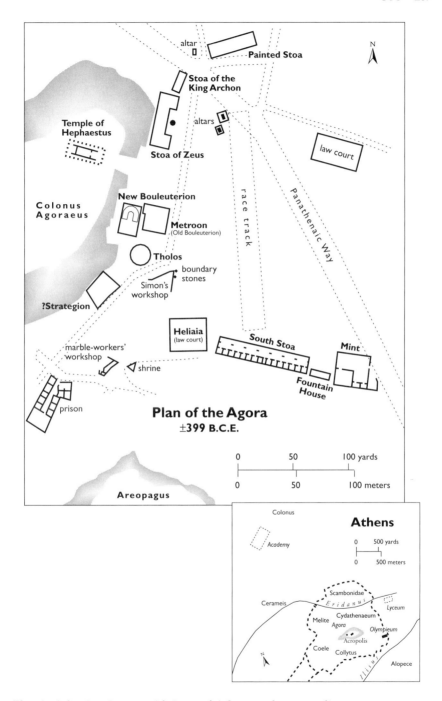

altar
Painted Stoa
N

Stoa of the
King Archon

Temple of
Hephaestus

altars

law court

Stoa of Zeus

Colonus
Agoraeus

New Bouleuterion

Metroon
(Old Bouleuterion)

Tholos

boundary
stones

Simon's
workshop

?Strategion

Heliaia
(law court)

South Stoa

Mint

race track

Panathenaic Way

marble-workers'
workshop

shrine

Fountain
House

prison

Plan of the Agora
±399 B.C.E.

| 0 | 50 | 100 yards |

| 0 | 50 | 100 meters |

Areopagus

Colonus

Athens

Academy

| 0 | 500 yards |

| 0 | 500 meters |

Scambonidae
Cerameis
Eridanus
Lyceum
Cydathenaeum
Melite
Agora
Olympieum
Acropolis
Coele
Collytus
Alopece
Ilissus

Plan 1. Athenian Agora, with inset of Athens and surrounding area.

of Cyrene s.v.) and finds it so mild with respect to the character of Socrates that "it is so far from weakening Plato's case that by implication it strengthens it" (xlviii).

When Socrates speaks of the comedy of Aristophanes as encouraging the belief that he "busies himself studying things in the sky and below the earth" (Pl. *Ap.* 19b–c), it is natural to think of Socrates on stage in the *Clouds*; but Aristophanes' lampooning of Socrates continued beyond *Clouds* to *Birds* in 414 (1280–3, 1553–5, including the coined verb, 'to socratize,' *sōkratein*) and to *Frogs* in 405 (1491–9).

In *Birds*, a herald praises the utopian Bird City as revered among earthlings: "Why, before you built this city all men were crazy about the Spartans: they wore their hair long, went hungry, never bathed, acted like Socrates, brandished batons" (1280–3, cf. Chaerephon s.v.). And the choral *strophe* beginning at 1553 in *Birds* is also accusing. In an underworld swamp, "unwashed Socrates conjures spirits" (ἄλουτος οὗ ψυχαγωγεῖ Σωκράτης); the pun is especially fine, given the contemporary view of Socratic dialectic as *psychagōgia* (lit. *psychē*-leading; cf. Teloh 1989, Howland 1993), but also because of its allusion to Aeschylus' *Psychagogoi*, a lost play in which Odysseus visits the underworld.

Nine years after *Birds*, in Aristophanes' *Frogs* 1491–9, the chorus sings,

> So what's stylish is not to sit
> beside Socrates and chatter,
> casting the arts aside
> and ignoring the best
> of the tragedian's craft.
> To hang around killing time
> in pretentious conversation
> and hairsplitting twaddle
> is the mark of a man who's lost his mind.

The comic poet Eupolis also spoofed Socrates, describing him as a sorry hairsplitter (fr. 386 [K 352]), and accusing him of stealing a wine ladle (*oinochoē*) at a party (fr. 395 [K 361]). Those frr., however, are not attributed to specific plays and cannot be dated more precisely than the 420s or early 410s.

Trial in 399. Favorinus states that he is quoting from the indictment preserved in the archive of the *polis*, the Metroön (i.e. the old *bouleutērion*, after the *boulē* moved into the new one; see Plan 1): "This indictment and affidavit is sworn by Meletus, the son of Meletus of Pitthos, against Socrates, the son of Sophroniscus of Alopece: Socrates is guilty of refusing to recognize the gods recognized by the state, and of introducing other new divinities. He is also guilty of corrupting the youth. The penalty demanded is death" (D. L. 2.40).

Citizens at least thirty years old volunteered for jury service at the beginning of the year, in midsummer; and a roster of six thousand potential jurymen was compiled. Who actually served in a particular trial—in the several civil and criminal courts of the city, with jury size determined by type of case—was probably determined by lot in 399, as it certainly was a little later in the 4th c., to help prevent the bribery that had characterized some of the trials of the 5th c. (see

Anytus I of Euonymon s.v.; Epicrates of Cephisia s.v.). Jury members were paid three *obols* per day from ≤425, just half what an able-bodied man could earn for a day's work, so the juries were dominated by the elderly and infirm, as Aristophanes depicts them in *Wasps* in 422. There is no hard evidence for juries with odd numbers in the 5th c., so that method of preventing tie votes may have been an innovation of the 4th c., but it has been argued (MacDowell 1978: 40) that references to juries of five hundred, the size of the jury for Socrates' trial, were even earlier understood to mean 501: in the mid-4th c., when we know the odd number had already been instituted, authors went on speaking loosely in round numbers, "five hundred." Much of the source material on Socrates' trial and execution is collected in Brickhouse and Smith (2002).

In the later tradition. Other entries in this prosopography include an abundance of references to Socrates that are not repeated or alluded to here. Among the more influential later references are Aristotle (*Meta.* 987b1–2, et al.); Athenaeus (184d–e); and Diogenes 2.18–47. *SSR* attempts to be comprehensive of contemporaneous and late antique sources in four vols., and provides an excellent starting place for research, but many passages are presented out of context and should be interpreted with great care. No doubt much Socratica has been lost: not only the works of Antisthenes and Aeschines, known now from others' quotations alone, but scores of dialogues from the hands of other Socratics that may have survived long enough to be catalogued by title, or may merely have been fabricated. See other entries s.vv. for evidence of prose production by members of the wider Socratic circle.

Socrates of Athens	Pl. *Tht.* 147c	present
[*PA* 13085 *LGPN2* 5 *RE* 6 *DPhA* 102 *PP*	Pl. *Sph.* 218b	present
Σωκράτης ὁ νεώτερος]	Pl. *Stm.*	speaker
b. mid 420s, † >360	[Pl.] *Ltr.* 11.358d–e	
"The Younger"	Aristot. *Meta.*	
	1036b25	

The young Socrates' date of birth is established by his youth in 399; Aristotle's remark on the comparison that the younger Socrates "used to make" puts him at the Academy sometime during the period 367–347, and—if *Letter* 11 has any relation to fact—he was ill in 360. The particular illness Socrates is said to have had, strangury (*stranguria*: strangled urine) is a condition in which an obstruction causes urine to be discharged spasmodically and painfully, drop by drop.

The name 'Socrates' was common: *LGPN2* lists 196, including four who predate Socrates of Alopece (the earliest is from the 6th c.), and as many as seven others whose lives overlapped his (four inscriptions are partially restored). There are some eighteen *more* Athenians who are apparently of the right age to be the younger Socrates. I have no reason whatever to think this is a fabricated character or a stand-in for someone else.

Solon of Athens, son of ?Execestides See App. II. *See stemma: Plato.*

Sophilus of Rhamnous See App. II.

Sophocles of Colonus, son of Sophilus (tragedian) See App. II.

Sophroniscus I of Alopece
[*PA* 13424 *LGPN2* 3 *PP* Σωφϱονίσϰος
Ἀλωπεϰῆθεν]
b. ≤500, † long before 424
wife: Phaenarete
father of Socrates
stonecutter (λιθουϱγοῦ)
See stemma: Socrates.

Pl. *Lch.* 181a et al. †
Pl. *Euthd.*
  297e–298b †
[Pl.] *G. Hp.* 298c
[Pl.] *Alc.* 131e, pat.
Xen. *Hell.* 1.7.15,
  pat.

We know little about Sophroniscus I. He was a close friend (fellow demesman) of Lysimachus II (*Lch.*), but appears chiefly as the patronymic of Socrates (D. L. 2.18, 2.40).

Sophroniscus II of Alopece, son of Socrates
[*PA* 13425 *LGPN2* 4 Σωφϱονίσϰος
Σωϰϱάτους Ἀλωπεϰῆθεν]
b. >410
mother: Xanthippe
brothers: Lamprocles II, Menexenus
See stemma: Socrates.

Pl. *Ap.* 34d *
Pl. *Phd.* 116b   present

Following the custom of the Athenians, Sophroniscus II received the name of a grandfather, in this case his paternal grandfather. What is unusual is that the name did not go to the first-born son, Lamprocles II s.v.

Sophroniscus of Paeania See App. II.

Sophrosyne, daughter of Dionysius I, and
  wife of Dionysius II, her half brother
[*LGPN3A* 4 Σωφϱοσύνα]
>396–>366/5
mother: Aristomache (sister of Dion)
siblings: Nysaeus, Hipparinus II, Arete (wife
  of Thearides and Dion); paternal half
  siblings: Dionysius II, Hermocritus II,
  Dicaeosyne (wife of Leptines I)
mother of Apollocrates
See stemma: Dion.

[Pl.] *Ltr.* 13.361a,
  unnamed *
GG 3.2.102–107
Plu. *Dion* 6

[Plato] commends Sophrosyne for taking care of him when he lived as a member of Dionysius II's household on his second visit to Sicily, and particularly for taking care of him when he was ill. He sends her a statue by Leochares s.v., transported by Leptines II, and sweet wine and honey for the children of the household.

Sosinomus of Athens, son of Aristonomus (banker) See App. II.

Speusippus of Myrrhinus, son of
  Eurymedon I
[*PA/APF* 12847 (3792.11D) *LGPN2* 6 *DPhA*
145 *OCD*³ *RE* 2 *PP* Σπεύσιππος
Εὐρυμέδοντος Μυρρινούσιος]
±407–339/8
mother: Potone
siblings: at least one sister
wife: his sister's daughter
father of ?Eurymedon II
friend of Dion
student and nephew of Plato
See stemma: Plato.

[Pl.] *Ltr.* 2.314e *
[Pl.] *Ltr.* 13 *
frr. in Tarán 1981
Ind. Acad. 1, 3, 9,
  31–32
Epi. fr. 10 (K 11)
Aristot. *Rh.* 1411a21,
  et al.
[Socr.] *Ep.* 30, 32, 33,
  35, 36
D. L., *passim*

Life. Having produced 521 pages on Plato's nephew, Speusippus, Tarán states disarmingly, "we are left with insufficient evidence to reconstruct more than the bare outline of Speusippus' life. Very little or nothing can be added to the following facts: he was the son of Plato's sister Potone and of Eurymedon of Myrrhinous; he was a member of the Academy and, at Plato's death, became its head; he was head of the school for eight years beginning in 348/7 B.C.; he dedicated statues of the *Charities* in the *temenos* of the Muses which Plato had set up in the Academy" (1981: 5). But Tarán also demonstrates in great detail something one suspects in several of the more famous persons encountered in Plato, that a tradition hostile to Speusippus grew up side by side with a sympathetic one, each made more extreme by the other. In the sympathetic tradition, Speusippus was particularly gregarious and charming, a good influence on the more staid Dion s.v.; his mobility problems were the result of the paralysis and pain that eventually led him to take his own life. In the hostile tradition, he was a philanderer with Axiothea and Lasthenia s.vv., and a stumbling drunkard who died of an infestation of lice. (Lice, by the way, *morbus pedicularis*, was one of the circulating explanations of Plato's death too—perhaps an oblique reference to the unwashed and bug-infested followers of Socrates that Aristophanes so often lampooned.)

Speusippus' birth is projected from his somewhat more reliably held death in 339/8, the second year of the 110th Olympiad (D. L. 4.14), and from his having been referred to as very old (γηραιὸς ὤν, D. L. 4.3) when he died. The *APF* and *LGPN2* date of birth for Speusippus, ±410, is probably too early, implying he lived to be seventy-one. Hicks (1925: 375) and Owen and Hornblower (*OCD*³) give 407, which is preferable. While dates of the deaths of prominent individuals appear often to have been noted and recorded accurately, Speusippus may have slipped from public view if he returned to the family property at Iphistiadae in illness; and his aged appearance might be accounted for by his increasingly debilitating paralysis, on which his younger contemporary, Aristotle, comments (*Rh.*; cf. D. L. 4.3 and [Pl.] *Ltr.* 2), the supposed reason why the headship of the Academy passed to Xenocrates some time before Speusippus' death. Speusippus is said to have accompanied Plato to Sicily in 361 ([Pl.] *Ltr.* 2), and said to have left some thirty memoirs and dialogues comprising 43,475 lines, purchased by Aristotle for three *talents* (D. L. 4.4–4.5). Aristotle mentions Speusippus several times, almost always on doctrinal matters.

Pseudo-Plato (*Ltr.* 13.361c–e, dated ≥365) makes a number of claims about Plato's family that apply—*if* true—to Speusippus as well: that Perictione, Speusippus' grandmother, was still alive; that Speusippus had married his niece, Potone's granddaughter; that two nieces of Plato (either Speusippus' siblings or first cousins) had died at about the same time, leaving four grandnieces whom Plato expected to provide with dowries. Eurymedon II, an executor named with Speusippus in Plato's will, was probably Speusippus' son but may have been his nephew *cum* brother-in-law.

In the later tradition and modern bibliography.   See Philostratus (*VA passim*); pseudo-Iamblichus (*TA* 82.10–85.23); Plutarch (*Mor.* 492a, *Dion* 17.22); Athenaeus (7.279e); Cicero (*Acad.* 1.4.17–18, *De nat.* 1.32); and the various ancient lives of Aristotle, quoted in Tarán, who collects both fragments (1981: 135–74) and testimonia (1981: 114–34) and provides thorough commentary. In prosopography, however, Tarán follows Burnet and *APF*.

Stephanus of Alopece, son of Thucydides I
[*PA*/*APF* 12884 (7268.3B) *LGPN2* 23 *PP*
Στέφανος Θουκυδίδου Ἀλωπεκῆθεν]
>475–>395
mother: sister of the wealthy Cimon II
brother: Melesias II
See stemma: Thucydides.

Pl. *Meno* 94b–c
[Pl.] *Virt.* 378a–c †
Polem. fr. 78
IG I³ 134

Stephanus' family was known for its wealth and political prominence on both sides of the family. Presumably in youth, Stephanus was a student of the wrestler, Eudorus s.v.; Stephanus' grandfather, Melesias I, had been a famous wrestler in his time. Stephanus was secretary of Council sometime after 415 (Polem., *IG*). By the time of pseudo-Plato, Stephanus and his brother, Melesias II s.v. (*Meno*), were dead, but well-known for their longevity (*Virt.*).

Stesagoras II of Laciadae, son of Cimon I See App. II. *See stemma: Thucydides.*

Stesagoras III of Laciadae See App. II.

Stesichorus of Himera, son of ?Euphemus (poet) See App. II.

Stesilaus of Athens   Pl. *Lch* 178a,
[*PA* 12905 *LGPN2* 3 Στησίλεως]   183c–184a *
active 420s
demonstrator of fighting in arms

Stesilaus is to the general as the sophist is to the philosopher: he puts on a display
of how to fight in arms (178a), invents new weapons (183d–e), and teaches his
skill to the young (179d–e). But Stesilaus cannot fight in a real battle, and his
newfangled weapons don't work. Laches s.v. is in a good position to know this
because, in the course of serving as general himself—presumably in 427/6 and
426/5 when he commanded the naval fleet in Sicily, Locri and Rhegium (Thu. 3; D.
S. 12)—he encountered in battle this same Stesilaus to whose display Lysimachus II
and Melesias II have now invited him. Laches' description of Stesilaus' slapstick
attempt to fight is perhaps the funniest passage in all of Plato (183c–184a).

Stesimbrotus of Thasos   Pl. *Ion* 530d *
[*LGPN1* 1 *RE* s.v. *DPhA* 160 *OCD*³ *PP PX*   Xen. *Smp.* 3.6
Στησιμβρότος]   frr. in *FGrH* 107
fl. late 5th c.

Historian, biographer, and Homeric critic who taught in Athens, criticized politicians and historians, and was a source for [Aristot.] *Ath. Pol.* Although mentioned
among rhapsodes in Plato's *Ion*, he appears to have been a literary critic, rather
than a performer, and is now included among historians.

Stratonicus of Athens (musician) See App. II.

Telauges of Samos   Aes. *Tel.* nos. 83–90
[*LGPN1* 1 *RE* s.v. Τηλαύγες]   [frr. 41–8 Dittmar]
?6–5th c.   D. L. 8.53, 55, 74
Pythagorean philosopher

The dialogue *Telauges* of Aeschines depicts Socrates and Critobulus in conversation
about asceticism with Telauges, a Pythagorean Burnet seemingly takes to have
lived in the time when Socrates was old enough that Critobulus could be a
participant too (1924: *Euthphr.* 2a1n). Diogenes identifies Telauges as the son of
Pythagoras (8.53), and also as the author of a letter commenting on Empedocles
(8.55, 74). The odds of his having had a real-life conversation with Socrates are

low, but they are zero for Critobulus, as Dittmar saw. *LGPN1* labels him of dubious historicity.

Telesippus of Cholarges, son of Hippocrates See App. II. *See stemma: Pericles.*

Temenus of Argos (legislator) See App. II.

Terillus of Syracuse	[Pl.] *Ltr.* 13.363c *
[Τήριλλος]	
son-in-law of Tison	
philosopher	

[Plato] requests that Dionysius II, unless he prefers someone else, give a present to Terillus, who makes the Sicily-Athens trip often, is a philosopher, and knows other things too. He is omitted from *LGPN3A*.

Terpsion of Megara	Pl. *Tht.*	speaker
[*LGPN2B* 1 *RE* 1 *PP* Τερψίων]	Pl. *Phd.* 59c	present
active late 5th–early 4th c.		
friend of Euclides		

Terpsion is represented as knowing Theaetetus well in 391, and of being interested in hearing the Socratic dialogue recorded by Euclides eight years before. He says he needs a rest because he has walked into the city of Megara from the surrounding rural area (*Tht.* 143a). This is almost humor, given that he is addressing his countryman, Euclides s.v., who has just walked 30 km. We know nothing further about Terpsion, but that has only paved the way for the later tradition to hypothesize; see pseudo-Socrates (*Ep.* 15.3, 21.1), Plutarch (*Mor.* 581a), et al. collected in *SSR* 2.VIB.

Teucrus (*metic*, stonemason) See App. II.

Thales of Miletus (philosopher) See App. II.

Theaetetus of Sunium, son of Euphronius	Pl. *Tht.*	speaker
[*PA* 6632, *LGPN2* 14 *PAA* 501840 *DPhA* 33	Pl. *Sph.*	speaker
OCD³ PP Θεαίτητος Εὐφρονίου Σουνιεύς]	Pl. *Stm.*	present
b. ±415, † spring of 391	Pap. 63–4	
student of Theodorus, Socrates	Procl. *Eucl.* 66.16	
associate of Plato, Euclides, Terpsion	Eucl. 10 schol. 62; 13	
mathematician, geometer	schol. 1	

Life and works.   If Theaetetus had been rich as well as brilliant, Davies (*APF*) might long ago have exploded the poignant fiction held by philosophers and historians of mathematics alike that Theaetetus taught mathematics in Plato's Academy from some time after the traditional date of its founding, 387, until his death in 369, and that Plato wrote the *Theaetetus* as a memorial to him when he died. Or maybe not, for myths are sometimes more resilient than truths. Kirchner (*PA*) stated in 1901 that Theaetetus was killed in the Corinthian war in 392, and Traill (*PAA*) has found no reason to alter the original evaluation of the evidence. I will explain below why I think 391 is more likely than 392, but let us look to Theaetetus' life before his death.

Theaetetus is represented in the dialogues as *meirakion*, but on the young side, for he is not fully grown (155b); and Socrates says to Theodorus, "Look at the company then. They are all children but you" where *paides* (*Tht.* 168d8) balances *meirakion* (168e2). The company is a group of late adolescents in a gymnasium who have had their geometry lesson and proceeded to their athletic exercise. In the introductory section of the *Theaetetus* (143e–144b), the geometry teacher, Theodorus s.v., describes Theaetetus' remarkable intellect, his quick mind and retentive memory, as the finest he has ever encountered in any human being; and he adds that Theaetetus' sharp intellect is accompanied by many other admirable qualities—gentleness, bravery, generosity, steadiness—so rarely found together that Theodorus previously thought the combination impossible. Yet the boy was in no danger of being anyone's beloved, for he was bug-eyed and snub-nosed, like Socrates, and further like Socrates, had no property: he was an orphan whose inheritance had been frittered away or squandered by trustees. Socrates knew Theaetetus' father, Euphronius, whom he describes as similarly gifted. The dialogue goes on to show just how mathematically precocious Theaetetus was.

It is important to distinguish what Theaetetus actually says in the dialogue from the mathematical developments attributed to him by later sources seeking the origins of what Euclid codified in *Elements*. As a known individual, Theaetetus was a handy hook on whom to hang later mathematical discoveries nascent in his remarks (or nascent in other dialogues, e.g. the mathematics curriculum in *R.* 7.524d–531e, or the "five regular solids" of *Ti.* 54d–55c, or the two means of *Ti.* 31b–32b, or the mean of *Prm.* 154b–d), then to infer he actually *made* the discoveries and articulated them fully to and with other working mathematicians in Plato's Academy in the fruitful decades before his death. While no one should hesitate to attribute to Theaetetus a surpassing mathematical intuition, there is scant evidence for much of what has come to be attributed to him. While Cherniss (1945: 66–8) is right to see the early Academy as devoted primarily to the study of mathematics (see below), the propaedeutic for dialectic, we know neither that Theaetetus was a participant in that activity nor, if he was, which later innovations and refinements were his, if any.

Theodorus' diagrammatic demonstration is discussed s.v. After having attended closely to the demonstration, the boys proposed to discover a general definition, a single term under which all the powers could be collected (Theaetetus generously included the young Socrates in his narration of the procedure, 147d). The boys succeeded, concluding, "any line which produces in square an oblong number we defined under the term 'power,' for the reason that although it is incommensurable with the former in length, it is commensurable in the plane figures which they respectively have the power to produce" (explained in its equivalent modern terminology by Burnyeat 1978: 494, and at PCW 164n2). This confident description marks a historical watershed in the problem of incommensurability. Theaetetus' second ground-breaking contribution was his insight that, "there is another distinction of the same sort with regard to solids" (148b, i.e. rational and irrational cube roots). Pappus, citing Aristotle's student, Eudemus, credits Theaetetus with developments in rational and irrational continuous quantities, as in Plato, but adds something new: that he "divided the more generally known irrational lines according to the different means, assigning the medial line to geometry, the binomial to arithmetic, and the apotome to harmony." The first scholium to book 13 of Euclid states that Theaetetus also added the octahedron and icosahedron to the Pythagoreans' cube, pyramid, and dodecahedron for a total of five regular solids. The provenance of these latter attributions is uncertain. Other less well-known mathematicians (see below) were at work, some of them in the Academy, and may have shared responsibility. Assuming all of it to be correctly attributed to Theaetetus, however, the question arises whether he could accomplish it all in less than a decade following Socrates' death.

In the 1910s, modern scholars (Vogt 1909–10, Sachs 1914) began to suppose that he could not. They found a later battle in Corinth, a famous one in 369, and attached Theaetetus' death to that one; the suggestion was immediately and eagerly accepted. One of the reasons for the enthusiasm was that a later date neatly fit the then-growing developmentalist movement (against which Raeder 1905 and Ritter 1910 were already cautioning), according to which the dialogue's content "proves" it was written just before the late *Sophist* and *Statesman*. And some people were attracted by the very idea of Plato's writing a moving obituary for an Academic colleague with whom he had been teaching for nearly twenty years. Historians of mathematics were pleased to be able to locate and date ancient mathematical developments within the Academy itself; Fowler (1999: 360) describes Theaetetus' death in 369 as "generally regarded as one fixed point, perhaps the only secure fixed point, in the shifting sands of the incommensurability issue" (at the same time doubting its security). Convenient and touching as it was, 369 raises two almost insuperable prosopographical problems (explicit in Thesleff 1990: 149–50): Athens was almost certainly not mustering forty-six-year-old academics for hoplite combat by 369; Theaetetus' skillful soldiering (142b–c) was far more likely to have been exhibited when he was of military age, twenty-four. Second, Euclides' 30-km. walk, from which he has just returned as the dialogue's frame begins, is more likely for a man of fifty-nine than a man of eighty-one. Further, the remark of Socrates that seems so prescient to Euclides and Terpsion, the query whether Theaetetus will live to grow up (142c–d), is appropriately applied to a man who dies before reaching thirty, but hardly for one who reaches forty-six.

Those who insist that Theaetetus was involved in the mathematics of the early decades of the Academy are invited to imagine that Theaetetus recovered from his wounds and dysentery and lived on for as long as they like (the year 369 becomes irrelevant when no battle is required to kill him off). If, however, Theaetetus died of his wounds, then the battle in which he was engaged was probably fought in the spring of 391, and I turn now to that minor issue.

By the spring of 393, Athens had reconstituted her empire, with the Spartans having been driven back to the Peloponnese with the help of the Persian Pharnabazus and the King's gold (Xen. *Hell.* 4.8.1–3; Demos. 20.69). By midsummer, the Athenians were rebuilding the long walls between Athens and the Piraeus under Conon's supervision. Corinth (see Map 1), nominally an Athenian ally, but suffering under Spartan incursions (Philoch. fr. 150; Demos. 4.24), revolted in March of 392. The revolt was quashed internally by mercenaries under Iphicrates. Xenophon says explicitly that, by this time, neither side was employing citizen armies anymore, but using mercenaries to prosecute their wars (*Hell.* 4.4.14). A Spartan effort to cut off Persian funding to Athens by making a separate peace with the King was foiled by the envoys of the Athenians and her allies in the summer of 392 (4.8.12–15—including Hermogenes s.v.). Meanwhile, exiles fleeing the Corinthian revolution invited a Spartan regiment under Praxitas within the long walls connecting Corinth to her port, Lechaeum. In the ensuing battle, it first appeared that the Spartans would be routed, but the tide turned and there was heavy loss of life among the panicked allies; the Spartans took control of the port, tore down a section of the long wall, stationed outposts, and returned home (Xen. *Hell.* 4.4.7–13; cf. the highly condensed D. S. 14.86.1–4). The war season was over without citizen involvement by Athenians, except by those impoverished enough to sign on as mercenaries (Aristoph. *Eccl.* 197).

In the winter of 392/1, Sparta called a general peace conference, the terms of which Athens rejected (Andoc. 3). With Iphicrates' contingent otherwise occupied (Xen. *Hell.* 4.4.15–16; D. S. 14.91.3), the Athenians then sent a full force (πανδημεί) including masons and builders to retake Lechaeum and rebuild the walls. Having moved quickly at first, the Athenians then slowed their efforts (Xen. *Hell.* 4.4.18). In the spring of 391, the Spartans set out under Agesilaus and his brother Teleutias against Argos, then turned and attacked Corinth. It was in this second battle, involving army regulars, that Theaetetus, aged twenty-four, was likely to have been mortally wounded. Theaetetus is thus no exception to the rule that mathematicians do most of their creative work while very young.

In the later tradition and modern bibliography.   We do not have, except embedded in the reports of later authors (esp. Pappus), the commentary of Eudemus, written in the latter half of the 4th c. B.C.E., i.e., pre-Euclid, though Proclus' summary at the head of Euclid's *Elements* appears to be based on it, probably at second hand. Proclus lists as the first mathematicians associated with Plato: Leodamas of Thasos s.v., Archytas of Taras s.v., and Theaetetus. Younger was Neoclides, whose student Leon collected an *Elements* and discovered the principle in use at *Meno* 86e–87b. Still younger was Eudoxus of Cnidos s.v.—who is the first said explicitly to have been an associate *of the Academy*. Amyclas (var. Amyntas), Menaechmus and his brother Dinostratus, Theudius of Magnesia, who arranged an *Elements*, appear to have been the next grouping by age, followed by Hermotimus of Colophon and Philip of Opus s.v. Proclus provides additional details about the achievements of most of them.

Extant mathematical commentaries on *Theaetetus* begin much later, with an anonymous commentary in the 2nd c. C.E., then Pappus in the 3rd c., and Iamblichus in the 4th c. The scholia to Euclid are of varying date. Burnyeat (1978), who cites several useful earlier modern sources, uses the dramatic features of the dialogue—the long-lived Theaetetus—to argue for the greatest possible participation by Theaetetus in mathematics until 369. Fowler (1999), more suspicious of the literary approach, devotes considerable attention to the dialogue in his second edition and cites a number of articles on the mathematics of *Theaetetus* that have appeared since Burnyeat. Diogenes (2.29) puts a different ending onto *Theaetetus:* Socrates sent Theaetetus away divinely inspired after a conversation about knowledge.

Theages of Anagyrus, son of Demodocus
[*PA* 6615 *LGPN2* 1 *PAA* 501640 *RE* 2 *DPhA*
28 *OCD*³ *PP* Θεάγης Δημοδόκου
Ἀναγράσιος]
brother: Paralius

Pl. *Ap.* 33e †
Pl. *R.* 496b *
[Pl.] *Thg.*   speaker
Ael. *VH* 4.15, 8.1

Theages is mentioned as an example of someone whose political ambition was thwarted by ill health that kept him studying philosophy (*R.*), and whose father's many official offices and honors would otherwise have made plausible a public career in Athens (*Thg*). Cf. Demodocus s.v.

Thearion of Athens
[*LGPN2* 1 *PAA* 501987 *PP* Θεαρίων]
fl. late 5th c.
well-known baker

Pl. *Grg.* 518b *
Aristoph. *Aiol.* fr. 1
  (K 1)
Aristoph. *Gery.* fr.
  177 (K 155)
Antipha. *Om.* fr. 174
  (K 176)
Ath. 112c–e

Thearion taught others to shape dough so that the baked loaves of bread would have animal forms (Antipha.).

Themistocles I of Phrearrhi, son of Neocles I
[*PA/APF* 6669 *LGPN2* 39 *PAA* 502610 *RE* 1
DPhA 43 *OCD*³ *PP PX* Θεμιστοκλῆς
(var. –θοκλῆς) Νεοκλέους Φρεάρριος]
±524–±459
mother: non-Athenian woman
one sibling, probably a brother (parent of
  Phrasicles)
wives: (1) Archippe, daughter of Lysander of
  Alopece; (2) unnamed
offspring: (1) five sons, including
  Cleophantus; (2) three daughters; two
  daughters with an unnamed woman
renowned political and military leader

Pl. *Grg.* 455e–519a,
  passim †
Pl. *Meno* 93d
Pl. *R.* 329e
[Pl.] *Thg.* 126a
[Pl.] *Ax.* 368d
[Pl.] *Virt.*
  376c–377d †
Aes. *Alc.* no. 42 (fr.
  1 Dittmar)
Aes. *Alc.* no. 48 (*P.
  Oxy.* 1608.1)
Aes. *Alc.* nos. 49–51
  (frr. 8–10 Dittmar)

Xen. *Mem.* 2.6.13,
3.6.2, 4.2.2
Xen. *Symp.* 8.39
inscriptions (see
below)
Hdt. 7–8, *passim*

Life and family.   Themistocles was a famous man from long ago by Plato's time
and even Socrates'; Thucydides adds that he was the most famous Athenian of
his own time as well (1.138.6). His family had cult income, and was affluent
enough to perform its due liturgies in the 5th c., but did not display its wealth
ostentatiously, and had neither public political activity to its credit, nor social
connections, that might have encouraged Themistocles' aspirations for a public
career. The tradition traced to Aeschines (no. 48) that Themistocles was renounced
and disinherited by his father is falsified by his later possession of the family
estate at Phrearrhi and by *ostraka* bearing his name that as often as not include
his patronymic, son of Neocles; but Plutarch's milder version of the disapproving
father, in which Neocles attempted to persuade his son to stay out of politics
since he would have to succeed entirely by his own devices (*Them.* 2.7), may
be based on similar considerations; *APF* points to Thucydides' comment that
Themistocles (1.38.3),

> displaying the very surest signs of natural ability, was far and away more
> worthy than anyone else of admiration for this quality. By native intelligence,
> without preparing or supplementing it by study, he was with the briefest
> deliberation the most effective in decisions about immediate situations and
> the best at conjecturing what would happen farthest into the future.

Even without a fancy education or rhetorical training, that is, Themistocles was
impressive—or impressive to Thucydides. Socrates implies that he deserved the
ostracism the city voted (*Grg.* 516d), criticizes his advice to Athens to build dock-
yards and harbors (519a), and finds fault with him as a father.

   Only one of Themistocles' ten children is likely to be of any interest: Cleophon-
tus follows the pattern, familiar in Plato, of being the passable son of a renowned
father; he was quite a skilled horseman, but not known for wisdom or goodness
(*Meno* 93c–e; cf. [Pl.] *Virt.*). Plutarch names and follows the other nine (*Them.*
32.1–3), one of whom, Diocles, was adopted by his maternal grandfather and took
Alopece as his deme, two half siblings married one another, another daughter
married Themistocles' nephew, Phrasicles, and reared Themistocles' youngest
daughter, Asia; Plutarch also records the marriages of the two daughters by a
third woman.

   Themistocles himself rose to wealth as well as fame; for the evidence of land,
horses, liturgies, politically motivated largesse, shrines, and sanctuaries (this last
based primarily on *IG* II^2 1035; see *APF* 6669.4–5). Themistocles' condemnation,
which resulted in the confiscation of his property, provided a public reckoning
that enabled Demosthenes (23.207, with Plu. *Them.* 22.2) to comment on the modest
size of his townhouse in Melite, and Critias IV (DK 88 fr. 45, with Theop. *hist.* fr.

86) to say that the three *talents* with which Themistocles began his career had increased to over a hundred by the time he was condemned. Even so, his wealth remained inferior to that of his longtime political rival, Cimon II s.v., but superior to the austere third in the rivalry, Aristides I s.v. Thucydides says that Themistocles' family secretly brought home his bones after his death in Persia (1.138.6), it being illegal to inter a criminal in Attic soil; his reputation was rehabilitated, however, enabling a tomb to be constructed in the city, probably in 393 (Pau. 1.1.2; Philoch. fr. 201; Pl. *com.* fr. 199 [K 183]; and Aristoph. *Eccl.* 1105–1111).

Career in brief.   Themistocles was eponymous archon in 493/2, during which time he directed the construction of the long walls to the Piraeus (Thu. 1.93.3). It can be inferred that he was rising into prominence as a political leader in the 480s, for he was often suggested for ostracism, though he avoided it then (Burn and Rhodes, *OCD*[3], count 2,264 separate *ostraka*; see the list in *PAA* including *Agora*, *Hesperia*, *Kera.*, *AM*, *IG*, and *SEG*). Ostracism was instituted to protect Athens from would-be tyrants, presumably as a part of Cleisthenes' reforms (see App. III), but the institution was not employed immediately or consistently. Nevertheless, the 480s was a period of enthusiasm for ostracism. If a man appeared to be gaining too much power, he could be exiled for a period of ten years (with or without his family) and lose neither his citizenship nor his property. Political factions appear to have promoted the practice and even to have organized some aspects of it: 190 'Themistocles' *ostraka* were found together in a well. On inspection of the handwriting, they proved to have been written by only ten to fourteen individuals who apparently intended to assist undecided voters at the polls. It was the fact that the system could be abused to dispose of rivals that led, but slowly, to its decline and abandonment (Camp 1986: 58–9).

In 483/2, Themistocles persuaded the Athenians to use profits from the silver mines at Laurium to enlarge the fleet, adding at least a hundred triremes (Hdt. 7.144; Thu. 1.14.3; [Aristot.] *Ath. Pol.* 22.7 adds a note of trickery to the account). According to Herodotus and later authors, Themistocles served as general against the Persians on land and at sea, earning admiration and honors primarily through strategies that worked politically and on the battlefield: in 480, he determined how to remove the Ionians and Carians from the Persian fleet, masterminded the evacuation of the city of Athens (*ML* 23.1), and tricked the Persians into entering the harbor at Salamis. When victory was certain for the Athenians, he sent a message currying favor with Xerxes by assisting his retreat. Diodorus and Plutarch fill in some missing years from 480 to 470 with public and liturgical activity, but it was in 470 that Themistocles was ostracized and went to Argos, from which he visited other cities.

It is Thucydides who takes up the story at this point (1.135.2). During a Spartan investigation of their own citizen, Pausanias, evidence is said to have emerged implicating Themistocles in treachery with the Persians. Sparta and Athens together sent retainers to Argos to apprehend him for trial in ±466 (Lewis *CAH* 5[2]: 106), but Themistocles had meanwhile escaped. Athens condemned him to death *in absentia* (Crater. fr. 11). Sparta hounded him on his circuitous flight to Persia where he supplicated to the new king, Artaxerxes I, reminding him that he had helped Xerxes to retreat after Salamis. Granted a year of grace in which to learn the language and ways of the Persians, he impressed the court when he was finally presented to the King, who ensured his income by making him governor of Magnesia, giving him Lampsacus (for its wine) and Myos as well. Thucydides insists against anecdotes then current that Themistocles died of disease.

In the later tradition.   Only Herodotus, fragments of other historians recorded mostly by Plutarch, and physical remains (*ostraka*, inscriptions) are contemporaneous, for Themistocles was long dead before the Socratics were born. A few citations from the late 5th and early 4th c. may contribute a broader view of how Themistocles was viewed in Athens by the time Plato was writing dialogues (Aristoph. *Knights* 813; Thu. 1, *passim*, Isocr. 15.233; Demos. 19.303). Both Plutarch and Nepos wrote biographies of Themistocles that have powerfully affected how his life has been understood since. He is mentioned in many other late antique sources as well, some of which are incorporated into citations of frr. of Aeschines above. See pseudo-Aristotle (*Ath. Pol.* 22–3); Diodorus (11, *passim*); Athenaeus (576c–d); and Dionysius (*AR* 6.34).

Theodorus of Byzantium   Pl. *Phdr.* 261c, 266e
[*PP* Θεόδωρος]   Aristot. *Rh.*, *passim*

Theodorus was a rhetorician who introduced a number of distinctions in forensic rhetoric (*Phdr.*), and more terms for rhetorical devices than there were genuine differences (Aristot. *Rh.* 1414b11–18). Aristotle mentions Theodorus more favorably as having altered the art of rhetoric generally (1400b16), and explains how Theodorus' rhetorical novelties were supposed to work in practice, surprising the listener (1412a25–b2). The later rhetorician of the same name from Gadara was tutor to the future Roman emperor, Tiberius.

Theodorus of Cyrene   Pl. *Tht.*   speaker
[*LPGN1* 43 *RE* 31 *DPhA* 61 *OCD³ PP PX*   Pl. *Sph.*   speaker
Θεόδωρος]   Pl. *Stm.*   speaker
fl. late 5th c.   Xen. *Mem.* 4.2.10
associate and friend of Protagoras
teacher of Theaetetus
geometer

Life.   Plato is said to have visited the mathematician Theodorus in Cyrene after Socrates' death (D. L. 3.6). Cyrene, the name for both the city and the area within which it was situated, including other settlements as well, was a major Greek colony in northern Africa, due south of the Peloponnese, founded by Thera in about 630. Plato's dialogues represent Theodorus as teaching in Athens in 399 while still having students in Cyrene as well, fitting the tradition that Plato went there to study more mathematics. Theodorus is not known as a mathematician in contemporaneous sources other than Plato, except Xenophon, whose comment is likely to be derivative from Plato's dialogues. Thus the historicity of Theodorus' contribution to the development of mathematics as reported by Plato has been questioned from time to time. (Bryson s.v. is another example of someone who made a single contribution—rather, for whom only one contribution is known.)

Works and modern bibliography.   As Theodorus' friend Protagoras said "man is the measure (*metron*) of all things," Theodorus is the measure (*metron*) of geometrical diagrams (*Tht.* 169a), and it is a diagram that he uses to address the problem of incommensurability by demonstrating what we would now call irrational numbers to Theaetetus and other young students (*Tht.* 147d), a demonstration interpolated in the text of Euclid at 10.117 (Thomas 1991: 110na). One ingenious diagram—showing why Theodorus cannot go higher than 17 with his diagrammatic procedure—is not often enough reproduced (see Thesleff 1990: 152, citing precedents in 1913 and 1941). Fowler (1999: 378–9n20), critical of a different diagrammatic approach (Artmann 1994), discusses two others, including one arithmetical proof that also must break down at 17. Burnyeat's note on the mathematics (PCW 164n2) is useful. See also the heated exchange on the matter in *Isis* between Burnyeat (1978), who privileges a literary context for the conversation, and Knorr (1979, with a reply from Burnyeat), whose approach is historical.

Prosopographical notes and the later tradition.   The Cyrenaic philosopher, Theodorus (D. L. 2.97–103), lived a century later than the geometer, i.e., at the end of 4th and beginning of the 3rd c.; Diogenes warns that they are separate individuals (2.103, where Plato's being Theodorus' student is stated in passing and deserves no credit), but testimonia collected in *SSR* 2.IVH show that the two have been persistently conflated since ancient times. See also Proclus (*Eucl.* 66.6–7, 118.7–8) and Iamblichus (*CMS* 77.24–78.1).

Theodorus of Samos, son of Telecles   Pl. *Ion* 533b
[*LGPN1* 187 *RE* 195 *OCD*[3] Θεόδωρος]   Hdt. 1.51, 3.41, 7.27
active ±550–520

By Socrates' time, Theodorus was well-known as a sculptor, architect, and inventor of tools who worked not only on Samos, but in Sparta and Ephesus as well, and whose smaller works in precious metals (notable in Herodotus) ended up in many places. Some of his architectural works (public buildings) were still standing, and his realistic bronze self-portrait was being exhibited, when Pliny was traveling around Greece, describing what he saw in the 1st c. c.e. (*HN* 34.183, 35.152, 36.90, 36.95).

Theodote of Athens   Xen. *Mem.* 3.11.1–18
[*LGPN2* 1 *PAA* 505035 *PX* Θεοδότη]   Ath. 220e; 535c,
active in the late 5th c.   574e, 588d
hetaira

Theodote was, reputedly, a beautiful *hetaira* in Athens to whose house Socrates goes with a companion; he converses with Theodote, while her mother is at her side, about how she can best attract men, and tells her to come to him to learn about potions and charms. She mentions that Cebes, Simmias, Apollodorus and

Antisthenes are among her visitors. In the later tradition (Ath.), the Theodote of Xenophon is said to have been a companion of Alcibiades III as well.

Theodotes of Syracuse   Pl. *Ltr.* 7.348c–349e *
[*PP* Θεοδότας]   [Pl.] *Ltr.* 3.318c,
friend of Dion   4.320e–321b *
friend of Heraclides   Plu. *Dion* 12
                                                    D. L. 3.21

This aristocrat assisted Plato in trying to save Heraclides' life, under threat from Dionysius II.

Theodotus of Athmonon, son of Theozotides I   Pl. *Ap.* 33e †
[*PA/APF* 6794 (6915) *LGPN2* 36 *PAA* 505325
PP Θεόδοτος Θεοζοτίδου Ἀθμονεύς]
±418–<399
brother: Nicostratus I

Theognis of Megara (poet) See App. II.

Theozotides I of Athmonon   Pl. *Ap.* 33e *
[*PA/APF* 6914 (6915) (*APF* 6914 = 6913)   Crat. fr. 489 (K 337)
LGPN2 2 *PAA* 507785 *PP* Θεοζοτίδης   Lys. frr. 8, 10
Ἀθμονεύς]   *SEG* 28.46.3
≤451–≥399   *IG* II² 5 + *SEG*
father of Nicostratus I, Theodotus   14.36.3, 11
democratic leader

Life.   Two frr. of Lysias mention the uncommon name 'Theozotides'; and Stroud (1971: 296–7) argues cogently for the identification of both frr. with Theozotides I of Plato's *Apology* and also with the proposer of a rider to a bill in 400 (*IG* II² 5). In fr. 8 (*P. Hib.*), Theozotides I (ms. var. Θεοδοτίδης) has lent a considerable sum of money to the accused, who has paid the loan with yet another loan from the man now prosecuting him.

Theozotides I, the opponent of Lysias' client who is the speaker of fr. 10, is an active democratic politician who has proposed a decree to extend the existing provision of pensions to orphans of *foreign* wars so that the sons of democratic Athenians killed in the *civil* war against the oligarchy would also be covered. The speaker objects to the limitation of the provision to the legitimate sons of Athenians, proposing that adopted and illegitimate sons (*nothoi*) be included as well. The decree addressed by fr. 10 has only recently come to light from excavations in the Athenian agora (*IG* II² 10)—Stroud published the text of the marble *stele* in 1971—making it certain that Theozotides won the case; otherwise the decree would not have been published. A second part of fr. 10 refers scathingly to what was probably a previous bill, also proposed by Theozotides, to raise the pay of mounted archers while decreasing that of the regular cavalry. Grenfell and Hunt (1919: 13.55) note that it is a democratic measure to reward nonaristocratic archers while punishing the *hippeis* class, but that the cavalry had in fact remained in the city under the oligarchy and done the bidding of the Thirty; Stroud (1971: 298) cites Xenophon (*Hell.* 3.1.4) and Lysias (16.6, 26.10) for the difficulties faced by *hippeis* in passing scrutiny for office under the democracy.

Prosopographical notes. *APF* removed the demotic of Cicunna (already "uncertain" in *PA*), adding that the most likely deme, Athmonon, so far "lacks the necessary prosopographical confirmation." *LGPN2* accepted Athmonon and added "cf. *PA* 6915." *PAA* gives no demotic for Theozotides but gives Athmonon for his sons. The confirmation is found in the son of Nicostratus I, who is the grandson of Theozotides I, Theozotides II: one of two inscriptions naming him provides the demotic (*IG* XII 5.542.35, a foreign decree), and the other the tribe Kekropis (which includes the deme Athmonon). Because the demotic passed through the male line, it is usually safe to argue from the grandson back to the paternal grandfather. Theozotides is missing from the *PP* index but appears on p. 223.

Theramenes of Stiria, son of Hagnon
[*PA/APF* 7234 *LGPN2* 7 *PAA* 513930 *RE* 7
*OCD*³ Θηραμένης Ἁγνῶνος Στειριεύς]
≤440–404
student of Prodicus
teacher of ?Isocrates
resilient politician of changing affiliation
Cf. stemma: Lysias.

[Pl.] *Ax.* 368d †
Aes. *Cal.* no. 73 (fr.
  34 Dittmar)
Aes. *Mil.* no. 77 (fr.
  37 Dittmar)
Xen. *Hell.* 1–2,
  passim
Thu. 8.68.4, 89.2,
  92.9
D. S. 13–14, *passim*
Eu., *Pol.* fr. 251 (K
  237)
Aristoph. *Frogs*
  533–541, 965–970
Aristoph. *Clouds* 361
  schol.
Lys. 12.62–78;
  13.9–19
P. Mich. 5982
[Aristot.] *Ath. Pol.*
  28.3–37.1, *passim*

Life. Theramenes' father, Hagnon, who appears in Aeschines' fragmentary *Milti-ades*, was a prominent general, a partisan of Pericles I, and a member of the *proboulē* after the Sicilian catastrophe, but there is no clear indication of wealth in his generation or his son's. Theramenes was a student of Prodicus, and was thus the butt of jokes (Eu., Aristoph. *Clouds*, *Frogs* 968–970) that he was really from Ceos and had merely been adopted by Hagnon. Theramenes is not known to have married, and neither his name nor his father's appears again in the ancient period in his deme, so the family may have been cut off with his death in 404.

With the Four Hundred in 411.   While serving as general, Theramenes was at first a leader in the establishment of the Four Hundred in 411 (Thu. 8.68.4), but then turned against that oligarchy. He lent his support instead to the relatively more democratic oligarchy of the Five Thousand (Thu. 8.89.2–8.94.1; [Aristot.] *Ath. Pol.* 32.2); the Platonic character with the same profile—*pro* then *contra*—is Clitophon s.v. Aristophanes will later link Theramenes and Clitophon in *Frogs* (965–967)—opportunists more clever than wise. Theramenes also supported the recall of Alcibiades III (D. S. 13.38.2) to the fleet. He did at least one other thing to retain the good will of the people in the retributive aftermath of the Four Hundred: he turned on Antiphon of Rhamnous s.v., his former co-leader, and succeeded in seeing him executed by the newly restored democracy (cf. Andron s.v.).

Theramenes continued to be elected as general. Diodorus chronicles his participation at Cyzicus in 410 (13.50.1–7) and on campaign through 408 (13.64.3, 13.66.1–3; cf. Xen. *Hell.* 1.3.8); but the claim that he returned to Athens with Alcibiades III in 407 has no contemporaneous source (cf. Plu. *Alc.* 32.4; Nep. *Alc.* 6.3).

At Arginusae in 406.   Theramenes was captain, perhaps *trierarch*, of a ship at the naval battle of Arginusae (see Exc. 2). Afterwards, when the fleet had failed to collect the casualties, and after the generals had been accused of negligence by Theramenes et al., Xenophon states that when Theramenes saw some of his *phratores* appearing in mourning and with shorn heads at the Apaturia festival, he persuaded them to attend the Assembly meeting that was to decide the fate of the generals, thus artificially exaggerating the number of actual mourners. Again according to Xenophon, Theramenes bribed Callixenus s.v. to make an illegal motion to try the generals *en masse* (1.7.8–9). Because these two details of Xenophon's version are nowhere corroborated, and because Theramenes, unlike Callixenus, was subject to no reprisals in the months after the trial, there is good reason to think that Xenophon was, as Andrewes (1974: 122) suggests, probably not guilty of such extensive deceit. While it is true that Aristophanes is not very negative toward him in the *Frogs* of 405 (lnn. 533–541), saying in effect that he was the sort of man who always knew how to stay on top, it is also true that Theramenes failed to pass scrutiny (*dokimasia*) for general that year although he had been elected for his tribe (Lys. 13.10).

As a member of the Thirty.   Theramenes was, at his own request, sent by the Athenians in 404 to negotiate with Lysander of Sparta, but he returned after more than three months with a settlement humiliating for Athens that had been imposed by the Spartan *ephors*, Lysander having no authority in the matter (Xen. *Hell.* 2.2.16–20; cf. Lys. 13.9–11). As Diodorus is silent about the embassy and its failure, Xenophon is silent about Theramenes' role in the establishment of the Thirty: Diodorus (14.3.5–7) credits Theramenes with openly but unsuccessfully opposing Lysander's advice to the Athenian Assembly to establish thirty rulers (14.3.5 –6), though Theramenes was himself one of those elected (14.4.1; cf. Exc. 3). Lysias, *contra* Diodorus, depicts Theramenes as Lysander's favorite, and blames

Theramenes himself for demanding rule by thirty men, backed up by an approving Lysander (Lys. 12.73–74). In the extant versions of events in the period soon after the Thirty had been established and began executing sycophants, Theramenes objected (Xen. 2.15–17; D. S. 14.4.4–5; [Aristot.] 36.1). But the executions continued and their scope only widened. Critias IV (Xen. 2.3.24–34), together with the rest of the Thirty, sought to achieve political stability by killing detractors and *metics*, thereby ensuring funds for their regime through confiscations. Xenophon reports that Theramenes objected again after the Three Thousand were selected (2.18; cf. [Aristot.] 36.1–2) and again when *metics* were being rounded up for execution (2.21–22)—putting him permanently at odds with the extremist leader of the Thirty, Critias IV.

In Xenophon's more detailed account (2.23–56; cf. D. S. 14.4.5–14.5.4; [Aristot.] 37.1), Critias IV, having privately arranged for Theramenes to be seized by armed guards at his command, called a meeting of the Council (*boulē*) in which he sought its support in condemning Theramenes. Critias IV skillfully mixed Theramenes' existing reputation for mercurial political alliances (Aristoph. *Frogs.*; Lys.) with darker claims more difficult to confirm or refute at this remove. Critias IV denounced Theramenes first for seeking his own advantage by constantly changing his political affiliation—pointing out that Theramenes was honored by the democrats before throwing in his lot with the Four Hundred, and calling him 'buskin' (κόθορνος at 2.3.31, a stage boot that fits either foot)—then accused Theramenes of dishonorable behavior after the Arginusae battle. When Theramenes defended himself against Critias IV's charges so eloquently that he was applauded by the *boulē*, Critias IV met separately with the Thirty, then told the *boulē* that, as their leader, he had to prevent their being deceived by Theramenes, whereupon he struck Theramenes' name from the roll of the Three Thousand, and condemned him to death in the name of the Thirty. Theramenes kept his sense of humor during the abduction and pending execution (Xen. *Hell.* 2.3.56). Diodorus' account ends with the following story, which seems to be one among many later attempts to make a controversial person appear better by associating him with Socrates:

> When the attendants came forward and were dragging him off, Theramenes bore his bad fortune with a noble spirit, since indeed he had had no little acquaintance with philosophy in company with Socrates; the multitude, however, in general mourned the ill-fortune of Theramenes, but had not the courage to come to his aid since a strong armed guard stood around him. Now Socrates the philosopher and two of his intimates ran forward and endeavoured to hinder the attendants. But Theramenes entreated them to do nothing of the kind; he appreciated, he said, their friendship and bravery, but as for himself, it would be the greatest grief if he should be the cause of the death of those who were so intimately associated with him. Socrates and his helpers, since they had no aid from anyone else and saw the intransigence of those in authority increasing, made no move. (D. S. 14.5.1–3)

In the later tradition and modern bibliography.   Theramenes remains controversial and resilient throughout ancient times. Early Xenophon shows hostility toward

Theramenes (1.7 and 2.2.16) and late Xenophon praises him (2.3, esp. 2.3.56), as does Diodorus (see esp. 13.38.2). "The Theramenes Papyrus" (*P. Mich.* tr. Peseley 1989: 30–1), seems to reply to the points made in Lysias 12.68–70 and 13 (Rhodes 1993: 22); Todd (2000: 115n4) calls it a "conscious rebuttal." Since Theramenes was dead when those speeches were written, one might think of *P. Mich.* as an early instance of what was to become a 4th c. rehabilitation of him that shows up in pseudo-Aristotle as well. Harding (1974), "The Myth of Theramenes," argues that Theramenes was not presented as a moderate until the 4th c. ([Aristot.] *Ath. Pol.*), but Rhodes' discussion of sources for the *Athenian Polity* rejects this notion, postulating instead that Theramenes was already a controversial character, and that the author of the *Athenian Polity*, generally oligarchic in orientation himself, thus found it necessary to justify the praise he heaped on Theramenes (1993: 15n75, 26). Roberts (1977: 109) seeks in part to vindicate Theramenes by exploring the underlying complexities of the Arginusae affair, on which Lang (1990) declares the question of Theramenes' motives and actions still open. Among the later claims sometimes deployed in contemporary scholarship is that Theramenes was a student of Socrates (D. S. 14.5). (Cf. Aristoph. *Wasps* 534–41 schol., *Lysistr.* 490 schol.; Ath. 218a, 220b; Poll. 7.91; Cic. *de Orat.* 2.93, *Tus. Dis.* 1.96; D. H. *Isoc.* 1; [Plu.] *LTO* 833e, 834a, 836f; Plu. *Nic.* 2.1, *Alc.* 31.1; Nep. *Alc.*; Polyae. 1.40.9.)

Thrasippus of Athens See App. II.

Thrasybulus of Collytus, son of Thrason See App. II.

Thrasybulus of Steria, son of Lycus See App. II. *See stemma: Nicias.*

Thrasyllus of Athens
[*PA* 7333 *LGPN2* 3 *PAA* 517480
*OCD*³ *RE* 2 *PP PX* Θράσυλλος]
?440s–406
democratic political and military leader

Pl. *Ap.* 32b,
    unnamed †
[Pl.] *Thg.* 129d
[Pl.] *Ax.* 368d,
    unnamed †
Xen. *Mem.* 1.1.18
Thu. 8.73.4–8.105.3,
    passim
Xen. *Hell.*
    1.1.7–1.7.34, *passim*
Hell. *Oxy.* 1.1.10,
    1.2.38
D. S.
    13.38.3–13.102.3,
    passim
Philoch. fr. 142
Lys. 21.7–8

Life. Thrasyllus was a hoplite at Samos who opposed the Samian oligarchs (Thu. 8.73) and emerged as a leader of the democratic faction (8.75.2–3). In exceptional circumstances, namely that the Athenian government was in the hands of the oligarchy of the Four Hundred in 411, the generals for the year were elected by the fleet rather than the *polis*, and Thrasyllus was elected—an example of able men rising under the democracy to positions of leadership (Thu. 8.76.2; D. S. 13.38.3). He continued to be elected general year after year, and to enjoy one military success after another—chronicled in Xenophon, Diodorus, and P. (See Alcibiades of Phegous s.v. for an encounter in 409.) Thrasyllus was still serving as general in 406, commanding the right wing of the fleet at Arginusae, when a storm prevented the casualties from being collected (see Exc. 2). He returned to Athens for trial and was executed for negligence.

In the later tradition. See Plutarch (*Alc.* 29.1–2), Dionysius of Halicarnassus (*Lys.* 21; cf. Lys. 32.7), and Pausanias (6.7.7).

Thrasymachus of Chalcedon
[*DPhA* 121 *OCD*³ *PP* Θρασύμαχος]
b. ±455
associates: Lysias, Clitophon
rhetorician and diplomat
Cf. stemma: Lysias.

Pl. *R.*   speaker
Pl. *Phdr.* 261c, 266c,
   267c–d, 269d, 271a
[Pl.] *Clt.* 406a
frr. in DK 85
Aristoph. *Banq.* fr.
   205.8 (K 198)
Eph. *Nau.* fr. 14 (K
   14)
Lys. 8.14–6
D. H. *Lys.* 6
D. H. *Dem.* 3

Life. Thrasymachus' *polis* was Chalcedon, an important trading port at the mouth of the Black Sea (modern Turkey, see Map 1). I figure his date of birth from his appearance as a "hairsplitter" in Aristophanes' *Banqueters* in 427, when he is unlikely to have been much less than thirty: since Aristophanes calls attention to him, he presumably had something of a reputation for rhetorical innovation already. This datum, however, must be balanced by his later career: if he delivered the speech Dionysius quotes, he was younger than fifty in 407. There is controversy, however, over whether Thrasymachus delivered the speech himself and, if so, when (see below). The date of birth I provide assumes that Thrasymachus was about twenty-eight in 427, and forty-eight in 407. Two years short of fifty made a difference: those over fifty spoke first in the Council and Assembly (Aes. *orat.* 1.23, 3.4).

Thrasymachus was a friend of the speaker of Lysias' undated *Against the Members of a* Sunousia—who *may* be Lysias himself (no explanation of this unique speech has achieved consensus)—where he is one of several men suspected of slander (cf. *Phdr.* 267d). If he was a rival of Plato in any sense, then the date of Ephippus' *Nauangus* (fr. 14), which implies it, needs to be narrowed closer to 380 than to 360. Neoptolemus of Paros, surveying epitaphs in Chalcedon in the 3rd

c. B.C.E. (some were probably cenotaphs), records: "Name: theta, rho, alpha, sigma, upsilon, mu, alpha, chi, omicron, sigma. Birthplace: Chalcedon. Profession: wisdom" (preserved in Ath. 454f).

Career. Thrasymachus was a rhetorician of some note, for there are numerous contemporaneous and later references to elements of his style. Besides the memorable representation of Thrasymachus notable for more than his diction in *Republic* (1.336b–354c), Socrates describes Thrasymachus' particular rhetorical skill to Phaedrus,

> As to the art of making speeches bewailing the evils of poverty and old age, the prize, in my judgment, goes to the mighty Chalcedonian. He it is also who knows best how to inflame a crowd and, once they are inflamed, how to hush them again with his words' magic spell, as he says himself. And let's not forget that he is as good at producing slander as he is at refuting it, whatever its source may be. As to the way of ending a speech, everyone seems to be in agreement, though some call it Recapitulation and others by some other name. (*Phdr.* 267c–d)

Socrates then lumps Thrasymachus with Lysias to warn Phaedrus that they are the wrong models for acquiring rhetorical skill (269d). In both dialogues, Thrasymachus is eager to make money (*R.* 1.337d, *Phdr.* 266c). (Plato keeps Thrasymachus in view throughout *R.*; see 5.450a–b, 6.498c–d, and 9.590d.)

It was as a diplomat in Athens on behalf of Chalcedon that Thrasymachus' rhetorical skills were tested most significantly. White (1995) presents an exceptionally strong case that Thrasymachus visited Athens for negotiations held in 407, after Chalcedon had mounted an unsuccessful revolt against imperial Athens, and that his diplomatic need to prevent harsh reprisals against his native city accounted for the actual speech preserved as DK fr. 1 (= D. H. *Dem.* 3) and gave potency and poignancy not only to Thrasymachus' position in *Republic* (cf. 351b) but to the fervor with which he defended it. Foregoing the usual stylistic approach to the substantial fragment, common since Dionysius, White's analysis of its content shows that its occasion was probably the diplomatic meeting that followed Alcibiades III's return to Athens in 407 and that Thrasymachus was "a consistent opponent of outside aggression and a champion of local autonomy" (1995: 308–9). White's is an important and convincing revision of the previously held view that the fragment, though written by Thrasymachus, was spoken by an Athenian after the Sicilian disaster, >413 (e.g. Ostwald *CAH* 5²: 348).

White argues further, however (citing Storey 1988), that the person spoofed in the *Banqueters* was not the Thrasymachus of *Republic*, but one of the *dramatis personae* of the play—who would have been a much younger man, born "about 440, and not much before 450 at the earliest" (1995: 315n27). Here White relies for a crucial premise on Dionysius who, writing in the 1st c. B.C.E., and giving the Aristotelian Theophrastus (4–3rd c. B.C.E.) as his source, said Thrasymachus was younger than Lysias, and put the latter's birth in 459 (i.e. fifteen years before the colony of Thurii was founded). While White considers later dates as well, settling on ±440 (1995: 324), he does not challenge Dionysius' ordering of the ages of the two men, and that leads to his conclusion about *Banqueters*: Thrasymachus' birth >440 would be too late for Aristophanes. But we do not know Dionysius' reasoning: if he surmised the relative ages of the two men from information available to him about their absolute ages, and if—as appears certain for Lysias s.v.—the information was unreliable, the relative order would fall away. That there were two prominent Chalcedonian rhetoricians named Thrasymachus in the second half of the 5th c. is less likely than that Thrasymachus was born ±455, accommodating not only Aristophanes and a revised Dionysius, but Plato's *Republic* and *Phaedrus*.

In the later tradition.   Most later references are about Thrasymachus' rhetorical innovations and style, though Cicero mentions also his speaking and writing about the material world (*De Orat.* 3.32.128). See also Aristotle (*S. Ref.* 183b29; *Rh.* 1404a3, 1409a2; 1413a7, quoted at Niceratus II s.v.); Dionysius (*Isae.* 20); Athenaeus (416a); Cicero (*Or.* 13.40); and the scholiast of Aristophanes' *Birds* (880). Several of these are quoted in DK.

Thucydides I of Alopece, son of Melesias I
[*PA*/*APF* 7268 *LGPN2* 7 *PAA* 515450 *OCD³ PP*
Θουκυδίδης Μελησίου Ἀλωπεκῆθεν]
≤508–>425
father of Melesias II, Stephanus and
  ?Hegesipyle II
important conservative political leader
See stemma: Thucydides.

Pl. *Lch.* 178a
Pl. *Meno* 94c
[Pl.] *Virt.* 376c–d †
Agora 25.1050–1
AM 106.151
Aristoph. *Ach.*
  676–718, & 703
  schol.
Aristoph. *Wasps*
  946–949
[Aristot.] *Ath. Pol.*
  28.2

Life.   Using the dramatic date of the *Laches* as a starting point for the age of Thucydides I's grandson and namesake, *APF* uses standard thirty-year generations to reach a birth date of ±500 for Thucydides I. That late date precludes his having fought at Marathon in 490, as Aristophanes implies he did (*Ach.* 696), so I date his birth ≤508. Aristophanes represents Thucydides as a "grey and bent old man," which suits the age of seventy-five suggested by *APF* 7268.2; but it also suits the eighty-three-year-old that my calculation yields. *APF* takes the reference to Marathon as symbolic, implying "nothing more chronologically specific than an attitude of mind." No. If one were looking for a reason to *doubt* that Thucydides I fought at Marathon, then such an argument might serve, but it is rather the case here that one should first attempt to locate the events that corroborate Lysimachus II's statement, "each of us has a great many fine things to say to the young men about his own father [i.e., about Thucydides I and Aristides I], things they achieved both in war and in peace in their management of the affairs both of their allies and of the city here" (Pl. *Lch.* 179c). To have fought at Marathon is that kind of fine thing. It is true, as *APF* points out, that other plays of the 420s likewise mention Marathon as a tag line to indicate nothing more than shared sympathy,

STEMMA: THUCYDIDES

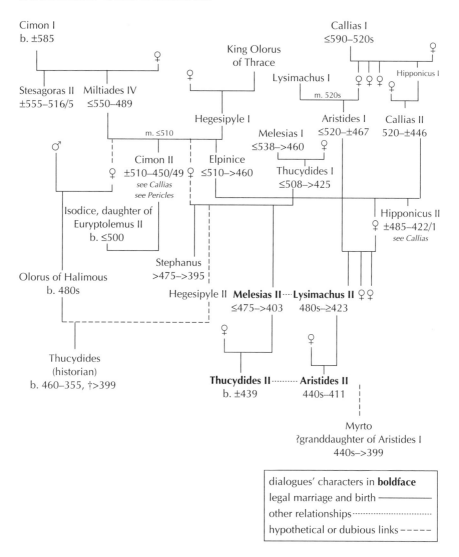

dialogues' characters in **boldface**	
legal marriage and birth ———————	
other relationships ··························	
hypothetical or dubious links – – – – –	

but the sheer length of the protest that Aristophanes offers on behalf of Thucydides I—in combination with Plato's statement—makes this a rather more persuasive defense than others.

Family.   Thucydides I is the son of one of the best-known wrestlers in antiquity, Melesias of Alopece, who was not only an Olympic victor himself, but was celebrated in Pindar's *Olympian Ode* 8 as a trainer, when he had trained his thirtieth victor; he is celebrated also in Pindar's *Nemean Odes* 4 and 6. There is controversy over whether Thucydides is brother-in-law or son-in-law to Cimon II (κηδεστής, [Aristot.] *Ath. Pol.* 28.2, can mean either), and both are possible using the dates that *APF* provides for the family. Because I give earlier dates of birth for both Thucydides I and Melesias II, two chronological problems (*APF* 7268.3) fall away. Thucydides cannot be the *son*-in-law of Cimon II and Isodice because a daughter of theirs would not be old enough to bear children until the decade after Melesias I's birth. Cimon II's unnamed sister, by my reckoning, can be about the *same* age as Thucydides rather than significantly older (see stemma). My dating also makes more likely the previously problematic connection between Thucydides I and the historian of that name.

Political career. In the period of Pericles I's prominence in Athens, Thucydides I was his primary rival. The rivalry came to a head over the massive building program undertaken by Pericles I on the Athenian acropolis, beginning about 447, but Thucydides I's ostracism in ?443 (*Agora* 25 for the *ostraka*) left Pericles I with a clear field. References in Aristophanes' *Acharnians* 703–712 and *Wasps* to a prosecution that Thucydides I botched by losing his tongue or becoming tongue-tied when he returned to Athens and attempted to regain public attention—thereby effectively scuttling his own career—have sometimes been supposed to be references to a prosecution of Anaxagoras s.v. Lacking contemporaneous corroboration, the notion builds on the antagonism between Pericles I and Thucydides I and a corresponding close association between Pericles I and Anaxagoras, on which Thucydides I supposedly hoped to capitalize. On the ostracism, see Krentz (1984).

Thucydides II of Alopece, son of Melesias II   Pl. *Lch.*   speaker
[*PA*/*APF* 7269 (7268.3) *LGPN2* 8 *PAA* 515455   [Pl.] *Thg.* 130a–b
PP Θουκυδίδης Μελησίου ᾿Αλωπεκῆθεν]
b. ±439
See stemma: Thucydides.

Thucydides II was ±15 at the time of *Laches*, set in 424, when his father is seeking a suitable teacher for him, hoping that he will distinguish himself as did his grandfather, Thucydides I. Socrates undertakes to teach both Thucydides II and his friend Aristides II (*Lch.* 200c–201c). Although Aristides II s.v. comes to a bad end, Thucydides II is reported still to be associating and disagreeing with Socrates in 409, the very approximate dramatic date of the pseudo-Platonic *Theages*.

Thucydides of Halimous, son of Olorus   Thu. *opera*
[*PA*/*APF* 7267 (7268.4–5) *LGPN2* 11 *PAA*   Mar. 17
515440 *RE* 12 *OCD*³ Θουκυδίδης ᾿Ολόρου
᾿Αλιμούσιος]
b. 460–355, † >399
mother: Hegesipyle II
father of ?Timotheus

historian of the Peloponnesian War
See stemma: Thucydides.

We know surprisingly little about the great historian. Polemon, in the 2nd c. B.C.E., recorded the historian's name, patronymic and demotic from a gravestone (or cenotaph), found near the Melite gate of Athens in the precinct of Cimon's family (Mar. 17). This contributes to the likelihood that Thucydides was in fact a descendent of Cimon I (see stemma), named for his maternal grandfather. The name 'Hegesipyle' is attributed to his mother because, *if* our understanding of his ascendants is correct, her maternal grandmother was Hegesipyle I. Beyond that, everything that can be said with certainty about Thucydides is known from his own comments in *The Peloponnesian War* (beginning at 1.1.1). Because Thucydides describes himself as having been of an age to understand events throughout the war, I date his birth ±460, which would make him about thirty when the war began; it is certain that he was born before 454 because he was elected general in 424 (4.104.4). He contracted plague at the beginning of the war, but recovered (2.48.3). He describes himself as influential in Thrace because of his goldmining interests there (4.105.1). As general, he arrived too late to save Amphipolis from Brasidas' attack (4.106.3) and was therefore exiled by the Athenians for twenty years (5.26.5), which he spent writing the history (5.26.1). Although he shows knowledge of how the war ended in 404 (5.26.1), and appears still to have been living in 399 (2.100.2), the history itself is incomplete, accounting for events only through the winter of 411 (8.109). Hellenistic biographers rely on no additional evidence, but they draw additional insecure inferences from *The Peloponnesian War*. (See late references in Pau. 1.23, Plu. *Cim.* 4, and D. H. *Thu.*)

Timaeus of Locri Epizephyrii   Pl. *Ti.*   speaker
[*LGPN3A* 24 *RE* 4 *DPhA* 149 *OCD*³   Pl. *Criti.*   speaker
PP Τίμαιος]   frr. in DK 49
active latter half of the 5th c.   Iamb. *VP* 267
Pythagorean

Prosopographical notes. Timaeus—well-born, rich, an astronomer and philosopher elected to high office in Locri—is unknown outside the dialogues: the historian of the same name who is a source for some of the 4th c. Sicilian material is about a century later. Iamblichus (*VP* 267 = DK 58 A, the catalogue of Pythagoreans) twice records 'Timaeus' among prominent Pythagoreans; in both cases DK cross-references the Timaeus of DK 49. The second instance immediately precedes the list of Locrian Pythagoreans; Lampert and Planeaux (1998: 92) follow Diels (DK⁶ 1: 345) in suggesting the copyist may have misplaced the name; but they add that Iamblichus' Locrian list includes a 'Timares' (Τιμάρης) which may be a corrupted 'Timaeus' and they emphasize that Cicero says twice that Plato studied with Timaeus of Locri (*De Fini.* and *Rep.*). One cannot rule out the possibility, however, that Cicero inferred the association from the dialogues.

Timarchus of ?Thebes   [Pl.] *Thg.* 129a–c †   speaker
[*PA* 13625 *LGPN2* 2 *PP* Τίμαρχος]
brother: Clitomachus

We know nothing of this would-be assassin of Nicias, son of Heroscamander, except what is in the *Theages*. Both Nicias and Timarchus' partner, Philemon, were assigned *PA* numbers on the strength of the dialogue, but may well be Thebans (see Dušanić 1990b: 65–70).

Timocrates of Thorae See App. II.

Timolaus of Cyzicus See App. II.

Timonides of Leucas (historian) See App. II.

Timotheus of Anaphlystus, son of Conon	[Pl.] *Ltr*. 13.363a
[*PA/APF* 13700 *LGPN2* 31	Xen. *Hell*. 5.4.63–66,
Τιμόθεος Κόνωνος Ἀναφλύστιος]	6.2.2, 3, 11
≤413–354/3	Isocr. 15.101–139,
brother: Cratinus	15.124–125
father of a daughter (who married	[Demos.] 49
Menestheus), and Conon	Philoch. fr. 223
friend of Isocrates, Plato	D. S. 15.29.7–16.21.4,
rich and famous general	*passim*

Life. Philochorus establishes the connections among Plato, Chabrias (see App. II), and Timotheus (see Dušanić 1995). For numerous inscriptions naming Timotheus, particularly for the performance of liturgies, see *APF*, updated and supplemented in *LGPN2*. For the great wealth of Conon, 17 *talents* of which Timotheus inherited, see *APF*; he had mortgaged it all by 373, partly to fund his military needs, and had become wealthy again by 362, though not wealthy enough to pay a one hundred-*talent* fine in 354/3.

In the later tradition. Timotheus appears in Aelian (*VH* 2.10, 18); Athenaeus (577a); Pausanias (6.3.16, an autopsy of statues in honor of Conon and Timotheus in Samos and Ephesus); and Nepos (*Tim.*).

Tisamenus of Athens See App. II.

Tisander II of Athens, son of Epilycus I See App. II. *See stemmata: Andocides, Callias, Pericles, Plato.*

Tisander of Aphidna, son of Cephisodorus	Pl. *Grg.* 487c *
[*PA/APF* 13459 (8410) *LGPN2* 14 *PP*	*IG* II² 1929.22
Τείσανδρος Κηφισοδώρου Ἀφιδναῖος]	

>445–≥380
associates: Callicles, Andron, Nausicydes

Life. Tisander was a member of one of Aphidna's well-known and wealthy families. His father, Cephisodorus, may have owned property to the north of, and adjacent to, the confiscated parcel of land of a member of the Thirty (*Agora* 19.2g.9, noted by Walbank 1982: 86, who cites *Grg.* 487c for Cephisodorus' son); he is listed by name on the confiscation *stele* for purposes of pinpointing the location of the seized property (cf. Plato's will s.v.). Walbank had noted already (1982: 78) that these properties were typically purchased by neighbors of the original owners, but he does not argue in this particular case that Cephisodorus bought the property. If Tisander's father was still a property owner in his own right in 403–2, however, it would be unwise to put Tisander's birth much earlier than that of his friend Andron (b. ±445). If born at about the same time, Tisander might have been sixty-five in 380, when he was perhaps one of the Thousand (*IG* dated ±380, *diadikasia*), but he may have been as much as a decade younger.

Prosopographical notes. This Tisander is a generation younger than the Tisander II (see App. II) who was a candidate for ostracism in 443. Neither *LGPN2* nor *PAA* have accepted Walbank's suggestion that the Cephisodorus on the *Agora* inscription is the father of Tisander.

Tisias of Syracuse   Pl. *Ltr.* 7.349c *
[*PP* Τισίας]
active 360s

Tisias was the leader of a band of lightly armed troops (*peltasts*) who sought the democratic leader Heraclides at Dionysius II's instigation.

Tisias of Syracuse (rhetorician) See App. II.

Tisias of Cephale, son of Tisimachus See App. II.

Tison of Syracuse   [Pl.] *Ltr.* 13.363c *
[*LGPN3A* 7 Τείσων]
father-in-law of Terillus
sometime city-steward in Syracuse

'Teison' at PCW 1676 is a misprint.

Tissaphernes of Sardis, son of Hydarnes (satrap) See App. II.

Tolmides of Athens, son of Tolmaeus (commander) See App. II.

Trophonius, son of Erginus (builder) See App. II.

Tychon, slave of Plato See App. II.

Tynnichus of Chalcis (poet) See App. II.

Tyrtaeus of Sparta (poet) See App. II.

[unnamed] of Aexone, son of Democrates I	Pl. *Ly.* 223a	present
b. >417		
brother: Lysis II		
See stemma: Lysis.		

[unnamed] of Alopece, son of Callias III	Pl. *Ap.* 20a *
[*APF* (7826.12C)]	Andoc. 1.125–127
b. ≥412	Met. *Phil.* fr. 14 (K
mother: Chrysilla	13)
paternal half brother: Hipponicus III	
See stemma: Callias.	

In Andocides IV's prejudiced account, Callias III threw out his wife, Chrysilla s.v., while she was pregnant with this son whose name is not known. After his birth, Chrysilla's family attempted to register him with his phratry but Callias III, who was officiating as a Ceryces priest, forbade it, swearing the infant was not his. Thus the child was for some time known as "Callias' *nothos*" (Met.). But years later, when the son was not an infant but a boy, Callias III took him before the phratry and swore he was his own son by his legal wife, Chrysilla, an Athenian woman. Thereafter, the boy could be treated like any other Athenian and should have had exactly the same rights of inheritance as his half brother, Hipponicus III. See s.v. for Callias III's attempt to secure a rich bride for this son.

[unnamed] of Athens, son of Demophon	Pl. *Ly.* 223a	present
b. >417		
brother: Menexenus		
cousin of Ctesippus of Paeania		

[unnamed] of Athens, wife of Pericles I,	Pl. *Prt.* 314e5–315a1
Hipponicus II	Plu. *Per.* 24.5
[*APF* (7826.9)]	
≤475–>440	

?parents: Megacles IV and Coesyra
?siblings: Megacles V and Dinomache
husbands: (1) Pericles I of Cholarges; (2)
  Hipponicus II of Alopece
offspring with (1): Xanthippus II, Paralus;
  with (2): Callias III, Hipparete I
See stemmata: Pericles, Callias, Alcibiades.

Life.   Pericles I's first wife, the mother of his two legitimate sons, was a close relation, possibly a first cousin, from whom he was divorced five years or more before Aspasia became his *de facto* wife. Hipponicus II was her second husband, with whom she had Callias III and Hipparete I. Because we know nothing else about her, a secondary literature has sprung up in an effort to identify her more clearly.

In the later tradition and modern bibliography.   It is generally accepted on Plato's evidence (*Prt.*) that Plutarch was mistaken about the order of this woman's two marriages when he asserted that the first wife of Pericles I had previously been married to Hipponicus II, though the order given by Plutarch still emerges periodically (e.g. MacDowell 1962). Plutarch also reports a third marriage for this woman, after her marriage to Pericles I. Recently, Cox (1998: 225n30 with 1989: 36n6) has reported a different adjustment that preserves Plutarch's order: Hipponicus II, after the birth of Callias III, divorced [unnamed] who then married Pericles I and bore two sons; and Hipponicus II, sometime after 450, married a woman who was later mother of Hipparete I. This alternative solution is barely possible: for Pericles I's eldest son to be born by 460, a date that makes plausible his marriage to a daughter of Tisander prior to his death in 429, Callias III would need to have been born *at least* a year before Xanthippus II; but Callias III was ambassador to Sparta in 371, unlikely for a man of eighty. Bicknell's similar alternative rests on the not-promising notion that an Athenian man might marry in his early twenties (1982: 248–9), highly unlikely in the 5th c. (see Critobulus s.v.). It seems preferable to take Plato's word over Plutarch's: this unnamed woman was first married to Pericles I and bore two sons, Xanthippus II and Paralus; afterwards, in about 455, she married Hipponicus II and bore Callias III and Hipparete I, the future wife of Alcibiades III s.vv.

In the same passage, Plutarch states that this unnamed woman was "near of kin" to Pericles I, which has led to a great deal of speculation. In Athenian society, where marriage between paternal half siblings was legal, and where marriage between first cousins, and between uncles and nieces, was especially common, "near" should not be further than first cousin. Megacles IV, Pericles I's maternal uncle, had a famous daughter, Dinomache, who was Pericles I's first cousin and the mother of Alcibiades III. Cromey (1984: 385–401) maintains that Pericles I's first wife was Dinomache, but this cannot work chronologically when Dinomache was certainly married to Clinias II from ≤450 to 446. Bicknell (1972) makes a persuasive case that Pericles I's first wife is likely to have been Dinomache's sister, and I have plotted that possibility on the family stemma. (Both articles contain useful references to modern bibliography on the topic.)

Finally, Plutarch says Pericles I s.v. "legally bestowed her upon another man, with her own consent, and himself took Aspasia, and loved her exceedingly." Because Plutarch mentions the two women in the same breath, the history of scholarship has largely followed suit, but it is unlikely that the divorce and the beginning of the relationship with Aspasia s.v. were linked; they appear to be separated by about five years ("at least five years"—*APF*). Cf. Kahn (1996: 8), "Pericles had previously been married to an Athenian woman of high station, mother of his two legitimate sons whom we meet in Plato's *Protagoras*. But he divorced her in order to take Aspasia as his semi-legal wife."

[unnamed] slave of Callias III of Alopece active ±433/2	Pl. *Prt.* 314d	speaker

This man, a eunuch, served as a doorman.

[unnamed] slave of Euclides of Megara active ±391	Pl. *Tht.* 143c	speaker

This slave read aloud Euclides' script
 (*biblion*).

[unnamed] slave of Meno active ±402	Pl. *Meno* 82b–85b	speaker

Meno's slave, like any male slave regardless of age, could expect to be called 'boy' (*pais*); nothing in the dialogue indicates his actual age except perhaps his readiness to participate in Socrates' demonstration and success at the task assigned him. Meno, who had brought several attendants with him from Thessaly (82a), would hardly be traveling with very old or very young slaves. Greek enslavement of other Greeks was not a new practice in 402, and Meno's words, "born in my household" cannot be taken literally: the epithet 'house-born' (*oikogenēs*) designated a class of privately owned slaves who worked as personal attendants and domestic servants, and not as craftsmen or field hands or miners; thus a house-born slave remained no less house-born when purchased by a third party. Important for the dialogue is that he speaks Greek, enough Greek to know what a square is without knowing what a diagonal is. His powers of inference are healthy, and, with practice, his knowledge of geometry would be inferior to no one's (85c).

[unnamed] slave of Polemarchus active 420s–410s	Pl. *R.* 327b	speaker

Although the great majority of Polemarchus' slaves were skilled metal workers who lived apart from the household (*chōris oikountes*), the slave who caught up with Socrates in the Piraeus and told him to wait was a personal attendant to Polemarchus. A rich young man was thought to require one or more such personal servants to assist him in his day-to-day affairs.

Xanthias
[*PA* 11151 *LGPN2* 8 *RE* 2 *PP* Ξανθίας]

Pl. *Meno* 94c
[Pl.] *Virt.* 378a †

This noted wrestler and trainer taught one of Thucydides I's sons.

Xanthippe of Athens, wife of Socrates of
Alopece
[*PA* 11155 *LGPN2* 1 *RE* 4 *PP PX*
Ξανθίππη Σωκράτους Ἀλωπεκῆθεν γυνή]
±440–>399
daughter of ?Lamprocles I
sons: Lamprocles II, Sophroniscus II,
Menexenus
See stemma: Socrates.

Pl. *Phd.* 60a, 116b   speaker
[Pl.] *Hal.* 8
[Pl.] *Epgr.* 8
Xen. *Symp.* 2.10 *
Xen. *Mem.* 2.2.1,
unnamed *
Aristoph. *Clouds*
60–67

Life. Nothing is certain about the family or background of Xanthippe (see Lamprocles I s.v.). I estimate her date of birth from her youngest child's being an infant or toddler in 399, when her oldest son is *meirakion* (*Ap.* 34d), just reaching manhood. She was probably not beyond forty when Socrates was seventy but, because Athenian women often married in early adolescence, she may have been thirty-five; and nothing physiological prevents her having been forty-five. Aristophanes' *Clouds* may provide an elaborate allusion to her name—whether to a real or a pretended upper-class connection, however, is impossible to determine from the context in which Strepsiades is speaking of his son, Phidippides: "After that, when this son was born to us, I mean to me and my high-class wife, we started to bicker over his name. She was for adding *hippos* to the name, Xanthippus or Chaerippus or Callippides, while I was for calling him Phidonides after his grandfather" (*Clouds*). Dover comments, "Xanthippos was the name of Perikles' father and of one of his sons, and also the name of the archon of 479/8; otherwise it was rare, and thus has much the same associations as 'Megakles' " (1968a: 102); Burnet (1911: *Phd.* 60n) saw aristocratic associations in both 'Xanthippe' and 'Lamprocles'; Brickhouse and Smith (1989: 15) add Socrates' third son, 'Menexenus'. If Socrates at the time of the *Clouds* in 423 had recently married the daughter of Lamprocles I, Aristophanes' joke is even better.

Plato's representation of Xanthippe is sympathetic, especially when compared to Xenophon and the later tradition. She is already with Socrates on the morning of the execution—their youngest child on her lap—when Socrates' friends arrive. The one thing she says is an expression of sadness that this will be Socrates' last conversation with his friends (*Phd.* 60a). Although Socrates asks Crito to let someone take her home, and although she weeps loudly, her behavior is expected—what is customary for women—and bears comparison to Apollodorus' later weeping and outburst (117d). Phaedo's remark to Echecrates (*Phd.* 116b) that the *women* of Socrates' household were brought to him in prison raises the question of what woman or women, other than Xanthippe, might be included. Although Xanthippe had been taken home earlier (60a–b), she may well have returned, not only because the prison is no great distance from Alopece, but because she had their youngest child, an infant, in her arms when led away earlier, yet all three children are presented to Socrates later; in that case one additional woman of the house requires identification. Less plausibly, she may have left the infant with another woman of the household and not returned, in which case there are two additional women members of the household about whom there is no information. Plato was not present, and speculation about the details here may seem feckless in view of the many possibilities. The war years had led to a burgeoning of women in Athenian households, and these women could also have been kinswomen of Xanthippe or other women displaced since the war. Cf. Myrto s.v. for the controversy over Socrates' "other wife."

But Xanthippe's critics have been loud and numerous. Xenophon (*Symp.* 2.10) is the source for the story that, in reply to Antisthenes' question why Xanthippe is allowed to go on being difficult, Socrates invoked the analogy of handling a spirited horse. At Xen. *Mem.* 2.2.1–14, Socrates finds his eldest son, Lamprocles II, annoyed with his mother; and Socrates counsels him didactically on the duties of parents and offspring.

In the later tradition and modern bibliography. Late authors take up Xenophon's version of matters, repeating a great deal of gossip (D. L. 2.26, 2.36–7; cf. Ael. *VH* 7.10, 9.29; and Ath. 219a). For Xanthippe's demotion to *hetaira*, see Fitton 1970, Woodbury 1973, and Bicknell 1974b, who offer more details from the later tradition.

Xanthippus I of Cholarges, son of Ariphron I See App. II. *See stemma: Pericles.*

Xanthippus II of Cholarges, son of Pericles I
[*PA/APF* 11170 (11811.3) *LGPN2* 8 *PP*
Ξάνθιππος Περικλέους Χολαργεύς]
b. ≤460–457, † 429
mother: [unnamed] kinswoman of Pericles I
  who later married Hipponicus II
siblings: full brother Paralus; maternal half
  brother Callias III; maternal half sister
  Hipparete I; paternal half brother
  Pericles II
wife: daughter of Tisander II
See stemma: Pericles.

Pl. *Prt.* 315a   present
Pl. *Meno* 94b
[Pl.] *Alc.* 118d–e
[Pl.] *Virt.*
  377d–378a †
IG I³ 49.14
Plu. *Per.* 36.1–3

Xanthippus II flanks Protagoras himself in the *Protagoras*. At the time the dialogue is set, he was not yet married, but would both marry and die about three years from its dramatic date (see App. I). He died in the plague at the outbreak of the Peloponnesian war (Plu.). Also set in that interim period is, according to Plutarch, an extended quarrel with his father over money that involved Xanthippus II's accusation that Pericles I had wasted a full day discussing with Protagoras whether—when one athlete accidentally killed another with a javelin—the javelin, the thrower, or the contest judges must be held responsible, *sensu strictu* (τὸν ὀρθότατον λόγον αἰτους χρή). On the name 'Xanthippus', see Xanthippe s.v.

Xenocrates of Chalcedon (Academy head) See App. II.

Xenophanes of Colophon (philosopher) See App. II.

Xenophon of Erchia, son of Gryllus I	Xen. *opera*
[*PA* 11307 *LGPN2* 22 *RE* 6 *DPhA* 18 *OCD*³	Aes. *Asp.* no. 70 (fr.
PP PX Ξενοφῶν Γρύλλου Ἐρχιεύς]	31 Dittmar)
±425–≥355	D. S. 14.37.1–4
mother: Diodora	
wife: Philesia	
father of Gryllus II, Diodorus	
student of Socrates	
mercenary and writer	

Life. The chief source for material about the life of Xenophon is his own *Anabasis*, in which he appears as a participant and where he makes reference to events that occurred after his return from Asia. His birth has usually been set 430–25 because he reports that his friend Proxenus of Boeotia was ±30 when beheaded by Tissaphernes in 401 (*Anab.* 2.6.20). Rallying Proxenus' captains afterwards, Xenophon twice acknowledged his own comparative youth (3.1.14, 25), implying that he was then somewhat younger than 30. Dillery (1998: 4) argues that Seuthes of Thrace's offer to exchange daughters with Xenophon (7.2.38) implies that Xenophon was older—old enough to have a daughter of twelve or thirteen—but Seuthes' offer is qualified, "if you have a daughter" (εἴ τις σοὶ ἔστι θυγάτηρ), so I infer Xenophon's approximate year of birth without that complication. If Xenophon had been born as early as 430–28, he could hardly have avoided service in the crucial naval battles of 406 and 405, when Athens' manpower shortage was acute, yet he represents himself as inexperienced in 401 (*Anab.* 3.1.4; cf. 3.1.14, 7.1.21); thus a date late in the range best fits the facts as they have come down to us.

Xenophon's family appears to have been affluent, probably of the *hippeis* class. His deme, Erchia, of the Aigeis tribe, lay east of Athens around the Hymettus mountains, 15 km. as the crow flies (see Map 2). Xenophon was an associate of Socrates and names a Socratic inner circle including Crito, Chaerephon, Chaerecrates, Hermogenes, Simmias, Cebes, Phaedondas, "and others who consorted with him not that they might shine in the courts or the assembly, but that they might become gentlemen, and be able to do their duty by house and household, and relatives and friends, and city and citizens. Of these not one, in youth or old age, did evil or incurred censure" (*Mem.* 1.2.48). Xenophon was apparently a superstitious religious man, often conducting sacrifices and reading signs (e.g., *Anab.* 5.3.4–10, 7.2.17 et al.). Xenophon's last known work, *Ways and Means*, was written with knowledge of the end of the Social War of 355, so his death was in or after that year.

Career. Although Xenophon writes critically of the Thirty (*Hell.* 2.3.11–2.4.10; *Mem.* 1.2.29–39), this is sometimes attributed to a late change of views, and it may well be. He is commonly said to have remained in the city during the rule of the Thirty, to have been included on the citizen roll of Three Thousand, and to have fought for the oligarchy in the battle at Munychia in 403 (see Rhodes 1993: 419). These claims are dubious, not only because of Xenophon's relative youth and inexperience in 401, but because of Xenophon's distance from the city and devotion to horses. He depicts himself as blooming rather late and reluctantly into public life.

In 401, before accepting the Boeotian Proxenus' invitation to join a mercenary expedition to Persia, Xenophon sought Socrates' advice. Socrates recommended consulting the god at Delphi about *whether* to undertake the journey; instead, Xenophon asked the god about the *best way* to do so, and thus incurred Socrates' criticism (*Anab.* 3.1.5–7). Xenophon says he agreed to accompany his friend Proxenus in the hope of becoming a friend of Cyrus; Xenophon was a companion, not a soldier, much less a captain or general (3.1.4–5). Like the other Greeks, Xenophon had been deceived by Cyrus about the purpose of the venture and did not know upon setting out that Cyrus intended to seize the throne of his brother, Artaxerxes II (3.1.10). Only after Cyrus had been killed in battle and the generals, including Proxenus, beheaded, with a ragtag mercenary army stranded deep in Persia, did Xenophon emerge as a natural leader of men (3.1.10–47). He held that role comfortably, however, leading the Ten Thousand, as they have come to be called, back through Asia to Byzantium (3.2–7.1.7).

From there, many of Cyrus' army began, piecemeal, to make their way back to Attica, and Xenophon too expected to return, well financed as a result of his Asian plundering. But the ordinary soldiers lacked provisions and depended on substantial aid from the governor of Byzantium. When a new governor arrived and began selling the stranded soldiers (7.2.6–7), Xenophon was instrumental in persuading the remaining army of Cyrus to enter service under Seuthes of Thrace (7.3.14). A Spartan army under Thibron arrived in 399 on its way to wage war against Tissaphernes (7.6.1), whereupon Seuthes gladly released the mercenaries into the service of the Spartans, ending the fifteen-month saga reported in *Anabasis*.

Xenophon remained with the Spartans for some time, through changes in leadership, and returned to Greece with the Spartan commander Agesilaus to put down a rebellion among Sparta's allies. This led to Xenophon's fighting with the Spartans against the Athenians and others in the battle of Coronea in 394. He was about that time exiled from Athens, most likely for his service to the Spartans (*Anab.* 5.3.6–7 with Dillery 1998: 4) who then provided him, their *proxenos*, with an estate near Olympia where Xenophon could ride and hunt at leisure (5.3.5). Here, at the age of about thirty-one, he apparently married and produced offspring. He suffered the loss of his estate to a Theban invasion in 370, and spent the remainder of his life in Corinth, despite formal reconciliation with Athens. His son Gryllus II was killed in battle in 362. Dillery (1998: 34) comments, "Late in life, when he was writing (or rewriting) several of the important works in his corpus, Xenophon came to believe that many of his most cherished beliefs about what contributed to successful community life were wrong."

Works. Some of the dialogues attributed to Xenophon by Diogenes bear the same titles as some of Plato's dialogues, contributing to the view (as old as Ath. 505c and D. L. 3.34) that Plato and Xenophon were rivals. Huss (1999) dates the writing of the *Symposium* in the second half of the 360s, enabling Xenophon to make use of much of the Socratica already available then—which he does. Noting his longevity, contemporary scholarship marks two distinct phases of Xenophon's style, often in the same work. Chroust (1957: 44–68) suggested, for example, that the *Memorabilia* begins at 1.3, with 1.1–2 added later as an introduction. Momigliano, however, an admirer of Xenophon's style, insists that the *Memorabilia* is one unitary whole (1993: 52, citing Erbse 1961: 257); he praises Xenophon's pioneering experimentation in biographical form, the fusion of fact and imagination, yet hardly knows what to make of Plato whom "we should all like to dismiss" (1993: 46). *Hellenica* is likewise usually divided into two parts, though there is controversy about where the break occurs (e.g., at 3.11 or at 2.3.9).

In addition to the works listed below, Xenophon wrote on revenue and taxation (*WM*), *On Horsemanship, Cavalry Commander, On Hunting, Agesilaus, Hiero, Constitution of the Spartans*, and the *Cyropaedia* or *Education of Cyrus* (of which the Athenian visitor's words at *Laws* 3.694c appear to be criticism).

work	content	persons
Anabasis 401–399 (15 mo.)	"ten thousand" Greek mercenaries followed Cyrus of Persia into Asia, were stranded, and followed Xenophon back home	Aristippus of Larissa, Meno, Socrates, Xenophon
Apology 399	the trial of Socrates, as told to Xenophon by Hermogenes	Anytus, Apollodorus of Phaleron, Hermogenes, Meletus II (accuser), Socrates
Hellenica 411–362	a partial history of Greece (many omissions), beginning where Thucydides left off and ending with the battle of Mantinea	Adeimantus of Scambonidae, Alcibiades III, Alcibiades of Phegous, Antiphon (son of Lysonides), Anytus, Archedemus, Aristocrates, Aristotle of Thorae, Callias III, Callixenus, Charicles, Charmides (son of Glaucon III), Critias IV, Erasistratus III, Euryptolemus, Hermocrates, Hermogenes, Leon, Meletus of Athens, Niceratus II, Nicias I, Pericles II, Phanosthenes, Socrates, Theramenes

work	content	persons
Memorabilia ±410–401	memories and imaginations of conversations between Socrates and a variety of people, at least partly (1.1–2) replying to Polycrates' discourse *Accusation of Socrates*	Acumenus, Alcibiades III, Anaxagoras, Antiphon (sophist), Antisthenes (Socratic), Antisthenes of Cytherus, Apollodorus of Phaleron, Archedemus, Aristarchus, Aristippus, Aristodemus, Aspasia, Cebes, Chaerephon, Chaerecrates, Charicles, Charmides (son of Glaucon III), Clito, Critias IV, Crito, Critobulus, Diodorus, Epigenes, Eutherus, Euthydemus (son of Diocles), Glaucon IV, Hermogenes, Hippias, Hippocrates of Cholarges, Lamprocles II of Alopece, Meletus II, Nausicydes, Nicias I, Nicomachides, Parrhasius, Pericles I, Pericles II, Phaedondas, Pistias, Plato, Prodicus, Socrates, Themistocles, Theodorus, Theodote, Thrasyllus, Xenophon
Oeconomicus ±431	"How to Manage an Estate"—agriculture and household	Critobulus, Ischomachus, Chrysilla, Socrates
Symposium August of 422	conversations at a banquet at Callias III's house in the Piraeus honoring Autolycus	Antisthenes, Autolycus, Callias III, Charmides (son of Glaucon III), Critobulus, Hermogenes, Lycon, Niceratus II, Philippus, Socrates, Xanthippe, Xenophon

In the later tradition. A number of later sources also mention Xenophon (D. L. 2.48–59, 3.34; Ath. 427–428, 505c; Str. 9.403; Pau. 5.6.5; Plu. *Ages.* 9, 18, *Mor.* 605c). A scholium to Eusebius (2.110) is the source for Xenophon's mother's name.

Xenophon of Melite, son of Euripides See App. II. *See stemma: Phaedrus.*

Xerxes of Persia, son of Darius I (king) See App. II.

Zeno of Elea, son of ?Teleutagoras Pl. *Prm.* speaker
[*LGPN3A* 29 *RE* 1 *DPhA* 19 *OCD³ PP* Ζήνων] Pl. *Sph.* 216a
b. ±490 Pl. *Phdr.* 261d,
student and ?adoptive son of Parmenides unnamed
teacher of Callias of Aexone, Pythodorus [Pl.] *Alc.* 119a
philosopher DK 29

Life.   Zeno's father's name is given by Apollodorus (D. L. 9.25). His life is not attested in contemporaneous sources, so Plato's *Parmenides*, depicting an event, or possible event, before Plato's birth and after Zeno's death, turns out to be crucial to any biographical account, though any truth in Plato's account depends on the accuracy of his sources, now lost. Diogenes says Zeno flourished during the 79th Olympiad, 464–460; according to Plato, Zeno was a tall and handsome man of about forty in 450, the dramatic date of the dialogue (*Prm.* 127b; cf. App. I). Zeno had privately written a defense of Parmenides' views that had been secretly copied and broadcast by someone else, robbing Zeno of the decision whether to make the book known to others (128c–d). In the dialogue, Zeno reads that very book aloud, as he had on other occasions (127c–d), providing some insight into what publication entailed in classical Greece. Interesting statistical evidence has been produced by Ledger (1989: 166) that the long final section of *Parmenides*—from 138c—"is highly derivative, based probably on a Zenonian original, possibly even the work mentioned in the dialogue, but if not that precisely, then on some other production(s) of the Eleatic School." At a broader structural level, it is worth noting that the final *Parmenides* section has the form of Parmenides' extant fr. 8.

Diogenes tells a garbled story of Zeno's heroic death (9.26–27, citing Hera. Lemb.; Dem. Phal.; a *Successions of Philosophers* by an Antisthenes who is not the Socratic; and Her. *hist.*), bits of which appear also in other stories of other heroic deaths. Zeno, arrested following an attempt to overthrow a tyrant, whose identity is disputed, cleverly implicated the tyrant's friends, but also bit off the ear, or the nose, of his accuser; or perhaps Zeno roused the citizens, then bit off his own tongue and spat it at the tyrant, who either was then stoned by the citizens, or had Zeno thrown into a mortar and beaten to death.

In the later tradition.   Later authors tell a variety of versions of the story (cf. e.g., Plu. *Mor.* 505d, 1051c, 1126d). See testimonia in DK.

Zeuxippus of Heraclea (painting teacher) See App. II.

Zopyrus of Thrace   [Pl.] *Alc.* 122b
[*RE* 4 *OCD*³ Ζώπυρος]   Phae. nos. 8–11 &
Alcibiades III's elderly tutor   Rossetti (1980)

In the later tradition.   'Zopyrus' became the commonplace name for physiognomists through the late antique period, as a result of what Diogenes (2.105) says was a dialogue by Phaedo, now lost, in which Zopyrus "reads" from Socrates' features that he is both stupid and lustful. Socrates pronounces the judgment correct, but explains that he has defeated his natural vices through efforts of reason. (Cf. Kahn 1996: 10–2 & nn for a much fuller story, in which Zopyrus is an "oriental magus," based on Rossetti's additional frr.)

Appendix I
Dramatic Dates, Characters, Setting and Style

Plato, the consummate philosopher, was not preoccupied with dramatic dates, so one rarely expects exactness; the dialogues are replete with anachronisms. Moreover, Plato wrote in an era that dated many events by the names of games or festivals held at four-year intervals, or by annual festivals, or by the eponymous archons that changed annually—and where three independent calendars were in use that could not be calibrated to one another exactly (see *On Ancient Dates* in the Introduction). On the other hand, Plato often represents people he knew intimately: young men who were, as he was, a part of Socrates' circle, his own brothers (whose personalities are distinct even in translation) and their friends, and sometimes his own extended family and forebears. Without presuming anything about Plato's authorial intentions, I have assumed that we are on rather safer prosopographical ground when Plato is writing about people he knew than when he is reconstructing the distant past—not because he made accuracy a goal, which he may or may not have, but because his memory naturally informed his imagination (in no stronger a way than the commonsense description provided in the *Theaetetus*), requiring a deliberate decision to change what he remembered for some literary or other purpose. While I cannot deny that Plato *may* have done so, it will be obvious to any reader that no project of the kind I am undertaking would be worthwhile if Plato were first and foremost a literary artist rather than a philosopher. Because Plato was a philosopher who presented ideas and arguments embedded in a context of individual and social specificity, my task is to proceed with respect for that specificity absent a compelling reason to abandon it.

For most of the dialogues, dramatic dates arise as a matter of course from his representing family, friends, and circumstances as he imagined or remembered them: foreign visitors to a summer festival, conversations in a gymnasium with friends of his own age, or tagging along with his older brothers. The result is a temporal lattice that helps to guide one through the life of Socrates and others. The view that Plato deliberately manipulated time for literary purposes (e.g. Moors 1987: 24n4; Davies *APF* 8792.5) would imply an incipient historical realism against which he meant to be operating, but the evidence of manipulation diminishes the more one knows about the characters. The dialogues taken together exhibit a remarkable coherence: at their center are a few Athenian family groups from a handful of demes (see App. III and Map 2), and individuals who are often related by blood or marriage. I make the minimal assumption that Plato represented persons he knew, or knew of, in plausible situations. So, regardless of what he may have intended, which is none of my concern, his shorter dialogues just do have dramatic dates. It is not so simple with the long dialogues apparently composed over a number of years, for those are often internally inconsistent and incompatible with one another as well. In the case of *Republic, Timaeus-Critias,* and *Laws,* issues of how the dialogues were composed impinge on how they are related to one another, requiring another layer of discussion in those cases below.

What follows is the most likely story I can tell, but it may not be a true story, and it is not the whole story. *Beware* of two related perils: misleading precision and circularity. Even when exact dramatic dates are provided, even when festivals tell us the time of year, the determination of those dates is imbricated with the calculation of characters' ages and judgments about the reliability of sources, both of which are dependent on the arguments in the prosopographical primer, and both of which could be refined in light of new information. References to events and persons external to the dialogues prevent the procedure from being merely circular, but circularity remains a danger worth watching for in any enterprise on this sort.

Dialogues are listed below in the dramatic order of the main action of each, proceeding from Socrates' youth to his death. The six dialogues with dramatic frames—introductory, and sometimes intervening, passages set later than the main action—usually have two dramatic dates, one for the main action and one for the frame. In the interest in keeping the parts of the dialogues together, frames are treated under the dates of the main action rather than where their frame dates would place them chronologically. Dialogues in square brackets are not generally thought to have been written by Plato. Characters in square brackets indicate a *flashback* from the main action.

Dialogues with Definite Dramatic Dates

Parmenides
August 450

frame (set ±382):	Cephalus of Clazomenae	*narrator*
Athenian agora, then	Clazomenian friends	
at Antiphon's house	Adeimantus I of Collytus, son of Ariston	*speaker*
in Melite; narrated	Glaucon IV of Collytus, son of Ariston	*indirect speaker*
(126a–127a, 136d–e)	Antiphon II of Athens, son of Pyrilampes	*indirect speaker*

main action: house of	Pythodorus of Athens, son of Isolochus	*indirect speaker*
Pythadorus outside	Zeno of Elea, son of ?Teleutagoras	*speaker*
Athens' city walls in	Parmenides of Elea, son of Pyres	*speaker*
the Ceramicus at the	Aristotle of Thorae, son of Timocrates	*speaker*
time of the greater	Socrates of Alopece, son of Sophroniscus I	*speaker*
Panathenaea;	two others (129d, 136e)	*join in*
narrated		

The greater Panathenaea was held in Hekatombaion, the end of July and most of August. The official year 450/49, where Hekatombaion falls in the first part, has long been recognized as fitting Socrates' youth, given his relatively well-known date of birth, and the ages assigned to Parmenides and Zeno in the dialogue; but one cannot infer that such a meeting actually took place. The specificity of Plato's dialogue has been used to set dates of birth for Parmenides (*pace* D. L. 9.23) and Zeno, more often than the other way around. There is broad agreement about the date; see Fowler (1926: 195), Cornford (1950: 64), Guthrie (1978: 35), and Davison (1962: 154).

We hear the story from Cephalus, who heard it from Antiphon, who heard it from Pythadorus, who witnessed most of it and inferred some of it. We do not know how much time elapsed between the action described in the frame and Cephalus' account of it, which I treat as occurring within the same year, a conjecture. Antiphon II is described as no longer a young man but now like his grandfather (126c); but Adeimantus and Glaucon IV are still active. If Antiphon is, say, forty, the date is ±382, but this is obviously a very crude estimate.

Protagoras
±433/2

frame (set later in the	friend (probably mentioned at 362a)	*speaker*
day of the main	Socrates of Alopece, son of Sophroniscus I	*speaker*
action): unspecified	slave (310a)	
public place;	others (310a)	
dramatic (309a–310a)		

main action:	Hippocrates, son of Apollodorus	*speaker*
Socrates' room, the	Socrates of Alopece, son of Sophroniscus I	*narrator, speaker*
courtyard outside, the	unnamed slave, eunuch doorman (314c–d)	*speaker*
street, the house of	Callias III of Alopece, son of Hipponicus II	*speaker*
Callias III; narrated	Protagoras of Abdera	*speaker*
	Xanthippus of Cholarges, son of Pericles I	
	Paralus of Cholarges, son of Pericles I	
following Protagoras:	Charmides of Athens, son of Glaucon III	
	Philippides I of Paeania, son of Philomelus I	
	Antimoerus of Mende	
	a group of mostly foreigners (315a)	
	Hippias of Elis, son of Diopeithes	*speaker*

	Eryximachus of Athens, son of Acumenus	
seated around	Phaedrus of Myrrhinus, son of Pythocles	
Hippias:	Andron of Gargettus, son of Androtion I	
	Elians and other foreigners (315c)	
	Prodicus of Ceos	*speaker*
	Pausanias of Cerameis	
lying around	Agathon of Athens, son of Tisamenus	
Prodicus:	Adeimantus of Athens, son of Cepis	
	Adeimantus of Scambonidae, son	
	of Leucolophides	
	some others (315e)	
arriving separately:	Critias IV of Athens, son of Callaeschrus I	*speaker*
	Alcibiades III of Scambonidae, son of Clinias II	*speaker*

By the 1950s, the essential pieces were in place for determining the dramatic date of *Protagoras*. Guthrie accurately canvassed the issues that had previously been bones of contention: "The date at which the conversation is supposed to take place is in the late 430s. Pericles is still in power in Athens, and his sons (who were to die in the plague of 429) are still alive. The Peloponnesian War has not yet broken out, Alcibiades is a young man 'with his first beard' and the tragic poet Agathon is a mere boy. Socrates is perhaps thirty-six. The reference (at 327d) to a play of Phere-crates which is known to have been produced in 420 must be accepted as an anachronism of the incidental kind which Plato took no particular pains to avoid" (1956: 27). In approximate agreement are Lamb (1924: 87n1), Morrison (1941), and C. C. W. Taylor (1976: 64). A. E. Taylor's ≤433 (1956: 236) is a little unusual, but in the ballpark. Outside is Davison's <458 (1962: 154). A host of facts about the lives of other characters in the dialogue (s.vv.) can now be added to confirm Guthrie's date, while little has happened in the interim to challenge it, but there is controversy in the secondary literature nonetheless. Athenaeus (218b–e), who criticized dramatic elements of the *Protagoras* in the 2–3rd c. c.e., was systematically refuted by Morrison (1941), then resuscitated by Walsh (1984) and Wolfsdorf (1997: 230). Walsh noted two levels of material, one dated ±431 and the other >420, but interpreted the *later* material as primary, implying that Protagoras was on a second visit to Athens; the Peace of Nicias was in force, permitting Elean participation; and Hipponicus II was dead. Such a view wreaks havoc on fitting together the lives of the individuals in *Protagoras* coherently. Wolfsdorf, siding with Athenaeus against Morrison, concluded that no consistent dramatic date is possible. Morrison and Wolfsdorf, unaware of Plutarch's error concerning the order of the marriages of Pericles I's wife (*Per.* 36), perform a number of calculations for the births of her offspring.

[Alcibiades]
early 432

no setting; dramatic	Socrates of Alopece, son of Sophroniscus I	*speaker*
	Alcibiades III of Scambonidae, son of Clinias II	*speaker*

Alcibiades III says (Pl. *Smp.* 219e) that he went with Socrates on campaign to Potidaea, so he had turned twenty by the time Callias left Attica in the fall of 432 (see Socrates s.v.). Alcibiades III is "not yet twenty" (*Alc.* 123d), not yet old enough to fight beyond Attica's frontiers, so the dialogue is set before the expedition. Lamb (1927: 96) says "about 432"; Forde (1987: 222n2) and Howland (1990: 87n2) say 433. Late 433 would suit as well as early 432.

[Second Alcibiades]
early 432, or mid 429

on the way to an	Socrates of Alopece, son of Sophroniscus I	*speaker*
unnamed temple;	Alcibiades III of Scambonidae, son of Clinias II	*speaker*
dramatic		

There is no particular indication of dramatic date, but the two men do not seem to be on campaign during the conversation, so the dialogue is probably conceived to take place just after *Alcibiades* (i.e. before Potidaea), though it could also be after their return more than two and a half years later (after May of 429). Since Pericles I is still alive (143e), a date after August–September 429 is ruled out.

Charmides
May 429

palaestra of Taureas	Socrates of Alopece, son of Sophroniscus I	*narrator, speaker*
(a wrestling school	Chaerephon of Sphettus	*speaker*
near the stoa of the	Critias IV of Athens, son of Callaeschrus I	*speaker*
king archon);	Charmides of Athens, son of Glaucon III	*speaker*
narrated	many others (153c, 154a)	
	a slave (155b)	

The dialogue takes place upon Socrates' return from the devastating battle near Spartolus (Thu. 2.79) that followed the extended siege of Potidaea. Planeaux (1999) provides a detailed chronology of the events, demonstrating that Socrates and Alcibiades III were on campaign from the summer or fall of 432 to May of 429, nearly three years: what started out as an invading army (1.57, 1.61) became a besieging army (2.70), then a defeated army (2.79) before its return (see discussion at Socrates s.v.). Kahn (1996: 185n3, citing Thu. 1.63 and *HCT* 1) had already seen correctly that Socrates could not by 432 have *returned* to Athens from Potidaea, but maintained the view that *Charmides* is set in 432, a date he calls "not only fictive but fictitious as well." The date is just wrong. Near unanimous past agreement that the *Charmides* takes place after the initial battle of 432 (from Lamb 1927: 4 to PCW 639), as if the soldiers had marched back home after the first action of the campaign, before the siege, before Potidaea had surrendered, has always been untenable historically; the large number of inferences drawn from that "secure" date of 432 (with implications for deaths and births within Plato's family) are equally untenable.

Laches
winter 424

follows an exhibition	Lysimachus II of Alopece, son of Aristides I	*speaker*
of fighting in armor	Nicias I of Cydantidae, son of Niceratus I	*speaker*
by Stesilaus;	Laches of Aexone, son of Melanopus	*speaker*
dramatic	Aristides II of Alopece, son of Lysimachus II	*speaker*
	Thucydides II of Alopece, son of Melesias II	*speaker*
	Socrates of Alopece, son of Sophroniscus I	*speaker*
	Melesias II of Alopece, son of Thucydides I	*speaker*

For the limiting dates of 424–418, there has long been virtually universal agreement (Tatham 1888: xxi; Thesleff 1982: 93–4, with reservations; Emlyn-Jones 1996: 2–3): Socrates and Laches have returned from the battle at Delium waged in the fall of 424, from which the two men were comrades in retreat (181b); but Laches, who was killed in 418 leading the Athenians against the Spartans at Mantinea (Thu. 5.74), is still alive. Emlyn-Jones adds that "absence of any direct reference to any current conflict in the Peloponnesian War suggests some period during the 'Peace of Nikias,'" but that is too late for other dramatic considerations, and winter would serve present purposes as well as a period of truce; 424 was a year in which Sparta did not invade Attica to burn the crops. Schmid (1992: 183n1) puts the conversation before the premier of *Clouds* in 423 and the Athenian defeat at Amphipolis in 422—because neither is mentioned. Since Laches was not at Amphipolis (even though Socrates was), there would not have been any reason for that battle to arise in the context of the dialogue, but Schmid is surely right about the *Clouds* which is in any case the earlier event. By setting the dramatic date in the winter of 424, I am placing it after Socrates' return from Delium in the fall, but before the reopening of the sailing season in April, before the premier of *Clouds* and, it should be remembered from the same Dionysian festival, the *Connus* of Amipsias that also featured Socrates in some way and placed 2nd ahead of *Clouds* in a field of five plays (Henderson 1998c: 5 & n13). After 423, it would have been much more difficult for Lysimachus not to have realized that the Socrates of whom the boys so often spoke was the son of his friend and fellow demesman.

Cratylus
≤422

no setting; dramatic	Hermogenes of Alopece, son of Hipponicus II	*speaker*
	Cratylus of Athens, son of Smicrion	*speaker*
	Socrates of Alopece, son of Sophroniscus I	*speaker*

The dramatic date is before the death of Hipponicus II († 422/1) as discussed at Cratylus and Hermogenes s.vv., including references to the several modern contributions to the question. Attempts to set the dialogue nearer *Euthyphro* (e.g. Burnet's), taking the conversation represented in *Euthyphro* to be the very one mentioned in *Cratylus* (396d), have foundered.

[Clitophon]
421–416

no setting; dramatic	Socrates of Alopece, son of Sophroniscus I	*speaker*
	Clitophon of Athens, son of Aristonymus	*speaker*

Putting the dialogue here is a nod to characters of *Republic* and *Phaedrus* mentioned in *Clitophon*. The dramatic date is long before 411 and especially 404 when Clitophon's oligarchical sympathies will have come to fruition.

[Greater Hippias]
421–416

a public place in	Socrates of Alopece, son of Sophroniscus I	*speaker*
Athens; dramatic	Hippias of Elis, son of Diopeithes	*speaker*

Two items affecting dramatic date cannot be reconciled adequately with one another: Hippias speaks of Protagoras (282d7–e4) in ignorance that Socrates, he, and Protagoras all conversed together at Callias III's house when Protagoras visited Athens in ±433/2; yet Gorgias' official visit to Athens of 427 is already in the past (282b). Hippias' presence implies a period of peace, so a dramatic date between 421 and 416 (during the Peace of Nicias) has often been assigned (Taylor 1956: 29; Woodruff 1982: 94). Earlier estimates were less precise: citing Hippias' fame and Jowett's editors, Guthrie (1975: 177) said ≥435; Fowler (1926: note to 282b), "after the time of Gorgias' activity at Athens," i.e. >427.

[Lesser Hippias]
421–416, two days later

Phidostratus' school;	Eudicus of Athens, son of Apemantus	*speaker*
dramatic	Socrates of Alopece, son of Sophroniscus I	*speaker*
	Hippias of Elis, son of Diopeithes	*speaker*

Assuming that the speech Hippias has just delivered in the dialogue is the one he says he expects to present "the day after tomorrow" at Eudicus' request (*G. Hp.* 286b5–6), the dramatic date can be set two days after the imprecise date of the *Greater Hippias*. Even if it is a different speech, 421–416 still holds.

Phaedrus
418–416

along the Ilisus	Phaedrus of Myrrhinus, son of Pythocles	*speaker*
River, and under a	Socrates of Alopece, son of Sophroniscus I	*speaker*
plane tree; dramatic	[Lysias, son of Cephalus II]	*quoted speaker*

The dramatic date of the *Phaedrus* has been actively controversial for some time. Dover uses information about the life of Lysias—the orator's autobiographical speech (12) and other sources, including Lysias' appearances in Plato's dialogues—in search of an appropriate dramatic date for the *Phaedrus*. He tries out "earlier than 415" (1968b: 32–3), then "no possible dramatic date" (41–2), finally settling on "418–416" (43) to fit facts as he ably sifts them. Any date between late 415 and 407 is ruled out because of Phaedrus' involvement in the profanation of the mysteries and subsequent exile. Phaedrus s.v., whose life is more easily reconstructed than most, would have been in his mid-twenties at the time of the dialogue. Lysias (flashback to morning) would have been in his late twenties. Shawyer (1906: xxvi) sugggested 410, but without explanation. Hackforth (1952: 8) and Guthrie (1975: 297) assigned 411–404 because Polemarchus (†404) is alive; but Sophocles and Euripides (268c, † 405 and 406, respectively) were also alive. MacDowell (1962: 74) agrees with Hatzfeld (1939: 313–8) who "insists that Plato had no precise historical date in mind" for the dialogue. Nussbaum holds for literary reasons that Plato deliberately set the dialogue at no possible date (1986: 212–3 & nn24–5).

Symposium
February 416

frame (set ±400): in	Apollodorus of Phaleron	*narrator, speaker*
an unspecified place;	friend, a rich businessman	*speaker*
dramatic (172a–174a)	companions (173b–c)	
	[Glaucon IV of Collytus, son of Ariston]	*remembered speaker*
main action: moves	Aristodemus of Cydathenaeum	*narrator, speaker*
from a public place to	Socrates of Alopece, son of Sophroniscus I	*speaker*
Agathon's house; the	slave who ushers Aristodemus (174e)	
day after Agathon's	Agathon of Athens, son of Tisamenus	*speaker*
victory celebration	slave who cannot budge Socrates (175a)	*indirect speaker*
after winning first	slave who brings water (175a)	*speaker*
prize in tragedy at	Pausanias of Cerameis	
the Lenaean festival;	Aristophanes of Cydatheneum, son	*speaker*
narrated	of Philippus I	
	Eryximachus of Athens, son of Acumenus	*speaker*
	Phaedrus of Myrrhinus, son of Pythocles	*speaker*
	female *aulos*-player (sent to women 176e)	

flashback, ±440	[Diotima of Mantinea]	*remembered speaker*
	Alcibiades III of Scambonidae, son	
	of Clinias II	*speaker*
	revelers	*noise makers*
	female *aulos*-player (with revelers, 212c, d)	*shrieker*

Athenaeus (217a) sets the date of Agathon's first victory with his first tragedy as the Lenaean festival of the fourth year of the ninetieth Olympiad, 416, and that date has not been seriously disputed (see Lamb 1925: 78, Hamilton 1951: 9, Dover 1965: 2, Nehamas and Woodruff 1989: xi, and Blanckenhagen 1992). Bury noted, however (1973: lxvi, citing earlier sources), that the Dionysian festival would fit the text of *Symposium* 175e better than the Lenaean. The celebration took place near the end of a period in which Athens had enjoyed relative peace following April of 421, the Peace of Nicias; it includes some of the most renowned and some of the lowliest of Athenians at the very peak of Alcibiades III's career (216b). Within months, four of the party will have been accused of sacrilege (see Exc. 1), and Athens will have embarked on the catastrophic Sicilian campaign. Blanckenhagen (1992) fills in some of the historical details to make the dramatic frame all the more dramatic in view of the changes undergone by the characters in the interim.

The frame takes place between Apollodorus and an unnamed companion who has asked to hear the speeches given at the long-ago symposium. The companion requesting Apollodorus' narration has heard a version already from someone who heard a version from Phoenix s.v., son of Philippus (172b1–3). The original witness to the symposium, from whom Apollodorus heard it, was Aristodemus. Apollodorus agrees to retell what he told Glaucon IV two days earlier (flashback from frame). The lack of any further specification of Glaucon by demotic or patronymic makes it almost certain that the reference is to Plato's brother. The night's conversation that is about to be recited as the bulk of the dialogue took place when Apollodorus and Glaucon IV were very young, long ago (παίδων ὄντων ἡμῶν ἔτι, 173a)—the date we know to be February of 416. Glaucon IV's birth ≤429 makes him about thirteen at the time of the action, and Apollodorus of a similar age.

[Eryxias]
≤415

stoa of Zeus;	Socrates of Alopece, son of Sophroniscus I	*narrator, speaker*
narrated	Eryxias of Stiria	*speaker*
	Critias IV of Athens, son of Callaeschrus I	*speaker*
	Erasistratus III of Athens	*speaker*
flashback, two days	[Prodicus of Ceos]	*remembered speaker*
	[unnamed youth]	*remembered speaker*
	[gymnasium supervisor]	*remembered speaker*

The dialogue is introduced with a discussion of the wasp-like Syracusans and the importance of attacking their nest with a large force, reminiscent of the period just before Athens undertook the Sicilian campaign in 415; Erasistratus III s.v., born perhaps in the 440s, has just returned from what seems to have been an embassy to Sicily (as his uncle, Phaeax I s.v., is known to have undertaken in 422). The dialogue brings together two men who will later be members of the Thirty, and a probable relative of Critias IV (see stemma: Plato). The dramatic date of *Eryxias* is roughly compatible with another datum about Erasistratus III: that he was the defendant in Antiphon's speech 20 (see Demos s.v.), dated after Pyrilampes' death <413.

Ion
413

unspecified public	Socrates of Alopece, son of Sophroniscus I	*speaker*
place; dramatic	Ion of Ephesus	*speaker*

The *Ion* must be set during the Peloponnesian war (*Ion* 541c4–5) before the Ionian revolt of 412 (Thu. 8.15.1) because Ephesus was afterwards not under Athenian rule (*Ion* 541c3–4), as Woodruff (1983: 5) saw clearly. I narrow the date to 413 because Athens was faced with an acute shortage of leadership, materials, and manpower after the Sicilian disaster and sought creatively the means to effect a recovery. Famously, she replaced tribute with import-export duties and, notably, increased the use of *extra ordinem* commands: generals (*stratēgoi* in name) on discrete assignments who were not regular members of the board of ten generals elected by tribe and apparently did not have to be citizens (see Dover *HCT* 4.391–2). Socrates mentions three foreigners as "generals or other sorts of officials" for Athens (541c–d): Apollodorus of Cyzicus, Phanosthenes of Andros, and Heraclides of Clazomenae, whose careers are detailed s.vv.

Few dialogues have suffered more than *Ion* at the hands of scholars since the 18th c. c.e. It is a fine example of how Plato's straightforward statements could be bypassed in the pursuit of literary and developmentalist objectives that create anachronisms where the text has none. Moore (1974) offered a comprehensive treatment of these issues with abundant citations of previous literature, a definitive article that scholars have since taken into account (except Kahn 1981: 308n9, and 1996: 34, citing Méridier 1931: 24, which was excellent in its time), and that I forbear to reduce to summary.

Lysis
early spring ±409

a newly erected	Socrates of Alopece, son of Sophroniscus I	*narrator, speaker*
palaestra (wrestling	Hippothales of Athens, son of Hieronymus	*speaker*
school) outside the	Ctesippus of Paeania	*speaker*
east wall of Athens	others (203a)	
at the Panops spring,	Lysis II of Aexone, son of Democrates I	*speaker*

near the Eridanus	Menexenus of Athens, son of Demophon	*speaker*
River, during the	two slaves with foreign accents (223a)	*indirect speakers*
Hermaea; narrated	unnamed of Aexone, son of Democrates I	
	unnamed of Athens, son of Demophon	

Guthrie was half right to say of *Lysis*, "There is nothing to indicate the dramatic date, nor is it important" (1975: 135). If that dialogue alone were all we knew of Lysis, the statement would appear wholly right. But Lysis s.v. lived long enough that Plato's associates in the Academy may easily have been personally acquainted with him. At least in the case of the *Lysis*, Plato was writing about families and individuals known to him personally, many of whom were still living when the dialogues were written, some of whom—Lysis in particular—he may well have known from childhood as his own friends or the friends of his brothers. The chief datum of interest for determining the dramatic date of the *Lysis* is that the characters are younger than they are in the *Euthydemus*, a dialogue that offers substantial grist for dramatic date milling and includes Ctesippus from the *Lysis* (see below). Plato goes to some lengths to depict the characters of the *Lysis* plausibly as adolescents. A dramatic date of ±409 implies that Lysis and Menexenus are about thirteen and the older boys, Ctesippus and Hippothales, about fifteen or sixteen. The secondary literature notes two vague internal clues to the dramatic date, but both are compatible with ±409: Guthrie (1975: 135) says, "At the end (223b), Socrates describes himself as an 'old man,' but since he is talking, not very seriously, to two schoolboys of twelve or thirteen, one cannot attach much weight to this." Stroud (1984: 356n2) notes that Socrates mentions Darius II (r. 424–404) as if he is alive (211e).

Euthydemus
≥407

frame (set the next	Crito of Alopece	*speaker*
day): a quiet place;	Socrates of Alopece, son of Sophroniscus I	*speaker*
dramatic (271a–272e,		
290e–293a, 304b–		
305a)		

main action: in the	Socrates of Alopece, son of Sophroniscus I	*narrator, speaker*
Lyceum; narrated	Euthydemus of Chios and Thurii	*speaker*
	Dionysodorus of Chios and Thurii	*speaker*
	Clinias III of Scambonidae, son of Axiochus	*speaker*
	Ctesippus of Paeania	*speaker*
	Crito of Alopece (among onlookers, 271a)	
	several lovers of Clinias III (273a)	
	a crowd of onlookers (271a)	

The date I propose for the *Euthydemus* is based on the following considerations: (a) >409: There is overlap with characters from other dialogues, Ctesippus of *Lysis*, for example, though he is now older. In the *Lysis*, the youths are referred to as boys (παις, παιδες = 8 *TLG*) twice as often as they are referred to as young men (νεανισκ–, μειρακ–= 4 *TLG*); whereas the ratio is more than reversed for the *Euthydemus* (6 to 26). Because at least some of these characters were Plato's contemporaries who lived on to the middle of the 4th c., we should not be surprised that their descriptions are so vivid. Athens is at war, but these youths do not appear to have reached military age. One of the persons Plato would have known personally is Crito's son, Critobulus II s.v., who would become one of the wealthiest men of early 4th c. Athens. Critobulus' age is used by his father to calibrate the ages of Ctesippus s.v., and Clinias III s.v.—who is more mature (already *meirakion*), though apparently slightly younger than Critobulus (hence Crito's surprise). But all can be called young men (*neaniskoi*) at the time of the dialogue. (b) <415 or ≥407: Clinias III's father, Axiochus s.v., fled the *polis* when accused of profaning the mysteries (Andoc. 1.16; Exc. 1; cf. Taylor 1956: 90; *pace* Lamb 1925). Families were adversely affected when heads of households fled into exile and had all their possessions confiscated by the state, of which there is no hint in the dialogue. The year 407 has the additional feature of being when Alcibiades III returned to Athens for four months, almost certainly accompanied by Clinias III's father, so he was again on Athenians' minds. (c) >413: The expulsion of Athenians from Thurii occurred "a good many years" ago (271c, *pace* Guthrie 1975: 267 who notes rather the *founding* of Thurii in 444/3). Dionysidorus and Euthydemus fled Thurii (271c), a colony supported mainly by Athens, under circumstances well enough known that no further explanation was required; thus the brothers were probably subject to the general expulsion of Athenians and their sympathizers from Thurii in 413, at the end of the Athenian army's defeat in Sicily. The two have been in and around Attica for several years since then. (d) >411–≤404: Protagoras is probably dead (286c), but Alcibiades is alive (275b). See Guthrie (1975: 267) and Stanley (1986: 187–8n20, citing Méridier 1950: 139), but note the former passage is about the followers of Protagoras, not the man himself. On the latter point, Lamb (1925: 391) confuses Alcibiades II and III and sets the dialogue "a year or two before Socrates' death"). The secondary literature turns up further items of little use: (e) late in the available period: "Socrates is old enough for Crito to be afraid he is too old to learn (272b)" (Guthrie 1975: 267; cf. Stanley 1986: 177) although Crito and Socrates are the same age, and Socrates' age is a fluid thing: cf. *Ly.*, where the characters are only a little younger than in *Euthd.* but where Guthrie (1975: 135) discounts the remarks about age explicitly because of the youth of the other characters. (f) 430–420 dramatic date, without explanation (Jowett's editors 1953: 1.202nI; cf. Bicknell 1982: 242n23, citing Taylor 1956: 90–1: "not later than 416/15 and probably close to 420").

Meno
402

an unspecified public	Meno of Thessaly, son of Alexidemus	*speaker*
place; dramatic	Socrates of Alopece, son of Sophroniscus I	*speaker*

          several slaves attending Meno (82a)

          unnamed slave of Meno   *speaker*

          Anytus I of Euonymon, son of Anthemion I   *speaker*

The dramatic date of the dialogue is not in much dispute ("about 402" Lamb 1924: 263; "402" Guthrie 1956: 101; "403 or early 402" Guthrie 1975: 236). The restoration of the democracy in 403 marks the earliest possible date since Anytus holds office (90b). Meno is visiting Athens from Thessaly, and staying with Anytus before leaving in March of 401 on the campaign against Artaxerxes led by Cyrus and reported in Xenophon's *Anabasis*. I favor a date later in the 403–402 period because the early days of the restoration were turbulent, with negotiations toward a reconciliation agreement continuing well into 402, making it unlikely Athens would have attracted many visitors right away.

Menexenus
winter 401/0

off the agora;   Socrates of Alopece, son of Sophroniscus I   *speaker*

dramatic   Menexenus of Athens, son of Demophon   *speaker*

                [Aspasia of Miletus, daughter of Axiochus]   *quoted speaker*

Menexenus has grown up since *Lysis*, finished school, and become interested in rhetoric, though he is young enough that Socrates can still tease him (*Mx.* 234a–b), perhaps in his twenties. Menexenus' age has never been much of a consideration in dating this blatantly anachronistically dialogue, conceived in the secondary literature as having no possible dramatic date. Guthrie (1975: 313) exclaims, "This is the shock. It is Socrates who recites the speech, but the Peace of Antalcidas was concluded twelve or thirteen years after his death." What has kept *Menexenus* in the canon at all is that Aristotle paraphrases 235d at *Rhetoric* 1367b8, ". . . as Socrates used to say, it is not difficult to praise the Athenians to an Athenian audience," and at 1415b31, "For it is true, as Socrates says in the *Funeral Speech* [the ancient name for *Mx.*], that 'the difficulty is not to praise the Athenians at Athens but at Sparta.' "

    It is likely that Plato wrote the dialogue without the section of the internal speech running from 244b to 246a, carrying events beyond the death of Socrates and perhaps beyond the life of Aspasia (b. late 470s). It has long been noted that the Academy was involved in much writing of dialogues and editing of works that had varying degrees of Platonic core; and it is no special feat to add a couple of pages in the style of the existing *Menexenus* speech, to bring the work up to date for the Athenian audience, deprecated in the preface of the same work. The deletion of 244b–246a would mark a rhetorical improvement as well, leaving the speech to address, in order, the furthermost to the closest: the gods, the heroes, the war against barbarians (Persians), the war against other Greeks, and the civil war of the Athenians. To move from the final civil war with its discovery of "genuine kinship" and "firm friendship based on ties of blood" *backward* to war with other Greeks again before ending is a rhetorical lapse that need not be attributed to Plato himself. The dramatic date of 401/0 is warranted for historical reasons. Since Aspasia's speech (a flashback to the day before) makes reference to the oligarchs' resettlement in Eleusis (243e–244a), and since the Athenians held their annual festival in honor of the war dead in winter (Thu. 2.34), the winter of 401/0 would have been the first appropriate occasion for the oration to be represented dramatically. For additional bibliography on this controversial dialogue, some of it excellent, some fanciful, see Bloedow (1975), Loraux (1986), Ledger (1989: 163–4), Thomas (1989: ch. 4), Henry (1995: ch. 3), and Tsitsidiris (1998).

Theaetetus
spring 399

frame (spring 391):	Euclides of Megara	*speaker*
house of Euclides in	Terpsion of Megara	*speaker*
Megara; dramatic	a male slave of Euclides	*oral reader*
(142a–143c)		
main action: in a	Theodorus of Cyrene	*speaker*
gymnasium in	Theaetetus of Sunium, son of Euphronius	*speaker*
Athens; dramatic	Socrates of Alopece, son of Sophroniscus I	*speaker*
	Socrates of Athens (147d)	
	a few other youths (144c)	
	[Protagoras of Abdera]	*conjured speaker*

The dramatic date of the main action is known because, at the end of the dialogue (210d), Socrates says he is on his way to the stoa of the king archon (where the *Euthyphro* takes place); i.e. he has already received his summons to a pretrial hearing. But he also says he will meet Theodorus the next morning, and both are perfectly possible. When a plaintiff brought a complaint of impiety in Athens, four days were required for notification of the defendant before a preliminary hearing could be held in the court of the king archon. If the king archon found that the plaintiff had established cause, then details of the impending case were published on tablets in the agora, evidence was collected, one of the city's courts was assigned the case, and a date was set for trial. The time required for these matters varied but, as a citizen, Socrates was not imprisoned pending trial, so he could go about his philosophizing as usual. The trial was held in a court, not yet excavated or even identified. (In ordinary suits, the procedure was much the same except that the pretrial hearing was held before a magistrate.) An excellent discussion of the legal issues is Harrison's (1998: 2, ch. 2 §4: "Initiating Procedure"). So there is room for the *Sophist* and *Statesman* before the trial, and even room for Euclides s.v. to make several trips from Megara to Athens before Socrates' death (*Tht.* 143a).

The date of the dramatic frame involves a long and complex argument interwoven with the life of Theaetetus, and with scholarship from the early 20th c. (see Theaetetus s.v.). In brief, and in conformity with historians' views of the issues

(*PA, PAA*), Theaetetus was wounded in a well-known battle of the Corinthian war (in 391) while he was of military age, not in his mid-forties at a time when Athens' army was made up primarily of mercenaries (369).

Euthyphro
spring 399, later the same day

stoa of the king	Euthyphro of Prospalta	*speaker*
archon; dramatic	Socrates of Alopece, son of Sophroniscus I	*speaker*

Although the dating issues are much the same for *Euthyphro* as for *Theaetetus*, it is worth noting Burnet's three-part argument that a minimum five-year interlude between the death of the hireling and the resulting trial should not be considered unusual; he uses the argument to suggest further that the *Theaetetus* and *Euthyphro* are more likely to have taken place in 400 than in 399 (1924: *Euthphr.* 4c4n): (a) legal maneuvering by the defendant could extend the period between the initial charge and the trial by several years, and Euthyphro's relatives strongly opposed his action (*Euthphr.* 4d); (b) in 412 (the date of Antiph. 6), cases of homicide required three preliminary hearings in three separate months before a trial in the fourth month, a rule Burnet assumed still held in 400/399; and (c) there was almost no court activity while the legal code was being formally revised after the democracy was restored in 403. Burnet, citing pseudo-Aristotle (*Ath. Pol.* 40.4), thought the courts were inactive from 403 until 401/0, the archonship of Xenaenetus; but that is not so. MacDowell (1978: 47) uses Andocides IV's contemporaneous account (1.81–87; cf. MacDowell 1962: 194–9) to demonstrate that the two boards of lawmakers (*nomothetai*) completed their work for the archonship of Euclides, 403/2. Burnet's first point alone is sufficient to explain the delay before Euthyphro's father's trial, but MacDowell adds that (d) all *cleruch* cases may have been assigned a specific month on the court calendar which, if missed for any reason, caused a further year's delay (1978: 229–30); we do not know whether *cleruch* courts observed a rule of three preliminary hearings. In Socrates' case, however, (a) there was no maneuvering, (b) the case was not homicide (there is no extant information for *asebeia* charges), (c) the revision of the laws was accomplished in less than a year, and (d) no one involved in Socrates' case was a *cleruch*. *Theaetetus* and *Euthyphro* cannot be set more precisely than the spring of 399, implying an interval of as much as two months between the preliminary hearing and the trial.

Sophist
spring 399, the next day

in the Athenian	Theodorus of Cyrene	*speaker*
gymnasium where	Socrates of Alopece, son of Sophroniscus I	*speaker*
the Theaetetus *was*	Eleatic visitor	*speaker*
set; dramatic	Theaetetus of Sunium, son of Euphronius	*speaker*
	Socrates of Athens	
	others (217d)	

Statesman
spring 399, later the same day

the same (258a)	Socrates of Alopece, son of Sophroniscus I	*speaker*
	Theodorus of Cyrene	*speaker*
	Eleatic visitor	*speaker*
	Socrates of Athens	*speaker*
	Theaetetus of Sunium, son of Euphronius	

Apology
May–June 399

one of the several	Socrates of Alopece, son of Sophroniscus I	*speaker*
courts used by	Anytus I of Euonymon, son of Anthemion I	
Athens; trial speech	Meletus II of Pithus, son of Meletus I	*speaker*
with some dialogue	Lycon of Thoricus	
	jury, and many spectators	*hecklers, murmurers*
	[Callias III of Alopece, son	
	of Hipponicus II]	*remembered speaker*
	Chaerecrates of Sphettus, unnamed	
	Crito of Alopece	
	Critobulus II of Alopece, son of Crito	
	Lysanias of Sphettus	
	Aeschines of Sphettus, son of Lysanias	
	Antiphon of Cephisia	
	Epigenes of Cephisia, son of Antiphon	
	Nicostratus of Athmonon, son	
	of Theozotides I	
	Paralius of Anagyrus, son of Demodocus	
	Adeimantus I of Collytus, son of Ariston	
	Plato of Collytus, son of Ariston	
	Aeantodorus of Phaleron	
	Apollodorus of Phaleron	

The trial was held in the month of Thargelion, roughly May–June, i.e. the month when the Athenians sent their sacred "ship of Theseus" to Delos (*Phd.* 58a–b), and execution was forbidden in the *polis* until its return. The ship embarked on the day before the trial. The length of the trip could vary with the seas and winds, but happened to take thirty-one days in 399 (Xen. *Mem.* 4.8.2), so Socrates lived thirty days beyond his trial, if we take Xenophon literally.

Crito
June–July 399, twenty-eight or twenty-nine days after the trial

just before dawn at	Crito of Alopece	*speaker*
the prison southwest	Socrates of Alopece, son of Sophroniscus I	*speaker*
of the agora; dramatic		

The warder (43a), who will be a participant in *Phaedo*, has admitted the sleepless Crito into Socrates' cell before dawn. Crito had learned that Theseus' ship was at the cape, Sunium, and was thus expected to reach the Piraeus a day later, that is, later in the day that was dawning by the time Socrates woke. Socrates interpreted a dream he had had to mean that the ship would take two days to make its way from Sunium (44a–b)—and we do not know who, if either, turned out to be right, assuming Xenophon's "thirty days" to have been accurate.

Phaedo
June–July 399, one or two days later

frame (set a few weeks or months after the execution): Pythagorean community at Phlius; dramatic (57a–59c, 88c–89a, 102a–b, 117b)	Phaedo of Elis	*speaker*
	Echecrates of Phlius	*speaker*
main action: the same prison as before; narrated	Phaedo of Elis	*narrator, speaker*
	Socrates of Alopece, son of Sophroniscus I	*speaker*
	Xanthippe, wife of Socrates of Alopece	*speaker*
	warder, a public slave (59d–e, 116a–d)	*speaker*
	women of Socrates' household (may include Xanthippe)	
	Sophroniscus II of Alopece, son of Socrates	
	Lamprocles II of Alopece, son of Socrates	
	Menexenus of Alopece, son of Socrates	
	slave of Crito, fetches poisoner (117a)	
	poisoner, a public slave (117a–118a)	*speaker*
Athenians:	Apollodorus of Phaleron	*angry weeper*
	Critobulus II of Alopece, son of Crito	
	Crito of Alopece	*speaker*
	Hermogenes of Alopece, son of Hipponicus II	
	Epigenes of Cephisia, son of Antiphon	
	Aeschines of Sphettus, son of Lysanias	
	Antisthenes II of Athens, son of Antisthenes I	
	Ctesippus of Paeania	
	Menexenus of Athens, son of Demophon	
	some others (59b)	
Thebans:	Simmias of Thebes	*speaker*
	Cebes of Thebes	*speaker*
	Phaedondas of Thebes	
Megarians:	Euclides of Megara	
	Terpsion of Megara	

Dialogues with Problematic Dramatic Dates

Republic
throughout the Peloponnesian war

road up to Athens	Socrates of Alopece, son of Sophroniscus I	*narrator, speaker*
during the Bendis	Glaucon IV of Collytus, son of Ariston	*speaker*
festival, then at the	Polemarchus, son of Cephalus II	*speaker*
house of Polemarchus	unnamed slave of Polemarchus (1.327b)	*speaker*
in the Piraeus;	Adeimantus I of Collytus, son of Ariston	*speaker*
narrated	Niceratus II of Cydantidae, son of Nicias I	
	some others (1.327c)	
	Lysias, son of Cephalus II	
	Euthydemus, son of Cephalus II	
	Thrasymachus of Chalcedon	*speaker*
	Charmantides I of Paeania	
	Clitophon of Athens, son of Aristonymus	*speaker*
	Cephalus II of Syracuse, son of Lysanias	*speaker*

The version of *Republic* that has come down to us is not a seamless dialogue, and it was not edited from the standpoint of dramatic date; thus there would be jarring anachronisms if any of the candidate specific dates between 432 and 404 were assigned definitively. Before the dialogue was revised into its current shape, there was a freestanding version of the first book, *On Justice* or *Thrasymachus*; and there was a proto-*Republic* or *Ideal State* of two scrolls to which Xenophon objected (Gell. *NA* 14.3.3). Each had its own dramatic date considerations that must be treated separately before I return to the dating of the dialogue as a whole. Both segments have had supporters among philosophers: Vlastos' endorsement of the separate composition of *Republic* 1 has been influential (1991: 46–7; also Kraut 1992: xii); Kahn (1993) has held out against the view. Ryle (1966: 55–64) was an early and articulate supporter of an *Ideal State*. But the bulk of the work on the composition of the *Republic* text has fallen to philologists (Hermann 1839; Hirmer 1897: 592–8; Thesleff 1982). For additional bibliography and finer detail, see Nails (1998).

   On Justice or *Thrasymachus* was set in May–June of 424 or perhaps 421. Adeimantus I and Glaucon IV could not have been participants since they were children then. The Peloponnesian war was going on (1.350d), but there was an interval of peace during Thargelion, May–June, when the festival of Bendis was being inaugurated. Osborne (*NIA* 3: 27 & n33, citing Pečirka 1966) notes the high Athenian expectations of a pact with Thrace that characterized the *early* part of the war: Athenians hoped to win the favor of the Thracians by granting citizenship to Sadokos, son of King Sitalkes of Odrysian Thrace (Thu. 2.29.4–5, 2.67.2) before 430; the official acceptance of the cult of Bendis was a further effort at such influence. Aristophanes' *Acharnians*, produced in 425, shows Athens' continuing expectation of military support from Thrace (lnn. 141–50); and probably it was then that Sadokos visited Athens, presumably as a citizen. After 424, when Sadokos was killed in action, there was no further hope of assistance, and Thracians would not likely have visited Athens (cf. Moors 1987: 10 & nn21–3). However, (a) it is unclear that Lysias and Polemarchus had returned permanently from Thurii as early as 424, or for that matter before 413; (b) 424 provides an interval of relative peace almost by accident: Cleon's return from Pylos with Spartan prisoners of war dissuaded the Spartans from invading Attica that summer; and (c) there is considerable evidence for a much earlier introduction of Bendis, making 424 already too late by some estimates (Morgan 1992: 228 gives 429, congruent with the Athenian wooing of Sadokos). If the Bendis festival, like the characters Adeimantus I and Glaucon IV, was an addition to the original *Thrasymachus*, then the date should probably be May–June of 421, when the Peace of Nicias had just come into effect in April. The peace broke down incrementally through 416, but a dramatic date earlier in the period fits better the elderly characters Charmantides I and Cephalus († 421–415). The presence of Nicias I's son, Niceratus II, has sometimes been interpreted as a quiet salute to Nicias I as a peacemaker.

Proto-*Republic* or *Ideal State* comprised most of *Republic* 2–5; if Plato's brothers were its interlocutors, then any dramatic date—if it had a definite dramatic date—before ±411 would be inappropriate. Ryle (1966: 61) points out that the explicit summary of the ideal state offered at the beginning of the *Timaeus-Critias* "group" summarizes books 2–5 only, adding that a summary of the same material appears at the beginning of *Republic* 8, and that Aristotle summarizes the same material in *Politics* II. The two-scroll *Ideal State* thus appears to have been well known for some time before Plato composed the *Republic*. If the dramatic date of *Timaeus-Critias* is allowed to determine the dramatic date of *Ideal State*, then they all took place in August of 429 (see below) in which case *Ideal State* did not include Adeimantus I and Glaucon IV. Thesleff (1997) has canvassed the history of the topic, added fresh arguments, and ferreted out the parts of books 2, 3 and 5 that are summarized in other ancient sources. He concludes that the proto-*Republic* began at 2.369b, after the speeches of Adeimantus I and Glaucon IV, when Socrates takes over with concrete proposals (he lists specific passages through 5.474e at 1997: 151); these are the proposals Aristophanes so successfully transformed into farce in the *Assemblywomen* of 392 or 391 (see Nails 1995: 116–22).

When the *Republic* as we have it was composed, an important potentially datable detail was added, a reference to the battle at Megara in which Adeimantus I and Glaucon IV participated (2.368a), discussed s.vv., which establishes that Glaucon IV is at least (and probably about) twenty. The dramatic date of the *Republic* by that criterion is 408/7, not far from Zeller's (1876) suggestion of 409/8 or White's (1995: 324–5) arguments from prosopographical data on Thrasymachus s.v. for 407. But those dates are too late for Cephalus II and Damon (3.400b), and probably for Charmantides I. A prosopographically scrambled dialogue, something like Steve Allen's ingenious *Meeting of the Minds* early television series is what we have in the *Republic*: consistency for the family and friends of Cephalus in the first book, and also for Plato's brothers in the second, but an uncomfortable fit for the dialogue as a whole. Here is a smattering from the modern bibliography, not mentioned above: Moors (1987: 22), a "timeless dialogue"; Rankin (1964:

120), "424"; Nussbaum (1986: 136), "probably 422"; Howland (1993: xii), "421–420 approximate"; Lee (1955: 60), "just before 420"; Allan (1940: 20) and A. E. Taylor (1956: 264), "spring, 421"; Waterfield (1993: 327an), "about 420"; Dover (1968b: 53), "421–415" as a window; (Ferrari 2000: 1n3, 31n30), "June . . . between 431 and 411"; Shorey (1930: viii) and Boeckh (1874: 448), "411 or 410"; Campbell (1894: 3:2) and Voegelin (1957: 3:53n4), "411/10"; and Bloom (1968: 440n3), "probably around 411."

Timaeus-Critias
August 429

house of Critias III	Timaeus of Locri Epizephyrii	*speaker*
during the	Critias III of Athens, son of ?Leaïdes	*speaker*
Panathenaea;	Socrates of Alopece, son of Sophroniscus I	*speaker*
dramatic	Hermocrates I of Syracuse, son of Herman	*speaker*

The version of *Republic* to which *Timaeus-Critias* is a sequel is *Ideal City* or proto-*Republic* (see above). The details that have troubled commentators—two months separating the Bendis festival from the Panathenaea, different characters in the two dialogues, inadequate summary of *Republic*—all fall away. What remains is a dramatic date of 429 that implicitly applies equally to proto-*Republic*. If the date is pushed any further forward, Critias III becomes unreasonably old to be so spry (he is ninety-one). Jowett (or his editors in the Great Books edition) was so certain of the connection between *Republic* and *Timaeus-Critias* that he added the list of characters of *Timaeus* to those of *Republic* to indicate Socrates' audience for the narration. Bury (1929: 3) accepted the connection among the three dialogues, but Clay (1987: 143–6), Lee (1965: 23), and Cornford (1937: 4–5) did not, offering the objections I have listed. Cornford held that Socrates had many such discussions of the ideal state, not only the one that ended up as a dialogue.

Gorgias
throughout the Peloponnesian war

outside a public place	Gorgias of Leontini	*speaker*
where Gorgias has	Polus of Acragas (Sicily)	*speaker*
given a display and	Callicles of Acharnae	*speaker*
taken questions;	Chaerephon of Sphettus	*speaker*
dramatic	Socrates of Alopece, son of Sophroniscus I	*speaker*
	others (458b)	

Gorgias, like *Republic*, has a variety of indicators of dramatic date. Some commentators have subordinated some and featured others. Lamb (1925: 350n1), for example, took Socrates' mention of the Arginusae trial "last year" (473e) to set the date clearly at 405. But Dodds (1959: 17–8) was so thorough about the issues that his discussion can well be called definitive, and his conclusion is that Plato sets the dialogue "in no particular year." Dodds notes the following points. Pericles I died recently (503c2), suggesting soon >429; but not <427 because that is the year of Gorgias' first (and only attested) visit to Athens (D. S. 12.53). Plato's stepbrother, Demos s.v., is Callicles' beloved (481d), so the date should be ±422; that fits nicely with the prediction that Alcibiades III will be unfairly blamed by the democracy (519a), still ahead in 415 and again in 407. Archelaus of Macedonia (r. 413–399) has recently assumed power (470d); and Euripides' *Antiope* (probably produced in 408, but certainly not earlier than 411) is already known (485e).

Dialogues without Dramatic Dates
(in alphabetical order)

[Axiochus]	Clinias III of Scambonidae, son of Axiochus	*speaker*
near the Ilisus River,	Axiochus of Scambonidae, son	
on the way to the	of Alcibiades II	*speaker*
Cynosarges	Damon of Oe, son of Damonides	
gymnasium outside	Charmides of Athens, son of Glaucon III	
the city walls, then at	Socrates of Alopece, son of Sophroniscus I	*speaker*
the house of		
Axiochus; narrated		

The muddled indicators for a dramatic date are that Axiochus has been unwell, but he is not necessarily old (364b); that Clinias and Charmides are of an age to be in love with one another (364a), but the two were in fact born far apart, so this is implausible; and that Prodicus recently made a speech at Callias' house (366b). Bicknell (1982: 242n27) says, "the dialogue is set shortly after the trial of the Arginousai generals."

[Demodocus]	Demodocus of Anagyrus	*speaker*
no setting;	unnamed narrator (?Socrates)	*narrator, speaker*
monologue followed	several others	*indirect speakers*
by three narrated bits		

[Epinomis]	Athenian	*speaker*
no setting; dramatic	Clinias of Cnossus in Crete	*speaker*
	Megillus of Sparta	

[Halcyon]	Chaerephon of Sphettus	*speaker*
no setting; dramatic	Socrates of Alopece, son of Sophroniscus I	*speaker*

[Hipparchus]	a friend	*speaker*
no setting; dramatic	Socrates of Alopece, son of Sophroniscus I	*speaker*

Laws	Athenian visitor	*speaker*
road up from	Clinias of Cnossus	*speaker*
Cnossus to the grotto	Megillus of Sparta	*speaker*
of Dicte (temple of		
Zeus) on Mount Ida;		
dramatic		

This is not the place to argue that *Laws* contains little genuine Platonic material; what counts is that it is still widely regarded as genuine, especially among philosophers (but see Ryle's discussion of a proto-*Laws* 1966: 66; Nails and Thesleff forthcoming). The possible existence of a proto-*Laws* fits the view of Dušanić (1990a: 364–5) that—whatever one may decide about the authenticity of the whole—the date conceived for the dialogue was originally ±408 when the Spartan ambassador, Megillus s.v., was active.

[Minos]	a friend	*speaker*
no setting; dramatic	Socrates of Alopece, son of Sophroniscus I	*speaker*

[On Justice]	a friend	*speaker*
no setting; dramatic	Socrates of Alopece, son of Sophroniscus I	*speaker*

[On Virtue]	a friend	*speaker*
no setting; dramatic	Socrates of Alopece, son of Sophroniscus I	*speaker*

There is little information that could lead to a dramatic date although the dialogue quotes freely from the *Meno* and appears to have been set with that dialogue's background in mind: the friend was once in love with one of the sons of Pericles I (377d–e), both of whom died in 429—but this is not very helpful because a lover might be much older than his beloved. The sons of Thucydides I, born in the 470s, are both dead after living very long lives (378a), placing the dramatic date years after Socrates' death.

Philebus	Protarchus of Athens, son of Callias	*speaker*
no setting; begins	Philebus of ?Athens	*speaker*
and ends abruptly;	Socrates of Alopece, son of Sophroniscus I	*speaker*
dramatic		

Guthrie (1978: 198) notes only that there is almost no drama in the dialogue and that the historicity of both Philebus and Protarchus is debated in the literature.

[Rival Lovers]	a young boy	
Dionysus the	another young boy	
grammarian's school;	first rival	*speaker*
narrated	second rival	*speaker*
	Socrates of Alopece, son of Sophroniscus I	*narrator, speaker*

[Sisyphus]	Sisyphus of Pharsalus	*speaker*
no setting; dramatic	Socrates of Alopece, son of Sophroniscus I	*speaker*

[Theages]	Demodocus of Anagyrus	*speaker*
just off, then in, the	Theages of Anagyrus, son of Demodocus	*speaker*
stoa of Zeus;	Socrates of Alopece, son of Sophroniscus I	*speaker*
dramatic	[Timarchus of ?Thebes]	*remembered speaker*
	[Aristides II of Alopece, son	
	of Lysimachus II]	*remembered speaker*

One might put the dramatic date at about 409, but doing so involves so much anachronism and adjustment that it seems better to view the dialogue as set in no particular year in the last decade of Socrates' life. In favor of 409, one could mention (a) Sannio s.v., is with Thrasyllus on an Ionian expedition (129d; the fleet in fact sailed in the spring of 409); (b) in the past (130a–b) is a conversation with Aristides II († 411/10), and a quarrel with Thucydides II († 411); and (c) the Sicilian expedition of 415–413 is over. Archelaus' rule in Macedonia (124d) has ended; since his reign was 413–399, Socrates' participation in the conversation would necessitate a date of early 399. At the other extreme, a date of 429 or soon after is required for Charmides' period of being *kalos* (128e). We know too little about the lives of others who are mentioned to be able to establish dramatic dates from those: Prodicus, Gorgias († ±380), and Polus are alive (127e); Euathlus and Timarchus are dead, and Clitomachus is alive (129a–c).

Letters

My starting point in dating the letters was Bury (1929), which I adjusted, taking into account Morrow (1935), Harward (1976), Sanders (1987), and the refinement of dates for Plato's life s.v.

>383	[*Letter* 9]	to Archytas of Tarentum
>383	[*Letter* 12]	to Archytas of Tarentum
≥365	[*Letter* 13]	to Dionysius II of Syracuse
365–60	[*Letter* 5]	to Perdiccas III of Macedonia
≥360	[*Letter* 1]	to Dionysius II of Syracuse

>360	[*Letter* 2]	to Dionysius II Syracuse
>360	[*Letter* 11]	to Laodamas of ?Thasos
>360	[*Letter* 10]	to Aristodorus of Syracuse
≥357	[*Letter* 3]	to Dionysius II Syracuse
≥357	[*Letter* 4]	to Dion of Syracuse
>summer 354	*Letter* 7	to the friends of Dion of Syracuse
353/2	*Letter* 8	to the friends of Dion of Syracuse
±350	[*Letter* 6]	to Hermias of Atarneus and Erastus and Coriscus in nearby Scepsis

APPENDIX II
PERIPHERAL PERSONS

Listed below with very brief identifications are the persons mentioned in the dialogues and letters of Plato and other Socratics, and their homonyms, who do not meet the criteria for inclusion in the primer. Also listed below are persons who appear only in the stemmata of the persons of the prosopography. Gods, heroes, legendary figures, fictional characters, place names and festivals are not included. Roman numerals for related persons, as opposed to homonyms, are provided to prevent confusion among individuals orbiting Socrates and Plato; they follow those assigned by *APF*.

A

Acusilaus of Argos [*RE* 3 *OCD*³], compiler of genealogies (frr. in *FGrH* 2) (fl. early 5th c.)

Adeimantus II [*PA/APF* 198 (8792.10A) *LGPN2* 15], Plato's heir (D. L. 3.41)

Aeschines of Athens [*PA* 341 *LGPN2* 95 *RE* 3], of the Kekropis tribe, member of the Thirty (Xen. *Hell.* 2.3.2, 3.13)

Aeschines of Cothocidae [*PA/APF* 354 (14625.2) *LGPN2* 54 *RE* 15 Stephanis 90 *OCD*³], son of Atrometus I and Glaucothea, rhetorician (±397–±322) (*IG* II² 2408.7, *CEG* II 776)

Aeschylus of Eleusis [*PA* 442 *LGPN2* 20 *RE* 13 *OCD*³], renowned tragedian (?525/4–456/5)

Agamedes, master builder with his brother, Trophonius (fl. late 7th c.)

Agariste I of Sicyon [*APF* 9688.3A *RE* 1], daughter of Cleisthenes of Sicyon (tyrant), wife of Megacles II, mother of Hippocrates II, Cleisthenes of Athens, a daughter who married Pisistratus, *et al.* (Hdt. 6.126–127)

Agariste II of Alopece [*PA/APF* 92 (9688.10, 11811) *LGPN2* 2 *RE* 2], Alcmaeonid family: daughter of Hippocrates, sister of Megacles IV, wife of Xanthippus I of Cholarges s.v., mother of Ariphron II s.v., and Pericles I s.v.

Agis II of Sparta, son of Archidamus [*LGPN3A* 16 *RE* 2 Poralla² 26] and Lampido, Spartan king (Thu., Xen., D. S., *passim*) (r. 427/6–400/399)

Aglaeon of Athens, father of Leontius s.v.

Aglaophon of Thasos [*RE* s.v.], painter and father of painters (Aristophon and Polygnotus)

Alcetas of Macedonia [*RE* 2], brother of Perdiccas II, murdered for political gain by Archelaus

Alcibiades II of Scambonidae, son of Clinias I [*PA/APF* 597 *LGPN2* 22 *PAA* 121625], father of Clinias II, a daughter, and Axiochus, (*Agora* 25, Thu. 5–6, Lys. 14.39; [Andoc.] 4.34, *IG* I³ 424–430) (ostracized 460)

Alcmaeon I of Athens [*PA/APF* 651 (9688.2) *LGPN2* 1], son of Megacles I, commander at First Sacred War (from ±595), Olympic victor (592), gave his name to the wealthy and powerful Alcmaeonid dynasty, father of Megacles II and Alcmonides I (Hdt. 6.125.2, 5; *IG* I³ 1469.2; Isocr. 16.25)

Alcmonides I of Athens [*PA/APF* 653 (9688.3B) *LGPN2* 1], son of Alcmaeon I (*IG* I² 472 note) (mid 6th c.)

Alcmonides of Aphidna [*PA/APF* 654, 656 (9688.13) *LGPN2* 4], second husband of Agariste III s.v. (*IG* II² 1929.14; Andoc. 1.16)

Alexander, son of Alcetas [*RE* 19], Macedonian youth murdered for political gain by Archelaus

Alexidemus of Thessaly [*LGPN3B* 5], father of Meno s.v.

Alexippus of Athens [*PA* 547 *LGPN2* 1], nephew of Acumenus s.v., witnessed in favor of the claims of Andocides IV in 400 about events of 415 (Andoc. 1.18)

Amestris [*RE* 4], wife of Persian king Xerxes

Amiantus of Athens and Aegina [*LGPN2* 1], co-instigated Dioclides' perjury about mutilation of herms in 415 (Andoc. 1.65–66)

Amyclus of Heraclea, student of Plato (D. L. 3.46)

Amycus, famous boxer who developed the use of gloves

Amynander of Athens, contemporary of Solon, member of Critias' *phratry*

Anacharsis of Scythia, geometer (fl. 7–6th c.)

Anacreon of Teos [*RE* 1 *OCD*³], lyric poet (b. ≤570)

Anaximander of Miletus [*RE* 1], natural philosopher who posited the 'unlimited' as fundamental (frr. in DK 12) (†>547)

Anaximander, Homeric critic (Xen. *Sym.* 3.6) (fl. late 5th c.)

Andromachus [*FRA* 7429], slave of Archebiades, gave evidence on the performance of the mysteries (see Exc. 1; Andoc. 1.12–14, 1.28)

Androtion I of Gargettus [*PA/APF* 914 = 915 (913) *LGPN2* 2 *OCD*³], son of Andron, father of Andron s.v., wealthy Atthidographer, used as a source by [Aristot.] *Ath. Pol.*, student of Isocrates (*IG* II² 61.6–7, Demos. 22)

Antaeus, famous wrestler who used the trick of falling to the ground in order to win

Anthemion I of Euonymon [*PA/APF* 935 (1324) *LGPN2* 12], father of Anytus, rose from *thete* to *hippeus* class; tanner

Antiphates of Cytherus [*PA/APF* 1260, 1261 (1194) *LGPN2* 15], father of Antisthenes I s.v. (*IG* II² 1951, *Naval Catalogue*, 112, 154–6 [= *IG* I³ 1032.161, 251–253]; *IG* II² 1138.28, 1623.233–4, 2828; *SEG* 27.15.1)

Apollodorus of Athens [*PA* 1379 *LGPN2* 4 *PAA* 142300], father of Hippocrates s.v.

Apollophanes [*FRA* 7439], slave of Alcibiades III (*IG* I³ 426.12, dated 414/3: adult male)

Apolloniades [*FRA* 7441], household slave named in Plato's will (D. L. 3.42)

Archebiades of Athens [*PA* 2300], lover of Alcibiades IV s.v., accused of profaning the mysteries (Lys. 14.27; Andoc. 1.13)

Archelaus of Athens [*PA* 2339 *PAA* 209490 *OCD³*], considered first Athenian philosopher, followed Anaxagoras (frr. in DK 60; cf. Plu. *Mor.* 876d; D. L. 2.16–17, who calls him Socrates' teacher)

Archelaus of Macedonia [*OCD³*], legitimized son of Perdiccas II (r. 413–399), allied with Athens, patronized Agathon s.v.; assisted Andocides IV s.v.; famous for heinous crimes (Thu. 2.100.2)

Archenius of Athens [*LGPN2* 3] sea captain unknown except in Lys. 12.16

Archestratus of Phrearrhi [*PA* 2431 *LGPN2* 64] Plato's neighbor on the east of his Iphistiadae estate (D. L. 3.41)

Archestratus [*PA/APF* 2411 (9238) *PAA* 211225], son of Lycomedes, general commanding thirty ships and a thousand hoplites at Potidaea (Thu. 1.57.6, *IG* I³ 48.11) (fl. 430s)

Archidamus II of Sparta, son of Zeuxidamus [*LGPN3A* 22 *RE* 3 Poralla² 157], Spartan king (Hdt., Thu., Xen., D. S. *passim*) (r. ±469/8–427/6)

Archilochus of Paros [*LGPN1* 2 *RE* 2 supp. 11 *OCD³*], son of Enipo, Greek lyric poet (active mid 7th c.)

Arete [*RE* 3], daughter of Aristippus of Cyrene s.v., mother of Aristippus, associated with the Cyrenaic school of philosophy (fl. early 4th c.)

Aristarchus [*FRA* 7455], slave of Alcibiades III (*IG* I³ 426.14, 24, dated 414/3: shoemaker)

Aristocles of Athens [*PA/APF* 1847 (8792.9)], archon 605/4, likely paternal ancestor of Plato

Aristocles of Collytus [*PA/APF* 1870 (8792.9) *LGPN2* 48], father of Ariston s.v. (archon 605/4)

Aristogiton of Athens [*PA* 1772 *RE* 2], son of Cydimachus a creditor of Aeschines (Lys. fr. 1)

Aristogiton of Athens [*PA* 1777 *RE* 1 *OCD³*], with Harmodius, assassinated Hipparchus, brother of the tyrant Hippias in 514

Aristomachus [*FRA* 7465], slave of Alcibiades III (*IG* I³ 426, 44, dated 414/3: adult male)

Ariston, father of Hegesippus s.v.

Aristonymus of Athens [*LGPN2* 2], father of Clitophon s.v. (Pl. *R.* 328b, pat., [Pl.] *Clt.* 406, pat.)

Aristophon of Thasos [*LGPN1* 48 *RE* 9], son of Aglaophon, painter

Aristotle of Stagira [*DPhA* 414 *RE* 18 + supp. 7 'Peripatos' s.v. *OCD³*], son of Nicomachus, famous philosopher, student of Plato (*opera*) (384–322)

Artaxerxes I of Persia [*OCD³*], son of Xerxes and Amestris, king (r. 465–424)

Artaxerxes II of Persia [*OCD³*], son of Darius II and Parysatis, king (r. 405/4–359/8)

Artemis [*FRA* 7481], slave named as freed in Plato's will (D. L. 3.42)

Astylus, athlete famous for moderation

Axiochus of Miletus, father of Aspasia s.v.

Axiothea of Phlius [*LGPN3A* 1 *RE* 2], student of Plato, and later of Speusippus, said to have worn men's clothing (D. L. 3.46, 4.2)

B

Bias of Priene, mortal sage

Bictas [*FRA* 7513], household slave named in Plato's will (D. L. 3.42)

Brachyllus of ?Athens [*PA* 2927 *LGPN2* 2], married the sister of Lysias ([Demos.] 59.22), later Lysias' father-in-law

Brasidas of Sparta [*LGPN1A* 2 *RE* 1 Paralla² 177 *OCD³*], son of Tellis and Argileonis commander during the early part of the Peloponnesian war (465–422)

C

Callaeschrus of Eupyridae [*PA* 7760 *LGPN2* 12], *tamias* of Athena in 412/ 1, may have been a leader of the Four Hundred (Lys. 12.66; *IG* I² 249.229; 250.244; [287.178;] 288.202)

Callaeschrus of Athens [*PA* 7755 *LGPN2* 6], plaintiff for whom Lysias composed an *epidikasia*, for Antiphon's daughter (Lys. fr. 66; [Plu.] *LTO* 833a)

Calliades of Athens [*PA* 7774 *LGPN2* 9], father of Callias s.v.

Callias I of Alopece [*PA/APF* 7833 (7826.2)], son of Phaenippus, father of Hipponicus I, Olympic victor in 564 (Hdt. 6.121–2) (≤590–520s)

Callias II of Alopece [*PA/APF* 7825 (7826.5) *LGPN2* 82], son of Hipponicus I, father of Hipponicus II s.v., wealthy, politically and militarily active, married Elpinice (*IG* I³ 835, 876; *AM* 106.152) (520–±446)

Callimachus of Athens [*PA* 7996 *LGPN2* 11], litigious democrat who sued Patrocles *et al.* (Isocr. 18)

Callimachus of Athens [*PA* 7997 *LGPN2* 17], man from whom Plato bought his Eresidae estate, and one of six executors of Plato's will in 348/7 (D. L. 4.43)

Callippides, renowned tragic actor (Xen. *Symp.* 3.11) (fl. 5th c.)

Cambyses of Persia [*OCD³*], son of Cyrus I, king (r. 530–522), known as deranged

Ceph[——] [*FRA* 7770], slave of Axiochus of Scambonidae (*IG* I³ 430.26: ΚΕΦ[——], dated 414/3)

Cephisodorus of Aphidna [*PA/APF* 8363 (8410) *LGPN2* 54], father of Tisander s.v., (*IG* II² 1929.22, pat.)

Cepis of Athens [*PA* 8282 *LGPN2* 1], father of Adeimantus s.v.

Ceramon of Athens [*PA* 8266 *LGPN2* 1], a rich man with many mouths to feed (Xen. *Mem.* 2.7.3)

Cercyon, famous wrestler who used tricks to win

Chabrias of Aexone [*PA/APF* 15086 *LGPN2* 2 *OCD³*], son of Ctesippus I, Athenian general (sometimes commanding mercenaries), Academy regular, friend of Plato, father of Ctesippus II (Xen. *Hell.* 5.1; *IG* II²; Philoch. fr. 223; Demos. 20.81, 21.64; D. L. 3.20–24) (±420–356)

Charias [*FRA* 8138], slave of Alcibiades III (*IG* I³ 426.13, dated 414/3: maker of iron skewers and spits)

Charmantides II of Paeania [*PA/APF* 15502] son of Chaerestratus (see discussion at Charmantides I)

Chilon of Sparta [*LGPN3A* 3 *RE* 1 Poralla² 760], sage (Aristot. *Rh.* 1389b4, 14)

Clearchus of Heraclea Pontica [*RE* 4], student of Plato and Isocrates, seized control of Heraclea in 364/3 and was murdered in 353/2, wrote *Encomium on Plato* (D. L. 3.2)

Cleisthenes of Sicyon [*APF* 9688.3A *OCD³*], tyrant, led troops in First Sacred War, father of Agariste I (Hdt. 6.126–130; Aristot. *Pol.* 1315b; *FGrH* 90, fr. 61) (r. ±600–570)

Cleisthenes of Athens [*PA/APF* 8526 (9688.6) *LGPN2* 1 *OCD³*], son of Megacles II and Agariste I of Sicyon, archon under the tyrant Hippias in 525/4, after Hippias was overthrown, initiated political reforms, including the division of Attica into demes—local units that increased democratic participation (active 525/4–507)

Cleobulus of Lindos (Rhodes) [*LGPN1* 13 *RE* s.v.], son of Evagoras, sage, father of Eumetis and Cleobulina (6th c.)

Cleon of Cydathenaeum [*PA/APF* 8674 *LGPN2* 43 *OCD³*], son of Cleaenetus, pro-war democratic leader, tanner, general (Thu. 2–5, *passim*; Aristoph. *Knights*) (±470–422)

Cleopatra [*RE* 11], wife of Macedonian king Perdiccas II

Cleophantus of Phrearrhi [*PA* 8635], son of Themistocles s.v.

Clinias I of Athens [*PA/APF* 8510a (600) *LGPN2* 21], son of Alcibiades I, father of Alcibiades II, *trierarch* at Artemisium in 480 (Hdt. 8.17.1; *ARV²* 173.5) (b. ±525)

Coesyra of Eretria (*Euboea*), wife of Megacles IV

Conon of Anaphlystus [*PA/APF* 8707 (13700)], son of Timotheus, Athenian general with a career from 414–393, father of ?Cratinus, Timotheus (see Exc. 2; Thu. 7.31; Xen. *Hell., passim*)

Creophylus of Samos [*LGPN1* 1 *RE* s.v.], son of Astycles, one of the Homeridae (Pl. *R.* schol. gives origin Chios) (?8th c.)

Cresphontes of Messene [*RE* s.v.], early Lacedaemonian legislator

Crison of Himera, champion sprinter, famous for rigorous training that included sexual abstinence

Critias I of Athens [*PA/APF* 8789 (8792.3–5) *LGPN2* 1], son of ?Dropides I (archon ±598, i.e. between 600 and 596)

Critias II of Athens [*PA/APF* 8790 (8792.3–5) *LGPN2* 3 *PAA* 585295], son of Dropides II, father of Leaïdes, red-haired (Pl. *Chrm.* 157e–158a, *Ti.* 20e; Aristot. *Rh.* 1375b32; Procl. *in Tim.* 20e) (±600–>510)

Croesus of Lydia [*OCD³*], son of Alyattes, king (r. 560–546), name synonymous with wealth, conquered by Persians under Cyrus I

Cydias of Hermione, lyric poet (Pl. *Chrm.* 155d; Aristoph. *Clouds* 967 schol.)

Cypselus of Corinth [*RE* 12], son of Aetion and Labda, tyrant (Hdt. 5.92) (r. 657–627)

Cyrebus of Athens [*LGPN2* 1] rich baker (Xen. *Mem.* 2.7.6)

Cyrus I ("the Great") of Persia [*OCD³*], son of Cambyses I, conqueror, king (Xen. *Cyr.*) (†530)

Cyrus II of Persia [*OCD³*], son of Darius II and Parysatis, younger brother of Artaxerxes II, whom he sought to overthrow with the help of Greek mercenaries (Xen. *Anab.*) († 401)

D

Damnippus of Athens [*LGPN2* 1] friend of Lysias, unknown except at Lys. 12.12–15

Damonides of Oe [*PA/APF* 3144 (9688.13) *LGPN2* 1], father of Damon s.v., (Ath. 27.4; *AM* 106.150; Plu. *Per.* 9.2)

Darius I of Persia [*RE* 1 *OCD³*], son of Hystaspes, king (r. 521–486)

Darius II of Persia [*RE* 2 *OCD*³], son of Artaxerxes I, king (r. 424–404)

Datis of Media [*RE* 1], Persian commander at Marathon, sent by Darius I (Aristoph. *Peace* 289)

Demeas of Collytus [*PA* 3318 *LGPN2* 42], rich cape maker (Xen. *Mem.* 2.7.6)

Demetrius of Athens [*PA* 3334 *LGPN2* 10], the one of Plato's six executors in 348/7 who had a copy of the household inventory (D. L. 3.43, *IG* II² 4383)

Demetrius of Amphipolis, student of Plato (D. L. 3.46)

Demophon of Cholarges [*PA/APF* 3701 (11811.2) *LGPN2* 12], son of Hippocrates s.v. (Aristoph. *Clouds* 1001 schol.; Eu. *Dem.* fr. 112 [K 103]) (b. ≤424/3)

Demophon of Athens [*PA* 3692 *LGPN2* 1], father of Menexenus s.v.

Demosthenes of Aphidna [*PA/APF* 3585 *LGPN2* 16 *RE* 5 *OCD*³], son of Alcisthenes, long-serving general who indicted Alcibiades of Phegous (Thu. 3–8; D. S. 12–13) (±460–413)

Demosthenes of Paeania [*PA/APF* 3597 *LGPN2* 37 *RE* 6 *OCD*³], son of Demosthenes, famous orator and logographer (±384–322)

Demostratus of Xyrete [*PA* 3626, *LGPN2* 74], son of Androsthenes, owner of property south of Plato's estate in Eresidae (*IG* II² 1927.13; D. L. 3.42)

Diocles of Athens [*PA* 3982 *LGPN2* 5], father of Euthydemus s.v.

Diocles of Phlius [*LGPN3A* 17 *RE* 49] Pythagorean philosopher (4th c.)

Dioclides of Athens [*PA* 3973 *LGPN2* 3] falsely accused some forty-seven men in 315 of mutilating herms, confessed, was executed (Andoc. 1.37–67; Phryn. fr. 61 [K 58])

Diodorus of Erchia [*PA* 3941 *RE* 10 *LGPN2* 62], son of Xenophon s.v. and Philesia (*SEG* 33.932.14)

Diogiton of Athens [*PA/APF* 3788 (3885) *LGPN2* 1], *trierarch*, guardian of his brother's three orphaned children (Lys. 32) (b. ±460)

Diomnestus of Cydantidae [*PA* 4075 *LGPN2* 7], son of Diognetus s.v. (Lys. 18.21)

Dionysius [*FRA* 7568], household slave named in Plato's will (D. L. 3.42)

Diopompus, athlete famous for moderation

Dropides I of Athens [*PA/APF* 4572 (4574, 8792.1–4) *LGPN2* 1], father of Critias I, Dropides II (archon 645/4)

Dropides II of Athens [*PA/APF* 4573 (4574, 8792.1–4) *LGPN2* 2 *PAA* 375780], son of ?Dropides I, father of Critias II, (Pl. *Chrm.* 157e, pat., *Ti.* 20e–21b, *Criti.* 20e; Procl. *in Tim.* 20e) (eponymous archon in ?593/2)

E

Elpinice of Laciadae [*PA/APF* 4678 (8429.10, 7826.5) *LGPN2* 4], daughter of Miltiades IV and Hegesipyle I of Thrace, sister of Cimon II, wife of Callias II, divorced, mother of Hipponicus II s.v., (≤510–>460)

Empedocles of Acragas [*LGPN3A* 5 *RE* 3 *OCD*³], presocratic philosopher, DK 31 (±492–432)

Epeius, famous boxer who devised tricks to win bouts

Epicharmus of Syracuse [*OCD*³], comic poet (Pl. *Grg.* 505e schol.) (fl. early 5th c.)

Epilycus II [*PA/APF* 4925 (8429.4) *LGPN2* 5], son of Tisander II, married the daughter of

Ischomachus s.v., negotiated treaty with the Persians 424/3, died leaving heiress daughters (Andoc. 1.117, 3.29; ML 72.16) (b. ≤454, † 415–413)

Epimenides of Crete [*OCD³*], famous prophet and ascetic (fl. late 7th c.)

Erasinides of Athens [*PA* 5021 *LGPN2* 1] general 406/5 executed after Arginusae (Xen. *Mem.* 1.1.18, Xen. *Hell.* 1.5–1.7; *IG* I³ 102.5)

Erasistratus I of Acharnae [*PA/APF* 5024 (13921) *LGPN2* 3], father of Phaeax s.v. (*IG* I² 941.6) killed in action in 450

Erasistratus II of Acharnae [*PA/APF* 5026 (13921) *LGPN2*], son of Phaeax s.v. (*Agora* 25.653–6; *AM* 106.155)

Euaeon of Lampsacus, student of Plato (D. L. 3.46)

Euclides of Athens [*PA* 5677 *LGPN2* 12], gem-cutter who owed Plato 3 *minae* mid-4th c. (D. L. 3.42)

Euphronius of Sunium [*PA* 6114 *LGPN2* 30], father of Theaetetus s.v.

Euripides of Melite [*PA/APF* 5951 *LGPN2* 9], relative of Phaedrus s.v. (Thu. 2.70, 79; Lys. 19.14)

Eurybatus, linked to Phrynondas, and synonymous with villainy

Eurymedon I of Myrrhinus [*PA/APF* 5975 (8792.11D) *LGPN2* 6], married Potone s.v., father of Speusippus (D. L. 4.1); not the general who died in Sicily in 413 (*PA* 5973)

Eurymedon II of Myrrhinus [*APF* 8792.11D *LGPN2* 7], son of ?Speusippus, named executor and landowner in Plato's will in 348/7 (D. L. 3.42–43); not the man of that name who prosecuted Aristotle in 323 (*PA* 5972)

Euryptolemus II of Athens [*PA/APF* 5984 (9688.8) *LGPN2* 7], son of

Euryptolemus I, sibling to Isodice, Megacles VII, and Pisianax II (b. ≤500)

Eurysthenes of Sparta [*LGPN3A* 1 *RE* 3 Poralla² 331], son of Aristodemus and Argeia, one of the first two kings of Sparta, the other was his twin, Procles (Hdt. 6.52, 7.204)

G

Gelon of Syracuse and Gela [*LGPN3A* 13 *RE* 3 *OCD³*], son of Dinomenes, tyrant of Syracuse (±540–478, r. ±490–478)

Glaucon I of Cerameis [*PA/APF* 3026 (3027) *LGPN2* 21], father of Leagrus I and a ?daughter who married Critias III (b. ≤560)

Glaucon II of Cerameis [*PA/APF* 3027 *LGPN2* 22], son of Leagrus I, general, father of Leagrus II and a daughter who married Callias III (*kalos ARV²* 1580, dated 475–465; *ARV²* 1581 "the Nolan amphora" for a victory as *chorēgos*; Androt. fr. 38; Thu. 1.51.4, ML 61.19–20) (±490–>432)

Glaucon, famous rhapsode (*Ion* 530d)

Glauconides [*PAA* 277225] wanted to acquire fighting cocks for the *polis* (D. L. 2.30)

Gobryas of Persia, sage named for his grandfather

Gryllus I of Erchia [*PA* 3094 *LGPN2* 1], father of Xenophon s.v.

Gryllus II of Erchia [*PA* 3096 *LGPN2* 2], son of Xenophon s.v. and Philesia

Gyges of Lydia [*OCD³*], king (r. ±680–645), murdered King Candaules, married the queen, first to exploit gold from the Pactolus, conqueror, first to be called 'tyrant' in Greek (see Hdt. 1.8–1.14; Pl. *R.* 2.359d)

H

Hagnodorus of Amphitrope [*PA/APF* 143 (8792.6) *LGPN2* 1] implicated in the acts of the Thirty, and brother-in-law (κηδεστής) to Critias IV (Lys. 13.55)

Hagnon of Stiria [*PA/APF* 171 (7234) *LGPN2* 22], son of Nicias of Stiria, partisan of Pericles, father of Theramenes s.v. (Lys. 12.25; *AM* 106.148) (±470–410)

Harmodius of Aphidna [*PA* 2232], with Aristogiton, assassinated Hipparchus, brother of the tyrant Hippias in 514

Hegias of Athens [*PA* 6361 *LGPN2* 5] one of six executors of Plato's will in 348/7 (D. L. 3.43)

Heraclides of Athens, student of Plato (D. L. 3.46)

Heraclides of Pontus [*OCD³*], son of Euthyphro, student and associate of Plato, historian (see Heraclides Ponticus in *FHG* 2.197), *scholarch* of the Academy 361–360, writer of dialogues, 47 titles attributed to him (D. L. 3.46; 5.86–94) (4th c.)

Heraclitus of Ephesus [*OCD³*], son of Bloson, presocratic philosopher associated with change (DK 22) (fl. ±500)

Hermocritus I of Syracuse [*LGPN3A* 11 as 'Hermocrates'], father of Dionysius I, Leptines I, Thearidas, Thesta (Tod 2.108; Plu. *Dion* 21) (5th c.)

Hermodorus of Syracuse [*LGPN3A* 7 *RE* 5], student and biographer of Plato, said to have sold Plato's works in Sicily (D. L. 2.106, 3.6)

Herodicus of Leontini, son of Charmantides [*LGPN3A* 1], doctor, brother of Gorgias (5th c.)

Heroscamander of ?Thebes [*PA* 6535], father of Nicias s.v. (The name is not attested in *LGPN3B*.)

Hesiod of Ascra (Boeotia) [*OCD³*], poet of *Works and Days, Theogony* et al. (fl. ±700)

Hestiaeus of Perinthus, student of Plato (D. L. 3.46)

Hieronymus of Athens [*PA* 7553 *LGPN2* 1], father of Hippothales s.v.

Hipparchus of Athens [*PA/APF* 7598 (11793.3) *LGPN2* 1], son of Pisistratus, co-tyrant with Hippias 527–514, assassinated (*IG* I³ 502; 1470; Hdt.; Thu.; [Pl.] *Hipparch.* 228b–229d—only source for claim that Hipparchus was elder to Hippias)

Hipparete II [*PA/APF* 7589 (600.10) *LGPN2* 2], daughter of Alcibiades IV of Scambonidae s.v. (*IG* II² 7400)

Hippias of Athens [*PA/APF* 7605 (11793.4, 7) *LGPN2* 1 *OCD³*], son of Pisistratus, co-tyrant with Hipparchus 527–514, expelled (*IG* I³ 948; 1031.17; Hdt.; Thu.) (b. ≤570)

Hippocrates I of Athens [*PA/APF* 7626 (11793.2) *LGPN2* 1], father of Pisistratus (7th–6th c.)

Hippocrates II of Athens [*PA/APF* 7633 (9688.10) *LGPN2* 2], son of Megacles II and Agariste I of Sicyon, Alcmaeonid family, father of Megacles IV and Agariste II (Hdt. 6.131.2; *Agora* 25.628–39) (b. early 550s)

Hippocrates of Chios [*RE* 14 *OCD³*], important mathematical astronomer associated with the early Academy, (see Procl. *Eucl.* 66.4, 7) (fl. end of 5th c.)

Hippodamus of Miletus, planned the colony at Thurii 444/3

Holas [*FRA* 7918], slave of Axiochus of Scambonidae (*IG* I³ 430.7, dated 414/3)

Horomazes of Persia, father of Zoroaster

I

Ibycus of Rhegium [*OCD*³], lyric poet (fl. 6th c.)

Iccus of Tarentum, Olympic athlete famous for self-disciplined training regimen, considered wise

Iphicrates, general inspired by Socrates' cockfighting illustration (likely a confusion: the famous Athenian general is a century later) (D. L. 2.30)

Ismenias of Thebes [*LGPN3B* 9 *RE* 1], democratic leader who gave aid to the exiled Athenian democrats in 403 and took bribes from the Persians (*FGrH* 66.12; Pl. *R.* 336a, *Meno* 90a; Xen. *Hell.* 3.5.1) (active 404–382)

Isodice of Athens [*PA/APF* 7712 (9688.8, 8429.11 *LGPN2* 2], daughter of Euryptolemus I; wife of Cimon II; sibling to Euryptolemus II, Megacles VII, and Pisianax II; mother of Lacedaemonius, Oulius, Thettalus, Cimon III, Miltiades V, and Pisianax III (b. ≤500)

Isolochus of Athens [*PA* 7718 *LGPN2* 1], father of Pythadorus s.v.

L

Lampido of Sparta [*LGPN3A* 1 Poralla² 474], daughter of (king) Leotychidas II, first wife of (king) Archidamus II, mother of (king) Agis II; var. Lampito ([Pl.] *Alc.* 123e; Hdt. 6.71.2)

Lamprus of Athens [*LGPN2* 1 *RE* 2], famous musician and music teacher (Pl. *Mx.* 236a; Phryn. fr. 74 [K69])

Lasthenia of Mantinea [*LGPN3A* 1 ?= 2 *RE* 2], student of Plato and later of Speusippus (D. L. 3.46, 4.2)

Leagrus I of Cerameis [*PA/APF* 9028 (3027)], son of Glaucon I, general (*kalos ARV²* 1591–2; Hdt. 9.75) (±525–465/4)

Leagrus II of Cerameis [*PA/APF* 9029 (3027)], son of Glaucon II, involved in dispute over heiresses (Andoc. 1.117–21) (b. ± 436)

Leaïdes of Athens [*LGPN2* 1 (*APF* 8792.5)], son of Critias II, father of Critias III, known only from pat. on *ostrakon* (*Agora* 25.608–9) (b. ±565)

Leodamas I of Acharnae [*PA/APF* 9076 (13921) *LGPN2* 2], son of Phaeax I s.v., criminal, and sympathizer with the Thirty (Aristot. *Rh.* 1400a30; Lys. 26.13–14)

Leogoras II of Cydathenaeum [*PA/ APF* 9075 (828.6) *LGPN2* 7], son of Andocides III, accused by Dioclides of mutilating herms, but saved by his son, Andocides IV s.v. (Andoc. 1.22, 40, 146; *AM* 106.152)

Leosthenes of Athens [*PA* 9142] one of Plato's six executors in 348/7; Lamian war hero (D. L. 3.42–43)

Leotychides II of Sparta [Poralla² 488], king (Hdt. 6–8, *passim*) (r. ±491/ 0–469/8)

Leucolophides of Scambonidae [*PA* 9061, *LGPN2* 2] father of Adeimantus s.v. (*IG* I³ 426.10, 43, 106, 141, 185, 190; 430.10, 27)

Lichas (not Lichias) of Sparta [*LGPN3A* 6 Poralla² 492 *RE* 3 *OCD*³], son of Archesilaus, entertained foreign guests at festivals (Xen. *Mem.* 1.2.61) (fl. 421–411)

Lycurgus of Sparta [*LGPN3A* 4 *RE* s.v. *OCD*³ Poralla² 499], famous legislator (Pl. *Laws*)

Lydus [*FRA* 7809], slave of Pherecles of Themicus, accused many citizens of profaning the Eleusinian mysteries in 415 (Andoc. 1.18)

Lysander of Sparta [*LGPN3A* 9 *OCD*³ Poralla² 504], son of Aristocritus, general in command during the defeat of Athens in 404 (±440–395)

Lysanias of Syracuse [*LGPN3A* 68], father of Cephalus s.v. ([Plu.] *LTO* 835c)

Lysicles [*PA* 9417 *LGPN2* 4 *RE* 2], general, democratic leader and stockbreeder, married Aspasia s.v. after Pericles I's death (Aristoph. *Knights*; Thu. 3.19.1–2) († 428)

Lysimachus I of Alopece [*PA/APF* 9504 (1695.1) *LGPN2* 36], father of Aristides I s.v. (*Agora* 25.21–88; *AM* 106.149)

Lysimachus of Athens [*PA* 9490 *LGPN2* 10] named in a legal argument in 402, involving Patrocles s.v. (Isocr. 18.7)

M

Megacles II of Athens [*PA/APF* 9692 (9688.3) *LGPN2* 3 *OCD*³], son of Alcmaeon I, husband of Agariste I, father of Cleisthenes, Hippocrates, et al., powerful and wealthy Alcmaeonid family (Hdt. 1.59–62, 6.126–31; [Aristot.] *Ath. Pol.* 13.4; schol. Aristoph. *Wasps* 1223) (b. ±600, active 575–±556)

Megacles IV of Alopece [*PA/APF* 9695 (9688.10) *LGPN2* 16 ?= 4], son of Hippocrates, father of Dinomache s.v., ostracized 487/6, (*IG* I³ 297.15; 298.27, 35; 299.42 f.; 322.38; 323.45, 51; 324.59; 349.59; 350.65; *Agora* 25, 628–39; [Aristot.] *Ath. Pol.* 22.5; Pindar *Pythian* 7.15)

Megacles V of Alopece [*PA/APF* 9697 (9688.11) *LGPN2* 17], son of Megacles IV and Coesyra of Eritrea, father of ?Megacles VI (*IG* I³ 297.15; 298.27, 35; 299.42; 322.38; 323.45, 51; 324.59; 349.58 f.; 350.65; *Agora* 19, plate 2d.19; plate 2e.?3]

Megacles VI of ?Alopece [*PA/APF* 9690 (9688.11 *LGPN2* 19], son of ?Megacles V, (*ARV*² 1599, dated 440–430)

Megacles VII of ?Sunium [*APF* (9688.11)], son of Euryptolemus I, sibling of Isodice, Euryptolemus II, and Pisianax II (b. ≤500)

Melanippides of Melos [*LGPN1* 1 *RE* 1], dithyrambic poet (Xen. *Mem.* 1.4.3) (6–5th c.)

Meles of Athens [*PA* 9802 *LGPN2* 2 Stephanis 1630], son of Pisias, famous lyre player, but poor singer, father of Cinesias s.v. (Pher. *Agr.* fr. 6 [K 6])

Melesias I of Alopece [*PA/APF* 9812], famous wrestler and trainer on Aegina, father of Thucydides I (Pindar, *Olympian Ode* 8, *Nemean Odes* 4, 6) (≤538–>460)

Melissus of Samos [*LGPN1* 2 *RE* 4 *OCD*³], presocratic philosopher in the Parmenidean tradition (DK 30) (fl. 5th c.)

Menedemus, student of Plato (Epi. fr. 10.2 [K 11])

Menedemus of Eretria [*RE* 9 *OCD*³], student of Stilpo, then Phaedo (D. L. 2.125–44)

Menon of Athens [*PA* 10069 *LGPN2* 7] rich cloak maker (Xen. *Mem.* 2.7.6)

Metaneira [*LGPN2* 1 *RE* 3], slave of Nicarete, *hetaira* of Lysias s.v. ([Demos.] 59.19–23; Ath. 107e, 584f), fl. late 4th c.

Metrobius of Athens [*PA* 10133
LGPN2 1 ?= 3], father of Connus s.v.
(Crat. *Arch.* fr. 1 [K 1])

Metrodorus of Lampsacus, Homeric
rhapsode specializing in allegory,
student of Anaxagoras (Epicurean
philosopher of the same name and
deme lived almost a century later)
(fl. late 5th c.)

Mithaecus of Syracuse [*LGPN3A* 1 *RE*
s.v.], author of a book on Sicilian
pastry

Myson of Chen, sage (*Prt.* 343a)

N

Niceratus I of Athens [*PA/APF* 10740
(10808) *LGPN2* 25], father of Nicias I
s.v., Diognetus s.v., and Eucrates
s.v., invested heavily in silver
mining, leaving great wealth in land
and slaves to three sons (*IG* I³
369.20, 370.20, 50, 470.13?, *IDélos*
104–127.7, *Agora* 25.648) (b. ±500)

Nicias II of Cydantidae [*PA/APF*
10809 (10808) *LGPN2* 96], son of
Niceratus II s.v., married a daughter
of Thrasybulus (*IG* II² 1627.201,
1629.494–5, 834, 1631.189, 1690.2; *IG*
VII 4254.28; *SEG* 39.171.3; Lys. 18.10,
19.47; Aristoph. *Eccl.* 427–8; *Agora*
19P5) (≤409–>350)

Nysaeus of Syracuse [*LGPN3A* 1 *RE*
2], son of Dionysius II and
Aristomache, tyrant of Syracuse (r.
351–346) (Plu. *Dion*; *GG* 3.2.102–7)
(±385–>346)

O

Oenopides of Chios [*LGPN1* 1 *OCD³*],
mathematical astronomer, credited
with discovering Eucl. 1.12 and 1.23,
the obliquity of the ecliptic, "great
year" *et al.* (DK 41) (fl. 5th c.)

Orthagoras of Thebes [*LGPN3B* 1 *RE*
3 Stephanis 1957], *aulos* teacher in
Athens (Pl. *Prt.* 318c–d) (active late
5th c.)

P

Pausanias I of Sparta [*LGPN3A* 32 *RE*
25 *OCD³* Poralla² 595], son of
Cleombrotus, general (Hdt. 9; Thu.
1.95, 131–4) (±510–469)

Pausanias II of Sparta [*LGPN3A* 34 *RE*
26 *OCD³* Poralla² 596], son of
Pleistoanax, Agiad king, grandson
of Pausanias I, minor at the
outbreak of the Peloponnesian wars
(r. 445–426, 408–395)

Perdiccas II of Macedonia [*OCD³*],
king (r. ±450–413) promoted the
revolt at Potidaea

Periander of Corinth [*LGPN3A* 8 *RE* 1
OCD³], son of Cypselus and Crateia,
oppressive tyrant (±627–587)

Pericles III of Cholarges [*PA/APF*
11810 (11811.2) *LGPN2* 4 *RE* 3], son
of Hippocrates s.v. (Aristoph. *Clouds*
1001 schol.; Eu. *Dem.* fr. 112 [K 103])
(b. ≤424/3)

Pherecles of Themacus (Attica) [*PA*
14191 *LGPN2* 7], son of
Pherenicaeus, accused in 415 of
profaning the Eleusinian mysteries
with others in his house (*IG* I³
426.83, listed among the condemned;
Andoc. 1.17, 19, 22, 35)

Pherecrates of Athens [*PA* 14195
LGPN2 1 *OCD³* *PP*], comic poet with
victories 440–430 (*PCG*; *IG* II²
2325.56, 122)

Philemonides of Athens [*PA* 14264],
father of Philemon s.v.

Philesia [*PA* 14286 *LGPN2* 1], wife of Xenophon of Erchia (D. L. 2.52)

Philippus I of Athens [*PA* 14399 *LGPN2* 87], father of Aristophanes

Philippus of Chollidae [*PA* 14417 *LGPN2* 58], Plato's neighbor to the west at his Iphistiadae estate (D. L. 3.41)

Philippus of Mende = Philip of Opus [*RE* 42 *OCD³*], astronomer, Plato's student, editor of the *Laws*, author of the *Epinomis* (D. L. 3.37; Procl. *Eucl.* 67.24 for Mende) (fl. 350)

Philolaus of Croton (or Tarentum) [*LGPN3A* 4 *RE* s.v. + supp. 13 *OCD³*], influential Pythagorean philosopher (DK 44) (±470–±390)

Philomelus of Paeania [*PA/APF* 14669 (14670) *LGPN2* 7], son of Philippides I, father of Philippides II s.vv. (±420–336/5)

Phocylides of Miletus, elegiac poet who wrote mostly epigrams (fl. mid 6th c.)

Phrychs [*FRA* 8132], slave of Alcibiades III (*IG* I³ 426.11, dated 414/3)

Phrynichus of Athens [*PA* 15008 *LGPN2* 1 *OCD³*], son of Polyphrasmon, tragedian (frr. in *TGrF* 1².69–79) (fl. late 6th, early 5th c.)

Phrynichus of Athens [*PA* 15006 *LGPN2* 3 *RE* 7 *OCD³*], son of Eunomides, comic poet (*PCG*; *IG* II² 2325.61, 124) (active ≥434–400)

Phrynichus of Diradiotae [*PA* 15011 *LGPN2* 16 *RE* 3], son of Stratonides, leader of the Four Hundred, assassinated in 411 (Thu. 8)

Phrynion of Phlius [*LGPN3A* 2], father of Echecrates s.v.

Phrynondas, linked to Eurybatus, and synonymous with villainy (Aristoph. *Thesm.* 861, Isocr. 18.57)

Pindar of Cynoscephalae (Boeotia) [*RE* 20 *OCD³*], lyric poet celebrating athletic victories (*opera*) (±518–>446)

Pisianax II of ?Sunium [*PA* 11775 + 11776 (*APF* 9688.8) *LGPN2* 6], son of Euryptolemus I, sibling of Isodice, Megacles VII, and Euryptolemus II, father of Euryptolemus III s.v.

Pisias of Athens [*PA* 11777 *LGPN2* 1], father of Meles s.v. (Aristoph. *Birds* 766)

Pisistratus [*PA/APF* 11791(11793) *LGPN2* 2 ?= 1) *OCD³*], son of Hippocrates, archon epon. 669/8, (Hdt. 1.59–64; Thu. 6.54–5; *AO* p. 28; [Aristot.] *Ath. Pol.* 13–17, 22) (active 565–>550)

Pittacus of Mytilene [*OCD³*], political leader, sage, advocate of the rule of law (±650–570)

Polyaratus of Cholarges [*PA/APF* 11907 *LGPN2* 7], wealthy public official with a marriageable daughter ([Demos.] 40.24) (†399)

Polyclitus of Argos [*OCD³*], sculptor in bronze, treatises on proportion, modeling, musculature et al. (Xen. *Mem.* 1.4.3) (active ±460–410)

Polycrates of Samos [*LGPN1* 56 *OCD³*], son of Aeaces, tyrant (r. ±535–±522) (Hdt. 3.39–60)

Polydamas of Thessaly, muscular athlete who won the pancration competition at the Olympic Games in 408 (Pl. *R.* 1.338c–d)

Polygnotus of Thasos and Athens [*LGPN1* 5 *RE* 1 *OCD³*], son and student of Aglaophon, famous painter of the stoa poikile (painted stoa), naturalized as an Athenian citizen in 460 (*NIA*: 3.23)

Procles of Sparta [*LGPN3A* 5 *RE* 3 Poralla² 644], son of Aristodemus and Argeia, one of the first two kings of Sparta, the other was his twin, Eurysthenes (Hdt. 6.52, 8.131)

Pulytion of Athens [*PA* 12154 *LGPN2* 1], rich man in whose house the mysteries were performed ([Pl.] *Eryx*. 400b; Andoc. 1.12, 14; Isocr. 16.6; Pher. *Hyp*. fr. 64 [K 58]; Plu. *Alc*. 19, 22; Paus. 1.2.5)

Pythocles of Myrrhinus [*PA/APF* 12447 (5951) *LGPN2* 25], father of Phaedrus s.v. (*IG* I³ 422.229 pat., 426.102 pat.) (b. ?480s)

Python of Aenus, student of Plato (D. L. 3.46)

R

Rhinon of Paeania [*PA/APF* 12532 *LGPN2* 3], son of Charicles, member of Board of Ten and negotiator of the reconciliation agreement in 403 (Aes. *Rhi*. fr. 82; [Aristot.] *Ath. Pol.* 38; Isocr. 18.6.8)

S

Sappho of Mytilene (Lesbos) [*LGPN1* 4 *RE* s.v. supp. *OCD³*], lyric poet (fl. late 7th c.)

Satyrus [*FRA* 7985–6], slave of Alcibiades III (*IG* I³ 426.15, and 430.28, dated 414/3: shoemaker)

Scellias II of Athens [*PA/APF* 12727 (1904) *LGPN2* 1], son of Aristocrates I, father of Aristocrates II s.v., tribe Kekropis

Scopas of Thessaly [*LGPN3B* 10 *RE* Skopadai s.v.] son of Creon (fl. 7–6th c.)

Simonides of Ceos [*LGPN1* 3 *RE* 2 *OCD³*], son of Leoprepes, lyric poet (*opera*; Xen. *Hiero*) (±558–468)

Smicrion of Athens, father of Cratylus s.v.

Solon of Athens [*PA/APF* 12806 (8792) *LGPN2* 1 *RE* 1 *OCD³*], son of ?Execestides, democratic leader and legislator, sage, poet; related to Dropides II (Pl. *Chrm*. 155a, *Ti*. 20e) (Hdt.) (b. 630–25, † 559) cf. App. III

Sophilus of Rhamnous [*PA* 12821 *LGPN2* 33 *OCD³*], father of Antiphon s.v.

Sophocles of Colonus [*PA* 12834 *LGPN2* 17 *OCD³*], son of Sophilus, renowned tragedian (±497–405)

Sophroniscus of Paeania [*LGPN2* 5], ?father of Agathocles s.v. (*IG* II² 7019)

Sosinomus of Athens [*PA* 13265 *LGPN2* 1], son of Aristonomus, banker, creditor of Aeschines (Lys. fr. 1; Demos. 36.20)

Stesagoras II of Laciadae [*PA/APF* 12896 8429.8A *RE* 2 *LGPN2* 6], son of Cimon I, father of Miltiades VI (Aes. *Mil*. no. 77 = fr. 37 Dittmar, pat.) (±555–516/5)

Stesagoras III of Laciadae [*LGPN2* 7 *APF* 8429.15], father of Miltiades VI (Aes. *Mil*. no. 77 = fr. 37 Dittmar, pat.) (5th c.)

Stesichorus of Himera [*LGPN3A* 2 *RE* 1 *OCD³*], son of ?Euphemus, lyric poet (active 600–550)

Stratonicus of Athens [*LGPN2* 1 *RE* 4 *OCD³*], famous performing musician and music teacher ("frr." in Athenaeus; Philetaerus *Oinopion* fr. 14 [K 14.15]) (±410–±360)

T

Telesippus of Cholarges [*PA/APF* 13541 (11811.2) *LGPN2* 7], son of Hippocrates s.v. (Aristoph. *Clouds* 1001 schol.; Eu. *Dem*. fr. 112 [K 103] b. ≤424/3)

Temenus of Argos [*OCD³*], early Lacedaemonian legislator (var. Temenos is a misprint at PCW: 1372)

Teucrus [*LGPN2* 5 ?= 6], *metic*, a.k.a. Teucer, who accused Athenians and himself in the profanation of the Eleusinian mysteries, and others in the mutilation of herms in 415 (Andoc. 1.15, 28, 35, 52, 59, 67; Phryn. fr. 61 [K 58]) stonemason employed on the Erechtheum in 408: *IG* I³ 476.20–1, 96, 214, 324)

Thales of Miletus [*OCD³*], said to be the first natural philosopher, engineer, political leader of Ionians, sage, astronomer: predicted eclipse of 585 (Hdt. 1.74.2; DK 11)

Theognis of Megara [*LGPN3B* 7 *RE* 1 *OCD³*], elegiac poet (7–6th c.)

Thrasippus of Athens [*PA* 7292 *LGPN2* 4] one of Plato's six executors in 348/7 (D. L. 3.43)

Thrasybulus of Collytus [*PA/APF* 7305 *LGPN2* 14], son of Thrason, supported Alcibiades III's dismissal in 407/6, *trierarch*, democratic leader (Xen. *Hell.* 5.11.26; Lys. 26.23; *IG* I² 43.77, 1634.4) (≤430–>373/2)

Thrasybulus of Steria [*PA/APF* 7310 *LGPN2* 22 *OCD³*], son of Lycus, democratic leader, opposed the Four Hundred from the fleet in Samos, *trierarch* in 411 and 406, supported the recall of Alcibiades III in 411, organized and led the overthrow of the Thirty in 403 (*IG* II² 10 = *NIA* D6.3–4, *IG* II² 28.8; Lys. 28, Isocr. 18; Thu. 8; Xen. *Hell.* 1–4; *SEG* 12.84) (440s–388)

Timocrates of Thorae [*PA* 13744 *LGPN2* 97], father of Aristotle s.v. (Thu. 3.105.3; *AM* 106.149)

Timolaus of Cyzicus, student of Plato (D. L. 3.46)

Timonides of Leucas [*LGPN3A* 3 *RE* s.v.], student of Plato, friend of Speusippus, historian of Dion's liberation of Syracuse, source for Plutarch (frr. in *FGrH* 561) (4th c. B.C.E.)

Tisamenus of Athens [*PA* 13441 *LGPN2* 2], father of Agathon s.v. (schol. Aristoph. *Frogs* 83; schol. Pl. *Smp.* 172a)

Tisander II of Athens [*PA/APF* 13458 (8429.4) *LGPN2* 4], son of Epilycus I, father of Epilycus II and three daughters who married prominently, candidate for ostracism in 443 (*IG* I² 911.4) (b. ±490)

Tisias of Syracuse [*LGPN3A* 14 *RE* 6 *OCD³*], rhetorician older than Gorgias

Tisias of Cephale [*PA/APF* 13479 *LGPN2* 14], son of Tisimachus, brother-in-law of Charicles s.v., cheated by Alcibiades III (*IG* I³ 370.29, 32; Thu. 5.84.3; Isocr. 16)

Tissaphernes of Sardis [*RE* s.v. *OCD³*], son of Hydarnes, satrap (r. ±413–395) who impinged on Greek interests in western Anatolia (Aes. *Alc.* no 42)

Tolmides of Athens [*PA* 13879 *RE* 1 *LGPN2* 1 *OCD³*], son of Tolmaeus, commander defeated at Coronea († 447) (Xen. *Mem.* 3.5.4)

Trophonius [*OCD³*], son of Erginus, master builder of temples and treasuries, later Apollonian cult figure (fl. late 7th c.)

Tychon [*FRA* 8088], household slave named in Plato's will (D. L. 3.42)

Tynnichus of Chalcis [*OCD³*], poet known for his paean (fl. ?early 5th c.)

Tyrtaeus of Sparta [Poralla² 709 *LGPN3A* 3 *RE* 1 *OCD³* Stephanis

2443], elegiac poet using martial themes (fl. mid 7th c.)

X

Xanthippus I of Cholarges [*PA/APF* 11169 (11811.1) *LGPN2* 7 *OCD³*], son of Ariphron I, father of Ariphron II and Pericles I s.vv., and a daughter (*Agora* 25.651–2, 1053–69; *AM* 106.150, 154, 155) († mid-470s)

Xenocrates of Chalcedon [*OCD³*], student of Plato, and third head of the Academy (D. L. 3.46, 4.6–15)

Xenophanes of Colophon [*OCD³*], presocratic philosopher, epistemologist (DK 21) (±570–>478)

Xenophon of Melite [*PA/APF* 11313 (5951) *LGPN2* 35], son of Euripides, *hipparch*, general, related to Phaedrus s.v., in command when Potidaea surrendered (*IG* I³ 48.45, 511; *IG* I² 400; Androt. fr. 38; Thu. 2.70, 79) (†429)

Xerxes of Persia [*OCD³*], son of Darius I, king (r. 486–465), invaded Greece, defeated at Salamis, made Themistocles a governor

Z

Zeuxippus of Heraclea (s. Italy) [*OCD³* as var. 'Zeuxis' *PP PX*], famous painting teacher residing in Athens (Pl. *Prt.* 318b–c; Xen. *Sym.* 4.63) (active 5th c.)

APPENDIX III
ATHENIAN AFFILIATION:
DEMES, PHRATRIES,
CLANS ET AL.

It was in the deme that each eighteen-year-old Athenian male was presented by his natural or adopted father to fellow demesmen (*dēmotai*), underwent scrutiny (*dokimasia*) to ascertain that his parents were lawfully married and that he was indeed of age, was entered onto the citizen roll (*lēxiarchikon grammateion*), and thereby made eligible—subject to age or class restrictions on certain offices—for the many tasks of government determined by lot or required of all citizens. Local (deme) eligibility was prior to and necessary for Athenian (*polis*) eligibility. The process normally began not at deme level, but when a year's cohort of male infants was formally presented at the Apaturia festival celebrated by the phratries—less numerous than demes (one phratry might include several demes in an area), and more religious than political in effect. Various stages in a boy's life were marked by additional rites at the Apaturia (a quadrennial festival called the Brauronia for very young girls is not well understood). As Whitehead puts the matter of deme affiliation in *The Demes of Attica*, "Indisputably the most crucial of the functions of a deme assembly was its control over its own membership. It was crucial because, in the absence of centralized lists of all citizens, becoming a *dēmotēs* and becoming a *politēs* [citizen] were effectively one and the same act; conversely, a man could prove his citizen-status, if need be, only by proving his membership of a deme" (1986: 97).

Before the Cleisthenic reform of 508/7 in which the deme became the formal unit of Attic political activity, the kinship groups or clans (*genē*), claiming ancestry to heroes and gods, and controlling many sacred functions, were the seats of political power. Within the clan, the *oikos* or household had its own purview. Brotherhoods and clubs (phratries and *hetaireai*) also wielded great influence. There is evidence that the deme system of Attica often followed pre-existing clan and club outlines, as well as existing geographical ones (Whitehead 1986: 25n86 and 31n117–118)—allowing what would turn out to be the West's principal democratic innovation to be and to seem as natural and as normal as possible. Plato's dialogues provide reason to believe that the strength of both clan and club continued to be felt into the fifth and fourth centuries, alongside or overlapping the deme system of political organization. Plato's own family and those of the characters in the dialogues show the important role that marrying within the extended family continued to play in the preservation of estates. Nor should that be surprising. Lacey wrote of the family as "the most central and enduring institution of Greek society" (1968: 9), and Patterson's more recent work has only made that statement all the better supported (cf. the ancillary anthropological evidence gathered by Cox 1998, and the various works of Humphreys). Patterson takes a special interest in the innovations offered in Plato's *Laws* that address existing Athenian problems with inheritance of property, marriage, and adultery (1998: 103–5, 133–7).

Cleisthenes' reform, or so it is reasonably hypothesized, involved an initial period in which every man registered in his home village (*kōmas*), presumably followed by a period of scrutiny, allowing the definite determination of a group of fellow demesmen for each of the 139 population centers, demes, in Attica. In each deme, the demesmen were all to be identified by their given names together with their shared demotic, usually the adjectival form of the deme. This was apparently meant to supplant the aristocratic use of patronymics, one's father's name as a surname, with its consequent ancestral one-upmanship; but simple replacement seems never to have become widespread, and the practice evolved into a three-name compromise wherein one's given name was followed by one's patronymic and one's demotic. "The long-term result of this," says Whitehead (1986: 71), "clear to any reader of the literature of the fifth and fourth centuries— especially Thucydides, Aristophanes, Plato, and the orators—was that an individual's choice of demotic or patronymic could become an issue and an expression of class, status, and political values." No doubt. But it need not be an expression of any of these: Plato's *Laches* 179a–181c explores positive aspects of the use of both the demotic and the patronymic. Moreover, assigning the same surname (demotic) to hundreds or even thousands of people in the same deme made it virtually impossible to distinguish individuals, regardless of their political leanings, especially because it was so common to name sons for grandfathers: several cousins could all have the name of their common grandfather, all at the same time, with only their patronymics to distinguish them. A tendency to marry within one's deme (Cox 1998: *passim*) made the problem slightly worse. Demesmen were expected to have special regard for, and responsibilities to, one another by virtue of that relationship alone, as many contemporaneous references make clear. Whitehead's chapter, "Deme Society" (1986: 223–52), is rich with examples of such responsibilities from Aristophanes and from Plato.

As a further step in the Cleisthenic reform, once the numbers of members of each deme had been reported nationally—perhaps a duty of the deme heads (*dēmarchoi*)—and scrutinized, there resulted a sorting of all the demes into ten groups of roughly equal population, the ten *tribes* (*phylai*), named for traditional heroes, that remained unchanged until 307/6.

Erechtheis I	Leontis IV	Hippothontis VIII
Aigeis II	Akamantis V	Aiantis IX
Pandionis III	Oineis VI	Antiochis X
	Kekropis VII	

Each tribe had at least one deme from each of the three *trittyes*: city, coastal, and inland, thereby ensuring each tribe access to commerce, trade, and production. The number of demes per tribe varied from six (Aiantis) to twenty (Aegis), but the *number* of demes per tribe was insignificant politically: the 139 demes provided names from their rolls as required in proportion to their populations, but demes were combined in such a way that each *tribe* had a stable membership of fifty on the Athenian Council (*boulē*). Although the numbers for some poorly documented tribes do not quite add up to fifty, the general picture is rendered with admirable clarity by Traill (1986: 125–40) and Whitehead (1986: 369–73). Large demes produced a larger number of names each year—e.g., Acharnae (Oineis VI) provided twenty-two—while some others were so small that they provided one name in alternate years. See Map 2.

Demes had some of the powers associated with local governments anywhere. They issued decrees in their own right: granting honors, contracting leases, regulating religious festivals, establishing local ordinances and prohibitions, and dedicating statues; they collected revenues, kept accounts, conducted and underwent audits; they made provisions for officers of the deme (only the *dēmarch* was universal). But the demes also had central governmental functions: because the only path to political participation was through citizenship in a deme, their function of registering and scrutinizing members—initially, the sons, adopted sons, and (more controversially) *nothoi* of existing member citizens, but later newly enfranchised metics who had been admitted to a deme—was crucial; demes provided Athenian Council members; and they implemented Athenian decrees (e.g., Andoc. 1.97, that oaths be taken). While numbers and the procedures appear to have remained remarkably consistent for centuries, that appearance may be the result of our meager record for the period preceding the second half of the fourth century.

Change of residence altered neither one's tribe nor one's deme, so by the fourth century (from which sufficient epigraphical and topographical information is available to allow a few careful generalizations), men from outlying demes domiciled in the city (*asty*) of Athens and its suburban (*proastion*) districts retained their affiliations and returned to their own demes for certain assemblies and rites. Thus one cannot assume that men in the dialogues whose demotic identifies them as on the citizens' roll in some remote part of Attica actually resided outside Athens itself. It was very common for citizens to have a house in the city as well as one in a rural deme, the rural one often providing income for both through farming, trade, mining, etc. In fact, the *Laws* (745e) prescribes just this arrangement for its citizens: two plots for each, one close to the center of the *polis*, and one in a rural area. There is evidence (Demos. 57, dated 346/5) that some demes eventually came to hold their meetings in the city where many of their members presumably lived, but the assumption is that deme meetings were normally held in the agora or theater of the deme itself.

Deme affiliation was strictly inherited by sons from their fathers. Despite the crucial role of women in religion and cult, Whitehead (1986: 77) does not put the point too strongly when he says, "women were simply ignored by the deme system and, through it, by the *polis* itself . . . A Kleisthenic deme was technically an all-male entity." Thus women appear in the record, when they do at all, as daughter of x, or wife of x, where x carries the man's demotic. Nevertheless,

Pericles I's citizenship laws of 451/0—requiring Athenian status for *both* parents of candidate youths—make it abundantly clear that the lineage of the female was a fact to be reckoned with (cf. Patterson 1990: 41; Cohen 2000: 44–60). It girds the practice of presenting prospective brides to one's phratry at the Apaturia festival (Lambert 1993: 178–89). Of course, the lineage of females had always been of crucial importance in contracting marriages, especially those with the purpose of concentrating wealth within families or of effecting dynastic alliances. It is presumably for this kind of reason that paternal half siblings could marry lawfully in Athens, but not maternal half siblings—despite the view of Aristotle (*Gen. An.* 738b20–27, cf. Aeschylus' *Eumenides* 657ff.) that it was the male who implanted the fetus in the female who merely provided nutrition and gave birth. Interestingly, the situation was the opposite in Sparta, where *only* maternal half siblings could marry legally. Under Athenian law, the father's side of the family, first of all the eldest paternal uncle, had first claim on an heiress, and it was fairly common for a man to adopt sons, if he had none, as husbands for his daughters (Harrison 1998: 1.23; this and other degrees-of-kinship relations are neatly illustrated in Patterson 1998).

Ordinarily, "An Athenian citizen was an Athenian citizen because, both logically and chronologically prior to that, he was a demesman of Alopeke or Themakos or wherever it might be" (Whitehead 1986: 258). Lambert's *The Phratries of Attica* argues a parallel case for the importance of phratry membership, concluding, "being a citizen involved membership and participation in the activities of a phratry, and failure to belong could be adduced in a court of law as evidence against legitimate Athenian descent, and therefore against the rights to inherit property and to exercise the privileges of citizenship" (1993: 238). Phratries appear in this study primarily through the Apaturia festival celebrated annually in October or early November when (a) males born in the previous year were presented by their fathers or guardians to their phratries, with each father swearing the son was his by an Athenian woman to whom he was lawfully married; (b) boys who had reached the end of their fifteenth year were again presented to the phratry and had their hair cut; girls *may* have been presented by their fathers (c) females were presented to the phratry by their prospective husbands to ensure that the phratry member (*phratōr*) was marrying a potential bearer of legitimate offspring, i.e. that she was the daughter of Athenian parents (Lambert 1993: 237–9; Garland 1990: 179–83).

Naturalization, through a decree of Council, was also possible, though the record is spotty for how deme or phratry membership was obtained with or after citizenship. A man could become a naturalized Athenian citizen in a number of ways, and the practice became far more common as the Peloponnesian war dragged on and the shortage of manpower became critical. As Osborne (*NIA*: 1.5) points out, the bestowing of honors to foreigners and metics was a significant part of political life, and the highest honor that could be granted was citizenship in Athens. Important instances for the people of Plato's dialogues include: (a) Extraordinary service to the *polis*; (cf. Andoc. 2.23, *NIA*, *passim*). (b) For manning a ship bound for Arginousae in 406, the Athenians promised even slaves citizenship (D. S. 13.97.1, *NIA* 3.33–37, including a number of contemporaneous references; see esp., Aristoph. *Frogs* with its role of the slave Xanthias and direct advice from the playwright to Athenians). (c) Patroclides' decree of 405 restored citizenship to previously disfranchised oligarchs (Andoc. 1.73–79). (d) The Samians were specially singled out for citizenship following Aegospotami in 405 (*IG* I³ 127, *NIA* 1.33, 2.25). (e) Thrasybulus' decree of 403, honoring service with him in restoring the democracy and including slaves, was overturned as unconstitutional ([Aristot.] *Ath. Pol.* 40.2, Aes. *orat.* 3.195, *P. Oxy.* 15.142 [no. 1800 frr. 6, 7], *NIA* 2.26–43, 3.39), but Archinus' decree of 401/0, honoring service with Thrasybulus in the period before the occupation of Piraeus, was successful, leading to the enfranchisement of some foreigners as well as metics (*IG* II² 10, *NIA* 1.37–41, 2.26–43). (f) Nicomenes' decree limited Pericles I's citizenship laws ([Aristot.] *Ath. Pol.* 26.4; Plu. *Per.* 37.2–5) to persons born after 403/2, thereby enfranchising men born to Athenian fathers and foreign mothers in the period after 451/0 (schol. Aes. *orat.* 1.39).

Metics, resident aliens, might rarely appear in a deme decree (e.g., *IG* I³ 244C4–10, dated 460, permitted Scambonidae *metics* to participate in a sacrifice), but this indicated nothing more than that demes might take an interest in the particular *metics* who were, as required by law, registered to live within their boundaries. Registration was compulsory since it made possible the collection of taxes from such men. Official documents would include a *metic's* deme of registration, but "in no sense was a metic a *member* of his deme of residence" (Whitehead 1986: 84). However, most especially in the latter half of the Peloponnesian war and its aftermath, as Athens enfranchised more *metics* and slaves who were willing to help in the prosecution of the war and, later, the overthrow of the Thirty, the newly enfranchised sought membership in demes (thereby tribes) and phratries— unless these were exceptionally allocated by the *polis* (cf. *IG* I³ 127.33–34 for the Samian case)—and were formally added to the citizen rolls in the demes. Until Pericles I's citizenship laws of 451/0, the children of naturalized citizens—since to be granted citizenship was to be honored by the *polis*—were treated exactly like ordinary citizens; afterwards, such children were required to have Athenian mothers along with their naturalized fathers to become citizens in their own right. It is interesting to note that more than 80 percent of Athenian *metics* resided in the few demes Melite, Piraeus, Collytus, Alopece, Cydathenaeum, Scambonidae, Ciriadae and Eleusis (Whitehead 1986: 83). On the accompanying map of Attica (Map 2), the high *metic* populations of those demes is invisible because only citizens were included in the counts that determined representation on the Council.

There were voluntary affiliations as well. Young upper-class men often joined *hetaireai*, clubs that were ostensibly social, providing opportunities for friends to eat and drink together, usually in private homes; much less common were *synōmosiai*, secret societies, conspiratorial bands, the members of which swore mutually binding oaths. In the late 5th c., however, *hetaireai* were comprised of politically like-minded men who sought to further the political careers of their outstanding members, and who acted in unison in cases of ostracism or election. The mutilation of the herms in 415, for example, was planned and carried out by Andocides IV's club (1.67), though the large numbers of men accused suggests that the affair was coordinated by more than one *hetaireia*. Thucydides explicitly blames the *hetaireai* for their role in bringing about the oligarchical revolution of 411 (8.54.4).

For an interesting comparison to 5th and early 4th c. Athens, note that Plato's *Laws* provides for four Solonic property-based classes with mobility dependant on increase and decrease of property (744c). However, having already emphasized that the very wealthy can be neither good (742e) nor happy (743c), limitations on poverty and wealth are established: on poverty, everyone shall have at least the universal *allotment*—two plots with houses, and all the furnishings and equipment necessary to make a living from them; and for wealth, no more than four times the value of the allotment (744e). Whereas the Athens of Plato's time had Cleisthenic divisions into ten tribes named for heroes, Plato's *Laws* divides the population into twelve tribes (745d–e) named for twelve gods. Whereas Cleisthenes had divided the country into thirty areas (ten each of urban, coastal, and inland *trittyes*—then assigned at least one of each kind to the tribes supposedly *by lot* ([Aristot.] *Ath. Pol.* 21.4), Plato's division attempts rational assignments to even out the good and bad qualities of the various regions with respect to production and trade. Another way in which the *Laws* preserves the spirit of the original Cleisthenic reform is by leaving a certain freedom of association: traditional hereditary priesthoods were left intact (though inheritance beyond the value of the allotment was forbidden); and citizens could choose their phratry affiliations, subject to scrutiny, and their clan, chiefly through marriage (cf. [Aristot.] *Ath. Pol.* 21.6). Although women were to be full citizens in Magnesia, the Cretan colony described in *Laws*, they are still treated as property in the part of the dialogue devoted to marriage regulations; and metics could never under any circumstances become citizens.

For the locations of demes, and the certainty with which the locations are known, I have relied on Traill (1986 and collegial correspondence); for the character of the deme system, on Traill (1986) and Whitehead (1986); for the history of the deme, on Ostwald (1969) and Andrewes (1977); for the phratry, on Lambert (1993); for clan divisions and the liturgical class, on *APF*; for metics, on Whitehead (1977) and *NIA*; for the calendar, on Woodhead (1992).

Athenians, *metics*, and their dependents below appear in Plato's dialogues or are mentioned there as living at the time of the dialogue. Persons in parentheses have their primary listings elsewhere. Place names are located on the accompanying map of Attica (Map 2).

City Trittyes

deme (partial): **Acharnae (Acharnai)**
tribe: **VI Oineis**
location: site SW of Menidi, enclave of an inland segment (certain)

Callicles

deme: **Alopece (Alopeke)**
tribe: **X Antiochis**

location: Katsipodi (general area certain)

Archestratus, son of Crito
Aristides II, son of Lysimachus II
Callias III, son of Hipponicus II (cf. Piraeus, Melite)
Chaeredemus
Crito
Critobulus, son of Crito

Hermogenes, son of Hipponicus II
Hipponicus II, son of Callias II
Hipponicus III, son of Callias III
Lamprocles II, son of Socrates
Lysimachus II, son of Aristides I
Melesias II, son of Thucydides I
Menexenus, son of Socrates
Patrocles, son of Chaeredemus
Phaenarete, wife of Sophroniscus I
Socrates, son of Sophroniscus I
Sophroniscus II, son of Socrates
Stephanus, son of Thucydides I
Thucydides II, son of Melesias II
[unnamed], slave of Callias III
[unnamed], son of Callias III
[unnamed], wife of Hipponicus II
Xanthippe, wife of Socrates

deme: **Cerameis (Kerameis)**
tribe: **V Akamantis**
location: NW of Dipylon gate (certain)

    Pausanias

deme: **Cholarges (Cholargos)**
tribe: **V Akamantis**
location: near Kato Liosia (probable
  from the findspot of a grave marker)

    Ariphron II, son of Xanthippus I
    Cf. Aspasia of Miletus, resident
    Nausicydes
    Paralus, son of Pericles I
    Pericles I, son of Xanthippus I
    Xanthippus, son of Pericles I

deme: **Coele (Koile)**
tribe: **VIII Hippothontis**
location: SW of the Pnyx (certain)

    Archinus

deme: **Collytus (Kollytos)**
tribe: **II Aegis (Aigeis)**
location: SW of the Agora and S of
  the Areopagus (certain)

    Adeimantus I, son of Ariston
    (Charmides, son of Glaucon III,
      owned a house by the
      Olympieum)
    (Epicrates of Cephisia, owned a
      house by the Olympieum)
    Glaucon IV, son of Ariston
    (Morychus, son of Lachemorus,
      owned a house by the
      Olympieum)
    Plato, son of Ariston

deme: **Cydathenaeum
(Kydathenaion)**
tribe: **III Pandionis**
location: N of Acropolis (certain)

    Aristodemus
    Aristophanes, son of Philippus I

deme: **Euonymon**
tribe: **I Erechtheis**
location: Trachones (probable)

    Anytus I, son of Anthemion I

deme: **Melite**
tribe: **VII Kekropis**
location: W of agora (certain)

    (Antiphon II, son of Pyrilampes,
      resident)
    (Callias III of Alopece, part-time
      resident)

deme: **Oe**
tribe: **VI Oineis**

location: 3 km. E and .5 km. N of
Koropi (Kakovoyiannis 1998, certain
from deme cemetery)

Damon, son of Damonides
Lamachus, son of Xenophanes

deme: **Phaleron**
tribe: **IX Aeantis (Aiantis)**
location: near Old Phaleron (general
area certain)

Aeantodorus
Apollodorus

deme: **Piraeus (Peiraieus)**
tribe: **VIII Hippothontis**
location: Mynychia (certain)

(Callias III of Alopece, part-time
resident)
Cephalus II of Syracuse, son of
Lysanius, *metic*
Euthydemus, son of Cephalus II,
metic
(Lysias, son of Cephalus II,
resident, *metic*, naturalized
Athenian)
Polemarchus, son of Cephalus II,
metic
[unnamed], slave of Polemarchus

deme: **Rhamnous**
tribe: **IX Aeantis (Aiantis)**
location: Rhamnous, enclave of
another segment (certain)

Antiphon, son of Sophilus

deme: **Scambonidae (Skambonidai)**
tribe: **IV Leontis**
location: N part of the city (probable)

Adeimantus, son of Leucolophides
Alcibiades III, son of Clinias II
Axiochus, son of Alcibiades II
Clinias III, son of Axiochus
Clinias IV, son of Clinias II

INLAND *TRITTYES*

deme: **Aphidnae**
tribe: **IX Aeantis (Aiantis)**
location: Kotroni (certain)

Tisander, son of Cephisodorus

deme: **Athmonon**
tribe: **VII Kekropis**
location: Amarousion (certain)

Nicostratus, son of Theozotides I
Theozotides I

deme: **Cephisia (Kephisia)**
tribe: **I Erechtheis**
location: Kephisia (certain)

Antiphon
Epicrates (cf. Collytus)
Epigenes, son of Antiphon

deme: **Ceramicus (Oion Kerameikon)**
tribe: **IV Leontis**
location: unknown, outside the city
wall

Pythodorus, son of Isolochus,
resident

deme: **Cydantidae (Kydantidai)**
tribe: **II Aegis (Aigeis)**
location: near Mendeli Monestery
(likely)

Diognetus, son of Niceratus I
Eucrates, son of Niceratus I
Niceratus II, son of Nicias I
Nicias I, son of Niceratus I

deme: **Erchia**
tribe: **II Aegis (Aigeis)**
location: S of Spata (certain)

Isocrates, son of Theodorus

deme: **Gargettus (Gargettos)**
tribe: **II Aegis (Aigeis)**
location: Ieraka (certain)

Andron, son of Androtion I

demes: **Paeania, Upper and Lower**
tribe: **III Pandionis**
location: Upper, site N of Liopesi
(certain);
Lower, site at E outskirts of Liopesi
(very probable)

Charmantides I
Ctesippus
Philippides I, son of Philomelus I

deme (or city *trittys*): **Pithus (Pithos)**
tribe: **VII Kekropis**
location: unknown (cf. Traill 1986:
135n33)

Meletus II, son of Meletus I

deme: **Prospalta**
tribe: **V Akamantis**
location: site NW of Kalyvia (certain)

Euthyphro of Prospalta

deme: **Sphettus (Sphettos)**
tribe: **V Akamantis**

location: NW of Koropi, below
Christos Chapel (certain)

Aeschines, son of Lysanias
Chaerecrates
Chaerephon
Lysanias

deme: **Thorae (Thorai)**
tribe: **X Antiochis**
location: Ag. Demetrios, Trapuria,
enclave of another segment
(probable)

Aristotle, son of Timocrates

COASTAL *TRITTYES*

deme: **Aexone (Aixone)**
tribe: **VII Kekropis**
location: Glyphada (certain)

Laches, son of Melanopus
Lysis II, son of Democrates I
[unnamed], son of Democrates I

deme: **Anagyrus (Anagyrou)**
tribe: **I Erechtheis**
location: Vari (virtually certain)

Demodocus
Paralius, son of Demodocus
Theages, son of Demodocus

deme: **Myrrhinus**
tribe: **III Pandionis**
location: Merenda (certain)

Phaedrus, son of Pythocles

deme: **Sunium**
tribe: **Leontis**

location: upper Agrileza valley
(general area certain, site probable)

Theaetetus, son of Euphronius

deme: **Thoricus (Thorikos)**
tribe: **V Akamantis**
location: Thorikos (certain)

Lycon

deme: **Thria**
tribe: **VI Oineis**
location: site SE of Aspropyrgos
(probable)

Morychus, son of Lachemorus (cf.
Collytus)

Naturalized Citizens

Apollodorus of Cyzicus
Heraclides of Clazomenae
Lysias, son of Cephalus II of Syracuse
Phanosthenes of Andros

Attic Deme Unknown

Acumenus
Adeimantus, son of Cepis
Agathon, son of Tisamenus
Antiphon II, son of Pyrilampes (cf.
Melite)

Antisthenes II, son of Antisthenes I
Aristocrates II, son of Scellius II
Charmides, son of Glaucon III (cf.
Melite)
Cinesias, son of Meles
Clitophon, son of Aristonymus
Connus, son of Metrobius
Cratylus, son of Smicrion
Critias III, son of Leaïdes
Critias IV, son of Callaeschrus I
Demos, son of Pyrilampes
Dion
Eryximachus, son of Acumenus
Euthydemus, son of Diocles
Hippocrates, son of Apollodorus
Hippothales, son of Hieronymus
Leontius, son of Aglaeon
Menexenus, son of Demophon
Miccus
Phason, son of Apollodorus
Phidias, son of Charmides
Philebus
Phoenix, son of Philip
Protarchus, son of Callias
Pyrilampes, son of Antiphon I
Pythodorus, son of Isolochus (cf.
Cerameis)
Sarambus
Satyrus, slave of Hippocrates
Socrates ("The Younger")
Stesilaus
Thearion
[unnamed], son of Demophon

APPENDIX IV
CHRONOLOGY OF THE
PERIOD OF THE PLATONIC
DIALOGUES AND LETTERS

Most of the Athenian historical dates are based on *CAH* 5² and *CAH* 6², though supplemented with *HCT*, Rhodes (1993) *et al.*; other dates derive from sources listed in Abbreviations, Ancient Texts, and Translations at the beginning of this volume, except for those of Plato's dialogues and letters, rationalized in Appendix I: Dramatic Dates, Characters, Setting, and Style.

Athenian History	Biography/Litigation
451 Pericles I's citizenship law; Five Years' Truce with Sparta	451 b. Alcibiades III; Cimon returns to Athens
	450/49 † Cimon
449 ?Peace of Callias	
448 Spartan invasion of Attica	
448–447 irregularities of tribute payment	
446 loss of battle at Coronea; Spartan invasion of Attica	446 Alcibiades III orphaned
	±446 b. Charmides
446–445 Thirty Years' Peace	
444–443 foundation of Thurii	
	?443 ostracism of Thucydides, Melesias' son
	438 Phidias prosecuted, leaves Athens
437 Pericles I's Pontic expedition	
437–436 Amphipolis founded	
	±436 † Empedocles; b. Isocrates; prosecution of Anaxagoras
433 alliance with Corcyra; decrees of Callias	±433 Protagoras in Athens
432 (April) revolt at Potidaea; (early summer) Archestratus responds; (fall) Callias responds; siege of Plataea begins; conference at Sparta	
431 war begins; Peloponnesian invasion of Attica; fleet in the Peloponnese	431 *cleruchy* on Aegina established
430 Peloponnesian invasion of Attica; plague breaks out; Pericles I sails to Peloponnese; Pericles I deposed, fined; (winter) Potidaea surrenders; battle near Spartolus	
429 (May) troops return from Potidaea	429 (August–September) death of Pericles I
428 Peloponnesian invasion of Attica; revolt of Mytilene; property tax	
427 Peloponnesian invasion of Attica; fall of Mytilene; fall of Plataea	427 Gorgias' embassy to Athens
426 Nicias at Melos	

Arts and Letters	Dialogues' Dramatic Dates
±450–430 Phidias, Polyclitus fl.	
	450 (August) *Parmenides*
447 work on Parthenon begins	
442 comedy added to Lenaea	
438 Euripides, *Alcestis*; Athena of Phidias dedicated	
437 work on Propylaea begins	
	±433/2 *Protagoras*
	432 [*Alcibiades*]
	[*Second Alcibiades*]
431 Euripides, *Medea*	
±430 classical grave-relief series begins; Cratinus, *Thraltae*	
430 or 429 Cratinus, *Dionysalexandros*	
≤429–428 Callias, *Pedētai*	429 (May) *Charmides*
428 Euripides, *Hippolytus*	
427 Aristophanes, *Banqueters*	
426 Aristophanes, *Babylonians*	

Athenian History	Biography/Litigation
425 Peloponnesian invasion of Attica; Pylos fortified; Spartan peace offer refused; reassessment of tribute	±425 b. Xenophon
424 raid on Laconia; battle of Delium; Spartans capture Amphipolis	424 exile of Thucydides (historian)
423 (April) one-year truce begins	424/3 b. Plato
422 battle of Amphipolis; peace negotiations	422 † Cleon, † Brasidas
421(April) Peace of Nicias; fifty-year alliance with Sparta	
	420 † Protagoras
419 Alcibiades III in Peloponnese battle of Mantinea	419 Nicias I, Alcibiades III generals
418–417 fifty-year alliance (Sparta & Argos)	418 † Laches; Antiphon fr. 30, *Invective against Alcibiades*
417 alliance with Argos	
416 subjugation of Melos	
415 mutilation of herms; fleet sails for Sicily; recall and flight of Alcibiades III; fleet arrives in Sicily	
414 Spartan invasion of Argive lands; Eurymedon sails to Sicily	414 † Lamachus; Spartans under Gylippus arrive in Sicily
413 second expedition reaches Sicily; catastrophic defeat in Sicily; *proboulē* established; Spartans renew war, seize Decelea; 5% duty substituted for tribute	<413 Antiphon fr. 20, *Prosecution of Erasistratus in a Case about Peacocks*
412 revolt of subject allies (e.g., Naxos); Sparta & Persia make treaty	412 Antiphon 6, *On the Chorus-boy*
411 *proboulē* increased by twenty; revolution of the Four Hundred; government of the Five Thousand; fleet at Samos recalls Alcibiades III	411 execution of Antiphon of Rhamnous
410 democracy restored; Spartan peace offers refused	

Arts and Letters	Dialogues' Dramatic Dates
425 Aristophanes, *Acharnians*	
±425–395 Zeuxis painter	
424 Aristophanes, *Knights*	424 (winter) *Laches*
424–415 Eupolis, *Baptae*	
423 Aristophanes, *Clouds*; Amipsias, *Connus*; Cratinus, *Pytinē*; Phrynichus, *Connus*	
422 Aristophanes, *Wasps*	≤422 *Cratylus*
421 Aristophanes, *Peace*; Eupolis *Flatterers, Maricas*	421–416 [*Clitophon*] [*Greater Hippias*] [*Lesser Hippias*]
±420–400 Parrhasius painter	
420 Eupolis, *Autolycus*; *Poleis*; Pherecrates, *Savages*	
	418–416 *Phaedrus*
<415 Antiphon 3, *Second Tetralogy*	416 *Symposium*
415 Euripides, *Troades*	≤415 [*Eryxias*]
>415 Pherecrates, *Hypnos* or *Panuchis*	
414 Aristophanes, *Birds*; Phrynichus, *Monotropus*	
	413 *Ion*
<412 Plato *comicus*, *Pisander*	
412 Euripides, *Helen*; Euripides, *Andromeda*	
±412 Eupolis, *Demes*	
411 Aristophanes, *Lysistrata*, *Thesmophoriazusae*	
410–405 Metagenes, *Philothytes*	

Athenian History	Biography/Litigation
409 battle at Megara	409 Lysias fr. 9, *For Eryximachus*
	408 Euripides and Agathon leave Athens
407 loss of battle at Notium	407 Alcibiades III in Athens (4 months)
406 (October) Arginusae naval victory; trial of the generals	406 Alcibiades III withdraws permanently; † Euripides; † Sophocles
405 Aegospotami naval battle lost	405 Dionysius I becomes tyrant
405–404 siege of Athens	
404 (spring) defeat of Athens; long walls destroyed; (summer) the Thirty established; Spartan aid arrives; reign of terror begins; Three Thousand selected; citizenry disarmed; Phyle occupied by Thrasybulus (winter) oligarchs secure Eleusis	404 † Alcibiades III; executions of Polemarchus, Niceratus, Leon, Autolycus (1,500 citizens); Theramenes executed
403 (spring) battle of Munychia; Ten replace Thirty, seek Spartan aid; Spartans arrive (summer) reconciliation talks; (autumn) return of the exiles; democracy restored	403 † Critias IV; † Charmides
	>403 Lysias 24, *For the Disabled Man;* fr. 11, *Concerning Antiphon's Daughter*
	403/2 Lysias 12, *Against Eratosthenes;* 21, *On a Charge of Accepting Bribes*
402–400 Spartan war against Elis	402 Isocrates 18, *Against Callimachus*
	>402 Lysias fr. 9, *For Eryximachus;* fr. 10, *Against Theozotides*
401 oligarchic state at Eleusis suppressed (March) Xenophon's mercenary campaign under Cyrus (*Anabasis*)	400 Andocides 1, *On the Mysteries*
	400–399 [Lysias] 6, *Against Andocides*
	≥400 Lysias 25, *On a Charge of Overthrowing the Democracy;* 32, *Against Diogeiton*
399 Xenophon's Ten Thousand reach Byzantium, join the Spartans	399 (May–July) trial and execution of Socrates
	≥399 Lysias 13, *Against Agoratus;* 30, *Against Nicomachus*
	>399 Lysias fr. 1, *Against Aeschines the Socratic*

Arts and Letters	Dialogues' Dramatic Dates
409–406/5 completion of Erechtheum, new *bouleutērion*	±409 (early spring) *Lysis*
409 Sophocles, *Philoctetes*	
408 Euripides, *Orestes*; Aristophanes *Plutus*	
	≥407 *Euthydemus*
405 Aristophanes, *Frogs*	
>403 Archippus *Fishes*	
	402 *Meno*
401 Sophocles *Oedipus at Colonus* (*posthumously*)	401/0 (winter) *Menexenus*
	±400 *Symposium* frame
>400 Metagenes, *Sophists*	399 (spring) *Theaetetus, Euthyphro, Sophist, Statesman* (May–June) *Apology* (June–July) *Crito, Phaedo*

Athenian History	Biography/Litigation
	397–396 Isocrates fr. 16, *On the Team of Horses*
	±396 Antisthenes opens school
	≤395 Lysias 18, *On the Property of Nicias' Brother*
395 (summer) outbreak of Corinthian War work on Athenian long walls begun	395 Lysias 14–5, *Against Alcibiades 1–2*
	395–387 Lysias 27, *Against Epicrates*
	394 Isocrates 20, *Against Lochites*
394 (spring) battle of Nemea; (August) battles of Cnidus, Coronea	>394 Lysias 3, *Against Simon*
	≥394 Xenophon exiled by Athens
393 Dionysius I honored at Athens	393 † Phaedrus
392 (March) Corinthian revolution Argos subsumes Corinth (summer) Spartans capture Lechaeum and destroy its walls to Corinth	
392/1 (winter) peace conference at Sparta; Lechaeum retaken and walls rebuilt	391 Andocides 3, *On the Peace with Sparta*; Athenian peace negotiators exiled
391(spring) Spartans recapture Lechaeum	(spring) † Theaetetus
	≥391–385 Isocrates 11, *Busiris*
	390 Isocrates opens school
	>389 Lysias 28, *Against Ergocles*
386 King's Peace concluded at Sparta	
	≥385 Lysias 19, *Property of Aristophanes*
	384/3 Plato visits Sicily; Lysias 10, *Against Theomnestus*
	383 Plato establishes Academy
	382 Lysias 26, *Against Euandrus*
378 (spring) second Athenian League formed; declares war on Sparta	
369 alliance with Sparta	

Arts and Letters	Dialogues' Dramatic Dates
>394 [Lysias] 2, *Funeral Speech*	
392 or 391 Aristophanes, *Assemblywomen*	
	391 (spring) *Theaetetus* frame
390 Isocrates, *Against the Sophists*	
±390 Temple of Apollo, Bassae	
388 Aristophanes, *Plutus*²	
386 Old Tragedy introduced at Dionysia	
	>383 [*Letters* 9, 12]
	±382 *Parmenides* frame
370 Isocrates 10, *Encomium on Helen*	

History of Syracuse/Athens	Biography/Litigation
	367 (spring) † Dionysius I; succession of Dionysius II; Aristotle joins Plato's Academy
	367/6 † Callias III
	366 (sailing season) Plato visits Syracuse; Eudoxus *scholarch* of the Academy; exile of Dion begins
	361–360 Plato visits Syracuse; Heraclides of Pontus *scholarch* of the Academy
	360 (summer) Dion, Plato, and Heraclides of Syracuse at Olympia
360–357 Dion and Heraclides gather support and funds	
357 Dion retakes Syracuse	
356 Dion deposed by assembly, is recalled, besieges Ortygia	≥356 † Aeschines
355 (autumn) Apollocrates abandons Ortygia	355 Dion reunited with family
	>355 † Xenophon
354–352 (13 months) Callippus tyrant of Syracuse	354 (summer) Dion assassinated
352 Hipparinus II overthrows Callippus	352 † Hipparinus II
351–346 Nysaeus tyrant of Syracuse	≤350 † Lysis
	348/7 † Plato; Speusippus *scholarch* of Academy

Arts and Letters	Dates of [Plato's] Letters
368 Isocrates Let. 1 to Dionysius II	
	365–360 [*Letter* 5]
	≥365 [*Letter* 13]
	≥360 [*Letter* 1]
	>360 [*Letters* 2, 10, 11]
±357 Isocrates 7, *Areopagiticus*	
	≥357 [*Letters* 3, 4]
355 Xenophon, *Ways and Means*; Isocrates 8, *On the Peace*	
354–353 Isocrates 15, *Antidosis*	
	>354 (summer) *Letter* 7
	353/2 *Letter* 8
	±350 [*Letter* 6]

GLOSSARY

Greek technical terms without exact English equivalents (e.g., 'amphidromia'), and English technical terms for Greek words (e.g., 'metic'), that are not ordinarily found in English dictionaries are included below. A few Greek words that have found their way into English (e.g., 'agora'), and are thus no longer italicized, and English words used systematically herein to translate particular Greek terms (e.g., 'Assembly' for 'ecclēsia') are also provided.

agora   market area, meeting place

amphidromia   ceremony in which a five-day-old infant was carried around the hearth and admitted to the *oikos*

anchisteia   those entitled to inherit; next-of-kin

antidosis   a court action in which a citizen required to perform a liturgy charged another citizen with having greater wealth; if the suit was successful, the defendant had the choice of exchanging properties with the plaintiff or performing the liturgy himself

archetheoros   man who managed and maintained (as a "tax" or liturgy) a delegation or deputation to the athletic games (Olympic, Isthmian, Pythian, or Nemean)

archon   (also *archōn*, pl. archons) one of ten state officials with highest administrative responsibility for religious and judicial matters in the *polis*, including conducting preliminary inquests and presiding over jury trials; in the late 5th and 4th c., a Board of Ten archons was chosen by lot annually, one per tribe, from among an elected shortlist (in other periods, there were nine); eligibility was limited to the three highest of the four citizen classes (the king-archon, *archōn basileus*, who handled homicide and impiety cases, and the archon who gave his name to the year, "eponymous archon," are often mentioned separately from the Board)

asebeia   in law, culpable impiety

Assembly   *ecclēsia*, in Athens under the democracy, the sovereign authority of the state and largest official body of the government, comprised of all four citizen classes

astoi   residents, locals (masc. s. *astos*; fem. s. *astē*) (cf. *politai*)

asty   city, urban area (cf. *proastion*)

atimia   disfranchisement

aulos   (pl. *auloi*) pipe-like wooden musical instrument consisting of one or two cylindrical tubes with holes for fingering notes, and with a separate mouthpiece for each tube, each fitted with either a single or double reed; a band around the head supported the mouthpiece(s) while he played one pipe with each hand, his cheeks puffed out characteristically so he could inhale and blow at the same time ("circular breathing"; cf. contemporary north African and Middle Eastern double-*auloi*, and the Sardinian triple-*aulos*, called a '*launeddas*')

beloved   *erōmenos*

biblion   scroll, paper (often translated 'book')

Board of Ten   see 'archon'

boulē   Council of the *polis*; in Athens, five hundred men (fifty per tribe) with everyday responsibility for the administration of the state; each tribe's contingent served as *prytaneis*, presidents, for a period of 35 or 36 days (one tenth of the year)

bouleutērion   building in which the *boulē* met; the new *bouleutērion*, just west of the old, was constructed in the last quarter of the 5th c. (see Plan 1)

bouleutēs   (pl. *-tai*, *-tae*) councilman, member of the *boulē*

Ceramicus   general name for the area west of the walled *asty* where pottery was produced; Oion Ceramicus was an inland deme of unknown location

chorēgia   tax (festival liturgy) requiring a man to finance a dithyrambic, comic, or tragic dramatic choral production

chorēgos   (pl. *chorēgoi*) man who undertook the *chorēgia*

chōris   distinct, apart

cithara   (also *kithara*) stringed instrument with two arms of equal length, a sound-box (from a tortoise shell or wood), and a crossbar; when plucked, it probably sounded more like a gut-stringed banjo than like a harp; its sound carried farther than a lyre's so it was used in public performances

cleros   (pl. *cleroi*) allotment of land; in law, estate of the deceased

cleruch   (also *kleruch*) special type of colonist provided with a *cleros* in a conquered territory by the state, allowing him to retain his Athenian citizenship while residing outside Attica

cleruchy   colony on conquered territory, in which colonists keep their original citizenship

club   *hetaireia*

Council   *boulē*

dadouchia   hereditary and sacred office of torchbearer for the Eleusinian mysteries *daimonion*   divinity inferior to a god (used of Socrates' "divine or spiritual sign," *Ap.* 31d)

dekatē   naming ceremony held on the tenth day after birth

dekazein   type of jury bribe allegedly invented by Anytus s.v.

dēmarch   (pl. *dēmarchoi*) chief officer of the deme

deme   (pl. demes) precinct, political district in which a citizen was registered; also, neighborhood, area of Attica (cf. App. III)

dēmos   the people, the citizen body

dēmotēs   (pl. *dēmotai*) demesman, man of the deme (cf. *politēs*)

demotic   *dēmotikon*, deme name, attached to one's own name like a surname (cf. App. III)

dexiōsis   handshake motif seen on many gravestones

diadikasia   in law, a court hearing to determine which of rival claimants would receive an *epiklēros*

didaskalos   producer, teacher of actors in a play

dikē   in law, a case

dokimasia   public scrutiny; in Athens, the examination of (a) public officials, selected initially by lot, to ensure their suitability for office, and (b) males in their eighteenth year as part of their enrollment as citizens of the deme

drachma   (pl. *drachmae,* abbr. *dr.*) standard unit of currency: the daily wage for a skilled worker

Athenian Currency
1 *drachma* = 6 *obols*
100 *drachmae* = 600 *obols* = 1 *mina*
6,000 *drachmae* = 36,000 *obols* = 60 *minae* = 1 *talent*

ecclēsia   (also *ekklēsia*) assembly; in Athens, the Assembly of citizens, having final authority in all decisions before the *polis*

eisangelia   in law, a term applied to a variety of types of suits, but having in common that the prosecutor suffered no penalty for dropping the suit before trial, or for receiving only a few votes from the jury (thus a favorite suit of sycophants)

eisphora   *ad hoc* tax on wealth for the prosecution of war

endeixis   in law, an action against a person for exercising rights to which s/he is not entitled

enkektēmenoi   men owning land within a deme

ephebe   (also *ephēbos*, pl. *ephebes*, *ephēboi*)   after ±370 in Athens, male citizen of eighteen, undertaking two years of military training

ephor   (pl. *ephors*) important Spartan political official (variations used in other Doric *poleis*): five were elected annually from among men who wished to stand; they ruled with the *gerousia* and had special responsibility for overseeing the two kings

epidikasia   court procedure in which a man appears before the archon to claim the right to inheritable property, often by marriage to an *epiklēros*

epiklēros   (pl. *epiklēroi*) unmarried female without living brothers at the time of her father's death, "heiress" without rights to the estate (cf. Callias III s.v.)

epistatēs   citizen chosen by lot to preside over the Prytanes (executive committee) of the Council for one day

erastēs   lover, senior in a hypothetical or actual homosexual relationship

erōmenos   beloved, junior in a hypothetical or actual homosexual relationship (cf. *paidika, pais*)

euergetēs   benefactor, honorific term used in inscriptions

Eupatrid   descendant of the early ruling caste of Attica

euthunai   public examination of the conduct of public officials, audit

general   *stratēgos*

genos   (pl. *genē*) clan, kinship group, e.g. those claiming a common ancestor; extended family

gerousia   Spartan institution comprising twenty-eight members over age sixty

graphē   literally, 'writing'; in law, an indictment in a public case

graphē paranomōn   indictment charging unconstitutional legislation

gymnasiarchos   liturgy requiring the training and maintenance of a team of relay runners

hēnia   leather thong (e.g. bootlace, rein)

hermocopidae   herm mutilators (a comic coinage from Aristoph. *Lysistr.* 1094)

hetaira   female companion, cf. *pallakē* and *pornē*

hetaireia   (pl. *hetaireai*) club, voluntary association, professional guild; in Athens, association of young, upper-class men serving both social and political purposes, where some were also *synōmosiai*

hetairos   (pl. *hetairoi*) male companion, friend, comrade

hipparch   cavalry commander

hippeus   (pl. *hippeis*) knight, man of the second citizen class; in the pl., class of knights, also cavalry *hoplite*   a heavily armed foot soldier

horos   (pl. *horai*) boundary stone

isonomia   political equality

isoteleia   status carrying partial citizen privileges including special tax status

kalos   beautiful, also a designation for pottery on which the word appears with the name of someone, usually a youth; also fine, noble

King   (a.k.a. Great King) king of Persia

klaros, kleruch,   etc. see *cleros, cleruch,* etc.

klēros   (pl. *klēroi*) allotment of land (e.g. in *Laws, the polis* is comprised of exactly 5,040 *klēroi*, each of which is indivisible and inalienable)

kōmē   (pl. *kōmai*) village (unwalled), district, neighborhood

kōmōidoumenos   person lampooned in comedy

kothornos   boot used in the production of tragedies that fits either foot

kylix   ceramic cup

kyrios   in law, a guardian, the person with authority to dispose of property or manage the affairs of a minor (woman, child, slave)

lēxiarchikon grammateion   citizen roll on which males were registered in their eighteenth year after presentation by a relative and scrutiny by demesmen

liturgy   service or tax to the state, ordinarily costing so much that only the very wealthy were required to perform it

loutrophoros   gravestone in the form of a vase

lover   *erastēs*

meirakion   male of adult height, beginning to grow facial hair

metic   foreign resident of Athens

metron   standard, rule, measure

mētroxenos   person with a non-Athenian mother

mina   (pl. *minae*) monetary unit worth 100 *drachmas* (see chart at *drachma*)

neaniskos   male of adult height, beginning to grow facial hair

nomothetai   lawmakers, commissioners assigned to review and suggest changes in the laws, subject to further scrutiny and approval by the Assembly

nothos   (pl. *nothoi*, fem. *nothē*) in Athens, (a) child of a citizen male outside a legal marriage, and (b) at least after 451/0, child of a citizen male with a non-Athenian woman regardless of marriage status; often translated 'bastard,' the term did not apply to a child whose father was unknown

obol   (s. *obolos*, pl. *oboloi*) smallest monetary unit, worth 1/6 *drachma* (see chart at *drachma*)

oikogenēs   house-born, normally used to distinguish domestic from foreign-born slaves

oikos   household, including persons and property

oinochoē   wine ladle

orphanos   child of a deceased father, usually translated 'orphan' though the mother could still be alive

ostrakon   (also *ostracon*, pl. *ostraka*, –*ca*) a potsherd on which a man's name was scratched, used as a ballot when a voter supported ostracism for the named man (cf. Themistocles s.v.)

paidika   young object of homosexual desire (cf. *erōmenos*, *pais*)

pais   (pl. *paides*) child, boy, girl—referring to physical development, preadolescent; also, son, daughter; also, slave; in context, junior in a hypothetical or actual homosexual relationship (cf. *erōmenos*, *paidika*)

pallakē   concubine; cf. *hetaira*, *pornē*

patrios politeia   ancestral constitution, constitution of Cleisthenes

patronymic   (abb. pat.) name of one's father, attached as a surname to one's own (cf. App. III)

peltasts   lightly armed troops

pentakosiomedimnos   (pl. *pentakosiomedimnoi*) man of the highest citizen class; literally, five-hundred-*medimnos*-man, i.e. man whose income equals the value of 6,000 gallons of grain (a *medimnos* equals about 12 gallons); in the plural, highest citizen class (cf. App. III)

pharmakeia   the use of drugs, potions etc.

phratriarch   chief officer of the phratry

phratōr or *phratēr*   (pl. *phratores*) member of a phratry

phratry   (also *phratra*, *phratrē*, pl. phratries) brotherhood, association with hereditary membership and, usually, a specific locality (cf. App. III)

phylarch   commander of a tribe's cavalry contingent

phylē   (pl. *phylai*) tribe (cf. App. III)

polis   (pl. *poleis*) city-state

politai   citizens (masc. s. *politēs*; fem. s. *politis*—hypothetical) (cf. *astoi*, *dēmotēs*)

porch   *stoa*

pornē   prostitute; cf. *hetaira* and *pollakē*

praetor   military commander, an appointed rather than elected officer

proastion   suburban (cf. *asty*)

proboulē   in Athens, a commission of ten men over forty, established to investigate the Sicilian disaster (413); its number was increased by twenty and its duties extended to include the examination of the ancestral constitution (*patrios politeia*) in the period preceding the oligarchy of the Four Hundred (cf. *syngrapheis*)

proeisphora   form of taxation in which a group of citizens advances money to the *polis*

proxenos   (pl. *proxenoi*) citizen of one *polis* who acted as the local representative of another *polis* in political and commercial ways, honorary consul

prytaneis   Prytanes; literally, presidents; the fifty men of a single tribe serving as the executive committee of the 500-member Council for one-tenth of the year (s. *prytanis*, president, is often used as the equivalent of *epistatēs*, leading to confusion because each of the fifty is a *prytanis*, whereas only one at a time serves as *epistatēs*)

prytany   one-tenth part of the archon year, numbered consecutively (first *prytany*, second, etc.)

psiloi   lightly armed troops

rhapsode   man who recited poetry at festivals or on an itinerant basis

rhētōr   (pl. *rhētores*) rhetorician, orator: man who addressed the Assembly or courts, proposed decrees etc.

sacra   portion of the house (shrine or room) in which sacred objects were kept

scholarch   man in charge of a scholarly enterprise, e.g. head, or temporary head, of the Academy

secret societies   *synōmosiai* (cf. club)

sitophylax   grain inspector

stoa   porch, colonnade

stratēgos   (pl. *stratēgoi*) general, commander of the Athenian fighting forces or a part of it (one per tribe was elected annually, for a total of ten)

sycophant   commonly in legal contexts, a malicious plaintiff, or person bringing frivolous suits in hopes of being paid to keep matters out of court; often used of informers, slanderers, and sometimes of scoundrels more generally (cf. *eisangelia*)

symposiarch   man in charge of determining the proper proportion of wine to water at a symposium (banquet), monitoring the drunkenness of the guests

syngrapheis   board of commissioners appointed in 411 to consider changes in the ancestral constitution (*patrios politeia*), extension of the *proboulē*

synōmosiai   secret societies, conspiratorial associations whose members pledged allegiance with oaths (cf. *hetaireiai*)

talent   (also *talant*, abbrev. *tal.*)   monetary unit (see chart at *drachma*)

tamias   (pl. *tamiai*) treasurer, i.e. man chosen by lot from among the wealthiest citizens to serve on a board overseeing shrines—ten treasurers for each of two boards, one board for ten named gods and the other board for "the other gods"

taxiarch   commander of a tribe's *hoplites* or infantry

temenos   precinct; portion of land allocated to a particular purpose

thete   (pl. *thetes*) man of the lowest of the four citizen classes, too poor to purchase the armor of a hoplite for service in the army, so normally a rower aboard a warship

thiasos   male association smaller than a *phratry* and without hereditary membership

tholos   building beside the *bouleutērion* where the *boulē* took its meals while in session; it served also as the office of the Thirty (see Plan 1)

timēma   tax assessment

tribe   *phylē* (see App. III)

trierarch   man who paid the *trierarchy*, during the year in which the tax was being executed

trierarchy   tax requiring a man to furnish a trireme, including officers and crew as well as food and supplies, for a year

trireme   ship fitted with both sails and oarlocks, designed for maneuverability, battleship of the Peloponnesian war

trittys   (pl. *trittyes*) Cleisthenic division of the Attic demes (city, inland, and coastal)

xenos   (pl. *xenoi*, f. *xenē*) foreigner; guest; outsider

zeugitai   the third citizen class, hoplites

WORKS CITED
AND CONSULTED

See Abbreviations, Ancient Authors Texts, and Translations (front matter) for ancient authors and translators cited in the text. Dates enclosed in angle brackets, < >, are copyright dates.

Adam, J. 1926–1929. *The* Republic *of Plato*. Cambridge: CUP.

Adeleye, Gabriel 1973. "Theramenes and the Overthrow of the 'Four Hundred'." *Museum Africum* 2, 77–81.

———— 1974. "Critias: Member of the Four Hundred." *TAPA* 104, 1–9.

———— 1976. "Theramenes: The End of a Controversial Career." *Museum Africum* 5, 2–22.

Allan, D. J. 1954. "The Problem of Cratylus." *AJP* 75:3, 271–87.

Allan, D. J., ed. 1962 <1940>. *Plato:* Republic *Book I*. Methuen's Classical Texts. London: Methuen.

Andrewes, A[ntony] 1953. "The Generals in the Hellespont." *JHS* 73, 2–9.

———— 1974. "The Arginousai Trial." *Phoenix* 28, 112–22.

———— 1977. "Kleisthenes' Reform Bill." *CQ* 27, 241–8.

Andrewes, A[ntony] and D[avid] M[alcolm] Lewis 1957. "Note on the Peace of Nikias." *JHS* 77, 177–80.

Arnim, H. von 1896. *De Platonis Dialogis Quaestiones Chronologicae*. Vorlesungs- verzeichnis der Universität Rostock für das W.–Semester 1896.

Aurenche, O. 1974. *Les groupes d'Alcibiade, de Léogoras et de Teucros: remarques sur la vie politique athénienne en 415 avant J.C.* Collection d'études anciennes. Paris: Les Belles Lettres.

Avery, Harry C. 1963. "Critias and the Four Hundred." *CP* 58, 165–7.

———— 1982. "One Antiphon or Two?" *Hermes* 110, 145–58.

Badian, Ernst 1988. "Towards a Chronology of the Pentekontaetia down to the Renewal of the Peace of Callias." *Échoes du Monde Classique* 31, 289–320.

Balatsos, P. 1991. "Inscriptions from the Academy." *ZPE* 86, 145–54.

Bartoletti, V. and M. Chambers, edd. 1993. *Hellenica Oxyrhynchia*. 2nd edn. T.

Beazley, J[ohn] D[avidson] 1956. *Attic Black-Figure Vase Painters*. Oxford: Clarendon.

—— 1963. *Attic Red-Figure Vase-Painters*. 2nd edn. Oxford: Clarendon.

—— 1971. *Paralipomena: Additions to Attic Black-Figure Vase-Painters and to Attic Red-Figure Vase-Painters*. 2nd edn. Oxford: Clarendon.

—— 1989. *Beazley Addenda. Additional References to ABV, ARV² and Paralipomena*. 2nd edn., compiled by T. H. Carpenter. British Academy Publications. Oxford: OUP.

Beloch, Julius 1912–1927. *Griechische Geschichte*, 4 vols. in 8. 2nd edn. vols. 1, 2 Strasbourg: K. J. Trübner, 1912–1916; vols. 3, 4 Berlin and Leipzig: W. de Gruyter, 1922–1927.

Bergk, Theodor 1867. *De Simonidis Epigrammate in Cimonis Victoriam ad Eurymedontem*. Halae: Formis Hendeliis.

—— 1887. *Griechische Literaturgeschichte* IV. Berlin: Weidmann.

Bianco, Elisabetta 1992–1993. "L'Attualità di Alcibiade nel Dibattito Politico Ateniese All'inizio del IV Secolo a. C." *Rivista Storica dell'Antichità* 22–3, 7–23.

Bicknell, Peter J. 1966. "Dating the Eleatics." In *Essays in Honor of Francis Letters*, ed. M. Kelly, 1–14. Melbourne: Cheshire.

—— 1972. *Studies in Athenian Politics and Genealogy*. *Historia* supp. vol. 19. Wiesbaden: Steiner.

—— 1974a. "Athenian Politics and Genealogy; Some Pendants." *Historia* 23, 146–63.

—— 1974b. "Socrates' Mistress Xanthippe." *Apeiron* 8, 1–6.

—— 1975. "Alkibiades and Kleinias. A Study in Athenian Genealogy." *Museum Philologum Londiniense* (Amsterdam), 51–64.

—— 1982. "Axiochos Alkibiadou, Aspasia and Aspasios." *L'Antiquité Classique* 51, 240–50.

Blanckenhagen, Peter H. von 1992. "Stage and Actors in Plato's *Symposium*." *GRBS* 33, 51–68.

Bloedow, Edmund F. 1975. "Aspasia and the 'Mystery' of the *Menexenos*." *Wiener Studien* 9, 32–48.

Blondell, Ruby 2002. *The Play of Character in Plato's Dialogues*. Cambridge: CUP.

Bloom, Allan, tr. 1968. *The* Republic *of Plato*. New York and London: Basic Books.

Blumenthal, H. 1973. "Meletus the Accuser of Andocides and Meletus the Accuser of Socrates: One Man or Two?" *Philologus* 117, 169–78.

Boeckh, August 1874. *Gesammelte Kleine Schriften* 4. Leipzig: n.p. 7 vols. in 4.

Bousquet, Jean 1992. "Deux Épigrammes Grecques (Delphes, Ambracie)." *Bulletin de Correspondance Hellénique* 116, 585–606.

Brandwood, Leonard 1990. *The Chronology of Plato's Dialogues*. Cambridge: CUP.

Brickhouse, Thomas C. and Nicholas D. Smith 1989. *Socrates on Trial*. Princeton: PUP.

—— 1994. *Plato's Socrates*. New York: OUP.

—— 2002. *The Trial and Execution of Socrates: Sources and Controversies*. New York: OUP.

Broadbent, Molly 1968. *Studies in Greek Genealogy.* Leiden: E. J. Brill.

Brock, Roger 1989. "Athenian Oligarchs: The Numbers Game." *JHS* 109, 160–4.

Brumbaugh, Robert S. 1988. "Digression and Dialectic: The *7th Letter* and Plato's Literary Form." In *Platonic Writings/Platonic Readings,* ed. Charles Griswold, 84–92. New York: Routledge.

—— 1991. "Simon and Socrates." *AncPhil* 11: 151–2.

—— 1992. "An Academy Inscription." *AncPhil* 12, 171–2.

Brunt, P. A. 1993. "Plato's Academy and Politics." In *Studies in Greek History and Thought,* ed. P. A. Brunt. New York: OUP.

Buck, R. J. 1995. "The Character of Theramenes." *AHB* 9:1, 14–23.

Burnet, John 1914. *Greek Philosophy. Part I Thales to Plato.* London: Macmillan.

—— 1920. *Early Greek Philosophy.* 3rd edn. London: A. & C. Black.

Burnet, John, ed. 1911. *Plato's* Phaedo. Oxford: Clarendon. Citations herein are from the 1985 reissue.

—— 1924. *Plato's* Euthyphro, Apology of Socrates *and* Crito. Oxford: Clarendon. Citations herein are from the 1977 reissue.

Burnyeat, M[yles] F. 1978. "The Philosophical Sense of Theaetetus' Mathematics." *Isis* 69, 489–513.

Burnyeat, Myles [F.], ed. 1990. *The Theaetetus of Plato.* M. J. Levett, tr., rev. by Myles Burnyeat. Indianapolis: Hackett.

Bury, R. G., tr. 1929. *Timaeus, Critias, Cleitophon, Menexenus, Epistles.* Loeb.

—— 1973. The Symposium *of Plato.* 2nd edn. Cambridge: Heffner.

Camp, John M. 1992 <1986>. *The Athenian Agora: Excavations in the Heart of Classical Athens.* London: Thames and Hudson.

Campbell, Lewis 1867. *The* Sophistes *and* Politicus *of Plato.* Oxford: Clarendon.

—— 1894. *Plato's* Republic. Oxford: Clarendon.

Caponigri, A. Robert, ed. and tr. 1969. *Diogenes Laertius. Lives of the Philosophers.* Chicago: Henry Regnery.

Cartledge, Paul 1990. "Fowl Play: A Curious Lawsuit in Classical Athens (Antiphon frr. 57–9 Thalheim)." In *Nomos: Law, Politics and Society,* ed. Paul Cartledge, Paul Millett and Stephen Todd, 41–61. Cambridge: CUP.

Caven, Brian 1990. *Dionysius I: War-lord of Sicily.* New Haven: Yale University Press.

Chen, Ludwig C. H. 1992. *Acquiring Knowledge of the Ideas: A Study of Plato's Methods in the Phaedo, the Symposium and the Central Books of the Republic.* Palingenesia 35. Stuttgart: Steiner.

Cherniss, Harold F. 1945. *The Riddle of the Early Academy.* Berkeley: University of California Press.

Chroust, Anton-Hermann 1957. *Socrates Man and Myth: The Two Socratic Apologies of Xenophon.* London: Routledge & Kegan Paul.

Clay, Diskin 1987. "Gaps in the 'Universe' of the Platonic Dialogues." *Boston Area Colloquium on Ancient Philosophy* 3, 131–57.

────── 1988. "Reading the *Republic.*" In *Platonic Writings/Platonic Readings,* ed. Charles Griswold, 19–33. New York: Routledge.

────── 1994. "The Origins of the Socratic Dialogue." In *The Socratic Movement,* edited by Paul A. Vander Waerdt, 23–47. Ithaca: Cornell University Press.

Cloché, P. 1915. *La Restauration démocratique à Athènes en 403 avant J.-C.* Paris: Leroux.

Cobet, Carel Gabriel 1836. *Commentatio, qua continetur Prosopographia Xenophontea.* Lugduni Batavorum: S. et J. Luchtmans.

Cohen, David 1991. "Law, Social Control and Homosexuality in Classical Athens." In *Law, Sexuality and Society: The Enforcement of Morals in Classical Athens.* New York: CUP.

Cohen, Edward E. 2000. *The Athenian Nation.* Princeton: PUP.

Connor, W. R[obert] 1971. *New Politicians of Fifth-Century Athens.* Princeton: PUP.

────── 1989. "City Dionysia and Athenian Democracy." *CM* 40, 7–32.

────── 1991. "The Other 399: Religion and the Trial of Socrates" in *Georgica: Greek Studies in Honor of George Cawkwell.* Institute of Classical Studies *Bulletin* supp. 58, 49–56.

Cook, R. M. 1989. "The Francis-Vickers Chronology." *JHS* 109, 164–70.

Cooper, John M[adison], ed. 1997. *Plato, Complete Works.* D. S. Hutchinson, associate ed. Indianapolis: Hackett.

Cornford, Francis Macdonald 1937. *Plato's Cosmology.* Reprinted 1975. Indianapolis: Bobbs-Merrill.

────── 1950. *Plato and Parmenides: Parmenides' Way of Truth and Plato's Parmenides.* London: Routledge and Kegan Paul.

Coulter, James A. 1964. "The Relation of the Apology of Socrates to Gorgias' Defense of Palamedes and Plato's Critique of Gorgianic Rhetoric." *HSCP* 68, 269–303.

Coventry, Lucinda 1989. "Philosophy and Rhetoric in the *Menexenus.*" *JHS* 109, 1–15.

Cox, Cheryl Ann 1988. "Sisters, Daughters, and the Deme of Marriage: a Note." *JHS* 108, 185–8.

────── 1989. "Incest, Inheritance and the Political Forum in Fifth-Century Athens." *CJ* 85, 34–46.

────── 1998. *Household Interests: Property, Marriage Strategies, and Family Dynamics in Ancient Athens.* Princeton: PUP.

Cox, Patricia L. 1983. *Biography in Late Antiquity.* Berkeley: University of California Press.

Cromey, Robert D. 1984. "On Deinomache." *Historia* 33:4, 385–401.

Crook, J. 1998. "Socrates' Last Words: Another Look at an Ancient Riddle." *CQ* 48, 117–25.

Cropsey, Joseph 1986. "The Dramatic End of Plato's Socrates." *Interpretation* 14, 155–75.

Davidson, Donald 1985. "Plato's Philosopher." *London Review of Books* 1 August, 15–7.

Davies, John Kenyon 1971. *Athenian Propertied Families 600–300* B.C. Oxford: Clarendon.

Davison, J. A. 1962. "Literature and Literacy in Ancient Greece." *Phoenix* 16, 141–56 and 219–33.

Dellis, Ioannis 1992–1993. "Phaidon and the Elian School?" Ἀθῆναι, 237–56. In *A Minor Socratic School*. In Greek.

Derenne, Eudore 1930. *Les Procès d'Impiété Intentés aux Philosophes*. Bibliothèque de la Faculté de Philosophie et Lettres de l'Université de Liège 45. Liège: Vaillant-Carmanne.

Develin, Robert 1989. *Athenian Officials 684–321* B.C. (Cambridge: CUP).

Dickey, Eleanor 1996. *Greek Forms of Address: From Herodotus to Lucian*. Oxford: OUP.

Diels, Hermann and Walther Kranz 1951–1954. *Die Fragmente der Vorsokratiker, griechisch und Deutsch*. 7th edn. Berlin: Weidmann.

Dinsmoor, W[illiam] B[ell] 1931. *The Archons of Athens in the Hellenistic Age*. Cambridge, Ma.: American School of Classical Studies at Athens, Harvard University.

Dittenberger, W. 1902. "Die Familie des Alkibiades." *Hermes* 37, 1–13.

Dodds, E. R. 1959. *Plato's* Gorgias. Oxford: Clarendon.

Döring, Klaus 1972. *Die Megariker: Kommentierte Sammlung der Testimonien*. Amsterdam: Grüner.

Dover, Kenneth J[ames] 1950. "The Chronology of Antiphon's Speeches." *CQ* 44:1–2, 44–60.

———— 1965. "The Date of Plato's Symposium." *Phronesis* 10, 2–20.

———— 1968a. *Aristophanes* Clouds. Oxford: Clarendon.

———— 1968b. *Lysias and the* Corpus Lysiacum. Berkeley: University of California Press.

———— 1970. "Excursus: The Herms and the Mysteries." In *HCT* 4: 264–88.

———— 1976. "The Freedom of the Intellectual in Greek Society." *Talanta* 7, 24–54.

———— 1989 <1978>. *Greek Homosexuality*. Cambridge: HUP.

———— 1993. *Aristophanes* Frogs. Oxford: Clarendon.

Dow, Sterling 1963. "The Attic Demes Oa and Oe." *AJP* 84, 166–81.

Draheim, H. 1911. "Wer ist Kallikles? *Wochenschrift für Klassische Philologie*, 364–6.

Dümmler, Ferdinand 1889. *Beiträge zur Litteraturgeschichte der sokratischen Schulen*. Giessen: J. Ricker.

Düring, Ingemar 1987 <1941>. *Herodicus the Cratetean: A Study in Anti-Platonic Tradition*. Greek and Roman Philosophy 12. New York: Garland.

Dušanić, Slobodan 1980. "Plato's Academy and Timotheus' Policy, 365–359 B.C." *Chiron* 10, 111–44.

———— 1990a. *Исморија ц Полцмцка у Пламонобцм „Законцма"* Beograd: The Serbian Academy of Sciences and Arts. *History and Politics in Plato's* Laws: English summary, 359–89.

———— 1990b. "The *Theages* and the Liberation of Thebes in 378 B.C." *Teiresias* supp. 3, 65–70.

———— 1995. "The True Statesman of the *Statesman* and the Young Tyrant of the *Laws*: A Historical Comparison." In *Reading the Statesman: Proceedings of the III Symposium Platonicum,* ed. Christopher J. Rowe, 337–46. Sankt Augustin: Academia Verlag.

———— 1999. " Isocrates, the Chian Intellectuals, and the Political Context of the *Euthydemus.*" *JHS* 119, 1–16.

Dyer, Louis 1901. "Plato as a Playwright." *HSCP* 12, 165–80.

Edelstein, Ludwig 1966. *Plato's Seventh Letter. Philosophia Antiqua* 14. Leiden: E. J. Brill.

Edwards, Michael 1995. *Greek Orators.* Vol. 4, *Andocides.* Warminster: Aris & Phillips.

Ehrenberg, Victor 1974 <1943>. *The People of Aristophanes; A Sociology of Old Attic Comedy.* London: Methuen.

Ehrhardt, Christopher 1995. "Lysias on Theramenes." *AHB* 9:3–4, 125–6.

Ellis, Walter M. 1989. *Alcibiades.* New York: Routledge.

Else, G. F. 1972. "The Structure and Date of Book 10 of Plato's *Republic.*" *Abhandlungen der Heidelberger Akademie der Wissenschaften,* Philosophisch-historische Klasse 3.

Emlyn-Jones, C. J. 1996. *Laches.* London: Bristol Classical Press.

Erbse, H. 1961. "Die Architektonik im Aufbau von Xenophons Memorabilien." *Hermes* 89, 257–87.

Fairweather, Janet 1974. "Fiction in the Biographies of Ancient Writers." *Ancient Society* 5, 231–75.

Ferguson, J. 1967. "Plato, Protagoras and Democritus." *Bucknell Review* 15, 49–58.

Ferrari, G. [John] R. F., ed. 2000. *Plato* The Republic. Tom Griffith, tr. Cambridge: CUP.

Field, G. C. 1948. *Plato and His Contemporaries; A Study in Fourth-Century Life and Thought.* London: Methuen.

Fine, John V. A. 1983. *The Ancient Greeks: A Critical History.* Cambridge: HUP.

Finley, Moses I. 1968. "Plato and Practical Politics." In *Aspects of Antiquity,* ed. Moses I. Finley, 74–87. New York: Viking.

Fitton, J. W. 1970. "That Was No Lady, That Was. . . ." *CQ* n.s. 20, 56–66.

Forde, Stephen 1987. "On the *Alcibiades* I." In *The Roots of Political Philosophy: Ten Forgotten Socratic Dialogues,* ed. Thomas Pangle, 222–39. Ithaca: Cornell University Press.

Fowler, David 1999. *The Mathematics of Plato's Academy: A New Reconstruction.* 2nd edn. Oxford: Clarendon.

Fowler, H. N., tr. 1925. *Plato* The Statesman, Philebus. Loeb.

———— 1926. *Plato* Cratylus, Parmenides, Greater Hippias, Lesser Hippias. Loeb.

Fraser, P[eter] M[arshall] and E. Matthews, edd. 1987. *A Lexicon of Greek Personal Names*. Vol. 1. *The Agean Islands, Cyprus, Cyrenaica*. Oxford: Clarendon.

———— 1997. *A Lexicon of Greek Personal Names*. Vol. 3A. *The Peloponnese, Western Greece, Sicily and Magna Graecia*. Oxford: Clarendon.

French, Alfred 1993. "A Note on the Size of the Athenian Armed Forces in 431 B.C." *AHB* 7:2, 43–8.

———— 1994. "Pericles' Citizenship Law." *AHB* 8:3, 71–5.

Furley, William D. 1985. "The Figure of Euthyphro in Plato's Dialogue." *Phronesis* 30:2, 201–8.

———— 1996. *Andokides and the Herms: A Study of Crisis in Fifth-Century Religion*. London: *Bulletin of the Institute of Classical Studies*, supp. 65.

Gagarin, Michael, ed. 1997. *Antiphon: The Speeches*. Cambridge: CUP.

Gagarin, Michael, and Douglas M[aurice] MacDowell, trr. 1998. *Antiphon and Andocides*. Austin: University of Texas Press.

Garland, Robert 1990. *The Greek Way of Life from Conception to Old Age*. Ithaca: Cornell University Press.

———— 1992. *Introducing New Gods; The Politics of Athenian Religion*. Ithaca: Cornell University Press.

———— 2001. *The Greek Way of Death*. 2nd edn. London: Duckworth.

Gernet, L. and M. Bizos 1955. *Lysias: Discours*. 2 vols. Paris: Coll. Univ. France.

Giannantoni, Gabriele 1990. *Socratis et Socraticorum Reliquiae*. 4 vols. Elenchos 18. Naples: Bibliopolis.

Gigon, Olof 1953. *Kommentar zum Ersten Buch von Xenophons Memorabilien*. Basel: Reinhardt.

———— 1956. *Kommentar zum Zweiten Buch von Xenophons Memorabilien*. Basel: Reinhardt.

———— 1979. *Sokrates, Sein Bild in Dichtung und Geschichte*. 2nd edn. Bern: Francke.

Gil, L. 1962. "La Semblanza de Nicias en Plutarco." *Estudios Clásicos* 6, 404–50.

Gill, Christopher 1973. "The Death of Socrates." *CQ* 23, 25–8.

———— 1996. *Personality in Greek Epic, Tragedy and Philosophy: The Self in Dialogue*. Oxford: Clarendon.

Goldhill, Simon 1999. "The Seductions of the Gaze: Socrates and His Girlfriends." In *Kosmos: Essays on Order, Conflict and Community in Classical Athens*, ed. Paul Cartledge, Paul Millett, and Sitta von Reden, 105–24. Cambridge: CUP.

Gomme, A. W., A[ntony] Andrewes, and Kenneth J[ames] Dover 1948–1981. *A Historical Commentary on Thucydides*. 5 vols. Oxford: Clarendon.

Gosling, J. C. B., tr. 1975. *Plato* Philebus. Oxford: Clarendon.

Gould, J. P. A. 1980. "Law, Custom and Myth: Aspects of the Social Position of Women in Classical Athens." *JHS* 100, 38–59.

Goulet, R., ed. 1994– . *Dictionnaire des Philosophes Antiques II*. Paris: Centre National de la Recherche Scientifique.

Gray, Vivienne J. 1992. "Xenophon's Symposion: The Display of Wisdom." *Hermes* 120, 58–75.

Green, Peter 1991. "Rebooking the Flute Girls: A Fresh Look at the Chronological Evidence for the Fall of Athens and the ὀκτάμηνος ἀρχή of the Thirty." *AHB* (Calgary) 5:1–2, 1–16.

Gribble, David 1999. *Alcibiades and Athens: A Study in Literary Presentation.* Oxford: Clarendon.

Griswold, Charles L., Jr. 1999. "*E Pluribus Unum?* On the Platonic 'Corpus'." *AncPhil* 19, 361–97.

Groen van Prinsterer, W. 1823. *Prosopographia Platonica.* Lugduni Batavorum: Hazenberg.

Gronewald, Michael 1985. "Sokratischer Dialog." In *Kölner Papyri* 5, Papyrologica Coloniensia VII, ed. M. Gronewald, K. Maresch and W. Schäfer. Opladen: Abhandlungen der Rheinisch—Westfälischen Akademie der Wissenschaften, 41–53.

Grote, George 1888 <1875>. *Plato and the Other Companions of Socrates.* London: John Murray. 4 vols.

Guthrie, W[illiam] K[eith] C[hambers] 1956. *Plato* Protagoras *and* Meno. New York: Penguin.

——— 1969. *The Fifth-Century Enlightenment. A History of Greek Philosophy* 3. Cambridge: CUP.

——— 1971a. *The Sophists.* First published as part 1 of Guthrie 1969.

——— 1971b. *Socrates.* First published as part 2 of Guthrie 1969.

——— 1975. *Plato the Man and His Dialogues: Earlier Period.* 4. Cambridge: CUP.

——— 1978. *The Later Plato and the Academy. A History of Greek Philosophy* 5. Cambridge: CUP.

Habicht, Christian 1990. "Notes on Attic Prosopography Coincidence in Father-Son Pairs of Names." *Hesperia* 59:2, 459–62.

Hackforth, 1952. *Plato's* Philebus. Cambridge: CUP.

Halperin, David M. 1990a. *One Hundred Years of Homosexuality: And Other Essays on Greek Love.* New York: Routledge.

——— 1990b. "Why Is Diotima a Woman? Platonic Erōs and the Figuration of Gender." In *Before Sexuality: The Construction of Erotic Experience in the Ancient Greek World,* ed. David Halperin, John J. Winkler, and Froma I. Zeitlin, 257–308. Princeton: PUP.

Hamilton, Walter 1951. *Plato* The Symposium. New York: Penguin.

Hansen, Mogens Herman 1975. *Eisangelia: The Sovereignty of the People's Court in Athens in the Fourth Century* B.C. *and the Impeachment of Generals and Politicians.* Odense: Odense Universitetsforlag.

——— 1980. "Hvorfor Henrettede Athenerne Sokrates?" *Museum Tusculanum* (Copenhagen) 40:3, 55–82.

——— 1992. "A Magisterial Inventory of Athenian Officials." *CP* 87:1, 51–61.

———— 1996. "The Trial of Sokrates from the Athenian Point of View." In *Démocratie et Culture*, ed. M. Sakellariou, 137–70. Athens: Academy of Athens.

———— 2000. *A Comparative Study of Thirty City-State Cultures.* Copenhagen: C. A. Reitzels Forlag.

Harding, Phillip 1974. "The Theramenes Myth." *Phoenix* 28, 101–11.

———— 1976. "Androtion's Political Career." *Historia* 25:2, 186–200.

———— 1994. *Androtion and the Atthis.* Oxford: Clarendon.

Harrison, A. R. W. 1998 <1968, 1971>. *The Law of Athens.* Vol. 1: *The Family and Property.* Vol. 2: *Procedure.* 2nd edn., with foreword by Douglas M[aurice] MacDowell. Indianapolis: Hackett.

Harrison, E. L. 1967. "Plato's Manipulation of Thrasymachus." *Phoenix* 21, 27–39.

Harward, John 1932. *The Platonic Epistles.* Reprinted 1976. New York: Arno.

Hatzfeld, Jean 1937. "Le départ de l'expédition de Sicile et les Adonies de 415." *Revue des Études Grecques* 1, 293–303.

———— 1939. "Du nouveau sur Phèdre." *Revue des Études Anciennes* 41, 313–8.

———— 1951 <1940>. *Alcibiade: Étude sur l'histoire d'Athènes à la fin du Ve siècle.* 2nd edn. Paris: Presses Universitaires de France.

Hayek, Friedrich von 1978. "Freedom of Choice." Letters to the Editor of *The Times of London* August 3, 1978, p. 15.

Heath, Thomas [Little] 1921. *A History of Greek Mathematics.* 2 vols. Oxford: Clarendon.

Henderson, Jeffrey 1991. "Women and the Athenian Dramatic Festivals." *TAPA* 121, 133–47.

———— 1998a. "Attic Old Comedy, Frank Speech, and Democracy." In *Democracy, Empire, and the Arts in Fifth-Century Athens*, ed. Deborah Boedeker and Kurt Raaflaub, 255–73. Cambridge and London: HUP.

Henderson, Jeffrey, tr. 1998b. *Aristophanes* I: Acharnians, Knights. Loeb.

———— 1998c. *Aristophanes* II: Clouds, Wasps, Peace. Loeb.

———— 2000. *Aristophanes* III: Birds, Lysistrata, and Women at the Thesmophoria. Loeb.

———— 2002. *Aristophanes* IV: Frogs, Assemblywomen, and Wealth. Loeb.

Henry, A. S. 1974. "Charmides Son of Glaucon." *Rheinisches Museum* (Frankfurt) 117, 360–2.

Henry, Madeleine M. 1995. *Prisoner of History: Aspasia of Miletus and her Biographical Tradition.* New York: OUP.

Hermann, Karl Friedrich 1839. *Geschichte und System der Platonischen Philosophie.* Vol. 1 (no more published). Heidelberg: Winter.

Hertz, Martin 1867. *De Apollodoro statuario et philosopho.* Vratislavie: Typis Universitatis.

Hibeh Papyri 1906, 1955. Part I, Bernard P[yne] Grenfell and Arthur S. Hunt, edd.; Part 2, E. G. Turner and Marie-Thérèse Lenger, edd. London: Egypt Exploration Society.

Hicks, R[obert] D[rew], ed. and tr. 1972 <1925>. *Diogenes Laertius Lives of the Eminent Philosophers*. 2 vols. rev. Herbert S. Long. Loeb.

Hignett, C. 1952. *A History of the Athenian Constitution to the End of the Fifth Century* B.C. Oxford: Clarendon.

Hirmer, J. 1897. "Entstehung und Komposition der Platonischen Politeia." *Jahrbücher für Classische Philologie*, supp. 23, 579–678.

Hock, Ronald F. 1976. "Simon the Shoemaker as an Ideal Cynic." *GRBS* 17, 41–53.

Hoerber, R. G. 1968. "Plato's *Laches*." *CP* 63, 95–105.

Holzinger, C. von 1900. "Ueber Zweck, Veranlassung und Daitierung der Platonischen *Phaidros*." *Festschrift Johannes Vahlen, zum Siebengizsten Geburtstag*, ed. Wilhelm August Hartel et al., 665–92. Berlin: G. Reimer.

Howland, Jacob 1991. "Re-reading Plato: The Problem of Platonic Chronology." *Phoenix* 45:3, 189–214.

——— 1993. *The Republic: The Odyssey of Philosophy*. New York: Twayne.

——— 1998. *The Paradox of Political Philosophy: Socrates' Philosophic Trial*. Lanham: Rowman and Littlefield.

Hubbard, T. K. 1998. "Popular Perceptions of Elite Homosexuality in Classical Athens." *Arion* 6, 48–78.

Humbert, J. 1967. *Socrate et les Petits Socratiques*. Coll. Les grands penseurs. Paris: Presses Universitaires.

Humphreys, Sally C. 1978. *Anthropology and the Greeks*. London: Routledge and Kegan Paul.

——— 1983. *The Family, Women and Death: Comparative Studies*. London: Routledge and Kegan Paul. [2nd edn. Ann Arbor 1993.]

——— 1990. "Phrateres in Alopeke, and the Salaminioi." *ZPE* 83, 243–8.

Hunter, Virginia. 1997. "The Prison of Athens: A Comparative Perspective." *Phoenix* 51:3–4, 296–326.

Huss, Bernhard 1999a. "The Dancing Socrates and the Laughing Xenophon or The Other Symposium." *AJP* 120, 381–409.

——— 1999b. *Xenophons Symposion: Ein Kommentar*. Stuttgart and Leipzig: T.

Ingenkamp, H. G. 1967. "Laches, Nikias und platonische Lehre." *Rheinisches Museum* (Frankfurt) 110, 234–47.

Inscriptiones de Délos 1926–1972. A. Plassart, J. Coupry, F. Durrbach, P. Roussel and M. Launey, edd. 7 vols. Paris.

Inscriptiones Graecae 1981– . 3rd edn., vol. I, ed. David M[alcolm] Lewis. Second edition, vols. II–III, ed. Johannes Kirchner, Berlin, 1913–1940. Editio Minor, vol. I, ed. F. Hiller von Gärtingen, Berlin, 1924.

Jacoby, Felix 1902. *Apollodors Chronik*. Philologische Untersuchungen 16. Berlin: Weidmann.

——— 1949. *Atthis: The Local Chronicles of Ancient Athens*. Oxford: Clarendon.

——— 1950–1963 <1923>. *Die Fragmente der Griechischen Historiker*. 3 vols. in 15. Leiden: E. J. Brill.

Jaeger, Werner 1939. *Paideia: The Ideals of Greek Culture.* Vol. 1. Oxford: OUP.

Jatakari, Tuija 1990. "Der jüngerer Sokrates." *Arctos* 24, 29–45.

Jones, Nicholas F. 1999. *The Associations of Classical Athens: The Response to Democracy.* Oxford: OUP.

Jowett, Benjamin, tr. 1953. *The Dialogues of Plato translated into English.* Oxford: Clarendon.

Kagan, Donald 1981. *The Peace of Nicias and the Sicilian Expedition.* Ithaca: Cornell University Press.

——— 1987. *The Fall of the Athenian Empire.* Ithaca: Cornell University Press.

Kahn, Charles 1963. "Plato's Funeral Oration: The Motive of the *Menexenus*." *CP* 58, 220–34.

——— 1981. "Did Plato Write Socratic Dialogues?" *CQ* 31:2, 305–20.

——— 1988. "On the Relative Date of the *Gorgias* and the *Protagoras*." *Oxford Studies in Ancient Philosophy* 6, 69–102.

——— 1993. "Proleptic Composition in the *Republic*, or Why Book I Was Never a Separate Dialogue." *CQ* n.s. 43, 131–42.

——— 1994. "Aeschines on Socratic Eros." In *The Socratic Movement*, edited by Paul Vander Waerdt, 87–106. Ithaca: Cornell University Press.

——— 1996. *Plato and the Socratic Dialogue: The Philosophical Use of a Literary Form.* Cambridge: CUP.

Kakovoyiannis, Olga 1998. "Prosphata Euremata apo ten Perioche tou Demou Koropiou: Entopismos tou Archaiou Demou tes Oas." *[Proceedings of the] Conference of the Southeast Attic Association of Kalyvia* 7, 68–83. In modern Greek.

Kassel, Rudolf and Colin Austin 1983–91. *Poetae Comici Graeci.* 6 vols. Berlin: De Gruyter.

Katz, Marilyn 1992. "Ideology and 'the Status of Women' in Ancient Greece." In *History and Feminist Theory*, edited by A.-L. Shapiro, 70–97. History and Theory: Studies in the Philosophy of History 31. Updated and abbreviated for *Women in Antiquity: New Assessments*, edited by R. Hawley and B. Levick, 21–43. London and New York, n.p., 1995.

Keaney, J[ohn] J. 1980. "Plato, *Apology* 32c8–d3." *CQ* n.s. 30, 296–8.

Keen, Antony G. 1996. [Review of MacDowell 1995] *BMCR* 96.4.10.

Kerameikos; Ergebnisse der Ausgrabungen 1939– . Deutsches Archäologisches Institut. Berlin: de Gruyter.

Kierkegaard, Søren 1965. *The Concept of Irony, with Constant Reference to Socrates.* L. M. Capel, tr. New York: Harper & Row.

Kirchner, Johannes 1896. *Hermes* 31, 258–9, 1617.

——— 1901, 1903. *Prosopographia Attica.* 2 vols. Berlin: De Gruyter.

Kirk, Geoffrey S. 1951. "The Problem of Cratylus." *AJP* 72:3, 225–53.

Knorr, Wilbur Richard 1975. *The Evolution of the Euclidean Elements: A Study of the Theory of Incommensurable Magnitudes and Its Significance for Early Greek Geometry.* Dordrecht: Reidel.

———— 1979. "Methodology, Philology, and Philosophy, with a Reply by M. Burnyeat." *Isis* 70, 565–70.

Kock, Theodor 1880. *Comicorum Atticorum Fragmenta*. T.

Koerte, Alfred 1912. "Fragment einer Handschrift der Demen." *Hermes* 47, 277–313.

Köhler, Ulrich 1892. "Herakleides der Klazomenier." *Hermes* 27, 68–78.

———— 1896. "Attische Inschriften des Fuenften Jahrhunderts." *Hermes* 31, 136–54.

Kraut, Richard, ed. 1992. *Cambridge Companion to Plato*. Cambridge: CUP.

Krentz, Arthur A. 1983. "Dramatic Form and Philosophical Content in Plato's Dialogues." *Philosophy and Literature* 7, 32–47.

Krentz, Peter 1979. "*SEG* XXI, 80 and the Rule of the Thirty." *Hesperia* 48:1, 54–62.

———— 1980. "Foreigners against the Thirty: *IG* 2^2 10 Again." *Phoenix* 34, 289–306.

———— 1982. *The Thirty at Athens*, Ithaca and London: Cornell University Press.

———— 1984. "The Ostracism of Thoukydides, Son of Melesias." *Historia* 33, 499–504.

———— 1993. "Athens' Allies and the *Phallophoria*." *AHB* 7:1, 12–6.

Kühn, Josef-Hans 1967. "Die Amnestie von 403 v. Chr. im Reflex der 18 Isokrates-Rede." *Wiener Studien* 80, 31–73.

Lacey, W[alter] K[irkpatrick] 1968. *The Family in Classical Greece*. Ithaca: Cornell University Press.

Laing, Donald Rankin, Jr. 1965. *A New Interpretation of the Athenian Naval Catalogue IG II^2 1951*. Dissertation University of Cincinnati. Microfilm. *Dissertation Abstracts* 26 1966 3889.

Lamb, W. R. M., tr. 1924. *Plato Laches, Protagoras, Meno, Euthydemus*. Loeb.

———— 1925. *Plato Lysis, Symposium, Gorgias*. Loeb.

———— 1927. *Plato Charmides, Alcibiades I and II, Hipparchus, The Lovers, Theages, Minos, Epinomis*. Loeb.

———— 1930. *Plato Lysias*. Loeb.

Lambert, S. D. 1993. *The Phratries of Attica*. Ann Arbor: University of Michigan Press.

Lampert, Laurence and Christopher Planeaux 1998. "Who's Who in Plato's *Timaeus-Critias* and Why." *Review of Metaphysics* 52:1, 87–125.

Lang, Mable L. 1978. *Socrates in the Agora*. Excavations of the Athenian Agora Picture Book 17. Princeton: American School of Classical Studies at Athens.

———— 1990. "Illegal Execution in Ancient Athens." *Proceedings of the American Philosophical Society* 134, 24–9.

Lang, Paul 1911. *De Speusippi Academici Scriptis Accedunt Fragmenta*. Bonn: Typis C. Georgi Typographi Academici.

Lasserre, François 1966. *Die Fragmente des Eudoxos von Knidos*. Berlin: de Gruyter.

Ledger, Gerard R. 1989. *Re-Counting Plato: A Computer Analysis of Plato's Style*. Oxford: OUP.

Lee, Desmond, tr. 1955. *Plato: The Republic*. London and New York: Penguin.

———— 1965. *Plato Timaeus and Critias*. New York: Penguin.

Lefkowitz, Mary R. 1981. *The Lives of the Greek Poets.* Baltimore: Johns Hopkins Press.

Lesky, Albin 1966 <1957–1958>. *A History of Greek Literature.* James and Cornelis de Heer Willis, trr. New York: Thomas Y. Crowell Co.

Lessing, Gotthold Ephraim 1894. "Hamburgische Dramaturgie." In *Sämtliche Schriften*, Karl Lachmann. Briefe Antiquarischen. Stuttgart: Göschen.

Lewis, David M[alcolm] 1955. "Notes on Attic Inscriptions (II) XXIII. Who Was Lysistrata?" *Annual of the British School of Athens* 50, 1–36.

———— 1961. "Double Representation in the *Strategia*." *JHS* 81, 118–23.

———— 1966. "After the Profanation of the Mysteries." *Ancient Society and Institutions: Studies Presented to Victor Ehrenberg on his 75th Birthday.* Oxford: OUP, pp. 177–91. Also 1967, New York: Barnes & Noble.

———— 1993. "The Epigraphical Evidence for the End of the Thirty." In *Aristote et Athènes*, 223–9. Fribourg Séminaire d'Histoire ancienne. Fribourg (Suisse), 23–5 mai 1991: L'Université de Fribourg & Paris de Boccard.

Loening, Thomas C[lark] 1981. "The Autobiographical Speeches of Lysias and the Biographical Tradition." *Hermes* 109:3, 280–94.

———— 1987. *The Reconciliation Agreement of 403/402 B.C. in Athens. Hermes* Einzelschriften Heft 53. Wiesbaden: Franz Steiner.

Löper, R. 1896. "The Thirty Tyrants." *Zhurnal Ministerstva Narodnago Prosveshcheniya*, 90–101.

Loraux, Nicole 1986. *The Invention of Athens: The Funeral Oration in the Classical City*, tr. Alan Sheridan. Cambridge: HUP. Originally published as *L'invention d'Athènes: Histoire de l'oraison funèbre dans la "cité classique."* Mouton, 1981.

Lynch, John Patrick 1983. "The 'Academy Tablets' (*SEG* XIX, No. 37)." *ZPE* 52, 115–51.

MacDowell, Douglas M[aurice], ed. 1962. *Andokides On the Mysteries.* Oxford: Clarendon.

MacDowell, Douglas M[aurice] 1976a. [Review of Aurenche 1974] *JHS* 96, 226.

———— 1976b. "Bastards as Athenian Citizens." *CQ*, n.s. 26, 88–91.

———— 1978. *The Law in Classical Athens.* Ithaca: Cornell University Press.

———— 1995. *Aristophanes and Athens: An Introduction to the Plays.* Oxford: OUP.

Maidment, K. J., tr. 1941. *Minor Attic Orators in Two Volumes. I. Antiphon Andocides.* Loeb.

Majno, Guido 1975. *The Healing Hand: Man and Wound in the Ancient World.* Cambridge: HUP.

Mandela, Nelson Rolihlahla 1994. *Long Walk to Freedom.* Boston: Little, Brown.

Mannebach, Erich, ed. 1961. *Aristippi et Cyrenaicorum Fragmenta.* Leiden: E. J. Brill.

Mansfeld, J. 1979–1980. "The Chronology of Anaxagoras' Athenian Period and the Date of His Trial." *Mnemosyne* series 4: 32 (1979), 39–69; 33 (1980), 17–95.

Marr, J. L. 1971. "Andocides' Part in the Mysteries and Hermae Affairs 415 B.C." *CQ* 21, 326–38.

McCoy, W. James 1975. "The Identity of Leon." *American Journal of Philology* 96, 187–99.

McQueen, E. I., and Christopher J. Rowe 1989. "Phaedo, Socrates, and the Chronology of the Spartan War with Elis." *Méthexis* 2, 1–18.

Meiggs, Russell, and David Malcolm Lewis 1988. *A Selection of Greek Historical Inscriptions to the End of the Fifth Century.* Rev. edn. Oxford: Clarendon.

Mekler, Siegfried, ed. 1902. *Academicorum Philosophorum Index Herculanensis.* Berlin: Weidmann.

Méridier, Louis et al., edd. 1920–64. *Plato: Oeuvres Completes.* 13 vols. in 23. Loeb.

Meritt, Benjamin D[ean] 1961. "Greek Inscriptions." *Hesperia* 30, 205–92, and plates 33–61.

Meritt, Benjamin D[ean], and A[ntony] Andrewes 1951. "Athens and Neapolis." *Annual of the British School of Athens* 46, 200–9.

Meritt, Benjamin D[ean], and J[ohn] S[tuart] Traill 1975. *The Inscriptions: The Councillors.* Agora 15. Princeton: PUP.

Meyer, Eduard 1899. *Zur Geschichte des funften Jahrhunderts v. Chr.* Forschungen zur alten Geschichte 2. Halle: Max Niemeyer.

Miller, Mitchell H., Jr. 1980. *The Philosopher in Plato's Statesman.* The Hague: Nijhoff.

——— 1986. *Plato's Parmenides: The Conversion of the Soul.* Princeton: PUP.

Millett, Paul 1991. *Lending and Borrowing in Ancient Athens.* New York: CUP.

Mirhady, David C. and Yun Lee Too, trr. 2000. *Isocrates I.* Austin: University of Texas Press.

Momigliano, Arnaldo 1993. *The Development of Greek Biography.* Expanded edn. Cambridge: HUP.

Mommsen, August 1898. *Feste der Stadt Athen im altertum: Geordnet nach Attischem Kalender.* T.

Monoson, S. Sara 2000. *Plato's Democratic Entanglements: Athenian Politics and the Practice of Philosophy.* Princeton: PUP.

Montuori, Mario 1977–1978. "Di Aspasia Milesia." *Annali della Facoltà di Lettere e Filosofia della Università di Napoli* 20, 63–85. "Aspasia of Miletus." In *Socrates, An Approach,* tr. Marcus de la Pae Beresford, 201–26. Amsterdam: J. C. Gieben, 1988.

Moore, John D. 1974. "The Dating of Plato's *Ion.*" *GRBS* 15, 421–39.

Moors, Kent 1987. "The Argument Against a Dramatic Date for Plato's *Republic.*" *Polis* 7:1, 6–31.

Moretti, Luigi 1968–1990. *Inscriptiones Graecae Urbis Romae,* 4 vols. Rome, n.p.

Morgan, Michael L. 1992. "Plato and Greek Religion." In Kraut, ed. (1992: 227–47).

Morrison, J. S. 1941. "The Place of Protagoras in Athenian Public Life." *CQ* 35, 1–16.

Morrow, Glenn R[aymond] 1935. *Studies in the Platonic Epistles. Illinois Studies in Language and Literature* 18:3–4. Urbana: University of Illinois.

——— 1960. *Plato's Cretan City: An Historical Interpretation of Plato's* Laws. Princeton: PUP.

Müller, Karl Otfried 1975 <1848, 1849>. *Fragmenta Historicorum Graecorum*. Frankfurt: Unveränderter Nachdruck.

Munk, E. 1857. *Die Natürliche Ordnung der Platonischen Schriften*. Berlin: F. Dümmler Verlagsbuchhandlung.

Murray, Gilbert 1933. *Aristophanes: A Study*. Oxford: OUP.

Murray, Oswyn 1990. "The Affair of the Mysteries: Democracy and the Drinking Group." In *Sympotica: A Symposium on the* Symposion, ed. Oswyn Murray, 149–61. New York: OUP.

Nails, Debra 1995. *Agora, Academy, and the Conduct of Philosophy*. Dordrecht and Boston: Kluwer Academic Publishers.

———— 1998. "The Dramatic Date of Plato's *Republic*." *CJ* 93:4, 383–96.

Nails, Debra and Holger Thesleff forthcoming. "Early Academic Editing: Plato's *Laws*." In *The Laws: Selected Papers from the VI Symposium Platonicum*, ed. Samuel Scolnicov and Luc Brisson. Sankt Augustin: Academia.

Navia, Luis E. 2001. *Antisthenes of Athens: Setting the World Aright*. Westport: Greenwood.

Nehamas, Alexander, and Paul Woodruff, trr. 1989. *Plato,* Symposium. Indianapolis: Hackett.

Németh, György 1988. "Die Dreissig Tyrannen und die Athenische Prosopographie." *ZPE* 73, 181–94.

Neschke-Hentschke, Ada 1990. "Matériaux pour une Approche Philologique de l'herméneutique de Schleiermacher." In *La Naissance du Paradigme Herméneutique: Schleiermacher, Humboldt, Boeckh, Droysen*, 29–67. Cahiers de philologie. Universitaires de Lille: Lille Presses.

Nevett, Lisa C. 1999. *House and Society in the Ancient Greek World*. New York: CUP.

Nightingale, Andrea 1995. *Genres in Dialogue: Plato and the Construct of Philosophy*. Cambridge: CUP.

Notopoulos, James A. 1939. "The Name of Plato." *CP* 34, 135–45.

Nussbaum, Martha C[raven] 1986. *The Fragility of Goodness*. Cambridge: CUP. Rev. edn. 2001.

Oikonomides, Al. (?) N. 1976–1984. *Inscriptiones Atticae: Supplementum Inscriptionum Atticarum*. 5 vols. Chicago: Ares.

Ollier, F. 1961. *Xénophon Banquet*. Paris: Budé.

Olson, S. Douglas 1983. "The Identity of the Δεσπότης at *Ecclesiazusae* 1128 f." *GRBS* 24, 161–6.

O'Regan, Daphne Elizabeth 1992. *Rhetoric, Comedy, and the Violence of Language in Aristophanes' Clouds*. New York: OUP.

Osborne, Michael J. 1981–1983. *Naturalization in Athens*. 4 vols. in 3. Brussels: Paleis der Academiën.

Osborne, Michael J. and S. G. Byrne 1994. *A Lexicon of Greek Personal Names*. Vol. 2. *Attica*. Oxford: Clarendon.

———— 1996. *The Foreign Residents of Athens: An Annex to the* Lexicon of Greek Personal Names: Attica. Studia Hellenistica 33. Leuven: Peeters.

Osborne, Robin 1985a. *Demos: The Discovery of Classical Athens*. Cambridge Classical Studies. Cambridge: CUP.

———— 1985b. "The Erection and Mutilation of the Hermai." *Proceedings of the Cambridge Philological Society* 31, 47–73.

———— 1999. "Inscribing Performance." In *Performance Culture and Athenian Democracy*, ed. Simon Goldhill and Robin Osborne, 341–58. Cambridge: CUP.

Ostwald, Martin 1969. *Nomos and the Beginnings of the Athenian Democracy*. Oxford: Clarendon.

———— 1986. *From Popular Sovereignty to the Sovereignty of Law*. Berkeley: University of California Press.

Overbeck, J[ohannes] A[dolf] 1868. *Die antiken Schriftquellen zur Geschichte der bildenden Kunst*. Leipzig: Englemann.

Oxyrhynchus Papyri 1898–   . Bernard P[yne] Grenfell, Arthur S. Hunt, *et al.*, edd. London: Egypt Exploration Society.

Parker, Douglass, tr. 1969. [Aristophanes'] *The Congresswomen (Ecclesiazusae)* with introduction and notes. Ann Arbor: University of Michigan Press.

Parkin, Tim 1999. [Review of Patterson 1998.] *BMCR* 99.6.7.

Parmentier, L. 1926. "L'Age de Phèdre dans Le Dialogue de Platon." *Bulletin de l'Association Guillaume Budé* 10, 8–21.

Patterson, Cynthia B. 1981. *Pericles' Citizenship Law of 451–50 B.C.* Monographs in Classical Studies. New York: Arno Press.

———— 1990. "Those Athenian Bastards." *Classical Antiquity* 9, 40–73.

———— 1998. *The Family in Greek History*. Cambridge and London: HUP.

Pauly, August Friedrich von, G. Wissowa et al. 1894–1980. *Real-Encyclopädie der classischen Altertumswissenschaft*. 84 vols. Stuttgart: Metzler.

Payne, H. G. G. 1934. "Archaeology in Greece, 1933–34." *JHS* 54, 185–210.

Pečirka, Jan 1966. *The Formula for the Grant of Enktesis in Attic Inscriptions*. Acta Philosophica et Historica 15. Prague: Universitatis Carolinae.

Pendrick, Gerard 1987. "Once Again Antiphon the Sophist and Antiphon of Rhamnous." *Hermes* 115, 47–60.

Pesely, George E. 1989. "The Origin and Value of the Theramenes Papyrus." *AHB* 3:2, 29–35.

Petersen, J. C. W. 1880. *Quaestiones de Historia Gentium Atticarum* (diss. Kiel).

Pickard-Cambridge, Arthur Wallace, tr. 1912. *The Public Orations of Demosthenes*. 2 vols. Oxford: Clarendon.

Planeaux, Christopher 1999. "Socrates, Alcibiades, and Plato's ΤΑ ΠΟΤΕΙΔΕΑ-ΤΙΚΑ. Does the *Charmides* Have an Historical Setting? *Mnemosyne* 52:1, 72–7.

———— 2001a. "Socrates, an Unreliable Narrator? The Dramatic Setting of the *Lysis*." *CP* 96, 60–8.

———— 2001b. "The Date of Bendis' Entry into Attica." *CJ* 96.2, 165–92.

Plepelits, Karl 1970. *Die Fragmente der 'Demen' des Eupolis*. Vienna: Notring.

Pomeroy, Sarah B. 1997. *Families in Classical and Hellenistic Greece: Representations and Realities.* Oxford: OUP.

Poralla, Paul 1985. *A Prosopography of Lacedaemonians from the Earliest Times to the Death of Alexander the Great (X–323 B.C.).* 2nd edn. with an introduction, addenda and corrigenda by Alfred S. Bradford. Chicago: Ares.

Pritchett, W. K[endrick] 1953. "The Attic Stelai. Part I." *Hesperia* 22, 225–99 and plates 67–84.

——— 1961. "Five New Fragments of the Attic Stelai." *Hesperia* 30, 23–29 and plates 5–6.

——— 1969. "Two Illustrated Epigraphical Notes." *American Journal of Archaeology* 73, 367–70 and plate 95.

Raeder, Hans 1905. *Platons Philosophische Entwickelung.* Leipzig.

Rankin, Herbert David 1964. *Plato and the Individual.* London: Methuen.

——— 1986. *Anthisthenes Sokratikos* [sic]. Amsterdam: Hakkert.

——— 1993. "Socrates, Plato and Fiction." *Scholia* 2:45–55.

Raubitschek, Antony Erich 1939. "Leagros." *Hesperia* 8, 155–64.

——— 1941. "The Heroes of Phyle." *Hesperia* 10, 284–95.

——— 1949. *Dedications from the Athenian Akropolis: A Catalogue of the Inscriptions of the Sixth and Fifth Centuries B.C.* Cambridge: Archaeological Institute of America.

——— 1955. "Damon." *CM* 16, 78–83.

Reagan, James Thomas 1960. *The Material Substrates in the Platonic Dialogues.* Dissertation St. Louis University. Microfilm. *Dissertation Abstracts* 21 1960 3123.

Rhodes, P. J. 1972. "The Five Thousand in the Athenian Revolutions of 411 B.C." *JHS* 92, 115–27.

——— 1978. "Bastards as Athenian Citizens." *CQ* n.s. 28, 89–92.

——— 1993. *A Commentary on the Aristotelian* Athenaion Politeia. 2nd edn. Oxford: Clarendon.

Riddle, John M. 1992. *Contraception and Abortion from the Ancient World to the Renaissance.* Cambridge: HUP.

Riginos, Alice Swift 1976. *Platonica: The Anecdotes Concerning the Life and Writings of Plato.* Leiden: E. J. Brill.

Ritter, Constantin 1888. *Untersuchungen über Platon.* Stuttgart: Kohlhammer.

——— 1910. *Platon, sein Lieben, seine Schriften, seine Lehre.* 2 vols. Munich: Beck.

Roberts, Jennifer Tolbert 1977. "Arginusae Once Again." *The Classical World* 71, 107–11.

Robertson, N. 1976. "False Documents at Athens. Fifth Century History and Fourth Century Publicists." *Historical Reflections* (Ontario) 3, 3–25.

Rogers, B. B., tr. 1924. *Aristophanes* Ecclesiazusae. Loeb.

Romilly, Jacqueline de 1991 <1988>. *Great Sophists in Periclean Athens.* Janet Lloyd, tr. Oxford: Clarendon.

Rosenmeyer, Thomas G. 1948. "The Family of Critias." *AJP* 70, 404–10.

Rossetti, Livio 1973. " 'Socratica' in Fedone di Elide." *Studi Urbinati* 47, 364–81.

—— 1980. "Ricerche sui Dialoghi Socratici di Fedone e di Euclide." *Hermes* 108, 183–200.

Rowe, Christopher J. 1998. "Democracy and Sokratic-Platonic Philosophy." In *Democracy, Empire, and the Arts in Fifth-century Athens*, ed. Deborah Boedeker and Kurt Raaflaub, 241–53. Cambridge and London: HUP.

Ryan, Francis X. 1993. "The Eleusinian Cult and the Thirty." *La Parola del Passato. Rivista di Studi Antichi* 48, 66.

Ryle, Gilbert 1966. *Plato's Progress*. Cambridge: CUP.

Sachs, Eva 1914. *De Theaeteto Atheniensi Mathematico*. Dissertation. Berlin.

—— 1917. *Die Fünf Platonischen Körper*. Philologische Untersuchungen 24. Berlin: Weidemann.

Sakurai, Mariko 1992. "Property Confiscated by the Thirty Tyrants and the Restored Democracy of Athens." *Journal of Classical Studies* 40, 22–3. In Japanese with summary in English.

Salkever, Stephen 1993. "Socrates' Aspasian Oration: The Play of Philosophy and Politics in Plato's *Menexenus*." *American Political Science Review* 87:1, 133–46.

Sanders, L. J. 1987. *Dionysius I of Syracuse and Greek Tyranny*. London: Croom Helm.

—— 1992. "What Did Timaeus Think of Dion?" *Hermes* 120, 205–15.

—— 1994. "Nationalist Recommendations and Policies in the Seventh and Eighth Platonic Epistles." *AHB* 8:3, 76–85.

Saunders, A. N. W., tr. 1970. *Greek Political Oratory*. Harmondsworth: Penguin.

Saunders, Trevor J. 1986. "The RAND Corporation of Antiquity? Plato's Academy and Greek Politics." In *Studies in Honor of T. B. L. Webster*, ed. J. H. Bets, J. T. Hooker, and J. R. Green, vol. 1. Bristol: Bristol Classical Press.

Saxonhouse, Arlene 1983. "An Unspoken Theme in Plato's *Gorgias*: War." *Interpretation* 112:2, 139–69.

—— 1998. "Plato and the Problematical Gentleness of Democracy." In *Athenian Democracy and "Democracy, Equality, and Eidē": A Radical View from Book 8 of Plato's* Republic. *American Political Science Review* 92:2, 273–84.

Schleiermacher, Friedrich E. D. 1973 <1804>. *Introductions to the Dialogues of Plato*. W. Dobson, tr. New York: Arno Press.

Schmid, Walter T. 1992. *On Manly Courage: A Study of Plato's* Laches. Carbondale: Southern Illinois University Press.

Seager, Robin 1976. "After the Peace of Nicias: Diplomacy and Policy, 421–416 B.C." *CQ* 26, 249–69.

Sealey, Raphael 1975. "Constitutional Changes in Athens in 410 B.C." *California Studies in Classical Antiquity* (Berkeley) 8, 271–95.

—— 1993. *Demosthenes and His Times*. New York: OUP.

Sedley, David 1995. "The Dramatis Personae of Plato's *Phaedo*." *Proceedings of the British Academy* 85, 3–26.

Segal, Charles 1978. " 'The Myth Was Saved': Reflections on Homer and the Mythology of Plato's *Republic*." *Hermes* 106:2, 315–36.

Shapiro, H. A. 1986. "The Attic Deity Basile." *ZPE* 63, 134–6.

Shawyer, J. A., ed. 1906. *The* Menexenus *of Plato.* Oxford: Clarendon.

Shear, T[heodore] Leslie, Jr. 1963. "Koisyra: Three Women of Athens." *Phoenix* 17, 99–112.

——— 1994. *"Isonomous t'Athēnas epoiēsatēn:* The Agora and the Democracy." In *The Archaeology of Athens and Attica under the Democracy: Proceedings of an International Conference Celebrating 2,500 Years Since the Birth of Democracy in Greece, held at the American School of Classical Studies at Athens, December 4–6, 1992,* ed. W. D. E. Coulson, O. Palagia, T. L. Shear, Jr., H. A. Shapiro, and F. J. Frost. Oxbow Monograph 37, 225–48. Oxford: Oxbow.

——— 1997. "The Athenian Agora: Excavations of 1989–1993." *Hesperia* 66:4, 495–548 and plates 93–108.

Shorey, Paul, tr. 1930. *Plato* The Republic. Loeb.

Sider, David 1981. *The Fragments of Anaxagoras.* Beiträge zur klassischen Philologie 118. Meisenheim am Glan: Hain.

Siebeck, Hermann 1888. *Untersuchungen zur Philosophie der Griechen.* Freiburg: J. C. B. Mohr.

Simeterre, R. 1938. *La Théorie Socratique de la Vertu-science selon les Memorables de Xenophon.* Paris: P. Téqui.

Skemp, Joseph Bright 1987. *Plato: The Statesman.* 2nd edn. New York: Bristol Classical Press.

Smith, J. A. 1989. *Athens Under the Tyrants.* Bristol: Bristol Classical Press.

Snell, Bruno, Richard Kannicht, and S. Radt, edd. 1971–8. *Tragicorum Graecorum Fragmenta.* 4 vols. Göttingen: Vandenhoeck & Ruprecht.

Sommerstein, Alan H. 1996. *Frogs.* The Comedies of Aristophanes, vol. 9. Warminster: Aris & Phillips.

Sordi, M. 1981. "Teramene e il processo della Arginuse." *Aevum* 55, 3–12.

Sparshott, F. E. 1957. "Plato and Thrasymachus." *University of Toronto Quarterly* 54–61.

Sprague, Rosamond Kent 1976. *Plato's Philosopher-King: A Study of the Theoretical Background.* Columbia: University of South Carolina Press.

——— 2001 <1972>. *The Older Sophists: A Complete Translation by Several Hands of the Fragments in* Die Fragmente der Vorsokratiker *Edited by Diels-Kranz with a New Edition of Antiphon and of Euthydemus.* Indianapolis: Hackett.

Stadter, Philip A. 1989. *A Commentary on Plutarch's Pericles.* Chapel Hill: University of North Carolina.

——— 1993. "Péricles y los Intelectuales." *Polis* 5, 227–40.

Stanford, W. B. 1968. *Aristophanes: The Frogs.* 2nd edn. New York: St. Martin's Press.

Stanley, Phillip V. 1986. "The Family Connection of Alcibiades and Axiochus." *GRBS* 27, 173–86.

Steinberger, Peter 1996. "Who Is Cephalus?" *Political Theory* 24:2, 172–99.

Steinhart, Karl von 1873. *Platon's Leben.* Leipzig: Brockhaus.

Stenzel, Julius August Heinrich 1957 <1916>. "Literarische Form und Philosophische Gehalt des Platonischen Dialoges." In *Kleine Schriften zur Griechischen Philosophie*, 32–47. Darmstadt: Hermann Gentner Verlag.

Stephanis, I. E. 1988. *Dionysiakoi Technitai: Symvoles Sten Prosopographia tou Theatrou kai tes Mousikes ton Archaion Hellenon.* Herakleio: Panepistemiakes Ekdoseis Kretes.

Stewart, Andrew F. 1990. *Greek Sculpture. An Exploration.* New Haven and London: Yale University Press.

Stewart, Douglas J. 1972. "Socrates' Last Bath." *Journal of the History of Philosophy* 10, 253–59.

Stock, St. George William Joseph 1909. *The Ion of Plato.* Oxford: Clarendon.

Stokes, Michael C. 1986. *Plato's Socratic Conversations: Drama and Dialectic in Three Dialogues.* Baltimore: The Johns Hopkins University Press.

Storey, Ian C. 1988. "Thrasymachos at Athens: Aristophanes fr. 205 (*Daitales*)." *Phoenix* 42:3, 212–8.

—— 1990. "Dating and Re-Dating Eupolis." *Phoenix* 44, 1–30.

—— 1996. [Review of MacDowell 1995] *BMCR* 96.4.9.

—— 1997. [Review of Vickers 1997] *BMCR* 97.9.15.

Strassler, Robert B., ed. 1996. *The Landmark Thucydides.* New York: The Free Press.

Strauss, Leo 1964. *The City and the Man.* Chicago: University of Chicago Press.

—— 1966. *Socrates and Aristophanes.* New York: Basic Books.

Stroud, Ronald S. 1971. "Greek Inscriptions: Theozotides and the Athenian Orphans." *Hesperia* 40, 280–301.

—— 1984. "The Gravestone of Socrates' Friend, Lysis." *Hesperia* 53:3, 355–60 and plate 68.

Strycker, Émile de, and S. R. Slings. 1994. *Plato's Apology of Socrates: A Literary and Philosophical Study with a Running Commentary.* Mnemosyne. Leiden: E. J. Brill.

Suidae Lexicon 1928–1938. Ada Adler, ed. T.

Sundwall, Johannes 1910. *Nachträge zur Prosopographia Attica.* Helsingfors: n.p.

Süvern, J. W. 1826. *Über Aristophanes Wolken.* Berlin: Ferdinand Dümmler.

Tarán, Leonardo 1975. *Academica: Plato, Philip of Opus, and the Pseudo-Platonic Epinomis.* Memoirs of the American Philosophical Society 107. Philadelphia: American Philosophical Society.

—— 1981. *Speusippus of Athens: A Critical Study with a Collection of the Related Texts and Commentary.* Philosophia Antiqua 39. Leiden: E. J. Brill.

Tarrant, H. A. S. 1994. "Chronology and Narrative Apparatus in Plato's Dialogues." *Electronic Antiquity* 1.8.

—— 1995. "Plato's *Euthydemus* and the Two Faces of Socrates." *Prudentia* 27:2, 4–17.

Tatham, M. T. 1888. *The Laches of Plato.* London: Macmillan.

Taylor, A[lfred] E[dward] 1928. *A Commentary on Plato's Timaeus*. Oxford: Clarendon.

———— 1956. *Plato: The Man and His Work*. Cleveland: The World Publishing Co.

Taylor, C. C. W., tr. 1976. *Plato* Protagoras. Oxford: Clarendon.

Teloh, Henry 1986. *Socratic Education in Plato's Early Dialogues*. Notre Dame: University of Notre Dame.

Thalheim, Theodor Franz Artur 1913 <1901>. *Lysias*. T.

Thesleff, Holger 1967. *Studies in the Styles of Plato*. Acta Philosophica Fennica. Helsinki: Abo Akademi.

———— 1982. *Studies in Platonic Chronology*. Commentationes Humanarum Litterarum 70. Helsinki: Societas Scientiarum Fennica.

———— 1990. "Theaitetos and Theodorus." *Arctos* 24, 147–59.

———— 1997. "The Early Version of Plato's *Republic*." *Arctos* 31, 149–74.

Thomas, Ivor 1991. *Greek Mathematical Works*. Vol. 1, rev. edn. Loeb.

Thomas, Rosalind 1989. *Oral Tradition and the Written Record in Classical Athens*. Cambridge Studies in Oral and Literate Culture 18. Cambridge: CUP.

Thompson, Dorothy Burr 1960. "The House of Simon the Shoemaker." *Archaeology* 13, 234–40.

Thompson, Homer A. 1954. "Excavations in the Athenian Agora: 1953." *Hesperia* 23, 31–67 and plates 12–7.

———— 1955. "Activities in the Athenian Agora: 1954." *Hesperia* 24, 50–71 and plates 32, 33.

Thompson, Homer A., and R. E. Wycherley 1972. *The Agora of Athens*. Agora 14. Princeton: PUP.

Thompson, W. H. 1965. "Prosopographical Notes on Athena's Treasurers." *Hesperia* 34: 148–53.

Thompson, Wesley E. 1967. "The Marriage of First Cousins in Athenian Society." *Phoenix* 21, 273–82.

———— 1970. "The Kinship of Perikles and Alkibiades." *GRBS* 11, 27–33.

Thorp, J. 1992. "The Social Construction of Homosexuality." *Phoenix* 46, 54–61.

Tigerstedt, Eugène Napoleon 1977. *Interpreting Plato*. Uppsala: Almquist and Wiksell.

Tod, M[arcus] N[ieuhr] 1946, 1948. *A Selection of Greek Historical Inscriptions*. 2 vols. Oxford: Clarendon.

Todd, S. C., tr. 2000. *Lysias*. Austin: University of Texas Press.

Tomin, Julius 1987. "Socratic Midwifery." *CQ* 37: 97–102.

———— 1987–1988. "Aristophanes: A Lasting Source of Reference." *Proceedings of the Aristotelian Society* 88, 83–95.

Traill, J[ohn] S[tuart]. 1975. *The Political Organisation of Attica: A Study of the Demes, Trittyes, and Phylai and their Representation in the Athenian Council*. Hesperia supp. 14. Princeton: PUP.

────── 1982. *Studies in Attic Epigraphy, History, and Topography Presented to Eugene Vanderpool. Hesperia* supp. 19. Princeton: PUP.

────── 1986. *Demos and Trittys: Epigraphical and Topographical Studies in the Organization of Attica.* Toronto: Athenians.

────── 1994– . *Persons of Ancient Athens.* 20 vols. projected. Toronto: Athenians.

Travlos, Ioannes N. 1971. *Pictorial Dictionary of Ancient Athens.* London and New York: Praeger.

Tsitsidiris, Stavros 1998. *Platons Menexenos: Einleitung, Text und Kommentar.* T.

Tulin, Alexander 1998. [Review of Gagarin 1997] *BMCR* 98.6.19.

Tuplin, Christopher 1984. [Review of Krentz 1982] *JHS* 104, 242.

Ueberweg, F. 1861. *Untersuchungen über die Echtheit und Zeitfolge Platonischer Schriften und über die Hauptmomente aus Plato's Leben.* Wien: Gerold.

Untersteiner, Mario. 1954 <1948>. *The Sophists.* Kathleen Freeman, tr. Oxford: Blackwell.

Usher, S. 1968. "Xenophon, Critias and Theramenes." *JHS* 88, 128–35.

Vanderpool, Eugene 1949. "Some Ostraka from the Athenian Agora." *Hesperia* supp. 8: *Commemorative Studies in Honor of Theodore Leslie Shear,* 394–412, and plates 57–60.

────── 1952. "The Ostracism of the Elder Alcibiades." *Hesperia* 21, 1–8 and plate 1.

────── 1959. "Newsletter from Greece." *American Journal of Archaeology* 63, 279–80.

────── 1968. "New Ostraka from the Athenian Agora." *Hesperia* 37, 117–20.

Van Hook, Larue, tr. 1945. *Isocrates in Three Volumes.* Vol. 3. Loeb.

Vickers, Michael. 1993. "Alcibiades in Cloudedoverland." In *Nomodeiktes: Greek Studies in Honor of Martin Ostwald,* ed. Ralph M. Rosen and Joseph Farrell, 603–18. Ann Arbor: University of Michigan Press.

────── 1997. *Pericles on Stage: Political Comedy in Aristophanes' Early Plays.* Austin: University of Texas Press.

Vidal-Naquet, Pierre, "Plato, History and Historians." In *Politics Ancient and Modern,* ed. Pierre Vidal-Naquet, tr. Janet Lloyd. Cambridge: Polity.

Vischer, Wilhelm 1877. *Kleine Schriften* I. Leipzig: S. Hirzel.

Vlastos, Gregory 1975. "Plato's Testimony Concerning Zeno of Elea." *JHS* 95, 155–61.

────── 1991. *Socrates: Ironist and Moral Philosopher.* Cambridge: CUP.

Voegelin, Eric 1957. *Order and History.* Vol. 3. Baton Rouge: Louisiana State University Press.

Vogt, Heinrich 1909–10. "Die Entdeckungsgeschichte des Irrationalen nach Plato und anderen Quellen des 4. Jahrhunderts." *Bibliotheca Mathematica* 10, 97–155.

Wade-Gery, H. T. 1932. "Thucydides the Son of Melesias: A Study of Periklean Policy." *JHS* 52, 205–27.

Walbank, F. W. 1957–1979. *A Historical Commentary on Polybius.* 3 vols. Oxford: Clarendon.

Walbank, Michael B. 1978. *Athenian Proxenies of the Fifth Century* B.C. Toronto and Sarasota: S. Stevens.

——— 1982. "The Confiscation and Sale by the Poletai in 402/1 B.C. of the Property of the Thirty Tyrants." *Hesperia* 51:1, 74–98 and plates 27–8.

Walcot, Peter 1996 <1987>. "Plato's Mother and Other Terrible Women." In *Women in Antiquity* ed. Ian McAuslan and Peter Walcot, 114–33. Greece and Rome Studies 3. Oxford: OUP (for the Classical Association).

Wallace, M. B. 1970. "Early Greek *Proxenoi.*" *Phoenix* 24, 189–208.

Wallace, Robert W. 1992. "Charmides, Agariste and Damon: Andocides 1.16." *CQ* 42:2, 328–35.

Walsh, J. 1984. "The Dramatic Dates of Plato's *Protagoras* and the Lesson of *Arete.*" *CQ* 34, 101–6.

Waterfield, Robin, tr. 1993. *Plato* Republic. Oxford: OUP.

Weiner, N. O. 1969. *The Divided Line, the Convening Art and the Dramatic Structure of Plato's Republic.* Dissertation University of Texas. Microfilm. *Dissertation Abstracts* 30 1969 1604A.

Wellmann, Max 1901. *Die Fragmente der Sikelischen Ärzte.* Berlin: Weidmann.

White, Stephen A. 1995. "Thrasymachus the Diplomat." *CP* 90:4, 307–27.

Whitehead, David 1977. *The Ideology of the Athenian Metic. Proceedings of the Cambridge Philological Society*, supp. vol. 4.

——— 1980. "The Tribes of the Thirty Tyrants." *JHS* 100, 208–13.

——— 1982. "Notes on Athenian Demarchs." *ZPE* 47, 37–42.

——— 1982–1983. "Sparta and the Thirty Tyrants." *Ancient Society* 13–14, 105–30.

——— 1983. "Competitive Outlay and Community Profit: *Philotimia* in Democratic Athens." *CM* 34, 55–74.

——— 1986. *The Demes of Attica 508/7–ca. 250* B.C.: *A Political and Social Study.* Princeton: PUP.

——— 1988. "Athenians in Xenophon's Hellenica." *Liverpool Classical Monthly* 13: 145–7.

Wieland, W. 1982. *Platon und die Formen des Wissen.* Göttingen: Vandenhoeck and Ruprecht.

Wilamowitz-Möllendorff, Ulrich von 1919, 1920. *Platon.* 2 vols. Berlin: Wiedmann.

——— 1921. *Griechische Verskunst.* Berlin: Weidmann.

Winkler, John J. 1985. "The *Ephebes'* Song: *Tragoidia* and *Polis.*" In *Nothing to Do with Dionysos?*, ed. John J. Winkler and Froma I. Zeitlin. Princeton: PUP.

——— 1990. "Laying Down the Law: The Oversight of Men's Sexual Behavior in Classical Athens." In *Before Sexuality: The Construction of Erotic Experience in the Ancient Greek World,* ed. David Halperin, John J. Winkler, and Froma I. Zeitlin, 171–209. Princeton: PUP.

Winspear, A. D. and T. Silverberg 1960. *Who Was Socrates?* New York: Russell & Russell.

Wolfsdorf, D. 1997. "The Dramatic Date of Plato's *Protagoras.*" *Rheinisches Museum* (Frankfurt) 140, 223–30.

—— 1998. "The Historical Reader of Plato's *Protagoras.*" *CQ* 48, 126–34.

Woodbury, Leonard 1973. "Socrates and the Daughter of Aristides." *Phoenix* 27, 7–25.

Woodhead, A[rthur] Geoffrey 1992. *The Study of Greek Inscriptions.* 2nd edn. Norman: University of Oklahoma Press.

Woodruff, Paul, tr. 1982. *Plato,* Hippias Major. Indianapolis: Hackett.

—— 1983. *Plato, Two Comic Dialogues:* Ion *and* Hippias Major. Indianapolis: Hackett.

Wycherley, R. E. 1978. *The Stones of Athens.* Princeton: PUP.

Yunis, Harvey 1996. *Taming Democracy: Models of Political Rhetoric in Classical Athens.* Ithaca: Cornell University Press.

Zeller, Eduard 1885 <1875>. *Socrates and the Socratic Schools.* O. Reichel, tr. London: Longmans, Green and Co.

—— 1876. *Plato and the Older Academy.* Sarah Frances Alleyne and Alfred Goodwin, trr. London: Longmans, Green, and Co.

MAPS

Map 1. Greece and western Asia Minor.

B

*Black
Sea*

THRACE

Hebrus

Bosphorus

Selymbria Byzantium
●   ● ●Chalcedon
Abdera   Perinthus
●   ●

Propontis

Thasos   Aenus
●

Samothrace   CHERSONESE
            ●Lampsacus   ●Cyzicus
            Aegospotami
Lemnos   ●Abydus
         Hellespont ●Troy   Scepsis
                  Scamander ●

Aegean   TROAD

                 Assos
                 ●

Sea   Mytilene
        Lesbos ●   *Caicus*

            Arginusae Is.

                Hermus
                     LYDIA
Chios   ●Sardis
              ●Clazomenae
              ●Teos
                  Notium
Andros   Samos   ●
        ●Ephesus *Maeander*

Delos   ●Miletus
                      CARIA
Paros   Naxos

       Cos

         Cnidus
         ●

Rhodes

Crete ●Cnossos

B

a

b

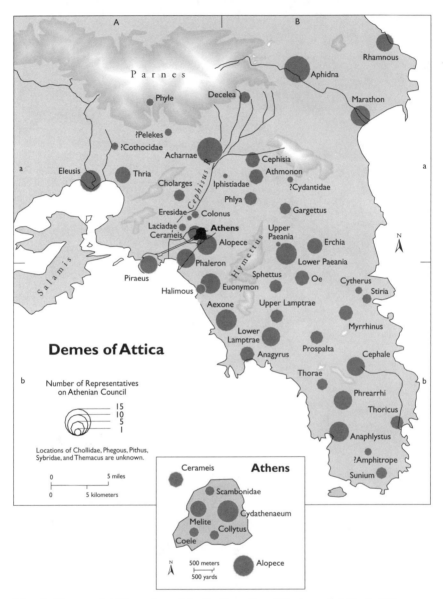

A

B

Rhamnous

P a r n e s

Aphidna

Phyle

Decelea

Marathon

?Pelekes

?Cothocidae

Acharnae

Cephisia

a

Eleusis

Thria

Cholarges

Iphistiadae

Athmonon

?Cydantidae

Phlya

Eresidae

Colonus

Gargettus

Laciadae

Cerameis

Athens

Upper
Paeania

Erchia

Alopece

Lower Paeania

Phaleron

Piraeus

Sphettus

Oe

Cytherus

Halimous

Euonymon

Stiria

Aexone

Upper Lamptrae

Lower
Lamptrae

Myrrhinus

Demes of Attica

Anagyrus

Prospalta

Cephale

Thorae

b

Number of Representatives
on Athenian Council

Phrearrhi

Thoricus

15
10
5
1

Anaphlystus

Locations of Chollidae, Phegous, Pithus,
Sybridae, and Themacus are unknown.

?Amphitrope

Cerameis

Athens

Sunium

0   5 miles

0   5 kilometers

Scambonidae

Cydathenaeum

Melite

Collytus

Coele

N

500 meters

Alopece

500 yards

Map 2. Demes of Attica relevant to the Socratics: fifty-two of Attica's 139 demes, with inset of the walled city of Athens.

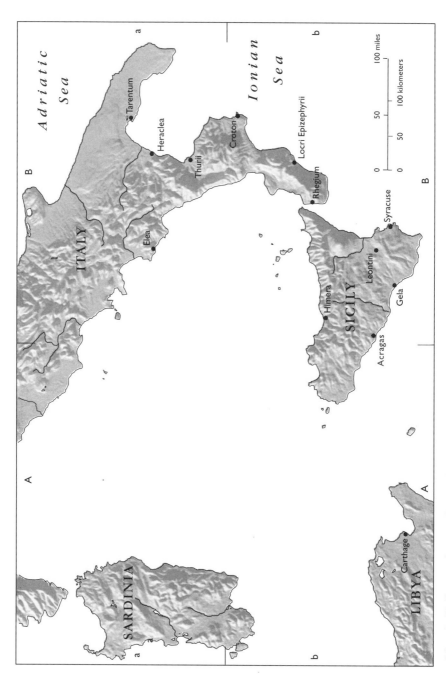

Map 3. Sicily, southern Italy, northern Libya.

Map Index

Place names, rivers and mountains are keyed to the three maps, each of which
is divided into quadrants, AB on the horizontal axis and ab on the vertical axis.
For example, the notation 1Ab means map 1, lower left quadrant.

INDEX OF
SELECTED TOPICS

Numbers in italics refer to maps and plan by page number. Introduction, text, and Appendices I and III are indexed.

A

agriculture, 4, 38, 41, 70, 97, 115, 177–8. *See also* farmers and herders

amnesty, 6, 28, 38, 44, 189, 192–3, 200, 219–22

architecture and city planning: dwellings, 11, 192, 279; garden at Academy, *267*, 248; public areas and buildings, *267*, 97, 225, 237, 265–8, 277, 279–80, 281, 292, 299; residences, *267*, *404*, 2, 9, 62, 70, 84, 91, 139–40, 143, 151, 170, 191, 196, 199, 208, 218, 233, 250, 251, 279, 295; residential patterns, *404*, 351, 352–6

arts and artists: literary criticism, 25, 39, 273; music, 8, 97, 103–4, 121–2, 168, 183, 198, 216, 259, 266, 273; painting, 10, 57, 218, 237, 253, 305; poetry (epic, lyric etc.), 23, 43, 91, 97–8, 106, 110–1, 120, 153, 165, 168, 175, 188, 195, 198, 201, 202, 206, 211, 241, 261, 262, 273, 283, 291, 296; pottery, 107, 195, 206; sculpture, 38, 39–40, 102, 157, 180, 184, 197, 202, 225, 236–7, 252, 271, 282, 294. *See also* comedy; performers; theatre

B

battles and campaigns: Aegospotami, *403*, 15, 185, 246, 301, 351; Amphipolis, *402*, 264–5, 312; Andros, *403*, 91, 235–6; Arginusae, *403*, 41, 47, 52, 64, 72, 79–80, 208, 228, 246, 265, 285, 288, 301; Argos, *402*, 181; Corinth, *402*, 72, 245, 275–7, 321; Coronea, 99, 101, 302; Delium, *402*, 13, 171, 181, 229, 245, 264–5, 312; Elis, *402*, 231; Mantinea, *402*, 181; Marathon, *402*, *404*, 48, 207, 290–1; Megara, *402*, 171, 245, 246, 325; Munychia (Piraeus), *402*, *404*, 92, 110, 219, 302; Notium, *403*, 15, 80, 185; Persia (against Artaxerxes II), 50, 204–5, 301–3, 319; Potidaea, *402*, 13, 74, 91, 264–5, 311; Pylos, 37, 214, 325; Salamis, *402*, *404*, 280; Sicily, against Carthage, *405*, 187, 253; Sicily, invasion of, *405*, 13–4, 17, 162, 182, 199, 215, 260, 316, 318; Syracuse, liberation of, *405*, 131–2, 135–6, 160, 167

birds, 73, 87, 124, 141, 164, 258. *See also* sports and games: cock-fighting

409

philosophy and philosophers, 23–5, 35–6, 42, 46, 50, 58, 126, 139, 140, 161, 202, 217, 231, 240, 247, 251, 273, 274, 278, 304–5. *See also* Pythagoreans

phratries, 7, 43, 95, 113, 128, 163–4, 228, 296, 347, 350, 352

poverty and wealth, 24, 46, 48, 68, 70, 117, 134, 140, 174, 177, 179, 264, 351–2. *See also* class

prisons and prisoners: debtors', 29; pending trial, 18, 20, 27, 79, 90, 109; political prisoners, 46, 148, 251; prisoners of war, 5, 59, 191, 198, 214, 231, 325; Socrates' imprisonment, *267*, 50, 115, 209, 261, 299, 320, 322–3

property: confiscation of, 4, 14–5, 16, 21, 22, 31, 33, 63, 92, 125, 127, 131, 142, 191–2, 232, 242, 279, 286, 295, 318; familial transfer of, 68, 84, 166, 107, 173, 251, 254, 352; mortgage of, 73, 294; redistribution of, 132, 352; restoration of, 220–1

prosopography, xl–xlviii, 2, 14, 22, 35, 76, 104, 120, 256, 308; generations in, xliii, 64–6, 107, 118–9, 234, 254, 290; sources in, xl–xli, 111–3

Pythagoreans 42, 44, 78, 82, 138, 139, 140, 175, 182, 187–8, 240, 260, 273, 293

R

religion, 17, 27, 98, 266; festivals, 19, 55–6, 95, 106, 120, 131, 161, 220, 285, 309, 314–5, 317, 320, 322–3, 324, 326, 347, 350; offices and cults, 70, 137, 163, 173, 174, 196, 279, 296, 347, 349, 352; sanctuaries, shrines, temples, 82, 131, 160, 171, 220, 249, 250, 265, 279, 311; prophecy, prophets, soothsayers, 141, 149, 152, 164, 301; visits from

underworld, 61, 226, 256, 320. *See also* phratries; sacrilege; theatre; trials and charges: impiety

rhetoric and rhetoricians, 6, 32, 43, 58, 83, 129, 139–40, 153, 156–7, 179, 188, 203, 226, 230, 252–3, 255, 281, 288–9, 295, 319; distinct from oratory, 179, distinct from philosophy, 157; distinct from sophistry, 32–3, 75–6, 179.

S

sacrilege, 17–20, 27, 143 315; Eleusinian mysteries, profanation of, 30, 314, 318; herms, mutilation of, 17, 20, 90, 146, 351. *See also* individual entries of persons implicated, listed on p. 18

sages, 94, 98, 156, 164, 209, 210, 243

slavery, 19, 72–3, 80, 134, 143, 162–3, 179, 213–4, 215, 231, 298, 302; prominent slave owners, 4, 9, 37, 64, 68, 84, 127, 172–3, 179, 210, 211, 212; slaves, biographical entries for, 161, 175, 191–2, 205, 208, 231, 248, 260, 298; slaves identified, 28, 41, 47, 53, 58, 66, 85, 87, 136, 174, 190, 241, 260, 296

sophistry: distinct from rhetoric, 32–3, 75–6, 179; students of, 30, 68; sophists, 66, 136–7, 152, 168, 189, 255, 256, 259, 266.

speechmaking, logography. *See* oratory

sports and games: athletes and trainers, 23, 29, 62, 85, 106, 137, 139, 144, 147, 164, 165, 175, 198, 206, 208, 253, 272, 275, 291, 299, 300–1, 311, 316; cockfighting, 72, 156, 206; Eleutherian games, 48; horses and horseracing, 13, 30, 31, 62, 88, 164, 195, 204, 279, 302; Olympics, 13, 21, 160, 291–2; Panathenaea, 62, 164, 259